FOURTH EDITION

Principles of MACROECONOMICS

A STREAMLINED APPROACH

THE McGRAW HILL SERIES IN ECONOMICS

SURVEY OF ECONOMICS

Brue, McConnell, and Flynn
Essentials of Economics
Fourth Edition

Guell
Issues in Economics Today
Ninth Edition

Mandel
M: Economics, The Basics
Fourth Edition

Schiller and Gebhardt
Essentials of Economics
Eleventh Edition

PRINCIPLES OF ECONOMICS

Asarta and Butters
Connect Master Principles of Economics

Colander
Economics, Microeconomics, and Macroeconomics
Eleventh Edition

Frank, Bernanke, Antonovics, and Heffetz
Principles of Economics, Principles of Microeconomics, Principles of Macroeconomics
Eighth Edition

Frank, Bernanke, Antonovics, and Heffetz
A Streamlined Approach for: Principles of Economics, Principles of Microeconomics, and Principles of Macroeconomics
Fourth Edition

Karlan and Morduch
Economics, Microeconomics, and Macroeconomics
Third Edition

McConnell, Brue, and Flynn
Economics, Microeconomics, and Macroeconomics
Twenty-Second Edition

McConnell, Brue, and Flynn
Brief Editions: Microeconomics and Macroeconomics
Third Edition

Samuelson and Nordhaus
Economics, Microeconomics, and Macroeconomics
Nineteenth Edition

Schiller and Gebhardt
The Economy Today, The Micro Economy Today, and The Macro Economy Today
Sixteenth Edition

Slavin
Economics, Microeconomics, and Macroeconomics
Twelfth Edition

ECONOMICS OF SOCIAL ISSUES

Guell
Issues in Economics Today
Ninth Edition

Register and Grimes
Economics of Social Issues
Twenty-First Edition

DATA ANALYTICS FOR ECONOMICS

Prince
Predictive Analytics for Business Strategy
First Edition

MANAGERIAL ECONOMICS

Baye and Prince
Managerial Economics and Business Strategy
Tenth Edition

Brickley, Smith, and Zimmerman
Managerial Economics and Organizational Architecture
Seventh Edition

Thomas and Maurice
Managerial Economics
Thirteenth Edition

INTERMEDIATE ECONOMICS

Bernheim and Whinston
Microeconomics
Second Edition

Dornbusch, Fischer, and Startz
Macroeconomics
Thirteenth Edition

Frank
Microeconomics and Behavior
Tenth Edition

ADVANCED ECONOMICS

Romer
Advanced Macroeconomics
Fifth Edition

MONEY AND BANKING

Cecchetti and Schoenholtz
Money, Banking, and Financial Markets
Sixth Edition

URBAN ECONOMICS

O'Sullivan
Urban Economics
Ninth Edition

LABOR ECONOMICS

Borjas
Labor Economics
Eighth Edition

McConnell, Brue, and Macpherson
Contemporary Labor Economics
Twelfth Edition

PUBLIC FINANCE

Rosen and Gayer
Public Finance
Tenth Edition

ENVIRONMENTAL ECONOMICS

Field and Field
Environmental Economics: An Introduction
Eighth Edition

INTERNATIONAL ECONOMICS

Appleyard and Field
International Economics
Ninth Edition

Pugel
International Economics
Seventeenth Edition

FOURTH EDITION

Principles of MACROECONOMICS

A STREAMLINED APPROACH

ROBERT H. FRANK

Cornell University

BEN S. BERNANKE

Brookings Institution [affiliated]

Former Chair, Board of Governors of the Federal Reserve System

KATE ANTONOVICS

University of California, San Diego

ORI HEFFETZ

Cornell University and Hebrew University of Jerusalem

Mc Graw Hill

PRINCIPLES OF MACROECONOMICS: A STREAMLINED APPROACH, FOURTH EDITION

Published by McGraw Hill LLC, 1325 Avenue of the Americas, New York, NY 10121.

This book is printed on acid-free paper.

1 2 3 4 5 6 7 8 9 LWI 26 25 24 23 22 21

ISBN 978-1-264-05865-5 (bound edition)
MHID 1-264-05865-9 (bound edition)
ISBN 978-1-264-05875-4 (loose-leaf edition)
MHID 1-264-05875-6 (loose-leaf edition)

Portfolio Director: *Anke Weekes*
Senior Product Developer: *Christina Kouvelis*
Marketing Manager: *Bobby Pearson*
Lead Content Project Manager: *Christine Vaughan*
Content Project Manager: *Emily Windelborn*
Senior Buyer: *Susan K. Culbertson*
Senior Designer: *Matt Diamond*
Senior Content Licensing Specialist: *Melissa Homer*
Cover Image: *Miroslava Hlavacova/Shutterstock*
Compositor: *Aptara®, Inc.*

Library of Congress Cataloging-in-Publication Data

Names: Frank, Robert H., author. | Bernanke, Ben, author. | Antonovics, Kate L., author. | Heffetz, Ori, 1973- author.
Title: Principle of macroeconomics : a streamlined approach / Robert H. Frank, Cornell University, Ben Bernanke, Brookings Institution, Former Chair, Board of Governors of the Federal Reserve System, Kate Antonovics, University of California, San Diego, Ori Heffetz, Cornell University and Hebrew University of Jerusalem.
Description: Fourth edition. | New York, NY : McGraw Hill LLC, [2022] | Includes index.
Identifiers: LCCN 2020058345 (print) | LCCN 2020058346 (ebook) | ISBN 9781264058655 (hardcover) | ISBN 9781264058754 (spiral bound) | ISBN 9781260590760 (hardcover) | ISBN 9781264058747 (ebook) | ISBN 9781264058778 (ebook other)
Subjects: LCSH: Macroeconomics.
Classification: LCC HB172.5 .F69 2021 (print) | LCC HB172.5 (ebook) | DDC 339–dc23
LC record available at https://lccn.loc.gov/2020058345
LC ebook record available at https://lccn.loc.gov/2020058346

mheducation.com/highered

DEDICATION

For Ellen

R. H. F.

For Anna

B. S. B.

For Fiona and Henry

K. A.

For Katrina, Eleanor, Daniel, and Amalia

O. H.

ABOUT THE AUTHORS

ROBERT H. FRANK

©Robert H. Frank

Robert H. Frank is the H. J. Louis Professor of Management and Professor of Economics, emeritus, at Cornell's Johnson School of Management, where he taught from 1972 to 2020. After receiving his B.S. from Georgia Tech in 1966, he taught math and science for two years as a Peace Corps Volunteer in rural Nepal. He received his M.A. in statistics in 1971 and his Ph.D. in economics in 1972 from The University of California at Berkeley. He also holds honorary doctorate degrees from the University of St. Gallen and Dalhousie University. During leaves of absence from Cornell, he has served as chief economist for the Civil Aeronautics Board (1978–1980), a Fellow at the Center for Advanced Study in the Behavioral Sciences (1992–1993), Professor of American Civilization at l'École des Hautes Études en Sciences Sociales in Paris (2000–2001), and the Peter and Charlotte Schoenfeld Visiting Faculty Fellow at the NYU Stern School of Business in 2008–2009. His papers have appeared in the *American Economic Review, Econometrica,* the *Journal of Political Economy,* and other leading professional journals, and for more than two decades, his economics columns appeared regularly in *The New York Times.*

Professor Frank is the author of a best-selling intermediate economics textbook–*Microeconomics and Behavior,* Tenth Edition (McGraw Hill, 2021). His research has focused on rivalry and cooperation in economic and social behavior. His books on these themes include *Choosing the Right Pond* (Oxford, 1985), *Passions Within Reason* (W. W. Norton, 1988), *What Price the Moral High Ground?* (Princeton, 2004), *Falling Behind* (University of California Press, 2007), *The Economic Naturalist* (Basic Books, 2007), *The Economic Naturalist's Field Guide* (Basic Books, 2009), *The Darwin Economy* (Princeton, 2011), *Success and Luck* (Princeton, 2016), and *Under the Influence* (Princeton, 2020), which have been translated into 24 languages. *The Winner-Take-All Society* (The Free Press, 1995), co-authored with Philip Cook, received a Critic's Choice Award, was named a Notable Book of the Year by *The New York Times,* and was included in *BusinessWeek*'s list of the 10 best books of 1995. *Luxury Fever* (The Free Press, 1999) was named to the Knight-Ridder Best Books list for 1999.

Professor Frank is a co-recipient of the 2004 Leontief Prize for Advancing the Frontiers of Economic Thought. He was awarded the Johnson School's Stephen Russell Distinguished Teaching Award in 2004, 2010, 2012, and 2018, and the School's Apple Distinguished Teaching Award in 2005. His introductory microeconomics course has graduated more than 7,000 enthusiastic economic naturalists over the years.

BEN S. BERNANKE

©Ben S. Bernanke

Professor Bernanke received his B.A. in economics from Harvard University in 1975 and his Ph.D. in economics from MIT in 1979. He taught at the Stanford Graduate School of Business from 1979 to 1985 and moved to Princeton University in 1985, where he was named the Howard Harrison and Gabrielle Snyder Beck Professor of Economics and Public Affairs and where he served as chair of the Economics Department. Professor Bernanke is currently a Distinguished Fellow in Residence with the Economic Studies Program at the Brookings Institution.

Professor Bernanke was sworn in on February 1, 2006, as chair and a member of the Board of Governors of the Federal Reserve System–his second term expired January 31, 2014. Professor Bernanke also served as chair of the Federal Open Market Committee, the Fed's principal monetary policymaking body. Professor Bernanke was also chair of the President's Council of Economic Advisers from June 2005 to January 2006.

Professor Bernanke's intermediate textbook, with Andrew Abel and Dean Croushore, *Macroeconomics,* Ninth Edition (Addison-Wesley, 2017), is a best seller in its field. He has authored numerous scholarly publications in macroeconomics, macroeconomic history, and finance. He has done significant research on the causes of the Great Depression, the role of financial markets and institutions in the business cycle, and measurement of the effects of monetary policy on the economy.

Professor Bernanke has held a Guggenheim Fellowship and a Sloan Fellowship, and he is a Fellow of the Econometric Society and of the American Academy of Arts and Sciences. He served as director of the Monetary Economics Program of the National Bureau of Economic Research (NBER) and as a member of the NBER's Business Cycle Dating Committee. From 2001 to 2004 he served as editor of the *American Economic Review,* and served as the president of the American Economic Association in 2019. Professor Bernanke's work with civic and professional groups includes having served two terms as a member of the Montgomery Township (N.J.) Board of Education.

KATE ANTONOVICS

©Kate Antonovics

Professor Antonovics received her B.A. from Brown University in 1993 and her Ph.D. in economics from the University of Wisconsin in 2000. Shortly thereafter, she joined the faculty in the Economics Department at the University of California, San

Diego. Professor Antonovics is also currently serving as the Provost of UC San Diego's Seventh College.

Professor Antonovics is known for her excellence in teaching and her innovative use of technology in the classroom. Her popular introductory-level microeconomics courses have regularly enrolled over 900 students each fall. She also teaches labor economics at both the undergraduate and graduate level. She has received numerous teaching awards, including the UCSD Department of Economics award for Best Undergraduate Teaching, the UCSD Academic Senate Distinguished Teaching Award, and the UCSD Chancellor's Associates Faculty Excellence Award in Undergraduate Teaching.

Professor Antonovics's research has focused on racial discrimination, gender discrimination, affirmative action, intergenerational income mobility, learning, and wage dynamics. Her papers have appeared in the *American Economic Review,* the *Review of Economics and Statistics,* the *Journal of Labor Economics,* and the *Journal of Human Resources.* She is a member of both the American Economic Association and the Society of Labor Economists.

ORI HEFFETZ

©Ori Heffetz

Professor Heffetz received his B.A. in physics and philosophy from Tel Aviv University in 1999 and his Ph.D. in economics from Princeton University in 2005. He is an Associate Professor of Economics at the Samuel Curtis Johnson Graduate School of Management at Cornell University, and at the Economics Department at the Hebrew University of Jerusalem.

Bringing the real world into the classroom, Professor Heffetz has created a unique macroeconomics course that introduces basic concepts and tools from economic theory and applies them to current news and global events. His popular classes are taken by hundreds of students every year on Cornell's Ithaca and New York City campuses and via live videoconferencing in dozens of cities across the United States, Canada, and Latin America.

Professor Heffetz's research studies the social and cultural aspects of economic behavior, focusing on the mechanisms that drive consumers' choices and on the links between economic choices, individual well-being, and policymaking. He has published scholarly work on household consumption patterns, individual economic decision making, and survey methodology and measurement. He was a visiting researcher at the Bank of Israel during 2011, is currently a Research Associate at the National Bureau of Economic Research (NBER), and serves on the editorial board of *Social Choice and Welfare.*

A LESS IS MORE FOCUS

Our fourth streamlined edition arrives in the midst of some of the most dramatic upheavals ever witnessed, both in the economy generally and in higher education in particular. The COVID-19 pandemic has produced levels of unemployment not seen since the Great Depression and has created dramatic changes in the ways we teach across educational institutions at every level.

These developments have reinforced our confidence in the instructional philosophy that motivated us to produce our first edition—the need to strip away clutter and focus more intensively on central concepts. This approach, we believe, is especially well suited for the new environment.

In earlier editions, we noted that although many millions of dollars are spent each year on introductory economics instruction in American colleges and universities, the return on this investment has been disturbingly low. Studies have shown, for example, that several months after having taken a principles of economics course, former students are no better able to answer simple economics questions than others who never even took the course. Most students, it seems, leave our introductory courses without having learned even the most important basic economic principles. Such dismal performance, never defensible, has become even more difficult to justify in the face of looming resource shortages in higher education.

The problem, in our view, has almost always been that courses try to teach students far too much. In the process, really important ideas get little more coverage than minor ones, and everything ends up going by in a blur. The human brain tends to ignore new information unless it comes up repeatedly. That's hardly surprising, since only a tiny fraction of the terabytes of information that bombard us each day is likely to be relevant for anything we care about. Only when something comes up a third or fourth time does the brain start laying down new circuits for dealing with it. Yet when planning their lectures, many instructors ask themselves, "How much can I cover today?" And because modern electronic media enable them to click through upwards of 100 PowerPoint slides in an hour, they feel they better serve their students when they put more information before them. But that's not the way learning works! Professors should instead be asking, "How much can my students absorb?"

Our approach to this text was inspired by our conviction that students will learn far more if we attempt to cover much less. Our basic premise is that a small number of basic ideas do most of the heavy lifting in economics, and that if we focus narrowly and repeatedly on those ideas, illustrating and applying them in numerous familiar contexts, students can actually master them in just a single semester. The enthusiastic reactions of users of previous editions of our textbook affirm the validity of this premise. Our emphasis throughout is on active learning. We ask students to apply basic economic ideas themselves to answer related questions, exercises, and problems.

ADAPTING TO CLASSROOM TRENDS

Baumol's cost disease refers to the tendency for costs to rise more rapidly for goods and services for which growth in labor productivity is either slow or nonexistent. It is thus no surprise that the cost of traditional methods of delivering classroom instruction has been rising so much faster than the cost of producing most manufactured goods.

Largely as a result of Baumol's cost disease, tuition increases have far exceeded even the rapid growth in the cost of health care. This is what we would expect if the dominant teaching model remains as it was a century ago, in which a learned instructor stands in front of a class reciting truths cataloged in an assigned text. But as the late Herb Stein once remarked, "If something cannot go on forever, it will stop." And so it is with rising tuitions. Universities are already facing strong pressure to moderate their rates of tuition growth, pressure that has been greatly exacerbated by the COVID-19 pandemic.

One result has been that much of the content that professors have traditionally delivered in live lecture will instead be delivered electronically. Indeed, technological advances have given today's students an unparalleled ability to access information via the Internet, YouTube, and social media.

If early experience is any indication, the "flipped-classroom" model is one of the most promising adaptations to this new environment. In this approach, students are expected to study basic concepts before coming to class and then deepen their understanding of them through structured classroom exercises and discussion. The logic of the flipped classroom is compelling because under this approach, students have access to instructors precisely when students are engaged in those activities that students find the most challenging (for example, problem solving and policy evaluation). Indeed, numerous studies have found that the flipped-classroom approach increases both student satisfaction and student learning.

A second adaptation, more pronounced in the wake of the COVID-19 lockdowns of March 2020, has been the move to remote instruction. The streamlined approach of this text is well suited for the goals of both the flipped-classroom and remote-instruction models. Rather than trying to bombard students with information they can easily access online, our book seeks to promote a deeper understanding of economics by focusing on core concepts. In addition, one of our central goals has been to create resources to help instructors promote student engagement outside the classroom. Some instructors may find these resources useful in completely overhauling the way they teach, while others may be interested in using them to make a few minor changes to their current courses.

In other words, this edition is intended to support a variety of teaching styles (and, indeed, our team of authors varies considerably in our pedagogical approach). The traditional approach has been to ask students to read the relevant sections from the textbook before coming to class. But instructors report that today's students are far less likely than their predecessors to complete such assignments. Stronger incentives can boost compliance. One effective approach assigns SmartBook chapters with adaptive questioning built in. Another administers brief tests at the start of class. These might involve two or three simple multiple-choice questions on the assigned material that are administered and graded electronically via audience response tools using smartphone apps.

Perhaps the biggest hurdle to effective implementation of the new teaching approaches has been a dearth of effective pre-class concept-delivery materials. To help fill this gap, we have created a library of short videos that focus on basic economic concepts. Many students have found these videos and animations engaging enough to watch even if they're not going to be tested on them, but we've also provided easily administered in-class questions that can boost compliance still further.

A big payoff in both the flipped-classroom and remote-instruction models comes from being able to use limited class time to discuss the concepts that students have studied before class. One approach begins by asking students to answer a multiple-choice question requiring application of a concept, and then reporting the frequencies with which students selected the various multiple-choice options. Students are then given a few moments to discuss the question—either with their neighbors in traditional classroom settings, or with fellow students in Zoom breakout rooms—before having an opportunity to change the answers they originally submitted. Professors then call on students who've offered both correct and incorrect answers to the question to defend their answers to the class and lead the ensuing discussion. We've spent considerable effort drafting the kinds of questions that reliably provoke animated discussions of this sort.

In summary, here are the resources we have developed to support the flipped-classroom and remote-instruction approaches, all available within McGraw Hill Connect® specific to the fourth edition:

Before Class (Exposure)

- **SmartBook® Adaptive Reading Assignments:** SmartBook contains the same content as the print book, but actively tailors that content to the needs of the individual through adaptive probing and integrated learning resources. Instructions can assign SmartBook reading assignments for points to create incentives for students to come to class prepared.
- **Learning Glass Lecture Videos:** A collection of brief instructional videos featuring the authors, Kate Antonovics and Ori Heffetz, utilize exciting learning glass technology to provide students with an overview of important economic concepts. Perfect for an introduction to basic concepts before coming to class, or as a quick review, these videos can be accessed as resources within SmartBook, or are available as standalone assignments within Connect.

In Class (Engagement)

- **Clicker Questions:** Classroom-tested by the authors, these multiple-choice questions are designed to facilitate discussion and group work in class.
- **Economic Naturalist Application-Focused Videos:** A known hallmark of this franchise, the Economic Naturalist examples are now available as an expanded set of short, engaging video vignettes within Connect and SmartBook.

After Class (Reinforcement)

- **Connect Exercises:** All end-of-chapter homework exercises are available to be assigned within Connect. Many of these exercises include algorithmic variations and require students to interact with the graphing and tool within the platform. **Worked Problem Videos,** available as hints within Connect, work through these problems to aid in student understanding of core economic concepts and offer assistance with more challenging material.
- **Test Bank Assessment:** Hundreds of multiple-choice questions are available for summative assessments of the chapter content. Select problems are now offered as an algorithmic alternative, providing even more variation.

All of the above assets can be implemented by instructors as preferred in order to satisfy as much or as little of the flipped-classroom approach as is desired.

KEY THEMES AND FEATURES

Economic Naturalism

Relying on examples drawn from familiar contexts, we encourage students to become "economic naturalists," people who employ basic economic principles to understand and explain what they observe in the world around them. An economic naturalist understands, for example, that infant safety seats are required in cars but not in airplanes because the marginal cost of space to accommodate these seats is typically zero in cars but often hundreds of dollars in airplanes. Scores of such examples are sprinkled throughout the text. Each one, we believe, poses a question that should make any curious person eager to learn the answer.

Our ultimate goal is to produce economic naturalists—people who see each human interaction as the result of an implicit or explicit cost-benefit calculation.

The economic naturalist sees mundane details of ordinary existence in a new light and becomes actively engaged in the attempt to understand them. Some representative examples follow:

- Why does the average Argentine hold more U.S. dollars than the average U.S. citizen?
- Why does news of inflation hurt the stock market?
- Why do almost all countries provide free public education?

Economic Naturalist Video Series: We are very excited to offer an expanded video series based on Economic Naturalist examples. A series of videos covering some of our favorite micro- and macro-focused examples can be used as part of classroom presentations, or assigned for homework along with accompanying questions within McGraw Hill Connect®. These fascinating, fun, and thought-provoking applications of economics in everyday life encourage students to think like an economist. Refer to the distinguishing features pages of the preface for additional information. You can view one of these dynamic videos here: http://econeveryday.com/why-do-cooked-rotisserie-chickens-cost-less-than-fresh-uncooked-chickens/

Active Learning Stressed

The only way to learn to hit an overhead smash in tennis is through repeated practice. The same is true for learning economics. Accordingly, we consistently introduce new ideas in the context of simple examples and then follow them with applications showing how they work in familiar settings. At frequent intervals, we pose self-tests that both test and reinforce the understanding of these ideas. The end-of-chapter questions and problems are carefully crafted to help students internalize and extend basic concepts, and are available within Connect as assignable content so that instructors can require students to engage with this material. Experience with earlier editions confirms that this approach really does prepare students to apply basic economic ideas to solve economic puzzles drawn from the real world.

Both the Economic Naturalist and Learning Glass videos and accompanying multiple-choice questions that test students' understanding of the principles illustrated in the videos have become valued tools for instructors who incorporate elements of the flipped-classroom approach in their teaching, or those who are relying more heavily on other forms of remote learning. Our less-is-more approach to topic coverage is also uniquely well suited to these new instructional approaches.

Cost-Benefit Focus

- *The cost-benefit principle, which tells us to take only those actions whose benefits exceed their costs, is the core idea behind the economic way of thinking.* Introduced in Chapter 1 and employed repeatedly thereafter, this principle is more fully developed here than in any other text. It underlies the argument for economic efficiency as an important social goal. Rather than speak of trade-offs between efficiency and other goals, we stress that maximizing economic surplus—that is, taking those actions whose benefits exceed their costs—facilitates the achievement of every goal we care about.
- One of the biggest hurdles to the fruitful application of cost-benefit thinking is to recognize and measure the relevant costs and benefits. Common decision pitfalls identified by 2002 Nobel Laureate Daniel Kahneman and others—such as the tendency to ignore implicit costs, the tendency not to ignore sunk costs, and the tendency to confuse average and marginal costs and benefits—are introduced early in Chapter 1 and invoked repeatedly in subsequent chapters.

Modern Macroeconomics

Both the Great Recession and the COVID-19 pandemic have renewed interest in cyclical fluctuations without challenging the importance of such long-run issues as growth, productivity, the evolution of real wages, and capital formation. Our treatment of these issues is organized as follows:

- A four-chapter treatment of *long-run issues,* followed by a modern treatment of *short-term fluctuations and stabilization policy,* emphasizes the important distinction between short- and long-run behavior of the economy.
- *Designed to allow for flexible treatment of topics,* these chapters are written so that short-run material (Chapters 9–11) can be used before long-run material (Chapters 5–8) with no loss of continuity.
- The analysis of aggregate demand and aggregate supply relates output to inflation, rather than to the price level, sidestepping the necessity of a separate derivation of the link between the output gap and inflation. The discussion of monetary policy has two parts. It starts with a standard supply and demand analysis of the market for money that is centered on the short-run interest rate. It then introduces the new tools of monetary policy, such as quantitative easing and forward guidance, that have been so important since 2008, and that again took center stage in the 2020 response to the pandemic.
- This book places a heavy emphasis on *globalization,* starting with an analysis of its effects on real wage inequality and progressing to such issues as the costs and benefits of trade, the role of capital flows in domestic capital formation, and the links between exchange rates and monetary policy.

CHANGES IN THE FOURTH EDITION

Changes Common to All Chapters

In all chapters, the narrative has been tightened. Many of the examples have been updated, with a focus on student-centered examples that connect to current topics such as the COVID-19 pandemic and the rise of the gig economy. The examples, self-tests, and the end-of-chapter material from the previous edition have been redesigned to provide more clarity and ease of use. Data have been updated throughout.

Chapter-by-Chapter Changes

Chapter 1

- Updated student-centered examples, such as Netflix, wireless keyboards, dogwalking, and Jeff Bezos
- New and updated end-of-chapter problems that reinforce the chapter's learning objectives
- Updated appendix on working with equations, graphs, and tables based on electric scooter rentals

Chapter 2

- Updated student-centered examples, such as digital versus print ads and Marvel Studio films
- New Economic Naturalist, "Why was there a shortage of toilet paper during the COVID-19 pandemic?"
- Three new end-of-chapter questions that reinforce the chapter's learning objectives, including a question related to the drop in crude oil prices during the COVID-19 pandemic

Chapter 3

- Updated discussion of growth that reflects higher Internet and cell phone penetration
- Updated discussion of recessions and expansions that mentions the COVID-19 economic disruptions

Chapter 4

- Updated discussion of the correlation between per capita GDP and health outcomes such as life expectancy that now mentions that within high-income countries, the relationship can even reverse, with examples of data from the U.S., Canada, and Japan
- Updated discussion of the development of real wages for production workers and for highly paid baseball players over time that is now linked together, in the context of a new discussion about increasing wage inequalities between the highest- and lowest-paid U.S. workers

Chapter 5

- Updated examples, data, and figures

Chapter 6

- Clarification throughout the chapter of the difference between trends in average incomes and trends in income inequality
- Updated discussion of globalization that now includes recent developments, including the political opposition to the Trans-Pacific Partnership trade agreement and the Trump administration's resistance to increased economic integration of the U.S. with China
- New Economic Naturalist, "Can new technology hurt workers?" that includes what was previously a paragraph on workers' resistance to new technology (with anecdotes on Ned Ludd and the tale of John Henry); the new EN highlights workers' concerns about automation, robotics, and artificial intelligence (AI)
- New Economic Naturalist, "How did the COVID-19 pandemic affect the demand for U.S. jobs?" that discusses the different effects the pandemic is having on different jobs in different sectors
- New discussion of European labor markets that highlights the deregulation in southern Europe following the global financial crisis and that, on some metrics, Europe's labor market does better than the U.S. labor market

Chapter 7

- Updates related to the COVID-19 economic downturn that include the discussion of U.S. household saving early in the chapter and the discussion of the U.S. government deficit later in the chapter
- New Economic Naturalist, "Why have real interest rates declined globally in recent decades?" that discusses the combination of higher global saving and lower global investment that helps explain the downward trend in real interest rates

Chapter 8

- New discussion of the Fed's role in stabilizing financial markets and as lender of last resort, which took center stage in recent episodes of financial panic; the discussion covers Section 13(3) landing during the 2008 and 2020 crises
- Updates related to recent U.S.-China trade frictions, in the discussion of the saving rate and the trade deficit
- Updates related to the COVID-19 pandemic and financial markets

Chapter 9

- Updates related to the COVID-19 downturn

- Revised Economic Naturalist 9.3 that includes discussion of the gig economy in the context of the natural rate of unemployment in the U.S.
- Revised Economic Naturalist 9.5 that discusses the U.S. government's response to the COVID-19 pandemic and covers details of the Coronavirus Aid, Relief, and Economic Security (CARES) Act of 2020 and their economic rationale
- Other COVID-19-related updates

Chapter 10

- Updates related to COVID-19: in the context of banks' excess reserves, in the context of the Fed's quick cuts of the federal funds rate, in the context of quantitative easing (QE) and the Fed's special landing in 2020, and in the context of the Fed's return to forward guidance in 2020; the chapter highlights the unprecedented speed and severity of the pandemic's economic hit, and therefore the unprecedented speed and size of the policy response
- Revisions throughout the chapter that reflect recent developments in thinking about QE, forward guidance, and other methods; when introduced in 2008, these methods were viewed as "unconventional" and "temporary"; the chapter now observes that such methods are increasingly recognized as a "new normal"

Chapter 11

- Updates to Economic Naturalist 11.5 to cover the Fed's unprecedented response to COVID-19
- Updated the chapter title to accurately reflect chapter coverage

Chapter 12

- Updated student-centered examples, such as interior designer Kelly Wearstler
- Revised Economic Naturalist that discusses the U.S.-China trade war that started in 2018, highlighting that there is more to trade than the exchange of goods and services and its supply and demand analysis in this chapter; also covers issues such as intellectual property and national security

Chapter 13

- New Economic Naturalist, "What is a safe haven currency?" (such as the U.S. dollar, the Swiss franc, and the Japanese yen), and how currencies tend to appreciate in periods of uncertainty; includes specific examples from the 2008 global financial crisis and the 2020 global COVID-19 crisis
- Updated Economic Naturalist 13.5 that covers the IMF's COVID-19-related landing in early 2020

ORGANIZED LEARNING IN THE FOURTH EDITION

Chapter Learning Objectives

Students and professors can be confident that the organization of each chapter surrounds common themes outlined by four to seven learning objectives listed on the first page of each chapter. These objectives, along with AACSB and Bloom's Taxonomy Learning Categories, are connected to all test bank questions and end-of-chapter material to offer a comprehensive, thorough teaching and learning experience. Reports available within Connect allow instructors to easily output data related to student performance across chapter learning objectives, AACSB criteria, and Bloom's Taxonomy Learning Categories.

Assurance of Learning Ready

Many educational institutions today are focused on the notion of assurance of learning, an important element of some accreditation standards. *Principles of Macroeconomics, A Streamlined Approach, 4/e,* is designed specifically to support your assurance of learning initiatives with a simple, yet powerful, solution. Instructors can use Connect to easily query for learning objectives that directly relate to the objectives of the course and then use the reporting features of Connect to aggregate student results in a similar fashion, making the collection and presentation of assurance of learning data simple and easy.

AACSB Statement

The McGraw Hill Companies is a proud corporate member of AACSB International. Recognizing the importance and value of AACSB accreditation, the authors of *Principles of Macroeconomics, A Streamlined Approach, 4/e,* have sought to recognize the curricula guidelines detailed in AACSB standards for business accreditation by connecting questions in the test bank and end-of-chapter material to the general knowledge and skill guidelines found in AACSB standards.

It is important to note that the statements contained in *Principles of Macroeconomics, A Streamlined Approach, 4/e,* are provided only as a guide for the users of this text.

A NOTE ON THE WRITING OF THIS EDITION

Ben Bernanke was sworn in on February 1, 2006, as chair and a member of the Board of Governors of the Federal Reserve System, a position to which he was reappointed in January 2010. From June 2005 until January 2006, he served as chair of the President's Council of Economic Advisers. These positions have allowed him to play an active role in making U.S. economic policy, but the rules of government service restricted his ability to participate in the preparation of previous editions. Since his second term as chair of the Federal Reserve has completed, we are happy to share that Ben is actively involved in the revision of the macro portion of this edition.

ACKNOWLEDGMENTS

Our thanks first and foremost go to our portfolio director, Anke Weekes, and our senior product developer, Christina Kouvelis. Anke encouraged us to think deeply about how to improve the book and helped us transform our ideas into concrete changes. Christina shepherded us through the revision process with intelligence, sound advice, and good humor. We are grateful as well to the production team, whose professionalism (and patience) was outstanding: Christine Vaughan, lead content project manager; Emily Windelborn, content project manager; Matt Diamond, senior designer; and all of those who worked on the production team to turn our manuscript into the book you see now. Finally, we also thank Bobby Pearson, marketing manager, for getting our message into the wider world.

Special thanks to Peggy Dalton Verner, Frostburg State University, for her energy, creativity, and help in refining the assessment material in both the text and Connect; Sukanya Kemp, University of Akron, for her detailed accuracy check of the learning glass and economic naturalist videos; Alvin Angeles and team at the University of California, San Diego, for their efforts in the production and editing of the learning glass videos; and Kevin Bertotti and the team at ITVK for their creativity in transforming Economic Naturalist examples into dynamic and engaging video vignettes.

Finally, our sincere thanks to the following teachers and colleagues, whose thorough reviews and thoughtful suggestions led to innumerable substantive improvements to *Principles of Macroeconomics, A Streamlined Approach, 4/e.*

Mark Abajian, *San Diego Mesa College*
Richard Agesa, *Marshall University*
Seemi Ahmad, *Dutchess Community College*
Donald L. Alexander, *Western Michigan University*
Chris Azevedo, *University of Central Missouri*
Narine Badasyan, *Murray State University*
Sigridur Benediktsdottir, *Yale University*
Robert Blewett, *St. Lawrence University*
Brian C. Brush, *Marquette University*
Colleen Callahan, *American University*
Giuliana Campanelli Andreopoulos, *William Paterson University*
J. Lon Carlson, *Illinois State University*
David Chaplin, *Northwest Nazarene University*
Joni Charles, *Texas State University*
Anoshua Chaudhuri, *San Francisco State University*
Nan-Ting Chou, *University of Louisville*
Maria Luisa Corton, *University of South Florida–St. Petersburg*
Manabendra Dasgupta, *University of Alabama at Birmingham*
Craig Dorsey, *College of DuPage*
Dennis Edwards, *Coastal Carolina University*
Tracie Edwards, *University of Missouri–St. Louis*
Roger Frantz, *San Diego State University*
Mark Frascatore, *Clarkson University*
Amanda Freeman, *Kansas State University*
Greg George, *Macon State College*
Seth Gershenson, *Michigan State University*
Amy D. Gibson, *Christopher Newport University*
Rajeev Goel, *Illinois State University*
Mehdi Haririan, *Bloomsburg University of Pennsylvania*
Susan He, *Washington State University*
John Hejkal, *University of Iowa*
Kuang-Chung Hsu, *Kishwaukee College*
Greg Hunter, *California State University–Pomona*
David W. Johnson, *University of Wisconsin–Madison*
Derek Johnson, *University of Connecticut*
Sukanya Kemp, *University of Akron*
Brian Kench, *University of Tampa*
Fredric R. Kolb, *University of Wisconsin–Eau Claire*
Daniel D. Kuester, *Kansas State University*
Valerie Lacarte, *American University*
Donald J. Liu, *University of Minnesota–Twin Cities*
Ida Mirzaie, *The Ohio State University*
Jelena Nikolic, *Northeastern University*
Anthony A. Noce, *State University of New York (SUNY)–Plattsburgh*

Diego Nocetti, *Clarkson University*
Stephanie Owings, *Fort Lewis College*
Dishant Pandya, *Spalding University*
Martin Pereyra, *University of Missouri*
Tony Pizelo, *Northwest University*
Ratha Ramoo, *Diablo Valley College*
Thomas Rhoads, *Towson University*
Bill Robinson, *University of Nevada–Las Vegas*
Brian Rosario, *University of California–Davis*
Elyce Rotella, *Indiana University*
Jeffrey Rubin, *Rutgers University*
Naveen Sarna, *Northern Virginia Community College*
Sumati Srinivas, *Radford University*
Thomas Stevens, *University of Massachusetts*
Carolyn Fabian Stumph, *Indiana University* and *Purdue University–Fort Wayne*
Markland Tuttle, *Sam Houston State University*
David Vera, *California State University–Fresno*
Nancy Virts, *California State University–Northridge*
Gilbert J. Werema, *Texas Woman's University*
Elizabeth Wheaton, *Southern Methodist University*
William C. Wood, *James Madison University*

DISTINGUISHING FEATURES

Economic Naturalist Examples and Videos

Each Economic Naturalist example starts with a question to spark curiosity and interest in learning an answer. These examples fuel interest while teaching students to see economics in the world around them. Videos of select and new Economic Naturalist examples are denoted in the margin of the material to which they pertain. They are housed within Connect with accompanying questions. A full list of Economic Naturalist examples and videos can be found in the following pages.

The Economic Naturalist 11.1

What is the China trade shock?

The China trade shock, a term most commonly associated with economists David Autor, David Dorn, and Gordon Hanson, is used to describe the dramatic change in international trade patterns that resulted from China's rise as a major player in the global economy over the past few decades.

In a series of influential studies, these economists and their collaborators investigated the costs of the shock to U.S. workers. They found that employment has falle

ECONOMIC NATURALISM

connect

► Visit your instructor's Connect course and access your eBook to view this video.

Why does the light come on when you open the refrigerator door but not when you open the freezer?

With the rudiments of the cost-benefit framework under your belt, you are now in a position to become an "economic naturalist," someone who uses insights from economics to help make sense of observations from everyday life. People who have studied biology are able to observe and marvel at many details of nature that would otherwise have escaped their notice. For example, on a walk in the woods in early April, the novice may see only trees. In contrast, the biology student notices many different species of trees and understands why some are already in leaf while others still lie dormant. Likewise, the novice may notice that in some animal species males are much larger than females, but the biology student knows that pattern occurs only in species in which males take several mates. Natural selection favors larger males in those species because their greater size helps them prevail in the often bloody contests among males for access to females. In contrast, males tend to be roughly the same size as females in monogamous species, in which there is much less fighting for mates.

Numbered Examples

Throughout the text, numbered and titled examples are referenced and called out to further illustrate concepts. Our engaging questions and examples from everyday life highlight how each human action is the result of an implicit or explicit cost-benefit calculation.

EXAMPLE 1.3 Implicit Cost

Should you use your frequent-flyer coupon to fly to Cancun for spring break?

With spring break only a week away, you are still undecided about whether to go to Cancun with a group of classmates at the University of Iowa. The round-trip airfare from Cedar Rapids is $500, but you have a frequent-flyer coupon you could use for the trip. All other relevant costs for the vacation week at the beach total exactly $1,000. The most you would be willing to pay for the Cancun vacation is $1,350. That amount is your benefit of taking the vacation. Your only alternative use for your frequent-flyer coupon is for a trip to Boston the weekend after spring break to attend your brother's wedding. (Your coupon expires shortly thereafter.) If the Cedar Rapids–Boston round-trip airfare is $400, should you use your frequent-flyer coupon to fly to Cancun for spring break?

The Cost-Benefit Principle tells us that you should go to Cancun if the benefits of the trip exceed its costs. If not for the complication of the frequent-flyer coupon, solving this problem would be a straightforward matter of comparing your benefit from the week at the beach to the sum of all relevant costs. And because your airfare and other costs would add up to $1,500, or $150 more than your benefit from the trip, you would not go to Cancun.

But what about the possibility of using your frequent-flyer coupon to make the trip? Using it for that purpose might make the flight to Cancun seem free, suggesting you'd reap an economic surplus of $350 by making the trip. But doing so also would mean you'd have to fork over $400 for your airfare to Boston. So the implicit cost of using your coupon to go to Cancun is really $400. If you use it for that purpose, the trip still ends up being a loser because the cost of the vacation, $1,400, exceeds the benefit by $50. In cases like these, you're much more likely to decide sensibly if you ask yourself, "Should I use my frequent-flyer coupon for this trip or save it for an upcoming trip?"

Bkindler/E+/Getty Images

Is your flight to Cancun "free" if you travel on a frequent-flyer coupon?

SELF-TESTS

These self-test questions in the body of the chapter enable students to determine whether the preceding material has been understood and reinforce understanding before reading further. Detailed answers to the self-test questions are found at the end of each chapter.

SELF-TEST 1.5

Should a basketball team's best player take all the team's shots?

A professional basketball team has a new assistant coach. The assistant notices that one player scores on a higher percentage of her shots than other players. Based on this information, the assistant suggests to the head coach that the star player take *all* the shots. That way, the assistant reasons, the team will score more points and win more games.

On hearing this suggestion, the head coach fires her assistant for incompetence. What was wrong with the assistant's idea?

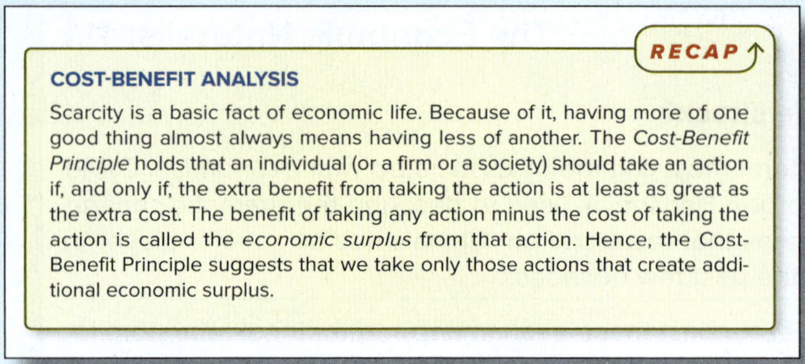

RECAP

COST-BENEFIT ANALYSIS

Scarcity is a basic fact of economic life. Because of it, having more of one good thing almost always means having less of another. The *Cost-Benefit Principle* holds that an individual (or a firm or a society) should take an action if, and only if, the extra benefit from taking the action is at least as great as the extra cost. The benefit of taking any action minus the cost of taking the action is called the *economic surplus* from that action. Hence, the Cost-Benefit Principle suggests that we take only those actions that create additional economic surplus.

Recap

Sprinkled throughout each chapter are Recap boxes that underscore and summarize the importance of the preceding material and key concept takeaways.

Worked Problem Videos

Brief videos work through end-of-chapter problems to aid in student understanding of core economic concepts and offer assistance with more challenging material. The videos are available as hints within Connect.

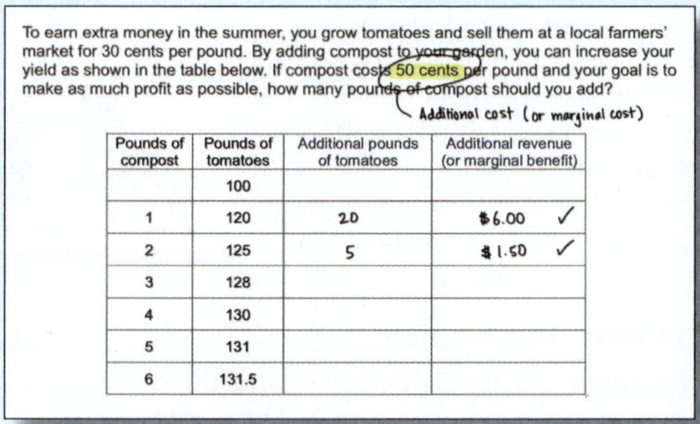

To earn extra money in the summer, you grow tomatoes and sell them at a local farmers' market for 30 cents per pound. By adding compost to your garden, you can increase your yield as shown in the table below. If compost costs 50 cents per pound and your goal is to make as much profit as possible, how many pounds of compost should you add?

Additional cost (or marginal cost)

Pounds of compost	Pounds of tomatoes	Additional pounds of tomatoes	Additional revenue (or marginal benefit)
	100		
1	120	20	$6.00 ✓
2	125	5	$1.50 ✓
3	128		
4	130		
5	131		
6	131.5		

LEARNING GLASS VIDEOS

Dozens of lecture videos featuring authors Kate Antonovics and Ori Heffetz utilize learning glass technology to provide you with an overview of important concepts. These videos can be accessed as resources within SmartBook® or as assignable content with questions via McGraw Hill Connect®.

ECONOMIC NATURALIST VIDEO SERIES

Commercial Banking: Why can it be more expensive to transfer funds between banks electronically than it is to send a check through the mail?

Comparative Advantage: Why are many products designed in one place yet assembled in another?

Cost Benefit 1: Why does the light come on when you open the refrigerator door but not when you open the freezer?

Cost Benefit 2: Why are child safety seats required in automobiles but not in airplanes?

Economy Strength and Currency Value: Does a strong currency imply a strong economy?

Human Capital: Why do almost all countries provide free education?

Inflation: Can inflation be too low?

Inflation and Cost of Living: Do official inflation figures overstate actual increases in our living costs?

Marginal Product of Labor: Why do female models earn so much more than male models?

Money and Its Uses: Is there such a thing as private, or communicably traded, money?

Saving: Why do American households save so little while Chinese households save so much?

Sources of Increasing Inequality: Why have the salaries of top earners been growing so much faster than everyone else's?

Supply and Demand: Why are rotisserie chickens less expensive than fresh chickens?

Tariffs: Why do consumers in the United States often pay more than double the world price for sugar?

The Demand for Money: Why does the average Argentine citizen hold more U.S. dollars than the average U.S. citizen?

ECONOMIC NATURALIST EXAMPLES

1.1 Why do many hardware manufacturers include more than $1,000 worth of "free" software with a computer selling for only slightly more than that?
1.2 Why don't auto manufacturers make cars without heaters?
1.3 Why do the keypad buttons on drive-up automated teller machines have Braille dots?
2.1 When the federal government implements a large pay increase for its employees, why do rents for apartments located near Washington Metro stations go up relative to rents for apartments located far away from Metro stations?
2.2 Why do major term papers go through so many more revisions today than in the 1970s?
2.3 Why do the prices of some goods, like airline tickets to Europe, go up during the months of heaviest consumption, while others, like sweet corn, go down?
2.4 Why was there a shortage of toilet paper during the COVID-19 pandemic?
4.1 Can nominal and real GDP ever move in different directions?
4.2 Every few years, there is a well-publicized battle in Congress over whether the minimum wage should be raised. Why do these heated legislative debates recur so regularly?
5.1 Why did West Germany and Japan recover so successfully from the devastation of World War II?
5.2 Why did U.S. labor productivity grow so rapidly in the late 1990s?
5.3 Why did medieval China stagnate economically?
5.4 Why do people work fewer hours today than their great-grandparents did?
5.5 Why do far fewer children complete high school in poor countries than in rich countries?
5.6 Why do almost all countries provide free public education?
6.1 Can new technology hurt workers?
6.2 How did the COVID-19 pandemic affect the demand for U.S. jobs?
7.1 How did many American households increase their wealth in the 1990s and 2000s while saving very little?
7.2 Why are racial and ethnic wealth disparities so persistent?
7.3 Why do Chinese households save so much?
7.4 Why do U.S. households save so little?
7.5 Why have real interest rates declined globally in recent decades?
8.1 From Ithaca Hours to Bitcoin: What is private money, communally created money, and open-source money?
8.2 Why did the banking panics of 1930–1933 reduce the national money supply?
8.3 What happens to national economies during banking crises?
8.4 Why did the U.S. stock market rise sharply and fall sharply in the 1990s and again in the 2000s?
8.5 Why is the U.S. trade deficit so large?
9.1 Do economic fluctuations affect presidential elections?
9.2 How was the 2020 recession called?
9.3 Why has the natural rate of unemployment in the United States declined?
9.4 Will new technologies eliminate menu costs?
9.5 Does military spending stimulate the economy?
9.6 Why did the federal government temporarily cut taxes in 2001, 2009, and 2020?
10.1 Why does the average Argentine hold more U.S. dollars than the average U.S. citizen?
10.2 How did the Fed respond to recession and the terrorist attacks in 2001?
10.3 Why did the Fed raise interest rates 17 times in a row between 2004 and 2006?
10.4 Why does news of inflation hurt the stock market?
10.5 Should the Federal Reserve respond to changes in asset prices?
10.6 What is the Taylor rule?
11.1 How did inflation get started in the United States in the 1960s?
11.2 Why did oil price increases cause U.S. inflation to escalate in the 1970s but not in the 2000s and 2010s?
11.3 Why was the United States able to experience rapid growth and low inflation in the latter part of the 1990s?
11.4 How was inflation conquered in the 1980s?
11.5 Can inflation be too low?

The following ancillaries are available for quick download and convenient access via the Instructor Resource material available through McGraw Hill Connect®.

Solutions Manual

Prepared by the authors with assistance from Peggy Dalton Verner, Frostburg State University, this manual provides detailed answers to the end-of-chapter review questions and problems.

Test Bank

The test bank has been carefully revised and reviewed for accuracy. Hundreds of questions have been categorized by chapter learning objectives, AACSB learning categories, Bloom's Taxonomy objectives, and level of difficulty. Select problems are now offered as an algorithmic alternative, providing even more variation.

Test Builder in Connect

Available within Connect, Test Builder is a cloud-based tool that enables instructors to format tests that can be printed or administered within an LMS. Test Builder offers a modern, streamlined interface for easy content configuration that matches course needs, without requiring a download.

Test Builder allows you to:

- access all test bank content from a particular title.
- easily pinpoint the most relevant content through robust filtering options.
- manipulate the order of questions or scramble questions and/or answers.
- pin questions to a specific location within a test.
- determine your preferred treatment of algorithmic questions.
- choose the layout and spacing.
- add instructions and configure default settings.

Test Builder provides a secure interface for better protection of content and allows for just-in-time updates to flow directly into assessments.

PowerPoints

Presentation slides contain a detailed, chapter-by-chapter review of the important ideas presented in the textbook, accompanied by animated graphs and slide notes. You can edit, print, or rearrange the slides to fit the needs of your course.

Remote Proctoring and Browser-Locking Capabilities

Mc Graw Hill connect® + proctorio

New remote proctoring and browser-locking capabilities, hosted by Proctorio within Connect, provide control of the assessment environment by enabling security options and verifying the identity of the student.

Seamlessly integrated within Connect, these services allow instructors to control students' assessment experience by restricting browser activity, recording students' activity, and verifying students are doing their own work.

Instant and detailed reporting gives instructors an at-a-glance view of potential academic integrity concerns, thereby avoiding personal bias and supporting evidence-based claims.

FOR MORE INFORMATION ABOUT CONNECT AND ITS AVAILABLE RESOURCES, REFER TO THE PAGES THAT FOLLOW.

Because learning changes everything.®

Connect Economics Asset Alignment with Bloom's Taxonomy

Principles of Macroeconomics: A Streamlined Approach, 4e

We Take Students Higher

As a learning science company we create content that supports higher order thinking skills. Within Connect®, we tag assessments accordingly so you can filter your search, assign it, and receive reporting on it. These content asset types can be associated with one or more levels of Bloom's Taxonomy.

The chart below shows a few of the key assignable economics assets with *McGraw Hill Connect* aligned with Bloom's Taxonomy. Take your students higher by assigning a variety of applications, moving them from simple memorization to concept application.

Higher Order Thinking Skills

	SmartBook 2.0	ECON Adaptive Math Prep	Videos	Exercises	Interactive Graphs	Application-Based Activities	ECON Everyday Current Events Blog*	Writing Assignment Plus
CREATE								✓
EVALUATE						✓	✓	✓
ANALYZE				✓	✓	✓	✓	✓
APPLY		✓	✓	✓	✓	✓	✓	✓
UNDERSTAND	✓	✓	✓	✓	✓	✓	✓	✓
REMEMBER	✓	✓	✓	✓	✓	✓	✓	✓

Lower Order Thinking Skills

* Outside of Connect.

SmartBook 2.0

Adaptively aids students to study more efficiently by highlighting where in the chapter to focus, asking review questions and pointing them to passages in the text until they understand. Assignable and assessable.

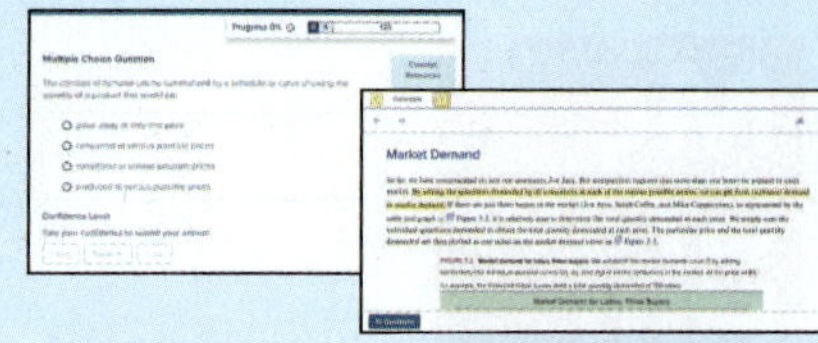

Adaptive Econ Prep

Math and graphing preparedness assignments help students refresh important prerequisite topics necessary to be successful in economics. New Adaptive Econ Prep Tool provides students just-in-time math remediation that is prerequisite to success in Principles of Economics courses and adapts to each student.

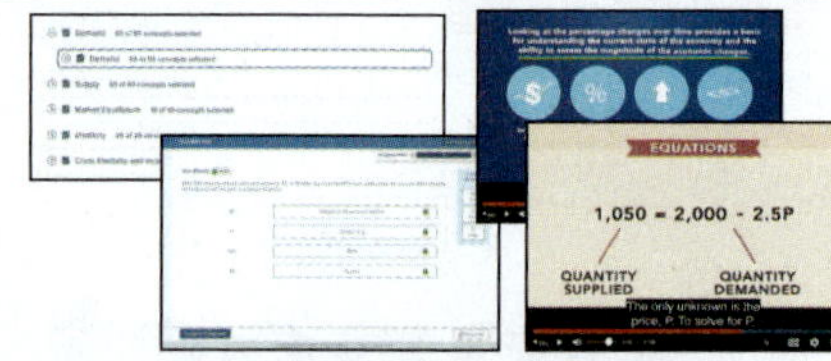

Videos

Worked examples and real-world application videos help students learn economics. **Learning Glass videos** reinforce challenging topics featuring the authors and innovative learning glass technology. **Economic Naturalist videos** bring examples to life showing interesting applications of economic concepts. **Worked Problem videos** work through select end-of-chapter questions for extra help and guidance through challenging material.

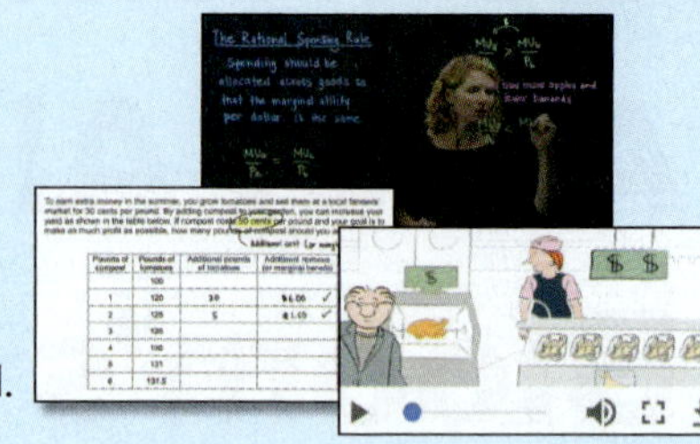

Exercises

Exercises with algorithmic variations provide ample opportunities for students to practice and hone quantitative skills. Graphing Exercises provide opportunities for students to draw, interact with, manipulate, and analyze graphs.

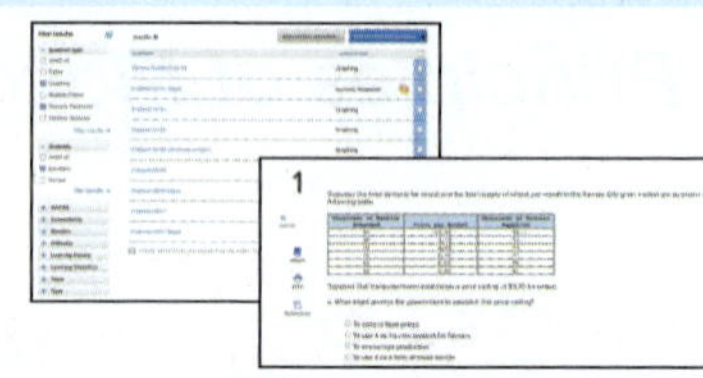

Interactive Graphs

Interactive Graphs provide visual displays of real data and economic concepts for students to manipulate. All graphs are accompanied by assignable assessment questions and feedback to guide students through the experience of learning to read and interpret graphs and data.

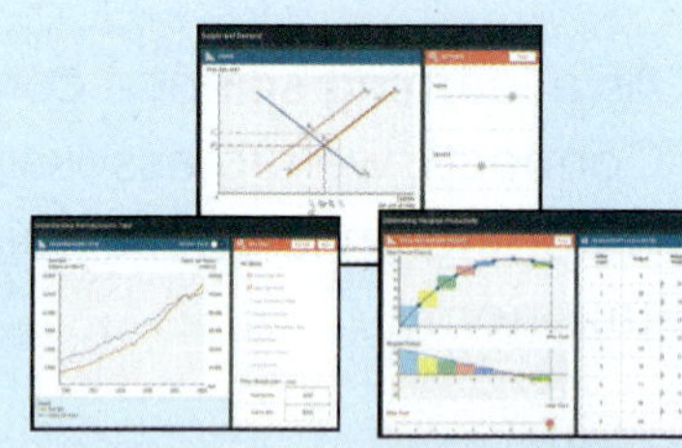

Application-Based Activities

Immersive real-life scenarios engage students and put them in the role of everyday economists. Students practice their economic thinking and problem-solving skills as they apply course concepts and see the implications of their decisions as they go. Each activity is designed as a 15-minute experience, unless students eagerly replay for a better outcome.

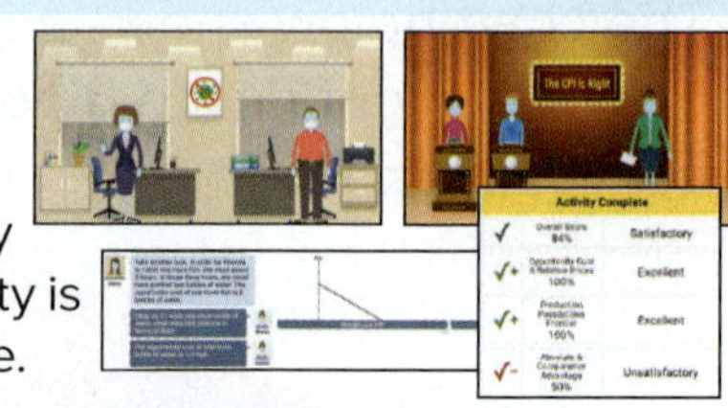

ECON Everyday Blog*

Our ECON Everyday blog saves instructors time bringing current, student-centered content into their course all semester long. Short articles, written for principles-level students, are tagged by topic to bring currency into your course. We also provide discussion questions to help you drive the conversation forward. Visit www.econeveryday.com and subscribe for updates. (*Outside of Connect.)

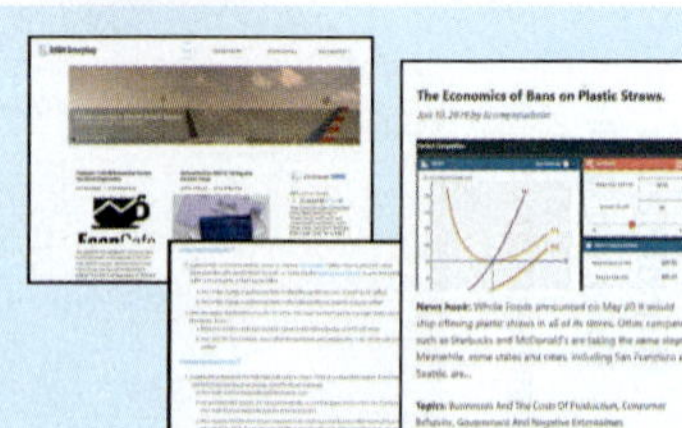

Writing Assignment Plus

Writing Assignment Plus delivers a learning experience that helps students improve their written communication skills and conceptual understanding. Faculty can assign, monitor, grade, and provide feedback on writing projects efficiently. Built-in grammar and writing review helps students improve writing quality while an originality check helps students correct central plagiarism before submission. End result? Improved workplace skills of writing in critical thinking.

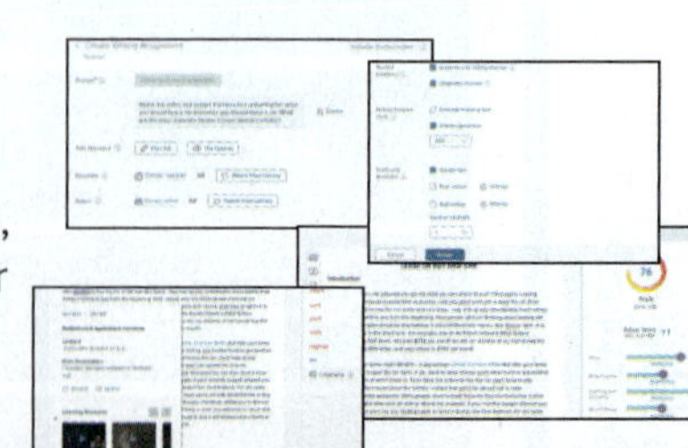

For more information, please visit: **www.mheducation.com/highered/economics**

SUPPORT AT every step

Students: Get Learning That Fits You

Effective tools for efficient studying

Connect is designed to make you more productive with simple, flexible, intuitive tools that maximize your study time and meet your individual learning needs. Get learning that works for you with Connect.

Study anytime, anywhere

Download the free ReadAnywhere app and access your online eBook or SmartBook 2.0 assignments when it's convenient, even if you're offline. And since the app automatically syncs with your eBook and SmartBook 2.0 assignments in Connect, all of your work is available every time you open it. Find out more at **www.mheducation.com/readanywhere**

"I really liked this app—it made it easy to study when you don't have your text-book in front of you."

- Jordan Cunningham, Eastern Washington University

Calendar: owattaphotos/Getty Images

Everything you need in one place

Your Connect course has everything you need—whether reading on your digital eBook or completing assignments for class, Connect makes it easy to get your work done.

Learning for everyone

McGraw Hill works directly with Accessibility Services Departments and faculty to meet the learning needs of all students. Please contact your Accessibility Services Office and ask them to email accessibility@mheducation.com, or visit **www.mheducation.com/about/accessibility** for more information.

Top: Jenner Images/Getty Images, Left: Hero Images/Getty Images, Right: Hero Images/Getty Images

COMPARISON GUIDE FOR FRANK, BERNANKE, ANTONOVICS, AND HEFFETZ PRODUCTS

Principles of Economics provides enhanced coverage and offers more topics and mathematical rigor. *Principles of Economics: A Streamlined Approach* is a stripped-down version of the big book featuring core content with a less-is-more approach. See which product is right for you!

Comparison Guide

<table>
<tr><th colspan="4">Principles of Economics, 8th edition</th><th colspan="4">Principles of Economics: A Streamlined Approach, 4th edition</th></tr>
<tr><th>Chapter Title</th><th>Econ 8e</th><th>Micro 8e</th><th>Macro 8e</th><th>Chapter Title</th><th>Streamlined 4e Econ</th><th>Streamlined 4e Micro</th><th>Streamlined 4e Macro</th></tr>
<tr><td>Thinking Like an Economist</td><td>1</td><td>1</td><td>1</td><td>Thinking Like an Economist</td><td>1</td><td>1</td><td>1</td></tr>
<tr><td>Comparative Advantage</td><td>2</td><td>2</td><td>2</td><td></td><td></td><td></td><td></td></tr>
<tr><td>Supply and Demand</td><td>3</td><td>3</td><td>3</td><td>Supply and Demand</td><td>2</td><td>2</td><td>2</td></tr>
<tr><td>Elasticity</td><td>4</td><td>4</td><td rowspan="2"></td><td rowspan="2">Demand and Elasticity</td><td rowspan="2">3</td><td rowspan="2">3</td><td rowspan="2"></td></tr>
<tr><td>Demand</td><td>5</td><td>5</td></tr>
<tr><td>Perfectly Competitive Supply</td><td>6</td><td>6</td><td></td><td>Perfectly Competitive Supply</td><td>4</td><td>4</td><td></td></tr>
<tr><td>Efficiency, Exchange, and the Invisible Hand in Action</td><td>7</td><td>7</td><td></td><td>Efficiency, Exchange, and the Invisible Hand in Action</td><td>5</td><td>5</td><td></td></tr>
<tr><td>Monopoly, Oligopoly, and Monopolistic Competition</td><td>8</td><td>8</td><td></td><td>Monopoly, Oligopoly, and Monopolistic Competition</td><td>6</td><td>6</td><td></td></tr>
<tr><td>Games and Strategic Behavior</td><td>9</td><td>9</td><td></td><td>Games and Strategic Behavior</td><td>7</td><td>7</td><td></td></tr>
<tr><td>An Introduction to Behavioral Economics</td><td>10</td><td>10</td><td></td><td>An Introduction to Behavioral Economics (NEW)</td><td>8</td><td>8</td><td></td></tr>
<tr><td>Externalities, Property Rights, and the Environment</td><td>11</td><td>11</td><td></td><td>Externalities and Property Rights</td><td>9</td><td>9</td><td></td></tr>
<tr><td>The Economics of Information</td><td>12</td><td>12</td><td rowspan="2"></td><td rowspan="2">Using Economics to Make Better Policy Choices</td><td rowspan="2">10</td><td rowspan="2">10</td><td rowspan="2"></td></tr>
<tr><td>Labor Markets, Poverty, and Income Distribution</td><td>13</td><td>13</td></tr>
<tr><td>Public Goods and Tax Policy</td><td>14</td><td>14</td><td></td><td></td><td></td><td></td><td></td></tr>
<tr><td>International Trade and Trade Policy</td><td>15</td><td>15</td><td>16</td><td>International Trade and Trade Policy</td><td>11</td><td>11</td><td>12</td></tr>
<tr><td>Macroeconomics: The Bird's-Eye View of the Economy</td><td>16</td><td></td><td>4</td><td>Macroeconomics: The Bird's Eye View of the Economy</td><td>12</td><td></td><td>3</td></tr>
<tr><td>Measuring Economic Activity: GDP and Unemployment</td><td>17</td><td></td><td>5</td><td rowspan="2">Measuring Economic Activity: GDP, Unemployment, and Inflation</td><td rowspan="2">13</td><td rowspan="2"></td><td rowspan="2">4</td></tr>
<tr><td>Measuring the Price Level and Inflation</td><td>18</td><td></td><td>6</td></tr>
<tr><td>Economic Growth, Productivity, and Living Standards</td><td>19</td><td></td><td>7</td><td>Economic Growth, Productivity, and Living Standards</td><td>14</td><td></td><td>5</td></tr>
<tr><td>The Labor Market: Workers, Wages, and Unemployment</td><td>20</td><td></td><td>8</td><td>The Labor Market: Workers, Wages, and Unemployment</td><td>15</td><td></td><td>6</td></tr>
<tr><td>Saving and Capital Formation</td><td>21</td><td></td><td>9</td><td>Saving and Capital Formation</td><td>16</td><td></td><td>7</td></tr>
<tr><td>Money, Prices, and the Federal Reserve</td><td>22</td><td></td><td>10</td><td rowspan="2">Money, the Federal Reserve, and Global Financial Markets</td><td rowspan="2">17</td><td rowspan="2"></td><td rowspan="2">8</td></tr>
<tr><td>Financial Markets and International Capital Flows</td><td>23</td><td></td><td>11</td></tr>
<tr><td>Short-Term Economic Fluctuations: An Introduction</td><td>24</td><td></td><td>12</td><td rowspan="2">Short-Term Economic Fluctuations and Fiscal Policy</td><td rowspan="2">18</td><td rowspan="2"></td><td rowspan="2">9</td></tr>
<tr><td>Spending and Output in the Short Run</td><td>25</td><td></td><td>13</td></tr>
<tr><td>Stabilizing the Economy: The Role of the Fed</td><td>26</td><td></td><td>14</td><td>Stabilizing the Economy: The Role of the Fed</td><td>19</td><td></td><td>10</td></tr>
<tr><td>Aggregate Demand, Aggregate Supply, and Inflation</td><td>27</td><td></td><td>15</td><td>Aggregate Demand, Aggregate Supply, and Inflation</td><td>20</td><td></td><td>11</td></tr>
<tr><td>Exchange Rates and the Open Economy</td><td>28</td><td></td><td>17</td><td>Exchange Rates and the Open Economy</td><td>21</td><td></td><td>13</td></tr>
</table>

BRIEF CONTENTS

CONTENTS

FOURTH EDITION

Principles of MACROECONOMICS

A STREAMLINED APPROACH

1

Thinking Like an Economist

LEARNING OBJECTIVES

After reading this chapter, you should be able to:

LO1 Explain why having more of any good thing necessarily requires having less of something else.

LO2 Explain and apply the Cost-Benefit Principle, which says that an action should be taken if, but only if, its benefit is at least as great as its cost.

LO3 Discuss three important pitfalls that occur when applying the Cost-Benefit Principle inconsistently.

LO4 Explain why if you want to predict people's behavior, a good place to start is by examining their incentives.

How many students are in your introductory economics class? Some classes have just 20 or so. Others average 35, 100, or 200 students. At some schools, introductory economics classes may have as many as 2,000 students. What size is best?

If cost were no object, the best size might be a single student. Think about it: the whole course, all term long, with just you and your professor! Everything could be custom-tailored to your own background and ability. You could cover the material at just the right pace. The tutorial format also would promote close communication and personal trust between you and your professor. And your grade would depend more heavily on what you actually learned than on your luck when taking multiple-choice exams. Let's suppose, for the sake of discussion, that students have been shown to learn best in the tutorial format.

Why, then, do so many introductory classes still have hundreds of students? The simple reason is that costs *do* matter. They matter not just to the university administrators who must build classrooms and pay faculty salaries, but also to *you*. The direct cost of providing you with your own personal introductory economics course might easily top $50,000. *Someone* has to pay these costs. In private universities, a large share of the cost would be recovered directly from higher tuition payments. In state universities, the burden would be split between higher tuition payments and higher tax payments. But, in either case, the course would be unaffordable for most students.

With larger classes, of course, the cost per student goes down. For example, an introductory economics course with 300 students might cost as little as $200 per student. But a class that large could easily compromise the quality of the learning environment. Compared to the custom tutorial format, however, it would be dramatically more affordable.

In choosing what size introductory economics course to offer, then, university administrators confront a classic economic trade-off. In making the class larger, they risk lowering the quality of instruction—a bad thing. At the same time, they reduce costs and hence the tuition students must pay—a good thing.

Are small classes "better" than large ones?

economics the study of how people make choices under conditions of scarcity and of the results of those choices for society

In this chapter, we'll introduce some simple ideas that will help you understand and explain patterns of behavior you observe in the world around you. These principles also will help you avoid three pitfalls that plague decision makers in everyday life.

ECONOMICS: STUDYING CHOICE IN A WORLD OF SCARCITY

Even in rich societies like the United States, *scarcity* is a fundamental fact of life. There is never enough time, money, or energy to do everything we want to do or have everything we'd like to have. **Economics** is the study of how people make choices under conditions of scarcity and of the results of those choices for society.

In the class-size example just discussed, a motivated economics student might definitely prefer to be in a class of 20 rather than a class of 100, everything else being equal. But other things, of course, are not equal. Students can enjoy the benefits of having smaller classes, but only at the price of having less money for other activities. The student's choice inevitably will come down to the relative importance of competing activities.

That such trade-offs are widespread and important is one of the core principles of economics. Although we have boundless needs and wants, the resources available to us are limited. So having more of one good thing usually means having less of another.

Inherent in the idea of a trade-off is the fact that choice involves compromise between competing interests. Economists resolve such trade-offs by using cost-benefit analysis, which is based on the disarmingly simple principle that an action should be taken if, and only if, its benefits exceed its costs. We call this statement the *Cost-Benefit Principle,* a core principle of economics.

With this principle in mind, let's think about our class-size question again. Imagine that classrooms come in only two sizes—100-seat lecture halls and 20-seat classrooms—and that your university currently offers introductory economics courses to classes of 100 students. Question: Should administrators reduce the class size to 20 students? Answer: Reduce if, and only if, the value of the improvement in instruction outweighs its additional cost.

This rule sounds simple. But to apply it we need some way to measure the relevant costs and benefits, a task that's often difficult in practice. If we make a few simplifying assumptions, however, we can see how the analysis might work. On the cost side, the primary expense of reducing class size from 100 to 20 is that we'll now need five professors instead of just one. We'll also need five smaller classrooms rather than a single big one, and this too may add slightly to the expense of the move. Let's suppose that classes with 20 cost $1,000 per student more than those with 100. Should administrators switch to the smaller class size? If they apply the Cost-Benefit Principle, they will realize that *doing so makes sense only if the value of attending the smaller class is at least $1,000 per student greater than the value of attending the larger class.*

Would you (or your family) be willing to pay an extra $1,000 for a smaller class? If not, and if other students feel the same way, then sticking with the larger class size makes sense. But if you and others would be willing to pay the extra tuition, then reducing the class size makes good economic sense.

Notice that the "best" class size, from an economic point of view, will generally not be the same as the "best" size from the point of view of an educational psychologist. That's because the economic definition of "best" takes into account both the benefits *and* the costs of different class sizes. The psychologist ignores costs and looks only at the learning benefits of different class sizes.

In practice, of course, different people feel differently about the value of smaller classes. People with high incomes, for example, tend to be willing to pay more for the advantage. That helps explain why average class size is smaller, and tuition higher, at private schools whose students come predominantly from high-income families.

The cost-benefit framework for thinking about the class-size problem also suggests a possible reason for the gradual increase in average class size that has been taking place in American colleges and universities. During the last 30 years, professors' salaries have risen sharply, making smaller classes more costly. During the same period, median family income—and hence the willingness to pay for smaller classes—has remained roughly constant. When the cost of offering smaller classes goes up but willingness to pay for smaller classes does not, universities shift to larger class sizes.

Chip Somodevilla/Getty Images

If Jeff Bezos saw a $100 bill lying on the sidewalk, would it be worth his time to pick it up?

Scarcity and the trade-offs that result also apply to resources other than money. Jeff Bezos is one of the richest people on Earth. His wealth is estimated at more than $180 billion. That's more than the combined wealth of the poorest 54 percent of Americans. Bezos could buy more houses, cars, vacations, and other consumer goods than he could possibly use. Yet he, like the rest of us, has only 24 hours each day and a limited amount of energy. So even he confronts trade-offs. Any activity he pursues—whether it be building his business empire or redecorating his mansion—uses up time and energy that he could otherwise spend on other things. Indeed, someone once calculated that the value of Bezos's time is so great that pausing to pick up a $100 bill from the sidewalk simply wouldn't be worth his while.

APPLYING THE COST-BENEFIT PRINCIPLE

In studying choice under scarcity, we'll usually begin with the premise that people are **rational,** which means they have well-defined goals and try to fulfill them as best they can. The Cost-Benefit Principle is a fundamental tool for the study of how rational people make choices.

rational person someone with well-defined goals who tries to fulfill those goals as best he or she can

As in the class-size example, often the only real difficulty in applying the cost-benefit rule is to come up with reasonable measures of the relevant benefits and costs. Only in rare instances will exact dollar measures be conveniently available. But the cost-benefit framework can lend structure to your thinking even when no relevant market data are available.

To illustrate how we proceed in such cases, the following example asks you to decide whether to perform an action whose cost is described only in vague, qualitative terms.

EXAMPLE 1.1 Comparing Costs and Benefits

Should you walk downtown to save $10 on a $25 wireless keyboard?

Imagine you are about to buy a $25 wireless keyboard at the nearby campus store when a friend tells you that the same keyboard is on sale at a downtown store for only $15. If the downtown store is a 30-minute walk away, where should you buy the keyboard?

The Cost-Benefit Principle tells us that you should buy it downtown if the benefit of doing so exceeds the cost. The benefit of taking any action is the dollar value of everything you gain by taking it. Here, the benefit of buying downtown is exactly $10, because that's the amount you'll save on the price of the keyboard. The cost of taking any action is the dollar value of everything you give up by taking it. Here, the cost of buying downtown is the dollar value you assign to the time and trouble it takes to make the trip. But how do we estimate that value?

One way is to perform the following hypothetical auction. Imagine that a stranger has offered to pay you to do an errand that involves the same walk downtown (perhaps to drop off a package for her at the post office). If she offered you a payment of, say, $1,000, would you accept? If so, we know that your cost of walking downtown and back must be less than $1,000. Now imagine her offer being reduced in small increments until you finally refuse the last offer. For example, if you'd agree to walk downtown and back for $9 but not for $8.99, then your cost of making the trip is $9. In this case, you should buy the keyboard downtown because the $10 you'll save (your benefit) is greater than your $9 cost of making the trip.

But suppose your cost of making the trip had been greater than $10. In that case, your best bet would have been to buy the keyboard from the nearby campus store. Confronted with this choice, different people may choose differently, depending on how costly they think it is to make the trip downtown. But although there is no uniquely correct choice, most people who are asked what they would do in this situation say they would buy the keyboard downtown.

Economic Surplus

economic surplus the benefit of taking an action minus its cost

Suppose that in Example 1.1 your "cost" of making the trip downtown was $9. Compared to the alternative of buying the keyboard at the campus store, buying it downtown resulted in an **economic surplus** of $1, the difference between the benefit of making the trip and its cost. In general, your goal as an economic decision maker is to choose those actions that generate the largest possible economic surplus. This means taking all actions that yield a positive total economic surplus, which is just another way of restating the Cost-Benefit Principle.

Note that the fact that your best choice was to buy the keyboard downtown doesn't imply that you *enjoy* making the trip, any more than choosing a large class means that you prefer large classes to small ones. It simply means that the trip is less unpleasant than the prospect of paying $10 extra for the keyboard. Once again, you've faced a trade-off. In this case, the choice was between a cheaper keyboard and the free time gained by avoiding the trip.

Opportunity Cost

opportunity cost the value of what must be forgone to undertake an activity

Of course, your mental auction could have produced a different outcome. Suppose, for example, that the time required for the trip is the only time you have left to study for a difficult test the next day. Or suppose you are watching one of your favorite shows on Netflix, or that you are tired and would love a short nap. In such cases, we say that the **opportunity cost** of making the trip—that is, the value of what you must sacrifice to walk downtown and back—is high and you are more likely to decide against making the trip.

Strictly speaking, your opportunity cost of engaging in an activity is the value of everything you must sacrifice to engage in it. For instance, if seeing a movie requires not only that you buy a $10 ticket, but also that you give up a $20 dogwalking job that you would have been willing to do for free, then the opportunity cost of seeing the film is $30.

Under this definition, *all* costs—both implicit and explicit—are opportunity costs. Unless otherwise stated, we will adhere to this strict definition.

We must warn you, however, that some economists use the term *opportunity cost* to refer only to the implicit value of opportunities forgone. Thus, in the example just discussed, these economists wouldn't include the $10 ticket price when calculating the opportunity cost of seeing the film. But virtually all economists would agree that your opportunity cost of not doing the dogwalking job is $20.

In the previous example, if watching another hour of your favorite show on Netflix is the most valuable opportunity that conflicts with the trip downtown, the opportunity cost of making the trip is the dollar value you place on pursuing that opportunity. It is the largest amount you'd be willing to pay to avoid watching your show at another time. Note that the opportunity cost of making the trip is not the combined value of *all* possible activities you could have pursued, but only the value of your *best* alternative—the one you would have chosen had you not made the trip.

Throughout the text we'll pose self-tests like the one that follows. You'll find that pausing to answer them will help you master key concepts in economics. Because doing these self-tests isn't very costly (indeed, many students report that they're actually fun), the Cost-Benefit Principle indicates that it's well worth your while to do them.

SELF-TEST 1.1

You would again save $10 by buying the wireless keyboard downtown rather than at the campus store, but your cost of making the trip is now $12, not $9. By how much would your economic surplus be smaller if you bought the keyboard downtown rather than at the campus store?

The Role of Economic Models

Economists use the Cost-Benefit Principle as an abstract model of how an idealized rational individual would choose among competing alternatives. (By "abstract model" we mean a simplified description that captures the essential elements of a situation and allows us to analyze them in a logical way.) A computer model of a complex phenomenon like climate change, which must ignore many details and includes only the major forces at work, is an example of an abstract model.

Noneconomists are sometimes harshly critical of the economist's cost-benefit model on the grounds that people in the real world never conduct hypothetical mental auctions before deciding whether to make trips downtown. But this criticism betrays a fundamental misunderstanding of how abstract models can help explain and predict human behavior. Economists know perfectly well that people don't conduct hypothetical mental auctions when they make simple decisions. All the Cost-Benefit Principle really says is that a rational decision is one that is explicitly or implicitly based on a weighing of costs and benefits.

Most of us make sensible decisions most of the time, without being consciously aware that we are weighing costs and benefits, just as most people ride a bike without being consciously aware of what keeps them from falling. Through trial and error, we gradually learn what kinds of choices tend to work best in different contexts, just as bicycle riders internalize the relevant laws of physics, usually without being conscious of them.

Even so, learning the explicit principles of cost-benefit analysis can help us make better decisions, just as knowing about physics can help in learning to ride a bicycle. For instance, when a young economist was teaching his oldest son to ride a bike, he followed the time-honored tradition of running alongside the bike and holding onto his son, then giving him a push and hoping for the best. After several hours and painfully skinned elbows and knees, his son finally got it. A year later, someone pointed out that the trick to riding a bike is to turn slightly in whichever direction the bike is leaning. Of course! The economist passed this information along to his second son, who learned to ride almost instantly. Just as knowing a little physics can help you learn to ride a bike, knowing a little economics can help you make better decisions.

RECAP

COST-BENEFIT ANALYSIS

Scarcity is a basic fact of economic life. Because of it, having more of one good thing almost always means having less of another. The *Cost-Benefit Principle* holds that an individual (or a firm or a society) should take an action if, and only if, the extra benefit from taking the action is at least as great as the extra cost. The benefit of taking any action minus the cost of taking the action is called the *economic surplus* from that action. Hence, the Cost-Benefit Principle suggests that we take only those actions that create additional economic surplus.

THREE IMPORTANT DECISION PITFALLS[1]

Rational people will apply the Cost-Benefit Principle most of the time, although probably in an intuitive and approximate way, rather than through explicit and precise calculation. Knowing that rational people tend to compare costs and benefits enables economists to predict their likely behavior. As noted earlier, for example, we can predict that students from wealthy families are more likely than others to attend colleges that offer small classes. (Again, while the cost of small classes is the same for all families, their benefit, as measured by what people are willing to pay for them, tends to be higher for wealthier families.)

Yet researchers have identified situations in which people tend to apply the Cost-Benefit Principle inconsistently. In these situations, the Cost-Benefit Principle may not predict behavior accurately. But it proves helpful in another way, by identifying specific strategies for avoiding bad decisions.

Pitfall 1: Measuring Costs and Benefits as Proportions Rather Than Absolute Dollar Amounts

As the next example makes clear, even people who seem to know they should weigh the pros and cons of the actions they are contemplating sometimes don't have a clear sense of how to measure the relevant costs and benefits.

EXAMPLE 1.2 **Comparing Costs and Benefits**

Should you walk downtown to save $10 on a $2,020 laptop computer?

You are about to buy a $2,020 laptop computer at the nearby campus store when a friend tells you that the same computer is on sale at a downtown store for only $2,010. If the downtown store is half an hour's walk away, where should you buy the computer?

Assuming that the laptop is light enough to carry without effort, the structure of this example is exactly the same as that of Example 1.1. The only difference is that the price of the laptop is dramatically higher than the price of the wireless keyboard. As before, the benefit of buying downtown is the dollar amount you'll save, namely, $10. And because it's exactly the same trip, its cost also must be the

[1]The examples in this section are inspired by the pioneering research of Daniel Kahneman and the late Amos Tversky. Kahneman was awarded the 2002 Nobel Prize in Economics for his efforts to integrate insights from psychology into economics. You can read more about this work in Kahneman's brilliant 2011 book, *Thinking Fast and Slow* (New York: Macmillan).

same as before. So if you are perfectly rational, you should make the same decision in both cases. Yet when people are asked what they would do in these situations, the overwhelming majority say they'd walk downtown to buy the keyboard but would buy the laptop at the campus store. When asked to explain, most of them say something like, "The trip was worth it for the keyboard because you save 40 percent, but not worth it for the laptop because you save only $10 out of $2,020."

This is faulty reasoning. The benefit of the trip downtown is not the *proportion* you save on the original price. Rather, it is the *absolute dollar amount* you save. The benefit of walking downtown to buy the laptop is $10, exactly the same as for the wireless keyboard. And because the cost of the trip must also be the same in both cases, the economic surplus from making both trips must be exactly the same. That means that a rational decision maker would make the same decision in both cases. Yet, as noted, most people choose differently.

The pattern of faulty reasoning in the decision just discussed is one of several decision pitfalls to which people are often prone. In the discussion that follows, we will identify two additional decision pitfalls. In some cases, people ignore costs or benefits that they ought to take into account. On other occasions they are influenced by costs or benefits that are irrelevant.

SELF-TEST 1.2

Which is more valuable: saving $100 on a $2,000 plane ticket to Tokyo or saving $90 on a $200 plane ticket to Chicago?

Pitfall 2: Ignoring Implicit Costs

Sherlock Holmes, Arthur Conan Doyle's legendary detective, was successful because he saw details that most others overlooked. In *Silver Blaze*, Holmes is called on to investigate the theft of an expensive racehorse from its stable. A Scotland Yard inspector assigned to the case asks Holmes whether some particular aspect of the crime requires further study. "Yes," Holmes replies, and describes "the curious incident of the dog in the nighttime." "The dog did nothing in the nighttime,"[2] responds the puzzled inspector. But, as Holmes realized, that was precisely the problem! The watchdog's failure to bark when Silver Blaze was stolen meant that the watchdog knew the thief. This clue ultimately proved the key to unraveling the mystery.

Just as we often don't notice when a dog fails to bark, many of us tend to overlook the implicit value of activities that fail to happen. As discussed earlier, however, intelligent decisions require taking the value of forgone opportunities properly into account.

The opportunity cost of an activity, once again, is the value of all that must be forgone in order to engage in that activity. If buying a wireless keyboard downtown means not watching another hour of your favorite show on Netflix, then the value to you of watching the show is an implicit cost of the trip. Many people make bad decisions because they tend to ignore the value of such forgone opportunities. To avoid overlooking implicit costs, economists often translate questions like "Should I walk downtown?" into ones like "Should I walk downtown or watch another hour of my favorite show?"

Implicit costs are like dogs that fail to bark in the night. Many of us tend to overlook activities that fail to happen.

[2]Arthur Conan Doyle, "The Adventure of Silver Blaze," *The Memoirs of Sherlock Holmes* (London: George Newnes Ltd., 1893).

EXAMPLE 1.3 Implicit Cost

Should you use your frequent-flyer coupon to fly to Cancun for spring break?

With spring break only a week away, you are still undecided about whether to go to Cancun with a group of classmates at the University of Iowa. The round-trip airfare from Cedar Rapids is $500, but you have a frequent-flyer coupon you could use for the trip. All other relevant costs for the vacation week at the beach total exactly $1,000. The most you would be willing to pay for the Cancun vacation is $1,350. That amount is your benefit of taking the vacation. Your only alternative use for your frequent-flyer coupon is for a trip to Boston the weekend after spring break to attend your brother's wedding. (Your coupon expires shortly thereafter.) If the Cedar Rapids–Boston round-trip airfare is $400, should you use your frequent-flyer coupon to fly to Cancun for spring break?

The Cost-Benefit Principle tells us that you should go to Cancun if the benefits of the trip exceed its costs. If not for the complication of the frequent-flyer coupon, solving this problem would be a straightforward matter of comparing your benefit from the week at the beach to the sum of all relevant costs. And because your airfare and other costs would add up to $1,500, or $150 more than your benefit from the trip, you would not go to Cancun.

But what about the possibility of using your frequent-flyer coupon to make the trip? Using it for that purpose might make the flight to Cancun seem free, suggesting you'd reap an economic surplus of $350 by making the trip. But doing so also would mean you'd have to fork over $400 for your airfare to Boston. So the implicit cost of using your coupon to go to Cancun is really $400. If you use it for that purpose, the trip still ends up being a loser because the cost of the vacation, $1,400, exceeds the benefit by $50. In cases like these, you're much more likely to decide sensibly if you ask yourself, "Should I use my frequent-flyer coupon for this trip or save it for an upcoming trip?"

Bkindler/E+/Getty Images

Is your flight to Cancun "free" if you travel on a frequent-flyer coupon?

We cannot emphasize strongly enough that the key to using the Cost-Benefit Principle correctly lies in recognizing precisely what taking a given action prevents us from doing. Self-Test 1.3 illustrates this point by modifying the details of Example 1.3 slightly.

SELF-TEST 1.3

Refer to given information in Example 1.3, but this time your frequent-flyer coupon expires in a week, so your only chance to use it will be for the Cancun trip. Should you use your coupon?

Pitfall 3: Failing to Think at the Margin

When deciding whether to take an action, the only relevant costs and benefits are those that would occur as a result of taking the action. Sometimes people are influenced by costs they ought to ignore. Other times they compare the wrong costs and benefits. *The only costs that should influence a decision about whether to take an action are those we can avoid by not taking the action. Similarly, the only benefits we should consider are those that would not occur unless the action were taken.* As a practical matter, however, many decision makers appear to be influenced by costs or benefits that would have occurred no matter what. Thus, people are often influenced by **sunk costs**—costs that are beyond recovery at the moment a decision is made. For example, money spent on a nontransferable, nonrefundable airline ticket is a sunk cost.

sunk cost a cost that is beyond recovery at the moment a decision must be made

As the following example illustrates, sunk costs must be borne *whether or not an action is taken,* so they are irrelevant to the decision of whether to take the action.

EXAMPLE 1.4 Sunk Cost

How much should you eat at an all-you-can-eat restaurant?

Sangam, an Indian restaurant in Philadelphia, offers an all-you-can-eat lunch buffet for $10. Customers pay $10 at the door, and no matter how many times they refill their plates, there is no additional charge. One day, as a goodwill gesture, the owner of the restaurant tells 20 randomly selected guests that they can eat at the all-you-can-eat buffet for free. The remaining guests pay the usual price. If all diners are rational, will those who are able to eat at the buffet for free consume a different amount of food, on average, than those who have to pay $10 for the buffet?

Having eaten their first helping, diners in each group confront the following question: "Should I go back for another helping?" For rational diners, if the benefit of doing so exceeds the cost, the answer is yes; otherwise it is no. Note that at the moment of decision, the $10 charge for the lunch is a sunk cost. Those who paid it have no way to recover it. Thus, for both groups, the (extra) cost of another helping is exactly zero. And because the people who received the free lunch were chosen at random, there's no reason their appetites or incomes should be any different from those of other diners. The benefit of another helping thus should be the same, on average, for people in both groups. And because their respective costs and benefits are the same, the two groups should eat the same number of helpings, on average.

Psychologists and economists have experimental evidence, however, that people in such groups do *not* eat similar amounts.[3] In particular, those who have to pay for the all-you-can-eat buffet tend to eat substantially more than those for whom the buffet is free. People in the former group somehow seem determined to "get their money's worth." Their implicit goal is apparently to minimize the average cost per bite of the food they eat. Yet minimizing average cost is not a particularly sensible objective. The irony is that diners who are determined to get their money's worth usually end up eating too much.

The fact that the cost-benefit criterion failed the test of prediction in Example 1.4 does nothing to invalidate its advice about what people *should* do. If you are letting sunk costs influence your decisions, you can do better by changing your behavior.

In addition to paying attention to costs and benefits that should be ignored, people often use incorrect measures of the relevant costs and benefits. This error often occurs when we must choose the *extent* to which an activity should be pursued (as opposed to choosing whether to pursue it at all). We can apply the Cost-Benefit Principle in such situations by repeatedly asking the question, "Should I increase the level at which I am currently pursuing the activity?"

marginal cost the increase in total cost that results from carrying out one additional unit of an activity

marginal benefit the increase in total benefit that results from carrying out one additional unit of an activity

In attempting to answer this question, the focus should always be on the benefit and cost of an *additional* unit of activity. To emphasize this focus, economists refer to the cost of an additional unit of activity as its **marginal cost.** Similarly, the benefit of an additional unit of the activity is its **marginal benefit.**

When the problem is to discover the proper level for an activity, the cost-benefit rule is to keep increasing the level as long as the marginal benefit of the activity

[3]See, for example, Richard Thaler, "Toward a Positive Theory of Consumer Choice," *Journal of Economic Behavior and Organization* 1, no. 1 (1980).

exceeds its marginal cost. As the following example illustrates, however, people often fail to apply this rule correctly.

EXAMPLE 1.5 Focusing on Marginal Costs and Benefits

Should SpaceX expand its launch program from four launches per year to five?

SpaceX accountants have estimated that the gains from the company's jumbo rocket launch program are currently $24 billion a year (an average of $6 billion per launch) and that its costs are currently $20 billion a year (an average $5 billion per launch). On the basis of these estimates, they have recommended that the company increase its number of launches. Should SpaceX CEO Elon Musk follow their advice?

average cost the total cost of undertaking *n* units of an activity divided by *n*

average benefit the total benefit of undertaking *n* units of an activity divided by *n*

To discover whether the advice makes economic sense, we must compare the marginal cost of a launch to its marginal benefit. The accountants' estimates, however, tell us only the **average cost** and **average benefit** of the program. These are, respectively, the total cost of the program divided by the number of launches and the total benefit divided by the number of launches.

Knowing the average benefit and average cost per launch for all rockets launched thus far is simply not useful for deciding whether to expand the program. Of course, the average cost of the launches undertaken so far *might* be the same as the cost of adding another launch. But it also might be either higher or lower than the marginal cost of a launch. The same holds true regarding average and marginal benefits.

Suppose, for the sake of discussion, that the benefit of an additional launch is in fact the same as the average benefit per launch thus far, $6 billion. Should SpaceX add another launch? Not if the cost of adding the fifth launch would be more than $6 billion. And the fact that the average cost per launch is only $5 billion simply does not tell us anything about the marginal cost of the fifth launch.

Suppose, for example, that the relationship between the number of rockets launched and the total cost of the program is as described in Table 1.1. The average cost per launch (third column) when there are four launches would then be $20 billion/4 = $5 billion per launch, just as the accountants reported. But note in the second column of the table that adding a fifth launch would raise costs from $20 billion to $32 billion, making the marginal cost of the fifth launch $12 billion. So if the benefit of an additional launch is $6 billion, increasing the number of launches from four to five would make absolutely no economic sense.

TABLE 1.1
How Total Cost Varies with the Number of Launches

Number of launches	Total cost ($ billions)	Average cost ($ billion/launch)
0	0	0
1	3	3
2	7	3.5
3	12	4
4	20	5
5	32	6.4

The following example illustrates how to apply the *Cost-Benefit Principle* correctly in this case.

EXAMPLE 1.6 Focusing on Marginal Costs and Benefits

How many rockets should SpaceX launch?

SpaceX must decide how many rockets to launch. The benefit of each launch is estimated to be $6 billion, and the total cost of the program again depends on the number of launches as shown in Table 1.1. How many rockets should SpaceX launch?

SpaceX should continue to launch its jumbo rockets as long as the marginal benefit of the program exceeds its marginal cost. In this example, the marginal benefit is constant at $6 billion per launch, regardless of the number of rockets launched. SpaceX should thus keep launching rockets as long as the marginal cost per launch is less than or equal to $6 billion.

Applying the definition of marginal cost to the total cost entries in the second column of Table 1.1 yields the marginal cost values in the third column of Table 1.2. (Because marginal cost is the change in total cost that results when we change the number of launches by one, we place each marginal cost entry midway between the rows showing the corresponding total cost entries.) Thus, for example, the marginal cost of increasing the number of launches from one to two is $4 billion, the difference between the $7 billion total cost of two launches and the $3 billion total cost of one launch.

TABLE 1.2
How Marginal Cost Varies with the Number of Launches

Number of launches	Total cost ($ billions)	Marginal cost ($ billion/launch)
0	0	
		3
1	3	
		4
2	7	
		5
3	12	
		8
4	20	
		12
5	32	

As we see from a comparison of the $6 billion marginal benefit per launch with the marginal cost entries in the third column of Table 1.2, the first three launches satisfy the cost-benefit test, but the fourth and fifth launches do not. SpaceX should thus launch three rockets.

SELF-TEST 1.4

If the marginal benefit of each launch had been not $6 billion but $9 billion, how many rockets should SpaceX have launched?

The cost-benefit framework emphasizes that the only relevant costs and benefits in deciding whether to pursue an activity further are *marginal* costs and benefits—measures that correspond to the *increment* of activity under consideration. In many contexts, however, people seem more inclined to compare the *average* cost and benefit of the activity. As Example 1.5 made clear, increasing the level of an activity may not be justified, even though its average benefit at the current level is significantly greater than its average cost.

SELF-TEST 1.5

Should a basketball team's best player take all the team's shots?

A professional basketball team has a new assistant coach. The assistant notices that one player scores on a higher percentage of her shots than other players. Based on this information, the assistant suggests to the head coach that the star player take *all* the shots. That way, the assistant reasons, the team will score more points and win more games.

On hearing this suggestion, the head coach fires her assistant for incompetence. What was wrong with the assistant's idea?

RECAP

THREE IMPORTANT DECISION PITFALLS

1. **The pitfall of measuring costs or benefits proportionally.** Many decision makers treat a change in cost or benefit as insignificant if it constitutes only a small proportion of the original amount. Absolute dollar amounts, not proportions, should be employed to measure costs and benefits.
2. **The pitfall of ignoring implicit costs.** When performing a cost-benefit analysis of an action, it is important to account for all relevant costs, including the implicit value of alternatives that must be forgone in order to carry out the action. A resource (such as a frequent-flyer coupon) may have a high implicit cost, even if you originally got it "for free," if its best alternative use has high value. The identical resource may have a low implicit cost, however, if it has no good alternative uses.
3. **The pitfall of failing to think at the margin.** When deciding whether to perform an action, the only costs and benefits that are relevant are those that would result from taking the action. It is important to ignore sunk costs—those costs that cannot be avoided even if the action isn't taken. Even though a ticket to a concert may have cost you $100, if you've already bought it and cannot sell it to anyone else, the $100 is a sunk cost and shouldn't influence your decision about whether to go to the concert. It's also important not to confuse average costs and benefits with marginal costs and benefits. Decision makers often have ready information about the total cost and benefit of an activity, and from these it's simple to compute the activity's average cost and benefit. A common mistake is to conclude that an activity should be increased if its average benefit exceeds its average cost. The Cost-Benefit Principle tells us that the level of an activity should be increased if, and only if, its *marginal* benefit exceeds its *marginal* cost.

Some costs and benefits, especially marginal costs and benefits and implicit costs, are important for decision making, while others, like sunk costs and average costs and benefits, are essentially irrelevant. This conclusion is implicit in our original statement of the Cost-Benefit Principle (an action should be taken if, and only if, the extra benefits of taking it exceed the extra costs).

NORMATIVE ECONOMICS VERSUS POSITIVE ECONOMICS

The examples discussed in the preceding section make the point that people *sometimes* choose irrationally. We must stress that our purpose in discussing these examples was not to suggest that people *generally* make irrational choices. On the contrary, most people appear to choose sensibly most of the time, especially when their decisions are important or familiar ones. The economist's focus on rational choice thus offers not only useful advice about making better decisions, but also a basis for predicting and explaining human behavior. We used the cost-benefit approach in this way when discussing how rising faculty salaries have led to larger class sizes. And as we will see, similar reasoning helps explain human behavior in virtually every other domain.

The Cost-Benefit Principle is an example of a **normative economic principle,** one that provides guidance about how we *should* behave. For example, according to the Cost-Benefit Principle, we should ignore sunk costs when making decisions about the future. As our discussion of the various decision pitfalls makes clear, however, the Cost-Benefit Principle is not always a **positive,** or **descriptive, economic principle,** one that describes how we actually *will* behave. As we saw, the Cost-Benefit Principle can be tricky to implement, and people sometimes fail to heed its prescriptions.

normative economic principle one that says how people should behave

positive (or **descriptive**) **economic principle** one that predicts how people will behave

That said, we stress that knowing the relevant costs and benefits surely does enable us to predict how people will behave much of the time. If the benefit of an action goes up, it is generally reasonable to predict that people will be more likely to take that action. And conversely, if the cost of an action goes up, the safest prediction will be that people will be less likely to take that action.

When the Cost-Benefit Principle helps us predict people's behavior, it also acts as a positive economic principle. The principle stresses that the relevant costs and benefits usually help us predict behavior, but at the same time does not insist that people behave rationally in each instance. For example, if the price of heating oil were to rise sharply, we would invoke the Cost-Benefit Principle to say that people *should* turn down their thermostats. And although some may not follow that advice, the Cost-Benefit Principle would also predict that average thermostat settings *will* in fact go down.

ECONOMICS: MICRO AND MACRO

By convention, we use the term **microeconomics** to describe the study of individual choices and of group behavior in individual markets. **Macroeconomics,** by contrast, is the study of the performance of national economies and of the policies that governments use to try to improve that performance. Macroeconomics tries to understand the determinants of such things as the national unemployment rate, the overall price level, and the total value of national output.

microeconomics the study of individual choice under scarcity and its implications for the behavior of prices and quantities in individual markets

macroeconomics the study of the performance of national economies and the policies that governments use to try to improve that performance

Our focus in this chapter is on issues that confront the individual decision maker, whether that individual confronts a personal decision, a family decision, a business decision, a government policy decision, or indeed any other type of decision. Further on, we'll consider economic models of groups of individuals such as all buyers or all sellers in a specific market. Later still we'll turn to broader economic issues and measures.

No matter which of these levels is our focus, however, our thinking will be shaped by the fact that, although economic needs and wants are effectively unlimited, the material and human resources that can be used to satisfy them are finite. Clear thinking about economic problems must therefore always take into account the idea of trade-offs—the idea that having more of one good thing usually means having less of another. Our economy and our society are shaped to a substantial degree by the choices people have made when faced with trade-offs.

THE APPROACH OF THIS TEXT

Choosing the number of students to register in each class is just one of many important decisions in planning an introductory economics course. Another concerns which topics to include on the course syllabus. There's a virtually inexhaustible set of issues that might be covered in an introductory course, but only limited time in which to cover them. There's no free lunch. Covering some inevitably means omitting others.

All textbook authors are forced to pick and choose. A textbook that covered *all* the issues would take up more than a whole floor of your campus library. It is our firm view that most introductory textbooks try to cover far too much. One reason that each of us was drawn to the study of economics is that a relatively short list of the discipline's core ideas can explain a great deal of the behavior and events we see in the world around us. So rather than cover a large number of ideas at a superficial level, our strategy is to focus on this short list of core ideas, returning to each entry again and again, in many different contexts. This strategy will enable you to internalize these ideas remarkably well in the brief span of a single course. And the benefit of learning a small number of important ideas well will far outweigh the cost of having to ignore a host of other, less important ones.

A second important element in our philosophy is a belief in the importance of active learning. In the same way that you can learn Spanish only by speaking and writing it, or tennis only by playing the game, you can learn economics only by *doing* economics. And because we want you to learn how to do economics, rather than just to read or listen passively as the authors or your instructor does economics, we'll make every effort to encourage you to stay actively involved.

For example, instead of just telling you about an idea, we'll usually first motivate the idea by showing you how it works in the context of a specific example. Often, these examples will be followed by self-tests for you to try, as well as applications that show the relevance of the idea to real life. Try working the self-tests *before* looking up the answers (which are at the back of the corresponding chapter).

Think critically about the applications: Do you see how they illustrate the point being made? Do they give you new insight into the issue? Work the problems at the end of the chapters and take extra care with those relating to points that you don't fully understand. Apply economic principles to the world around you. (We'll say more about this when we discuss economic naturalism below.) Finally, when you come across an idea or example that you find interesting, tell a friend about it. You'll be surprised to discover how much the mere act of explaining it helps you understand and remember the underlying principle. The more actively you can become engaged in the learning process, the more effective your learning will be.

ECONOMIC NATURALISM

With the rudiments of the cost-benefit framework under your belt, you are now in a position to become an "economic naturalist," someone who uses insights from economics to help make sense of observations from everyday life. People who have studied biology are able to observe and marvel at many details of nature that would otherwise have escaped their notice. For example, on a walk in the woods in early April, the novice may see only trees. In contrast, the biology student notices many different species of trees and understands why some are already in leaf while others still lie dormant. Likewise, the novice may notice that in some animal species males are much larger than females, but the biology student knows that pattern occurs only in species in which males take several mates. Natural selection favors larger males in those species because their greater size helps them prevail in the often bloody contests among males for access to females. In contrast, males tend to be roughly the same size as females in monogamous species, in which there is much less fighting for mates.

connect

▸ Visit your instructor's Connect course and access your eBook to view this video.

Why does the light come on when you open the refrigerator door but not when you open the freezer?

Learning a few simple economic principles broadens our vision in a similar way. It enables us to see the mundane details of ordinary human existence in a new light. Whereas the uninitiated often fail even to notice these details, the economic naturalist not only sees them, but also becomes actively engaged in the attempt to understand them. Let's consider a few examples of questions economic naturalists might pose for themselves.

The Economic Naturalist 1.1

Why do many hardware manufacturers include more than $1,000 worth of "free" software with a computer selling for only slightly more than that?

The software industry is different from many others in the sense that its customers care a great deal about product compatibility. When you and your classmates are working on a project together, for example, your task will be much simpler if you all use the same word-processing program. Likewise, an executive's life will be easier at tax time if her financial software is the same as her accountant's.

The implication is that the benefit of owning and using any given software program increases with the number of other people who use that same product. This unusual relationship gives the producers of the most popular programs an enormous advantage and often makes it hard for new programs to break into the market.

Recognizing this pattern, Intuit Corp. offered computer makers free copies of *Quicken*, its personal financial-management software. Computer makers, for their part, were only too happy to include the program because it made their new computers more attractive to buyers. *Quicken* soon became the standard for personal financial-management programs. By giving away free copies of the program, Intuit "primed the pump," creating an enormous demand for upgrades of *Quicken* and for more advanced versions of related software. Thus, *TurboTax*, Intuit's personal income-tax software, has become the standard for tax-preparation programs.

Inspired by this success story, other software developers have jumped onto the bandwagon. Most hardware now comes bundled with a host of free software programs. Some software developers are even rumored to *pay* computer makers to include their programs!

connect

▶ Visit your instructor's Connect course and access your eBook to view this video.

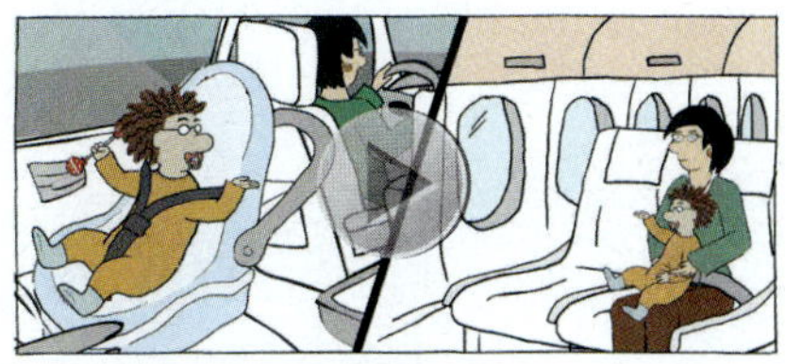

Why are child safety seats required in automobiles but not in airplanes?

The Economic Naturalist 1.1 illustrates a case in which the *benefit* of a product depends on the number of other people who own that product. As the next Economic Naturalist demonstrates, the *cost* of a product may also depend on the number of others who own it.

The Economic Naturalist 1.2

Why don't auto manufacturers make cars without heaters?

Virtually every new car sold in the United States today has a heater. But not every car has a satellite navigation system. Why this difference?

One might be tempted to answer that, although everyone *needs* a heater, people can get along without navigation systems. Yet heaters are of limited use in places like Hawaii and Southern California.

Although heaters cost extra money to manufacture and are not useful in all parts of the country, they do not cost *much* money and are useful on at least a few days each year in most parts of the country. As time passed and people's incomes grew, manufacturers found that people were ordering fewer and fewer cars without heaters. At some point it actually became cheaper to put heaters in *all* cars, rather than bear the administrative expense of making some cars with heaters and others without. No doubt a few buyers would still order a car without a heater if they could save some money in the process, but catering to these customers is just no longer worth it.

Similar reasoning explains why certain cars today cannot be purchased without a satellite navigation system. Buyers of the 2020 BMW 750i, for example, got one whether they wanted it or not. Most buyers of this car, which sells for more than $85,000, have high incomes, so the overwhelming majority of them would have chosen to order a navigation system had it been sold as an option. Because of the savings made possible when all cars are produced with the same equipment, it would have actually cost BMW more to supply cars for the few who would want them without navigation systems.

Buyers of the least-expensive makes of car have much lower incomes on average than BMW 750i buyers. Accordingly, most of them have more pressing alternative uses for their money than to buy navigation systems for their cars, and this explains why some inexpensive makes continue to offer navigation systems only as options. But as incomes continue to grow, new cars without navigation systems will eventually disappear.

The insights afforded by The Economic Naturalist 1.2 suggest an answer to the following strange question:

The Economic Naturalist 1.3

Why do the keypad buttons on drive-up automated teller machines have Braille dots?

Why do the keypad buttons on drive-up automated teller machines have Braille dots?

Braille dots on elevator buttons and on the keypads of walk-up automated teller machines enable blind people to participate more fully in the normal flow of daily activity. But even though blind people can do many remarkable things, they cannot drive automobiles on public roads. Why, then, do the manufacturers of automated teller machines install Braille dots on the machines at drive-up locations?

The answer to this riddle is that once the keypad molds have been manufactured, the cost of producing buttons with Braille dots is no higher than the cost of producing smooth buttons. Making both would require separate sets of molds and two different types of inventory. If the patrons of drive-up machines found buttons with Braille dots harder to use, there might be a reason to incur these extra costs. But since the dots pose no difficulty for sighted users, the best and cheapest solution is to produce only keypads with dots.

The preceding example was suggested by Cornell student Bill Tjoa, in response to the following assignment:

SELF-TEST 1.6

In 500 words or less, use cost-benefit analysis to explain some pattern of events or behavior you have observed in your own environment.

There is probably no more useful step you can take in your study of economics than to perform several versions of the assignment in Self-Test 1.6. Students who do so almost invariably become lifelong economic naturalists. Their mastery of economic concepts not only does not decay with the passage of time, but it actually grows stronger. We urge you, in the strongest possible terms, to make this investment!

SUMMARY

- Economics is the study of how people make choices under conditions of scarcity and of the results of those choices for society. Economic analysis of human behavior begins with the assumption that people are rational—that they have well-defined goals and try to achieve them as best they can. In trying to achieve their goals, people normally face trade-offs: Because material and human resources are limited, having more of one good thing means making do with less of some other good thing. *(LO1)*
- Our focus in this chapter has been on how rational people make choices among alternative courses of action. Our basic tool for analyzing these decisions is cost-benefit analysis. The Cost-Benefit Principle says that a person should take an action if, and only if, the benefit of that action is at least as great as its cost. The benefit of an action is defined as the largest dollar amount the person would be willing to pay in order to take the action. The cost of an action is defined as the dollar value of everything the person must give up in order to take the action. *(LO2)*
- In using the cost-benefit framework, we need not presume that people choose rationally all the time. Indeed, we identified three common pitfalls that plague decision makers in all walks of life: a tendency to treat small proportional changes as insignificant, a tendency to ignore implicit costs, and a tendency to fail to think at the margin—for example, by failing to ignore sunk costs or by failing to compare marginal costs and benefits. *(LO3)*
- Often the question is not whether to pursue an activity but rather how many units of it to pursue. In these cases, the rational person pursues additional units as long as the marginal benefit of the activity (the benefit from pursuing an additional unit of it) exceeds its marginal cost (the cost of pursuing an additional unit of it). *(LO4)*
- Microeconomics is the study of individual choices and of group behavior in individual markets, while macroeconomics is the study of the performance of national economics and of the policies that governments use to try to improve economic performance.

KEY TERMS

average benefit
average cost
economic surplus
economics
macroeconomics
marginal benefit
marginal cost
microeconomics
normative economic principle
opportunity cost
positive (or descriptive) economic principle
rational person
sunk cost

REVIEW QUESTIONS

1. A friend of yours on the tennis team says, "Private tennis lessons are definitely better than group lessons." Explain what you think she means by this statement. Then use the Cost-Benefit Principle to explain why private lessons are not necessarily the best choice for everyone. *(LO2)*
2. True or false: Your willingness to drive downtown to save $30 on a new appliance should depend on what fraction of the total selling price $30 is. Explain. *(LO3)*
3. Why might someone who is trying to decide whether to see a movie be more likely to focus on the $10 ticket price than on the $20 he or she would fail to earn by not dogwalking? *(LO3)*
4. Many people think of their air travel as being free when they use frequent-flyer coupons. Explain why

these people are likely to make wasteful travel decisions. *(LO3)*

5. Is the nonrefundable tuition payment you made to your university this semester a sunk cost? How would your answer differ if your university were to offer a full tuition refund to any student who dropped out of school during the first two months of the semester? *(LO3)*

PROBLEMS

1. Suppose your school is considering whether to spend $20 million building a new state-of-the-art recreation facility. All of the students agree that the existing facility is in disrepair and that a new facility would be much nicer. Despite this, however, when students are asked to vote on whether they would like the school to build the new recreation facility, over 78 percent vote no. Why might such a large fraction of students vote no even though they all agree that a new recreation facility would be much nicer than the existing one? *(LO1)*
2. Suppose the most you would be willing to pay to have a freshly washed car before going out on a date is $6. The smallest amount for which you would be willing to wash someone else's car is $3.50. You are going out this evening and your car is dirty. How much economic surplus would you receive from washing it? *(LO2)*
3. To earn extra money in the summer, you grow tomatoes and sell them at a local farmers' market for 30 cents per pound. By adding compost to your garden, you can increase your yield as shown in the accompanying table. If compost costs 50 cents per pound and your goal is to make as much profit as possible, how many pounds of compost should you add? *(LO2)*

Pounds of compost	Pounds of tomatoes
	100
1	120
2	125
3	128
4	130
5	131
6	131.5

4.* You and your friend Jamal have identical tastes. At 2 p.m., you go to the local Ticketmaster outlet and buy a nonrefundable $30 ticket to a basketball game to be played that night in Syracuse, 50 miles north of your home in Ithaca. Jamal plans to attend the same game, but because he cannot get to the Ticketmaster outlet, he plans to buy his ticket at the game. Tickets sold at the game cost only $25 because they carry no Ticketmaster surcharge. (Many people nonetheless pay the higher price at Ticketmaster, to be sure of getting good seats.) At 4 p.m., an unexpected snowstorm begins, making the prospect of the drive to Syracuse much less attractive than before (but ensuring the availability of good seats). If both you and Jamal are rational, is one of you more likely to attend the game than the other? *(LO2)*

5. Kenya is a mushroom farmer. She invests all her spare cash in additional mushrooms, which grow on otherwise useless land behind her barn. The mushrooms double in weight during their first year, after which time they are harvested and sold at a constant price per pound. Kenya's friend Fatima asks Kenya for a loan of $200, which she promises to repay after one year. How much interest will Fatima have to pay Kenya in order for Kenya to recover her opportunity cost of making the loan? Explain briefly. *(LO3)*
6. Suppose that in the last few seconds you devoted to question 1 on your physics exam you earned 4 extra points, while in the last few seconds you devoted to question 2 you earned 10 extra points. You earned a total of 48 and 12 points, respectively, on the two questions, and the total time you spent on each was the same. If you could take the exam again, how–if at all–should you reallocate your time between these questions? *(LO3)*
7. Monica and Rachel have the same preferences and incomes. Just as Monica arrived at the theater to see a play, she discovered that she had lost the $10 ticket she had purchased earlier. Rachel also just arrived at the theater planning to buy a ticket to see the same play when she discovered that she had lost a $10 bill from her wallet. If both Monica and Rachel are rational and both still have enough money to pay for a ticket, is one of them more likely than the other to go ahead and see the play anyway? *(LO3)*
8. Residents of your city are charged a fixed weekly fee of $6 for garbage collection. They are allowed to put out as many cans as they wish. The average household disposes of three cans of garbage per week under this plan. Now suppose that your city changes to a "tag" system. Each can of garbage to be collected must have a tag affixed to it. The tags cost $2 each and are not reusable. What effect do you think the introduction of

*Denotes more difficult problem.

the tag system will have on the total quantity of garbage collected in your city? Explain briefly. *(LO4)*

9. Once a week, Hector purchases a six-pack of cola and puts it in his refrigerator for his two children. He invariably discovers that all six cans are gone on the first day. Jin also purchases a six-pack of cola once a week for his two children, but unlike Hector, he tells them that each may drink no more than three cans per week. If the children use cost-benefit analysis each time they decide whether to drink a can of cola, explain why the cola lasts much longer at Jin's house than at Hector's. *(LO4)*

10.* Suppose there is only one electric scooter company in Adriana's hometown. Currently, the company charges 20 cents per minute, and there is no fee to unlock a scooter. The scooter company is considering changing its pricing plan so that it would charge $1 to unlock a scooter and 10 cents per minute. If Adriana never takes a ride that lasts less than 10 minutes, then what will happen to the average length of her rides if the scooter company switches to the new pricing plan? Explain. *(LO4)*

11.* The meal plan at University A lets students eat as much as they like for a fixed fee of $500 per semester. The average student there eats 250 pounds of food per semester. University B charges $500 for a book of meal tickets that entitles the student to eat 250 pounds of food per semester. If the student eats more than 250 pounds, he or she pays $2 for each additional pound; if the student eats less, he or she gets a $2 per pound refund. If students are rational, at which university will average food consumption be higher? Explain briefly. *(LO4)*

ANSWERS TO SELF-TESTS

1.1 The benefit of buying the wireless keyboard downtown is again $10 but the cost is now $12, so your economic surplus would be $2 smaller than if you'd bought it at the campus store. *(LO2)*

1.2 Saving $100 is $10 more valuable than saving $90, even though the percentage saved is much greater in the case of the Chicago ticket. *(LO3)*

1.3 Since you now have no alternative use for your coupon, the opportunity cost of using it to pay for the Cancun trip is zero. That means your economic surplus from the trip will be $1,350 − $1,000 = $350 > 0, so you should use your coupon and go to Cancun. *(LO3)*

1.4 The marginal benefit of the fourth launch is $9 billion, which exceeds its marginal cost of $8 billion, so the fourth launch should be added. But the fifth launch should not, because its marginal cost ($12 billion) exceeds its marginal benefit ($9 billion). *(LO3)*

1.5 If the star player takes one more shot, some other player must take one less. The fact that the star player's *average* success rate is higher than the other players' does not mean that the probability of making her *next* shot (the marginal benefit of having her shoot once more) is higher than the probability of another player making her next shot. Indeed, if the best player took all her team's shots, the other team would focus its defensive effort entirely on her, in which case letting others shoot would definitely pay. *(LO3)*

1.6 Answers will vary.

*Denotes more difficult problem.

APPENDIX

Working with Equations, Graphs, and Tables

Although many of the examples and most of the end-of-chapter problems in this book are quantitative, none requires mathematical skills beyond rudimentary high school algebra and geometry. In this brief appendix, we review some of the skills you'll need for dealing with these examples and problems.

One important skill is to be able to read simple verbal descriptions and translate the information they provide into the relevant equations or graphs. You'll also need to be able to translate information given in tabular form into an equation or graph, and sometimes you'll need to translate graphical information into a table or equation. Finally, you'll need to be able to solve simple systems with two equations and two unknowns. The following examples illustrate all the tools you'll need.

USING A VERBAL DESCRIPTION TO CONSTRUCT AN EQUATION

We begin with an example that shows how to construct a billing equation for a ride on an electric scooter from a verbal description of the billing plan.

EXAMPLE 1A.1 A Verbal Description

An electric scooter company charges $1 to unlock a scooter plus 20 cents per minute. Write an equation that describes your bill for riding this scooter.

An **equation** is a simple mathematical expression that describes the relationship between two or more **variables,** or quantities, that are free to assume different values in some range. The most common type of equation we'll work with contains two types of variables: **dependent variables** and **independent variables**. In this example, the dependent variable is the dollar amount of your scooter bill and the independent variable is the variable on which your bill depends, namely, the number of minutes you ride the scooter. Your bill also depends on the $1 fee to unlock the scooter and the 20 cents per minute charge. But, in this example, those amounts are **constants**, not variables. A constant, also called a **parameter**, is a quantity in an equation that is fixed in value, not free to vary. As the terms suggest, the dependent variable describes an outcome that depends on the value taken by the independent variable.

Once you've identified the dependent variable and the independent variable, choose simple symbols to represent them. In algebra courses, X is typically used to represent the independent variable and Y the dependent variable. Many people find it easier to remember what the variables stand for, however, if they choose symbols that are linked in some straightforward way to the quantities that

equation a mathematical expression that describes the relationship between two or more variables

variable a quantity that is free to take a range of different values

dependent variable a variable in an equation whose value is determined by the value taken by another variable in the equation

independent variable a variable in an equation whose value determines the value taken by another variable in the equation

constant (or parameter) a quantity that is fixed in value the variables represent. Thus, in this example, we might use B to represent your scooter *bill* in dollars and T to represent the total *time* in minutes of your ride.

Having identified the relevant variables and chosen symbols to represent them, you are now in a position to write the equation that links them

$$B = 1 + 0.20T, \tag{1A.1}$$

where B is your scooter bill in dollars and T is the number of minutes you spend riding the scooter. The fee to unlock the scooter (1) and the charge per minute (0.20) are parameters in this equation. Note the importance of being clear about the units of measure. Because B represents the scooter bill in dollars, we must also express the fee to unlock the scooter and the per-minute charge in dollars, which is why the latter number appears in Equation 1A.1 as 0.20 rather than 20. Equation 1A.1 follows the normal convention in which the dependent variable appears by itself on the left-hand side while the independent variable or variables and constants appear on the right-hand side.

Once we have the equation for the scooter bill, we can use it to calculate how much you'll owe as a function of the number of minutes you spend riding. For example, if you ride the scooter for 16 minutes, you can calculate your scooter bill by simply substituting 16 minutes for T in Equation 1A.1

$$B = 1 + 0.20(16) = 4.20. \tag{1A.2}$$

Your scooter bill when you ride for 16 minutes is thus equal to $4.20.

SELF-TEST 1A.1

Under the scooter billing plan described in Example 1A.1, how much would you owe for a 22-minute ride?

GRAPHING THE EQUATION OF A STRAIGHT LINE

The next example shows how to portray the billing plan described in Example 1A.1 as a graph.

EXAMPLE 1A.2 Graphing an Equation

Construct a graph that portrays the scooter billing plan described in Example 1A.1, putting your total bill, in dollars, on the vertical axis and the length of your ride, in minutes, on the horizontal axis.

The first step in responding to this instruction is the one we just took, namely, to translate the verbal description of the billing plan into an equation. When graphing an equation, the normal convention is to use the vertical axis to represent the dependent variable and the horizontal axis to represent the independent variable. In Figure 1A.1, we therefore put B on the vertical axis and T on the horizontal axis. One way to construct the graph shown in the figure is to begin by plotting the bill values that correspond to several different ride lengths. For example, someone who rides for 10 minutes would have a bill of $B = 1 + 0.20(10) = \$3$. Thus, in Figure 1A.1 the value of 10 minutes on the horizontal axis corresponds to a bill of $3 on the vertical axis (point A). Someone who rides for 15 minutes would have a bill of

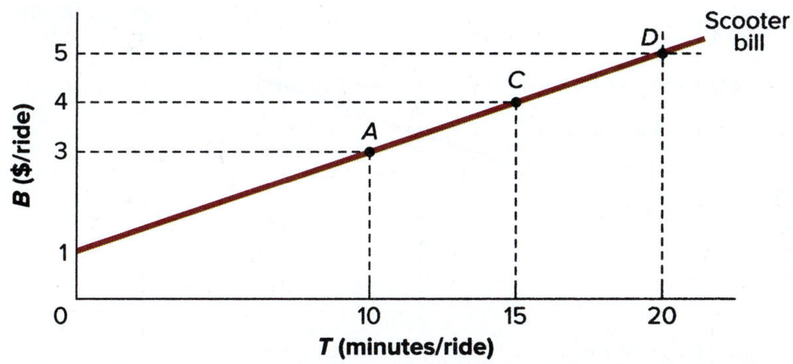

FIGURE 1A.1

The Scooter Billing Plan in Example 1A.1.

The graph of the equation $B = 1 + 0.20T$ is the straight line shown. Its vertical intercept is 1 and its slope is 0.20.

$B = 1 + 0.20(15) = \$4$, so the value of 15 minutes on the horizontal axis corresponds to \$4 on the vertical axis (point *C*). Similarly, someone who rides for 20 minutes would have a bill of $B = 1 + 0.20(20) = \$5$, so the value of 20 minutes on the horizontal axis corresponds to \$5 on the vertical axis (point *D*). The line joining these points is the graph of the billing Equation 1A.1.

As shown in Figure 1A.1, the graph of the equation $B = 1 + 0.20T$ is a straight line. The parameter 1 is the **vertical intercept** of the line—the value of *B* when $T = 0$, or the point at which the line intersects the vertical axis. The parameter 0.20 is the **slope** of the line, which is the ratio of the **rise** of the line to the corresponding **run**. The ratio rise/run is simply the vertical distance between any two points on the line divided by the horizontal distance between those points. For example, if we choose points *A* and *C* in Figure 1A.1, the rise is $4 - 3 = 1$ and the corresponding run is $15 - 10 = 5$, so rise/run $= 1/5 = 0.20$. More generally, for the graph of any equation $Y = a + bX$, the parameter *a* is the vertical intercept and the parameter *b* is the slope.

vertical intercept in a straight line, the value taken by the dependent variable when the independent variable equals zero

slope in a straight line, the ratio of the vertical distance the straight line travels between any two points ***(rise)*** to the corresponding horizontal distance ***(run)***

DERIVING THE EQUATION OF A STRAIGHT LINE FROM ITS GRAPH

The next example shows how to derive the equation for a straight line from a graph of the line.

EXAMPLE 1A.3 Deriving an Equation from a Graph

Figure 1A.2 shows the graph of the billing plan for an electric scooter company. What is the equation for this graph? How much is the fee to unlock a scooter under this plan? How much is the charge per minute?

The slope of the line shown is the rise between any two points divided by the corresponding run. For points *A* and *C*, rise $= 3.50 - 3 = 0.50$ and run $= 15 - 10 = 5$, so the slope equals rise/run $= 0.50/5 = 0.10$. And since the horizontal intercept of the line is 2, its equation must be given by

$$B = 2 + 0.10T. \tag{1A.3}$$

Under this plan, the fee to unlock a scooter is the value of the bill when $T = 0$, which is \$2. The charge per minute is the slope of the billing line, 0.10, or 10 cents per minute.

FIGURE 1A.2

Another Scooter Billing Plan.

The vertical distance between points *A* and *C* is 3.50 − 3 = 0.50 units, and the horizontal distance between points *A* and *C* is 15 − 10 = 5, so the slope of the line is 0.50/5 = 0.10. The vertical intercept (the value of *B* when *T* = 0) is 2. So the equation for the billing plan shown is *B* = 2 + 0.10*T*.

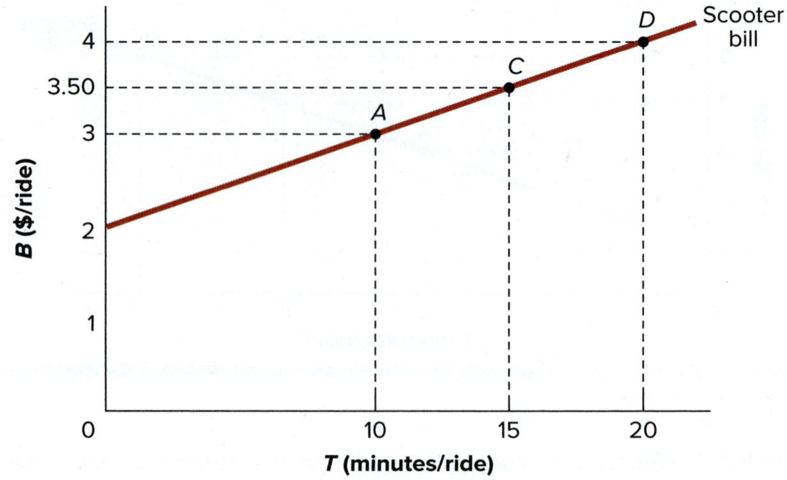

SELF-TEST 1A.2

Write the equation for the billing plan shown in the accompanying graph. How much does it cost to unlock a scooter? What is the charge per minute?

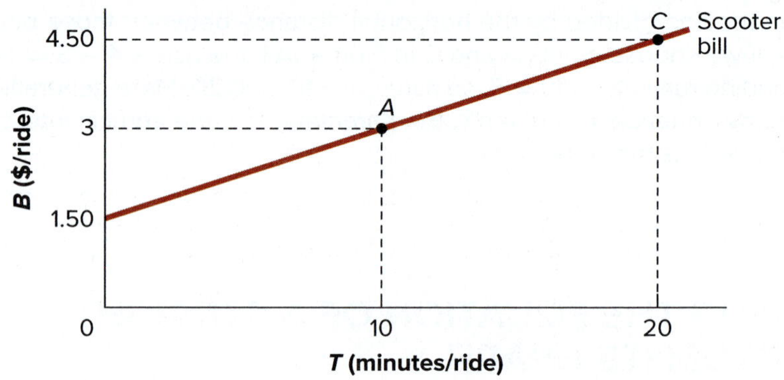

CHANGES IN THE VERTICAL INTERCEPT AND SLOPE

The next two examples and self-tests provide practice in seeing how a line shifts with a change in its vertical intercept or slope.

EXAMPLE 1A.4 Change in Vertical Intercept

Show how the billing plan whose graph is in Figure 1A.2 would change if the fee to unlock a scooter were increased from $2 to $3.

An increase in the fee to unlock a scooter from $2 to $3 would increase the vertical intercept of the billing plan by $1 but would leave its slope unchanged. An increase in the fee to unlock a scooter thus leads to a parallel upward shift in the billing plan by $1, as shown in Figure 1A.3. For any given number of minutes the new bill will be $1 higher than the old bill. Thus, a 10-minute ride cost $3 under the original plan

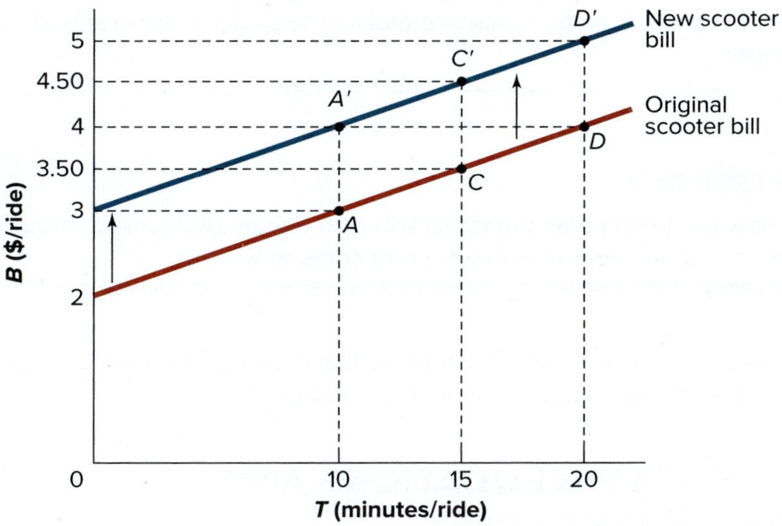

FIGURE 1A.3

The Effect of an Increase in the Vertical Intercept.

An increase in the vertical intercept of a straight line produces an upward parallel shift in the line.

(point *A*) but $4 under the new plan (point *A*′). A 15-minute ride cost $3.50 under the original plan (point *C*), but $4.50 under the new plan (point *C*′). And a 20-minute ride cost $4 under the original plan (point *D*), but $5 under the new plan (point *D*′).

SELF-TEST 1A.3

Show how the billing plan whose graph is in Figure 1A.2 would change if the fee to unlock a scooter were reduced from $2 to $1.

EXAMPLE 1A.5 Change in Slope

Show how the billing plan whose graph is in Figure 1A.2 would change if the charge per minute were increased from 10 cents to 20 cents.

Because the fee to unlock a scooter is unchanged, the vertical intercept of the new billing plan continues to be 2. But the slope of the new plan, shown in

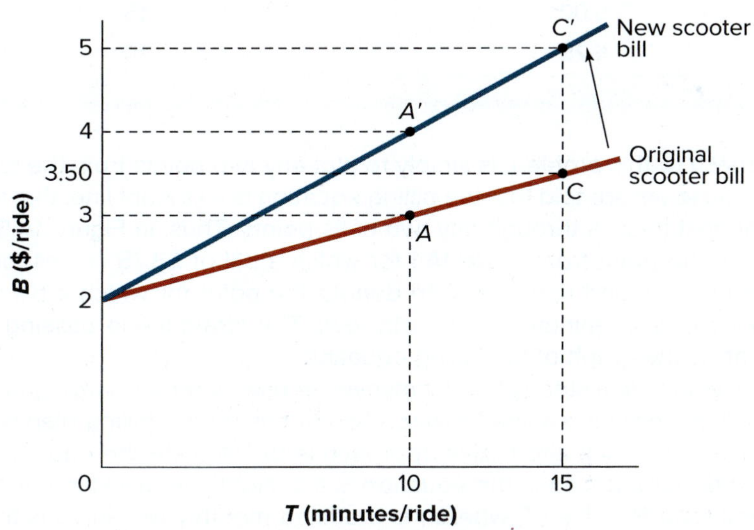

FIGURE 1A.4

The Effect of an Increase in the Charge per Minute.

Because the fixed monthly fee continues to be $2, the vertical intercept of the new plan is the same as that of the original plan. With the new charge per minute of 20 cents, the slope of the billing plan rises from 0.10 to 0.20.

Figure 1A.4, is 0.20, or twice the slope of the original plan. More generally, in the equation $Y = a + bX$, an increase in b makes the slope of the graph of the equation steeper.

SELF-TEST 1A.4

Show how the billing plan whose graph is in Figure 1A.2 would change if the charge per minute were reduced from 10 cents to 5 cents.

Self-Test 1A.4 illustrates the general rule that in an equation $Y = a + bX$, a reduction in b makes the slope of the graph of the equation less steep.

CONSTRUCTING EQUATIONS AND GRAPHS FROM TABLES

The next example and self-test show how to transform tabular information into an equation or graph.

EXAMPLE 1A.6 Transforming a Table to a Graph

Table 1A.1 shows four points from a scooter billing equation. If all points on this billing equation lie on a straight line, find the vertical intercept of the equation and graph it. What is the fee to unlock a scooter? What is the charge per minute? Calculate the total bill for a 30-minute ride.

TABLE 1A.1
Points on a Scooter Billing Plan

Total bill ($/ride)	Length of ride (minutes/ride)
2.50	5
3.75	10
5.00	15
6.25	20

One approach to this problem is simply to plot any two points from the table on a graph. Because we are told that the billing equation is a straight line, that line must be the one that passes through any two of its points. Thus, in Figure 1A.5 we use A to denote the point from Table 1A.1 for which a bill of \$3.75 corresponds to a 10-minute ride (second row) and C to denote the point for which a bill of \$6.25 corresponds to a 20-minute ride (fourth row). The straight line passing through these points is the graph of the billing equation.

Unless you have a steady hand, however, or use extremely large graph paper, the method of extending a line between two points on the billing plan is unlikely to be very accurate. An alternative approach is to calculate the equation for the billing plan directly. Because the equation is a straight line, we know that it takes the general form $B = f + sT$, where f is the fixed monthly fee and s is the slope.

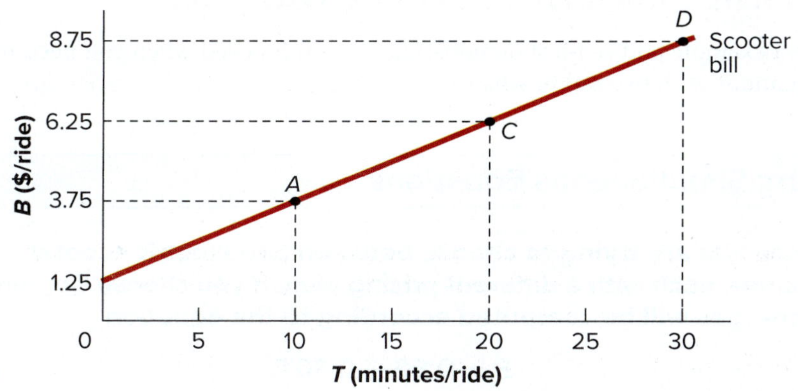

FIGURE 1A.5

Plotting the Scooter Billing Plan from a Sample of Points. Point *A* is taken from row 2, Table 1A.1, and point *C* from row 4. The billing plan is the straight line that passes through these points.

Our goal is to calculate the vertical intercept f and the slope s. From the same two points we plotted earlier, *A* and *C*, we can calculate the slope of the billing plan as $s = \text{rise/run} = 2.50/10 = 0.25$.

So all that remains is to calculate f, the fee to unlock a scooter. At point *C* on the billing plan, the total bill is \$6.25 for 20 minutes, so we can substitute $B = 6.25$, $s = 0.25$, and $T = 20$ into the general equation $B = f + sT$ to obtain

$$6.25 = f + 0.25(20), \tag{1A.4}$$

or

$$6.25 = f + 5, \tag{1A.5}$$

which solves for $f = 1.25$. So the billing equation must be

$$B = 1.25 + 0.25T. \tag{1A.6}$$

For this billing equation, the fee to unlock a scooter is \$1.25, the charge per minute is 25 cents (\$0.25/minute), and the total bill for a 30-minute ride is $B = 1.25 + 0.25(30) = \$8.75$, just as shown in Figure 1A.5.

SELF-TEST 1A.5

The following table shows four points from a scooter billing plan.

Total bill ($/ride)	Length of ride (minutes/ride)
2.50	5
4.25	10
6.00	15
7.75	20

If all points on this billing plan lie on a straight line, find the vertical intercept of the corresponding equation without graphing it. What is the fee to unlock a scooter? What is the charge per minute? How much would the charges be for a 30-minute ride?

SOLVING SIMULTANEOUS EQUATIONS

The next example and self-test demonstrate how to proceed when you need to solve two equations with two unknowns.

EXAMPLE 1A.7 Solving Simultaneous Equations

Suppose you are trying to choose between two electric scooter companies, each with a different pricing plan. If you choose Company 1, your charges will be computed according to the equation

$$B = 0.50 + 0.30T, \tag{1A.7}$$

where B is again your bill in dollars and T is the length of your ride in minutes. If you choose Company 2, your bill will be computed according to the equation

$$B = 2 + 0.15T. \tag{1A.8}$$

How many minutes long would your ride have to be to make Company 2 cheaper?

Company 1 has the attractive feature of a relatively low fee to unlock a scooter, but also the unattractive feature of a relatively high rate per minute. In contrast, Company 2 has a relatively high fee to unlock a scooter but a relatively low rate per minute. Someone who wanted to make a short ride (for example, 4 minutes) would do better under Company 1 (bill = \$1.70) than under Company 2 (bill = \$2.60) because the low fee to unlock a scooter for Company 1 would more than compensate for its higher rate per minute. Conversely, someone who wanted to make a long ride (say, 15 minutes) would do better under Company 2 (bill = \$4.25) than under Company 1 (bill = \$5.00) because Company 2's lower rate per minute would more than compensate for its higher fee to unlock a scooter.

Our task here is to find the break-even ride length, which is ride length for which the bill is the same under the two plans. One way to answer this question is to graph the two billing plans and see where they cross. At that crossing point, the two equations are satisfied simultaneously, which means that the length of the rides will be the same, as will the bills.

In Figure 1A.6, we see that the graphs of the two plans cross at A, where both yield a bill of \$3.50 for a 10-minute ride. The break-even ride length for these two

FIGURE 1A.6

The Break-Even Volume of Ride Length.

For 10-minute rides, your bill will be the same under both plans. For longer rides, Company 2 is cheaper; Company 1 is cheaper for shorter rides.

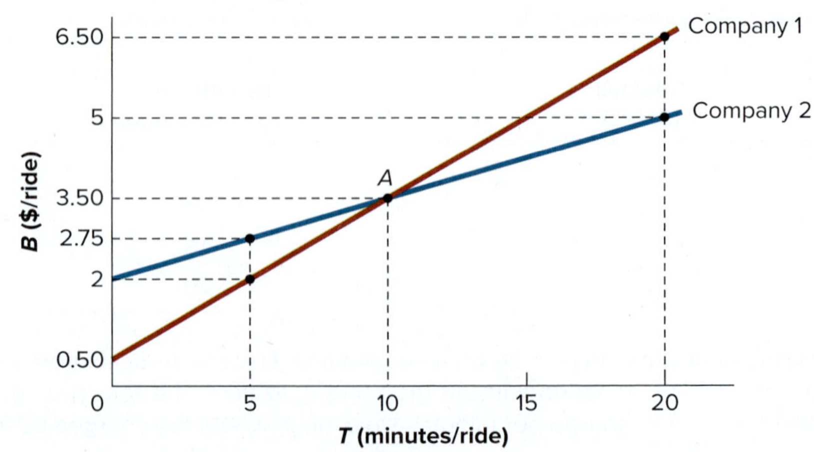

companies is thus 10 minutes. If the length of your ride is longer than that, you will save money by choosing Company 2. For example, if you take a 20-minute ride, your bill under Company 2 ($5) will be $1.50 cheaper than under Company 1 ($6.50). Conversely, if you ride for less than 10 minutes, you will do better under Company 1. For example, if you take a 5-minute ride, your bill under Company 1 ($2) will be 75 cents cheaper than under Company 2 ($2.75). For 10-minute rides, the two companies cost exactly the same ($3.50).

The question posed here also may be answered algebraically. As in the graphical approach just discussed, our goal is to find the point (T, B) that satisfies both billing equations simultaneously. As a first step, we rewrite the two billing equations, one on top of the other, as

$$B = 0.50 + 0.30T \qquad \text{(Company 1).}$$
$$B = 2 + 0.15T \qquad \text{(Company 2).}$$

As you'll recall from high school algebra, if we subtract the terms from each side of one equation from the corresponding terms of the other equation, the resulting differences must be equal. So if we subtract the terms on each side of the Company 2 equation from the corresponding terms in the Company 1 equation, we get

$$\begin{array}{ll} B = 0.50 + 0.30T & \text{(Company 1).} \\ -B = -2 - 0.15T & \text{(}-\text{Company 2).} \\ \hline 0 = -1.5 + 0.15T & \text{(Company 1} - \text{Company 2).} \end{array}$$

Finally, we solve the last equation (Company 1 − Company 2) to get $T = 10$.

Plugging $T = 10$ into either plan's equation, we then find $B = 3.50$. For example, Company 1's equation yields $0.5 + 0.30(10) = 3.50$, as does Company 2's $2 + 0.15(10) = 3.50$.

Because the point $(T, B) = (10, 3.50)$ lies on the equations for both plans simultaneously, the algebraic approach just described is often called the *method of simultaneous equations*.

SELF-TEST 1A.6

Suppose you are trying to choose between two electric scooter companies. If you choose Company 1, your bill will be computed according to the equation

$$B = 0.20 + 0.40T \qquad \text{(Company 1),}$$

where B is again your bill in dollars and T is the length of your ride in minutes. If you choose Company 2, your bill will be computed according to the equation

$$B = 5 + 0.10T \qquad \text{(Company 2).}$$

Use the algebraic approach described in the preceding example to find the break-even ride length for these plans.

KEY TERMS

constant (or parameter)
dependent variable
equation
independent variable
rise
run
slope
variable
vertical intercept

ANSWERS TO APPENDIX SELF-TESTS

1A.1 To calculate your bill for a 22-minute ride, substitute 22 minutes for T in Equation 1A.1 to get $B = 1 + 0.20(22) = \$5.40$.

1A.2 Calculating the slope using points A and C, we have rise $= 4.50 - 3 = 1.50$ and run $= 20 - 10 = 10$, so rise/run $= 1.5/10 = 0.15$. And since the horizontal intercept of the line is 1.5, its equation is $B = 1.5 + 0.15T$. Under this plan, the fee to unlock a scooter is \$1.50 and the charge per minute is the slope of the billing line, 0.15, or 15 cents per minute.

1A.3 A \$1 reduction in the fee to unlock a scooter would produce a downward parallel shift in the billing plan by \$1.

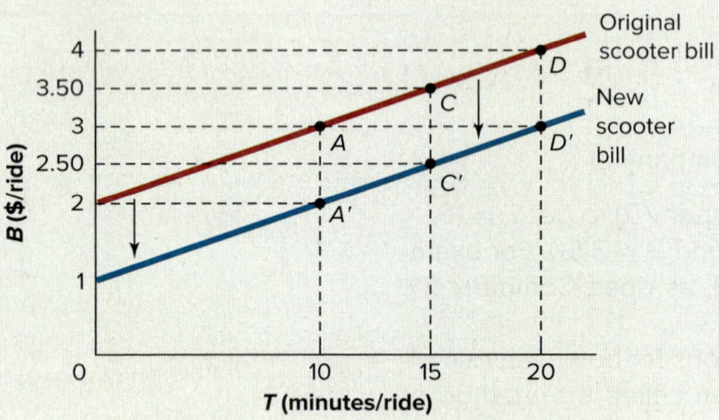

1A.4 With the fee to unlock a scooter unchanged, the vertical intercept of the new billing plan continues to be 2. The slope of the new plan is 0.05, half the slope of the original plan.

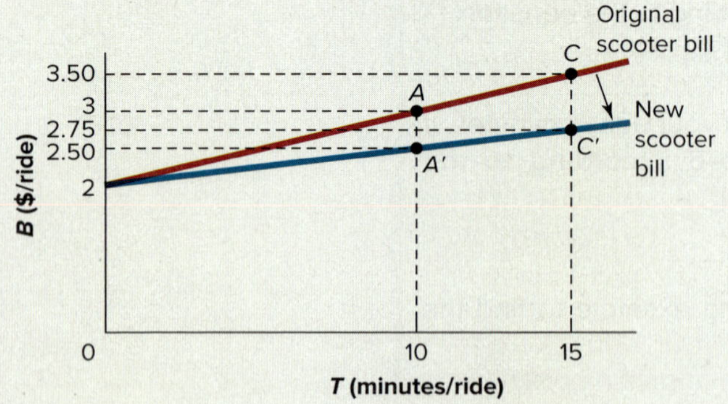

1A.5 Let the billing equation be $B = f + sT$, where f is the fee to unlock a scooter and s is the slope. From the first two points in the table, calculate the slope s = rise/run $= 1.75/5 = 0.35$. To calculate f, we can use the information in the first row of the table to write the billing equation as $2.50 = f + 0.35(5)$ and solve for $f = 0.75$. So the billing equation must be $B = 0.75 + 0.35T$. For this billing equation, the fee to unlock a scooter is 75 cents, the charge per minute is 35 cents, and the total bill for a 30-minute ride is $B = 0.75 + 0.35(30) = \$11.25$.

1A.6 Subtracting the Company 2 equation from the Company 1 equation yields the equation

$$0 = -4.8 + 0.30T \qquad \text{(Company 1} - \text{Company 2)},$$

which solves for $T = 16$. So if you ride for more than 16 minutes, you'll do better with Company 2.

2

Supply and Demand

LEARNING OBJECTIVES

After reading this chapter, you should be able to:

LO1 Describe how the demand and supply curves summarize the behavior of buyers and sellers in the marketplace.

LO2 Discuss how the supply and demand curves interact to determine equilibrium price and quantity.

LO3 Illustrate how shifts in supply and demand curves cause prices and quantities to change.

LO4 Explain why markets in equilibrium tend to leave no unexploited opportunities available to individuals.

The stock of foodstuffs on hand at any moment in New York City's grocery stores, restaurants, and private kitchens is sufficient to feed the area's 10 million residents for at most a week or so. Since most of these residents have nutritionally adequate and highly varied diets, and since almost no food is produced within the city proper, provisioning New York requires that millions of pounds of food and drink be delivered to locations throughout the city each day.

No doubt many New Yorkers, buying groceries at their favorite local markets or eating at their favorite Italian restaurants, give little or no thought to the nearly miraculous coordination of people and resources required to feed city residents on a daily basis. But near-miraculous it is, nevertheless. Even if the supplying of New York City consisted only of transporting a fixed collection of foods to a given list of destinations each day, it would be quite an impressive operation, requiring at least a small (and well-managed) army to carry out.

Yet the entire process is astonishingly more complex than that. For example, the system must somehow ensure that not only *enough* food is delivered to satisfy New Yorkers' discriminating palates, but also the *right kinds* of food. There can't be too much pheasant and not enough smoked eel, or too much bacon and not enough eggs, or too much caviar and not enough canned tuna, and so on. Similar judgments must be made *within* each category of food and drink: there must be the right amount of Swiss cheese and the right amounts of provolone, gorgonzola, and feta.

But even this doesn't begin to describe the complexity of the decisions and actions required to provide our nation's largest city with its daily bread. Someone has to decide where each particular type of food gets produced, and how, and by whom. Someone must decide how much of each type of food gets delivered to *each* of the tens of thousands of restaurants and grocery stores in the city. Someone must determine whether the deliveries should be made in big trucks or small ones, arrange that the trucks be in the right place at the right time, and ensure that gasoline and qualified drivers be available.

Thousands of individuals must decide what role, if any, they will play in this collective effort. Some people—just the right number—must choose to drive food delivery trucks rather than trucks that deliver lumber. Others—again, just the right number—must become the mechanics who fix these trucks rather than carpenters who build houses. Others must become farmers rather than architects or bricklayers. Still others must become chefs in upscale restaurants, or flip burgers at McDonald's, instead of becoming plumbers or electricians.

Yet despite the almost incomprehensible number and complexity of the tasks involved, somehow the supplying of New York City manages to get done remarkably smoothly. Oh, a grocery store will occasionally run out of flank steak or a diner will sometimes be told that someone else has just ordered the last serving of roast duck. But if episodes like these stick in memory, it is only because they are rare. For the most part, New York's food delivery system—like that of every other city in the country—functions so seamlessly that it attracts virtually no notice.

The situation is strikingly different in New York City's rental housing market. According to one estimate, growth in the city's population has long outstripped growth in the city's supply of housing units (with the exception of a recent surge in construction of ultra-luxury condominiums).[1] As a result, America's most densely populated city has been experiencing a protracted housing shortage. Yet, paradoxically, in the midst of this shortage, apartment houses are being demolished; and in the vacant lots left behind, people from the neighborhoods are planting flower gardens!

New York City is experiencing not only a growing shortage of rental housing, but also chronically strained relations between landlords and tenants. In one all-too-typical case, for example, a photographer living in a loft on the Lower East Side waged an eight-year court battle with his landlord that generated literally thousands of pages of legal documents. "Once we put up a doorbell for ourselves," the photographer recalled, "and [the landlord] pulled it out, so we pulled out the wires to his doorbell."[2] The landlord, for his part, accused the photographer of obstructing his efforts to renovate the apartment. According to the landlord, the tenant preferred that the apartment remain in substandard condition since that gave him an excuse to withhold rent payments.

Melissamn/Shutterstock

Thinkstock/Jupiter Images

Why does New York City's food distribution system work so much better than its housing market?

Same city, two strikingly different patterns: In the food industry, goods and services are available in wide variety and people (at least those with adequate income) are generally satisfied with what they receive and the choices available to them. In contrast, in the rental housing industry, chronic shortages and chronic dissatisfaction are rife among both buyers and sellers. Why this difference?

The brief answer is that New York City relies on a complex system of administrative rent regulations to allocate housing units but leaves the allocation of food essentially in the hands of market forces—the forces of supply and demand. Although intuition might suggest otherwise, both theory and experience suggest that the seemingly chaotic and unplanned outcomes of market forces, in most cases, can do a better job of allocating economic resources than can (for example) a government agency, even if the agency has the best of intentions.

In this chapter we'll explore how markets allocate food, housing, and other goods and services, usually with remarkable efficiency despite the complexity of the tasks. To be sure, markets are by no means perfect, and our stress on their virtues is to some extent an attempt to counteract what most economists view as an

[1]For additional information see www.citylab.com/equity/2017/05/is-housing-catching-up/528246/.
[2]John Tierney, "The Rentocracy: At the Intersection of Supply and Demand," *New York Times Magazine*, May 4, 1997, p. 39.

underappreciation by the general public of their remarkable strengths. But, in the course of our discussion, we'll see why markets function so smoothly most of the time and why bureaucratic rules and regulations rarely work as well in solving complex economic problems.

To convey an understanding of how markets work is a major goal of this course, and in this chapter we provide only a brief introduction and overview. As the course proceeds, we'll discuss the economic role of markets in considerably more detail, paying attention to some of the problems of markets as well as their strengths.

WHAT, HOW, AND FOR WHOM? CENTRAL PLANNING VERSUS THE MARKET

No city, state, or society—regardless of how it is organized—can escape the need to answer certain basic economic questions. For example, how much of our limited time and other resources should we devote to building housing, how much to the production of food, and how much to providing other goods and services? What techniques should we use to produce each good? Who should be assigned to each specific task? And how should the resulting goods and services be distributed among people?

In the thousands of different societies for which records are available, issues like these have been decided in essentially one of two ways. One approach is for all economic decisions to be made centrally, by an individual or small number of individuals on behalf of a larger group. For example, in many agrarian societies throughout history, families or other small groups consumed only those goods and services that they produced for themselves, and a single clan or family leader made most important production and distribution decisions. On an immensely larger scale, the economic organization of the former Soviet Union (and other communist countries) was also largely centralized. In so-called centrally planned communist nations, a central bureaucratic committee established production targets for the country's farms and factories, developed a master plan for how to achieve the targets (including detailed instructions concerning who was to produce what), and set up guidelines for the distribution and use of the goods and services produced.

Neither form of centralized economic organization is much in evidence today. When implemented on a small scale, as in a self-sufficient family enterprise, centralized decision making is certainly feasible. For the reasons discussed in the preceding chapter, however, the jack-of-all-trades approach was doomed once it became clear how dramatically people could improve their living standards by specialization—that is, by having each individual focus his or her efforts on a relatively narrow range of tasks. And with the fall of the Soviet Union and its satellite nations in the late 1980s, there are now only three communist economies left in the world: Cuba, North Korea, and China. The first two of these appear to be on their last legs, economically speaking, and China has largely abandoned any attempt to control production and distribution decisions from the center. The major remaining examples of centralized allocation and control now reside in the bureaucratic agencies that administer programs like New York City's rent controls—programs that are themselves becoming increasingly rare.

At the beginning of the twenty-first century, we are therefore left, for the most part, with the second major form of economic system, one in which production and distribution decisions are left to individuals interacting in private markets. In the so-called capitalist, or free-market, economies, people decide for themselves which careers to pursue and which products to produce or buy. In fact, there are no *pure* free-market economies today. Modern industrial countries are more properly described as "mixed economies." Their goods and services are allocated by a combination of free markets, regulation, and other forms of collective control. Still, it makes sense to refer to such systems as free-market economies because people are for the most part free to start businesses, shut them down, or sell them. And within broad limits, the distribution of goods and services is determined by individual preferences backed by individual purchasing power, which in most cases comes from the income people earn in the labor market.

In country after country, markets have replaced centralized control for the simple reason that they tend to assign production tasks and consumption benefits much more effectively. The popular press and conventional wisdom often assert that economists disagree about important issues. (As someone once quipped, "If you lay all the economists in the world end to end, they still wouldn't reach a conclusion.") The fact is, however, that there is overwhelming agreement among economists about a broad range of issues. A substantial majority believes that markets are the most effective means for allocating society's scarce resources. For example, a recent survey found that more than 90 percent of American professional economists believe that rent regulations like the ones implemented by New York City do more harm than good. That the stated aim of these regulations—to make rental housing more affordable for middle- and low-income families—is clearly benign was not enough to prevent them from wreaking havoc on New York City's housing market. To see why, we must explore how goods and services are allocated in private markets and why nonmarket means of allocating goods and services often do not produce the expected results.

BUYERS AND SELLERS IN MARKETS

market the market for any good consists of all buyers or sellers of that good

Beginning with some simple concepts and definitions, we will explore how the interactions among buyers and sellers in markets determine the prices and quantities of the various goods and services traded. We begin by defining a market: the **market** for any good consists of all the buyers and sellers of that good. So, for example, the market for pizza on a given day in a given place is just the set of people (or other economic actors such as firms) potentially able to buy or sell pizza at that time and location.

In the market for pizza, sellers comprise the individuals and companies that either do sell—or might, under the right circumstances, sell—pizza. Similarly, buyers in this market include all individuals who buy—or might buy—pizza.

Why do Claude Monet's paintings sell for so much more than Pierre-Auguste Renoir's?

The Metropolitan Museum of Art, New York, H. O. Havemeyer Collection, Bequest of Mrs. H. O. Havemeyer, 1929

In most parts of the country, a decent pizza can still be had for less than \$10. Where does the market price of pizza come from? Looking beyond pizza to the vast array of other goods that are bought and sold every day, we may ask, "Why are some goods cheap and others expensive?" Aristotle had no idea. Nor did Plato, or Copernicus, or Newton. On reflection, it is astonishing that, for almost the entire span of human history, not even the most intelligent and creative minds on Earth had any real inkling of how to answer that seemingly simple question. Even Adam Smith, the Scottish moral philosopher whose *Wealth of Nations* launched the discipline of economics in 1776, suffered confusion on this issue.

Smith and other early economists (including Karl Marx) thought that the market price of a good was determined by its cost of production. But although costs surely do affect prices, they cannot explain why one of Claude Monet's paintings sells for so much more than one of Pierre-Auguste Renoir's.

Stanley Jevons and other nineteenth-century economists tried to explain price by focusing on the value people derived from consuming different goods and services. It certainly seems plausible that people will pay a lot for a good they value highly. Yet willingness to pay cannot be the whole story, either. Deprive a person in the desert of water, for example, and he will be dead in a matter of hours, and yet water sells for less than a penny a gallon. By contrast, human beings can get along perfectly well without gold, and yet gold sells for more than $1,800 an ounce.

Cost of production? Value to the user? Which is it? The answer, which seems obvious to today's economists, is that both matter. Writing in the late nineteenth century, the British economist Alfred Marshall was among the first to show clearly how costs and value interact to determine both the prevailing market price for a good and the amount of it that is bought and sold. Our task in the pages ahead will be to explore Marshall's insights and gain some practice in applying them. As a first step, we introduce the two main components of Marshall's pathbreaking analysis: the demand curve and the supply curve.

A Pierre-Auguste Renoir painting.
Source: Courtesy of National Gallery of Art, Washington

The Demand Curve

In the market for pizza, the **demand curve** for pizza is a simple schedule or graph that tells us how many slices people would be willing to buy at different prices. By convention, economists usually put price on the vertical axis of the demand curve and quantity on the horizontal axis.

A fundamental property of the demand curve is that it is downward-sloping with respect to price. For example, the demand curve for pizza tells us that as the price of pizza falls, buyers will buy more slices. Thus, the daily demand curve for pizza in Chicago on a given day might look like the curve seen in Figure 2.1. (Although economists usually refer to demand and supply "curves," we often draw them as straight lines in examples.)

demand curve a schedule or graph showing the quantity of a good that buyers wish to buy at each price

The demand curve in Figure 2.1 tells us that when the price of pizza is low—say, $2 per slice—buyers will want to buy 16,000 slices per day, whereas they will want to buy only 12,000 slices at a price of $3 and only 8,000 at a price of $4. The demand curve for pizza—as for any other good—slopes downward for multiple reasons. Some have to do with the individual consumer's reactions to price changes. Thus, as pizza becomes more expensive, a consumer may switch to chicken sandwiches, hamburgers, or other foods that substitute for pizza. This is called the **substitution effect** of a price change. In addition, a price increase reduces the quantity demanded because it reduces purchasing power: a consumer simply can't afford to buy as many slices of pizza at higher prices as at lower prices. This is called the **income effect** of a price change.

substitution effect the change in the quantity demanded of a good that results because buyers switch to or from substitutes when the price of the good changes

income effect the change in the quantity demanded of a good that results because a change in the price of a good changes the buyer's purchasing power

Another reason the demand curve slopes downward is that consumers differ in terms of how much they're willing to pay for the good. The Cost-Benefit Principle tells us that a given person will buy the good if the benefit she expects to receive from

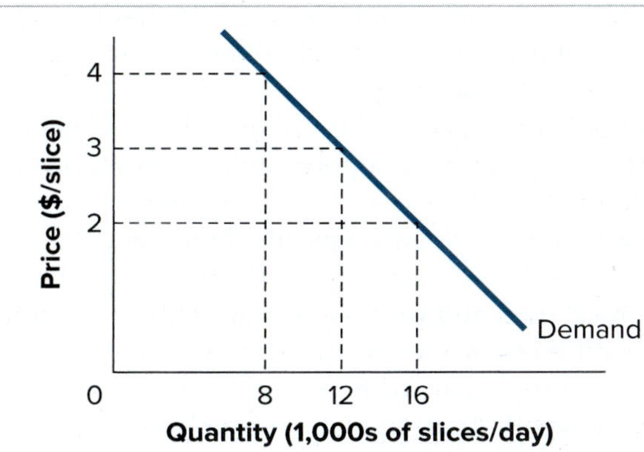

FIGURE 2.1

The Daily Demand Curve for Pizza in Chicago.

The demand curve for any good is a downward-sloping function of its price.

buyer's reservation price the largest dollar amount the buyer would be willing to pay for a good

it exceeds its cost. The benefit is the **buyer's reservation price,** the highest dollar amount she'd be willing to pay for the good. The cost of the good is the actual amount that the buyer actually must pay for it, which is the market price of the good. In most markets, different buyers have different reservation prices. So, when the good sells for a high price, it will satisfy the cost-benefit test for fewer buyers than when it sells for a lower price.

To put this same point another way, the fact that the demand curve for a good is downward-sloping reflects the fact that the reservation price of the marginal buyer declines as the quantity of the good bought increases. Here the marginal buyer is the person who purchases the last unit of the good sold. If buyers are currently purchasing 12,000 slices of pizza a day in Figure 2.1, for example, the reservation price for the buyer of the 12,000th slice must be $3. (If someone had been willing to pay more than that, the quantity demanded at a price of $3 would have been more than 12,000 to begin with.) By similar reasoning, when the quantity sold is 16,000 slices per day, the marginal buyer's reservation price must be only $2.

We defined the demand curve for any good as a schedule telling how much of it consumers wish to purchase at various prices. This is called the *horizontal interpretation* of the demand curve. Using the horizontal interpretation, we start with price on the vertical axis and read the corresponding quantity demanded on the horizontal axis. Thus, at a price of $4 per slice, the demand curve in Figure 2.1 tells us that the quantity of pizza demanded will be 8,000 slices per day.

The demand curve also can be interpreted in a second way, which is to start with quantity on the horizontal axis and then read the marginal buyer's reservation price on the vertical axis. Thus, when the quantity of pizza sold is 8,000 slices per day, the demand curve in Figure 2.1 tells us that the marginal buyer's reservation price is $4 per slice. This second way of reading the demand curve is called the *vertical interpretation*.

SELF-TEST 2.1

In Figure 2.1, what is the marginal buyer's reservation price when the quantity of pizza sold is 10,000 slices per day? For the same demand curve, what will be the quantity of pizza demanded at a price of $2.50 per slice?

The Supply Curve

supply curve a graph or schedule showing the quantity of a good that sellers wish to sell at each price

In the market for pizza, the **supply curve** is a simple schedule or graph that tells us, for each possible price, the total number of slices that all pizza vendors would be willing to sell at that price. What does the supply curve of pizza look like? The answer to this question is based on the logical assumption that suppliers should be willing to sell additional slices as long as the price they receive is sufficient to cover their opportunity cost of supplying them. Thus, if what someone could earn by selling a slice of pizza is insufficient to compensate her for what she could have earned if she had spent her time and invested her money in some other way, she will not sell that slice. Otherwise, she will.

Just as buyers differ with respect to the amounts they are willing to pay for pizza, sellers also differ with respect to their opportunity cost of supplying pizza. For those with limited education and work experience, the opportunity cost of selling pizza is relatively low (because such individuals typically do not have a lot of high-paying alternatives). For others, the opportunity cost of selling pizza is of moderate value, and for still others—like rock stars and professional athletes—it is prohibitively high. In part because of these differences in opportunity cost among people, the daily supply curve of pizza will be *upward-sloping* with respect to price. As an illustration, see Figure 2.2, which shows a hypothetical supply curve for pizza in the Chicago market on a given day.

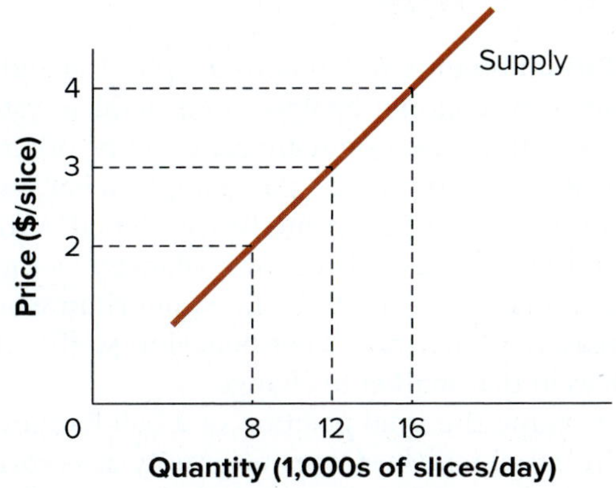

FIGURE 2.2

The Daily Supply Curve of Pizza in Chicago.

At higher prices, sellers generally offer more units for sale.

The reason the supply curve slopes upward may be seen as a consequence of the fact that as we expand the production of pizza, we turn first to those whose opportunity cost of producing pizza is lowest, and only then to others with a higher opportunity cost.

Like the demand curve, the supply curve can be interpreted either horizontally or vertically. Under the horizontal interpretation, we begin with a price and then go over to the supply curve to read the quantity that sellers wish to sell at that price on the horizontal axis. For instance, at a price of $2 per slice, sellers in Figure 2.2 wish to sell 8,000 slices per day.

Under the vertical interpretation, we begin with a quantity and then go up to the supply curve to read the corresponding marginal cost on the vertical axis. Thus, if sellers in Figure 2.2 are currently supplying 12,000 slices per day, the opportunity cost of the marginal seller is $3 per slice. In other words, the supply curve tells us that the marginal cost of producing the 12,000th slice of pizza is $3. (If someone could produce a 12,001st slice for less than $3, she would have an incentive to supply it, so the quantity of pizza supplied at $3 per slice would not have been 12,000 slices per day to begin with.) By similar reasoning, when the quantity of pizza supplied is 16,000 slices per day, the marginal cost of producing another slice must be $4. The **seller's reservation price** for selling an additional unit of a good is her marginal cost of producing that good. It is the smallest dollar amount for which she would not be worse off if she sold an additional unit.

seller's reservation price the smallest dollar amount for which a seller would be willing to sell an additional unit, generally equal to marginal cost

SELF-TEST 2.2

In Figure 2.2, what is the marginal cost of a slice of pizza when the quantity of pizza sold is 10,000 slices per day? For the same supply curve, what will be the quantity of pizza supplied at a price of $3.50 per slice?

RECAP

DEMAND AND SUPPLY CURVES

The *market* for a good consists of the actual and potential buyers and sellers of that good. For any given price, the *demand curve* shows the quantity that demanders would be willing to buy and the *supply curve* shows the quantity that suppliers of the good would be willing to sell. Suppliers are willing to sell more at higher prices (supply curves slope upward) and demanders are willing to buy less at higher prices (demand curves slope downward).

MARKET EQUILIBRIUM

equilibrium a balanced or unchanging situation in which all forces at work within a system are canceled by others

The concept of **equilibrium** is employed in both the physical and social sciences, and it is of central importance in economic analysis. In general, a system is in equilibrium when all forces at work within the system are canceled by others, resulting in a balanced or unchanging situation. In physics, for example, a ball hanging from a spring is said to be in equilibrium when the spring has stretched sufficiently that the upward force it exerts on the ball is exactly counterbalanced by the downward force of gravity. In economics, a market is said to be in equilibrium when no participant in the market has any reason to alter his or her behavior, so that there is no tendency for production or prices in that market to change.

equilibrium price and **equilibrium quantity** the price and quantity at the intersection of the supply and demand curves for the good

If we want to determine the final position of a ball hanging from a spring, we need to find the point at which the forces of gravity and spring tension are balanced and the system is in equilibrium. Similarly, if we want to find the price at which a good will sell (which we will call the **equilibrium price**) and the quantity of it that will be sold (the **equilibrium quantity**), we need to find the equilibrium in the market for that good. The basic tools for finding the equilibrium in a market for a good are the supply and demand curves for that good. For reasons we will explain, the equilibrium price and equilibrium quantity of a good are the price and quantity at which the supply and demand curves for the good intersect. For the hypothetical supply and demand curves shown earlier for the pizza market in Chicago, the equilibrium price will therefore be $3 per slice, and the equilibrium quantity of pizza sold will be 12,000 slices per day, as shown in Figure 2.3.

Note that at the equilibrium price of $3 per slice, both sellers and buyers are "satisfied" in the following sense: buyers are buying exactly the quantity of pizza they wish to buy at that price (12,000 slices per day) and sellers are selling exactly the quantity of pizza they wish to sell (also 12,000 slices per day). And since they are satisfied in this sense, neither buyers nor sellers face any incentives to change their behavior.

market equilibrium occurs in a market when all buyers and sellers are satisfied with their respective quantities at the market price

Note the limited sense of the term *satisfied* in the definition of **market equilibrium.** It doesn't mean that sellers would be displeased to receive a price higher than the equilibrium price. Rather, it means only that they're able to sell all they wish to sell at that price. Similarly, to say that buyers are satisfied at the equilibrium price doesn't mean that they wouldn't be happy to pay less than that price. Rather, it means only that they're able to buy exactly as many units of the good as they wish to at the equilibrium price.

Note also that if the price of pizza in our Chicago market were anything other than $3 per slice, either buyers or sellers would be frustrated. Suppose, for example, that the price of pizza were $4 per slice, as shown in Figure 2.4. At that price, buyers wish to buy only 8,000 slices per day, but sellers wish to sell 16,000. And since no one can force someone to buy a slice of pizza against her wishes, this means that buyers will buy only the 8,000 slices they wish to buy. So when price exceeds the

FIGURE 2.3

The Equilibrium Price and Quantity of Pizza in Chicago.

The equilibrium price and quantity of a product are the values that correspond to the intersection of the supply and demand curves for that product.

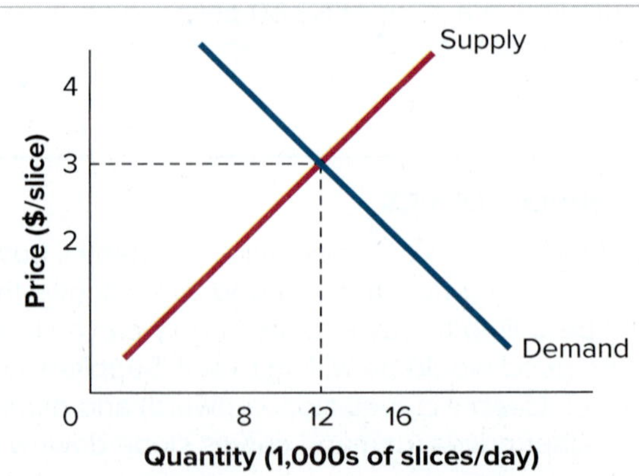

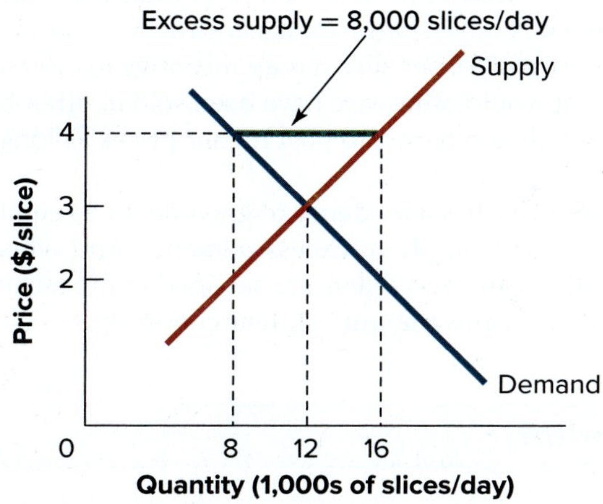

FIGURE 2.4

Excess Supply.

When price exceeds equilibrium price, there is excess supply, or surplus, the difference between quantity supplied and quantity demanded.

equilibrium price, it is sellers who end up being frustrated. At a price of $4 in this example, they are left with an **excess supply**, or **surplus**, of 8,000 slices per day.

Conversely, suppose that the price of pizza in our Chicago market were less than the equilibrium price—say, $2 per slice. As shown in Figure 2.5, buyers want to buy 16,000 slices per day at that price, whereas sellers want to sell only 8,000. And since sellers cannot be forced to sell pizza against their wishes, this time it is the buyers who end up being frustrated. At a price of $2 per slice in this example, they experience an **excess demand**, or **shortage**, of 8,000 slices per day.

An extraordinary feature of private markets for goods and services is their automatic tendency to gravitate toward their respective equilibrium prices and quantities. The mechanisms by which the adjustment happens are implicit in our definitions of excess supply and excess demand. Suppose, for example, that the price of pizza in our hypothetical market was $4 per slice, leading to excess supply as shown in Figure 2.4. Because sellers are frustrated in the sense of wanting to sell more pizza than buyers wish to buy, sellers have an incentive to take whatever steps they can to increase their sales. The simplest strategy available to them is to cut their price slightly. Thus, if one seller reduced her price from $4 to, say, $3.95 per slice, she would attract many of the buyers who had been paying $4 per slice for pizza supplied by other sellers. Those sellers, in order to recover their lost business, would then have an incentive to match the price cut. But notice that if all sellers lowered their prices to $3.95 per slice, there would still be considerable excess supply. So sellers would face continuing incentives to cut their prices. This pressure to cut prices won't go away until prices fall all the way to $3 per slice.

excess supply (or **surplus**) the amount by which quantity supplied exceeds quantity demanded when the price of the good exceeds the equilibrium price

excess demand (or **shortage**) the amount by which quantity demanded exceeds quantity supplied when the price of a good lies below the equilibrium price

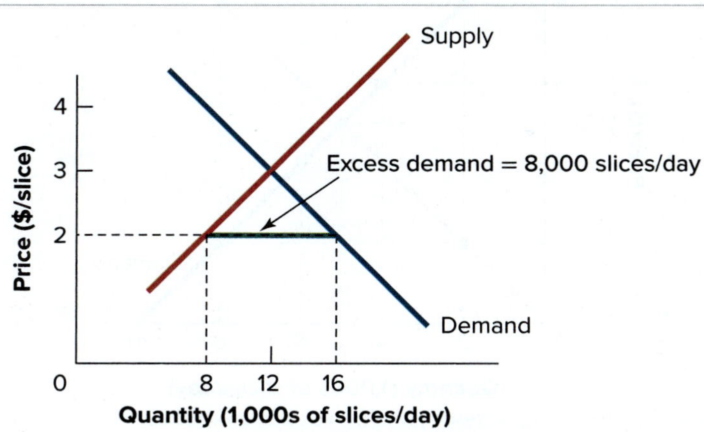

FIGURE 2.5

Excess Demand.

When price lies below equilibrium price, there is excess demand, the difference between quantity demanded and quantity supplied.

Conversely, suppose that price starts out less than the equilibrium price—say, $2 per slice. This time it is buyers who are frustrated. A person who can't get all the pizza she wants at a price of $2 per slice has an incentive to offer a higher price, hoping to obtain pizza that would otherwise have been sold to other buyers. And sellers, for their part, will be only too happy to post higher prices as long as queues of frustrated buyers remain.

The upshot is that price has a tendency to gravitate to its equilibrium level under conditions of either excess supply or excess demand. And when price reaches its equilibrium level, both buyers and sellers are satisfied in the technical sense of being able to buy or sell precisely the amounts of their choosing.

EXAMPLE 2.1 Market Equilibrium

Samples of points on the demand and supply curves of a pizza market are provided in Table 2.1. Graph the demand and supply curves for this market and find its equilibrium price and quantity.

TABLE 2.1
Points along the Demand and Supply Curves of a Pizza Market

Demand for Pizza		Supply of Pizza	
Price ($/slice)	Quantity demanded (1,000s of slices/day)	Price ($/slice)	Quantity supplied (1,000s of slices/day)
1	8	1	2
2	6	2	4
3	4	3	6
4	2	4	8

The points in the table are plotted in Figure 2.6 and then joined to indicate the supply and demand curves for this market. These curves intersect to yield an equilibrium price of $2.50 per slice and an equilibrium quantity of 5,000 slices per day.

FIGURE 2.6
Graphing Supply and Demand and Finding Equilibrium Price and Quantity.
To graph the demand and supply curves, plot the relevant points given in the table and then join them with a line. Equilibrium price and quantity occur at the intersection of these curves.

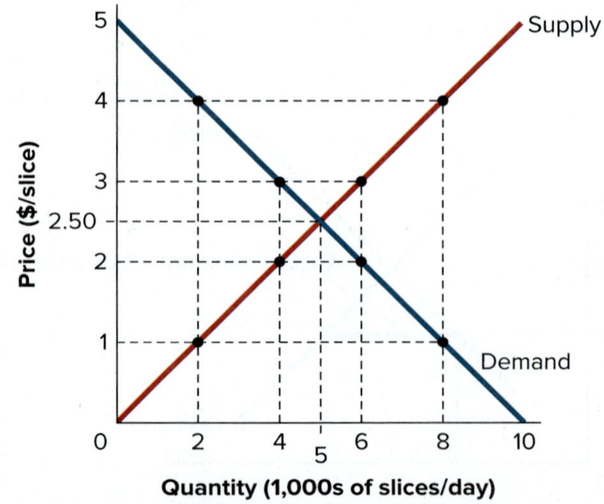

We emphasize that market equilibrium doesn't necessarily produce an ideal outcome for all market participants. Thus, in Example 2.1, market participants are satisfied with the amount of pizza they buy and sell at a price of $2.50 per slice, but for a poor buyer this may signify little more than that he *can't* buy additional pizza without sacrificing other more highly valued purchases.

Indeed, buyers with extremely low incomes often have difficulty purchasing even basic goods and services, which has prompted governments in almost every society to attempt to ease the burdens of the poor. Yet the laws of supply and demand cannot simply be repealed by an act of the legislature. In the next section, we'll see that when legislators attempt to prevent markets from reaching their equilibrium prices and quantities, they often do more harm than good. Fortunately, there are other, more effective, ways of providing assistance to families in need.

Rent Controls Reconsidered

Consider again the market for rental housing units in New York City and suppose that the demand and supply curves for one-bedroom apartments are as shown in Figure 2.7. This market, left alone, would reach an equilibrium monthly rent of $1,600, at which 2 million one-bedroom apartments would be rented. Both landlords and tenants would be satisfied, in the sense that they would not wish to rent either more or fewer units at that price.

This wouldn't necessarily mean, of course, that all is well and good. Many potential tenants, for example, might simply be unable to afford a rent of $1,600 per month and thus be forced to remain homeless (or to move out of the city to a cheaper location). Suppose that, acting purely out of benign motives, legislators made it unlawful for landlords to charge more than $800 per month for one-bedroom apartments. Their stated aim in enacting this law was that no person should have to remain homeless because decent housing was unaffordable.

But note in Figure 2.8 that when rents for one-bedroom apartments are prevented from rising above $800 per month, landlords are willing to supply only 1 million apartments per month, 1 million fewer than at the equilibrium monthly rent of $1,600. Note also that at the controlled rent of $800 per month, tenants want to rent 3 million one-bedroom apartments per month. (For example, many people who would have decided to live in New Jersey rather than pay $1,600 a month in New York will now choose to live in the city.) So when rents are prevented from rising above $800 per month, we see an excess demand for one-bedroom apartments of 2 million units each month. Put another way, the rent controls result in a housing shortage of 2 million units each month. What is more, the number of apartments actually available *declines* by 1 million units per month.

If the housing market were completely unregulated, the immediate response to such a high level of excess demand would be for rents to rise sharply. But here the law

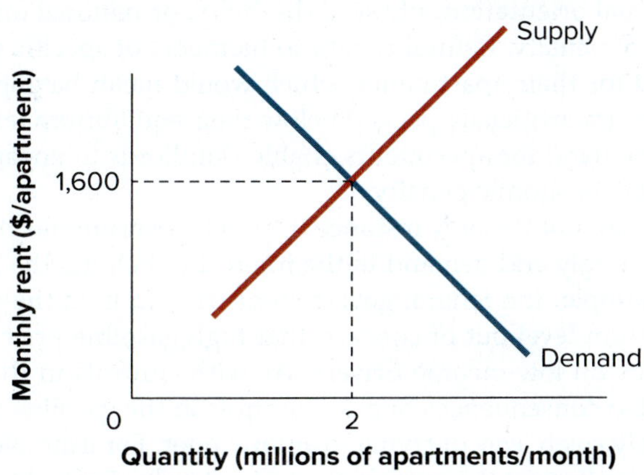

FIGURE 2.7

An Unregulated Housing Market.

For the supply and demand curves shown, the equilibrium monthly rent is $1,600 and 2 million apartments will be rented at that price.

FIGURE 2.8

Rent Controls.

When rents are prohibited from rising to the equilibrium level, the result is excess demand in the housing market.

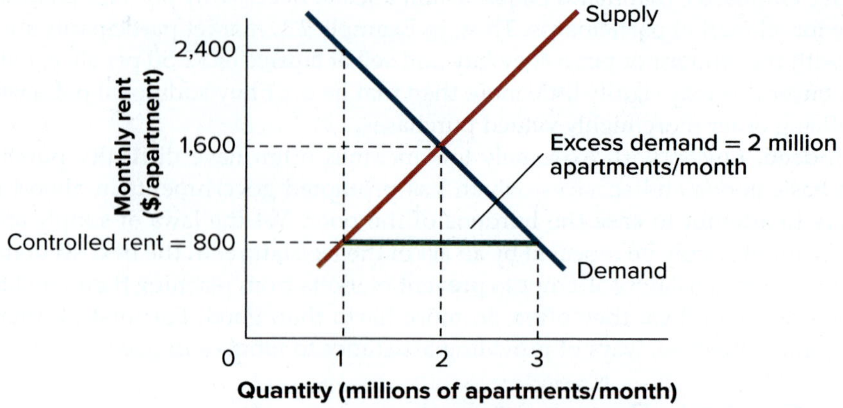

prevents them from rising above $800. Many other ways exist, however, in which market participants can respond to the pressures of excess demand. For instance, owners will quickly learn that they are free to spend less on maintaining their rental units. After all, if there are scores of renters knocking at the door of each vacant apartment, a landlord has considerable room to maneuver. Leaking pipes, peeling paint, broken furnaces, and other problems are less likely to receive prompt attention—or, indeed, any attention at all—when rents are set well below market-clearing levels.

Nor are reduced availability of apartments and poorer maintenance of existing apartments the only difficulties. With an offering of only 1 million apartments per month, we see in Figure 2.8 that there are renters who'd be willing to pay as much as $2,400 per month for an apartment. This pressure will almost always find ways, legal or illegal, of expressing itself. In New York City, for example, it is not uncommon to see "finder's fees" or "key deposits" as high as several thousand dollars. Owners who cannot charge a market-clearing rent for their apartments also have the option of converting them to condominiums or co-ops, which enables them to sell their assets for prices much closer to their true economic value.

Even when rent-controlled apartment owners don't hike their prices in these various ways, serious misallocations result. For instance, ill-suited roommates often remain together despite their constant bickering because each is reluctant to reenter the housing market. Or a widow might steadfastly remain in her seven-room apartment even after her children have left home because it is much cheaper than alternative dwellings not covered by rent control. It would be much better for all concerned if she relinquished that space to a larger family that valued it more highly. But under rent controls, she has no economic incentive to do so.

There's also another more insidious cost of rent controls. In markets without rent controls, landlords cannot discriminate against potential tenants on the basis of race, religion, sexual orientation, physical disability, or national origin without suffering an economic penalty. Refusal to rent to members of specific groups would reduce the demand for their apartments, which would mean having to accept lower rents. When rents are artificially pegged below their equilibrium level, however, the resulting excess demand for apartments enables landlords to engage in discrimination with no further economic penalty.

Rent controls are not the only instance in which governments have attempted to repeal the law of supply and demand in the interest of helping the poor. During the late 1970s, for example, the federal government tried to hold the price of gasoline below its equilibrium level out of concern that high gasoline prices imposed unacceptable hardships on low-income drivers. As with controls in the rental housing market, unintended consequences of price controls in the gasoline market made the policy an extremely costly way of trying to aid the poor. For example, gasoline shortages resulted in long lines at the pumps, a waste not only of valuable time, but also of gasoline as cars sat idling for extended periods.

In their opposition to rent controls and similar measures, are economists revealing a total lack of concern for the poor? Although this claim is sometimes made by those who don't understand the issues, or who stand to benefit in some way from government regulations, there is little justification for it. *Economists simply realize that there are much more effective ways to help poor people than to try to give them apartments and other goods at artificially low prices.*

One straightforward approach would be to give the poor additional income and let them decide for themselves how to spend it. True, there are also practical difficulties involved in transferring additional purchasing power into the hands of the poor—most importantly, the difficulty of targeting cash to the genuinely needy without weakening others' incentives to fend for themselves. But there are practical ways to overcome this difficulty. For example, for far less than the waste caused by price controls, the government could afford generous subsidies to the wages of the working poor and could sponsor public-service employment for those who are unable to find jobs in the private sector.

Regulations that peg prices below equilibrium levels have far-reaching effects on market outcomes. The following self-test asks you to consider what happens when a price control is established at a level above the equilibrium price.

SELF-TEST 2.3

In the rental housing market whose demand and supply curves are shown below, what will be the effect of a law that prevents rents from rising above $1,200 per month?

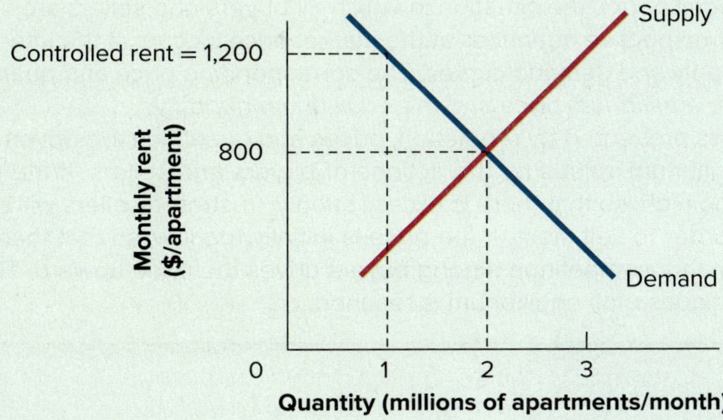

Pizza Price Controls?

The sources of the contrast between the rent-controlled housing market and the largely unregulated food markets in New York City can be seen more vividly by trying to imagine what would happen if concern for the poor led the city's leaders to implement price controls on pizza. Suppose, for example, that the supply and demand curves for pizza are as shown in Figure 2.9 and that the city imposes a **price ceiling** of $2 per slice, making it unlawful to charge more than that amount. At $2 per slice, buyers want to buy 16,000 slices per day, but sellers want to sell only 8,000.

price ceiling a maximum allowable price, specified by law

At a price of $2 per slice, every pizza restaurant in the city will have long queues of buyers trying unsuccessfully to purchase pizza. Frustrated buyers will behave rudely to clerks, who will respond in kind. Friends of restaurant managers will begin to get preferential treatment. Devious pricing strategies will begin to emerge (such as the $2 slice of pizza sold in combination with a $5 cup of Coke). Pizza will be made from poorer-quality ingredients. Rumors will begin to circulate about sources of black-market pizza. And so on.

FIGURE 2.9

Price Controls in the Pizza Market.

A price ceiling below the equilibrium price of pizza would result in excess demand for pizza.

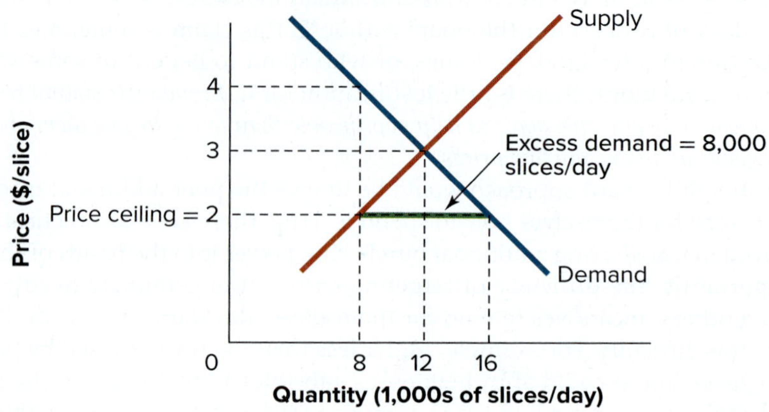

The very idea of not being able to buy a pizza seems absurd, yet precisely such things happen routinely in markets in which prices are held below the equilibrium levels. For example, prior to the collapse of communist governments, it was considered normal in those countries for people to stand in line for hours to buy bread and other basic goods, while the politically connected had first choice of those goods that were available.

RECAP

MARKET EQUILIBRIUM

Market equilibrium, the situation in which all buyers and sellers are satisfied with their respective quantities at the market price, occurs at the intersection of the supply and demand curves. The corresponding price and quantity are called the *equilibrium price* and the *equilibrium quantity*.

Unless prevented by regulation, prices and quantities are driven toward their equilibrium values by the actions of buyers and sellers. If the price is initially too high, so that there is excess supply, frustrated sellers will cut their price in order to sell more. If the price is initially too low, so that there is excess demand, competition among buyers drives the price upward. This process continues until equilibrium is reached.

PREDICTING AND EXPLAINING CHANGES IN PRICES AND QUANTITIES

change in the quantity demanded a movement along the demand curve that occurs in response to a change in price

change in demand a shift of the entire demand curve

If we know how the factors that govern supply and demand curves are changing, we can make informed predictions about how prices and the corresponding quantities will change. But when describing changing circumstances in the marketplace, we must take care to recognize some important terminological distinctions. For example, we must distinguish between the meanings of the seemingly similar expressions **change in the quantity demanded** and **change in demand.** When we speak of a "change in the quantity demanded," this means the change in the quantity that people wish to buy that occurs in response to a change in price. For instance, Figure 2.10(a) depicts an increase in the quantity demanded that occurs in response to a reduction in the price of tuna. When the price falls from \$2 to \$1 per can, the quantity demanded rises from 8,000 to 10,000 cans per day. By contrast, when we speak of a "change in demand," this means a *shift in the entire demand curve*. For example, Figure 2.10(b) depicts an increase in demand, meaning that at every price the quantity demanded is higher than before. In summary, a "change in the quantity demanded" refers to a movement *along* the demand curve and a "change in demand" means a *shift* of the entire curve.

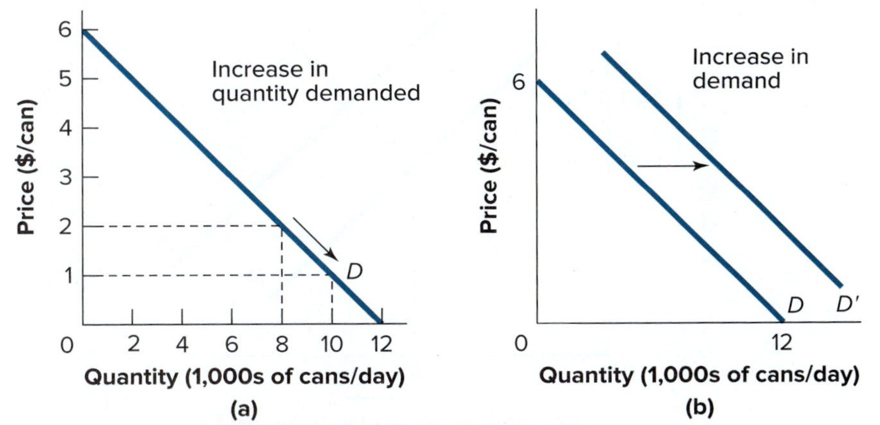

FIGURE 2.10

An Increase in the Quantity Demanded versus an Increase in Demand.

(a) An increase in quantity demanded describes a downward movement along the demand curve as price falls. (b) An increase in demand describes an outward shift of the demand curve.

A similar terminological distinction applies on the supply side of the market. A **change in supply** means a shift in the entire supply curve, whereas a **change in the quantity supplied** refers to a movement along the supply curve.

change in supply a shift of the entire supply curve

change in the quantity supplied a movement along the supply curve that occurs in response to a change in price

Alfred Marshall's supply and demand model is one of the most useful tools of the economic naturalist. Once we understand the forces that govern the placements of supply and demand curves, we're suddenly in a position to make sense of a host of interesting observations in the world around us.

Shifts in Demand

To get a better feel for how the supply and demand model enables us to predict and explain price and quantity movements, it's helpful to begin with a few simple examples. The first one illustrates a shift in demand that results from events outside the particular market itself.

EXAMPLE 2.2 Complements

What will happen to the equilibrium price and quantity of tennis balls if court-rental fees decline?

Let the initial supply and demand curves for tennis balls be as shown by the curves *S* and *D* in Figure 2.11, where the resulting equilibrium price and quantity are $1 per ball and 40 million balls per month, respectively. Tennis courts and tennis balls are what economists call **complements,** goods that are more valuable when used in combination than when used alone. Tennis balls, for example, would be of little value if there were no tennis courts on which to play. (Tennis balls would still have *some* value even without courts—for example, to the parents who pitch them to their children for batting practice.) As tennis courts become cheaper to use, people will respond by playing more tennis, and this will increase their demand for tennis balls. A decline in court-rental fees will thus shift the demand curve for tennis balls rightward to *D*′. (A "rightward shift" of a demand curve also can be described as an "upward shift." These distinctions correspond, respectively, to the horizontal and vertical interpretations of the demand curve.)

complements two goods are complements in consumption if an increase in the price of one causes a leftward shift in the demand curve for the other (or if a decrease causes a rightward shift)

Note in Figure 2.11 that, for the illustrative demand shift shown, the new equilibrium price of tennis balls, $1.40, is higher than the original price and the new equilibrium quantity, 58 million balls per month, is higher than the original quantity.

FIGURE 2.11

The Effect on the Market for Tennis Balls of a Decline in Court-Rental Fees.

When the price of a complement falls, demand shifts right, causing equilibrium price and quantity to rise.

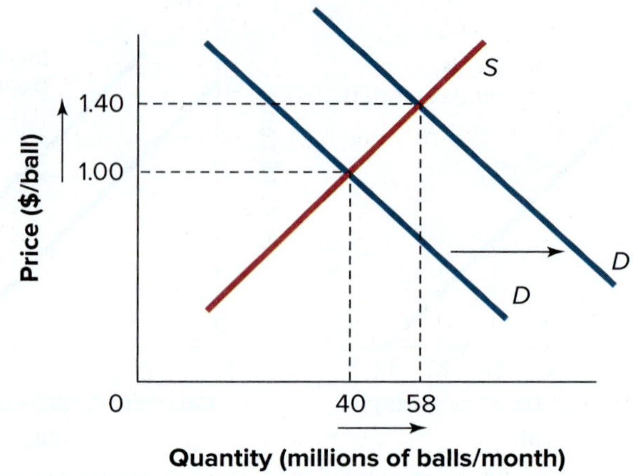

EXAMPLE 2.3 Substitutes

What will happen to the equilibrium price and quantity of print ads as the price of digital ads falls?

Most businesses purchase a mix of digital and print ads to promote their products. Suppose the initial supply and demand curves print ads are as shown by the curves *S* and *D* in Figure 2.12, and the resulting equilibrium price and quantity are denoted *P* and *Q*. Print ads and digital ads are examples of what economists call **substitutes,** meaning that, in many applications at least, the two serve similar functions. (Many noneconomists would call them substitutes, too. Economists don't *always* choose obscure terms for important concepts!) When two goods or services are substitutes, a decrease in the price of one will cause a leftward shift in the demand curve for the other. (A "leftward shift" in a demand curve can also be described as a "downward shift.") Diagrammatically, the demand curve for print ads shifts from *D* to *D'* in Figure 2.12.

substitutes two goods are substitutes in consumption if an increase in the price of one causes a rightward shift in the demand curve for the other (or if a decrease causes a leftward shift)

FIGURE 2.12

The Effect on the Market for Print Ads of a Decline in the Price of Digital Ads.

When the price of a substitute falls, demand shifts left, causing equilibrium price and quantity to fall.

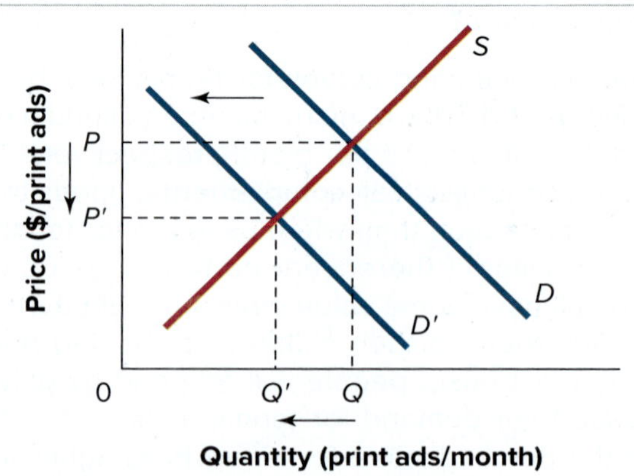

As the figure shows, both the new equilibrium price, *P'*, and the new equilibrium quantity, *Q'*, are lower than the initial values, *P* and *Q*. Cheaper digital ads probably won't put print advertising companies out of business, but it will definitely lead to a drop in sales.

To summarize, economists define goods as substitutes if an increase in the price of one causes a rightward shift in the demand curve for the other. By contrast, goods are complements if an increase in the price of one causes a leftward shift in the demand curve for the other.

The concepts of substitutes and complements enable you to answer questions like the one posed in Self-Test 2.4.

connect

▸ Visit your instructor's Connect course and access your eBook to view this video.

Why are rotisserie chickens less expensive than fresh chickens?

SELF-TEST 2.4

How will a decline in airfares affect intercity bus fares and the price of hotel rooms in resort communities?

Demand curves are shifted not just by changes in the prices of substitutes and complements but also by other factors that change the amounts people are willing to pay for a given good or service. One of the most important such factors is income.

The Economic Naturalist 2.1

When the federal government implements a large pay increase for its employees, why do rents for apartments located near Washington Metro stations go up relative to rents for apartments located far away from Metro stations?

For the citizens of Washington, D.C., a substantial proportion of whom are government employees, it's more convenient to live in an apartment located 1 block from the nearest subway station than to live in one that is 20 blocks away. Conveniently located apartments thus command relatively high rents. Suppose the initial demand and supply curves for such apartments are as shown in Figure 2.13. Following a federal pay raise, some government employees who live in less convenient apartments will be willing and able to use part of their extra income to bid for more conveniently located apartments, and those who already live in such apartments will be willing and able to pay more to keep them. The effect of the pay raise is thus to shift the demand curve for conveniently located apartments to the right, as indicated by the demand curve labeled D'. As a result, both the equilibrium price and quantity of such apartments, P' and Q', will be higher than before.

Who gets to live in the most conveniently located apartments?

FIGURE 2.13

The Effect of a Federal Pay Raise on the Rent for Conveniently Located Apartments in Washington, D.C.

An increase in income shifts demand for a normal good to the right, causing equilibrium price and quantity to rise.

It might seem natural to ask how there could be an increase in the number of conveniently located apartments, which might appear to be fixed by the constraints of geography. But we must never underestimate the ingenuity of sellers when they confront an opportunity to make money by supplying more of something that people want. For example, if rents rose sufficiently, some landlords might respond by converting warehouse space to residential use. Or perhaps people with cars who do not place high value on living near a subway station might sell their co-op apartments to landlords, thereby freeing them for people eager to rent them. (Note that these responses constitute movements along the supply curve of conveniently located apartments, as opposed to shifts in that supply curve.)

When incomes increase, the demand curves for most goods will behave like the demand curve for conveniently located apartments, and in recognition of that fact, economists have chosen to call such goods **normal goods.**

normal good a good whose demand curve shifts rightward when the incomes of buyers increase and leftward when the incomes of buyers decrease

Not all goods are normal goods, however. In fact, the demand curves for some goods actually shift leftward when income goes up. Such goods are called **inferior goods.**

inferior good a good whose demand curve shifts leftward when the incomes of buyers increase and rightward when the incomes of buyers decrease

When would having more money tend to make you want to buy less of something? In general, this happens with goods for which there exist attractive substitutes that sell for only slightly higher prices. Apartments in unsafe, inconveniently located neighborhoods are an example. Most residents would choose to move out of such neighborhoods as soon as they could afford to, which means that an increase in income would cause the demand for such apartments to shift leftward.

SELF-TEST 2.5

How will a large pay increase for federal employees affect the rents for apartments located far away from Washington Metro stations?

Ground beef with high fat content is another example of an inferior good. For health reasons, most people prefer grades of meat with low fat content, and when they do buy high-fat meats it's usually a sign of budgetary pressure. When people in this situation receive higher incomes, they usually switch quickly to leaner grades of meat.

Preferences, or tastes, are another important factor that determines whether the purchase of a given good will satisfy the Cost-Benefit Principle. The release of each Marvel Studio film appears to kindle a powerful preference among children for Marvel action figures. When these films are released, the demand for Marvel action figures shifts sharply to the right. And the same children who can't get enough Marvel action figures suddenly lose interest in their other toys, whose respective demand curves shift to the left.

Expectations about the future are another factor that may cause demand curves to shift. If Apple users hear a credible rumor, for example, that a cheaper or significantly upgraded model will be introduced next month, the demand curve for the current model is likely to shift leftward.

Shifts in the Supply Curve

The preceding examples involved changes that gave rise to shifts in demand curves. Next, we'll look at what happens when supply curves shift. Because the supply curve is based on costs of production, anything that changes production costs will shift the supply curve, resulting in a new equilibrium quantity and price.

EXAMPLE 2.4 Increasing Opportunity Cost

What will happen to the equilibrium price and quantity of skateboards if the price of fiberglass, a substance used for making skateboards, rises?

Suppose the initial supply and demand curves for skateboards are as shown by the curves *S* and *D* in Figure 2.14, resulting in an equilibrium price and quantity of

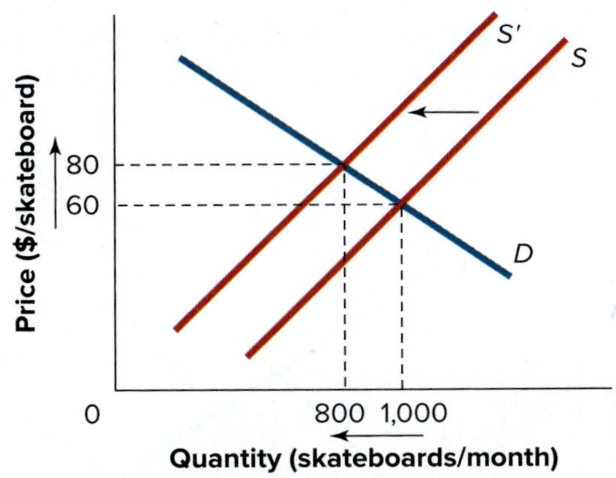

FIGURE 2.14

The Effect on the Skateboard Market of an Increase in the Price of Fiberglass.

When input prices rise, supply shifts left, causing equilibrium price to rise and equilibrium quantity to fall.

$60 per skateboard and 1,000 skateboards per month, respectively. Since fiberglass is one of the materials used to produce skateboards, the effect of an increase in its price is to raise the marginal cost of producing skateboards. How will this affect the supply curve of skateboards?

Recall that the supply curve is upward-sloping because when the price of skateboards is low, only those potential sellers whose marginal cost of making skateboards is low can sell boards profitably, whereas at higher prices, those with higher marginal costs also can enter the market profitably. So if the cost of one of the materials used to produce skateboards rises, the number of potential sellers who can profitably sell skateboards at any given price will fall. And this, in turn, implies a leftward shift in the supply curve for skateboards. Note that a "leftward shift" in a supply curve also can be viewed as an "upward shift" in the same curve. The first corresponds to the horizontal interpretation of the supply curve, while the second corresponds to the vertical interpretation. We will use these expressions to mean exactly the same thing. The new supply curve (after the price of fiberglass rises) is the curve labeled *S′* in Figure 2.14.

Does an increase in the cost of fiberglass have any effect on the demand curve for skateboards? The demand curve tells us how many skateboards buyers wish to purchase at each price. Any given buyer is willing to purchase a skateboard if her reservation price for it exceeds its market price. And since each buyer's reservation price, which is based on the benefits of owning a skateboard, does not depend on the price of fiberglass, there should be no shift in the demand curve for skateboards.

In Figure 2.14, we can now see what happens when the supply curve shifts leftward and the demand curve remains unchanged. For the illustrative supply curve shown, the new equilibrium price of skateboards, $80, is higher than the original price, and the new equilibrium quantity, 800 per month, is lower than the original quantity. (These new equilibrium values are merely illustrative. There is insufficient information provided in the example to determine their exact values.) People who don't place a value of at least $80 on owning a skateboard will choose to spend their money on something else.

The effects on equilibrium price and quantity run in the opposite direction whenever marginal costs of production decline, as illustrated in the next example.

EXAMPLE 2.5 Reduction of Marginal Cost

What will happen to the equilibrium price and quantity of new houses if the wage rate of carpenters falls?

Suppose the initial supply and demand curves for new houses are as shown by the curves *S* and *D* in Figure 2.15, resulting in an equilibrium price of

FIGURE 2.15

The Effect on the Market for New Houses of a Decline in Carpenters' Wage Rates.

When input prices fall, supply shifts right, causing equilibrium price to fall and equilibrium quantity to rise.

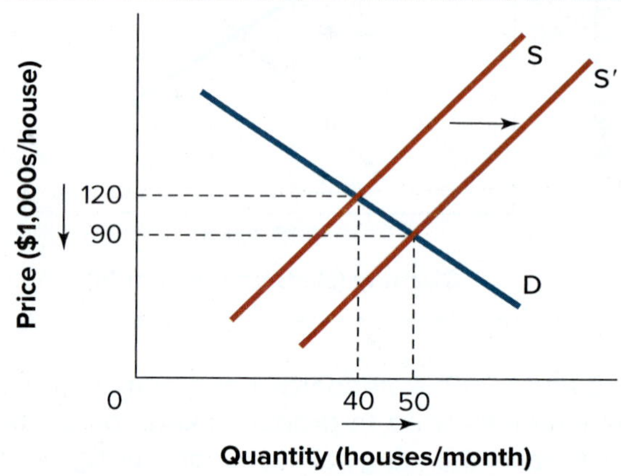

$120,000 per house and an equilibrium quantity of 40 houses per month, respectively. A decline in the wage rate of carpenters reduces the marginal cost of making new houses, and this means that, for any given price of houses, more builders can profitably serve the market than before. Diagrammatically, this means a rightward shift in the supply curve of houses, from *S* to *S′*. (A "rightward shift" in the supply curve also can be described as a "downward shift.")

Does a decrease in the wage rate of carpenters have any effect on the demand curve for houses? The demand curve tells us how many houses buyers wish to purchase at each price. Because carpenters are now earning less than before, the maximum amount that they are willing to pay for houses may fall, which would imply a leftward shift in the demand curve for houses. But because carpenters make up only a tiny fraction of all potential home buyers, we may assume that this shift is negligible. Thus, a reduction in carpenters' wages produces a significant rightward shift in the supply curve of houses, but no appreciable shift in the demand curve.

We see from Figure 2.15 that the new equilibrium price, $90,000 per house, is lower than the original price and the new equilibrium quantity, 50 houses per month, is higher than the original quantity.

Examples 2.4 and 2.5 involved changes in the cost of a material, or input, in the production of the good in question—fiberglass in the production of skateboards and carpenters' labor in the production of houses. As the following example illustrates, supply curves also shift when technology changes.

The Economic Naturalist 2.2

Why do major term papers go through so many more revisions today than in the 1970s?

Students in the dark days before word processors were in widespread use could not make even minor revisions in their term papers without having to retype their entire manuscript from scratch. The availability of word-processing technology has, of course, radically changed the picture. Instead of having to retype the entire draft, now only the changes need be entered.

In Figure 2.16, the curves labeled *S* and *D* depict the supply and demand curves for revisions in the days before word processing, and the curve *S′* depicts the supply curve for revisions today. As the diagram shows, the result is not only a sharp decline in the price per revision, but also a corresponding increase in the equilibrium number of revisions.

Why does written work go through so many more revisions now than in the 1970s?

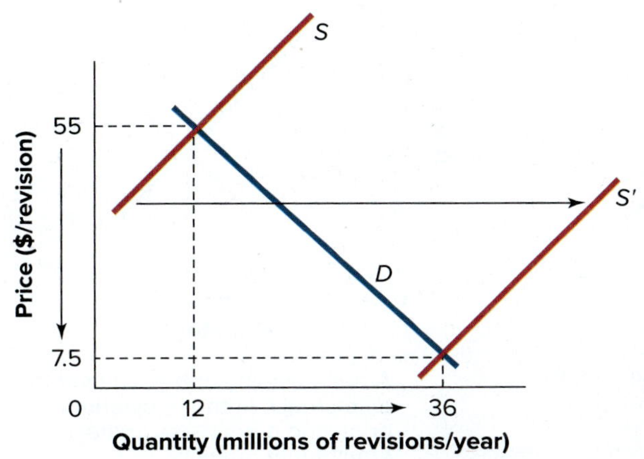

FIGURE 2.16

The Effect of Technical Change on the Market for Term-Paper Revisions.

When a new technology reduces the cost of production, supply shifts right, causing equilibrium price to fall and equilibrium quantity to rise.

Note that in The Economic Naturalist 2.2 we implicitly assumed that students purchased typing services in a market. In fact, however, many students type their own term papers. Does that make a difference? Even if no money actually changes hands, students pay a price when they revise their term papers—namely, the opportunity cost of the time it takes to perform that task. Because technology has radically reduced that cost, we would expect to see a large increase in the number of term-paper revisions even if most students type their own work.

Changes in input prices and technology are two of the most important factors that give rise to shifts in supply curves. In the case of agricultural commodities, weather may be another important factor, with favorable conditions shifting the supply curves of such products to the right and unfavorable conditions shifting them to the left. (Weather also may affect the supply curves of nonagricultural products through its effects on the national transportation system.) Expectations of future price changes also may shift current supply curves, as when the expectation of poor crops from a current drought causes suppliers to withhold supplies from existing stocks in the hope of selling at higher prices in the future. Changes in the number of sellers in the market also can cause supply curves to shift.

Four Simple Rules

For supply and demand curves that have the conventional slopes (upward-sloping for supply curves, downward-sloping for demand curves), the preceding examples illustrate the four basic rules that govern how shifts in supply and demand affect equilibrium prices and quantities. These rules are summarized in Figure 2.17.

FIGURE 2.17

Four Rules Governing the Effects of Supply and Demand Shifts.

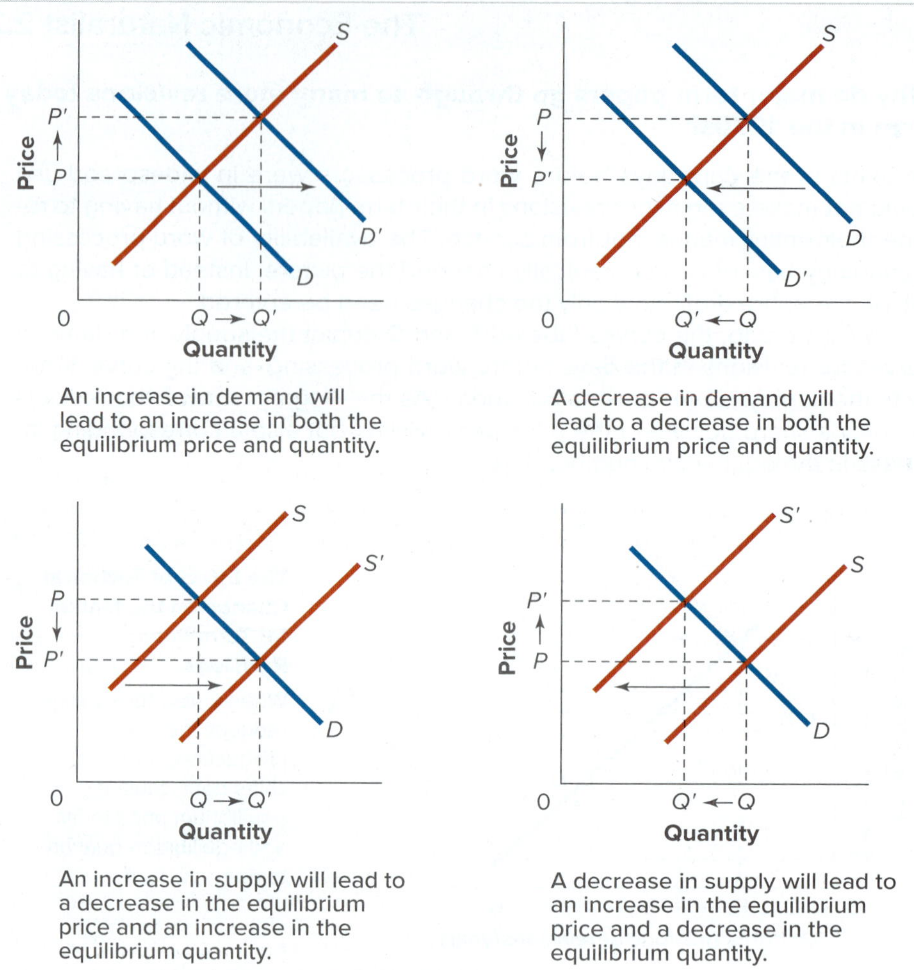

RECAP

FACTORS THAT SHIFT SUPPLY AND DEMAND

Factors that cause an increase (rightward or upward shift) in demand:

1. A decrease in the price of complements to the good or service.
2. An increase in the price of substitutes for the good or service.
3. An increase in income (for a normal good).
4. An increased preference by demanders for the good or service.
5. An increase in the population of potential buyers.
6. An expectation of higher prices in the future.

When these factors move in the opposite direction, demand will shift left.

Factors that cause an increase (rightward or downward shift) in supply:

1. A decrease in the cost of materials, labor, or other inputs used in the production of the good or service.
2. An improvement in technology that reduces the cost of producing the good or service.
3. An improvement in the weather (especially for agricultural products).
4. An increase in the number of suppliers.
5. An expectation of lower prices in the future.

When these factors move in the opposite direction, supply will shift left.

The qualitative rules summarized in Figure 2.17 hold for supply or demand shifts of any magnitude, provided the curves have their conventional slopes. But as the next example demonstrates, when both supply and demand curves shift at the same time, the direction in which equilibrium price or quantity changes will depend on the relative magnitudes of the shifts.

EXAMPLE 2.6 Shifts in Supply and Demand

How do shifts in *both* demand and supply affect equilibrium quantities and prices?

What will happen to the equilibrium price and quantity in the corn tortilla chip market if both of the following events occur: (1) researchers prove that the oils in which tortilla chips are fried are harmful to human health and (2) the price of corn harvesting equipment falls?

The conclusion regarding the health effects of the oils will shift the demand for tortilla chips to the left because many people who once bought chips in the belief that they were healthful will now switch to other foods. The decline in the price of harvesting equipment will shift the supply of chips to the right because additional farmers will now find it profitable to enter the corn market. In Figure 2.18(a) and 2.18(b), the original supply and demand curves are denoted by *S* and *D*, while the new curves are denoted by *S′* and *D′*. Note that in both panels the shifts lead to a decline in the equilibrium price of chips.

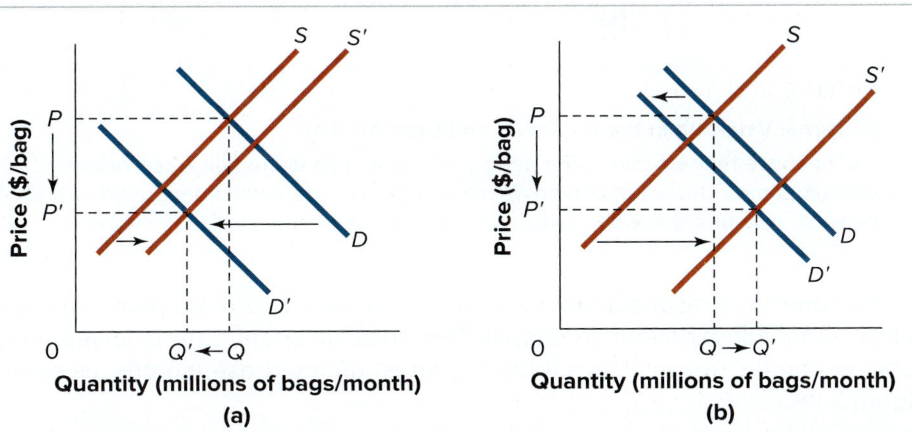

FIGURE 2.18

The Effects of Simultaneous Shifts in Supply and Demand.

When demand shifts left and supply shifts right, equilibrium price falls, but equilibrium quantity may either rise (b) or fall (a).

But note also that the effect of the shifts on equilibrium quantity cannot be determined without knowing their relative magnitudes. Taken separately, the demand shift causes a decline in equilibrium quantity, whereas the supply shift causes an increase in equilibrium quantity. The net effect of the two shifts thus depends on which of the individual effects is larger. In Figure 2.18(a), the demand shift dominates, so equilibrium quantity declines. In Figure 2.18(b), the supply shift dominates, so equilibrium quantity goes up.

The following Self-Test 2.6 asks you to consider a simple variation on the problem posed in the previous example.

SELF-TEST 2.6

What will happen to the equilibrium price and quantity in the corn tortilla chip market if both of the following events occur: (1) researchers discover that a vitamin found in corn helps protect against cancer and heart disease and (2) a swarm of locusts destroys part of the corn crop?

The Economic Naturalist 2.3

Why do the prices of some goods, like airline tickets to Europe, go up during the months of heaviest consumption, while others, like sweet corn, go down?

Why are some goods cheapest during the months of heaviest consumption, while others are most expensive during those months?

Seasonal price movements for airline tickets are primarily the result of seasonal variations in demand. Thus, ticket prices to Europe are highest during the summer months because the demand for tickets is highest during those months, as shown in Figure 2.19(a), where the *w* and *s* subscripts denote winter and summer values, respectively.

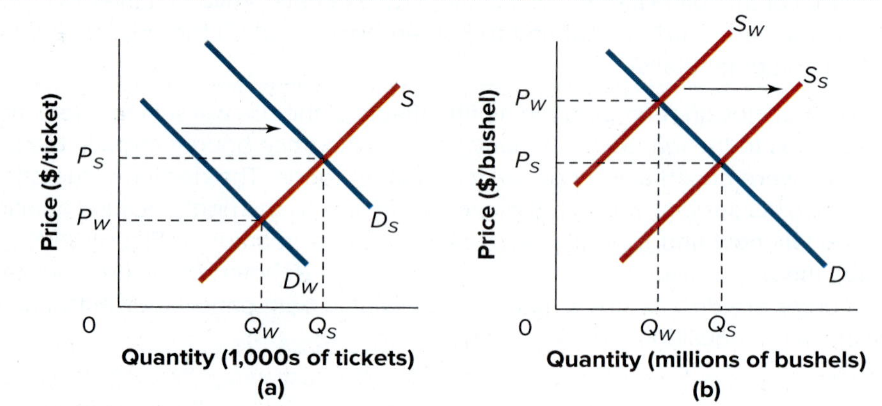

FIGURE 2.19

Seasonal Variation in the Air Travel and Corn Markets.

(a) Prices are highest during the period of heaviest consumption when heavy consumption is the result of high demand. (b) Prices are lowest during the period of heaviest consumption when heavy consumption is the result of high supply.

By contrast, seasonal price movements for sweet corn are primarily the result of seasonal variations in supply. The price of sweet corn is lowest in the summer months because its supply is highest during those months, as seen in Figure 2.19(b).

EFFICIENCY AND EQUILIBRIUM

Markets represent a highly effective system of allocating resources. When a market for a good is in equilibrium, the equilibrium price conveys important information to potential suppliers about the value that potential demanders place on that good. At the same time, the equilibrium price informs potential demanders about the opportunity cost of supplying the good. This rapid, two-way transmission of information is the reason that markets can coordinate an activity as complex as supplying New York City with food and drink, even though no one person or organization oversees the process.

But are the prices and quantities determined in market equilibrium socially optimal, in the sense of maximizing total economic surplus? That is, does equilibrium in unregulated markets always maximize the difference between the total benefits and total costs experienced by market participants? As we'll see, the answer is it depends: a market that is out of equilibrium, such as the rent-controlled New York housing market, always creates opportunities for individuals to arrange transactions that will increase their individual economic surplus. As we'll also see, however, a market for a good that is in equilibrium makes the largest possible contribution to total economic surplus only when its supply and demand curves fully reflect all costs and benefits associated with the production and consumption of that good.

Cash on the Table

In economics we assume that all exchange is purely voluntary. This means that a transaction cannot take place unless the buyer's reservation price for the good exceeds the seller's reservation price. When that condition is met and a transaction takes place, both parties receive an economic surplus. The **buyer's surplus** from the transaction is the difference between his or her reservation price and the price he or she actually pays. The **seller's surplus** is the difference between the price he or she receives and his or her reservation price. The **total surplus** from the transaction is the sum of the buyer's surplus and the seller's surplus. It is also equal to the difference between the buyer's reservation price and the seller's reservation price.

buyer's surplus the difference between the buyer's reservation price and the price he or she actually pays

seller's surplus the difference between the price received by the seller and his or her reservation price

total surplus the difference between the buyer's reservation price and the seller's reservation price

Suppose there is a potential buyer whose reservation price for an additional slice of pizza is \$4 and a potential seller whose reservation price is only \$2. If this buyer purchases a slice of pizza from this seller for \$3, the total surplus generated by this exchange is \$4 − \$2 = \$2, of which \$4 − \$3 = \$1 is the buyer's surplus and \$3 − \$2 = \$1 is the seller's surplus.

A regulation that prevents the price of a good from reaching its equilibrium level unnecessarily prevents exchanges of this sort from taking place, and in the process reduces total economic surplus. Consider again the effect of price controls imposed in the market for pizza. The demand curve in Figure 2.20 tells us that if a price ceiling of \$2 per slice were imposed, only 8,000 slices of pizza per day would be sold. At that quantity, the vertical interpretations of the supply and demand curves tell us that a buyer would be willing to pay as much as \$4 for an additional slice and that a seller would be willing to sell one for as little as \$2. The difference—\$2 per slice—is the additional economic surplus that would result if an additional slice were produced and sold. As noted earlier, an extra slice sold at a price of \$3 would result in an additional \$1 of economic surplus for both buyer and seller.

When a market is out of equilibrium, it's always possible to identify mutually beneficial exchanges of this sort. When people have failed to take advantage of all mutually beneficial exchanges, we often say that there's **"cash on the table"**—the economist's metaphor for unexploited opportunities. When the price in a market is below the equilibrium price, there's cash on the table because the reservation price of sellers (marginal cost) will always be lower than the reservation price of buyers. In the absence of a law preventing buyers from paying more than \$2 per slice,

cash on the table an economic metaphor for unexploited gains from exchange

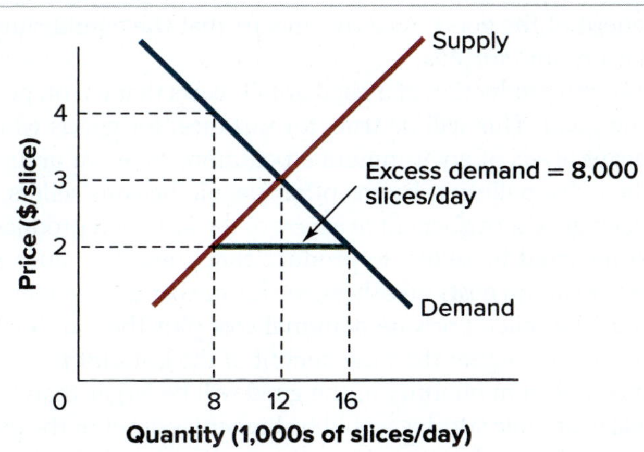

FIGURE 2.20

Price Controls in the Pizza Market.

A price ceiling below the equilibrium price of pizza would result in excess demand for pizza.

restaurant owners would quickly raise their prices and expand their production until the equilibrium price of $3 per slice were reached. At that price, buyers would be able to get precisely the 12,000 slices of pizza they want to buy each day. All mutually beneficial opportunities for exchange would have been exploited, leaving no more cash on the table.

It should be no surprise that buyers and sellers in the marketplace have an uncanny ability to detect the presence of cash on the table. It is almost as if unexploited opportunities give off some exotic scent triggering neurochemical explosions in the olfactory centers of their brains. The desire to scrape cash off the table and into their pockets is what drives sellers in each of New York City's thousands of individual food markets to work diligently to meet their customers' demands. That they succeed to a far higher degree than participants in the city's rent-controlled housing market is plainly evident. Whatever flaws it might have, the market system moves with considerably greater speed and agility than any centralized allocation mechanisms yet devised. But as we emphasize in the following section, this does not mean that markets *always* lead to the greatest good for all.

Smart for One, Dumb for All

socially optimal quantity the quantity of a good that results in the maximum possible economic surplus from producing and consuming the good

The **socially optimal quantity** of any good is the quantity that maximizes the total economic surplus that results from producing and consuming the good. From the Cost-Benefit Principle, we know that we should keep expanding production of the good as long as its marginal benefit is at least as great as its marginal cost. This means that the socially optimal quantity is that level for which the marginal cost and marginal benefit of the good are the same.

When the quantity of a good is less than the socially optimal quantity, boosting its production will increase total economic surplus. By the same token, when the quantity of a good exceeds the socially optimal quantity, reducing its production will increase total economic surplus. **Efficiency,** or **economic efficiency,** occurs when all goods and services in the economy are produced and consumed at their respective socially optimal levels.

efficiency (or **economic efficiency**) a condition that occurs when all goods and services are produced and consumed at their respective socially optimal levels

Efficiency is an important social goal. Failure to achieve efficiency means that total economic surplus is smaller than it could have been. Movements toward efficiency make the total economic pie larger, making it possible for everyone to have a larger slice.

Is the market equilibrium quantity of a good efficient? That is, does it maximize the total economic surplus received by participants in the market for that good? When the private market for a given good is in equilibrium, we can say that the cost *to the seller* of producing an additional unit of the good is the same as the benefit *to the buyer* of having an additional unit. If all costs of producing the good are borne directly by sellers, and if all benefits from the good accrue directly to buyers, it follows that the market equilibrium quantity of the good will equate the marginal cost and marginal benefit of the good. And this means that the equilibrium quantity also maximizes total economic surplus.

But sometimes the production of a good entails costs that fall on people other than those who sell the good. This will be true, for instance, for goods whose production generates significant levels of environmental pollution. As extra units of these goods are produced, the extra pollution harms other people besides sellers. In the market equilibrium for such goods, the benefit *to buyers* of the last good produced is, as before, equal to the cost incurred by sellers to produce that good. But since producing that good also imposes pollution costs on others, we know that the *full* marginal cost of the last unit produced—the seller's private marginal cost plus the marginal pollution cost borne by others—must be higher than the benefit of the last unit produced. So, in this case, the market equilibrium quantity of the good will be larger than the socially optimal quantity. Total economic surplus would be higher if output of the good were lower. Yet neither sellers nor buyers have any incentive to alter their behavior.

The Economic Naturalist 2.4

Why was there a shortage of toilet paper during the COVID-19 pandemic?

During the COVID-19 pandemic many consumers in search of toilet paper arrived at their local grocery stores only to be faced with empty shelves. If prices are supposed to adjust to equate the quantity supplied and the quantity demanded, then why was there a shortage of toilet paper during the pandemic?

Faced with the public health crisis brought about COVID-19 many, if not most, consumers in the United States stocked up on essential items such as toilet paper. Indeed, some consumers purchased excessive quantities of these items, and this type of hoarding behavior received much of the blame for the shortage of toilet paper during the pandemic.

But there is another important factor as well. The toilet paper market in the United States is divided into two distinct segments. There is a market for the lower-quality commercial-grade toilet paper, typically used in restaurants, schools, workplaces and other public venues, and a separate market for the higher-quality consumer-grade toilet paper, generally used in people's homes. Even though the overall use of toilet paper did not substantially change during the pandemic, there was a large shift away from commercial-grade toilet paper toward consumer-grade toilet paper. That is, the widespread stay-at-home orders led to a sharp decrease in the demand for commercial-grade toilet paper, and an equally abrupt increase in the demand for consumer-grade toilet paper, and toilet paper producers, who are accustomed to relatively stable demand, had difficulty adjusting to this rapid change.

Of course, in normal times, an increase in demand would not lead to a shortage. Instead we would expect prices to rise. During times of emergency, however, both social norms and price gouging laws limit retailers' ability to raise prices. Thus while the demand for consumer-grade toilet paper surged during the pandemic (both because of hoarding and the shift away from commercial-grade toilet paper), prices did not adjust, leading to empty shelves and anxious consumers.

Another possibility is that people other than those who buy a good may receive significant benefits from it. For instance, when someone purchases a vaccination against measles from her doctor, she not only protects herself, but also makes it less likely that others will catch this disease. From the perspective of society as a whole, we should keep increasing the number of vaccinations until their marginal cost equals their marginal benefit. The marginal benefit of a vaccination is the value of the protection it provides the person vaccinated *plus* the value of the protection it provides all others. Private consumers, however, will choose to be vaccinated only if the marginal benefit *to them* exceeds the price of the vaccination. In this case, then, the market equilibrium quantity of vaccinations will be smaller than the quantity that maximizes total economic surplus. Again, however, individuals would have no incentive to alter their behavior.

Situations like the ones just discussed provide examples of behaviors that we may call "smart for one but dumb for all." In each case, the individual actors are behaving rationally. They are pursuing their goals as best they can, and yet there remain unexploited opportunities for gain from the point of view of the whole society. The difficulty is that these opportunities cannot be exploited by individuals acting alone. In subsequent chapters, we will see how people can often organize collectively to exploit such opportunities.

RECAP

EFFICIENCY AND EQUILIBRIUM

When the supply and demand curves for a good reflect all significant costs and benefits associated with the production and consumption of that good, the market equilibrium will result in the largest possible economic surplus. But if people other than buyers benefit from the good, or if people other than sellers bear costs because of it, market equilibrium need not result in the largest possible economic surplus.

SUMMARY

- The demand curve is a downward-sloping line that tells what quantity buyers will demand at any given price. The supply curve is an upward-sloping line that tells what quantity sellers will offer at any given price. *(LO1)*
- Alfred Marshall's model of supply and demand explains why neither cost of production nor value to the purchaser (as measured by willingness to pay) is, by itself, sufficient to explain why some goods are cheap and others are expensive. To explain variations in price, we must examine the interaction of cost and willingness to pay. As we've seen in this chapter, goods differ in price because of differences in their respective supply and demand curves. *(LO2)*
- Market equilibrium occurs when the quantity buyers demand at the market price is exactly the same as the quantity that sellers offer. The equilibrium price–quantity pair is the one at which the demand and supply curves intersect. In equilibrium, market price measures both the value of the last unit sold to buyers and the cost of the resources required to produce it. *(LO2)*
- When the price of a good lies above its equilibrium value, there is an excess supply of that good. Excess supply motivates sellers to cut their prices and price continues to fall until equilibrium price is reached. When price lies below its equilibrium value, there is excess demand. With excess demand, frustrated buyers are motivated to offer higher prices and the upward pressure on prices persists until equilibrium is reached. A remarkable feature of the market system is that, relying only on the tendency of people to respond in self-interested ways to market price signals, it somehow manages to coordinate the actions of literally billions of buyers and sellers worldwide. When excess demand or excess supply occurs, it tends to be small and brief, except in markets where regulations prevent full adjustment of prices. *(LO2)*
- The basic supply and demand model is a primary tool of the economic naturalist. Changes in the equilibrium price of a good, and in the amount of it traded in the marketplace, can be predicted on the basis of shifts in its supply or demand curves. The following four rules hold for any good with a downward-sloping demand curve and an upward-sloping supply curve.
  1. An increase in demand will lead to an increase in equilibrium price and quantity.
  2. A reduction in demand will lead to a reduction in equilibrium price and quantity.
  3. An increase in supply will lead to a reduction in equilibrium price and an increase in equilibrium quantity.
  4. A decrease in supply will lead to an increase in equilibrium price and a reduction in equilibrium quantity. *(LO3)*
- Incomes, tastes, population, expectations, and the prices of substitutes and complements are among the factors that shift demand schedules. Supply schedules, in turn, are primarily governed by such factors as technology, input prices, expectations, the number of sellers, and, especially for agricultural products, the weather. *(LO3)*
- The efficiency of markets in allocating resources does not eliminate social concerns about how goods and services are distributed among different people. For example, we often lament the fact many buyers enter the market with too little income to buy even the most basic goods and services. Concern for the well-being of the poor has motivated many governments to intervene in a variety of ways to alter the outcomes of market forces. Sometimes these interventions take the form of laws that peg prices below their equilibrium levels. Such laws almost invariably generate harmful, if unintended, consequences. Programs like rent-control laws, for example, lead to severe housing shortages, black marketeering, and a rapid deterioration of the relationship between landlords and tenants. *(LO4)*
- If the difficulty is that the poor have too little money, the best solution is to discover ways of boosting their incomes directly. The law of supply and demand cannot be repealed by the legislature. But legislatures do have the capacity to alter the underlying forces that

govern the shape and position of supply and demand schedules. *(LO4)*

- When the supply and demand curves for a good reflect all significant costs and benefits associated with the production and consumption of that good, the market equilibrium price will guide people to produce and consume the quantity of the good that results in the largest possible economic surplus. This conclusion, however, does not apply if others, besides buyers, benefit from the good (as when someone benefits from his neighbor's purchase of a vaccination against measles) or if others besides sellers bear costs because of the good (as when its production generates pollution). In such cases, market equilibrium does not result in the greatest gain for all. *(LO4)*

KEY TERMS

buyer's reservation price
buyer's surplus
cash on the table
change in demand
change in supply
change in the quantity demanded
change in the quantity supplied
complements
demand curve
efficiency (or economic efficiency)
equilibrium
equilibrium price and equilibrium quantity
excess demand (or shortage)
excess supply (or surplus)
income effect
inferior good
market
market equilibrium
normal good
price ceiling
seller's reservation price
seller's surplus
socially optimal quantity
substitutes
substitution effect
supply curve
total surplus

REVIEW QUESTIONS

1. Explain the distinction between the horizontal and vertical interpretations of the demand curve. *(LO1)*
2. Why isn't knowing the cost of producing a good sufficient to predict its market price? *(LO2)*
3. In recent years, a government official proposed that gasoline price controls be imposed to protect the poor from rising gasoline prices. What evidence could you consult to discover whether this proposal was enacted? *(LO2)*
4. Distinguish between the meaning of the expressions "change in demand" and "change in the quantity demanded." *(LO3)*
5. Give an example of behavior you have observed that could be described as "smart for one but dumb for all." *(LO4)*

PROBLEMS

connect

1. How would each of the following affect the U.S. market supply curve for corn? *(LO1)*
   a. A new and improved crop rotation technique is discovered.
   b. The price of fertilizer falls.
   c. The government offers new tax breaks to farmers.
   d. A tornado sweeps through Iowa.
2. Indicate how you think each of the following would shift demand in the indicated market. *(LO1)*
   a. The incomes of buyers in the market for Adirondack vacations increase.
   b. Buyers in the market for pizza read a study linking pepperoni consumption to heart disease.
   c. Buyers in the market for gas-powered cars learn of an increase in the price of electric cars (a substitute for gas-powered cars).
   d. Buyers in the market for electric cars learn of an increase in the price of electric cars.
3. An Arizona student claims to have spotted a UFO over the desert outside of Tucson. How will this claim affect the *supply* (not the quantity supplied) of binoculars in Tucson stores? *(LO1)*
4. Suppose that when milk sells for $4.50 per gallon, the quantity of milk demanded is 3,250 gallons per day and the quantity of milk supplied is 3,860 gallons per day. Will the equilibrium price of milk be greater than, less than, or equal to $4.50 per gallon? Explain. *(LO2)*
5. State whether the following pairs of goods are complements, or substitutes, or both. *(LO3)*
   a. Washing machines and dryers.
   b. Tennis rackets and tennis balls.

c. Birthday cake and birthday candles.
d. Cloth diapers and disposable diapers.

6. How will an increase in the birth rate affect the equilibrium price of land? *(LO3)*
7. What will happen to the equilibrium price and quantity of beef if the price of chickenfeed increases (assume that chicken and beef are substitutes)? *(LO3)*
8. How will a new law mandating an increase in required levels of automobile insurance affect the equilibrium price and quantity in the market for new automobiles? *(LO3)*
9. Predict what will happen to the equilibrium price and quantity of oranges if the following events take place. *(LO3)*
   a. A study finds that a daily glass of orange juice reduces the risk of heart disease.
   b. The price of grapefruit falls drastically.
   c. The wage paid to orange pickers rises.
   d. Exceptionally good weather provides a much greater than expected harvest.
10. Suppose the current issue of *The New York Times* reports an outbreak of mad cow disease in Nebraska, as well as the discovery of a new breed of chicken that gains more weight than existing breeds that consume the same amount of food. How will these developments affect the equilibrium price and quantity of chickens sold in the United States? *(LO3)*
11. Twenty-five years ago, tofu was available only from small businesses operating in predominantly Asian sections of large cities. Today tofu has become popular as a high-protein health food and is widely available in supermarkets throughout the United States. At the same time, tofu production has evolved to become factory-based using modern food-processing technologies. Draw a diagram with demand and supply curves depicting the market for tofu 25 years ago and the market for tofu today. Given the information above, what does the demand–supply model predict about changes in the volume of tofu sold in the United States between then and now? What does it predict about changes in the price of tofu? *(LO3)*
12. For each of the following statements about a market equilibrium identify whether the statement is always true, never true, or sometimes true. *(LO4)*
   a. A market equilibrium maximizes total economic surplus.
   b. A market equilibrium exploits all gains achievable through collective action.
   c. A market equilibrium leaves no unexploited opportunities for individuals.
13. In March 2020, global crude oil prices tumbled from over $50 a barrel to below $23 per barrel, bringing prices to their lowest level in nearly two decades. This precipitous drop in crude oil prices was fueled by two major shocks to the oil market. First, the COVID-19 pandemic led to a massive reduction in all forms of travel as large numbers of people around the world were advised to shelter in place. Second, Russia, Saudi Arabia, and a number of other major oil-producing nations typically reach collective agreements to limit the world supply of oil in order to keep prices high, but these negotiations broke down in March 2020, prompting a sharp increase in oil production. Using a supply and demand graph, show how each of these factors affected the market price and quantity of crude oil. *(LO3)*

ANSWERS TO SELF-TESTS

2.1 At a quantity of 10,000 slices per day, the marginal buyer's reservation price is $3.50 per slice. At a price of $2.50 per slice, the quantity demanded will be 14,000 slices per day. *(LO1)*

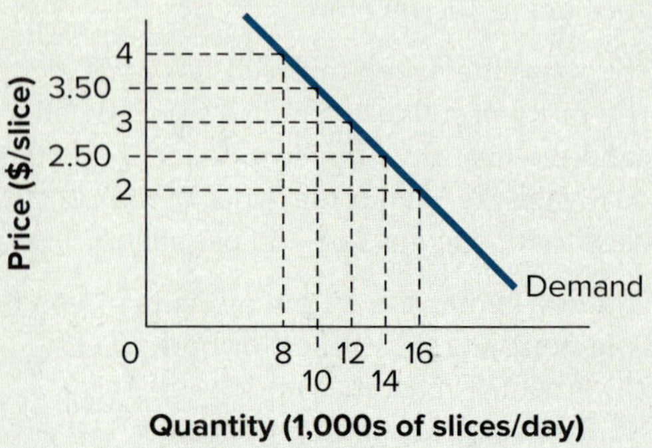

2.2 At a quantity of 10,000 slices per day, the marginal cost of pizza is $2.50 per slice. At a price of $3.50 per slice, the quantity supplied will be 14,000 slices per day. *(LO1)*

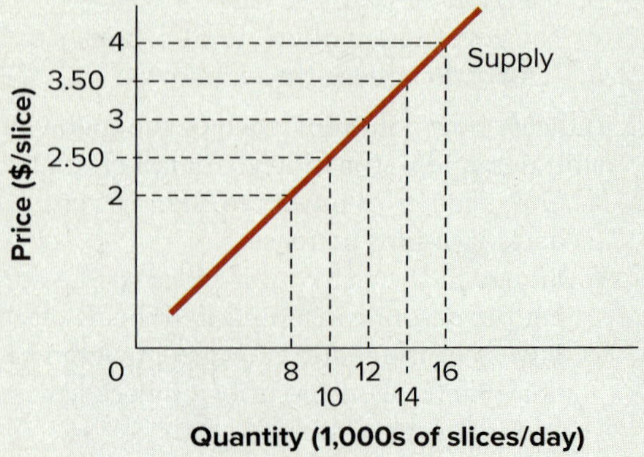

2.3 Because landlords are permitted to charge less than the maximum rent established by rent-control laws, a law that sets the maximum rent at $1,200 will have no effect on the rents actually charged in this market, which will settle at the equilibrium value of $800 per month. *(LO2)*

2.4 Travel by air and travel by intercity bus are substitutes, so a decline in airfares will shift the demand for bus travel to the left, resulting in lower bus fares and fewer bus trips taken. Travel by air and the use of resort hotels are complements, so a decline in airfares will shift the demand for resort hotel rooms to the right, resulting in higher hotel rates and an increase in the number of rooms rented. *(LO3)*

2.5 Apartments located far from Washington Metro stations are an inferior good. A pay increase for federal workers will thus shift the demand curve for such apartments downward, which will lead to a reduction in their equilibrium rent. *(LO3)*

2.6 The vitamin discovery shifts the demand for tortilla chips to the right and the crop losses shift the supply of tortilla chips to the left. Both shifts result in an increase in the equilibrium price of tortilla chips. But depending on the relative magnitude of the shifts, the equilibrium quantity of tortilla chips may either rise (top figure) or fall (bottom figure). *(LO3)*

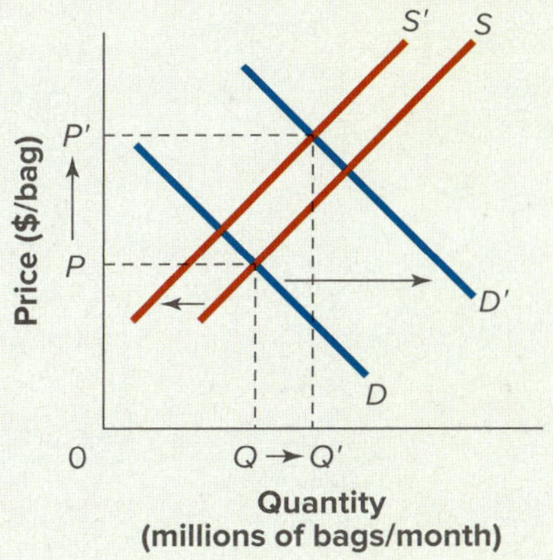

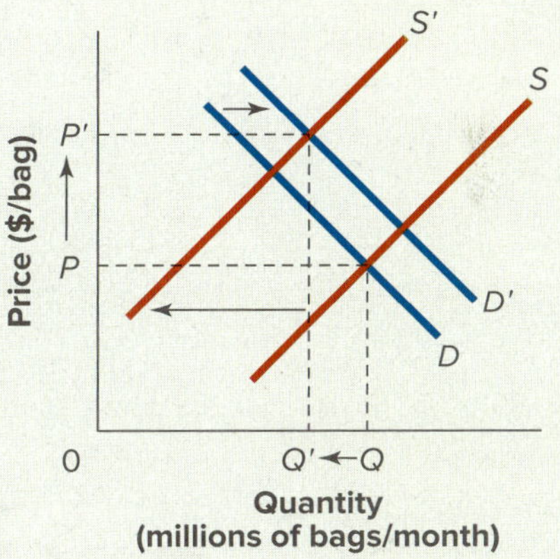

APPENDIX

The Algebra of Supply and Demand

In the text of this chapter, we developed supply and demand analysis in a geometric framework. The advantage of this framework is that many find it an easier one within which to visualize how shifts in either curve affect equilibrium price and quantity.

It is a straightforward extension to translate supply and demand analysis into algebraic terms. In this brief appendix, we show how this is done. The advantage of the algebraic framework is that it greatly simplifies computing the numerical values of equilibrium prices and quantities.

Consider, for example, the supply and demand curves in Figure 2A.1, where P denotes the price of the good and Q denotes its quantity. What are the equations of these curves?

The equation of a straight-line demand curve must take the general form $P = a + bQ^d$, where P is the price of the product (as measured on the vertical axis), Q^d is the quantity demanded at that price (as measured on the horizontal axis), a is the vertical intercept of the demand curve, and b is its slope. For the demand curve shown in Figure 2A.1, the vertical intercept is 16 and the slope is −2. So the equation for this demand curve is

$$P = 16 - 2Q^d. \qquad (2A.1)$$

Similarly, the equation of a straight-line supply curve must take the general form $P = c + dQ^s$, where P is again the price of the product, Q^s is the quantity supplied at that price, c is the vertical intercept of the supply curve, and d is its slope. For the supply curve shown in Figure 2A.1, the vertical intercept is 4 and the slope is also 4. So the equation for this supply curve is

$$P = 4 + 4Q^s. \qquad (2A.2)$$

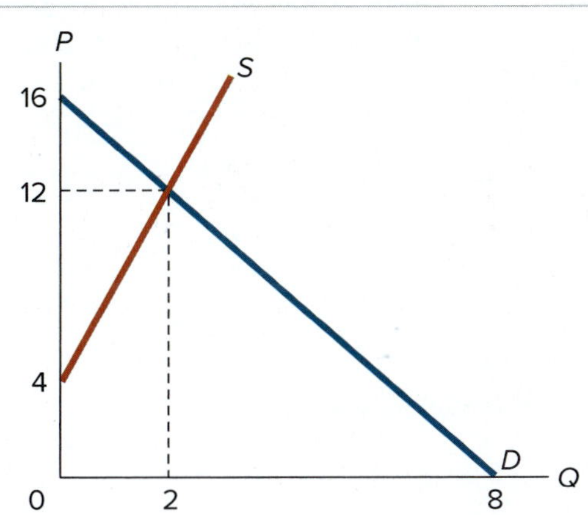

FIGURE 2A.1

Supply and Demand Curves.

If we know the equations for the supply and demand curves in any market, it is a simple matter to solve them for the equilibrium price and quantity using the method of simultaneous equations. The following example illustrates how to apply this method.

EXAMPLE 2A.1 Simultaneous Equations

If the supply and demand curves for a market are given by $P = 4 + 4Q^s$ and $P = 16 - 2Q^d$, respectively, find the equilibrium price and quantity for this market.

In equilibrium, we know that $Q^s = Q^d$. Denoting this common value as Q^*, we may then equate the right-hand sides of Equations 2A.1 and 2A.2 and solve

$$4 + 4Q^* = 16 - 2Q^*, \tag{2A.3}$$

which yields $Q^* = 2$. Substituting $Q^* = 2$ back into either the supply or demand equation gives the equilibrium price $P^* = 12$.

Of course, having already begun with the graphs of Equations 2A.1 and 2A.2 in hand, we could have identified the equilibrium price and quantity by a simple glance at Figure 2A.1. (That is why it seems natural to say that the graphical approach helps us visualize the equilibrium outcome.) As the following Self-Test 2A.1 illustrates, the advantage of the algebraic approach to finding the equilibrium price and quantity is that it is much less painstaking than having to produce accurate drawings of the supply and demand schedules.

SELF-TEST 2A.1

Find the equilibrium price and quantity in a market whose supply and demand curves are given by $P = 2Q^s$ and $P = 8 - 2Q^d$, respectively.

ANSWER TO APPENDIX SELF-TEST

2A.1 Let Q^* denote the equilibrium quantity. Since the equilibrium price and quantity lie on both the supply and demand curves, we equate the right-hand sides of the supply and demand equations to obtain

$$2Q^* = 8 - 2Q^*,$$

which solves for $Q^* = 2$. Substituting $Q^* = 2$ back into either the supply or demand equation gives the equilibrium price $P^* = 4$.

3

Macroeconomics: The Bird's-Eye View of the Economy

LEARNING OBJECTIVES

After reading this chapter, you should be able to:

LO1 Discuss the broad issues that macroeconomists study and the types of data they use and interpret.

LO2 Identify the three major types of macroeconomic policy and discuss the difference between positive and normative analyses of macroeconomic policy.

LO3 Understand the difference between microeconomics and macroeconomics and how aggregation is used.

In 1929, the economy of the United States slowed dramatically. Between August 1929 and the end of 1930, the nation's factories and mines, facing sharp declines in sales, cut their production rates by a remarkable 31 percent. These cutbacks in turn led to mass layoffs: Between 1929 and 1930, the number of people without jobs almost tripled, from about 3 percent of the workforce to nearly 9 percent.[1] Financial markets were equally shaky. The stock market crashed in October 1929, and stocks lost nearly a third of their value in just three weeks.

At first, policymakers and the general public (except for those people who had put their life savings into the stock market) were concerned but not panic stricken. Americans remembered that the nation had experienced a similar slowdown only eight years earlier, in 1921–1922. That episode had ended quickly, apparently on its own, and the decade that followed (popularly known as the Roaring Twenties) had been one of unparalleled prosperity. But the fall in production and the rise in unemployment that began in 1929 continued into 1931. In the spring of 1931, the economy seemed to stabilize briefly, and President Herbert Hoover optimistically proclaimed that "prosperity is just around the corner." But in mid-1931, the economy went into an even steeper dive. What historians now call the Great Depression had begun in earnest.

Labor statistics tell the story of the Great Depression from the worker's point of view. Unemployment was extremely high throughout the 1930s, despite government attempts to reduce it through large-scale public employment programs. At the worst point of the Depression, in 1933, one out of every four American workers was unemployed. Joblessness declined gradually to 17 percent of the workforce by 1936 but remained stuck at that level through 1939. Of those lucky enough to have jobs, many were able to work only part-time, while others worked for near-starvation wages.

[1]The source for these and most other pre-1960 statistics cited in this chapter is the U.S. Bureau of the Census, *Historical Statistics of the United States: Colonial Times to 1970* (Washington, D.C., 1975).

In some other countries, conditions were even worse. In Germany, which had never fully recovered from its defeat in World War I, nearly a third of all workers were without jobs, and many families lost their savings as major banks collapsed. Indeed, the desperate economic situation was a major reason for Adolf Hitler's election as chancellor of Germany in 1933. Introducing extensive government control over the economy, Hitler rearmed the country and ultimately launched what became the most destructive war in history, World War II.

How could such an economic catastrophe have happened? One often-heard hypothesis is that the Great Depression was caused by wild speculation on Wall Street, which provoked the stock market crash. But though stock prices may have been unrealistically high in 1929, there is little evidence to suggest that the fall in stock prices was a major cause of the Depression. A similar crash in October 1987, when stock prices fell a record 23 percent in one day—an event comparable in severity to the crash of October 1929—did not slow the economy significantly. Another reason to doubt that the 1929 stock market crash caused the Great Depression is that, far from being confined to the United States, the Depression was a worldwide event, affecting countries that did not have well-developed stock markets at the time.

What *did* cause the Great Depression, then? Today most economists who have studied the period blame *poor economic policymaking* both in the United States and in other major industrialized countries. Of course, policymakers did not set out to create an economic catastrophe. Rather, they fell prey to misconceptions of the time about how the economy worked. In other words, the Great Depression, far from being inevitable, *might have been avoided*—if only the state of economic knowledge had been better. From today's perspective, the Great Depression was to economic policymaking what the voyage of the *Titanic* was to ocean navigation.

One of the few benefits of the Great Depression was that it forced economists and policymakers of the 1930s to recognize that there were major gaps in their understanding of how the economy works. This recognition led to the development of a new subfield within economics, called macroeconomics. *Macroeconomics* is the study of the performance of national economies and the policies governments use to try to improve that performance.

This chapter will introduce the subject matter and some of the tools of macroeconomics. Although understanding episodes like the Great Depression and, more recently, the Great Recession remains an important concern of macroeconomists, the field has expanded to include the analysis of many other aspects of national economies. Among the issues macroeconomists study are the sources of long-run economic growth and development, the causes of high unemployment, and the factors that determine the rate of inflation. Appropriately enough in a world in which economic "globalization" preoccupies businesspeople and policymakers, macroeconomists also study how national economies interact. Since the performance of the national economy has an important bearing on the availability of jobs, the wages workers earn, the prices they pay, and the rates of return they receive on their saving, it's clear that macroeconomics addresses bread-and-butter issues that affect virtually everyone.

macroeconomic policies government actions designed to affect the performance of the economy as a whole

In light of the nation's experience during the Great Depression, macroeconomists are particularly concerned with understanding how *macroeconomic policies* work and how they should be applied. **Macroeconomic policies** are government actions designed to affect the performance of the economy as a whole (as opposed to policies intended to affect the performance of the market for a particular good or service, such as sugar or haircuts). The hope is that by understanding more fully how government policies affect the economy, economists can help policymakers do a better job—and avoid serious mistakes, such as those that were made during the Great Depression. On an individual level, educating people about macroeconomic policies and their effects will make for a better-informed citizenry, capable of making well-reasoned decisions in the voting booth.

THE MAJOR MACROECONOMIC ISSUES

We defined macroeconomics as the study of the performance of the national economy as well as the policies used to improve that performance. Let's now take a closer look at some of the major economic issues that macroeconomists study.

Economic Growth and Living Standards

Although the wealthy industrialized countries (such as the United States, Canada, Japan, and the countries of western Europe) are certainly not free from poverty, hunger, and homelessness, the typical person in those countries enjoys a *standard of living* better than at any previous time or place in history. By **standard of living,** we mean the degree to which people have access to goods and services that make their lives easier, healthier, safer, and more enjoyable. People with a high living standard enjoy more and better consumer goods: technologically advanced cars, laptop and tablet computers, smartphones, and the like. But they also benefit from a longer life expectancy and better general health (the result of high-quality medical care, good nutrition, and good sanitation), from higher literacy rates (the result of greater access to education), from more time and opportunity for cultural enrichment and recreation, from more interesting and fulfilling career options, and from better working conditions. Of course, having more of one good thing means having less of another. But higher incomes make these choices much less painful than they would be otherwise. Choosing between a larger apartment and a nicer car is much easier than choosing between feeding your children adequately and sending them to school, the kind of hard choice people in the poorest nations face.

standard of living the degree to which people have access to goods and services that make their lives easier, healthier, safer, and more enjoyable

Americans sometimes take their standard of living for granted, or even as a "right." But we should realize that the way we live today is radically different from the way people have lived throughout most of history. The current standard of living in the United States is the result of several centuries of sustained *economic growth,* a process of steady increase in the quantity and quality of the goods and services the economy can produce. The basic equation is simple: The more we can produce, the more we can consume. Of course, not everyone in a society shares equally in the fruits of economic growth and economists are rightly concerned by the increase in economic inequality that has sometimes accompanied economic growth. That said, in most cases growth brings an improvement in the average person's standard of living.

To get a sense of the extent of economic growth over time, examine Figure 3.1, which shows how the output of the U.S. economy has increased since 1929. (We discuss the measure of output used here, real gross domestic product, in the next chapter.) Although output fluctuates at times, the overall trend has been unmistakably upward. Indeed, in 2019 the output of the U.S. economy was more than 16 times what it was in 1929 and more than 4 times its level in 1965. What caused this remarkable economic growth? Can it continue? Should it? These are some of the questions macroeconomists try to answer.

One reason for the growth in U.S. output over the last century has been the rapid growth of the U.S. population, and hence the number of workers available. Because of population growth, increases in *total* output cannot be equated with improvements in the general standard of living. Although increased output means that more goods and services are available, increased population implies that more people are sharing those goods and services. Because the population changes over time, output *per person* is a better indicator of the average living standard than total output.

Figure 3.2 shows output per person in the United States since 1929 (the blue line). Note that the long-term increase in output per person is smaller than the increase in total output shown in Figure 3.1 because of population growth. Nevertheless, the gains made over this long period are still impressive: In 2019, a typical U.S. resident consumed more than six times the quantity of goods and services available to a typical resident at the onset of the Great Depression. To put this increase into perspective, according

FIGURE 3.1

Output of the U.S. Economy, 1929–2019.

The output of the U.S. economy has increased by more than 16 times since 1929 and by more than 4 times since 1965.

Source: https://fred.stlouisfed.org/series/GDPCA.

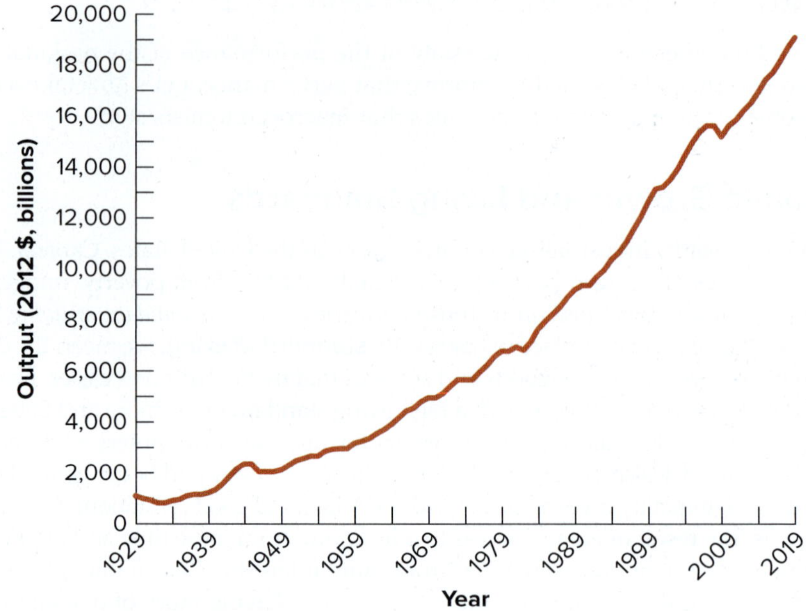

to the U.S. Census Bureau, in 2016, 87 percent of U.S. households reported that they owned a computer (desktop, laptop, notebook, tablet) or a smartphone, and 77 percent reported Internet access (home subscription or mobile broadband plan). And in 2019, 96 percent of Americans owned a cell phone. These goods and services, now available to so many people, could hardly be imagined a few decades ago.

Nor has the rise in output been reflected entirely in increased availability of consumer goods. For example, as late as 1960, only 41 percent of U.S. adults over age 25 had completed high school, and less than 8 percent had completed four years of college. Today, about 89 percent of the adult population have at least a high school diploma, and about 32 percent have a college degree. More than

FIGURE 3.2

Output per Person and per Worker in the U.S. Economy, 1929–2019.

The red line shows the output per worker in the U.S. economy since 1929, and the blue line shows output per person. Both have risen substantially. Relative to 1929, output per person today is more than six times greater, and output per worker is more than five times greater.

Sources: U.S. Bureau of Economic Analysis, Bureau of Labor Statistics, U.S. Census Bureau.

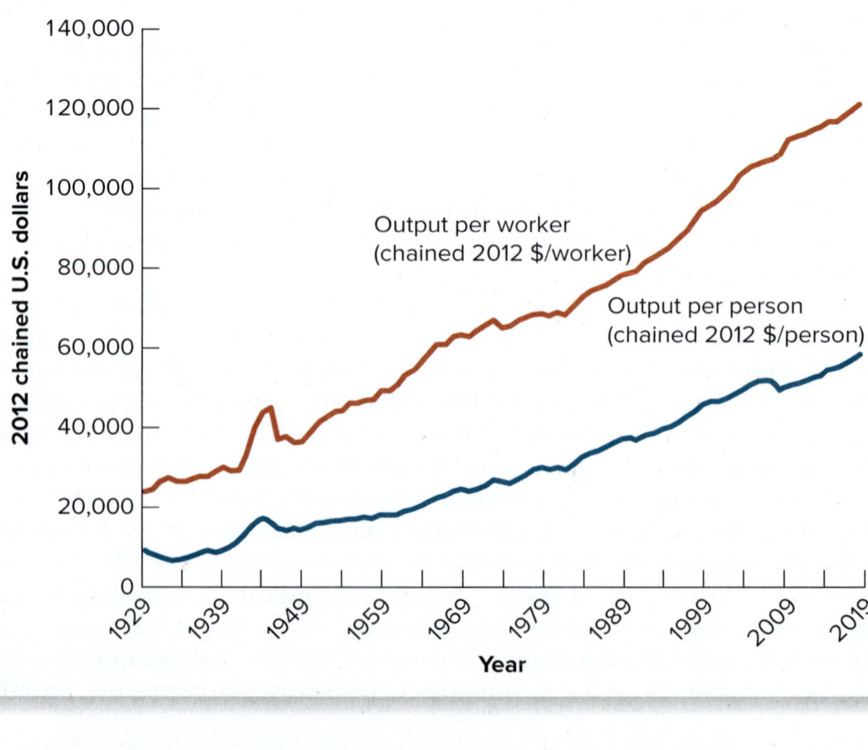

two-thirds of the students currently leaving high school will go on to college. Higher incomes, which allow young people to continue their schooling rather than work to support themselves and their families, are a major reason for these increases in educational levels.

Productivity

While growth in output per person is closely linked to changes in what the typical person can *consume*, macroeconomists are also interested in changes in what the average worker can *produce*. Figure 3.2 shows how output per employed worker (that is, total output divided by the number of people working) has changed since 1929 (red line). The figure shows that in 2019 a U.S. worker could produce more than five times the quantity of goods and services produced by a worker at the beginning of the Great Depression, despite the fact that the workweek is now much shorter than it was over 90 years ago.

Economists refer to output per employed worker as **average labor productivity.** As Figure 3.2 shows, average labor productivity and output per person are closely related. This relationship makes sense—as we noted earlier, the more we can produce, the more we can consume. Because of this close link to the average living standard, average labor productivity and the factors that cause it to increase over time are of major concern to macroeconomists.

average labor productivity output per employed worker

Although the long-term improvement in output per worker is impressive, the *rate* of improvement has slowed somewhat since the 1970s. Between 1950 and 1973 in the United States, output per employed worker increased by more than 2 percent per year. But from 1974 to 1995, the average rate of increase in output per worker was close to 1 percent per year. From 1996 to 2007, the pace of productivity growth picked up again, to nearly 2 percent per year before slowing down again to around 1 percent per year since 2008. Slowing productivity growth leads to less rapid improvement in living standards because the supply of goods and services cannot grow as quickly as it does during periods of rapid growth in productivity. Identifying the causes of productivity slowdowns and speedups is thus an important challenge for macroeconomists.

The current standard of living in the United States is not only much higher than in the past but also much higher than in many other nations today. Why have many of the world's countries, including both the developing nations of Asia, Africa, and Latin America and some formerly communist countries of eastern Europe, for many decades not enjoyed the same rates of economic growth as the industrialized countries? How can a country's rate of economic growth be improved? Once again, these are questions of keen interest to macroeconomists.

EXAMPLE 3.1 Productivity and Living Standards

How do China's productivity and output per person compare with those of the United States?

According to data from the World Bank (http://data.worldbank.org), in 2018 the value of the output of the U.S. economy was about $20,494 billion. In the same year, the estimated value of the output of the People's Republic of China was $13,608 billion (U.S.). The populations of the United States and China in 2018 were about 327 million and 1,393 million, respectively, while the numbers of employed workers in the two countries were, respectively, approximately 159 million and 756 million.

Find output per person and average labor productivity for the United States and China in 2018. What do the results suggest about comparative living standards in the two countries?

Output per person is simply total output divided by the number of people in an economy, and average labor productivity is output divided by the number of employed workers. Doing the math we get the following results for 2018.

	United States	**China**
Output per person	\$ 62,673	\$ 9,769
Average labor productivity	\$128,893	\$18,000

Note that, although the total output of the Chinese economy is more than 65 percent that of the U.S. output, output per person and average labor productivity in China are each less than 16 and 14 percent, respectively, of what they are in the United States. Thus, though the Chinese economy is predicted in the next 10 or 15 years to catch up with or surpass the U.S. economy in total output, for the time being there remains a large gap in productivity. This gap translates into striking differences in the average person's living standard between the two countries—in access to consumer goods, health care, transportation, education, and other benefits of affluence.

Recessions and Expansions

Economies do not always grow steadily; sometimes they go through periods of unusual strength or weakness. A look back at Figure 3.1 shows that although output generally grows over time, it does not always grow smoothly. Particularly striking is the decline in output during the Great Depression of the 1930s, followed by the sharp increase in output during World War II (1941–1945). But the figure shows many more moderate fluctuations in output as well.

Slowdowns in economic growth are called *recessions*; particularly severe economic slowdowns, like the one that began in 1929, are called *depressions*. In the United States, major recessions occurred in 1973–1975, 1981–1982, and 2007–2009 (find those recessions in Figure 3.1). More modest downturns occurred in 1990–1991 and 2001. Time will tell how the latest recession, that started in 2020 due to the COVID-19 pandemic, will compare with the depression and these recessions.

During recessions economic opportunities decline: Jobs are harder to find, people with jobs are less likely to get wage increases, profits are lower, and more companies go out of business. Recessions are particularly hard on economically disadvantaged people, who are most likely to be thrown out of work and have the hardest time finding new jobs.

Sometimes the economy grows unusually quickly. These periods of rapid economic growth are called *expansions*, and particularly strong expansions are called *booms*. During an expansion, jobs are easier to find, more people get raises and promotions, and most businesses thrive.

The alternating cycle of recessions and expansions raises some questions that are central to macroeconomics. What causes these short-term fluctuations in the rate of economic growth? Can government policymakers do anything about them? Should they try? These questions are discussed further in Chapter 9, *Short-Term Economic Fluctuations and Fiscal Policy*.

Unemployment

The *unemployment rate*, the fraction of people who would like to be employed but can't find work, is a key indicator of the state of the labor market. When the unemployment rate is high, work is hard to find, and people who do have jobs typically find it harder to get promotions or wage increases.

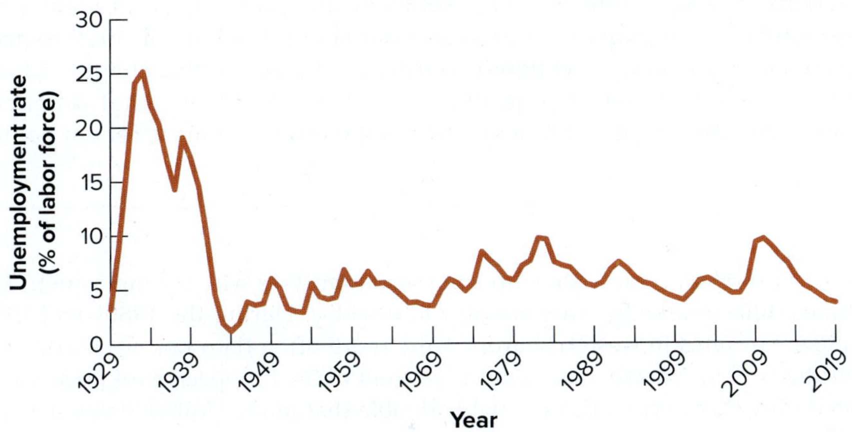

FIGURE 3.3

The U.S. Unemployment Rate, 1929–2019.

The unemployment rate is the percentage of the labor force that is out of work. Unemployment spikes upward during recessions and depressions, but the unemployment rate is always above zero, even in good times.

Source: Bureau of Labor Statistics, http://data.bls.gov.

Figure 3.3 shows the unemployment rate in the United States since 1929. Unemployment rises during recessions—note the dramatic spike in unemployment during the Great Depression, as well as the increases in unemployment during the 1973–1975, 1981–1982, and 2007–2009 recessions. But even in the so-called good times, such as the late 1990s and the late 2010s, some people are unemployed. Why does unemployment rise so sharply during periods of recession? And why are there always unemployed people, even when the economy is booming?

EXAMPLE 3.2 Unemployment and Recessions

By how much did unemployment increase during five recent U.S. recessions?

Using monthly data on the national civilian unemployment rate, find the increase in the unemployment rate between the onset of recession in November 1973, January 1980, July 1990, January 2001, and December 2007 and the peak unemployment rate in the following years. Compare these increases in unemployment to the increase during the Great Depression.

Unemployment data are collected by the U.S. Bureau of Labor Statistics (BLS) and can be obtained from the BLS website (www.bls.gov/bls/unemployment.htm). Periodic publications include the *Survey of Current Business*, the *Federal Reserve Bulletin*, and *Economic Indicators*. Monthly data from the BLS website yield the following comparisons.

Unemployment rate at beginning of recession (%)	Peak unemployment rate (%)	Increase in unemployment rate (%)
4.8 (Nov. 1973)	9.0 (May 1975)	+4.2
6.3 (Jan. 1980)	10.8 (Nov./Dec. 1982)	+4.5
5.5 (July 1990)	7.8 (June 1992)	+2.3
4.1 (Jan. 2001)	6.3 (June 2003)	+2.2
5.0 (Dec. 2007)	10.0 (Oct. 2009)	+5.0

Unemployment increased significantly following the onset of each recession, although the impact of the 1990 and 2001 recessions on the labor market was clearly less serious than that of the 1973, 1980, and 2007 recessions. (Actually, the 1980 recession was a "double dip"—a short recession in 1980, followed by a longer one in 1981–1982.) In comparison, during the Great Depression the unemployment rate rose from about 3 percent in 1929 to about 25 percent in 1933, as we mentioned in the introduction to this chapter. Clearly, the 22 percentage point change in the unemployment rate that Americans experienced in the Great Depression dwarfs the effects of more recent postwar recessions.

One question of great interest to macroeconomists is why unemployment rates sometimes differ markedly from country to country. During the 1980s and 1990s, unemployment rates in western Europe were more often than not measured in the "double digits." On average, more than 10 percent of the European workforce was out of a job during that period, a rate roughly double that in the United States. The high unemployment was particularly striking, because during the 1950s and 1960s, European unemployment rates were generally much lower than those in the United States. Most recently, following the 2008 global financial crisis, the euro area's unemployment rate has been close to or in the double digits much of the time, with dramatic differences between countries within the common currency area. What explains these differences in the unemployment rate in different countries at different times? The measurement of unemployment will be discussed further in the next chapter.

SELF-TEST 3.1

Find the most recent unemployment rates for France, Germany, Spain, and the United Kingdom, and compare them to the most recent unemployment rate for the United States. A useful source is the home page of the Organization for Economic Cooperation and Development (OECD), an organization of industrialized countries (www.oecd.org). See also the OECD's publication *Main Economic Indicators*. Is unemployment still lower in the United States than in western Europe?

Inflation

Another important economic statistic is the rate of *inflation*, which is the rate at which prices in general are increasing over time. As we will discuss in Chapter 4, *Measuring Economic Activity: GDP, Unemployment, and Inflation,* inflation imposes a variety of costs on the economy. And when the inflation rate is high, people on fixed incomes, such as pensioners who receive a fixed dollar payment each month, can't keep up with the rising cost of living.

In recent years, inflation has been relatively low in the United States, but that has not always been the case (see Figure 3.4 for data on U.S. inflation since 1929). During the 1970s, inflation was a major problem; in fact, many people told poll takers that inflation was "public enemy number one." Why was inflation high in the 1970s, and why is it relatively low today? What difference does it make to the average person?

As with unemployment rates, the rate of inflation can differ markedly from country to country. For example, during the 1990s, the inflation rate averaged 3 percent per year in the United States, but the nation of Ukraine averaged over 400 percent annual inflation for the whole decade. And in 2008, when annual inflation in the United States was less than 4 percent, the percentage rate of inflation in Zimbabwe was estimated in the hundreds of millions, and then billions, and quickly rising! What accounts for such large differences in inflation rates among countries?

Inflation and unemployment are often linked in policy discussions. One reason for this linkage is the oft-heard argument that unemployment can be reduced only at the cost of higher inflation and that inflation can be reduced only at the cost of

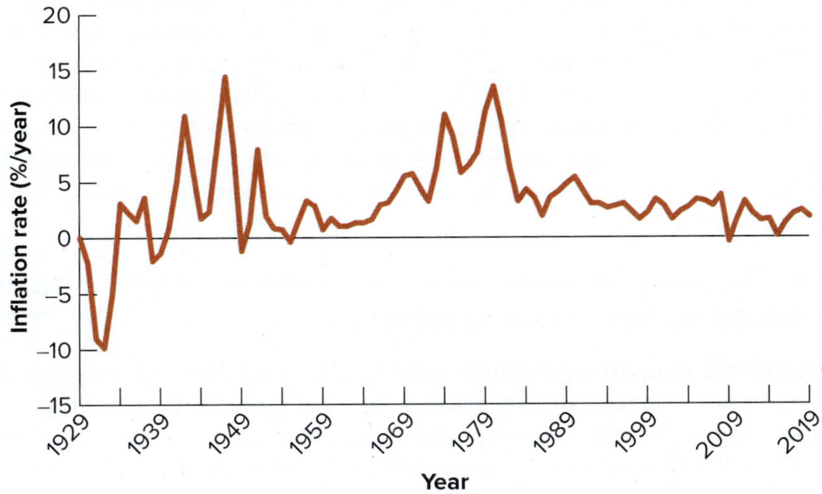

FIGURE 3.4

The U.S. Inflation Rate, 1929–2019.

The U.S. inflation rate has fluctuated over time. Inflation was high in the 1970s but has been quite low recently.

Source: Bureau of Labor Statistics, http://data.bls.gov.

higher unemployment. Must the government accept a higher rate of inflation to bring down unemployment, and vice versa?

Economic Interdependence among Nations

National economies do not exist in isolation but are increasingly interdependent. The United States, because of its size and the wide variety of goods and services it produces, is one of the most self-sufficient economies on the planet. Even so, in 2019 the United States exported about 12 percent of all the goods and services it produced, and imported from abroad 15 percent of the goods and services that Americans used. Merely 50 years earlier, in 1969, neither figure was above 5 percent.

Sometimes international flows of goods and services become a matter of political and economic concern. For example, some politicians maintain that low-priced imports threaten the farming and manufacturing jobs of their constituents. Are free-trade agreements, in which countries agree not to tax or otherwise block the international flow of goods and services, a good or bad thing?

A related issue is the phenomenon of *trade imbalances,* which occur when the quantity of goods and services that a country sells abroad (its *exports*) differs significantly from the quantity of goods and services its citizens buy from abroad (its *imports*). Figure 3.5

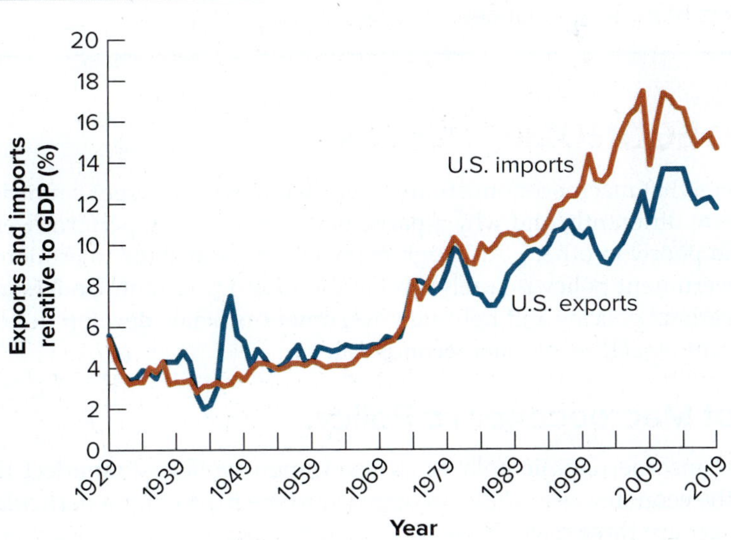

FIGURE 3.5

Exports and Imports as a Share of U.S. Output, 1929–2019.

The blue line shows U.S. exports of goods as a percentage of U.S. output. The red line shows U.S. imports of goods relative to U.S. output. For much of its history, the United States has exported more than it imported, but over the past decades, imports have greatly outstripped exports.

Sources: Import data: https://fred.stlouisfed.org/series/IMPGSA; export data: https://fred.stlouisfed.org/series/EXPGSA.

shows U.S. exports and imports since 1929, measured as a percentage of the economy's total output. Prior to the 1970s, the United States generally exported more than it imported. (Notice the major export boom that occurred after World War II, when the United States was helping reconstruct Europe.) Since the 1970s, however, imports to the United States have outstripped exports, creating a situation called a *trade deficit*. Other countries—China, for example—export much more than they import. A country such as China is said to have a *trade surplus*. What causes trade deficits and surpluses? Are they harmful or helpful?

RECAP

THE MAJOR MACROECONOMIC ISSUES

- ***Economic growth and living standards.*** Over the last century, the industrialized nations have experienced remarkable economic growth and improvements in living standards. Macroeconomists study the reasons for this extraordinary growth and try to understand why growth rates vary markedly among nations.
- ***Productivity.*** Average labor productivity, or output per employed worker, is a crucial determinant of living standards. Macroeconomists ask: What causes slowdowns and speedups in the rate of productivity growth?
- ***Recessions and expansions.*** Economies experience periods of slower growth (recessions) and more rapid growth (expansions). Macroeconomists examine the sources of these fluctuations and the government policies that attempt to moderate them.
- ***Unemployment.*** The unemployment rate is the fraction of people who would like to be employed but can't find work. Unemployment rises during recessions, but there are always unemployed people even during good times. Macroeconomists study the causes of unemployment, including the reasons why it sometimes differs markedly across countries.
- ***Inflation.*** The inflation rate is the rate at which prices in general are increasing over time. Questions macroeconomists ask about inflation include: Why does inflation vary over time and across countries? Must a reduction in inflation be accompanied by an increase in unemployment, or vice versa?
- ***Economic interdependence among nations.*** Modern economies are highly interdependent. Related issues studied by macroeconomists include the desirability of free-trade agreements and the causes and effects of trade imbalances.

MACROECONOMIC POLICY

We have seen that macroeconomists are interested in why different countries' economies perform differently and why a particular economy may perform well in some periods and poorly in others. Although many factors contribute to economic performance, government policy is surely among the most important. Understanding the effects of various policies and helping government officials develop better policies are important objectives of macroeconomists.

Types of Macroeconomic Policy

We defined macroeconomic policies as government policies that affect the performance of the economy as a whole, as opposed to the market for a particular good or service. There are three major types of macroeconomic policy: *monetary policy, fiscal policy,* and *structural policy*.

The term **monetary policy** refers to the determination of the nation's money supply. (Cash and coin are the basic forms of money, although as we will see, modern economies have other forms of money as well.) For reasons that we will discuss in later chapters, most economists agree that changes in the money supply affect important macroeconomic variables, including national output, employment, interest rates, inflation, stock prices, and the international value of the dollar. In virtually all countries, monetary policy is controlled by a government institution called the *central bank*. The Federal Reserve System, often called the Fed for short, is the central bank of the United States.

monetary policy determination of the nation's money supply

Fiscal policy refers to decisions that determine the government's budget, including the amount and composition of government expenditures and government revenues. The balance between government spending and taxes is a particularly important aspect of fiscal policy. When government officials spend more than they collect in taxes, the government runs a *deficit*, and when they spend less, the government's budget is in *surplus*. As with monetary policy, economists generally agree that fiscal policy can have important effects on the overall performance of the economy. For example, many economists believe that the large deficits run by the federal government during the 1980s were harmful to the nation's economy. Likewise, many would say that the balancing of the federal budget that occurred during the 1990s contributed to the nation's strong economic performance during that decade. Since the early 2000s, the federal budget has moved once again into deficit. The deficit increased dramatically during and after the 2007–2009 recession.

fiscal policy decisions that determine the government's budget, including the amount and composition of government expenditures and government revenues

Finally, the term **structural policy** includes government policies aimed at changing the underlying structure, or institutions, of the nation's economy. Structural policies come in many forms, from minor tinkering to ambitious overhauls of the entire economic system. The move away from government control of the economy and toward a more market-oriented approach in many formerly communist countries, such as Poland, the Czech Republic, and Hungary, is a large-scale example of structural policy. Many developing countries have tried similar structural reforms. Supporters of structural policy hope that, by changing the basic characteristics of the economy or by remaking its institutions, they can stimulate economic growth and improve living standards.

structural policy government policies aimed at changing the underlying structure, or institutions, of the nation's economy

SELF-TEST 3.2

The Congressional Budget Office (CBO) is the government agency that is charged with projecting the federal government's surpluses or deficits. From the CBO's home page (www.cbo.gov), find the most recent value of the federal government's surplus or deficit and the CBO's projected values for the next five years. How do you think these projections are likely to affect congressional deliberations on taxation and government spending?

Positive versus Normative Analyses of Macroeconomic Policy

Macroeconomists are frequently called upon to analyze the effects of a proposed policy. For example, if Congress is debating a tax cut, economists in the Congressional Budget Office or the Treasury may be asked to prepare an analysis of the likely effects of the tax cut on the overall economy, as well as on specific industries, regions, or income groups. An objective analysis aimed at determining only the economic consequences of a particular policy—not whether those consequences are desirable—is called a **positive analysis.** In contrast, a **normative analysis** includes recommendations on whether a particular policy *should* be implemented. While a positive analysis is supposed to be objective and scientific, a normative analysis

positive analysis addresses the economic consequences of a particular event or policy, not whether those consequences are desirable

normative analysis addresses the question of whether a policy *should* be used; normative analysis inevitably involves the values of the person doing the analysis involves the *values* of the person or organization doing the analysis—conservative, liberal, or middle-of-the-road.

While pundits often joke that economists cannot agree among themselves, the tendency for economists to disagree is exaggerated. When economists do disagree, the controversy often centers on normative judgments (which relate to economists' personal values) rather than on positive analysis (which reflects objective knowledge of the economy). For example, liberal and conservative economists might agree that a particular tax cut would increase the incomes of the relatively wealthy (positive analysis). But they might vehemently disagree on whether the policy *should* be enacted, reflecting their personal views about whether wealthy people deserve a tax break (normative analysis).

The next time you hear or read about a debate over economic issues, try to determine whether the differences between the two positions are primarily *positive* or *normative*. If the debate focuses on the actual effects of the event or policy under discussion, then the disagreement is over positive issues. But if the main question has to do with conflicting personal opinions about the *desirability* of those effects, the debate is normative. The distinction between positive and normative analyses is important, because objective economic research can help resolve differences over positive issues. When people differ for normative reasons, however, economic analysis is of less use.

SELF-TEST 3.3

Which of the following statements are positive and which are normative? How can you tell?

a. A tax increase is likely to lead to lower interest rates.
b. Congress should increase taxes to reduce the inappropriately high level of interest rates.
c. A tax increase would be acceptable if most of the burden fell on those with incomes over $250,000.
d. Higher tariffs (taxes on imports) are needed to protect American jobs.
e. An increase in the tariff on imported steel would increase employment of American steelworkers.

RECAP

MACROECONOMIC POLICY

Macroeconomic policies affect the performance of the economy as a whole. The three types of macroeconomic policy are monetary policy, fiscal policy, and structural policy. *Monetary policy*, which in the United States is under the control of the Federal Reserve System, refers to the determination of the nation's money supply. *Fiscal policy* involves decisions about the government budget, including its expenditures and tax collections. *Structural policy* refers to government actions to change the underlying structure or institutions of the economy. Structural policy can range from minor tinkering to a major overhaul of the economic system, as with the formerly communist countries that converted to market-oriented systems.

The analysis of a proposed policy can be positive or normative. A *positive analysis* addresses the policy's likely economic consequences but not whether those consequences are desirable. A *normative analysis* addresses the question of whether a proposed policy *should* be used. Debates about normative conclusions inevitably involve personal values and thus generally cannot be resolved by objective economic analysis alone.

AGGREGATION

In Chapter 1, *Thinking Like an Economist,* we discussed the difference between *macroeconomics,* the study of national economies, and *microeconomics,* the study of individual economic entities, such as households and firms, and the markets for specific goods and services. The main difference between the fields is one of perspective: Macroeconomists take a "bird's-eye view" of the economy, ignoring the fine details to understand how the system works as a whole. Microeconomists work instead at "ground level," studying the economic behavior of individual households, firms, and markets. Both perspectives are useful—indeed essential—to understanding what makes an economy work.

Although macroeconomics and microeconomics take different perspectives on the economy, the basic tools of analysis are much the same. In the chapters to come you will see that macroeconomists apply the same principles as microeconomists in their efforts to understand and predict economic behavior. Even though a national economy is a much bigger entity than a household or even a large firm, the choices and actions of individual decision makers ultimately determine the performance of the economy as a whole. So, for example, to understand saving behavior at the national level, the macroeconomist must first consider what motivates an individual family or household to save.

SELF-TEST 3.4

Which of the following questions would be studied primarily by macroeconomists? By microeconomists? Explain.

a. Does increased government spending lower the unemployment rate?
b. Does Google's dominance of Internet searches harm consumers?
c. Would a school voucher program improve the quality of education in the United States? (Under a voucher program, parents are given a fixed amount of government aid, which they may use to send their children to any school, public or private.)
d. Should government policymakers aim to reduce inflation still further?
e. Why is the average rate of household saving low in the United States?
f. Does the increase in the number of consumer products being sold over the Internet threaten the profits of conventional retailers?

While macroeconomists use the core principles of economics to understand and predict individual economic decisions, they need a way to relate millions of individual decisions to the behavior of the economy as a whole. One important tool they use to link individual behavior to national economic performance is **aggregation,** the adding up of individual economic variables to obtain economywide totals.

aggregation the adding up of individual economic variables to obtain economywide totals

For example, macroeconomists don't care whether consumers drink Pepsi or Coke, go to the movie theater or stream videos, or drive a convertible or a sport-utility vehicle. These individual economic decisions are the province of microeconomics. Instead, macroeconomists add up consumer expenditures on all goods and services during a given period to obtain *aggregate,* or total, consumer expenditure. Similarly, a macroeconomist would not focus on plumbers' wages versus electricians' but would concentrate instead on the average wage of all workers. By focusing on aggregate variables, like total consumer expenditures or the average wage, macroeconomists suppress the mind-boggling details of a complex modern economy to see broad economic trends.

EXAMPLE 3.3 Aggregation (Part 1): A National Crime Index

Is crime in the United States getting better or worse?

To illustrate not only why aggregation is needed, but also some of the problems associated with it, consider an issue that is only partly economic: crime. Suppose policymakers want to know whether *in general* the problem of crime in the United States is getting better or worse. How could an analyst obtain a statistical answer to that question?

Police keep detailed records of the crimes reported in their jurisdictions, so in principle a researcher could determine precisely how many purse snatchings occurred last year on New York City subways. But data on the number of crimes of each type in each jurisdiction would produce stacks of computer output. Is there a way to add up, or aggregate, all the crime data to get some sense of the national trend?

Law enforcement agencies such as the FBI use aggregation to obtain national *crime rates*, which are typically expressed as the number of "serious" crimes committed per 100,000 population. For example, the FBI reported that in 2015, some 9.2 million serious crimes (both violent crimes and property crimes) occurred in the United States (www.fbi.gov). Dividing the number of crimes by the U.S. population in 2015, which was about 321 million, and multiplying by 100,000 yields the crime rate for 2015, equal to about 2,860 crimes per 100,000 people. This rate represented a substantial drop from the crime rate in 2000, which was about 4,100 crimes per 100,000 people. So aggregation (the adding up of many different crimes into a national index) indicates that, in general, serious crime decreased in the United States between 2000 and 2015.

Although aggregation of crime statistics reveals the "big picture," it may obscure important details. The FBI crime index lumps together relatively minor crimes such as petty theft with very serious crimes such as murder and rape. Most people would agree that murder and rape do far more damage than a typical theft, so adding together these two very different types of crimes might give a false picture of crime in the United States. For example, although the U.S. crime rate fell 30 percent between 2000 and 2015, the murder rate fell by less than 12 percent. Because murder is the most serious of crimes, the reduction in crime between 2000 and 2015 was probably less significant than the change in the overall crime rate indicates. The aggregate crime rate glosses over other important details, such as the fact that the most dramatic reductions in crime occurred in urban areas. This loss of detail is a cost of aggregation, the price analysts pay for the ability to look at broad economic or social trends.

EXAMPLE 3.4 Aggregation (Part 2): U.S. Exports

How can we add together Kansas grain with Hollywood movies?

The United States exports a wide variety of products and services to many different countries. Kansas farmers sell grain to Russia, Silicon Valley programmers sell software to France, and Hollywood movie studios sell entertainment the world over. Suppose macroeconomists want to compare the total quantities of American-made goods sold to various regions of the world. How could such a comparison be made?

Economists can't add bushels of grain, lines of code, and movie tickets—the units aren't comparable. But they can add the *dollar values* of each—the revenue farmers earned from foreign grain sales, the royalties programmers received for their exported software, and the revenues studios reaped from films shown abroad. By comparing the dollar values of U.S. exports to Europe, Asia, Africa, and other regions in a particular year, economists are able to determine which regions are the biggest customers for American-made goods.

RECAP

AGGREGATION

Macroeconomics, the study of national economies, differs from microeconomics, the study of individual economic entities (such as households and firms) and the markets for specific goods and services. Macroeconomists take a "bird's-eye view" of the economy. To study the economy as a whole, macroeconomists make frequent use of aggregation, the adding up of individual economic variables to obtain economywide totals. For example, a macroeconomist is more interested in the determinants of total U.S. exports, as measured by total dollar value, than in the factors that determine the exports of specific goods. A cost of aggregation is that the fine details of the economic situation are often obscured.

STUDYING MACROECONOMICS: A PREVIEW

This chapter introduced many of the key issues of macroeconomics. In the chapters to come we will look at each of these issues in more detail. We will start with the *measurement* of economic performance, including key variables like the level of economic activity, the extent of unemployment, and the rate of inflation. Obtaining quantitative measurements of the economy, against which theories can be tested, is the crucial first step in answering basic macroeconomic questions like those raised in this chapter.

Next, we will study economic behavior over relatively long periods of time. We will examine economic growth and productivity improvement, the fundamental determinants of the average standard of living in the long run. We will then discuss the long-run determination of employment, unemployment, and wages; and study saving and its link to the creation of new capital goods, such as factories and machines. The role played in the economy by money, and its relation to the rate of inflation and to the central bank, will then be discussed, as will both domestic and international financial markets and their role in allocating saving to productive uses, in particular their role in promoting international capital flows.

John Maynard Keynes, a celebrated British economist, once wrote, "In the long run, we are all dead." Keynes's statement was intended as an ironic comment on the tendency of economists to downplay short-run economic problems on the grounds that "in the long run," the operation of the free market will always restore economic stability. Keynes, who was particularly active and influential during the Great Depression, correctly viewed the problem of massive unemployment, whether "short run" or not, as the most pressing economic issue of the time.

So why start our study of macroeconomics with the long run? Keynes's comment notwithstanding, long-run economic performance is extremely important, accounting for most of the substantial differences in living standards and economic well-being the world over. Furthermore, studying long-run economic behavior provides important background for understanding short-term fluctuations in the economy.

We turn to those short-term fluctuations by first providing background on what happens during recessions and expansions, as well as some historical perspective, before discussing one important source of short-term economic fluctuations, variations in aggregate spending. We will also show how, by influencing aggregate spending, fiscal policy may be able to moderate economic fluctuations. The second major policy tool for stabilizing the economy, monetary policy, will then be discussed, along with the circumstances under which macroeconomic policymakers may face a short-term trade-off between inflation and unemployment.

The international dimension of macroeconomics will be highlighted throughout the discussion. We will introduce topics such as exchange rates between national currencies and discuss how they are determined and how they affect the workings of the economy and macroeconomic policy.

SUMMARY

- Macroeconomics is the study of the performance of national economies and of the policies governments use to try to improve that performance. Here are some of the broad issues macroeconomists study. *(LO1)*
  - Sources of economic growth and improved *living standards*.
  - Trends in *average labor productivity,* or output per employed worker.
  - Short-term fluctuations in the pace of economic growth (recessions and expansions).
  - Causes and cures of unemployment and inflation.
  - Economic interdependence among nations.
- To help explain differences in economic performance among countries, or in economic performance in the same country at different times, macroeconomists study the implementation and effects of macroeconomic policies. *Macroeconomic policies* are government actions designed to affect the performance of the economy as a whole. Macroeconomic policies include *monetary policy* (the determination of the nation's money supply), *fiscal policy* (relating to decisions about the government's budget), and *structural policy* (aimed at affecting the basic structure and institutions of the economy). *(LO2)*
- In studying economic policies, economists apply both *positive analysis* (an objective attempt to determine the consequences of a proposed policy) and *normative analysis* (which addresses whether a particular policy *should* be adopted). Normative analysis involves the values of the person doing the analysis. *(LO2)*
- Macroeconomics is distinct from microeconomics, which focuses on the behavior of individual economic entities and specific markets. Macroeconomists make heavy use of *aggregation,* which is the adding up of individual economic variables into economywide totals. Aggregation allows macroeconomists to study the "big picture" of the economy, while ignoring fine details about individual households, firms, and markets. *(LO3)*

KEY TERMS

aggregation
average labor productivity
fiscal policy
macroeconomic policies
monetary policy
normative analysis
positive analysis
standard of living
structural policy

REVIEW QUESTIONS

1. How did the experience of the Great Depression motivate the development of the field of macroeconomics? *(LO1)*
2. Generally, how does the standard of living in the United States today compare to the standard of living in other countries? To the standard of living in the United States a century ago? *(LO1)*
3. Why is average labor productivity a particularly important economic variable? *(LO1)*
4. True or false: Economic growth within a particular country generally proceeds at a constant rate. Explain. *(LO1)*
5. True or false: Differences of opinion about economic policy recommendations can always be resolved by objective analysis of the issues. Explain. *(LO2)*
6. What type of macroeconomic policy (monetary, fiscal, structural) might include each of the following actions? *(LO2)*
   a. A broad government initiative to reduce the country's reliance on agriculture and promote high-technology industries.
   b. A reduction in income tax rates.
   c. Provision of additional cash to the banking system.

d. An attempt to reduce the government budget deficit by reducing spending.
e. A decision by a developing country to reduce government control of the economy and to become more market-oriented.

7. Baseball statistics, such as batting averages, are calculated and reported for each individual player, for each team, and for the league as a whole. What purposes are served by doing this? Relate to the idea of aggregation in macroeconomics. *(LO3)*

PROBLEMS

connect

1. Over the next 50 years the Japanese population is expected to decline, while the fraction of the population that is retired is expected to increase sharply. What are the implications of these population changes for total output and average living standards in Japan, assuming that average labor productivity continues to grow? What if average labor productivity stagnates? *(LO1)*
2. Is it possible for average living standards to rise during a period in which average labor productivity is falling? Discuss, using a numerical example for illustration. *(LO1)*
3. The Bureau of Economic Analysis, or BEA, is a government agency that collects a wide variety of statistics about the U.S. economy. From the BEA's website (www.bea.gov), find data for the most recent year available on U.S. exports and imports of goods and services. Is the United States running a trade surplus or deficit? Calculate the ratio of the surplus or deficit to U.S. exports. *(LO1)*
4. Which of the following statements are positive and which are normative? *(LO2)*
   a. If the Federal Reserve raises interest rates, demand for housing is likely to fall.
   b. The Federal Reserve should raise interest rates to keep inflation at an acceptably low level.
   c. Stock prices are likely to fall over the next year as the economy slows.
   d. A reduction in the capital gains tax (the tax on profits made in the stock market) would lead to a 10 to 20 percent increase in stock prices.
   e. Congress should not reduce capital gains taxes without also providing tax breaks for lower-income people.
5. Which of the following would be studied by a macroeconomist? By a microeconomist? *(LO3)*
   a. The worldwide operations of General Motors.
   b. The effect of government subsidies on sugar prices.
   c. Factors affecting average wages in the U.S. economy.
   d. Inflation in developing countries.
   e. The effects of tax cuts on consumer spending.

ANSWERS TO SELF-TESTS

3.1 Your answer will depend upon the current unemployment rate available at the OECD website. *(LO1)*

3.2 Your answer will depend upon the current CBO budget data. *(LO2)*

3.3 a. Positive. This is a prediction of the effect of a policy, not a value judgment on whether the policy should be used.
b. Normative. Words like *should* and *inappropriately* express value judgments about the policy.
c. Normative. The statement is about the desirability of certain types of policies, not their likely effects.
d. Normative. The statement is about desirability of a policy.
e. Positive. The statement is a prediction of the likely effects of a policy, not a recommendation on whether the policy should be used. *(LO2)*

3.4 a. Macroeconomists. Government spending and unemployment are aggregate concepts pertaining to the national economy.
b. Microeconomists. Google, though large, is an individual firm.
c. Microeconomists. The issue relates to the supply and demand for a specific service, education.
d. Macroeconomists. Inflation is an aggregate, economywide concept.
e. Macroeconomists. Average saving is an aggregate concept.
f. Microeconomists. The focus is on a relatively narrow set of markets and products rather than on the economy as a whole. *(LO3)*

4

Measuring Economic Activity: GDP, Unemployment, and Inflation

"Real GDP increased 2.2 percent in the fourth quarter, according to the U.S. Bureau of Economic Analysis . . ."

"Total nonfarm payroll employment increased by 209,000 in July, and the unemployment rate was little changed at 4.3 percent, the U.S. Bureau of Labor Statistics reported today . . ."

"Inflation appears subdued as the consumer price index registered an increase of only 0.1 percent last month . . ."

News reports like these fill the airwaves and the web—some TV and radio stations and some websites carry nothing else. In fact, all kinds of people are interested in economic data. The average person hopes to learn something that will be useful in a business decision, a financial investment, or a career move. The professional economist depends on economic data in much the same way that a doctor depends on a patient's vital signs—pulse, blood pressure, and temperature—to make an accurate diagnosis. To understand economic developments and to be able to give useful advice to policymakers, businesspeople, and financial investors, an economist simply must have up-to-date, accurate data. Political leaders and policymakers also need economic data to help them in their decisions and planning.

Interest in measuring the economy, and attempts to do so, date back as far as the mid-seventeenth century, when Sir William Petty (1623–1687) conducted a detailed survey of the land and wealth of Ireland. The British government's purpose in commissioning the survey was to determine the capacity of the Irish people to pay taxes to the Crown. But Petty used the opportunity to measure a variety of social and economic variables and went on to conduct pioneering studies of wealth, production, and population in several other countries. He was a firm believer in the idea that

LEARNING OBJECTIVES

After reading this chapter, you should be able to:

LO1 Explain how economists define an economy's output.

LO2 Apply the production, expenditure, and income methods for measuring GDP to analyze economic activity.

LO3 Define and compute nominal GDP and real GDP.

LO4 Define and calculate the unemployment rate and the participation rate.

LO5 Explain how the consumer price index (CPI) is constructed and use it to calculate the inflation rate.

LO6 Show how the CPI is used to adjust dollar amounts to eliminate the effects of inflation.

LO7 Discuss the quality adjustment bias in measuring inflation.

LO8 Distinguish between inflation and relative price changes in order to find the true costs of inflation.

scientific progress depends first and foremost on accurate measurement, an idea that today's economists endorse.

Not until the twentieth century, though, did economic measurement come into its own. World War II was an important catalyst for the development of accurate economic statistics because its very outcome was thought to depend on the mobilization of economic resources. Two economists, Simon Kuznets in the United States and Richard Stone in the United Kingdom, developed comprehensive systems for measuring a nation's output of goods and services, which were of great help to Allied leaders in their wartime planning. Kuznets and Stone each received a Nobel Prize in Economics for their work, which became the basis for the economic accounts used today by almost all the world's countries. The governments of the United States and many other countries now collect and publish a wealth of statistics covering all aspects of their economies.

In this chapter, we will discuss how economists measure three basic macroeconomic variables that arise frequently in analyses of the state of the economy: the *gross domestic product* (or *GDP*), the *rate of unemployment*, and the *rate of inflation*. The first two of these statistics, GDP and the unemployment rate, both measure the overall level of economic activity in a country. The third statistic, the inflation rate, measures how fast prices change in a country.

Measuring economic activity might sound like a straightforward and uncontroversial task, but that is not the case. Indeed, the basic measure of a nation's output of goods and services—the gross domestic product, or GDP—has been criticized on many grounds. Some critics have complained that GDP does not adequately reflect factors such as the effect of economic growth on the environment or the rate of resource depletion. Because of problems like these, they charge, policies based on GDP statistics are likely to be flawed. Unemployment statistics have also been the subject of some controversy. By the end of this chapter, you will understand how official measures of output and unemployment are constructed and used and will have gained some insight into these debates over their accuracy. In particular, you will understand how these statistics are defined and measured, and you will be able to discuss the strengths and limitations of the definitions as well as the measurement difficulties that governments face when turning the definitions into actual, published estimates. You will see, for example, what goes into the calculation of a nation's GDP and, importantly, what is left out. So next time you hear or read about the most recent economic statistics, you will avoid misinterpreting them.

Understanding the strengths and limitations of economic data is the first critical step toward becoming an intelligent user of economic statistics, as well as a necessary background for careful economic analysis in the chapters to come.

GROSS DOMESTIC PRODUCT: MEASURING THE NATION'S OUTPUT

Chapter 3, *Macroeconomics: The Bird's-Eye View of the Economy,* emphasized the link between an economy's output of goods and services and its living standard. We noted that high levels of output per person, and per worker, are typically associated with a high standard of living. But what, exactly, does "output" mean? To study economic growth and productivity scientifically, we need to be more precise about how economists define and measure an economy's output.

The most frequently used measure of an economy's output is called the *gross domestic product,* or *GDP*. **Gross domestic product (GDP)** is intended to measure how much an economy produces in a given period, such as a quarter (three months) or a year. More precisely, GDP is the market value of the final goods and services produced in a country during a given period. To understand this definition, let's take it apart and examine each of its parts separately. The first key phrase in the definition is "market value."

gross domestic product (GDP) the market value of the final goods and services produced in a country during a given period

Market Value

A modern economy produces many different goods and services, from dental floss (a good) to acupuncture (a service). Macroeconomists are not interested in this kind of detail, however; rather, their goal is to understand the behavior of the economy as a whole. For example, a macroeconomist might ask: "Has the overall capacity of the economy to produce goods and services increased over time? If so, by how much?"

To be able to talk about concepts like the "total output" or "total production"—as opposed to the production of specific items like dental floss—economists need to *aggregate* the quantities of the many different goods and services into a single number. They do so by adding up the *market values* of the different goods and services the economy produces. **Market value** is the selling prices of goods and services in the open market. We use these prices because they are the prices at which buyers and sellers agree to make their transactions. Examples 4.1 and 4.2 will illustrate the process.

market value the selling prices of goods and services in the open market

EXAMPLE 4.1 Orchardia's GDP, Part 1

What is Orchardia's GDP?

In the imaginary economy of Orchardia, total production is 4 apples and 6 bananas. To find the total output of Orchardia, we could add the number of apples to the number of bananas and conclude that total output is 10 pieces of fruit. But what if this economy also produced 3 pairs of shoes? There really is no sensible way to add apples and bananas to shoes.

Suppose though that we know that apples sell for $0.25 each, bananas for $0.50 each, and shoes for $20.00 a pair. Then the market value of this economy's production, or its GDP, is equal to

$$(4 \text{ apples} \times \$0.25/\text{apple}) + (6 \text{ bananas} \times \$0.50/\text{banana}) + (3 \text{ pairs of shoes} \times \$20.00/\text{pair}) = \$64.00.$$

Notice that when we calculate total output this way, the more expensive items (the shoes) receive a higher weighting than the cheaper items (the apples and bananas). Since, in general, the amount people are willing to pay for an item is an indication of the economic benefit they expect to receive from it, market values provide a convenient way for aggregating output into one number.

EXAMPLE 4.2 Orchardia's GDP, Part 2

What is Orchardia's new GDP?

Now suppose instead that Orchardia were to produce 3 apples, 3 bananas, and 4 pairs of shoes at the same prices as in the preceding example. What is its GDP now?

Now the Orchardian GDP is equal to

$$(3 \text{ apples} \times \$0.25/\text{apple}) + (3 \text{ bananas} \times \$0.50/\text{banana}) + (4 \text{ pairs of shoes} \times \$20.00/\text{pair}) = \$82.25.$$

Notice that Orchardian GDP is higher in Example 4.2 than in Example 4.1, even though two of the three goods (apples and bananas) are being produced in smaller quantities than before. The reason is that the good whose production has increased (shoes) has a much higher market value than the goods whose production has decreased (apples and bananas).

SELF-TEST 4.1

Suppose Orchardia produces the same quantities of the three goods at the same prices as in Example 4.1. In addition, it produces five oranges at $0.30 each. What is the GDP of Orchardia now?

Market values provide a convenient way to add together, or aggregate, the many different goods and services produced in a modern economy. A drawback of using market values, however, is that not all economically valuable goods and services are bought and sold in markets. For example, the unpaid work of a homemaker, although it is of economic value, is not sold in markets and so isn't counted in GDP. But paid housekeeping and child-care services, which are sold in markets, do count. As a result, new moms or dads who decide to take an extended unpaid leave from work and dedicate all their time and energy to providing for their newborn's physical, cognitive, and emotional development in the first months of the child's life may be making a priceless contribution to the health and well-being (including economic) of a society in the present and future; yet their decision is likely to make present GDP smaller because it withdraws activity from markets. Example 4.3 illustrates some of the pitfalls that the distinction between market and nonmarket value creates.

EXAMPLE 4.3 Women's Labor Force Participation and GDP Measurement

How has GDP been affected by women joining the labor force?

The percentage of adult American women working, or seeking work, outside the home increased dramatically in the second half of the twentieth century, from less than 35 percent in 1950 to about 60 percent in 2019 (see Figure 4.1). This trend has led to a substantial increase in the demand for paid day care and housekeeping services as working wives and mothers require more help at home. How have these changes affected measured GDP?

FIGURE 4.1

Percentages of American Men and Women over Age 16 Working or Seeking Work outside the Home, 1950–2019.

The fraction of American women working outside the home rose by about 25 percentage points between 1950 and 2019, while the fraction of men working outside the home declined.

Source: Bureau of Labor Statistics, www.bls.gov/cps.

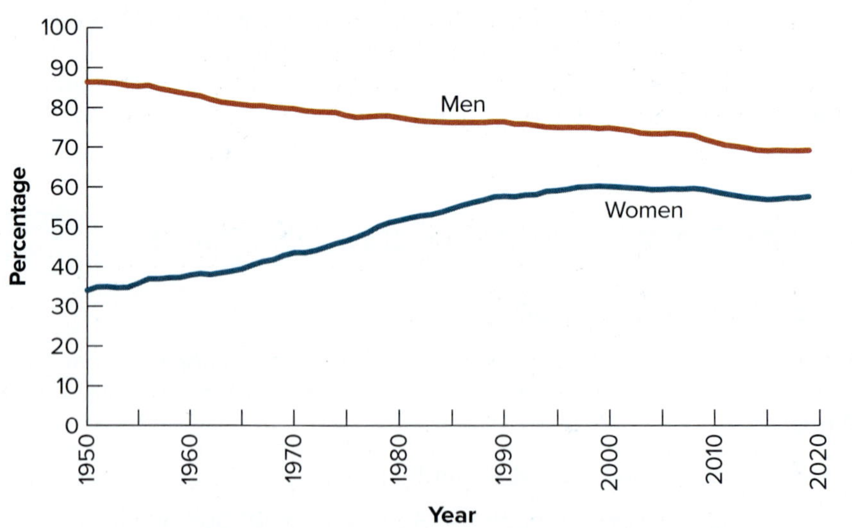

The entry of many women into the labor market has raised measured GDP in two ways. First, the goods and services that women produce in their new jobs have contributed directly to increasing GDP. Second, the fact that paid workers took over previously unpaid housework and child-care duties has increased measured GDP by the amount paid to those workers. The first of these two changes represents a genuine increase in economic activity, but the second reflects a transfer of existing economic activities from the unpaid sector to the market sector (moreover, it is possible that this transfer lowered the quality of these activities). Overall, then, the increase in measured GDP associated with increased participation in the labor force by women probably overstates the actual increase in economic activity.

Although homemaking activities are excluded from measured GDP, in a few cases, goods and services that are not sold in markets are included in GDP. By far the most important are the goods and services provided by federal, state, and local governments. The protection provided by the army and navy, the transportation convenience of the interstate highway system, and the education provided by the public school system are examples of publicly provided goods and services that are not sold in markets.

As market prices for publicly provided goods and services do not exist, economic statisticians add to the GDP the *costs* of providing those goods and services as rough measures of their economic value. For example, to include public education in the GDP, the statisticians add to GDP the salaries of teachers and administrators, the costs of textbooks and supplies, and the like. Similarly, the economic value of the national defense establishment is approximated, for the purposes of measuring GDP, by the *costs* of defense: the pay earned by soldiers and sailors, the costs of acquiring and maintaining weapons, and so on.

While approximating value by looking at costs is much better than ignoring nonmarket goods and services altogether, it is far from perfect: A more efficient government could deliver *more value* at a *lower cost*. For example, as a report by the Organization for Economic Cooperation and Development (OECD)[1] suggests, the children in countries whose governments spend *less* (per child) than other governments do not always show worse outcomes on indicators such as health and safety, educational well-being, and quality of school life. In fact, using cost as a substitute for market value means that every dollar a government spends adds a dollar to GDP regardless of how efficiently or wastefully it is spent!

With a few exceptions, like publicly provided goods and services, GDP is calculated by adding up market values. However, not all goods and services that have a market value are counted in GDP. As we will see next, GDP includes only those goods and services that are the end products of the production process, called *final goods and services*. Goods and services that are used up in the production process are not counted in GDP.

Why was the female labor force participation rate in 2019 more than 70 percent greater than in 1950?

Final Goods and Services

Many goods are used in the production process. For instance, before a baker can produce a loaf of bread, grain must be grown and harvested and then ground into flour. The flour is then used along with other ingredients to make bread. Of the three major goods that are produced during this process—the grain, the flour, and the bread—only the bread is used by consumers. Because producing the bread is the ultimate purpose of the process, the bread is called a *final good*. In general, a **final good or service** is the end product of a process, the product or service that consumers actually use. The goods or services produced on the way toward making the final product—here, the grain and the flour—are called **intermediate goods or services.**

final goods or services goods or services consumed by the ultimate user; because they are the end products of the production process, they are counted as part of GDP

intermediate goods or services goods or services used up in the production of final goods and services and therefore not counted as part of GDP

Since we are interested in measuring only those items that are of direct economic value, *only final goods and services are included in GDP*. Intermediate goods and services are *not* included. To illustrate, suppose that the grain from the previous example has a market value of $0.50 (the price the milling company paid for the grain). The grain is then ground into flour, which has a market value of $1.20 (the price the baker paid for the flour). Finally, the flour is made into a loaf of fine French bread,

[1]OECD, *Doing Better for Children*, 2009. See also coverage in *The Economist*, "The Nanny State," September 3, 2009.

worth $2.00 at the local store. In calculating the contribution of these activities to GDP, would we want to add together the values of the grain, the flour, and the bread? No, because the grain and flour are intermediate goods, valuable only because they can be used to make bread. So in this example, the total contribution to GDP is $2.00, the value of the loaf of bread, the final product.

Example 4.4 illustrates the same distinction but this time with a focus on services.

EXAMPLE 4.4 GDP for the Barber and His Assistant

How do we count a haircut in GDP?

Your barber charges $10 for a haircut. In turn, the barber pays his assistant $2 per haircut in return for sharpening the scissors, sweeping the floor, and other chores. For each haircut given, what is the total contribution of the barber and his assistant, taken together, to GDP?

The answer to this problem is $10, the price, or market value, of the haircut. The haircut is counted in GDP because it is the final service, the one that actually has value to the final user. The services provided by the assistant have value only because they contribute to the production of the haircut; thus they are not counted in GDP.

Example 4.5 illustrates that the same good can be either intermediate or final, depending on how it is used.

EXAMPLE 4.5 A Good That Can Be Either Intermediate or Final

What is an intermediate good?

Farmer Brown produces $100 worth of milk. He sells $40 worth of milk to his neighbors and uses the rest to feed his pigs, which he sells to his neighbors for $120. What is Farmer Brown's contribution to the GDP?

The final goods in this example are the $40 worth of milk and the $120 worth of pigs sold to the neighbors. Adding $40 and $120, we get $160, which is Farmer Brown's contribution to the GDP. Note that part of the milk Farmer Brown produced serves as an intermediate good and part as a final good. The $60 worth of milk that is fed to the pigs is an intermediate good, and so it is not counted in GDP. The $40 worth of milk sold to the neighbors is a final good, and so it is counted.

capital good a long-lived good that is used in the production of other goods and services

A special type of good that is difficult to classify as intermediate or final is a *capital good*. A **capital good** is a long-lived good, which is itself produced and used to produce other goods and services. Factories and machines are examples of capital goods. Houses and apartment buildings, which produce dwelling services, are also a form of capital goods. Capital goods do not fit the definition of final goods since their purpose is to produce other goods. On the other hand, they are not used up during the production process, except over a very long period, so they are not exactly intermediate goods either. For purposes of measuring GDP, economists have agreed to classify newly produced capital goods as final goods. Otherwise, a country that invested in its future by building modern factories and buying new machines would be counted as having a lower GDP than a country that devoted all its resources to producing consumer goods.

We have established the rule that only final goods and services (including newly produced capital goods) are counted in GDP. Intermediate goods and services, which are used up in the production of final goods and services, are not counted. In practice, however, this rule is not easy to apply because the production process often stretches over several periods. To illustrate, recall the earlier example of the grain that was milled into flour, which in turn was baked into a loaf of French bread. The contribution of the whole process to GDP is $2.00, the value of the bread (the final product). Suppose, though, that the grain and the flour were produced near the end of the year 2019 and the bread was baked early the next year in 2020. In this case, should we attribute the $2.00 value of the bread to the GDP for the year 2019 or to the GDP for the year 2020?

Neither choice seems quite right because part of the bread's production process occurred in each year. Part of the value of the bread should probably be counted in the year 2019 GDP and part in the year 2020 GDP. But how should we make the split? To deal with this problem, economists determine the market value of final goods and services indirectly, by adding up the *value added* by each firm in the production process. The **value added** by any firm equals the market value of its product or service minus the cost of inputs purchased from other firms. As we'll see, summing the value added by all firms (including producers of both intermediate and final goods and services) gives the same answer as simply adding together the value of final goods and services. The value-added method thus eliminates the problem of dividing the value of a final good or service between two periods.

value added for any firm, the market value of its product or service minus the cost of inputs purchased from other firms

To illustrate this method, let's revisit the example of the French bread, which is the result of multiple stages of production. We have already determined that the total contribution of this production process to GDP is $2.00, the value of the bread. Let's show now that we can get the same answer by summing value added. Suppose that the bread is the ultimate product of three corporations: ABC Grain Company Inc. produces grain, General Flour produces flour, and Hot'n'Fresh Baking produces the bread. If we make the same assumptions as before about the market value of the grain, the flour, and the bread, what is the value added by each of these three companies?

ABC Grain Company produces $0.50 worth of grain, with no inputs from other companies, so ABC's value added is $0.50. General Flour uses $0.50 worth of grain from ABC to produce $1.20 worth of flour. The value added by General Flour is thus the value of its product ($1.20) less the cost of purchased inputs ($0.50), or $0.70. Finally, Hot'n'Fresh Baking buys $1.20 worth of flour from General Flour and uses it to produce $2.00 worth of bread. So the value added by Hot'n'Fresh is $0.80. These calculations are summarized in Table 4.1.

TABLE 4.1
Value Added in Bread Production

Company	Revenues	− Cost of purchased inputs	= Value added
ABC Grain	$0.50	$0.00	$0.50
General Flour	$1.20	$0.50	$0.70
Hot'n'Fresh	$2.00	$1.20	$0.80
Total			$2.00

You can see that summing the value added by each company gives the same contribution to GDP, $2.00, as the method based on counting final goods and services only. Basically, the value added by each firm represents the portion of the value of the final good or service that the firm creates in its stage of production. Summing the value added by all firms in the economy yields the total value of final goods and services, or GDP.

This example also illustrates how the value-added method solves the problem of production processes that bridge two or more periods. Suppose that the grain and flour are produced during the year 2019 but the bread is not baked until 2020. Using the value-added method, the contribution of this production process to the year 2019 GDP is the value added by the grain company plus the value added by the flour company, or $1.20. The contribution of the production process to the year 2020 GDP is the value added by the baker, which is $0.80. Thus part of the value of the final product, the bread, is counted in the GDP for each year, reflecting the fact that part of the production of the bread took place in each year.

SELF-TEST 4.2

Amy's card shop receives a shipment of Valentine's Day cards in December 2019. Amy pays the wholesale distributor of the cards a total of $500. In February 2020 she sells the cards for a total of $700. What are the contributions of these transactions to GDP in the years 2019 and 2020?

We have now established that GDP is equal to the market value of final goods and services. Let's look at the last part of the definition, "produced in a country during a given period."

Produced in a Country during a Given Period

The word *domestic* in the term *gross domestic product* tells us that GDP is a measure of economic activity within a given country. Thus, only production that takes place within the country's borders is counted. For example, the GDP of the United States includes the market value of *all* cars produced within U.S. borders, even if they are made in foreign-owned plants. However, cars produced in Mexico by a U.S.-based company like General Motors are *not* counted.

What about cars that are produced in the United States from parts that are produced in Mexico? The *value-added* method introduced earlier could again be used to suggest an answer. Recall that we used this method to divide the market value of a product that was produced over two years into its contribution to the GDP of each of the years. Similarly, we can use this method to divide the value of a product that was produced in part in two different countries into its contribution to each country's GDP. Revisiting our French bread example, suppose now that ABC Grain Company produces the grain in Mexico. General Flour buys $0.50 worth of grain from ABC in Mexico, imports it to the United States, and uses it to produce $1.20 worth of flour (in the U.S.). Finally, Hot'n'Fresh Baking buys $1.20 worth of flour from General Flour and uses it to produce $2.00 worth of bread (in the U.S.). Using the value-added method, Table 4.1 suggests that the total value of the bread, $2.00, is divided across the two countries' national accounts: $0.50 is included in Mexico's GDP (the value of the grain produced in Mexico), and $1.50 is included in the United States' GDP (the value added in the U.S.).

We have seen that GDP is intended to measure the amount of production that occurs during a given period, such as the calendar year. For this reason, only goods and services that are actually produced during a particular year are included in the GDP for that year. Example 4.6 and Self-Test 4.3 demonstrate this point.

EXAMPLE 4.6 The Sale of a House and GDP

Does the sale of an existing home count in GDP?

A 20-year-old house is sold to a young family for $200,000. The seller pays the real estate agent a 6 percent commission, or $12,000. What is the contribution of this transaction to GDP?

Because the house was not produced during the current year, its value is *not* counted in this year's GDP. (The value of the house was included in the GDP 20 years earlier, the year the house was built.) In general, purchases and sales of existing assets, such as old houses or used cars, do not contribute to the current year's GDP. However, the $12,000 fee paid to the real estate agent represents the market value of the agent's services in helping to sell the house and helping the family make the purchase. Since those services were provided during the current year, the agent's fee *is* counted in current-year GDP.

SELF-TEST 4.3

Lotta Doe sells 100 shares of stock in Benson Buggywhip for $50 per share. She pays her broker a 2 percent commission for executing the sale. How does Lotta's transaction affect the current-year GDP?

RECAP

MEASURING GDP

Gross domestic product (GDP) equals the market value

- GDP is an aggregate of the market values of the many goods and services produced in the economy.
- Goods and services that are not sold in markets, such as unpaid housework, are not counted in GDP. An important exception is goods and services provided by the government, which are included in GDP at the government's cost of providing them.

of final goods and services

- Final goods and services (which include capital goods, such as factories and machines) are counted in GDP. Intermediate goods and services, which are used up in the production of final goods and services, are not counted.
- In practice, the value of final goods and services is determined by the value-added method. The value added by any firm equals the firm's revenue from selling its product minus the cost of inputs purchased from other firms. Summing the value added by all firms in the production process yields the value of the final good or service.

produced in a country during a given period.

- Only goods and services produced within a nation's borders are included in GDP.
- Only goods and services produced during the current year (or the portion of the value produced during the current year) are counted as part of the current-year GDP.

METHODS FOR MEASURING GDP

GDP is a measure of the quantity of goods and services *produced* by an economy. But any good or service that is produced will also be *purchased* and used by some economic agent—a consumer buying Christmas gifts or a firm investing in new machinery, for example. For many purposes, knowing not only how much is produced, but who uses it and how, is important. Furthermore, when an economic agent purchases a good or a service, that agent's spending is some other economic agent's *income*. For some purposes, it is also important to track this income from the production of goods and services.

The Expenditure Method for Measuring GDP

Economic statisticians divide the users of the final goods and services that make up the GDP for any given year into four categories: *households, firms, governments,* and the *foreign sector* (that is, foreign purchasers of domestic products). They assume that all the final goods and services that are produced in a country in a given year will be purchased and used by members of one or more of these four groups. Furthermore, the amounts that purchasers spend on various goods and services should be equal to the market values of those goods and services. As a result, GDP can be measured with equal accuracy by either of two methods: (1) adding up the market values of all the final goods and services that are produced domestically or (2) adding up the total amount spent by each of the four groups on final goods and services and subtracting spending on imported goods and services. The values obtained by the two methods will be the same.

Corresponding to the four groups of final users are four components of expenditure: consumption, investment, government purchases, and net exports. That is, households consume, firms invest, governments make government purchases, and the foreign sector buys the nation's exports. Table 4.2 gives the dollar values for each of these components for the U.S. economy in 2019. As the table shows, GDP for the United States in 2019 was about $21.4 trillion, roughly $65,200 per person. Detailed definitions of the components of expenditure, and their principal subcomponents, follow. As you read through them, refer to Table 4.2 to get a sense of the relative importance of each type of spending.

TABLE 4.2
Expenditure Components of U.S. GDP, 2019 ($ billions)

			Percentage
Consumption		**14,562.7**	68%
Durable goods	1,526.8		
Nondurable goods	2,978.1		
Services	10,057.7		
Investment		**3,743.9**	17%
Business fixed investment	2,878.1		
Residential investment	797.5		
Inventory investment	68.3		
Government purchases		**3,753.0**	18%
Net exports		**−631.9**	−3%
Exports	2,504.3		
Imports	3,136.1		
Total: Gross domestic product		**21,427.7**	100%

Source: U.S. Bureau of Economic Analysis, www.bea.gov.

consumption expenditure (or **consumption**) spending by households on goods and services such as food, clothing, and entertainment

Consumption expenditure, or simply **consumption,** is spending by households on goods and services such as food, clothing, and entertainment. Consumption expenditure is subdivided into three subcategories:

- *Consumer durables* are long-lived consumer goods such as cars and furniture. Note that new houses are not treated as consumer durables but as part of investment.
- *Consumer nondurables* are shorter-lived goods like food and clothing.
- *Services,* a large component of consumer spending, include everything from haircuts and taxi rides to legal, financial, and educational services.

investment spending by firms on final goods and services, primarily capital goods and housing

Investment is spending by firms on final goods and services, primarily capital goods and housing. Investment is divided into three subcategories:

- *Business fixed investment* is the purchase by firms of new capital goods such as machinery, factories, and office buildings. (Remember that for the purposes of calculating GDP, long-lived capital goods are treated as final goods rather than as intermediate goods.) Firms buy capital goods to increase their capacity to produce.

- *Residential investment* is construction of new homes and apartment buildings. For GDP accounting purposes, residential investment is treated as an investment by the business sector, which then sells the homes to households.
- *Inventory investment* is the addition of unsold goods to company inventories. In other words, the goods that a firm produces but doesn't sell during the current period are treated, for accounting purposes, as if the firm had bought those goods from itself. (This convention guarantees that production equals expenditure.) Inventory investment can be positive or negative, depending on whether the value of inventories on hand rises or falls over the course of the year. In 2009, for example, inventories fell, and the *inventory investment* component contributed a negative value to GDP.

People often refer to purchases of financial assets, such as stocks or bonds, as "investments." That use of the term is different from the definition we give here. A person who buys a share of a company's stock acquires partial ownership of the *existing* physical and financial assets controlled by the company. A stock purchase does not usually correspond to the creation of *new* physical capital, however, and so is not investment in the sense we are using the term in this chapter. We will generally refer to purchases of financial assets, such as stocks and bonds, as "financial investments," to distinguish them from a firm's investment in new capital goods, such as factories and machines.

Government purchases are purchases by federal, state, and local governments of final goods, such as fighter planes, and services, such as teaching in public schools. Government purchases do *not* include *transfer payments,* which are payments made by the government in return for which no current goods or services are received. Examples of transfer payments (which, again, are *not* included in government purchases) are Social Security benefits, unemployment benefits, pensions paid to government workers, and welfare payments. Interest paid on the government debt is also excluded from government purchases.

government purchases purchases by federal, state, and local governments of final goods and services; government purchases do not include transfer payments, which are payments made by the government in return for which no current goods or services are received, nor do they include interest paid on the government debt

Net exports equal exports minus imports.

net exports exports minus imports

- *Exports* are domestically produced final goods and services that are sold abroad.
- *Imports* are purchases by domestic buyers of goods and services that were produced abroad. Since imports are included in consumption, investment, and government purchases but do not represent spending on domestic production, they must be subtracted. Imports are subtracted from exports to find the net amount of spending on domestically produced goods and services. A shorthand way of adding exports and subtracting imports is to add net exports, which equals exports minus imports.

A country's net exports reflect the net demand by the rest of the world for its goods and services. Net exports can be negative since imports can exceed exports in any given year. As Table 4.2 shows, the United States had significantly greater imports than exports in 2019.

The relationship between GDP and expenditures on goods and services can be summarized by an equation. Let

$$\begin{aligned} Y &= \text{gross domestic product, or output} \\ C &= \text{consumption expenditure} \\ I &= \text{investment} \\ G &= \text{government purchases} \\ NX &= \text{net exports.} \end{aligned}$$

Using these symbols, we can write that GDP equals the sum of the four types of expenditure algebraically as

$$Y = C + I + G + NX.$$

EXAMPLE 4.7 Measuring GDP by Production and by Expenditure

Do we get the same GDP using two different methods?

An economy produces 1,000,000 automobiles valued at $15,000 each. Of these, 700,000 are sold to consumers, 200,000 are sold to businesses, 50,000 are sold to the government, and 25,000 are sold abroad. No automobiles are imported. The automobiles left unsold at the end of the year are held in inventory by the auto producers. Find GDP in terms of (a) the market value of production and (b) the components of expenditure. You should get the same answer both ways.

The market value of the production of final goods and services in this economy is 1,000,000 autos times $15,000 per auto, or $15 billion.

To measure GDP in terms of expenditure, we must add spending on consumption, investment, government purchases, and net exports. Consumption is 700,000 autos times $15,000, or $10.5 billion. Government purchases are 50,000 autos times $15,000, or $0.75 billion. Net exports are equal to exports (25,000 autos at $15,000, or $0.375 billion) minus imports (zero), so net exports are $0.375 billion.

But what about investment? Here we must be careful. The 200,000 autos that are sold to businesses, worth $3 billion, count as investment. But notice too that the auto companies produced 1,000,000 automobiles but sold only 975,000 (700,000 + 200,000 + 50,000 + 25,000). Hence 25,000 autos were unsold at the end of the year and were added to the automobile producers' inventories. This addition to producer inventories (25,000 autos at $15,000, or $0.375 billion) counts as inventory investment, which is part of total investment. Thus total investment spending equals the $3 billion worth of autos sold to businesses plus the $0.375 billion in inventory investment, or $3.375 billion.

Recapitulating, in this economy consumption is $10.5 billion, investment (including inventory investment) is $3.375 billion, government purchases equal $0.75 billion, and net exports are $0.375 billion. Summing these four components of expenditure yields $15 billion—the same value for GDP that we got by calculating the market value of production.

SELF-TEST 4.4

Extending Example 4.7, suppose that 25,000 of the automobiles purchased by households are imported rather than domestically produced. Domestic production remains at 1,000,000 autos valued at $15,000 each. Once again, find GDP in terms of (a) the market value of production and (b) the components of expenditure.

GDP and the Incomes of Capital and Labor

The GDP can be thought of equally well as a measure of total production or as a measure of total expenditure–either method of calculating the GDP gives the same final answer. There is yet a third way to think of the GDP, which is as the *incomes of capital and labor.*

Whenever a good or service is produced or sold, the revenue from the sale is distributed to the workers and the owners of the capital involved in the production of the good or service. Thus, except for some technical adjustments that we will ignore, GDP also equals labor income plus capital income.

- *Labor income* comprises wages, salaries, and the incomes of the self-employed.
- *Capital income* is made up of payments to owners of physical capital (such as factories, machines, and office buildings) and intangible capital (such as copyrights and patents). The components of capital income include items such as profits earned by business owners, the rents paid to owners of land or buildings, interest received by bondholders, and the royalties received by the holders of copyrights or patents.

How much of GDP is labor income versus capital income? Answering this question is not a simple task. Consider, for example, the income of a self-employed person (who owns his or her work equipment) or the income of a small-business owner: How much of their incomes should we count as labor income, and how much should we count as capital income? Economists do not always agree on the answers, and different estimation methods result in somewhat different numbers. For our purposes, as a rough approximation, we will think of labor income as being equal to about 75 percent of GDP and of capital income as equal to about 25 percent of GDP.

Both labor income and capital income are to be understood as measured prior to payment of taxes; ultimately, of course, a portion of both types of income is captured by the government in the form of tax collections.

Figure 4.2 may help you visualize the three equivalent ways of thinking about GDP: the market value of production, the total value of expenditure, and the sum of labor income and capital income. The figure also roughly captures the relative importance of the expenditure and income components. In 2019, about 68 percent of expenditure was consumption spending, about 18 percent was government purchases, and the rest was investment spending and net exports. (Actually, as Table 4.2 shows, net exports have been negative in recent years, reflecting the U.S. trade deficit.) As we mentioned, we think of labor income as being about 75 percent of total income, with capital income making up the rest.

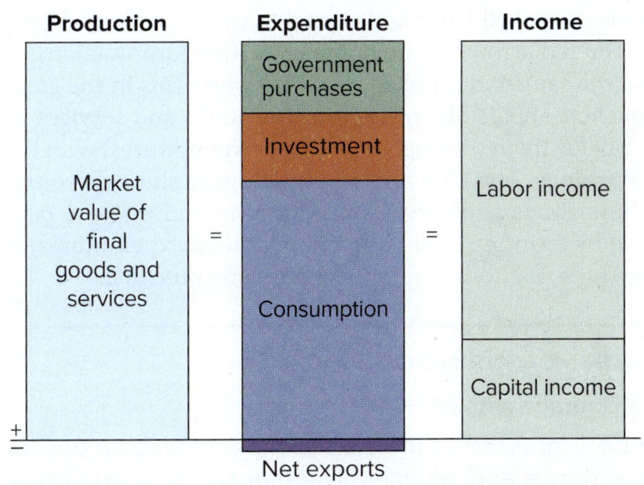

FIGURE 4.2

The Three Faces of GDP. The GDP can be expressed equally well as (1) the market value of production, (2) total expenditure (consumption, investment, government purchases, net exports), or (3) total income (labor income and capital income).

Figure 4.2 can be also viewed in the context of what is called a *circular flow diagram* of the economy. Such a diagram is drawn in Figure 4.3. It depicts a simplified economy where consumption, C, is the only component of GDP—not a bad simplified model of the U.S. economy, where C accounts for more than two-thirds of GDP (as discussed, it was roughly 68 percent in 2019). The left panel of Figure 4.3 conveys the economy as a flow of resources from households to firms, accompanied by a flow of final goods and services from firms to households. The *production* approach to measuring GDP would amount to counting that flow of goods and services (the blue arrow on the left in Figure 4.3) produced in a country in a given time period.

The right panel of Figure 4.3 conveys the economy as a flow of spending, paid by households to firms, in return for goods and services, and a flow of income, paid by firms to households, in return for resources such as labor and capital. The *expenditure* approach to measuring GDP would amount to counting the former (the blue arrow on the right), and the *income* approach would amount to counting the latter (the red arrow on the right) in a country in a given time period. As the diagram suggests, all three methods should yield the same GDP figures because, in principle, everything that is produced (and is therefore counted with the production method) is bought by some buyer (and is therefore counted with the expenditure method), and that buyer's spending is, in turn, someone else's income (counted with the income method).

FIGURE 4.3

Two Circular Flow Diagrams.

The left panel shows that households supply labor and capital to firms, which use those resources to produce goods and services for households. The right panel shows that households receive income from firms for the resources they supply, which they then spend on goods and services from firms.

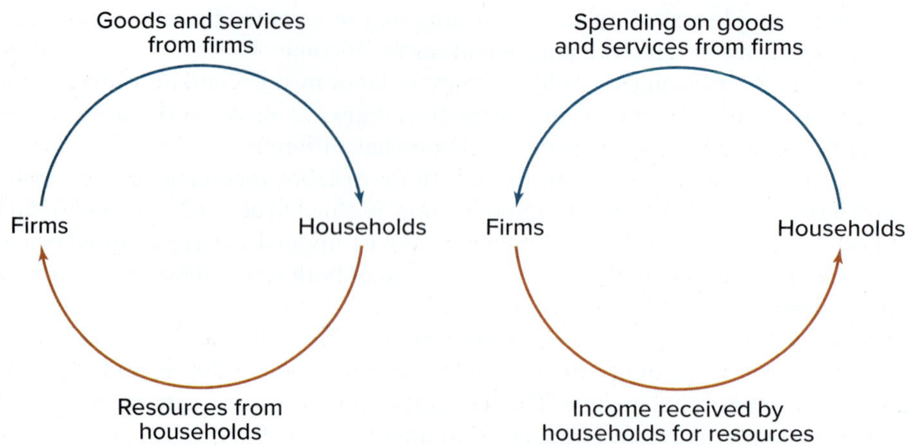

Figure 4.3 suggests a simple story that captures much—though far from all—of what is going on in the more complex U.S. economy. In this story, there are two main players in the economy—households and firms—and there are two main markets where these players trade: the market for production inputs and the market for goods and services. In the mornings, households meet firms in the market for production inputs (or for resources), sell labor and capital to those firms, and get paid labor and capital income. The red arrows in the figure show these transactions. In the evenings (and weekends), the same households meet the same firms in the goods and services market, and now households buy from firms the goods and services produced in the mornings, and pay for them (through household expenditures) with the same income earned in the mornings. The blue arrows in the figure show these transactions. The total value of these goods and services produced in a given time period—GDP—can thus be measured by counting total production, or total expenditures, or total income. In principle, the three methods would yield the same outcome.

RECAP

METHODS FOR MEASURING GDP

Expenditure Components of GDP

- GDP can be expressed as the sum of expenditures on domestically produced final goods and services. The four types of expenditure that are counted in the GDP, and the economic groups that make each type of expenditure, are as follows.

Type of expenditure	Who makes the expenditure?	Examples
Consumption	Households	Food, clothes, haircuts, new cars
Investment	Business firms	New factories and equipment, new houses, increases in inventory stocks
Government purchases	Governments	New school buildings, new military hardware, salaries of soldiers and government officials
Net exports, or exports minus imports	Foreign sector	Exported manufactured goods, legal or financial services provided by domestic residents to foreigners

Incomes of Capital and Labor

- GDP also equals labor income plus capital income.

NOMINAL GDP VERSUS REAL GDP

As a measure of the total production of an economy over a given period, such as a particular year, GDP is useful in comparisons of economic activity in different places. For example, GDP data for the year 2019, broken down state by state, could be used to compare aggregate production in New York and California during that year. However, economists are interested in comparing levels of economic activity not only in different *locations* but *over time* as well. For example, a president who is running for reelection on the basis of successful economic policies might want to know by how much output in the U.S. economy had increased during his or her term.

Using GDP to compare economic activity at two different points in time may give misleading answers, however, as the following example shows. Suppose, for the sake of illustration, that the economy produces only pizzas and calzones. The prices and quantities of the two goods in the years 2016 and 2020, the beginning and end of the president's term, are shown in Table 4.3. If we calculate GDP in each year as the market value of production, we find that the GDP for 2016 is (10 pizzas × \$10/pizza) + (15 calzones × \$5/calzone) = \$175. The GDP for 2020 is (20 pizzas × \$12/pizza) + (30 calzones × \$6/calzone) = \$420. Comparing the GDP for the year 2016 to the GDP for the year 2020, we might conclude that it is 2.4 times greater (\$420/\$175).

Can you see what is wrong with this conclusion? The quantities of both pizzas and calzones produced in the year 2020 are exactly twice the quantities produced in the year 2016. If economic activity, as measured by actual production of both goods, exactly doubled over the four years, why do the calculated values of GDP show a greater increase?

The answer, as you also can see from the table, is that prices as well as quantities rose between 2016 and 2020. Because of the increase in prices, the *market value* of production grew more over those four years than the *physical volume* of production. So in this case, GDP is a misleading gauge of economic growth during the president's term because the physical quantities of the goods and services produced in any given year, not the dollar values, are what determine people's economic well-being. Indeed, if the prices of pizzas and calzones had risen 2.4 times between 2016 and 2020 with no changes in the quantities of pizzas and calzones produced, GDP would have risen 2.4 times as well, with no increase in physical production! In that case, the claim that the economy's (physical) output had more than doubled during the president's term would obviously be wrong.

As this example shows, if we want to use GDP to compare economic activity at different points in time, we need some method of excluding the effects of price changes. In other words, we need to adjust for inflation. To do so, economists use a common set of prices to value quantities produced in different years. The standard approach is to pick a particular year, called the *base year,* and use the prices from that year to calculate the market value of output. When GDP is calculated using the prices from a base year, rather than the current year's prices, it is called *real GDP,* to indicate that it is a measure of real physical production. **Real GDP** is GDP adjusted for inflation. To distinguish real GDP, in which quantities produced are valued at base-year prices, from GDP valued at current-year prices, economists refer to the latter measure as **nominal GDP.**

real GDP a measure of GDP in which the quantities produced are valued at the prices in a base year rather than at current prices; real GDP measures the actual *physical volume* of production

nominal GDP a measure of GDP in which the quantities produced are valued at current-year prices; nominal GDP measures the *current dollar value* of production

TABLE 4.3
Prices and Quantities in 2016 and 2020

	Quantity of pizzas	Price of pizzas	Quantity of calzones	Price of calzones
2016	10	\$10	15	\$5
2020	20	\$12	30	\$6

EXAMPLE 4.8 Calculating the Change in Real GDP over a Four-Year Span

How much did real GDP grow over a four-year span?

Using data from Table 4.3 and assuming that 2016 is the base year, find real GDP for the years 2020 and 2016. By how much did real output grow between 2016 and 2020?

To find real GDP for the year 2020, we must value the quantities produced that year using the prices in the base year, 2016. Using the data in Table 4.3,

Year 2020 real GDP = (Year 2020 quantity of pizzas × Year 2016 price of pizzas) + (Year 2020 quantity of calzones × Year 2016 price of calzones)

= (20 × \$10) + (30 × \$5)

= \$350.

The real GDP of this economy in the year 2020 is \$350.

What is the real GDP for 2016? By definition, the real GDP for 2016 equals 2016 quantities valued at base-year prices. The base year in this example happens to be 2016, so real GDP for 2016 equals 2016 quantities valued at 2016 prices, which is the same as nominal GDP for 2016. In general, in the base year, real GDP and nominal GDP are the same. We already found nominal GDP for 2016, \$175, so that is also the real GDP for 2016.

We can now determine how much real production has actually grown over the four-year period. Since real GDP was \$175 in 2016 and \$350 in 2020, the physical volume of production doubled between 2016 and 2020. This conclusion makes sense—Table 4.3 shows that the production of both pizzas and calzones exactly doubled over the period. By using real GDP, we have eliminated the effects of price changes and obtained a reasonable measure of the actual change in physical production over the four-year span.

Of course, the production of all goods will not necessarily grow in equal proportion, as in the previous example. Self-Test 4.5 asks you to find real GDP when pizza and calzone production grow at different rates.

SELF-TEST 4.5

Suppose production and prices of pizzas and calzones in 2016 and 2020 are as follows.

	Quantity of pizzas	Price of pizzas	Quantity of calzones	Price of calzones
2016	10	\$10	15	\$5
2020	30	\$12	30	\$6

These data are the same as those in Table 4.3, except that pizza production has tripled rather than doubled between 2016 and 2020. Find real GDP in 2020 and 2016, and calculate the growth in real output over the four-year period. (Continue to assume that 2016 is the base year.)

After you complete Self-Test 4.5, you will find that the growth in real GDP between 2016 and 2020 reflects a sort of average of the growth in physical production of pizzas and calzones. Real GDP therefore remains a useful measure of overall physical production, even when the production of different goods and services grows at different rates.

The Economic Naturalist 4.1

Can nominal and real GDP ever move in different directions?

In most countries, both nominal and real GDP increase in almost every year. It is possible, however, for them to move in opposite directions. The last time this happened in the United States was 2007–2008. Using 2009 as a base year, real GDP fell by 0.3 percent, from $14.87 trillion in 2007 to $14.83 trillion in 2008. This reflected an overall reduction in the physical quantities of goods and services produced. Nominal GDP, however, rose by 1.7 percent, from $14.48 trillion to $14.72 trillion, over the same period because prices rose by more than quantities fell.

The preceding example also illustrates the fact that nominal GDP will be *less* than real GDP if prices during the current year are less than prices during the base year. This will generally be the case when the current year is earlier than the base year.

Could real GDP ever rise during a year in which nominal GDP fell? Once again, the answer is yes. For example, this could happen when a country experiences economic growth and falling prices (deflation) at the same time. This actually happened in Japan during several years in the 1990s.

The method of calculating real GDP just described was followed for many decades by the Bureau of Economic Analysis (BEA), the U.S. government agency responsible for GDP statistics. However, in recent decades, the BEA has adopted a more complicated procedure of determining real GDP, called *chain weighting*. The new procedure makes the official real GDP data less sensitive to the particular base year chosen. However, the chain-weighting and traditional approaches share the basic idea of valuing output in terms of base-year prices, and the results obtained by the two methods are generally similar.

Real GDP, Economic Growth, and Economic Well-Being

In Chapter 5, *Economic Growth, Productivity, and Living Standards,* we will discuss the costs and benefits of economic growth, which in practice means growth in real GDP per person. In that context we will ask the question of whether a growing real GDP is necessarily equated with greater economic well-being.

Now that you understand how real GDP is defined and what it measures, you can see why it is not the same as economic well-being–it was intended as a measure of the volume of economic activity in a given place at a given time (as Figures 4.2 and 4.3 illustrate). Real GDP does not measure everything that has economic value–in particular, it excludes many things that do not have *market* value (because they are not traded in markets), including leisure time and nonmarket services such as parenting, unpaid homemaking, and volunteer services. As we will discuss in the next chapter, GDP also does not measure things like economic inequality, environmental quality, and quality-of-life indicators such as a low crime rate.

But real GDP is *related* to economic well-being: After all, the things it is aimed to measure–the volume of production of private-sector goods and services and of government services—are valued by people and improve the quality of their lives. This association of GDP with many things that people value, including a higher material standard of living, better health, and longer life expectancies, led many people to emigrate to higher-GDP countries and has motivated policymakers to try to increase their nations' rates of GDP growth.

RECAP

NOMINAL GDP VERSUS REAL GDP

- Real GDP is calculated using the prices of goods and services that prevailed in a base year rather than in the current year. Nominal GDP is calculated using current-year prices. Real GDP is GDP adjusted for inflation; it may be thought of as measuring the physical volume of production. Comparisons of economic activity at different times should always be done using real GDP, not nominal GDP.
- Although GDP is not the same as economic well-being, it is positively associated with many things that people value, including a higher material standard of living, better health, and longer life expectancies. This relationship between real GDP and economic well-being has led many people to emigrate from poor nations in search of a better life and has motivated policymakers to try to increase their nations' rates of economic growth.

UNEMPLOYMENT AND THE UNEMPLOYMENT RATE

In assessing the level of economic activity in a country, economists look at a variety of statistics. Besides real GDP, one statistic that receives a great deal of attention, both from economists and from the general public, is the rate of unemployment. The unemployment rate is a sensitive indicator of conditions in the labor market. When the unemployment rate is low, jobs are secure and relatively easier to find. Low unemployment is often associated with improving wages and working conditions as well, as employers compete to attract and retain workers.

We will discuss labor markets and unemployment in detail in Chapter 6, *The Labor Market: Workers, Wages, and Unemployment.* This section will explain how the unemployment rate and some related statistics are defined and measured. It will close with a discussion of the costs of unemployment, both to the unemployed and to the economy as a whole.

Measuring Unemployment

In the United States, defining and measuring unemployment is the responsibility of the Bureau of Labor Statistics, or BLS. Each month the BLS surveys about 60,000 randomly selected households. Each person in those households who is 16 years or older is placed in one of three categories:

1. *Employed.* A person is employed if he or she worked full-time or part-time (even for a few hours) during the past week or is on vacation or sick leave from a regular job.
2. *Unemployed.* A person is unemployed if he or she did not work during the preceding week but made some effort to find work (for example, by going to a job interview) in the past four weeks.

3. *Out of the labor force.* A person is considered to be out of the labor force if he or she did not work in the past week and did not look for work in the past four weeks. In other words, people who are neither employed nor unemployed (in the sense of looking for work but not being able to find it) are "out of the labor force." Full-time students, unpaid homemakers, retirees, and people unable to work because of disabilities are examples of people who are out of the labor force.

Based on the results of the survey, the BLS estimates how many people in the whole country fit into each of the three categories. The working-age population is the sum of these three categories, and consists of the population age 16 and over.[2]

To find the unemployment rate, the BLS must first calculate the size of the *labor force*. The **labor force** is defined as the total number of employed and unemployed people in the economy (the first two categories of respondents to the BLS survey). The **unemployment rate** is then defined as the number of unemployed people divided by the labor force. Notice that people who are out of the labor force (because they are in school, have retired, or are disabled, for example) are not counted as unemployed and thus do not affect the unemployment rate. In general, a high rate of unemployment indicates that the economy is performing poorly.

Another useful statistic is the **participation rate,** or the percentage of the working-age population in the labor force (that is, the percentage that is either employed or looking for work). Figure 4.1 showed participation rates for American women and men since 1950. The participation rate is calculated by dividing the labor force by the working-age (16 years and older) population.[3]

Table 4.4 illustrates the calculation of key labor market statistics, using data based on the BLS survey for November 2019. In that month unemployment was 3.5 percent of the labor force. The participation rate was 63.2 percent; that is, almost two out of every three adults had a job or were looking for work.

labor force the total number of employed and unemployed people in the economy

unemployment rate the number of unemployed people divided by the labor force

participation rate the percentage of the working-age population in the labor force (that is, the percentage that is either employed or looking for work)

TABLE 4.4
U.S. Employment Data, November 2019 (in millions)

Employed	158.59
Plus:	
Unemployed	5.81
Equals: Labor force	164.40
Plus:	
Not in labor force	95.62
Equals:	
Working-age (over 16) population	260.02

Unemployment rate = Unemployed/Labor force = 5.81/164.40 = 3.5%

Participation rate = Labor force/Working-age population = 164.40/260.02 = 63.2%

Source: Bureau of Labor Statistics, www.bls.gov.

[2]See www.bls.gov/cps/cps_htgm.htm for complete details on how the government collects and categorizes these data.

[3]We note that different governmental agencies use slightly different definitions of the participation rate. In particular, the numbers underlying the figures, tables, and discussion in this chapter (including Figure 4.1, Figure 4.4, Table 4.4, etc.) are published by the U.S. Bureau of Labor Statistics (BLS), which defines participation rate as "the labor force as a percent of the civilian noninstitutional population." The civilian noninstitutional population includes only those working-age (16+) people "who are not inmates of institutions (for example, penal and mental facilities, homes for the aged), and who are not on active duty in the Armed Forces."

FIGURE 4.4

The U.S. Unemployment Rate, 1965–2019.

The unemployment rate—the fraction of the U.S. labor force that is unemployed—was just above 4 percent in the late 1990s. Unemployment rose to 6 percent in 2003 due to a recession and then decreased to just above 4.5 percent in 2007. During the 2007–2009 recession unemployment increased dramatically. From 2010 to 2019 it declined from its 2010 peak of 9.6 percent to a trough of 3.7 percent—the lowest recorded rate in 50 years.

Source: Bureau of Labor Statistics, www.bls.gov.

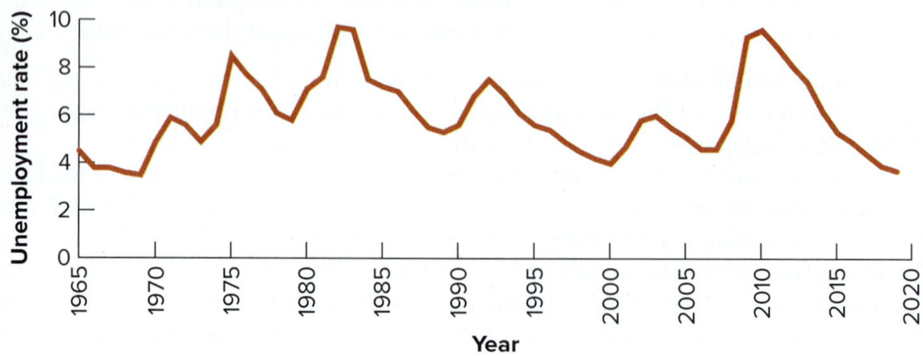

Figure 4.4 shows the U.S. unemployment rate since 1965. Unemployment rates were exceptionally low—just below and just above 4 percent—in the late 1960s, the late 1990s, and the late 2010s. By this measure, the latter part of the 1990s was an exceptionally good time for American workers. However, unemployment rose in 2001–2002 as the nation fell into recession, then declined to a low of 4.6 percent, and then more than doubled during the 2007–2009 recession. From 2010 to 2019, unemployment declined, reflecting the economic recovery. In the last few months of 2019, the unemployment rate was the lowest it has been since May 1969—over 50 years earlier. Figure 4.4 stops at 2019—the last year for which we have full-year unemployment data right now—but as you already know, in early 2020 the COVID-19 pandemic hit the U.S. economy; by mid-2020, the monthly unemployment rate jumped to levels not seen since the Great Depression. We will discuss these economic upswings (or expansions) and downswings (recessions) and their relationship with unemployment in greater detail in Chapter 9, *Short-Term Economic Fluctuations and Fiscal Policy*.

SELF-TEST 4.6

Following are November 2019 BLS U.S. employment data for African Americans.

Employed	19.527 million
Unemployed	1.135 million
Not in the labor force	12.523 million

Find the labor force, the working-age population, the unemployment rate, and the participation rate for African Americans and compare your results to those in Table 4.4.

The Costs of Unemployment

Unemployment imposes *economic, psychological,* and *social* costs on a nation. From an economic perspective, the main cost of unemployment is the output that is lost because the workforce is not fully utilized. Much of the burden of the reduced output is borne by the unemployed themselves, whose incomes fall when they are not working and whose skills may deteriorate from lack of use. However, society at large also bears part of the economic cost of unemployment. For example, workers who become unemployed are liable to stop paying taxes and start receiving government support payments, such as unemployment benefits. This net drain on the government's budget is a cost to all taxpayers.

The *psychological* costs of unemployment are felt primarily by unemployed workers and their families. Studies show that lengthy periods of unemployment can lead to a loss of self-esteem, feelings of loss of control over one's life, depression, and even suicidal behavior.[4] The unemployed worker's family is likely to feel increased psychological stress, compounded by the economic difficulties created by the loss of income.

The *social* costs of unemployment are a result of the economic and psychological effects. People who have been unemployed for a while tend not only to face severe financial difficulties, but also to feel anger, frustration, and despair. Not surprisingly, increases in unemployment tend to be associated with increases in crime, domestic violence, alcoholism, drug abuse, and other social problems. The costs created by these problems are borne not only by the unemployed but by society in general, as more public resources must be spent to counteract these problems—for example, by hiring more police to control crime or increasing spending on social services.

The Duration of Unemployment

In assessing the impact of unemployment on jobless people, economists must know how long individual workers have been without work. Generally, the longer a person has been out of work, the more severe are the economic and psychological costs that person will face. People who are unemployed for only a few weeks, for example, are not likely to suffer a serious reduction in their standard of living, experience psychological problems such as depression or loss of self-esteem, and have their skills deteriorate (in turn reducing future earnings)—at least not to the same extent as someone who has been out of work for months or years.

In its surveys, therefore, the BLS asks respondents how long they have been unemployed. A period during which an individual is continuously unemployed is called an **unemployment spell;** it begins when the worker becomes unemployed and ends when the worker either finds a job or leaves the labor force. (Remember, people outside the labor force are not counted as unemployed.) The length of an unemployment spell is called its **duration.** The duration of unemployment rises during recessions, reflecting the greater difficulty of finding work during those periods.

unemployment spell a period during which an individual is continuously unemployed

duration the length of an unemployment spell

At any given time, a substantial fraction of unemployed workers have been unemployed for six months or more; we will refer to this group as the *long-term unemployed*. Long-term unemployment creates the highest economic, psychological, and social costs, both for the unemployed themselves and for society as a whole.

When the economy is not in a recession, most unemployment spells are relatively short. For example, in November 2019, 34 percent of the unemployed had been out of work for just 5 weeks or less, another 30 percent had been unemployed for 5 to 14 weeks, and about 36 percent of the unemployed had been without a job for more than 14 weeks (about three months). However, during the latest recession, unemployment spells grew longer. For example, in August 2020, 17 percent of the unemployed had been out of work for 5 weeks or less, 23 percent had been unemployed for 5 to 14 weeks, and 60 percent of the unemployed had been searching for work without any success for more than 14 weeks.

Even these statistics are a bit deceptive, however, because short unemployment spells can arise from two very different patterns of labor market experience. Some

[4]For a survey of the literature on the psychological effects of unemployment, see William Darity Jr. and Arthur H. Goldsmith, "Social Psychology, Unemployment and Macroeconomics," *Journal of Economic Perspectives* 10 (Winter 1996), pp. 121–140.

people have short unemployment spells that end in their finding a stable long-term job. For the most part, these workers, whom we will refer to as the *short-term unemployed,* do not typically bear a high cost of unemployment. But other workers have short unemployment spells that typically end either in their withdrawal from the labor force or in a short-term or temporary job that soon leaves the worker unemployed again. Workers whose unemployment spells are broken up by brief periods of employment or withdrawals from the labor force are referred to as the *chronically unemployed.* In terms of the costs of unemployment, the experience of these workers is similar to that of the long-term unemployed.

The Unemployment Rate versus "True" Unemployment

Like GDP measurement, unemployment measurement has its critics. Most of them argue that the official unemployment rate understates the true extent of unemployment. They point in particular to two groups of people who are not counted among the unemployed: so-called *discouraged workers* and *involuntary part-time workers.*

discouraged workers people who say they would like to have a job but have not made an effort to find one in the past four weeks

Discouraged workers are people who say they would like to have a job but have not made an effort to find one in the past four weeks. Often, discouraged workers tell the survey takers that they have not searched for work because they have tried without success in the past or because they are convinced that labor market conditions are such that they will not be able to find a job. Because they have not sought work in the past four weeks, discouraged workers are counted as being out of the labor force rather than unemployed. Some observers have suggested that treating discouraged workers as unemployed would provide a more accurate picture of the labor market.

involuntary part-time workers people who say they would like to work full-time but are able to find only part-time work

Involuntary part-time workers are people who say they would like to work full-time but are able to find only part-time work. Because they do have jobs, involuntary part-time workers are counted as employed rather than unemployed. These workers are sometimes referred to as *underemployed* or part-time workers for economic reasons. Some economists have suggested that these workers should be counted as partially unemployed.

In response to these criticisms, since the 1990s, the BLS has been releasing special unemployment rates that include estimates of the number of discouraged workers and involuntary part-time workers. In November 2019, when the official unemployment rate was 3.5 percent (see Table 4.4), the BLS calculated that if both discouraged workers and involuntary part-time workers were counted as unemployed, the unemployment rate would have been 6.9 percent. So the problem of discouraged and underemployed workers appears to be fairly significant.

Whether in an official or adjusted version, the unemployment rate is a good overall indicator of labor market conditions. A high unemployment rate tends to be bad news even for those people who are employed, since raises and promotions are hard to come by in a "slack" labor market. We will discuss the causes and cures of unemployment at some length in Chapter 6, *The Labor Market: Workers, Wages, and Unemployment,* and subsequent chapters.

THE CONSUMER PRICE INDEX AND INFLATION

When discussing nominal GDP versus real GDP we demonstrated how one could convert a nominal quantity—a quantity that is measured in dollars (or other currency units)—into a real quantity—a quantity that is adjusted for inflation. We demonstrated how, by working with real quantities such as real GDP, economists can compare economic activity across different years without letting changes in prices muddy the picture. The simple example we used was an economy that produced only corn, so measuring the price level and inflation in that economy amounted to measuring the price of one good (corn) and its rate of change over time. But what is the price level in an economy, such as the U.S. economy, that produces many goods and services?

The basic tool economists use to measure the price level in the U.S. economy is the *consumer price index,* or *CPI* for short. The CPI is a measure of the "cost of living" during a particular period. Specifically, the **consumer price index (CPI)** for any period measures the cost in that period of a standard set, or basket, of goods and services *relative* to the cost of the same basket of goods and services in a fixed year, called the *base year.*

consumer price index (CPI) for any period, a measure of the cost in that period of a standard basket of goods and services relative to the cost of the same basket of goods and services in a fixed year, called the *base year*

To illustrate how the CPI is constructed, suppose the government has designated 2015 as the base year. Assume for the sake of simplicity that in 2015 a typical American family's monthly household budget consisted of spending on just three items: rent on a two-bedroom apartment, hamburgers, and movie tickets. In reality, of course, families purchase hundreds of different items each month, but the basic principles of constructing the CPI are the same no matter how many items are included. Suppose too that the family's average monthly expenditures in 2015, the base year, were as shown in Table 4.5.

TABLE 4.5
Monthly Household Budget of the Typical Family in 2015 (Base Year)

Item	Cost (in 2015)
Rent, two-bedroom apartment	$750
Hamburgers (60 at $2.00 each)	120
Movie tickets (10 at $7.00 each)	70
Total expenditure	$940

Now let's fast-forward to the year 2020. Over that period, the prices of various goods and services are likely to have changed; some will have risen and some fallen. Let's suppose that by the year 2020 the rent that our family pays for their two-bedroom apartment has risen to $945. Hamburgers now cost $2.50 each, and the price of movie tickets has risen to $8.00 each. So, in general, prices have been rising.

By how much did the family's cost of living increase between 2015 and 2020? Table 4.6 shows that if the typical family wanted to consume the *same basket of goods and services* in the year 2020 as they did in the year 2015, they would have to spend $1,175 per month, or $235 more than the $940 per month they spent in 2015. In other words, to live the same way in the year 2020 as they did in the year 2015, the family would have to spend 25 percent more ($235/$940) each month. So, in this example, the cost of living for the typical family rose 25 percent between 2015 and 2020.

TABLE 4.6
Cost of Reproducing the 2015 (Base-Year) Basket of Goods and Services in Year 2020

Item	Cost (in 2020)	Cost (in 2015)
Rent, two-bedroom apartment	$ 945	$750
Hamburgers (60 at $2.50 each)	150	120
Movie tickets (10 at $8.00 each)	80	70
Total expenditure	$1,175	$940

The government—actually, the Bureau of Labor Statistics (BLS), the same agency that is responsible for determining the unemployment rate—calculates the official consumer price index (CPI) using essentially the same method. The first step in deriving the CPI is to pick a base year and determine the basket of goods and services that were consumed by the typical family during that year. In practice, the government learns how consumers allocate their spending through a detailed survey, called the Consumer Expenditure Survey, in which randomly selected families record every purchase they make and the price they paid over a given month. (Quite a task!) Let's call the basket of goods and services that results the *base-year basket*. Then, each month BLS employees visit thousands of stores and conduct numerous interviews to determine the current prices of the goods and services in the base-year basket.[5]

The CPI in any given year is computed using the formula

$$\text{CPI} = \frac{\text{Cost of base-year basket of goods and services in current year}}{\text{Cost of base-year basket of goods and services in base year}}.$$

Returning to the example of the typical family that consumes three goods, we can calculate the CPI in the year 2020 as

$$\text{CPI in year 2020} = \frac{\$1{,}175}{\$940} = 1.25.$$

In other words, in this example, the cost of living in the year 2020 is 25 percent higher than it was in 2015, the base year. Notice that the base-year CPI is always equal to 1.00 since in that year the numerator and the denominator of the CPI formula are the same. The CPI for a given period (such as a month or year) measures the cost of living in that period *relative* to what it was in the base year.

The BLS multiplies the CPI by 100 to get rid of the decimal point. If we were to do that here, the year 2020 CPI would be expressed as 125 rather than 1.25, and the base-year CPI would be expressed as 100 rather than 1.00. However, many calculations are simplified if the CPI is stated in decimal form, so we will not adopt the convention of multiplying it by 100.

EXAMPLE 4.9 Calculating the CPI

How do we measure the typical family's cost of living?

Suppose that in addition to the three goods and services the typical family consumed in 2015, they also bought four sweaters at $30 each. In the year 2020, the same sweaters cost $50 each. The prices of the other goods and services in 2015 and 2020 were the same as in Table 18.2. With this additional item, what was the change in the family's cost of living between 2015 and 2020?

In the example in the text, the cost of the base-year (2015) basket was $940. Adding four sweaters at $30 each raises the cost of the base-year basket to $1,060. What does this same basket (including the four sweaters) cost in 2020? The cost of the apartment, the hamburgers, and the movie tickets is $1,175, as before. Adding the cost of the four sweaters at $50 each raises the total cost of the basket to $1,375. The CPI equals the cost of the basket in 2020 divided by the cost of the basket in 2015 (the base year), or $1,375/$1,060 = 1.30. We conclude that the family's cost of living rose 30 percent between 2015 and 2020.

SELF-TEST 4.7

Returning to the three-good example in Tables 4.5 and 4.6, find the year 2020 CPI if the rent on the apartment falls from $750 in 2015 to $600 in 2020. The prices for hamburgers and movie tickets in the two years remain the same as in the two tables.

[5]More details on how the Bureau of Labor Statistics constructs the CPI are available at www.bls.gov/cpi/questions-and-answers.htm.

The CPI does not measure the price of a specific good or service. Indeed, it has no units of measurement at all since the dollars in the numerator of the fraction cancel with the dollars in the denominator. Rather, the CPI is an *index*. The *value* of an index in a particular year has meaning only in comparison with the value of that index in another year. Thus, a **price index** measures the average price of a class of goods or services relative to the price of those same goods or services in a base year. The CPI is an especially well-known price index, one of many economists use to assess economic trends. For example, because manufacturers tend to pass on increases in the prices of raw materials to their customers, economists use indexes of raw materials' prices to forecast changes in the prices of manufactured goods. Other indexes are used to study the rate of price change in energy, food, health care, and other major sectors.

price index a measure of the average price of a given class of goods or services relative to the price of the same goods or services in a base year

SELF-TEST 4.8

The consumer price index captures the cost of living for the "typical" or average family. Suppose you were to construct a personal price index to measure changes in your own cost of living over time. In general, how would you go about constructing such an index? Why might changes in your personal price index differ from changes in the CPI?

Inflation

The CPI provides a measure of the average *level* of prices relative to prices in the base year. *Inflation,* in contrast, is a measure of how fast the average price level is *changing* over time. The **rate of inflation** is defined as the annual percentage rate of change in the price level, as measured, for example, by the CPI. Suppose that the CPI has a value of 1.25 in the year 2019 and a value of 1.27 in the year 2020. The rate of inflation between 2019 and 2020 is the percentage increase in the price level, or the increase in the price level (0.02) divided by the initial price level (1.25), which is equal to 1.6 percent.

rate of inflation the annual percentage rate of change in the price level, as measured, for example, by the CPI

EXAMPLE 4.10 Calculating Inflation Rates: 1972–1976

How do we calculate the inflation rate using the CPI?

CPI values for the years 1972 through 1976 are shown in the following table. Find the rates of inflation between 1972 and 1973, 1973 and 1974, 1974 and 1975, and 1975 and 1976.

Year	CPI
1972	0.418
1973	0.444
1974	0.493
1975	0.538
1976	0.569

The inflation rate between 1972 and 1973 is the percentage increase in the price level between those years, or $(0.444 - 0.418)/0.418 = 0.026/0.418 = 0.062 =$ 6.2 percent. Do the calculations on your own to confirm that inflation during each of the next three years was 11.0, 9.1, and 5.8 percent, respectively. During the 1970s, inflation rates were much higher than the 1.5 to 3 percent inflation rates that have prevailed in most years during the past quarter century.

SELF-TEST 4.9

Following are CPI values for the years 1929 through 1933. Find the rates of inflation between 1929 and 1930, 1930 and 1931, 1931 and 1932, and 1932 and 1933.

Year	CPI
1929	0.171
1930	0.167
1931	0.152
1932	0.137
1933	0.130

How did inflation rates in the 1930s differ from those of the 1970s?

SELF-TEST 4.10

CPI values for the years 2015 to 2019 are shown here. Calculate the inflation rate for each year.

Year	CPI
2015	2.37
2016	2.40
2017	2.45
2018	2.51
2019	2.56

deflation a situation in which the prices of most goods and services are falling over time so that inflation is negative

The results of the calculations for Self-Test 4.9 include some examples of *negative* inflation rates. A situation in which the prices of most goods and services are falling over time so that inflation is negative is called **deflation.** The early 1930s was the last time the United States experienced significant deflation. Japan experienced relatively mild deflation during the past two decades. As Self-Test 4.10 demonstrates, most recently in the U.S. inflation rates have been low but not negative.

ADJUSTING FOR INFLATION

The CPI is an extremely useful tool. Not only does it allow us to measure changes in the cost of living; it also can be used to adjust economic data to eliminate the effects of inflation. In this section, we will see how the CPI can be used to convert quantities measured at current dollar values into real terms, a process called *deflating*. We also will see that the CPI can be used to convert real quantities into current-dollar terms, a procedure called *indexing*. Both procedures are useful not only to economists but to anyone who needs to adjust payments, accounting measures, or other economic quantities for the effects of inflation.

Deflating a Nominal Quantity

nominal quantity a quantity that is measured in terms of its current dollar value

An important use of the CPI is to adjust **nominal quantities**—quantities measured at their current dollar values—for the effects of inflation. To illustrate, suppose we know that the typical family in a certain metropolitan area had a total income of $40,000 in 2015 and $44,000 in 2020. Was this family economically better off in the year 2020 than in 2015?

Without any more information than this, we might be tempted to say yes. After all, their income rose by 10 percent over the five-year period. But prices also might have been rising, as fast as or faster than the family's income. Suppose the prices of the goods and services the family consumes rose 25 percent over the same period. Since the family's income rose only 10 percent, we would have to conclude that the family is worse off, in terms of the goods and services they can afford to buy, despite the increase in their *nominal,* or current-dollar, income.

We can make a more precise comparison of the family's purchasing power in 2015 and 2020 by calculating their incomes in those years in *real* terms. In general, a **real quantity** is one that is measured in physical terms—for example, in terms of quantities of goods and services. To convert a nominal quantity into a real quantity, we must divide the nominal quantity by a price index for the period, as shown in Table 4.7. The calculations in the table show that in *real* or purchasing power terms, the family's income actually *decreased* by $4,800, or 12 percent of their initial real income of $40,000, between 2015 and 2020.

real quantity a quantity that is measured in physical terms—for example, in terms of quantities of goods and services

TABLE 4.7
Comparing the Real Values of a Family's Income in 2015 and 2020

Year	Nominal family income	CPI	Real family income = Nominal family income/CPI
2015	$40,000	1.00	$40,000/1.00 = $40,000
2020	$44,000	1.25	$44,000/1.25 = $35,200

The problem for this family is that though their income has been rising in nominal (dollar) terms, it has not kept up with inflation. Dividing a nominal quantity by a price index to express the quantity in real terms is called **deflating the nominal quantity.** (Be careful not to confuse the idea of deflating a nominal quantity with deflation, or negative inflation. The two concepts are different.)

deflating (a nominal quantity) the process of dividing a nominal quantity by a price index (such as the CPI) to express the quantity in real terms

Dividing a nominal quantity by the current value of a price index to measure it in real or purchasing power terms is a very useful tool. It can be used to eliminate the effects of inflation from comparisons of any nominal quantity—workers' wages, health care expenditures, the components of the federal budget—over time. Why does this method work? In general, if you know both how many dollars you have spent on a given item and the item's price, you can figure out how many of the item you bought (by dividing your expenditures by the price). For example, if you spent $100 on hamburgers last month and hamburgers cost $2.50 each, you can determine that you purchased 40 hamburgers. Similarly, if you divide a family's dollar income or expenditures by a price index, which is a measure of the average price of the goods and services they buy, you will obtain a measure of the real quantity of goods and services they purchased. Such real quantities are sometimes referred to as *inflation-adjusted* quantities.

EXAMPLE 4.11 Babe Ruth versus Stephen Strasburg

Who earned more, Babe Ruth or Stephen Strasburg?

In 1930, the great baseball player Babe Ruth earned a salary of $80,000. When it was pointed out to him that he had earned more than President Hoover, Ruth replied, with some justification, "I had a better year than he did." In 2019, the highest-paid baseball player was Stephen Strasburg, a star pitcher for the Washington

Nationals. His salary was $38.3 million. Adjusting for inflation, whose salary was higher, Ruth's or Strasburg's?

To answer this question, we need to know that the CPI (using the average of 1982–1984 as the base year) was 0.167 in 1930 and as of November 2019, it was 2.57 (for simplicity, we will treat this figure as if it were the annual 2019 figure). Dividing Babe Ruth's salary by 0.167, we obtain approximately $479,000, which is Ruth's salary "in 1982–1984 dollars." In other words, to enjoy the same purchasing power during the 1982–1984 period as in 1930, the Babe would have needed a salary of $479,000. Dividing Strasburg's 2019 salary by the November 2019 CPI, 2.57, yields a salary of $14.9 million in 1982–1984 dollars. We can now compare the salaries of the two players. Although adjusting for inflation brings the two figures closer together (since part of Strasburg's higher salary compensates for the increase in prices between 1930 and 2019), in real terms Strasburg's salary was still more than 31 times Ruth's salary. Incidentally, Strasburg's salary was also more than 95 times the U.S. president's salary.

real wage the wage paid to workers measured in terms of purchasing power; the real wage for any given period is calculated by dividing the nominal (dollar) wage by the CPI for that period

Clearly, in comparing wages or earnings at two different points in time, we must adjust for changes in the price level. Doing so yields the **real wage**—the wage measured in terms of real purchasing power. The real wage for any given period is calculated by dividing the nominal (dollar) wage by the CPI for that period.

SELF-TEST 4.11

In 2001, Barry Bonds of the San Francisco Giants hit 73 home runs, breaking the previous single-season home run record and becoming the current record holder. Bonds earned $10.3 million in 2001. In that year the CPI was 1.77. How did Bonds's real earnings compare to Ruth's and Strasburg's real salaries?

Indexing to Maintain Buying Power

The consumer price index also can be used to convert real quantities to nominal quantities. Suppose, for example, that in the year 2020 the government paid certain Social Security recipients $1,000 per month in benefits. Let's assume that Congress would like the buying power of these benefits to remain constant over time so that the recipients' standard of living is unaffected by inflation. To achieve that goal, at what level should Congress set the monthly Social Security benefit in the year 2025?

The nominal, or dollar, benefit Congress should pay in the year 2025 to maintain the purchasing power of retired people depends on how much inflation has taken place between 2020 and 2025. Suppose that the CPI has risen 20 percent between 2020 and 2025. That is, on average the prices of the goods and services consumers buy have risen 20 percent over that period. For Social Security recipients to "keep up" with inflation, their benefit in the year 2025 must be $1,000 + 0.20($1,000) = $1,200 per month, or 20 percent more than it was in 2020. In general, to keep purchasing power constant, the dollar benefit must be increased each year by the percentage increase in the CPI.

indexing the practice of increasing a nominal quantity each period by an amount equal to the percentage increase in a specified price index; indexing prevents the purchasing power of the nominal quantity from being eroded by inflation

The practice of increasing a nominal quantity according to changes in a price index to prevent inflation from eroding purchasing power is called **indexing.** In the case of Social Security, federal law provides for the automatic indexing of benefits. Each year, without any action by Congress, benefits increase by an amount equal to the percentage increase in the CPI. Some labor contracts are indexed as well so that wages are adjusted fully or partially for changes in inflation (see Example 4.12).

EXAMPLE 4.12 An Indexed Labor Contract

How much do workers get paid when they have an indexed contract?

A labor contract provides for a first-year wage of \$12.00 per hour and specifies that the real wage will rise by 2 percent in the second year of the contract and by another 2 percent in the third year. The CPI is 1.00 in the first year, 1.05 in the second year, and 1.10 in the third year. Find the dollar wage that must be paid in the second and third years of the contract.

Because the CPI is 1.00 in the first year, both the nominal wage and the real wage are \$12.00. Let W_2 stand for the nominal wage in the second year. Deflating by the CPI in the second year, we can express the real wage in the second year as $W_2/1.05$. The contract says that the second-year real wage must be 2 percent higher than the real wage in the first year, so $W_2/1.05 = \$12.00 \times 1.02 = \$12.24$. Multiplying through by 1.05 to solve for W_2, we get $W_2 = \$12.85$, the nominal wage required by the contract in the second year. In the third year, the nominal wage W_3 must satisfy the equation $W_3/1.10 = \$12.24 \times 1.02 = \$12.48$. (Why?) Solving this equation for W_3 yields \$13.73 as the nominal wage that must be paid in the third year.

SELF-TEST 4.12

In 1950, the minimum wage prescribed by federal law was \$0.75 per hour. In 2019, it was \$7.25 per hour. The CPI was 0.24 in 1950 and 2.56 in 2019. The minimum wage is not indexed to inflation, but suppose it had been starting in 1950. What would the nominal minimum wage have been in 2019?

The Economic Naturalist 4.2

Every few years, there is a well-publicized battle in Congress over whether the minimum wage should be raised. Why do these heated legislative debates recur so regularly?

Because the minimum wage is not indexed to inflation, its purchasing power falls as prices rise. Congress must therefore raise the nominal minimum wage periodically to keep the real value of the minimum wage from eroding. Ironically, despite the public's impression that Congress has raised the nominal minimum wage steeply over the years, the real minimum wage has fallen almost 30 percent since 1970.

Why doesn't Congress index the minimum wage to the CPI and eliminate the need to reconsider it so often? Evidently, some members of Congress prefer to hold a highly publicized debate on the issue every few years—perhaps because it mobilizes both advocates and opponents of the minimum wage to make campaign donations to those members who represent their views.

RECAP

METHODS TO ADJUST FOR INFLATION

Deflating. To correct a nominal quantity, such as a family's dollar income, for changes in the price level, divide it by a price index such as the CPI. This process expresses the nominal quantity in terms of real purchasing power. If nominal quantities from two different years are deflated by a price index with the same base year, the purchasing power of the two deflated quantities can be compared.

Indexing. To ensure that a nominal payment, such as a Social Security benefit, represents a constant level of real purchasing power, increase the nominal quantity each year by a percentage equal to the rate of inflation for that year.

INFLATION MEASUREMENT AND QUALITY CHANGE

You may have concluded that measuring inflation is straightforward, but as with GDP and the unemployment rate, the issue is not free from controversy. Indeed the question of whether U.S. inflation is properly measured has been the subject of serious debate. Because the CPI is one of the most important U.S. economic statistics, the issue is far from academic. Policymakers pay close attention to the latest inflation numbers when deciding what actions to take. Furthermore, because of the widespread use of indexing, changes in the CPI directly impact the government's budget. For example, if the CPI rises by 3 percent during a given year, by law Social Security benefits—which are a significant part of the federal budget—increase automatically by 3 percent. Many other government payments and private contracts, such as union labor contracts, are indexed to the CPI as well.

One of the difficulties in measuring inflation is that in practice, government statisticians cannot always adjust adequately for changes in the *quality* of goods and services. Suppose a new laptop computer has 20 percent more memory, computational speed, and data storage capacity than last year's model. Suppose too for the sake of illustration that its price is 20 percent higher. Has there been inflation in computer prices? Economists would say no; although consumers are paying 20 percent more for a computer, they are getting a 20 percent better machine. The situation is really no different from paying 20 percent more for a pizza that is 20 percent bigger. However, because quality change is difficult to measure precisely and because they have many thousands of goods and services to consider, government statisticians often miss or understate changes in quality. In general, whenever statisticians fail to adjust adequately for improvements in the quality of goods or services, they will tend to overstate inflation. This type of overstatement is called *quality adjustment bias*.

One important consequence of quality adjustment bias, and of an overstated rate of inflation in general, is an *under*estimation of the true improvement in living standards over time. If the typical family's nominal income increases by 3 percent per year, and inflation is reported to be 3 percent per year, economists would conclude that American families are experiencing no increase in their real income. But if the "true" inflation rate, adjusting for quality improvements, is really 2 percent per year, then the family's real income is actually rising by 1 percent per year (the 3 percent increase in nominal income minus 2 percent inflation).

connect

▶ Visit your instructor's Connect course and access your eBook to view this video.

Do official inflation figures overstate actual increases in our living costs?

The Bureau of Labor Statistics (the agency responsible for calculating the CPI) makes significant efforts to adjust for quality and avoid overstating inflation. In spite of these efforts, in recent years some economists have argued that the problem of quality adjustment bias has in fact been getting *worse*. For example, some argue that as the U.S. economy shifts from producing computer hardware to producing software and digital content, accurately measuring quality change becomes increasingly harder.

An extreme example of quality adjustment bias can occur whenever a totally new good becomes available. For instance, the introduction of the first effective AIDS drugs significantly increased the quality of medical care received by AIDS patients. In practice, however, quality improvements that arise from totally new products are likely to be poorly captured by the CPI, if at all. The problem is that because the new good was not produced in the base year, there is no base-year price with which to compare the current price of the good. Government statisticians use various approaches to correct for this problem, such as comparing the cost of the new drug to the cost of the next-best therapies. But such methods are necessarily imprecise and open to criticism.

THE COSTS OF INFLATION: NOT WHAT YOU THINK

In the late 1970s, when inflation was considerably higher than it is now, the public told poll takers that they viewed it as "public enemy number one"—that is, as the nation's most serious problem. Although U.S. inflation rates have not been very high in recent years, today many Americans remain concerned about inflation or the threat of inflation. Why do people worry so much about inflation? Detailed opinion surveys often find that many people are confused about the meaning of inflation and its economic effects. When people complain about inflation, they are often concerned primarily about relative price changes. Before describing the true economic costs of inflation, which are real and serious, let's examine this confusion people experience about inflation and its costs.

We need first to distinguish between the *price level* and the *relative price* of a good or service. The **price level** is a measure of the overall level of prices at a particular point in time as measured by a price index such as the CPI. Recall that the inflation rate is the percentage change in the price level from year to year. In contrast, a **relative price** is the price of a specific good or service *in comparison to* the prices of other goods and services. For example, if the price of oil were to rise by 10 percent while the prices of other goods and services were rising on average by 3 percent, the relative price of oil would increase. But if oil prices rise by 3 percent while other prices rise by 10 percent, the relative price of oil would decrease. That is, oil would become cheaper relative to other goods and services, even though it has not become cheaper in absolute terms.

price level a measure of the overall level of prices at a particular point in time as measured by a price index such as the CPI

relative price the price of a specific good or service *in comparison to* the prices of other goods and services

Public opinion surveys suggest that many people are confused about the distinction between inflation, which is an increase in the overall *price level*, and an increase in a specific *relative price*. Suppose that supply disruptions in the Middle East were to double the price of gas at the pump, leaving other prices unaffected. Appalled by the increase in gasoline prices, people might demand that the government do something about "this inflation." But while the increase in gas prices hurts consumers, is it an example of inflation? Gasoline is only one item in a consumer's budget, one of the thousands of goods and services that people buy every day. Thus, the increase in the price of gasoline might affect the overall price level, and hence the inflation rate, only slightly. In this example, inflation is not the real problem. What upsets consumers is the change in the *relative price* of gasoline, particularly compared to the price of labor (wages). By increasing the cost of using a car, the increase in the relative price of gasoline reduces the income people have left over to spend on other things.

Again, changes in relative prices do *not* necessarily imply a significant amount of inflation. For example, increases in the prices of some goods could well be counterbalanced by decreases in the prices of other goods, in which case the price level and the inflation rate would be largely unaffected. Conversely, inflation can be high without affecting relative prices. Imagine, for instance, that all prices in the economy, including wages and salaries, go up exactly 10 percent each year. The inflation rate is 10 percent, but relative prices are not changing. Indeed, because wages (the price of labor) are increasing by 10 percent per year, people's ability to buy goods and services is unaffected by the inflation.

These examples show that changes in the price level (inflation) and changes in the relative prices of specific goods are two quite different issues. The public's tendency to confuse the two is important because the remedies for the two problems are different. To counteract changes in relative prices, the government would need to implement policies that affect the supply and demand for specific goods. In the case of an increase in oil prices, for example, the government could try to restore supplies by mediating the peace process in the Middle East, or it could try to encourage the development of alternative sources of energy. To counteract inflation, however, the government must resort (as we will see) to changes in macroeconomic policies such as monetary or fiscal policies. If, in confusion, the public forces the government to adopt anti-inflationary policies when the real problem is a relative price change, the economy could actually be hurt by the effort. Here is an important example of why economic literacy is important—to both policymakers and the general public.

EXAMPLE 4.13 The Price Level, Relative Prices, and Inflation

Has the price of oil risen faster or slower than the price level?

Suppose the value of the CPI is 1.20 in the year 2018, 1.32 in 2019, and 1.40 in 2020. Assume also that the price of oil increases 8 percent between 2018 and 2019 and another 8 percent between 2019 and 2020. What is happening to the price level, the inflation rate, and the relative price of oil?

The price level can be measured by the CPI. Since the CPI is higher in 2019 than in 2018 and higher still in 2020 than in 2019, the price level is rising throughout the period. Since the CPI increases by 10 percent between 2018 and 2019, the inflation rate between those years is 10 percent. However, the CPI increases only about 6 percent between 2019 and 2020 ($1.40/1.32 \approx 1.06$), so the inflation rate decreases to about 6 percent between those years. The decline in the inflation rate implies that although the price level is still rising, it is doing so at a slower pace than the year before.

The price of oil rises 8 percent between 2018 and 2019. But because the general inflation over that period is 10 percent, the relative price of oil—that is, its price *relative to all other goods and services*—falls by about 2 percent ($8\% - 10\% = -2\%$). Between 2019 and 2020, the price of oil rises by another 8 percent, while the general inflation rate is about 6 percent. Hence, the relative price of oil rises between 2019 and 2020 by about 2 percent ($8\% - 6\%$).

The True Costs of Inflation

Having dispelled the common confusion between inflation and relative price changes, we are now free to address the true economic costs of inflation. There are a variety of such costs, each of which tends to reduce the efficiency of the economy. Five of the most important are discussed here.

First, inflation raises the cost of holding cash to consumers and businesses. Consider a miser with $10,000 in $20 bills under his mattress. What happens to the buying power of his hoard over time? If inflation is zero so that on average the prices of goods and services are not changing, the buying power of the $10,000 does not change over time. At the end of a year the miser's purchasing power is the same as it was at the beginning of the year. But suppose the inflation rate is 10 percent. In that case, the purchasing power of the miser's hoard will fall by 10 percent each year. After a year, he will have only $9,000 in purchasing power. In general, the higher the rate of inflation, the less people will want to hold cash because of the loss of purchasing power that they will suffer. So when faced with high inflation, people will take actions to try to "economize" on their cash holdings. For example, instead of drawing out enough cash for a month the next time they visit the bank, they will draw out only enough to last a week. Similarly, businesses will reduce their cash holdings by sending employees to the bank more frequently, or by installing computerized systems to monitor cash usage. To deal with the increase in bank transactions required by consumers and businesses trying to use less cash, banks will need to hire more employees and expand their operations.

The costs of more frequent trips to the bank, new cash management systems, and expanded employment in banks are real costs. They use up resources, including time and effort, that could be used for other purposes. Traditionally, the costs of economizing on cash have been called *shoe-leather costs*—the idea being that shoe leather is worn out during extra trips to the bank. Shoe-leather costs probably are not a significant problem in the United States today, where inflation is only 2 to 3 percent per year. But in economies with high rates of inflation, they can become quite significant.

A second real cost of inflation is that it leads to *noise in the price system.* In Chapter 2, *Supply and Demand,* we described the remarkable economic coordination that is necessary to provide the right amount and the right kinds of food to New Yorkers every day. This feat is not orchestrated by some Food Distribution Ministry staffed by bureaucrats. It is done much better than a ministry ever could by the workings of free markets, operating without central guidance.

How do free markets transmit the enormous amounts of information necessary to accomplish complex tasks like the provisioning of New York City? The answer is through the price system. When the owners of French restaurants in Manhattan cannot find sufficient quantities of chanterelles, a particularly rare and desirable mushroom, they bid up its market price. Specialty food suppliers notice the higher price for chanterelles and realize that they can make a profit by supplying more chanterelles to the market. At the same time, price-conscious diners will shift to cheaper, more available mushrooms. The market for chanterelles will reach equilibrium only when there are no more unexploited opportunities for profit, and both suppliers and demanders are satisfied at the market price. Multiply this example a million times, and you will gain a sense of how the price system achieves a truly remarkable degree of economic coordination.

When inflation is high, however, the subtle signals that are transmitted through the price system become more difficult to interpret, much in the way that static, or "noise," makes a radio message harder to interpret. With high inflation, market participants cannot easily tell—without information on the prices of other goods and services—whether a price increase of a certain mushroom reflects a relative price change (to which they have incentives to respond) or merely a general increase in the price level (that is, inflation). Since this information takes time and effort to collect, suppliers' and demanders' responses to price changes are likely to be slower and more tentative. This reduction in the efficiency of the market system imposes real economic costs.

A third cost of inflation is that it leads to *distortions of the tax system.* In spite of the fact that just as some government expenditures, such as Social Security benefits, are indexed to inflation, many taxes are also indexed. However, many provisions of the tax code have not been indexed, either because of lack of political support or because of the complexity of the task. As a result, inflation can produce unintended changes in the taxes people pay, which in turn may cause them to change their behavior in economically undesirable ways.

Yet another concern about inflation is that it may *arbitrarily redistribute wealth* from one group to another. Consider a group of union workers who signed a contract setting their wages for the next three years. If those wages are not indexed to inflation, then the workers will be vulnerable to upsurges in the price level. Suppose, for example, that inflation is much higher than expected over the three years of the contract. In that case the buying power of the workers' wages—their real wages—will be less than anticipated when they signed the contract. If inflation had been *lower* than expected, the workers would have enjoyed greater purchasing power than they anticipated and the employer would have been the loser.

Another example of the redistribution caused by inflation takes place between borrowers (debtors) and lenders (creditors), whenever the borrowing (or lending) contract is not indexed. *In general, unexpectedly high inflation rates help borrowers at the expense of lenders,* because borrowers are able to repay their loans in less valuable dollars. Unexpectedly low inflation rates, in contrast, help lenders and hurt borrowers by forcing borrowers to repay in dollars that are worth more than expected when the loan was made.

Although redistributions caused by inflation do not directly destroy wealth, but only transfer it from one group to another, they are still bad for the economy. Our economic system is based on incentives. For it to work well, people must know that if they work hard, save some of their income, and make wise financial investments, they will be rewarded in the long run with greater real wealth and a better standard of living. Some observers have compared a high-inflation economy to a casino, in which wealth is distributed largely by luck—that is, by random fluctuations in the inflation rate. In the long run, a "casino economy" is likely to perform poorly, as its unpredictability discourages people from working and saving. (Why bother if inflation can take away your savings overnight?) Rather, a high-inflation economy encourages people to use up resources in trying to anticipate inflation and protect themselves against it.

The fifth and final cost of inflation we will examine is its tendency to *interfere with the long-run planning* of households and firms. Many economic decisions take place within a long time horizon. Planning for retirement, for example, may begin when workers are in their twenties or thirties. And firms develop long-run investment and business strategies that look decades into the future.

Clearly, high and erratic inflation can make long-term planning difficult. Suppose, for example, that you want to enjoy a certain standard of living when you retire. How much of your income do you need to save to make your dreams a reality? That depends on what the goods and services you plan to buy will cost 30 or 40 years from now. With high and erratic inflation, even guessing what your chosen lifestyle will cost by the time you retire is extremely difficult. You may end up saving too little and having to compromise on your retirement plans; or you may save too much, sacrificing more than you need to during your working years. Either way, inflation will have proved costly.

In summary, inflation damages the economy in a variety of ways. Some of its effects are difficult to quantify and are therefore controversial. But most economists agree that a low and stable inflation rate is instrumental in maintaining a healthy economy.

RECAP

THE TRUE COSTS OF INFLATION

The public sometimes confuses changes in relative prices (such as the price of oil) with inflation, which is a change in the overall level of prices. This confusion can cause problems, because the remedies for undesired changes in relative prices and for inflation are different.

There are a number of true costs of inflation, which together tend to reduce economic growth and efficiency. These include:

- Shoe-leather costs, or the costs of economizing on cash (for example, by making more frequent trips to the bank or installing a computerized cash management system).
- "Noise" in the price system, which occurs when general inflation makes it difficult for market participants to interpret the information conveyed by prices.
- Distortions of the tax system, for example, when provisions of the tax code are not indexed.
- Unexpected redistributions of wealth, as when higher-than-expected inflation hurts wage earners to the benefit of employers or hurts creditors to the benefit of debtors.
- Interference with long-term planning, arising because people find it difficult to forecast prices over long periods.

SUMMARY

- The basic measure of an economy's output is *gross domestic product (GDP),* the market value of the final goods and services produced in a country during a given period. Expressing output in terms of market values allows economists to aggregate the millions of goods and services produced in a modern economy. *(LO1)*
- Only *final goods and services* (which include *capital goods*) are counted in GDP since they are the only goods and services that directly benefit final users. *Intermediate goods and services,* which are used up in the production of final goods and services, are not counted in GDP, nor are sales of existing assets, such as a 20-year-old house. Summing the value added by each firm in the production process is a useful method of determining the value of final goods and services. *(LO1)*
- GDP can also be expressed as the sum of four types of expenditure: *consumption, investment, government purchases,* and *net exports*. These four types of expenditure correspond to the spending of households, firms, the government, and the foreign sector, respectively. *(LO2)*
- To compare levels of GDP over time, economists must eliminate the effects of inflation. They do so by measuring the market value of goods and services in terms of the prices in a base year. GDP measured in this way is called *real GDP,* while GDP measured in terms of current-year prices is called *nominal GDP*. Real GDP should always be used in making comparisons of economic activity over time. *(LO3)*
- The unemployment rate, perhaps the best-known indicator of the state of the labor market, is based on surveys conducted by the Bureau of Labor Statistics. The surveys classify all respondents over age 16 as employed, unemployed, or not in the labor force. The *labor force* is the sum of employed and unemployed workers—that is, people who have a job or are looking for one. The *unemployment rate* is calculated as the number of unemployed workers divided by the labor force. The *participation rate* is the percentage of the working-age population that is in the labor force. *(LO4)*
- The costs of unemployment include the economic cost of lost output, the psychological costs borne by unemployed workers and their families, and the social costs associated with problems like increased crime and violence. The greatest costs are imposed by long *unemployment spells* (periods of unemployment). Critics of the official unemployment rate argue that it understates "true" unemployment by excluding *discouraged workers* and *involuntary part-time workers*. *(LO4)*
- The basic tool for measuring inflation is the *consumer price index (CPI)*. The CPI measures the cost of purchasing a fixed basket of goods and services in any period relative to the cost of the same basket of goods and services in a base year. The *inflation rate* is the annual percentage rate of change in the price level as measured by a *price index* such as the CPI. *(LO5)*
- The official U.S. inflation rate, based on the CPI, may overstate the true inflation rate because, for example, it may not adequately reflect improvements in the quality of goods and services. *(LO6)*
- A *nominal quantity* is a quantity that is measured in terms of its current dollar value. Dividing a nominal quantity such as a family's income or a worker's wage in dollars by a price index such as the CPI expresses that quantity in terms of real purchasing power. This procedure is called *deflating* the nominal quantity. If nominal quantities from two different years are deflated by a common price index, the purchasing power of the two quantities can be compared. To ensure that a nominal payment such as a Social Security benefit represents a constant level of real purchasing power, the nominal payment should be increased each year by a percentage equal to the inflation rate. This method of adjusting nominal payments to maintain their purchasing power is called *indexing*. *(LO6)*
- The public sometimes confuses increases in the *relative prices* for specific goods or services with inflation, which is an increase in the general price level. Since the remedies for a change in relative prices are different from the remedies for inflation, this confusion can cause problems. *(LO7)*
- Inflation imposes a number of true costs on the economy, including "noise" in the price system; distortions of the tax system; "shoe-leather" costs, which are the real resources that are wasted as people try to economize on cash holdings; unexpected redistributions of wealth; and interference with long-term planning. Because of these costs, most economists agree that sustained economic growth is more likely if inflation is low and stable. *(LO8)*

KEY TERMS

capital good
consumer price index (CPI)
consumption expenditure (or consumption)
deflating (a nominal quantity)
deflation
discouraged workers
duration (of an unemployment spell)
final goods or services
government purchases
gross domestic product (GDP)
indexing
intermediate goods or services
investment
involuntary part-time workers
labor force
market value
net exports
nominal GDP
nominal quantity
participation rate
price index
price level
rate of inflation
real GDP
real quantity
real wage
relative price
unemployment rate
unemployment spell
value added

REVIEW QUESTIONS

1. Why do economists use market values when calculating GDP? What is the economic rationale for giving high-value items more weight in GDP than low-value items? *(LO1)*
2. Give examples of each of the four types of aggregate expenditure. Which of the four represents the largest share of GDP in the United States? Can an expenditure component be negative? Explain. *(LO2)*
3. Sara's Rock Painting Stand painted 1,000 rocks last year and 1,200 rocks this year. She charged $4 per rock last year and $5 this year. If last year is taken as the base year, find Sara's contribution to both nominal GDP and real GDP in both years. Which measure would be better to use if you were trying to measure the change in Sara's productivity over the past year? Why? *(LO3)*
4. What are the costs of a high unemployment rate? Do you think providing more generous government benefits to the unemployed would increase these costs, reduce these costs, or leave them unchanged? Discuss. *(LO4)*
5. Explain why changes in the cost of living for any particular individual or family may differ from changes in the official cost-of-living index, the CPI. *(LO5)*
6. Why is it important to adjust for inflation when comparing nominal quantities (for example, workers' average wages) at different points in time? What is the basic method for adjusting for inflation? *(LO6)*
7. Give two reasons the official inflation rate may understate the "true" rate of inflation. Illustrate by examples. *(LO7)*
8. "It's true that unexpected inflation redistributes wealth, from creditors to debtors, for example. But what one side of the bargain loses, the other side gains. So from the perspective of the society as a whole, there is no real cost." Do you agree? Discuss. *(LO8)*

PROBLEMS

1. George and John, stranded on an island, use clamshells for money. Last year George caught 300 fish and 5 wild boars. John grew 100 bunches of bananas. In the two-person economy that George and John set up, fish sell for 3 clamshells each, boars sell for 10 clamshells each, and bananas go for 10 clamshells a bunch. George paid John a total of 30 clamshells for helping him dig bait for fishing, and he also purchased five of John's mature banana trees for 30 clamshells each. What is the GDP of George and John's island in terms of clamshells? *(LO1)*
2. How would each of the following transactions affect the GDP of the United States? *(LO1)*
   a. The U.S. government pays $1 billion in salaries for government workers.
   b. The U.S. government pays $1 billion to Social Security recipients.
   c. The U.S. government pays a U.S. firm $1 billion for newly produced airplane parts.
   d. The U.S. government pays $1 billion in interest to holders of U.S. government bonds.
   e. The U.S. government pays $1 billion to Saudi Arabia for crude oil to add to U.S. official oil reserves.
3. MNLogs harvested logs (with no inputs from other companies) from its property in northern Minnesota. It sold these logs to MNLumber for $1,500, and

MNLumber cut and planed the logs into lumber. MNLumber then sold the lumber for $4,000 to MNFurniture. MNFurniture used the lumber to produce 100 tables that it sold to customers for $70 each. *(LO1)*

a. Complete the following table to calculate the value added by each firm.

Company	Revenues	Cost of purchased inputs	Value added
MNLogs			
MNLumber			
MNFurniture			

b. Suppose that all of these transactions took place in 2019. By how much did GDP increase because of these transactions?

c. Suppose that MNLogs harvested the logs in October 2019 and sold them to MNLumber in December 2019. MNLumber then sold the finished lumber to MNFurniture in April 2020 and MNFurniture sold all 100 tables during the rest of 2020. By how much did GDP increase in 2019 and 2020 because of these transactions?

4. For each of the following transactions, state the effect both on U.S. GDP and on the four components of aggregate expenditure. *(LO2)*
   a. Your mother-in-law buys a new car from a U.S. producer.
   b. Your mother-in-law buys a new car imported from Sweden.
   c. Your mother-in-law's car rental business buys a new car from a U.S. producer.
   d. Your mother-in-law's car rental business buys a new car imported from Sweden.
   e. The U.S. government buys a new, domestically produced car for the use of your mother-in-law, who has been appointed the ambassador to Sweden.
5. Calculate the four components of expenditure and GDP for the following economy using data from the following table. *(LO2)*

Consumption expenditures	$550
Exports	75
Government purchases of goods and services	200
Construction of new homes and apartments	100
Sales of existing homes and apartments	200
Imports	50
Beginning-of-year inventory stocks	100
End-of-year inventory stocks	125
Business fixed investment	100
Government payments to retirees	100
Household purchases of durable goods	150

6. The nation of Potchatoonie produces hockey pucks, cases of root beer, and sandals. The following table lists prices and quantities of the three goods in the years 2017 and 2020. *(LO3)*

	Pucks		Root Beer		Sandals	
Year	Quantity	Price	Quantity	Price	Quantity	Price
2017	100	$5	300	$20	75	$20
2020	125	$9	325	$20	110	$25

Assume that 2017 is the base year. Find nominal GDP and real GDP for both years.

7. The following is a report from a BLS survey taker: "There were 65 people in the houses I visited, 10 of them children under 16; 25 people had full-time jobs, and 5 had part-time jobs. There were 10 retirees, 5 full-time homemakers, 5 full-time students over age 16, and 2 people who were disabled and cannot work. The remaining people did not have jobs but all said they would like one. One of these people had not looked actively for work for 3 months, however." Find the labor force, the unemployment rate, and the participation rate implied by the survey taker's report. *(LO4)*
8. Skyler is downloading labor market data for the most recent month, but her connection is slow and so far this is all she has been able to get.

Unemployment rate	5.9%
Participation rate	62.5%
Not in the labor force	63 million

Find the labor force, the working-age population, the number of employed workers, and the number of unemployed workers. *(LO4)*

9. Government survey takers determine that typical family expenditures each month in the year designated as the base year are as follows:

   25 pizzas at $10 each
   Rent of apartment, $600 per month
   Gasoline and car maintenance, $100
   Cell phone service, $50

   In the year following the base year, the survey takers determine that pizzas have risen to $11 each, apartment rent is $700, gasoline and maintenance have risen to $120, and phone service has dropped in price to $40. *(LO5)*
   a. Find the CPI in the subsequent year and the rate of inflation between the base year and the subsequent year.
   b. The family's nominal income rose by 5 percent between the base year and the subsequent year. Are they worse off or better off in terms of what their income is able to buy?

10. Here are values of the CPI (multiplied by 100) for each year from 2000 to 2010. For each year beginning with 2001, calculate the rate of inflation from the previous year. What happened to inflation rates over the 2000s? *(LO5)*

2000	122.7
2001	128.2
2002	132.3
2003	136.5
2004	140.2
2005	144.4
2006	148.9
2007	152.5
2008	155.0
2009	158.6
2010	164.2

11. According to the U.S. Census Bureau (www.census.gov), nominal income for the typical family of four in the United States (median income) was \$23,618 in 1985, \$34,076 in 1995, \$46,326 in 2005, and \$49,276 in 2010. In purchasing power terms, how did family income compare in each of those four years? You will need to know that the CPI (multiplied by 100, 1982–1984 = 100) was 107.6 in 1985, 152.4 in 1995, 195.3 in 2005, and 218.1 in 2010. *(LO6)*
12. A recent report found that the real entry-level wage for college graduates declined by 8 percent between 1990 and 1997. The nominal entry-level wage in 1997 was \$13.65 per hour. Assuming that the findings are correct, what was the nominal entry-level wage in 1990? You will need to use data from Problem 10. *(LO6)*
13. Imagine two economies, A and B. In Economy A, technological improvements are rare, and the basket of goods and services that households consume is essentially unchanged from one year to the next. In Economy B, technology improves fast, and every year households consume goods and services that are better than those consumed the year before (or that did not even exist previously, e.g., new drugs). In both economies, during the year 2015, the government measured inflation to be 2 percent, and nominal incomes also increased by 2 percent. *(LO7)*
    a. According to the official inflation figures, by how much did real incomes increase in each of the economies?
    b. If government statisticians missed or understated quality changes, in which of the two economies was inflation overstated? In which of the two was the true improvement in living standards understated?
14. The following table lists the actual per-gallon prices for unleaded regular gasoline for June of each year between 1978 and 1986, together with the values of the CPIs for those years. For each year from 1979 to 1986, find the CPI inflation rate and the change in the real price of gasoline, both from the previous year. Would it be fair to say that most of the changes in gas prices during this period were due to general inflation, or were factors specific to the oil market playing a role as well? *(LO5, LO8)*

Year	Gasoline price (\$/gallon)	CPI (1982–1984 = 1.00)
1978	0.663	0.652
1979	0.901	0.726
1980	1.269	0.824
1981	1.391	0.909
1982	1.309	0.965
1983	1.277	0.996
1984	1.229	1.039
1985	1.241	1.076
1986	0.955	1.136

ANSWERS TO SELF-TESTS

4.1 In the text, GDP was calculated to be \$64.00. If in addition Orchardia produces 5 oranges at \$0.30 each, GDP is increased by \$1.50 to \$65.50. *(LO1)*

4.2 The value added of the wholesale distributor together with the ultimate producers of the cards is \$500. Amy's value added–her revenue less her payments to other firms–is \$200. Since the cards were produced and purchased by Amy during the year 2019 (we assume), the \$500 counts toward year 2019 GDP. The \$200 in value added originating in Amy's card shop counts in year 2020 GDP since Amy actually sold the cards in that year. *(LO1)*

4.3 The sale of stock represents a transfer of ownership of part of the assets of Benson Buggywhip, not the production of new goods or services. Hence, the stock sale itself does not contribute to GDP. However, the broker's commission of \$100 (2 percent of the stock sale proceeds) represents payment for a current service and is counted in GDP. *(LO1)*

4.4 As in Example 4.7, the market value of domestic production is 1,000,000 autos times \$15,000 per auto, or \$15 billion.

Also as in Example 4.7, consumption is \$10.5 billion and government purchases are \$0.75 billion. However, because 25,000 of the autos that are purchased are imported rather than domestic, the domestic producers have unsold inventories at the end of the year of 50,000 (rather than 25,000 as in Example 4.7). Thus inventory investment is 50,000 autos times \$15,000, or \$0.75 billion, and total investment (autos purchased by businesses plus inventory investment) is \$3.75 billion. Because exports and imports are equal (both are 25,000 autos), net exports (equal to exports minus imports) are zero. Notice that because we subtract imports to get net exports, it is unnecessary also to subtract imports from consumption. Consumption is defined as total purchases by households, not just purchases of domestically produced goods.

Total expenditure is $C + I + G + NX =$ \$10.5 billion + \$3.75 billion + \$0.75 billion + 0 = \$15 billion, the same as the market value of production. *(LO2)*

4.5 Real GDP in the year 2020 equals the quantities of pizzas and calzones produced in the year 2020, valued at the market prices that prevailed in the base year 2016. So real GDP in 2020 = (30 pizzas × \$10/pizza) + (30 calzones × \$5/calzone) = \$450.

Real GDP in 2016 equals the quantities of pizzas and calzones produced in 2016, valued at 2016 prices, which is \$175. Notice that because 2016 is the base year, real GDP and nominal GDP are the same for that year.

The real GDP in the year 2020 is \$450/\$175, or about 2.6 times what it was in 2016. Hence the expansion of real GDP lies between the threefold increase in pizza production and the doubling in calzone production that occurred between 2016 and 2020. *(LO3)*

4.6 Labor force = Employed + Unemployed = 19.527 million + 1.135 million = 20.662 million.

Working-age population = Labor force + Not in labor force = 20.662 million + 12.523 million = 33.185 million.

Unemployment rate = Unemployed/Labor force = 1.135 million/20.662 million = 5.5%.

Participation rate = Labor force/Working-age population = 20.662 million/33.185 million = 62.3%.

In November 2019, African Americans represented approximately 13 percent of the U.S. labor force and the working-age population. Note that while the participation rate for African Americans is similar to that of the overall population, the unemployment rate for African Americans is substantially higher. *(LO4)*

4.7 The cost of the family's basket in 2015 remains at \$940, as in Table 4.5. If the rent on their apartment falls to \$600 in 2020, the cost of reproducing the 2015 basket of goods and services in 2020 is \$830 (\$600 for rent + \$150 for hamburgers + \$80 for movie tickets). The CPI for 2020 is accordingly \$830/\$940, or 0.883. So in this example, the cost of living fell nearly 12 percent between 2015 and 2020. *(LO5)*

4.8 To construct your own personal price index, you would need to determine the basket of goods and services that you personally purchased in the base year. Your personal price index in each period would then be defined as the cost of your personal basket in that period relative to its cost in the base year. To the extent that your mix of purchases differs from that of the typical American consumer, your cost-of-living index will differ from the official CPI. For example, if in the base year, you spent a higher share of your budget than the typical American on goods and services that have risen relatively rapidly in price, your personal inflation rate will be higher than the CPI inflation rate. *(LO5)*

4.9 The percentage changes in the CPI in each year from the previous year are as follows.

1930	−2.3% = (0.167 − 0.171)/0.171
1931	−9.0%
1932	−9.9%
1933	−5.1%

Negative inflation is called deflation. The experience of the 1930s, when prices were falling, contrasts sharply with the 1970s, during which prices rose rapidly. *(LO5)*

4.10 The percentage changes in inflation rates in each year from the previous year are as follows.

2016	1.3% = (2.40 − 2.37)/2.37
2017	2.1%
2018	2.4%
2019	2.0%

In the past few years, inflation has been nonnegative but low, in the 0–3 percent range. (Due to rounding, the inflation rates calculated above are slightly different from those published by the BLS.) *(LO5)*

4.11 Barry Bonds's real earnings, in 1982–1984 dollars, were \$10.3 million/1.77, or \$5.8 million. That is more than 12 times Babe Ruth's salary in 1930, but less than half of Stephen Strasburg's salary in 2019.

4.12 The increase in the cost of living between 1950 and 2019 is reflected in the ratio of the 2019 CPI to the 1950 CPI, or 2.56/0.24 = 10.66. That is, the cost of living in 2019 was over 10 times what it was in 1950. If the minimum wage were indexed to preserve its purchasing power, it would have been over 10 times higher in 2019 than in 1950, or 10.66 × \$0.75 = \$8.0. *(LO6)*

5

Economic Growth, Productivity, and Living Standards

One of us once attended a conference on the effects of economic growth and development on society. A speaker at the conference posed the following question: "Which would you rather be? An ordinary, middle-class American living today, or the richest person in America at the time of George Washington?"

A member of the audience spoke out immediately: "I can answer that question in one word. Dentistry."

The answer drew a laugh, perhaps because it reminded people of George Washington's famous wooden teeth. But it was a good answer. Dentistry in early America—whether the patient was rich or poor—was a primitive affair. Most dentists simply pulled a patient's rotten teeth, with a shot of whiskey for anesthetic.

Other types of medical care were not much better than dentistry. Eighteenth-century doctors had no effective weapons against tuberculosis, typhoid fever, diphtheria, influenza, pneumonia, and other communicable diseases. Such illnesses, now quite treatable, were major killers in Washington's time. Infants and children were particularly susceptible to deadly infectious diseases, especially whooping cough and measles. Even a well-to-do family often lost two or three children to these illnesses. Washington, an unusually large and vigorous man, lived to the age of 67, but the average life expectancy during his era was probably not much more than 40 years.

Medical care is not the only aspect of ordinary life that has changed drastically over the past two centuries. Author Stephen Ambrose, in his account of the Lewis and Clark expedition, described the limitations of transportation and communication in early America:

> A critical fact in the world of 1801 was that nothing moved faster than the speed of a horse. No human being, no manufactured item, no bushel of wheat, no side of beef (or any beef on the hoof for that matter), no letter, no information, no idea, order, or instruction of any kind moved faster, and, as far as Jefferson's contemporaries were able to tell, nothing ever would.

LEARNING OBJECTIVES

After reading this chapter, you should be able to:

LO1 Show how small differences in growth rates can lead to large differences in living standards.

LO2 Explain why GDP per capita is the product of average labor productivity and the proportion of the population that is employed and use this decomposition to discuss the sources of economic growth.

LO3 List the determinants of average labor productivity within a particular country and use these concepts to analyze per capita GDP differences across countries.

LO4 Discuss the relationships between real GDP and economic well-being.

LO5 Identify the costs of increasing economic growth.

LO6 Evaluate government policies that promote economic growth.

LO7 Analyze whether having finite resources implies that there are limits to growth.

> And except on a racetrack, no horse moved very fast. Road conditions in the United States ranged from bad to abominable, and there weren't very many of them. The best highway in the country ran from Boston to New York; it took a light stagecoach . . . three full days to make the 175-mile journey. The hundred miles from New York to Philadelphia took two full days.[1]

Today, New Yorkers can go to Philadelphia by train in slightly more than an hour. What would George Washington have thought of that? And how would nineteenth-century pioneers, who crossed the continent by wagon train, have reacted to the idea that their great-grandchildren would be able to have breakfast in New York and lunch the same day in San Francisco?

Would you rather be a rich person living in the eighteenth century or a middle-class person living in the twenty-first century?

No doubt you can think of other enormous changes in the way average people live, even over the past few decades. The Internet, mobile and cloud computing, tablets and smartphones have changed the ways people work and study in just a few years, for example. Though these changes are due in large part to scientific advances, scientific discoveries *by themselves* usually have little effect on most people's lives. New scientific knowledge leads to widespread improvements in living standards only when it is commercially applied. Better understanding of the human immune system, for example, has little impact unless it leads to new therapies or drugs. And a new drug will do little to help unless it is affordable to those who need it.

An illustration of this point—with both tragic and more optimistic aspects—is the AIDS epidemic in Africa. Although some new drugs that moderate the effects of the virus that causes AIDS were developed in the late 1990s, they were so expensive that they were of little practical value in poverty-stricken African nations grappling with the disease. And even if affordable, the drugs would have limited benefit without modern hospitals, trained health professionals, and adequate nutrition and sanitation. Nowadays, more than 20 years after the first effective treatments were developed, around a million people a year still die from AIDS. But this number is finally declining. The reversal resulted from a combination of the scientific discovery of new potential treatments *and* their effective implementation through international aid programs funded by industrialized countries.[2] In short, most improvements in a nation's living standard are the result not just of scientific and technological advances, but of an economic system that makes the benefits of those advances available to the average person.

In this chapter, we will explore the sources of economic growth and rising living standards in the modern world. We will begin by reviewing the remarkable economic growth in the industrialized countries, as measured by real GDP per person. Since the mid-nineteenth century (and earlier in some countries), a radical transformation in living standards has occurred in these countries. What explains this transformation? The key to rising living standards is a *continuing increase in average labor productivity,* which depends on several factors, from the skills and motivation workers bring to their jobs to the legal and social environment in which they work. We will analyze each of these factors and discuss its implications for government policies to promote growth. We will then discuss the costs of rapid economic growth and consider whether there may be limits to the amount of economic growth a society can achieve.

THE REMARKABLE RISE IN LIVING STANDARDS: THE RECORD

For millennia, the great majority of the world's inhabitants eked out a meager existence by tilling the soil. Only a small proportion of the population lived above the level of subsistence, learned to read and write, or traveled more than a few miles from

[1]Stephen E. Ambrose, *Undaunted Courage: Meriwether Lewis, Thomas Jefferson, and the Opening of the American West* [New York: Touchstone (Simon & Schuster), 1996], p. 52.
[2]For an interesting point of view, see "How Was the AIDS Epidemic Reversed?," *The Economist,* September 26, 2013.

their birthplaces. Large cities grew up, serving as imperial capitals and centers of trade, but the great majority of urban populations lived in dire poverty, subject to malnutrition and disease.

Then, about three centuries ago, a fundamental change occurred. Spurred by technological advances and entrepreneurial innovations, a process of economic growth began. Sustained over many years, this growth in the economy's productive capacity has transformed almost every aspect of how we live—from what we eat and wear to how we work and play.

The advances in health care and transportation mentioned in the beginning of this chapter illustrate only a few of the impressive changes that have taken place in people's material well-being over the past two centuries, particularly in industrialized countries like the United States. To study the factors that affect living standards systematically, however, we must go beyond anecdotes and adopt a specific measure of economic well-being in a particular country and time.

In Chapter 4, *Measuring Economic Activity: GDP, Unemployment, and Inflation,* we introduced the concept of real GDP as a basic measure of the level of economic activity in a country. Recall that, in essence, real GDP measures the physical volume of goods and services produced within a country's borders during a specific period, such as a quarter or a year. Consequently, real GDP *per person* provides a measure of the quantity of goods and services available to the typical resident of a country at a particular time. Although real GDP per person is certainly not a perfect indicator of economic well-being, as we will see later in this chapter, it is positively related to a number of pertinent variables, such as life expectancy, infant health, and literacy. Lacking a better alternative, economists have focused on real GDP per person as a key measure of a country's living standard and stage of economic development.

Figure 5.1, which reproduces the blue line from Figure 3.2, shows the remarkable growth in real GDP per person that occurred in the United States between 1929 and 2019. For comparison, Table 5.1 and Figure 5.2 show real GDP per person in eight countries in selected years from 1870 to 2010.

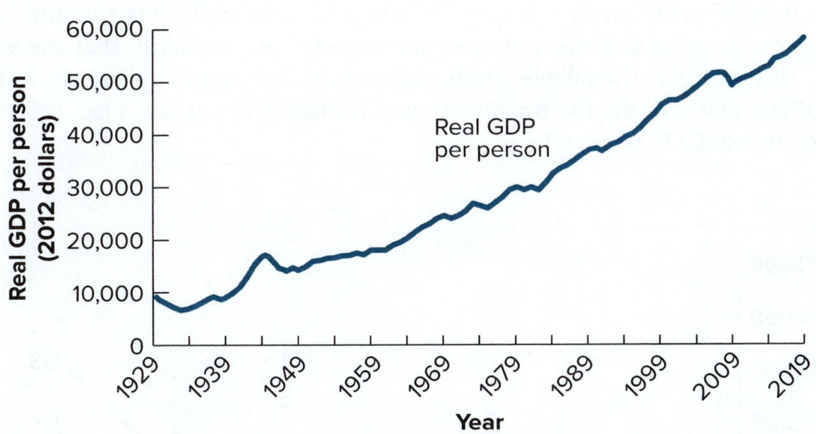

FIGURE 5.1

Real GDP per Person in the United States, 1929–2019.

The blue line shows the real GDP per person in the U.S. economy since 1929. Real GDP per person today is more than six times what it was in 1929.

Source: Bureau of Economic Analysis, www.bea.gov.

The data in Table 5.1 and Figure 5.2 tell a dramatic story. For example, in the United States (which was already a relatively wealthy industrialized country in 1870), real GDP per person grew more than 12-fold between 1870 and 2010. In Japan, real GDP per person grew almost 30 times over the same period. Underlying these statistics is an amazingly rapid process of economic growth and transformation, through which, in just a few generations, relatively poor agrarian societies became highly industrialized economies—with average standards of living that could scarcely have been imagined in 1870. As Figure 5.2 shows, a significant part of this growth has occurred since 1950, particularly in Japan and China. Further,

TABLE 5.1
Real GDP per Person in Selected Countries, 1870–2010

Country	1870	1913	1950	1980	1990	2010	Annual % change 1870–2010	Annual % change 1950–2010	Annual % change 1980–2010
United States	2,445	5,301	9,561	18,577	23,201	30,491	1.8	2.0	1.7
United Kingdom	3,190	4,921	6,939	12,931	16,430	23,777	1.4	2.1	2.1
Germany	1,839	3,648	3,881	14,114	15,929	20,661	1.7	2.8	1.3
Japan	737	1,387	1,921	13,428	18,789	21,935	2.5	4.1	1.6
China	530	552	448	1,061	1,871	8,032	2.0	4.9	7.0
Brazil	713	811	1,672	5,195	4,920	6,879	1.6	2.4	0.9
India	533	673	619	938	1,309	3,372	1.3	2.9	4.4
Ghana	439	781	1,122	1,157	1,062	1,922	1.1	0.9	1.7

Source: Angus Maddison, *The Maddison Project*, www.ggdc.net/maddison. Real GDP per person is measured in 1990 international dollars. "Germany" refers to West Germany in 1950 and 1980.

both China and India have grown significantly faster since 1990 than they did in earlier periods.

A note of caution is in order. The farther back in time we go, the less precise are historical estimates of real GDP. Most governments did not keep official GDP statistics until after World War II; production records from earlier periods are often incomplete or of questionable accuracy. Comparing economic output over a century or more is also problematic because many goods and services that are produced today were unavailable—indeed, inconceivable—in 1870. How many nineteenth-century horse-drawn wagons, for example, would be the economic equivalent of a BMW i8 plug-in hybrid sports car or a Boeing 787 Dreamliner jet? Despite the difficulty of making precise comparisons, however, we can say with certainty that the variety, quality, and quantity of available goods and services increased enormously in industrialized countries during the nineteenth and twentieth centuries, a fact reflected in the data on real GDP per capita.

FIGURE 5.2

Real GDP per Person in a Sample of Countries, 1870–2010.

The United States, the United Kingdom, and Germany began with high levels of GDP per person in 1870 and remained high-income countries throughout the period. Economic growth has been especially rapid between the 1950s and the 1980s in Japan and since 1980 in China and India. Ghana and the rest of sub-Saharan Africa experienced very low growth rates.

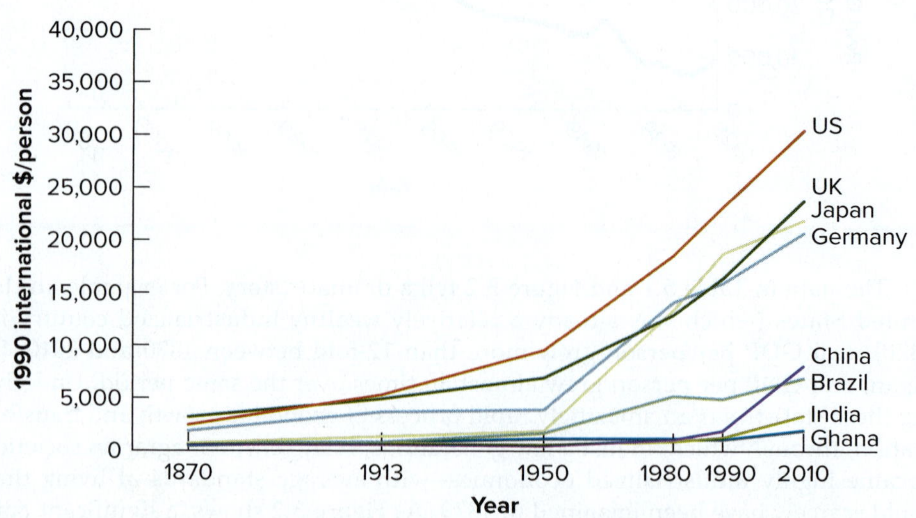

Why "Small" Differences in Growth Rates Matter

The last three columns of Table 5.1 show annual growth rates of real GDP per person for both the entire 1870–2010 period and two more recent periods. At first glance, these growth rates don't seem to differ much from country to country. For example, for the period 1870–2010, the highest growth rate is 2.5 percent (Japan) and the lowest is 1.1 percent (Ghana).

But consider the long-run effect of this seemingly "small" difference in annual growth rates. For example, in 1870 China's output per person was roughly 120 percent that of Ghana, yet by 2010 China had more than four times the output per person of Ghana. This widening of the gap between these two countries is the result of the difference between China's 2.0 percent annual growth rate and Ghana's 1.1 percent annual growth rate, maintained for almost 140 years. The fact that what seem to be small differences in growth rates can have large long-run effects results from what is called the *power of compound interest*. A good illustration of this power is the effect of compound interest on a bank deposit.

EXAMPLE 5.1 Compound Interest, Part 1

What is compound interest?

In 1820, one of your ancestors deposited \$10.00 in a checking account at 4 percent interest. Interest is compounded annually (so that interest paid at the end of each year receives interest itself in later years). Your ancestor's will specified that the account be turned over to his most direct descendant (you) in the year 2020. When you withdrew the funds in that year, how much was the account worth?

The account was worth \$10.00 in 1820; $\$10.00 \times 1.04 = \$10.40$ in 1821; $\$10.00 \times 1.04 \times 1.04 = \$10.00 \times (1.04)^2 = \$10.82$ in 1822; and so on. Since 200 years elapsed between 1820, when the deposit was made, and the year 2020, when the account was closed, the value of the account in the year 2020 was $\$10.00 \times (1.04)^{200}$, or $\$10.00 \times 1.04$ to the 200th power. Using a calculator, you will find that \$10.00 times 1.04 to the 200th power is \$25,507.50—a good return for a \$10.00 deposit!

Compound interest—an arrangement in which interest is paid not only on the original deposit but on all previously accumulated interest—is distinguished from *simple interest,* in which interest is paid only on the original deposit. If your ancestor's account had been deposited at 4 percent simple interest, it would have accumulated only 40 cents each year (4 percent of the original \$10.00 deposit), for a total value of $\$10.00 + 200 \times \$0.40 = \$90.00$ after 200 years. The tremendous growth in the value of his account came from the compounding of the interest—hence the phrase "the power of compound interest."

compound interest the payment of interest not only on the original deposit, but on all previously accumulated interest

EXAMPLE 5.2 Compound Interest, Part 2

What is the difference between 2 percent interest and 6 percent interest, compounded annually?

Refer to Example 5.1. What would your ancestor's \$10.00 deposit have been worth after 200 years if the annual interest rate had been 2 percent? 6 percent?

At 2 percent interest the account would be worth \$10.00 in 1820; $\$10.00 \times 1.02 = \$10.20$ in 1821; $\$10.00 \times (1.02)^2 = \$10.40$ in 1822; and so on. In the year 2020, the value of the account would be $\$10.00 \times (1.02)^{200}$, or \$524.85. If the interest rate were 6 percent, after 200 years the account would be worth $\$10.00 \times (1.06)^{200}$, or \$1,151,259.04. Let's summarize the results of Examples 5.1 and 5.2.

Interest rate (%)	Value of \$10 after 200 years
2	\$524.85
4	\$25,507.50
6	\$1,151,259.04

The power of compound interest is that even at relatively low rates of interest, a small sum, compounded over a long enough period, can greatly increase in value. A more subtle point, illustrated by this example, is that small differences in interest rates matter a lot. The difference between a 2 percent and a 4 percent interest rate doesn't seem tremendous, but over a long period of time it implies large differences in the amount of interest accumulated on an account. Likewise, the effect of switching from a 4 percent to a 6 percent interest rate is enormous, as our calculations show.

Economic growth rates are similar to compound interest rates. Just as the value of a bank deposit grows each year at a rate equal to the interest rate, so the size of a nation's economy expands each year at the rate of economic growth. This analogy suggests that even a relatively modest rate of growth in output per person—say, 1 to 2 percent per year—will produce tremendous increases in average living standard over a long period. And relatively small *differences* in growth rates, as in the case of Ghana and China, will ultimately produce very different living standards.

Economists employ a useful formula for approximating the number of years it will take for an initial amount to double at various growth or interest rates. The formula is 72 divided by the growth or interest rate. Thus, if the interest rate is 2 percent per year, it will take roughly $72/2 = 36$ years for the initial sum to double. If the interest rate is 4 percent, it will take roughly $72/4 = 18$ years. This formula is a good approximation only for small and moderate interest rates. Over the long run, then, the rate of economic growth is an extremely important variable. Hence, government policy changes or other factors that affect the long-term growth rate even by a small amount will have a major economic impact.

SELF-TEST 5.1

Suppose that real GDP per capita in the United States had grown at 2.5 percent per year, as Japan's did, instead of the actual 1.8 percent per year, from 1870 to 2010. How much larger would real GDP per person have been in the United States in 2010?

RECAP

THE REMARKABLE RISE IN LIVING STANDARDS

Real GDP per person, a basic indicator of living standards, has grown dramatically in the industrialized countries. This growth reflects the *power of compound interest:* Even a modest growth rate, if sustained over a long period of time, can lead to large increases in the size of the economy.

WHY NATIONS BECOME RICH: THE CRUCIAL ROLE OF AVERAGE LABOR PRODUCTIVITY

What determines a nation's economic growth rate? To get some insight into this vital question, we will find it useful to express real GDP per person as the product of two terms: average labor productivity and the share of the population that is working.

To do this, let Y equal total real output (as measured by real GDP, for example), N equal the number of employed workers, and POP equal the total population. Then real GDP per person can be written as Y/POP; **average labor productivity,** or output per employed worker, equals Y/N; and the share of the population that is working is N/POP. The relationship between these three variables is

average labor productivity output per employed worker

$$\frac{Y}{POP} = \frac{Y}{N} \times \frac{N}{POP},$$

which, as you can see by canceling out N on the right-hand side of the equation, always holds exactly. In words, this basic relationship is

Real GDP per person = Average labor productivity
× Share of population employed.

This expression for real GDP per person tells us something very basic and intuitive: The quantity of goods and services that each person can consume depends on (1) how much each worker can produce and (2) how many people (as a fraction of the total population) are working. Furthermore, because real GDP per person equals average labor productivity times the share of the population that is employed, real GDP per person can *grow* only to the extent that there is *growth* in worker productivity and/or the fraction of the population that is employed.

Figures 5.3 and 5.4 show the U.S. figures for the three key variables in the relationship above and for a fourth variable that was mentioned in Chapter 4, *Measuring Economic Activity: GDP, Unemployment, and Inflation* (the labor force participation rate), for the period 1960–2019. Figure 5.3, which reproduces part of Figure 3.2, shows both real GDP per person and real GDP per worker (average labor productivity). Figure 5.4 shows the portion of the entire U.S. population (not just the working-age population) that was employed, and the portion of the (civilian, noninstitutional) adult population (16+) that participated in the labor force during that period. Once again, we see that the expansion in output per person in the United States has been impressive. Between 1960 and 2019, real GDP per person in

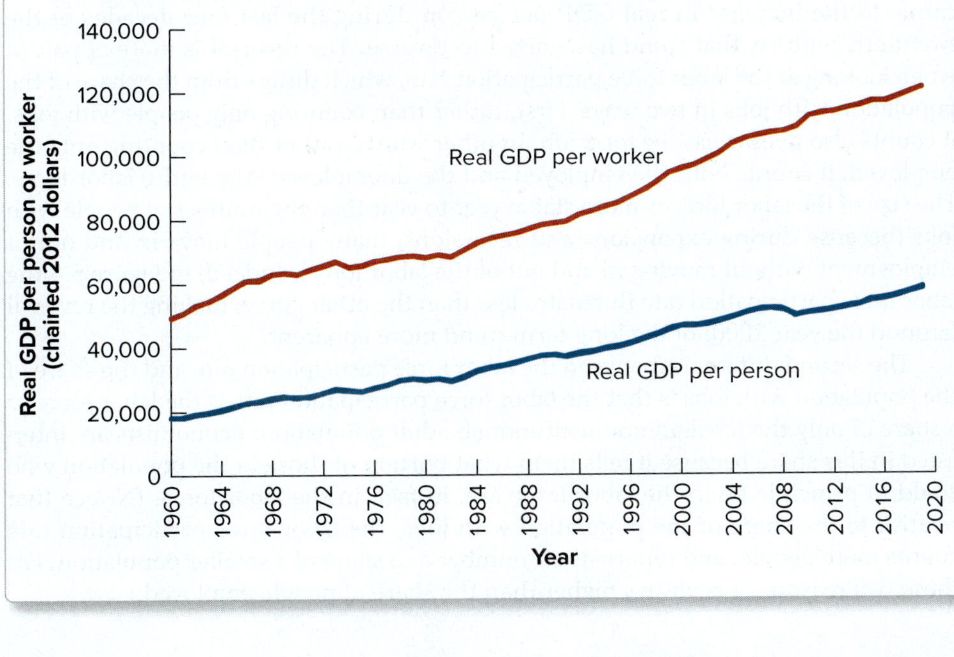

FIGURE 5.3

Real GDP per Person and Average Labor Productivity in the United States, 1960–2019.

Real GDP per person in the United States grew 222 percent between 1960 and 2019, and real GDP per worker (average labor productivity) grew by 144 percent.

Source: Federal Reserve Bank of St. Louis Economic Research, https://fred.stlouisfed.org.

FIGURE 5.4

Share of the U.S. Population Employed and Labor Force Participation Rate, 1960–2019.

The share of the U.S. population holding a job increased from 30 percent in 1960 to almost 47 percent in 2000 and was 46 percent in 2019. The labor force participation rate increased from 59 percent in 1960 to 67 percent in the late 1990s; since 2000, it has generally declined, falling below 63 percent in recent years.

Sources: BLS (CIVPART, PAYEMS), Census (POP), retrieved from FRED, Federal Reserve Bank of St. Louis, https://fred.stlouisfed.org.

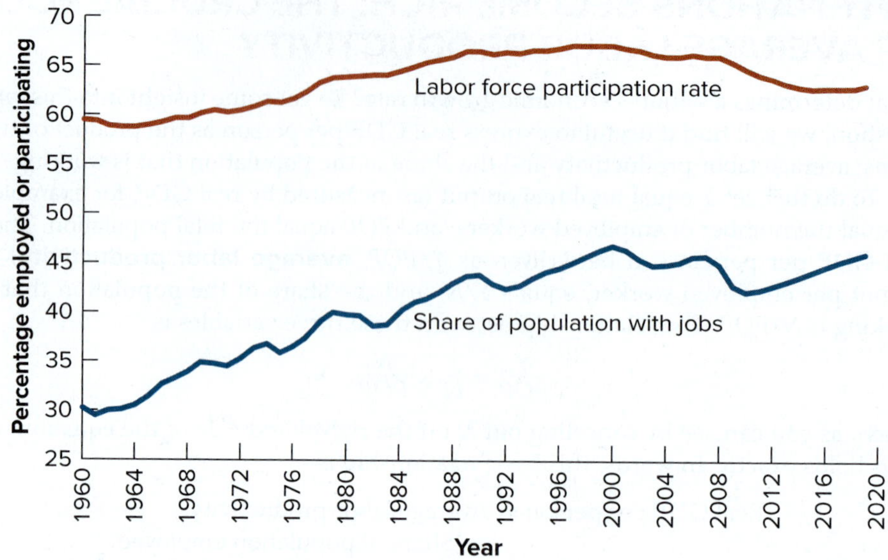

the United States more than tripled, growing by 222 percent. Thus in 2019, the average American enjoyed more than three times as many goods and services as in 1960. Figures 5.3 and 5.4 show that until the year 2000 or so, increases in both labor productivity and the share of the population holding a job contributed to this rise in living standard. But as Figure 5.4 shows, more recently things have changed.

Let's look a bit more closely at these two contributing factors, beginning with the share of the population that is employed. As Figure 5.4 shows, between 1960 and 2000, the number of people employed in the United States rose from 30 to almost 47 percent of the entire population, a remarkable increase. The growing tendency of women to work outside the home was the most important reason for this rise in employment. Another factor leading to higher rates of employment was an increase in the share of the general population that is of working age (ages 16 to 65). The coming of age of the "baby boom" generation, born in the years after World War II, and to a lesser extent the immigration of young workers from other countries helped cause this growth in the workforce.

Although the rising share of the U.S. population with jobs contributed significantly to the increase in real GDP per person during the last four decades of the twentieth century, that trend has started to reverse. The reversal is more apparent when looking at the labor force participation rate, which differs from the share of the population with jobs in two ways. First, rather than counting only people with jobs, it counts also people *looking* for a job. In other words, rather than counting only the employed, it counts both the employed and the unemployed—the entire labor force. The size of the labor force is more stable year to year than the number of people with jobs (because during expansions and recessions, many people move in and out of employment without moving in and out of the labor force). Indeed, in Figure 5.4 the labor force participation rate fluctuates less than the other curve, making the reversal (around the year 2000) of the long-term trend more apparent.

The second difference between the labor force participation rate and the share of the population with jobs is that the labor force participation rate is the labor force as a share of only the (civilian noninstitutional) adult population. Economists are interested in this share because it tells them what portion of those in the population who could in principle be in the labor force are, in fact, in the labor force. (Notice that relative to the share of the population with jobs, the labor force participation rate counts more people, and reports their number as a share of a smaller population. For these two reasons, it is always higher than the share of people employed.)

The labor force participation rate increased from below 60 percent in 1960 to more than 67 percent in the late 1990s, and then leveled off. Since 2000, it has decreased, and in 2014, it fell to below 63 percent—for the first time since 1977. Some of the factors that we discussed earlier when explaining the increase in employed people prior to 2000 also explain the decline after 2000. The baby boomers have been aging and have recently started retiring. The participation rate of women could not increase forever, and it eventually leveled off. But the aging population and women cannot be the whole explanation because participation has been on a long-term decline also among younger men. Economists are still trying to understand all the reasons. Potential explanations include young people staying longer in school—and spending more time on schoolwork while in school—and a decline in the demand for workers with certain skills and education. We will return to these issues in the next chapter, where we use supply and demand analysis to understand long-term trends in the labor market. For now, we note that the recent downward trends in Figure 5.4 are expected to continue in the future. In the long run, then, the improvement in living standards brought about by the rising share of Americans with jobs was transitory.

What about the other factor that determines output per person, average labor productivity? As Figure 5.3 shows, between 1960 and 2019, average labor productivity in the United States increased by 144 percent, accounting for a sizable share of the overall increase in GDP per person. In other periods, the link between average labor productivity and output per person in the United States has often been even stronger because, in most earlier periods, the share of the population holding jobs was more stable than it has been recently. (See Figure 3.2 for the behavior of real GDP per person and average labor productivity in the United States over the period 1929–2019.)

This quick look at recent data supports a more general conclusion. *In the long run, increases in output per person arise primarily from increases in average labor productivity.* In simple terms, the more people can produce, the more they can consume. To understand why economies grow, then, we must understand the reasons for increased labor productivity.

RECAP

THE CRUCIAL ROLE OF AVERAGE LABOR PRODUCTIVITY

Output per person equals average labor productivity times the share of the population that is employed. Since 1960, the share of the U.S. population with jobs has risen significantly, but it has declined since 2000. In the long run, increases in output per person and hence living standards arise primarily from increases in average labor productivity.

THE DETERMINANTS OF AVERAGE LABOR PRODUCTIVITY

What determines the productivity of the average worker in a particular country at a particular time? Popular discussions of this issue often equate worker productivity with the willingness of workers of a given nationality to work hard. Everything else being equal, a culture that promotes hard work certainly tends to increase worker productivity. But intensity of effort alone cannot explain the huge differences in average labor productivity that we observe around the world. For example, according to 2018 estimates from the International Labor Organization, average labor productivity in the United States is about 12 times what it is in Indonesia and 39 times what it is in Bangladesh, though there is little doubt that Indonesians and Bangladeshis work very hard.

In this section, we will examine six factors that appear to account for the major differences in average labor productivity, both between countries and between generations. Later in the chapter we will discuss how economic policies can influence these factors to spur productivity and growth.

Human Capital

To illustrate the factors that determine average labor productivity, we introduce two prototypical assembly-line workers, Lucy and Ethel.

EXAMPLE 5.3 Assembly-Line Productivity

CBS/Getty Images

How productive are these workers?

Are Lucy and Ethel more productive as a team or by themselves?

Lucy and Ethel have jobs wrapping chocolate candies and placing them into boxes. Lucy, a novice wrapper, can wrap only 100 candies per hour. Ethel, who has had on-the-job training, can wrap 300 candies per hour. Lucy and Ethel each work 40 hours per week. Find average labor productivity, in terms of candies wrapped per week and candies wrapped per hour, (a) for Lucy, (b) for Ethel, and (c) for Lucy and Ethel as a team.

We have defined average labor productivity in general terms as output per worker. Note, though, that the measurement of average labor productivity depends on the time period that is specified. For example, the data presented in Figure 5.3 tell us how much the average worker produces *in a year*. In this example we are concerned with how much Lucy and Ethel can produce *per hour* of work or *per week* of work. Any one of these ways of measuring labor productivity is equally valid, as long as we are clear about the time unit we are using.

Lucy's and Ethel's hourly productivities are given in the problem: Lucy can wrap 100 candies per hour and Ethel can wrap 300. Lucy's weekly productivity is (40 hours/week) × (100 candies wrapped/hour) = 4,000 wrapped candies per week. Ethel's weekly productivity is (40 hours/week) × (300 candies wrapped/hour), or 12,000 candies per week.

Together Lucy and Ethel can wrap 16,000 candies per week. As a team, their average weekly productivity is (16,000 candies wrapped)/(2 weeks of work), or 8,000 candies per week. Their average hourly productivity as a team is (16,000 candies wrapped)/(80 hours of work) = 200 candies per hour. Notice that, taken as a team, the two women's productivity lies midway between their individual productivities.

Ethel is more productive than Lucy because she has had on-the-job training, which has allowed her to develop her candy-wrapping skills to a higher level than Lucy's. Because of her training, Ethel can produce more than Lucy can in a given number of hours.

SELF-TEST 5.2

Suppose Ethel attends additional classes in candy wrapping and learns how to wrap 500 candies per hour. Find the output per week and output per hour for Lucy and Ethel, both individually and as a team.

human capital an amalgam of factors such as education, training, experience, intelligence, energy, work habits, trustworthiness, and initiative that affects the value of a worker's marginal product

Economists would explain the difference in the two women's performance by saying that Ethel has more *human capital* than Lucy. **Human capital** comprises the talents, education, training, and skills of workers. Workers with a large stock of human capital are more productive than workers with less training. For example, an auto mechanic who is familiar with computerized diagnostic equipment will be able to fix engine problems that less well-trained mechanics could not.

The Economic Naturalist 5.1

Why did West Germany and Japan recover so successfully from the devastation of World War II?

Germany and Japan sustained extensive destruction of their cities and industries during World War II and entered the postwar period impoverished. Yet within 30 years, both countries not only had been rebuilt, but had become worldwide industrial and economic leaders. What accounts for these "economic miracles"?

Many factors contributed to the economic recovery of West Germany and Japan from World War II, including the substantial aid provided by the United States to Europe under the Marshall Plan and to Japan during the U.S. occupation. Most economists agree, however, that high levels of human capital played a crucial role in both countries.

At the end of the war, Germany's population was exceptionally well educated, with a large number of highly qualified scientists and engineers. The country also had (and still does today) an extensive apprentice system that provided on-the-job training to young workers. As a result, Germany had a skilled industrial workforce. In addition, the area that became West Germany benefited substantially from an influx of skilled workers from East Germany and the rest of Soviet-controlled Europe, including 20,000 trained engineers and technicians. Beginning as early as 1949, this concentration of human capital contributed to a major expansion of Germany's technologically sophisticated, highly productive manufacturing sector. By 1960, West Germany was a leading exporter of high-quality manufactured goods, and its citizens enjoyed one of the highest standards of living in Europe.

Japan, which probably sustained greater physical destruction in the war than Germany, also began the postwar period with a skilled and educated labor force. In addition, occupying American forces restructured the Japanese school system and encouraged all Japanese to obtain a good education. Even more so than the Germans, however, the Japanese emphasized on-the-job training. As part of a lifetime employment system, under which workers were expected to stay with the same company their entire career, Japanese firms invested extensively in worker training. The payoff to these investments in human capital was a steady increase in average labor productivity, particularly in manufacturing. By the 1980s, Japanese manufactured goods were among the most advanced in the world and Japan's workers among the most skilled.

Although high levels of human capital were instrumental in the rapid economic growth of West Germany and Japan, human capital alone cannot create a high living standard. A case in point is Soviet-dominated East Germany, which had a level of human capital similar to West Germany's after the war but did not enjoy the same economic growth. For reasons we will discuss later in the chapter, the communist system imposed by the Soviets utilized East Germany's human capital far less effectively than the economic systems of Japan and West Germany.

Human capital is analogous to *physical capital* (such as machines and factories) in that it is acquired primarily through the investment of time, energy, and money. For example, to learn how to use computerized diagnostic equipment, a mechanic might need to attend a technical school at night. The cost of going to school includes not only the tuition paid but also the *opportunity cost* of the mechanic's time spent attending class and studying. The benefit of the schooling is the increase in wages the mechanic will earn when the course has been completed. We know by the cost-benefit principle that the mechanic should learn how to use computerized diagnostic equipment only if the benefits exceed the costs, including the opportunity costs. In general, then, we would expect to see people acquire additional education and skills when the difference in the wages paid to skilled and unskilled workers is significant.

Physical Capital

physical capital equipment and tools (such as machines and factories) needed to complete one's work

Workers' productivity depends not only on their skills and effort, but on the tools they have to work with. Even the most skilled surgeon cannot perform open-heart surgery without sophisticated equipment, and an expert software developer is of limited value without a computer. These examples illustrate the importance of **physical capital,** such as factories and machines. More and better capital allows workers to produce more efficiently, as Example 5.4 shows.

EXAMPLE 5.4 Physical Capital and Efficiency

Will the introduction of a candy-wrapping machine make Lucy and Ethel more productive?

Continuing with Example 5.3, suppose that Lucy and Ethel's boss acquires an electric candy-wrapping machine, which is designed to be operated by one worker. Using this machine, an untrained worker can wrap 500 candies per hour. What are Lucy's and Ethel's hourly and weekly outputs now? Will the answer change if the boss gets a second machine? A third?

Suppose for the sake of simplicity that a candy-wrapping machine must be assigned to one worker only. (This assumption rules out sharing arrangements, in which one worker uses the machine on the day shift and another on the night shift.) If the boss buys just one machine, she will assign it to Lucy. (Why? Solve Self-Test 5.3.) Now Lucy will be able to wrap 500 candies per hour, while Ethel can wrap only 300 per hour. Lucy's weekly output will be 20,000 wrapped candies (40 hours × 500 candies wrapped per hour). Ethel's weekly output is still 12,000 wrapped candies (40 hours × 300 candies wrapped per hour). Together they can now wrap 32,000 candies per week, or 16,000 candies per week each. On an hourly basis, average labor productivity for the two women taken together is 32,000 candies wrapped per 80 hours of work, or 400 candies wrapped per hour—twice their average labor productivity before the boss bought the machine.

With two candy-wrapping machines available, both Lucy and Ethel could use a machine. Each could wrap 500 candies per hour, for a total of 40,000 wrapped candies per week. Average labor productivity for both women taken together would be 20,000 wrapped candies per week, or 500 wrapped candies per hour.

What would happen if the boss purchased a third machine? With only two workers, a third machine would be useless: It would add nothing to either total output or average labor productivity.

SELF-TEST 5.3

Using the assumptions made in Examples 5.3 and 5.4, explain why the boss should give the single available candy-wrapping machine to Lucy rather than Ethel.

The candy-wrapping machine is an example of a *capital good,* which was defined in Chapter 4, *Measuring Economic Activity: GDP, Unemployment, and Inflation,* as a long-lived good, which is itself produced and used to produce other goods and services. Capital goods include machines and equipment (such as computers, earthmovers, or assembly lines) as well as buildings (such as factories or office buildings).

Capital goods like the candy-wrapping machine enhance workers' productivity. Table 5.2 summarizes the results from Examples 5.3 and 5.4. For each number of machines the boss might acquire (column 1), Table 5.2 gives the total weekly output of Lucy and Ethel taken together (column 2), the total number of hours worked by the two women (column 3), and average output per hour (column 4), equal to total weekly output divided by total weekly hours.

TABLE 5.2
Capital, Output, and Productivity in the Candy-Wrapping Factory

(1) Number of machines (capital)	(2) Total number of candies wrapped each week (output)	(3) Total hours worked per week	(4) Candies wrapped per hour worked (productivity)
0	16,000	80	200
1	32,000	80	400
2	40,000	80	500
3	40,000	80	500

Table 5.2 demonstrates two important points about the effect of additional capital on output. First, for a given number of workers, adding more capital generally increases both total output and average labor productivity. For example, adding the first candy-wrapping machine increases weekly output (column 2) by 16,000 candies and average labor productivity (column 4) by 200 candies wrapped per hour.

The second point illustrated by Table 5.2 is that the more capital is already in place, the smaller the benefits of adding extra capital. Notice that the first machine adds 16,000 candies to total output, but the second machine adds only 8,000. The third machine, which cannot be used since there are only two workers, does not increase output or productivity at all. This result illustrates a general principle of economics, called *diminishing returns to capital*. According to the principle of **diminishing returns to capital,** if the amount of labor and other inputs employed is held constant, then the greater the amount of capital already in use, the less an additional unit of capital adds to production. In the case of the candy-wrapping factory, diminishing returns to capital imply that the first candy-wrapping machine acquired adds more output than the second, which in turn adds more output than the third.

diminishing returns to capital if the amount of labor and other inputs employed is held constant, then the greater the amount of capital already in use, the less an additional unit of capital adds to production

Diminishing returns to capital are a natural consequence of firms' incentive to use each piece of capital as productively as possible. To maximize output, managers will assign the first machine that a firm acquires to the most productive use available, the next machine to the next most productive use, and so when many machines are available, all the highly productive ways of using them already have been exploited. Thus adding yet another machine will not raise output or productivity by very much. If Lucy and Ethel are already operating two candy-wrapping machines, there is little point to buying a third machine, except perhaps as a replacement or spare.

The implications of Table 5.2 can be applied to the question of how to stimulate economic growth. First, increasing the amount of capital available to the workforce will tend to increase output and average labor productivity. The more adequately equipped workers are, the more productive they will be. Second, the degree to which productivity can be increased by an expanding stock of capital is limited. Because of diminishing returns to capital, an economy in which the quantity of capital available to each worker is already very high will not benefit much from further expansion of the capital stock.

Land and Other Natural Resources

Besides capital goods, other inputs to production help make workers more productive, among them land, energy, and raw materials. Fertile land is essential to agriculture, and modern manufacturing processes make intensive use of energy and raw materials.

In general, an abundance of natural resources increases the productivity of the workers who use them. For example, a farmer can produce a much larger crop in a land-rich country like the United States or Australia than in a country where the soil is poor or arable land is limited in supply. With the aid of modern farm machinery and great expanses of land, today's American farmers are so productive that even though they constitute less than 1 percent of the workforce, they provide enough food not only to feed the country but to export to the rest of the world.

Although there are limits to a country's supply of arable land, many other natural resources, such as petroleum and metals, can be obtained through international markets. Because resources can be obtained through trade, countries need not possess large quantities of natural resources within their own borders to achieve economic growth. Indeed, a number of countries have become rich without substantial natural resources of their own, including Japan, Hong Kong, Singapore, and Switzerland. Just as important as possessing natural resources is the ability to use them productively—for example, by means of advanced technologies.

Technology

Besides human capital, physical capital, and natural resources, a country's ability to develop and apply new, more productive technologies will help determine its productivity. Consider just one industry, transportation. Two centuries ago, as suggested by the quote from Stephen Ambrose in the beginning of the chapter, the horse and wagon were the primary means of transportation—a slow and costly method indeed. But in the nineteenth century, technological advances such as the steam engine supported the expansion of riverborne transportation and the development of a national rail network. In the twentieth century, the invention of the internal combustion engine and the development of aviation, supported by the construction of an extensive infrastructure of roads and airports, have produced increasingly rapid, cheap, and reliable transport. Technological change has clearly been a driving force in the transportation revolution.

New technologies can improve productivity in industries other than the one in which they are introduced. Once farmers could sell their produce only in their local communities, for example. Now the availability of rapid shipping and refrigerated transport allows farmers to sell their products virtually anywhere in the world. With a broader market in which to sell, farmers can specialize in those products best suited to local land and weather conditions. Similarly, factories can obtain their raw materials wherever they are cheapest and most abundant, produce the goods they are most efficient at manufacturing, and sell their products wherever they will fetch the best price. Both these examples illustrate the principle of comparative advantage, that overall productivity increases when producers concentrate on those activities at which they are relatively most efficient.

Numerous other technological developments led to increased productivity, including advances in communication and medicine, the introduction of computer technology, and most recently the emergence of global networks that connect mobile computing, communication, and even health devices around the world. In fact, *most economists would probably agree that new technologies are the single most important source of productivity improvement* and, hence, of economic growth in general.

However, economic growth does not automatically follow from breakthroughs in basic science. To make the best use of new knowledge, an economy needs entrepreneurs who can exploit scientific advances commercially, as well as a legal and political environment that encourages the practical application of new knowledge.

SELF-TEST 5.4

A new kind of wrapping paper has been invented that makes candy wrapping quicker and easier. The use of this paper *increases* the number of candies a person can wrap by hand by 200 per hour, and the number of candies a person can wrap by machine by 300 per hour. Using the data from Examples 5.3 and 5.4, construct a table like Table 5.2 that shows how this technological advance affects average labor productivity. Do diminishing returns to capital still hold?

The Economic Naturalist 5.2

Why did U.S. labor productivity grow so rapidly in the late 1990s?

During the 1950s and 1960s, most industrialized countries experienced rapid growth in real GDP and average labor productivity. Between 1948 and 1973, for example, U.S. labor productivity grew by 2.5 percent per year.[3] Between 1973 and 1995, however, labor productivity growth in the United States fell by more than half to 1.1 percent per year. Other countries experienced similar productivity slowdowns, and many articles and books were written trying to uncover the reasons. Between 1995 and 2000, however, there was a rebound in productivity growth, particularly in the United States, where productivity grew 2.4 percent per year. What caused this resurgence in productivity growth? Can it be sustained?

Economists agree that the pickup in productivity growth between 1995 and 2000 was the product of rapid technological progress and increased investment in new information and communications technology (ICT). Research indicates that productivity grew rapidly in both those industries that *produced* ICT, such as silicon chips and fiber optics, and those industries that most intensively *used* ICT. The application of these advances had ripple effects in areas ranging from automobile production to retail inventory management. The rapid growth of the Internet, for example, made it possible for consumers to shop and find information online. But it also helped companies improve their efficiency by improving coordination between manufacturers and their suppliers. On the other hand, there was no acceleration in labor productivity growth in those industries that neither produced nor used much ICT.[4]

Although technological progress continued after 2000, productivity growth slowed to 1.5 percent per year from 2000 to 2007, and to 1.0 percent per year from 2007 to 2019. Why? While economists are still trying to understand all the reasons, it appears that the gains in productivity in the 1990s, which came from both improved production of ICT equipment and its use in ICT-intensive industries, were followed by smaller gains coming from broader application of ICT to other industries. It is also possible that the implosion of the NASDAQ (the "dot-com collapse") in 2000 and the mild recession of 2001 and, on a much larger scale, the global financial crisis and the recession of 2007–2009, contributed to slowing productivity growth. Indicators such as the number of new companies starting up and the amount invested in new technologies decreased somewhat during and following the 2001 recession and decreased dramatically during and following the 2007–2009 recession, impeding the introduction of new products and production techniques. In addition, the global financial crisis brought tighter credit conditions, making it difficult for companies to maintain or upgrade their equipment, and the high unemployment rates during and following the 2007–2009 recession may have caused the skills of some workers to deteriorate. If these factors are indeed the reason for the lower rates of productivity growth in recent years, then the higher rates of the late 1990s may return as the recovery from the crisis and the recession continues.

Optimists argue that advances in mobile computing, communications, biotechnology, and other ICT fields will allow productivity growth to return to the elevated rate of the late 1990s. Others are more cautious, arguing that the increases in productivity growth from these developments may be temporary rather than permanent. A great deal is riding on which view will turn out to be correct.

[3]Data refers to labor productivity growth in the nonfarm business sector and can be found at www.bls.gov.
[4]Kevin J. Stiroh, "Information Technology and the U.S. Productivity Revival: What Do the Industry Data Say?," *American Economic Review* 92 (December 2002), pp. 1559–1576.

Entrepreneurship and Management

entrepreneurs people who create new economic enterprises

The productivity of workers depends in part on the people who help decide what to produce and how to produce it: entrepreneurs and managers. **Entrepreneurs** are people who create new economic enterprises. Because of the new products, services, technological processes, and production methods they introduce, entrepreneurs are critical to a dynamic, healthy economy. In the late nineteenth and early twentieth centuries, individuals like Henry Ford and Alfred Sloan (automobiles), Andrew Carnegie (steel), John D. Rockefeller (oil), and J. P. Morgan (finance) played central roles in the development of American industry–and, not incidentally, amassed huge personal fortunes in the process. These people and others like them (including contemporary entrepreneurs like Bill Gates and Mark Zuckerberg) have been criticized for some of their business practices, in some cases with justification. Clearly, though, they and dozens of other prominent business leaders of the past century have contributed significantly to the growth of the U.S. economy. Henry Ford, for example, developed the idea of mass production, which lowered costs sufficiently to bring automobiles within reach of the average American family. Ford began his business in his garage, a tradition that has been maintained by thousands of innovators ever since. Larry Page and Sergey Brin, the cofounders of Google, revolutionized the way people conduct research by developing a method to prioritize the list of websites obtained in a search of the Internet.

Entrepreneurship, like any form of creativity, is difficult to teach, although some of the supporting skills, like financial analysis and marketing, can be learned in college or business school. How, then, does a society encourage entrepreneurship? History suggests that the entrepreneurial spirit will always exist; the challenge to society is to channel entrepreneurial energies in economically productive ways. For example, economic policymakers need to ensure that taxation is not so heavy, and regulation not so inflexible, that small businesses–some of which will eventually become big businesses–cannot get off the ground. Sociological factors may play a role as well. Societies in which business and commerce are considered to be beneath the dignity of refined, educated people are less likely to produce successful entrepreneurs (see The Economic Naturalist 5.3). In the United States, for the most part, business has been viewed as a respectable activity. Overall, a social and economic milieu that allows entrepreneurship to flourish appears to promote economic growth and rising productivity, perhaps especially so in high-technology eras like our own.

The Economic Naturalist 5.3

Why did medieval China stagnate economically?

The Sung period in China (A.D. 960–1270) was one of considerable technological sophistication; its inventions included paper, waterwheels, water clocks, gunpowder, and possibly the compass. Yet no significant industrialization occurred, and in subsequent centuries, Europe saw more economic growth and technological innovation than China. Why did medieval China stagnate economically?

According to research by economist William Baumol,[5] the main impediment to industrialization during the Sung period was a social system that inhibited entrepreneurship. Commerce and industry were considered low-status activities, not fit for an educated person. In addition, the emperor had the right to seize his subjects' property and to take control of their business enterprises—a right that greatly reduced his subjects' incentives to undertake business ventures. The most direct path

[5]W. Baumol, "Entrepreneurship: Productive, Unproductive, and Destructive," *Journal of Political Economy*, October 1990, pp. 893–921.

to status and riches in medieval China was to go through a system of demanding civil service examinations given by the government every three years. The highest scorers on these national examinations were granted lifetime positions in the imperial bureaucracy, where they wielded much power and often became wealthy, in part through corruption. Not surprisingly, medieval China did not develop a dynamic entrepreneurial class, and consequently, its scientific and technological advantages did not translate into sustained economic growth. China's experience shows why scientific advances alone cannot guarantee economic growth; to have economic benefits, scientific knowledge must be commercially applied through new products and new, more efficient means of producing goods and services.

EXAMPLE 5.5 Inventing the Personal Computer

Does entrepreneurship pay?

In 1975, Steve Jobs and Steve Wozniak were two 20-year-olds who designed computer games for Atari. They had an idea to make a computer that was smaller and cheaper than the closet-sized mainframes that were then in use. To set up shop in Steve Jobs's parents' garage and buy their supplies, they sold their two most valuable possessions, Jobs's used Volkswagen van and Wozniak's Hewlett-Packard scientific calculator, for a total of $1,300. The result was the first personal computer, which they named after their new company (and Jobs's favorite fruit): Apple. The rest is history. Clearly, Jobs's and Wozniak's average labor productivity as the inventors of the personal computer eventually became many times what it was when they designed computer games. Creative entrepreneurship can increase productivity just like additional capital or land.

Although entrepreneurship may be more glamorous, managers—the people who run businesses on a daily basis—also play an important role in determining average labor productivity. Managerial jobs span a wide range of positions, from the supervisor of the loading dock to the CEO (chief executive officer) at the helm of a *Fortune* 500 company. Managers work to satisfy customers, deal with suppliers, organize production, obtain financing, assign workers to jobs, and motivate them to work hard and effectively. Such activities enhance labor productivity. For example, in the 1970s and 1980s, Japanese managers introduced new production methods that greatly increased the efficiency of Japanese manufacturing plants. Among them was the *just-in-time* inventory system, in which suppliers deliver production components to the factory just when they are needed, eliminating the need for factories to stockpile components. Japanese managers also pioneered the idea of organizing workers into semi-independent production teams, which allowed workers more flexibility and responsibility than the traditional assembly line. Managers in the United States and other countries studied the Japanese managerial techniques closely and adopted many of them.

The Political and Legal Environment

So far we have emphasized the role of the private sector in increasing average labor productivity. But government too has a role to play in fostering improved productivity. One of the key contributions government can make is to provide a *political and legal environment* that encourages people to behave in economically productive ways—to work hard, save and invest wisely, acquire useful information and skills, and provide the goods and services that the public demands.

One specific function of government that appears to be crucial to economic success is the establishment of *well-defined property rights*. Property rights are well defined when the law provides clear rules for determining who owns what resources (through a system of deeds and titles, for example) and how those resources can be used. Imagine living in a society in which a dictator, backed by the military and the police, could take whatever he wanted, and regularly did so. In such a country, what incentive would you have to raise a large crop or to produce other valuable goods and services? Very little, since much of what you produced would likely be taken away from you. Unfortunately, in many countries of the world today, this situation is far from hypothetical.

Political and legal conditions affect the growth of productivity in other ways, as well. Political scientists and economists have documented the fact that *political instability* can be detrimental to economic growth. This finding is reasonable, since entrepreneurs and savers are unlikely to invest their resources in a country whose government is unstable, particularly if the struggle for power involves civil unrest, terrorism, or guerrilla warfare. On the other hand, a political system that promotes the *free and open exchange of ideas* will speed the development of new technologies and products. For example, some economic historians have suggested that the decline of Spain as an economic power was due in part to the advent of the Spanish Inquisition, which permitted no dissent from religious orthodoxy. Because of the Inquisition's persecution of those whose theories about the natural world contradicted Church doctrine, Spanish science and technology languished, and Spain fell behind more tolerant nations like the Netherlands.

SELF-TEST 5.5

A Bangladeshi worker who immigrates to America is likely to find that his average labor productivity is much higher in the United States than it was at home. The worker is, of course, the same person he was when he lived in Bangladesh. How can the simple act of moving to the United States increase the worker's productivity? What does your answer say about the incentive to immigrate?

RECAP

DETERMINANTS OF AVERAGE LABOR PRODUCTIVITY

Key factors determining average labor productivity in a country include:

- The skills and training of workers, called *human capital*.
- The quantity and quality of *physical capital*—machines, equipment, and buildings.
- The availability of land and other *natural resources*.
- The sophistication of the *technologies* applied in production.
- The effectiveness of *management* and *entrepreneurship*.
- The broad *social and legal environment*.

Labor productivity growth slowed throughout the industrialized world in the early 1970s and remained slow for more than two decades. Between 1995 and 2000, labor productivity rebounded (especially in the United States), largely because of advances in information and communication technology. Since then, labor productivity in the United States has again slowed. It remains to be seen if this recent slowdown is temporary (for example, due to factors that include the last financial crisis and recession) or the beginning of a new period of slower productivity growth.

REAL GDP AND ECONOMIC WELL-BEING

Government policymakers pay close attention to real GDP, often behaving as if the greater the real GDP, the better. However, real GDP is *not* the same as economic well-being. At best, it is an imperfect measure of economic well-being because, for the most part, it captures only those goods and services that are priced and sold in markets. Many factors that contribute to people's economic well-being are not priced and sold in markets and thus are largely or even entirely omitted from GDP. Maximizing real GDP is not, therefore, the right goal for government policymakers. Whether or not policies that increase GDP will also make people better off has to be determined on a case-by-case basis.

Why Real GDP Isn't the Same as Economic Well-Being

To understand why an increase in real GDP does not always promote economic well-being, let's look at some factors that are not included in GDP but do affect whether people are better off.

Leisure Time

Most Americans (and most people in other industrialized countries as well) work many fewer hours than their great-grandparents did 100 years ago. Early in the twentieth century, some industrial workers–steelworkers, for example–worked as many as 12 hours a day, 7 days a week. Today, the 40-hour workweek is typical. Also, Americans tend to start working later in life (after college or graduate school), and, in many cases, they are able to retire earlier. The increased leisure time available to workers in the United States and other industrialized countries–which allows them to pursue many worthwhile activities, including being with family and friends, participating in sports and hobbies, and pursuing cultural and educational activities–is a major benefit of living in a wealthy society. These extra hours of leisure are not priced in markets, however, and therefore are not reflected in GDP.

The Economic Naturalist 5.4

Why do people work fewer hours today than their great-grandparents did?

Americans start work later in life; retire earlier; and, in many cases, work fewer hours per week than people of 50 or 100 years ago. The *opportunity cost* of working less—retiring earlier, for example, or working fewer hours per week—is the earnings you forgo by not working. If you can, say, make $400 per week at a summer job in a department store, then leaving the job two weeks early to take a trip with some friends has an opportunity cost of $800. The fact that people are working fewer hours today suggests that their opportunity cost of forgone earnings is lower than their grandparents' and great-grandparents' opportunity cost. Why this difference?

We can use the cost-benefit principle to help us understand this phenomenon. Over the past century, rapid economic growth in the United States and other industrialized countries has greatly increased the purchasing power of the average worker's wages. In other words, the typical worker today can buy more goods and services with his or her hourly earnings than ever before. This fact would seem to suggest that the opportunity cost of forgone earnings (measured in terms of what those earnings can buy) is greater, not smaller, today than in earlier times. But because the buying power of wages is so much higher today than in the past,

Americans can achieve a reasonable standard of living by working fewer hours than they did in the past. Thus, while your grandparents may have had to work long hours to pay the rent or put food on the table, today the extra income from working long hours is more likely to buy relative luxuries, like nicer clothes or a fancier car. Because such discretionary purchases are easier to give up than basic food and shelter, the true opportunity cost of forgone earnings is lower today than it was 50 years ago. As the opportunity cost of leisure has fallen, Americans have chosen to enjoy more of it.

Nonmarket Economic Activities

Not all economically important activities are bought and sold in markets; with a few exceptions, such as government services, nonmarket economic activities are omitted from GDP. We mentioned earlier the examples of parenting and child-care services and unpaid housekeeping services. Another example is volunteer services, such as the volunteer fire and rescue squads that serve many small towns. The fact that these unpaid services are left out of GDP does *not* mean that they are unimportant. The problem is that because there are no market prices and quantities for unpaid services, estimating their market values is very difficult.

How far do economists go wrong by leaving nonmarket economic activities out of GDP? The answer depends on the type of economy being studied. Although nonmarket economic activities exist in all economies, they are particularly important in poor economies. For example, in rural villages of developing countries, people commonly trade services with each other or cooperate on various tasks without exchanging any money. Families in these communities also tend to be relatively self-sufficient, growing their own food and providing many of their own basic services. Because such nonmarket economic activities are not counted in official statistics, GDP data may substantially understate the true amount of economic activity in the poorest countries.

Closely related to nonmarket activities is the *underground economy,* which includes transactions that are never reported to government officials and data collectors. The underground economy encompasses both legal and illegal activities, from informal babysitting jobs to organized crime. For instance, some people pay temporary or part-time workers like housecleaners and painters in cash, which allows these workers to avoid paying taxes on their income. Economists who have tried to estimate the value of such services by studying how much cash the public holds have concluded that these sorts of transactions make up an important share of overall economic activity, even in advanced industrial economies.

Environmental Quality and Resource Depletion

China has experienced tremendous growth in real GDP. But in expanding its manufacturing base, it also has suffered a severe decline in air and water quality. Increased pollution certainly detracts from the quality of life, but because air and water quality are not bought and sold in markets, the Chinese GDP does not reflect this downside of its economic growth.

The exploitation of finite natural resources also tends to be overlooked in GDP. When an oil company pumps and sells a barrel of oil, GDP increases by the value of the oil. But the fact that there is one less barrel of oil in the ground, waiting to be pumped sometime in the future, is not reflected in GDP.

A number of efforts have been made to incorporate factors like air quality and resource depletion into a comprehensive measure of GDP. Doing so is difficult since it often involves placing a dollar value on intangibles, like having a clean river to swim in instead of a dirty one. But the fact that the benefits of environmental quality and resource conservation are hard to measure in dollars and cents does not mean that they are unimportant.

Quality of Life

What makes a particular town or city an attractive place to live? Some desirable features you might think of are reflected in GDP: spacious, well-constructed homes; good restaurants and stores; a variety of entertainment; and high-quality medical services. However, other indicators of the good life are not sold in markets and so may be omitted from GDP. Examples include a low crime rate, minimal traffic congestion, active civic organizations, and open space. Thus, citizens of a rural community may oppose the construction of a new shopping center because they believe it may have a negative effect on the quality of life—even though the new shopping center may increase local GDP.

Poverty and Economic Inequality

GDP measures the *total* quantity of goods and services produced and sold in an economy, but it conveys no information about who gets to enjoy those goods and services. Two countries may have identical GDPs but differ radically in the distribution of economic welfare across the population. Suppose, for example, that in one country—call it Equalia—most people have a comfortable middle-class existence; both extreme poverty and extreme wealth are rare. But in another country, Inequalia—which has the same real GDP as Equalia—a few wealthy families control the economy, and the majority of the population lives in poverty. While most people would say that Equalia has a better economic situation overall, that judgment would not be reflected in the GDPs of the two countries, which are the same.

In the United States, absolute poverty has been declining. Today, many families whose income is below today's official "poverty line" (in 2019, $25,750 for a family of four) own a television, a car, and in some cases their own home. Some economists have argued that people who are considered poor today live as well as many middle-class people did in the 1950s.

But, though absolute poverty seems to be decreasing in the United States, inequality of income has generally been rising. The chief executive officer of a large U.S. corporation may earn hundreds of times what the typical worker in the same firm receives. Psychologists tell us that people's economic satisfaction depends not only on their absolute economic position—the quantity and quality of food, clothing, and shelter they have—but also on what they have compared to what others have. If you own an old, beat-up car but are the only person in your neighborhood to have a car, you may feel privileged. But if everyone else in the neighborhood owns a luxury car, you are likely to be less satisfied. To the extent that such comparisons affect people's well-being, inequality matters as well as absolute poverty. Again, because GDP focuses on total production rather than on the distribution of output, it does not capture the effects of inequality.

But GDP Is Related to Economic Well-Being

You might conclude from the list of important factors omitted from the official figures that GDP is useless as a measure of economic welfare. Indeed, numerous critics have made that claim. Clearly, in evaluating the effects of a proposed economic policy, considering only the likely effects on GDP is not sufficient. Planners must also ask whether the policy will affect aspects of economic well-being that are not captured in GDP. Environmental regulations may reduce production of steel, for example, which reduces the GDP. But that fact is not a sufficient basis on which to decide whether such regulations are good or bad. The right way to decide such questions is to apply the cost-benefit principle: Are the benefits of cleaner air worth more to people than the costs the regulations impose in terms of lost output and lost jobs? If so, then the regulations should be adopted; otherwise, they should not.

Although looking at the effects of a proposed policy on real GDP is not the only basis on which to evaluate a policy, real GDP per person *does* tend to be positively associated with many things people value, including a high material standard of living, better health and life expectancies, and better education. We discuss next some of the ways in which a higher real GDP is associated with greater economic well-being.

Availability of Goods and Services

Obviously, citizens of a country with a high GDP are likely to possess more and better goods and services (after all, that is what GDP measures). On average, people in high-GDP countries enjoy larger, better-constructed, and more comfortable homes; higher-quality food and clothing; a greater variety of entertainment and cultural opportunities; better access to transportation and travel; better communications and sanitation; and other advantages. While social commentators may question the value of material consumption—and we agree that riches do not necessarily bring happiness or peace of mind—the majority of people in the world place great importance on achieving material prosperity. Throughout history people have made tremendous sacrifices and taken great risks to secure a higher standard of living for themselves and their families. In fact, to a great extent the United States was built by people who were willing to leave their native lands, often at great personal hardship, in hopes of bettering their economic condition.

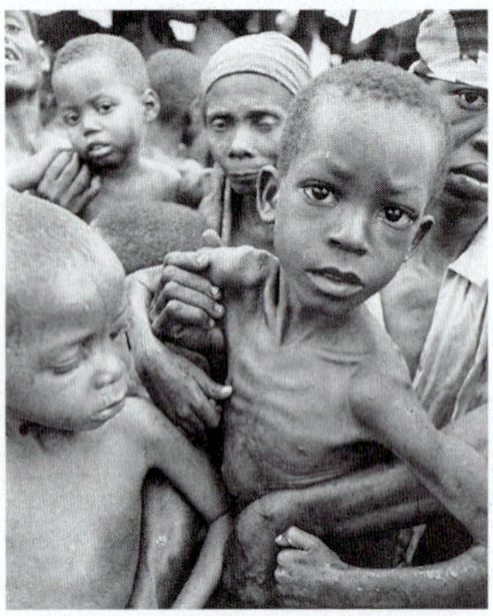
Bettmann/Getty Images

A child born in one of the low human development countries has almost an 8 percent chance of dying before his or her fifth birthday.

Health and Education

While some people question the value of an abundance of consumer goods and services, few question the value of literacy and education, and no one questions the value of having longer and healthier lives. Table 5.3 shows four groups of countries with radically different levels of GDP per person. Most noticeably, GDP per person in the countries with very high human development is more than 14 times that of the countries with low human development.[6]

How do these large differences in GDP relate to other measures of well-being? Table 5.3 shows that on some of the most basic measures of human welfare, the low human development countries fare much worse than the high human development countries. A child born in one of the countries with low human development

TABLE 5.3
GDP and Basic Indicators of Well-Being

Indicator and year	Very high human development	High human development	Medium human development	Low human development
GDP per person (U.S. dollars), 2018	40,019	14,669	6,279	2,704
Total population in group of countries (millions), 2018	1,532.1	2,857.7	2,245.3	923.2
Life expectancy at birth (years), 2018	79.5	75.1	69.3	61.3
Under-5 mortality rate (per 1,000 live births), 2017	6.2	16.1	44.5	76.6
Expected years of schooling (of children), 2018	16.4	13.8	11.7	9.3

Source: United Nations, *Human Development Report 2019*, http://hdr.undp.org/en/2019-report.

[6]GDP data in Table 5.3 use U.S. prices to value goods and services in low human development nations. Because basic goods and services tend to be cheaper in poor countries, this adjustment significantly increases measured GDP in those countries.

has almost an 8 percent chance of dying before his or her fifth birthday. Compare this with a 0.6 percent chance of dying before the fifth birthday in the countries with very high human development. A child born in a country with very high human development has a life expectancy of more than 79 years, compared to about 61 years in the low human development countries.

Table 5.3 shows that citizens of very high human development countries attend school for almost twice as many years as those in the low human development countries. Furthermore, data on years of schooling do not capture important differences in the quality of education available in rich and poor countries, as measured by indicators such as the educational backgrounds of teachers and student–teacher ratios.

The Economic Naturalist 5.5

Why do far fewer children complete high school in poor countries than in rich countries?

One possible explanation is that people in poor countries place a lower priority on getting an education than people in rich countries. This seems unlikely since immigrants from poor countries often put a heavy emphasis on education—though it may be that people who emigrate from poor countries are unrepresentative of the population as a whole.

An economic naturalist's explanation for the lower schooling rates in poor countries would rely not on cultural differences, but on differences in opportunity costs. In poor societies, most of which are heavily agricultural, children are an important source of labor. Sending children to school beyond a certain age imposes a high opportunity cost on the family. Children who are in school are not available to help with planting, harvesting, and other tasks that must be done if the family is to survive. In addition, the cost of books and school supplies imposes a major hardship on poor families. The Cost-Benefit Principle thus implies that children will stay at home rather than go to school. In rich, nonagricultural countries, school-age children have few work opportunities, and their potential earnings are small relative to other sources of family income. The low opportunity cost of sending children to school in rich countries is an important reason for the higher enrollment rates in those countries. It is probably also true that the benefits or returns from receiving an education are higher in rich countries, as there are more employment opportunities for people with education than in poor countries.

We close this discussion by noting that Table 5.3 compares fairly large groups of countries that are at very different stages of economic development. Looking in the *Human Development Report* at specific countries within each group, the relationship between GDP and health outcomes is often much weaker, and is sometimes strongly reversed. For example, within the group of countries with very high human development, GDP per person in the United States is $56,140–more than 28 percent higher than Canada's $43,602, and more than 37 percent higher than Japan's $40,799. But life expectancy at birth in the United States is 78.9 years–more than three years shorter than Canada's 82.3, and more than five and a half years shorter than Japan's 84.5![7]

[7]For a discussion of the recent drop in life expectancy in the United States in a broad economic and social context, see Anne Case and Angus Deaton, *Deaths of Despair and the Future of Capitalism* (Princeton, NJ: Princeton University Press, 2020).

RECAP

REAL GDP AND ECONOMIC WELL-BEING

- Real GDP is an imperfect measure of economic well-being. Among the factors affecting well-being omitted from real GDP are the availability of leisure time, nonmarket services such as unpaid homemaking and volunteer services, environmental quality and resource conservation, and quality-of-life indicators such as a low crime rate. The GDP also does not reflect the degree of economic inequality in a country. Because real GDP is not the same as economic well-being, proposed policies should not be evaluated strictly in terms of whether or not they increase the GDP.
- Although GDP is not the same as economic well-being, it is positively associated with many things that people value, including a higher material standard of living, better health, longer life expectancies, and higher rates of literacy and educational attainment. This relationship between real GDP and economic well-being has led many people to emigrate from poor nations in search of a better life and has motivated policymakers to try to increase their nations' rates of economic growth.

So far in this chapter we have said that while GDP is related to economic well-being, it is not the same as economic well-being. We said that therefore societies should not automatically strive for the highest possible rate of economic growth without also considering aspects of economic well-being that are not included in GDP. Even if we accept for the moment that increased output per person is always desirable, attaining a higher rate of economic growth does impose costs on society.

What are the costs of increasing economic growth? The most straightforward is the cost of creating new capital. We know that by expanding the capital stock we can increase future productivity and output. But, to increase the capital stock, we must divert resources that could otherwise be used to increase the supply of consumer goods. For example, to add more robot-operated assembly lines, a society must employ more of its skilled technicians in building industrial robots and fewer in developing medical assistance robots. To build new factories, more carpenters and lumber must be assigned to factory construction and less to finishing basements or renovating family rooms. In short, high rates of investment in new capital require people to tighten their belts, consume less, and save more—a real economic cost.

Should a country undertake a high rate of investment in capital goods at the sacrifice of consumer goods? The answer depends on the extent that people are willing and able to sacrifice consumption today to have a bigger economic pie tomorrow. In a country that is very poor, or is experiencing an economic crisis, people may prefer to keep consumption relatively high and savings and investment relatively low. The midst of a thunderstorm is not the time to be putting something aside for a rainy day! But in a society that is relatively well off, people may be more willing to make sacrifices to achieve higher economic growth in the future.

Consumption sacrificed to capital formation is not the only cost of achieving higher growth. In the United States in the nineteenth and early twentieth centuries, periods of rapid economic growth were often times in which many people worked extremely long hours at dangerous and unpleasant jobs. While those workers helped build the economy that Americans enjoy today, the costs were great in terms of reduced leisure time and, in some cases, workers' health and safety.

Other costs of growth include the cost of the research and development that is required to improve technology and the costs of acquiring training and skill (human capital). The fact that a higher living standard tomorrow must be purchased at the cost of current sacrifices is an example of how having more of one good thing usually means having less of another. Because achieving higher economic growth imposes real economic costs, we know from the cost-benefit principle that higher growth should be pursued only if the benefits outweigh the costs.

RECAP

THE COSTS OF ECONOMIC GROWTH

Economic growth has substantial costs, notably the sacrifice of current consumption that is required to free resources for creating new capital and new technologies. Higher rates of growth should be pursued only if the benefits outweigh the costs.

PROMOTING ECONOMIC GROWTH

If a society decides to try to raise its rate of economic growth, what are some of the measures that policymakers might take to achieve this objective? Here is a short list of suggestions, based on our discussion of the factors that contribute to growth in average labor productivity and, hence, output per person.

Policies to Increase Human Capital

Because skilled and well-educated workers are more productive than unskilled labor, governments in most countries try to increase the human capital of their citizens by supporting education and training programs. In the United States, government provides public education through high school and grants extensive support to postsecondary schools, including technical schools, colleges, and universities. Publicly funded early intervention programs like Head Start also attempt to build human capital by helping disadvantaged children prepare for school. To a lesser degree than some other countries, the U.S. government also funds job training for unskilled youths and retraining for workers whose skills have become obsolete.

The Economic Naturalist 5.6

Why do almost all countries provide free public education?

All industrial countries provide their citizens free public education through high school, and most subsidize college and other postsecondary schools. Why?

Americans are so used to the idea of free public education that this question may seem odd. But why should the government provide free education when it does not provide even more essential goods and services, such as food or medical care, for free, except to the most needy? Furthermore, educational services can be, and indeed commonly are, supplied and demanded on the private market, without the aid of the government.

An important argument for free or at least subsidized education is that the private demand curve for educational services does not include all the social benefits of education. For example, the democratic political system relies on an educated citizenry to operate effectively—a factor that an individual demander of educational services has little reason to consider. From a narrower economic perspective, we might argue that individuals do not capture the full economic returns from their schooling. For example, people with high human capital, and thus high earnings, pay more taxes—funds that can be used to finance government services and aid the less fortunate. Because

connect

▶ Visit your instructor's Connect course and access your eBook to view this video.

Why do almost all countries provide free public education?

of income taxation, the private benefit to acquiring human capital is less than the social benefit, and the demand for education on the private market may be less than optimal from society's viewpoint. Similarly, educated people are more likely than others to contribute to technological development, and hence to general productivity growth, which may benefit many other people besides themselves. Finally, another argument for public support of education is that poor people who would like to invest in human capital may not be able to do so because of insufficient income.

The late Nobel laureate Milton Friedman, among many economists, suggested that these arguments may justify government grants, called educational *vouchers*, to help citizens purchase educational services in the private sector, but they do *not* justify the government providing education directly, as through the public school system. Defenders of public education, on the other hand, argue that the government should have some direct control over education in order to set standards and monitor quality. What do you think?

Policies That Promote Saving and Investment

Average labor productivity increases when workers can utilize a sizable and modern capital stock. To support the creation of new capital, government can encourage high rates of saving and investment in the private sector. Many provisions in the U.S. tax code are designed expressly to stimulate households to save and firms to invest. For example, a household that opens an Individual Retirement Account (IRA) is able to save for retirement without paying taxes on either the funds deposited in the IRA or the interest earned on the account. (However, taxes are due when the funds are withdrawn at retirement.) The intent of IRA legislation is to make saving more financially attractive to American households. Similarly, at various times Congress has instituted an investment tax credit, which reduces the tax bills of firms that invest in new capital. Private-sector saving and investment are discussed in greater detail in Chapter 7, *Saving and Capital Formation*.

Government can contribute directly to capital formation through *public investment*, or the creation of government-owned capital. Public investment includes the building of roads, bridges, airports, dams, and, in some countries, energy and communications networks. The construction of the U.S. interstate highway system, begun during the administration of President Eisenhower, is often cited as an example of successful public investment. The interstate system substantially reduced long-haul transportation costs in the United States, improving productivity throughout the economy. Today, the web of computers and communications links we call the Internet is having a similar effect. This project, too, received crucial government funding in its early stages. Many research studies have confirmed that government investment in the *infrastructure*, the public capital that supports private-sector economic activities, can be a significant source of growth.

Policies That Support Research and Development

Productivity is enhanced by technological progress, which in turn requires investment in research and development (R&D). In many industries private firms have adequate incentive to conduct research and development activities. There is no need, for example, for the government to finance research for developing a better underarm deodorant.

But some types of knowledge, particularly basic scientific knowledge, may have widespread economic benefits that cannot be captured by a single private firm. The developers of the silicon computer chip, for example, were instrumental in creating huge new industries, yet they received only a small portion of the profits flowing from their inventions.

Because society in general, rather than the individual inventors, may receive much of the benefit from basic research, government may need to support basic research, as it does through agencies such as the National Science Foundation. The federal government also sponsors a great deal of applied research, particularly in military and space applications. To the extent that national security allows, the government can increase growth by sharing the fruits of such research with the private sector. For example, the Global Positioning System (GPS), which was developed originally for military purposes, is now available in most cell phones, helping people find their way almost anywhere.

The Legal and Political Framework

Although economic growth comes primarily from activities in the private sector, the government plays an essential role in providing the framework within which the private sector can operate productively. We have discussed the importance of secure property rights and a well-functioning legal system, of an economic environment that encourages entrepreneurship, and of political stability and the free and open exchange of ideas. Government policymakers should also consider the potential effects of tax and regulatory policies on activities that increase productivity, such as investment, innovation, and risk taking. Policies that affect the legal and political framework are examples of *structural macroeconomic policies*.

The Poorest Countries: A Special Case?

Radical disparities in living standards exist between the richest and poorest countries of the world (see Table 5.3 for some data). Achieving economic growth in the poorest countries is thus particularly urgent. Are the policy prescriptions of this section relevant to those countries, or are very different types of measures necessary to spur growth in the poorest nations?

To a significant extent, the same factors and policies that promote growth in richer countries apply to the poorest countries as well. Increasing human capital by supporting education and training, increasing rates of saving and investment, investing in public capital and infrastructure, supporting research and development, and encouraging entrepreneurship are all measures that will enhance economic growth in poor countries.

However, to a much greater degree than in richer countries, most poor countries need to improve the legal and political environment that underpins their economies. For example, many developing countries have poorly developed or corrupt legal systems, which discourage entrepreneurship and investment by creating uncertainty about property rights. Taxation and regulation in developing countries are often heavy-handed and administered by inefficient bureaucracies, to the extent that it may take months or years to obtain the approvals needed to start a small business or expand a factory. Regulation is also used to suppress market forces in poor countries; for example, the government, rather than the market, may determine the allocation of bank credit or the prices for agricultural products. Structural policies that aim to ameliorate these problems are important preconditions for generating growth in the poorest countries. But probably most important—and most difficult, for some countries—is establishing political stability and the rule of law. Without political stability, domestic and foreign savers will be reluctant to invest in the country, and economic growth will be difficult if not impossible to achieve.

Can rich countries help poor countries develop? Historically, richer nations have tried to help by providing financial aid through loans or grants from individual countries (foreign aid) or by loans made by international agencies, such as the World Bank. Experience has shown, however, that financial aid to countries that do not undertake structural reforms, such as reducing excessive regulation or improving the legal system, is of limited value. To make their foreign aid most effective, rich countries should help poor countries achieve political stability and undertake the necessary reforms to the structure of their economies.

RECAP

PROMOTING ECONOMIC GROWTH

Policies for promoting economic growth include policies to increase human capital (education and training); policies that promote saving and capital formation; policies that support research and development; and the provision of a legal and political framework within which the private sector can operate productively. Deficiencies in the legal and political framework (for example, official corruption or poorly defined property rights) are a special problem for many developing countries.

ARE THERE LIMITS TO GROWTH?

Earlier in this chapter, we saw that even relatively low rates of economic growth, if sustained for a long period, will produce huge increases in the size of the economy. This fact raises the question of whether economic growth can continue indefinitely without depleting natural resources and causing massive damage to the global environment. Does the basic truth that we live in a finite world of finite resources imply that, ultimately, economic growth must come to an end?

The concern that economic growth may not be sustainable is not a new one. An influential 1972 book, *The Limits to Growth,*[8] reported the results of computer simulations that suggested that unless population growth and economic expansion were halted, the world would soon be running out of natural resources, drinkable water, and breathable air. This book, and later works in the same vein, raises some fundamental questions that cannot be done full justice here. However, in some ways its conclusions are misleading.

One problem with the "limits to growth" thesis lies in its underlying concept of economic growth. Those who emphasize the environmental limits on growth assume implicitly that economic growth will always take the form of more of what we have now—more smoky factories, more polluting cars, more fast-food restaurants. If that were indeed the case, then surely there would be limits to the growth the planet can sustain.

But growth in real GDP does not necessarily take such a form. Increases in real GDP can also arise from new or higher-quality products. For example, not too long ago, tennis rackets were relatively simple items made primarily of wood. Today they are made of newly invented synthetic materials and designed for optimum performance using sophisticated computer simulations. Because these new high-tech tennis rackets are more valued by consumers than the old wooden ones, they increase the real GDP. Likewise, the introduction of new pharmaceuticals has contributed to economic growth, as have the expanded number of web-based services and apps. As people switch, for example, from frequent visits to the bank or the mall to frequent visits to the bank's or store's website (or mobile app), GDP may increase while the number of cars and of brick-and-mortar stores decreases. Thus, economic growth need not take the form of more and more of the same old stuff; it can mean newer, better, and perhaps cleaner and more efficient goods and services.

[8]Donella H. Meadows, Dennis L. Meadows, Jørgen Randers, and William W. Behrens III, *The Limits to Growth* (New York: New American Library, 1972).

A second problem with the "limits to growth" conclusion is that it overlooks the fact that increased wealth and productivity expand society's capacity to take measures to safeguard the environment. In fact, the most polluted countries in the world are not the richest but those that are in a relatively early stage of industrialization. At this stage countries must devote the bulk of their resources to basic needs—food, shelter, health care—and continued industrial expansion. In these countries, clean air and water may be viewed as a luxury rather than a basic need. In more economically developed countries, where the most basic needs are more easily met, extra resources are available to keep the environment clean. Thus continuing economic growth may lead to less, not more, pollution.

A third problem with the pessimistic view of economic growth is that it ignores the power of the market and other social mechanisms to deal with scarcity. During the oil-supply disruptions of the 1970s, newspapers were filled with headlines about the energy crisis and the imminent depletion of world oil supplies. Yet 40 years later, the world's known oil reserves are actually *greater* than they were in the 1970s.

Today's energy situation is so much better than was expected 40 years ago because the market went to work. Reduced oil supplies led to an increase in prices that changed the behavior of both demanders and suppliers. Consumers insulated their homes, purchased more energy-efficient cars and appliances, and switched to alternative sources of energy. Suppliers engaged in a massive hunt for new reserves, opening up major new sources in Latin America, China, the North Sea, and more recently North America's large shale oil deposits. In short, market forces solved the energy crisis, at least for now.

In general, shortages in any resource will trigger price changes that induce suppliers and demanders to deal with the problem. Simply extrapolating current economic trends into the future ignores the power of the market system to recognize shortages and make the necessary corrections. Government actions spurred by political pressures, such as the allocation of public funds to preserve open space or reduce air pollution, can be expected to supplement market adjustments.

Despite the shortcomings of the "limits to growth" perspective, most economists would agree that not all the problems created by economic growth can be dealt with effectively through the market or the political process. Probably most important, global environmental problems, such as the possibility of global warming or the ongoing destruction of rain forests, are a particular challenge for existing economic and political institutions. Many environmental-quality goods—living in a healthy environment with clean air and water, avoiding global warming, and avoiding deforestation—are desired by many people, but they are not bought and sold in markets and thus will not automatically reach their optimal levels through market processes. Nor can local or national governments effectively address problems that are global in scope. Unless international mechanisms are established for dealing with global environmental problems, these problems may become worse as economic growth continues.

RECAP

ECONOMIC GROWTH: ARE THERE LIMITS?

Some have argued that finite resources imply ultimate limits to economic growth. This view overlooks the facts that growth can take the form of better, rather than more, goods and services; that increased wealth frees resources to safeguard the environment; and that political and economic mechanisms exist to address many of the problems associated with growth. However, these mechanisms may not work well when environmental or other problems arising from economic growth are global in scope.

SUMMARY

- Over the past two centuries, the industrialized nations saw enormous improvements in living standards, as reflected in large increases in real GDP per person. Because of the power of *compound interest*, relatively small differences in growth rates, if continued over long periods, can produce large differences in real GDP per person and average living standards. Thus, the rate of long-term economic growth is an economic variable of critical importance. *(LO1)*
- Real GDP per person is the product of average labor productivity (real GDP per employed worker) and the share of the population that is employed. Growth in real GDP per person can occur only through growth in *average labor productivity*, in the share of the population that is working, or both. In the period from 1960 to 2000, increases in the share of the U.S. population holding a job contributed significantly to rising real GDP per person. But, as in most periods, the main source of the increase in real GDP per person was rising average labor productivity. *(LO2)*
- Among the factors that determine labor productivity are the talents, education, training, and skills of workers, or *human capital*; the quantity and quality of the *physical capital* that workers use; the availability of land and other natural resources; the application of technology to the production and distribution of goods and services; the effectiveness of *entrepreneurs* and managers; and the broad social and legal environment. Because of *diminishing returns to capital*, beyond a certain point expansion of the capital stock is not the most effective way to increase average labor productivity. Economists generally agree that new technologies are the most important single source of improvements in productivity. *(LO3)*
- Since the 1970s, the industrial world has experienced a slowdown in productivity growth. Productivity growth rebounded between 1995 and 2000, largely as a result of advances in information and communication technology, before slowing down again. *(LO3)*
- Real GDP per person is an imperfect measure of economic well-being. With a few exceptions, notably government purchases of goods and services (which are included in GDP at their cost of production), GDP includes only those goods and services sold in markets. It excludes important factors that affect people's well-being, such as the amount of leisure time available to them, the value of unpaid or volunteer services, the quality of the environment, quality of life indicators such as the crime rate, and the degree of economic inequality. *(LO4)*
- Real GDP is still a useful indicator of economic well-being, however. Countries with a high real GDP per person not only enjoy high average standards of living; they also tend to have higher life expectancies, low rates of infant and child mortality, and high rates of school enrollment and literacy. *(LO4)*
- Economic growth has costs as well as benefits. Prominent among them is the need to sacrifice current consumption to achieve a high rate of investment in new capital goods; other costs of growing more quickly include extra work effort and the costs of research and development. Thus, more economic growth is not necessarily better; whether increased economic growth is desirable depends on whether the benefits of growth outweigh the costs. *(LO5)*
- Among the ways in which government can stimulate economic growth are by adopting policies that encourage the creation of human capital; that promote saving and investment, including public investment in infrastructure; that support research and development, particularly in the basic sciences; and that provide a legal and political framework that supports private-sector activities. The poorest countries, with poorly developed legal, tax, and regulatory systems, are often in the greatest need of an improved legal and political framework and increased political stability. *(LO6)*
- Are there limits to growth? Arguments that economic growth must be constrained by environmental problems and the limits of natural resources ignore the fact that economic growth can take the form of increasing quality as well as increasing quantity. Indeed, increases in output can provide additional resources for cleaning up the environment. Finally, the market system, together with political processes, can solve many of the problems associated with economic growth. On the other hand, global environmental problems, which can be handled neither by the market nor by individual national governments, have the potential to constrain economic growth. *(LO7)*

KEY TERMS

average labor productivity
compound interest
diminishing returns to capital
entrepreneurs
human capital
physical capital

REVIEW QUESTIONS

1. What has happened to real GDP per person in the industrialized countries over the past century? What implications does this have for the average person? Are there implications for different countries in different regions (e.g., Japan versus Ghana)? *(LO1)*
2. Why do economists consider growth in average labor productivity to be the key factor in determining long-run living standards? *(LO2)*
3. What is *human capital*? Why is it economically important? How is new human capital created? *(LO3)*
4. You have employed five workers of varying physical strength to dig a ditch. Workers without shovels have zero productivity in ditchdigging. How should you assign shovels to workers if you don't have enough shovels to go around? How should you assign any additional shovels that you obtain? Using this example, discuss (a) the relationship between the availability of physical capital and average labor productivity and (b) the concept of diminishing returns to capital. *(LO3)*
5. Would you say that real GDP per person is a useful measure of economic well-being? Defend your answer. *(LO4)*
6. What are the costs of increasing economic growth? *(LO5)*
7. What major contributions can the government make to the goal of increasing average labor productivity? *(LO6)*
8. Discuss the following statement: "Because the environment is fragile and natural resources are finite, ultimately economic growth must come to an end." *(LO7)*

PROBLEMS

connect

1. Richland's real GDP per person is $40,000, and Poorland's real GDP per person is $20,000. However, Richland's real GDP per person is growing at 1 percent per year and Poorland's is growing at 3 percent per year. Compare real GDP per person in the two countries after 10 years and after 20 years. Approximately how many years will it take Poorland to catch up to Richland? *(LO1)*
2. Suppose labor productivity in the United States was $100,000 per worker in 2015. Calculate the value of labor productivity in the year 2035 (20 years later) if *(LO1)*
   a. productivity continues to grow by 3.1 percent per year.
   b. productivity growth falls to 1.4 percent per year. (*Note:* You do not need to know the actual values of average labor productivity in any year to solve this problem.)

   How much larger would labor productivity per worker be in 2035 with the higher growth rate as compared to the lower growth rate?
3. The "graying of America" will substantially increase the fraction of the population that is retired in the decades to come. To illustrate the implications for U.S. living standards, suppose that over the 56 years following 2016, the share of the population that is working returns to its 1960 level, while average labor productivity increases by as much as it did during 1960–2016. Under this scenario, what would be the net change in real GDP per person between 2016 and 2072? The following data will be useful. *(LO2)*

	Average labor productivity	Share of population employed
1960	$ 47,263	36.4%
2016	$110,384	46.8%

4. Consider the following table containing data for Germany and Japan on the ratio of employment to population in 1980 and 2010.

	1980	2010
Germany	0.33	0.52
Japan	0.48	0.49

   Using data from Table 5.1, find average labor productivity for each country in 1980 and 2010. How much of the increase in output per person in each country over the 1980 to 2010 period is due to increased labor productivity? To increased employment relative to population? *(LO2)*
5. Joanne has just completed high school and is trying to determine whether to go to community college for two years or go directly to work. Her objective is to maximize the savings she will have in the bank five years from now. If she goes directly to work she will earn $20,000 per year for each of the next five years. If she goes to community college, for each of the next two years she will earn nothing–indeed, she will have to borrow $6,000 each year to cover tuition and books. This loan must be repaid in full three years after graduation. If she graduates from community college, in each of the subsequent three years, her

wages will be $38,000 per year. Joanne's total living expenses and taxes, excluding tuition and books, equal $15,000 per year. *(LO3)*

a. Suppose for simplicity that Joanne can borrow and lend at 0 percent interest. On purely economic grounds, should she go to community college or work?
b. Does your answer to part a change if she can earn $23,000 per year with only a high school degree?
c. Does your answer to part a change if Joanne's tuition and books cost $8,000 per year?
d.* Suppose that the interest rate at which Joanne can borrow and lend is 10 percent per year, but other data are as in part a. Savings are deposited at the end of the year they are earned and receive (compound) interest at the end of each subsequent year. Similarly, the loans are taken out at the end of the year in which they are needed, and interest does not accrue until the end of the subsequent year. Now that the interest rate has risen, should Joanne go to college or go to work?

6. The Good'n'Fresh Grocery Store has two checkout lanes and four employees. Employees are equally skilled, and all are able either to operate a register (checkers) or bag groceries (baggers). The store owner assigns one checker and one bagger to each lane. A lane with a checker and a bagger can check out 42 customers per hour. A lane with a checker can check out only 25 customers per hour. *(LO3)*
   a. In terms of customers checked out per hour, what is total output and average labor productivity for the Good'n'Fresh Grocery Store?
   b. The owner adds a third checkout lane and register. Assuming that no employees are added, what is the best way to reallocate the workers to tasks? What is total output and average labor productivity (in terms of customers checked out per hour) now?
   c. Repeat part b for the addition of a fourth checkout lane, and a fifth. Do you observe diminishing returns to capital in this example?

7. Harrison, Carla, and Fred are housepainters. Harrison and Carla can paint 100 square feet per hour using a standard paintbrush, and Fred can paint 80 square feet per hour. Any of the three can paint 200 square feet per hour using a roller. *(LO3)*
   a. Assume Harrison, Carla, and Fred have only paintbrushes at their disposal. What is the average labor productivity, in terms of square feet per painter-hour, for the three painters taken as a team? Assume that the three painters always work the same number of hours.
   b. Repeat part a for the cases in which the team has one, two, three, or four rollers available. Are there diminishing returns to capital?
   c. An improvement in paint quality increases the area that can be covered per hour (by either brushes or rollers) by 20 percent. How does this technological improvement affect your answers to part b? Are there diminishing returns to capital? Does the technological improvement increase or reduce the economic value of an additional roller?

8. Hester's Hatchery raises fish. At the end of the current season, Hester has 1,000 fish in the hatchery. She can harvest any number of fish that she wishes, selling them to restaurants for $5 apiece. Because big fish make little fish, for every fish that she leaves in the hatchery this year she will have two fish at the end of next year. The price of fish is expected to be $5 each next year as well. Hester relies entirely on income from current fish sales to support herself. *(LO3)*
   a. How many fish should Hester harvest if she wants to maximize the growth of her stock of fish from this season to next season?
   b. Do you think maximizing the growth of her fish stock is an economically sound strategy for Hester? Why or why not? Relate to the text discussion on the costs of economic growth.
   c. How many fish should Hester harvest if she wants to maximize her current income? Do you think this is a good strategy?
   d. Explain why Hester is unlikely to harvest either all or none of her fish, but instead will harvest some and leave the rest to reproduce.

9. The government is considering a policy to reduce air pollution by restricting the use of "dirty" fuels by factories. In deciding whether to implement the policy, how, if at all, should the likely effects of the policy on real GDP be taken into account? *(LO4)*

10. We discussed how the opportunity cost of sending children to school affects the level of school enrollment across countries. The United Nations *Human Development Report 2019* reports the following data for per capita income in 2018 (in the equivalent of 2011 U.S. dollars). *(LO4)*

Canada	$43,602
Denmark	$48,836
Greece	$24,909
Lesotho	$ 3,244
Ethiopia	$ 1,782

Source: http://hdr.undp.org/en/countries.

   a. Which country would you expect to have the highest school enrollment rate? The lowest rate?
   b. Discuss what other factors besides GDP per capita a family might consider when applying the cost-benefit principle to the decision of whether or not to send a child to school.

*Denotes more difficult problem.

11. Discuss the following statement, using concrete examples where possible to illustrate your arguments: For advances in basic science to translate into improvements in standards of living, they must be supported by favorable economic conditions. *(LO3, LO6)*
12. Write a short essay evaluating the U.S. economy in terms of each of the six determinants of average labor productivity discussed in the text. Are there any areas in which the United States is exceptionally strong, relative to other countries? Areas where the United States is less strong than some other countries? Illustrate your arguments with numbers from the *Statistical Abstract of the United States* (available online at www.census.gov/library/publications/time-series/statistical_abstracts.html) and other sources, as appropriate. *(LO3, LO6)*

ANSWERS TO SELF-TESTS

5.1 If the United States had grown at the Japanese rate for the period 1870–2010, real GDP per person in 2010 would have been ($2,445) × $(1.025)^{140}$ = $77,556.82. Actual GDP per person in the United States in 2010 was $30,491, so at the higher rate of growth output per person would have been $77,556.82/$30,491 = 2.54 times higher. *(LO1)*

5.2 As before, Lucy can wrap 4,000 candies per week, or 100 candies per hour. Ethel can wrap 500 candies per hour, and working 40 hours weekly, she can wrap 20,000 candies per week. Together Lucy and Ethel can wrap 24,000 candies per week. Since they work a total of 80 hours between them, their output per hour as a team is 24,000 candies wrapped per 80 hours = 300 candies wrapped per hour, midway between their hourly productivities as individuals. *(LO3)*

5.3 Because Ethel can wrap 300 candies per hour by hand, the benefit of giving Ethel the machine is 500 − 300 = 200 additional candies wrapped per hour. Because Lucy wraps only 100 candies per hour by hand, the benefit of giving Lucy the machine is 400 additional candies wrapped per hour. So the benefit of giving the machine to Lucy is greater than of giving it to Ethel. Equivalently, if the machine goes to Ethel, then Lucy and Ethel between them can wrap 500 + 100 = 600 candies per hour, but if Lucy uses the machine the team can wrap 300 + 500 = 800 candies per hour. So output is increased by letting Lucy use the machine. *(LO3)*

5.4 Now, working by hand, Lucy can wrap 300 candies per hour and Ethel can wrap 500 candies per hour. With a machine, either Lucy or Ethel can wrap 800 candies per hour. As in Self-Test 5.3, the benefit of giving a machine to Lucy (500 candies per hour) exceeds the benefit of giving a machine to Ethel (300 candies per hour), so if only one machine is available, Lucy should use it.

The table analogous to Table 5.2 now looks like the following.

Relationship of Capital, Output, and Productivity in the Candy-Wrapping Factory

Number of machines (*K*)	Candies wrapped per week (*Y*)	Total hours worked (*N*)	Average hourly labor productivity (*Y/N*)
0	32,000	80	400
1	52,000	80	650
2	64,000	80	800
3	64,000	80	800

Comparing this table with Table 5.2, you can see that technological advance has increased labor productivity for any value of *K*, the number of machines available.

Adding one machine increases output by 20,000 candies wrapped per week, adding the second machine increases output by 12,000 candies wrapped per week, and adding the third machine does not increase output at all (because there is no worker available to use it). So diminishing returns to capital still hold after the technological improvement. *(LO3)*

5.5 Although the individual worker is the same person he was in Bangladesh, by coming to the United States he gains the benefit of factors that enhance average labor productivity in this country, relative to his homeland. These include more and better capital to work with, more natural resources per person, more advanced technologies, sophisticated entrepreneurs and managers, and a political-legal environment that is conducive to high productivity. It is not guaranteed that the value of the immigrant's human capital will rise (it may not, for example, if he speaks no English and has no skills applicable to the U.S. economy), but normally it will.

Since increased productivity leads to higher wages and living standards, on economic grounds, the Bangladeshi worker has a strong incentive to immigrate to the United States if he is able to do so. *(LO3)*

6

The Labor Market: Workers, Wages, and Unemployment

LEARNING OBJECTIVES

After reading this chapter, you should be able to:

LO1 Discuss five important trends that have characterized labor markets in the industrialized world in the past few decades.

LO2 Apply a supply and demand model to understand the labor market.

LO3 Explain how changes in the supply of and demand for labor account for trends in real wages and employment in the past few decades.

LO4 Differentiate among the three types of unemployment defined by economists and the costs associated with each.

Why are you reading this book?

Some readers, thinking about this question in broad terms, may answer: "To better understand the economy" or even "To better understand the world around me." Others, focusing more on the here and now, may answer: "Because it is required reading for my economics class," or even just "To pass the final exam!" Still other readers would offer other answers, or more than one answer.

For an economist, by reading this book (and, more generally, by taking a course or studying for a degree) you are increasing your *human capital*. The concept of human capital was introduced in Chapter 5, *Economic Growth, Productivity, and Living Standards*. We described it as comprising one's talents, education, training, and skills, and said that it is acquired primarily through the investment of time, energy, and money. We also said that workers with more human capital are more productive than those with less human capital. How have these productivity gaps changed over time? To what extent have they translated to income gaps between workers who managed to "keep up" with a modern labor market by acquiring the right skills and those unwilling or unable to do so?

We also examined the remarkable economic growth and increased productivity that have occurred in the industrialized world over the past two centuries. These developments have greatly increased the quantity of goods and services that the economy can produce. But we have not yet discussed how the fruits of economic growth are distributed. Has everyone benefited equally from economic growth and increased productivity? Or, as some writers suggest, is the population divided between those who have caught the "train" of economic modernization, enriching themselves in the process, and those who have been left at the station?[1]

To understand how economic growth and change affect different groups, we must turn to the labor market. Except for retirees and others receiving government support, most people rely almost entirely on wages and salaries to pay their bills and

[1]See, for example, Thomas L. Friedman, *The Lexus and the Olive Tree* (New York: Farrar, Straus & Giroux, 1999).

put something away for the future. Hence, it is in the labor market that most people will see the benefits of the economic growth and increasing productivity. This chapter describes and explains some important trends in the labor markets of industrial countries. Using a supply and demand model of the labor market, we focus first on several important trends in real wages and employment. In the second part of the chapter, we turn to the problem of unemployment, especially long-term unemployment. We will see that two key factors contributing to recent trends in wages, employment, and unemployment are the *globalization* of the economy, as reflected in the increasing importance of international trade, and ongoing *technological change*. By the end of the chapter, you will better understand the connection between these macroeconomic developments and the economic fortunes of workers and their families.

FIVE IMPORTANT LABOR MARKET TRENDS

In recent decades, at least five trends have characterized the labor markets of the industrialized world. We divide these trends into two groups: those affecting real wages and those affecting employment and unemployment.

Trends in Real Wages

1. Over the twentieth century, all industrial countries have enjoyed substantial growth in average real wages.

In the United States in 2018, on average, workers' yearly earnings could command more than twice as many goods and services as in 1960 and more than five times as much as in 1929, just prior to the Great Depression. Similar trends have prevailed in other industrialized countries.

2. Since the early 1970s, however, the rate of average real wage growth has slowed.

Though the post–World War II period has seen impressive increases in average real wages, the fastest rates of increase occurred during the 1960s and early 1970s. In the 13 years between 1960 and 1973, the buying power of workers' incomes rose at a rate of about 2.5 percent per year, a strong rate of increase. But from 1973 to 1995, real yearly earnings grew at only 0.9 percent per year. The good news is that from 1995 to 2007, the eve of the 2007–2009 recession, real earnings grew at 1.9 percent per year, despite a recession in 2001. However, since then earnings growth has slowed again: From 2007 to 2018, real earnings grew at only 0.8 percent per year, and for the whole 1973–2018 period, earnings grew at 1.1 percent a year. It remains to be seen whether a steeper upward trend in average earnings resumes in the next few years.

3. Furthermore, recent decades have brought a pronounced increase in wage inequality in the United States.

A growing gap in real wages between skilled and unskilled workers has been of particular concern. Indeed, the real wages of the least-skilled, least-educated workers have actually *declined* since the early 1970s, according to some studies. At the same time, the best-educated, highest-skilled workers have enjoyed continuing gains in real wages. Data from the *Bureau of Labor Statistics* for a recent year showed that, in the United States, the typical worker with a master's degree earned almost twice the income of a high school graduate and three times the income of a worker with less than a high school degree. Many observers worry that the United States is developing a "two-tier" labor market: plenty of good jobs at good wages for the well-educated and highly skilled, but less and less opportunity for those without schooling or skills.

Outside the United States, particularly in western Europe, the trend toward wage inequality has been much less pronounced. But, as we will see, employment trends in Europe have not been as encouraging as in the United States. Let's turn now to the trends in employment and unemployment.

Trends in Employment and Unemployment

4. In the United States, the number of people with jobs has grown substantially in the past 50 years. The rate of job growth has slowed recently.

In 1970, about 57 percent of the over-16 population in the United States had jobs. By 2000, total U.S. employment exceeded 136 million people, more than 64 percent of the over-16 population. Between 1980 and 2000, the U.S. economy created more than 37 million new jobs—an increase in total employment of 38 percent—while the over-16 population grew only 27 percent. The pace of new job creation has slowed since, dropping below the growth rate of the over-16 population: By late 2019, about 159 million people in the U.S. had jobs, about 61 percent of the over-16 population.

Similar job growth has been a more recent phenomenon in many other industrialized countries.

5. Compared with the U.S., western European countries have, in general, been suffering higher rates of unemployment during much of the past four decades.

In France, Italy, and Spain, for example, an average of 9.9, 9.6, and 16.6 percent of the workforce, respectively, was unemployed over the period 1990–2018, compared to just 5.9 percent in the United States. In that entire period, the unemployment rate was always lower in the United States than in Spain, and it was always lower in the U.S. than in France and Italy except for one relatively short period of time, in the aftermath of the 2008 global financial crisis. Since then, the unemployment gap between the U.S. and Europe increased again. By late 2019, when the unemployment rate in the U.S. was back down to around 3.5 percent—the lowest rate in 50 years—it was around 8.5 percent in France, more than 9.5 percent in Italy, and more than 14 percent in Spain. Figure 6.8, presented later in this chapter, shows recent unemployment rates in five western European countries. As we note there, in recent years, ongoing structural reforms have been improving the unemployment situation in Europe. We also note that by some labor market metrics, such as female participation, Europe does better than the United States.

Given the trend toward increasing wage inequality in the United States and the persistence of high unemployment in Europe, we may conclude that a significant fraction of the industrial world's labor force has not been sharing in the recent economic growth and prosperity.

What explains these trends in employment and wages? In the remainder of the chapter, we will show that a supply and demand analysis of the labor market can help explain these important developments.

RECAP

FIVE IMPORTANT LABOR MARKET TRENDS

1. Over a long period, average real wages have risen substantially both in the United States and in other industrialized countries.
2. Despite the long-term upward trend in real wages, real wage growth has slowed significantly in the United States since the early 1970s.
3. In the United States, wage inequality has increased dramatically in recent decades. The real wages of some unskilled workers have actually declined, while the real wages of skilled and educated workers have continued to rise.
4. Employment has grown substantially in the United States in recent decades. However, the rate of growth has slowed since 2000.
5. Since about 1980, western European nations have experienced very high rates of unemployment and low rates of job creation.

SUPPLY AND DEMAND IN THE LABOR MARKET

We have seen how supply and demand analysis can be used to determine equilibrium prices and quantities for individual goods and services. The same approach is equally useful for studying labor market conditions. In the market for labor, the "price" is the wage paid to workers in exchange for their services. The wage is expressed per unit of time—for example, per hour or per year. The "quantity" is the amount of labor firms use, which in this book we will generally measure by number of workers employed. Alternatively, we could state the quantity of labor in terms of the number of hours worked; the choice of units is a matter of convenience.

Who are the demanders and suppliers in the labor market? Firms and other employers demand labor in order to produce goods and services. Virtually all of us supply labor during some phase of our lives. Whenever people work for pay, they are supplying labor services at a price equal to the wage they receive. In this chapter, we will discuss both the supply of and demand for labor, with an emphasis on the demand side of the labor market. Changes in the demand for labor turn out to be key in explaining the aggregate trends in wages and employment described in the preceding section.

The labor market is studied by microeconomists as well as macroeconomists, and both use the tools of supply and demand. However, microeconomists focus on issues such as the determination of wages for specific types of jobs or workers. In this chapter, we take the macroeconomic approach and examine factors that affect aggregate, or economywide, trends in employment and wages.

Wages and the Demand for Labor

Let's start by thinking about what determines the number of workers employers want to hire at any given wage—that is, the demand for labor. As we will see, the demand for labor depends both on the productivity of labor and the price that the market sets on workers' output. The more productive workers are, or the more valuable the goods and services they produce, the greater the number of workers an employer will want to hire at any given wage.

Table 6.1 shows the relationship between output and the number of workers employed at the Banana Computer Company (BCC), which builds and sells computers. Column 1 of the table shows some different possibilities for the number of technicians BCC could employ in its plant. Column 2 shows how many computers the company can produce each year, depending on the number of workers employed. The more workers, the greater the number of computers BCC can produce. For the sake of simplicity, we assume that the plant, equipment, and materials the workers use to build computers are fixed quantities.

Column 3 of Table 6.1 shows the *marginal product* of each worker, the extra production that is gained by adding one more worker. Note that each additional worker adds less to total production than the previous worker did. The tendency for marginal product to decline as more and more workers are added is called *diminishing returns to labor.* The principle of **diminishing returns to labor** states that if the amount of capital and other inputs in use is held constant, then the greater the quantity of labor already employed, the less each additional worker adds to production.

diminishing returns to labor if the amount of capital and other inputs in use is held constant, then the greater the quantity of labor already employed, the less each additional worker adds to production

The principle of diminishing returns to labor is analogous to the principle of diminishing returns to capital discussed in Chapter 5, *Economic Growth, Productivity, and Living Standards.* The economic basis for diminishing returns to labor is the concept of increasing opportunity cost. A firm's managers want to use their available inputs in the most productive way possible. Hence, an employer who has one worker will assign that worker to the most productive job. If she hires a second worker, she will assign that worker to the second most productive job. The third worker will be given the third most productive job available, and so on. The greater the number of workers already employed, the lower the marginal product of adding another worker, as shown in Table 6.1.

If BCC computers sell for $3,000 each, then column 4 of Table 6.1 shows the *value of the marginal product* of each worker. The value of a worker's marginal product is the amount of extra revenue that the worker generates for the firm. Specifically, the value of the marginal product of each BCC worker is that worker's marginal product, stated in terms of the number of additional computers produced, multiplied by the price of output (here, $3,000 per computer). We now have all the information necessary to find BCC's demand for workers.

TABLE 6.1
Production and Marginal Product for Banana Computers

(1) Number of workers	(2) Computers produced per year	(3) Marginal product	(4) Value of marginal product (at $3,000/computer)
0	0		
		25	$75,000
1	25		
		23	69,000
2	48		
		21	63,000
3	69		
		19	57,000
4	88		
		17	51,000
5	105		
		15	45,000
6	120		
		13	39,000
7	133		
		11	33,000
8	144		

EXAMPLE 6.1 BCC's Demand for Labor

How many workers should BCC hire?

Suppose that the going wage for computer technicians is $60,000 per year. BCC managers know that this is the wage being offered by all their competitors, so they cannot hire qualified workers for less. How many technicians will BCC hire? What would the answer be if the wage were $50,000 per year?

BCC will hire an extra worker if and only if the value of that worker's marginal product (which equals the extra revenue the worker creates for the firm) exceeds the wage BCC must pay. The going wage for computer technicians, which BCC takes as given, is $60,000 per year. Table 6.1 shows that the value of the marginal product of the first, second, and third workers each exceeds $60,000. Hiring these workers will be profitable for BCC because the extra revenue each generates exceeds the wage that BCC must pay. However, the fourth worker's marginal product is worth only $57,000. If BCC's managers hired a fourth worker, they would be paying $60,000 in extra wages for additional output that is worth only $57,000. Since hiring the fourth worker is a money-losing proposition, BCC will hire only three workers. Thus the quantity of labor BCC demands when the going wage is $60,000 per year is three technicians.

If the market wage for computer technicians were $50,000 per year instead of $60,000, the fourth technician would be worth hiring since the value of the fourth technician's marginal product, $57,000, would be $7,000 more than the fourth technician's wages. The fifth technician would also be worth hiring since the fifth worker's marginal product is worth $51,000—$1,000 more than the going wage. The value of the marginal product of a sixth technician, however, is only $45,000, so hiring a sixth worker would not be profitable. When wages are $50,000 per year then, BCC's labor demand is five technicians.

SELF-TEST 6.1

Continuing with Example 6.1, how many workers will BCC hire if the going wage for technicians is $35,000 per year?

The lower the wage a firm must pay, the more workers it will hire. Thus the demand for labor is like the demand for other goods or services in that the quantity demanded rises as the price (in this case, the wage) falls. Figure 6.1 shows a hypothetical labor demand curve for a firm or industry, with the wage on the vertical axis and employment on the horizontal axis. All else being equal, the higher the wage, the fewer workers a firm or industry will demand.

FIGURE 6.1

The Demand Curve for Labor. The demand curve for labor is downward-sloping. The higher the wage, the fewer workers employers will hire.

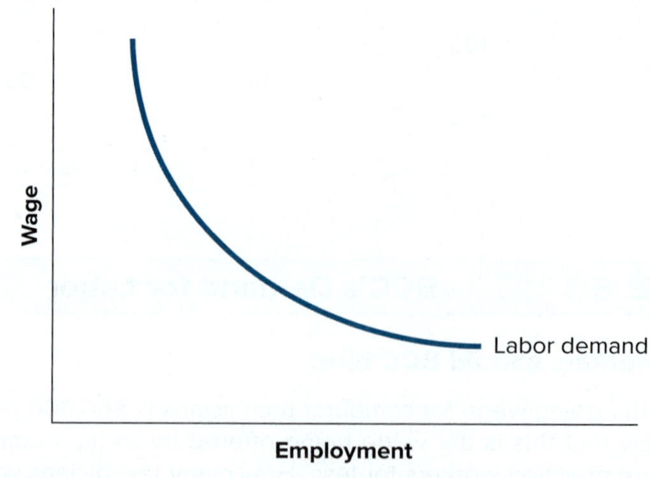

In our example thus far, we have discussed how labor demand depends on the *nominal,* or dollar, wage and the *nominal* price of workers' output. Equivalently, we could have expressed the wage and the price of output in *real* terms—that is, measured relative to the average price of goods and services. The wage measured relative to the general price level is the *real wage;* as we saw in Chapter 4, *Measuring Economic Activity: GDP, Unemployment, and Inflation,* the real wage expresses the wage in terms of its purchasing power. The price of a specific good or service measured relative to the general price level is called the *relative price* of that good or service. Because our main interest is in real rather than nominal wages, from this point on we will analyze the demand for labor in terms of the real wage and the relative price of workers' output, rather than in terms of nominal variables.

Shifts in the Demand for Labor

The number of workers that BCC will employ at any given real wage depends on the value of their marginal product, as shown in column 4 of Table 6.1. Changes in the economy that increase the value of workers' marginal product will increase the value of extra workers to BCC, and thus BCC's demand for labor at any given real wage. In other words, any factor that raises the value of the marginal product of BCC's workers will shift BCC's labor demand curve to the right.

Two main factors could increase BCC's labor demand:

1. An increase in the relative price of the company's output (computers).
2. An increase in the productivity of BCC's workers.

The next two examples illustrate both of these possibilities.

EXAMPLE 6.2 Relative Price and an Increase in Demand

Will BCC hire more workers if the price of computers rises?

Suppose an increase in the demand for BCC's computers raises the relative price of its computers to $5,000 each. How many technicians will BCC hire now, if the real wage is $60,000 per year? If the real wage is $50,000?

The effect of the increase in computer prices is shown in Table 6.2. Columns 1 to 3 of the table are the same as in Table 6.1. The number of computers a given number of technicians can build (column 2) has not changed; hence, the marginal product of particular technicians (column 3) is the same. But because computers can now be sold for $5,000 each instead of $3,000, the *value* of each worker's marginal product has increased by two-thirds (compare column 4 of Table 6.2 with column 4 of Table 6.1).

How does the increase in the relative price of computers affect BCC's demand for labor? Recall from Example 6.1 that when the price of computers was $3,000 and the going wage for technicians was $60,000, BCC's demand for labor was three workers. But now, with computers selling for $5,000 each, the value of the marginal product of each of the first seven workers exceeds $60,000 (Table 6.2). So if the real wage of computer technicians is still $60,000, BCC would increase its demand from three workers to seven.

Suppose instead that the going real wage for technicians is $50,000. In the previous example, when the price of computers was $3,000 and the wage was $50,000, BCC demanded five workers. But if computers sell for $5,000, we can see from column 4 of Table 6.2 that the value of the marginal product of even the eighth worker exceeds the wage of $50,000. So if the real wage is $50,000, the increase in computer prices raises BCC's demand for labor from five workers to eight.

TABLE 6.2

Production and Marginal Product for Banana Computers after an Increase in Computer Prices

(1) Number of workers	(2) Computers produced per year	(3) Marginal product	(4) Value of marginal product ($5,000/computer)
0	0		
		25	$125,000
1	25		
		23	115,000
2	48		
		21	105,000
3	69		
		19	95,000
4	88		
		17	85,000
5	105		
		15	75,000
6	120		
		13	65,000
7	133		
		11	55,000
8	144		

SELF-TEST 6.2

Refer to Example 6.2. How many workers will BCC hire if the going real wage for technicians is $100,000 per year and the relative price of computers is $5,000? Compare your answer to the demand for technicians at a wage of $100,000 when the price of computers is $3,000.

The general conclusion to be drawn from Example 6.2 is that *an increase in the relative price of workers' output increases the demand for labor,* shifting the labor demand curve to the right, as shown in Figure 6.2. A higher relative price for workers' output makes workers more valuable, leading employers to demand more workers at any given real wage.

FIGURE 6.2

A Higher Relative Price of Output Increases the Demand for Labor.

An increase in the relative price of workers' output increases the value of their marginal product, shifting the labor demand curve to the right.

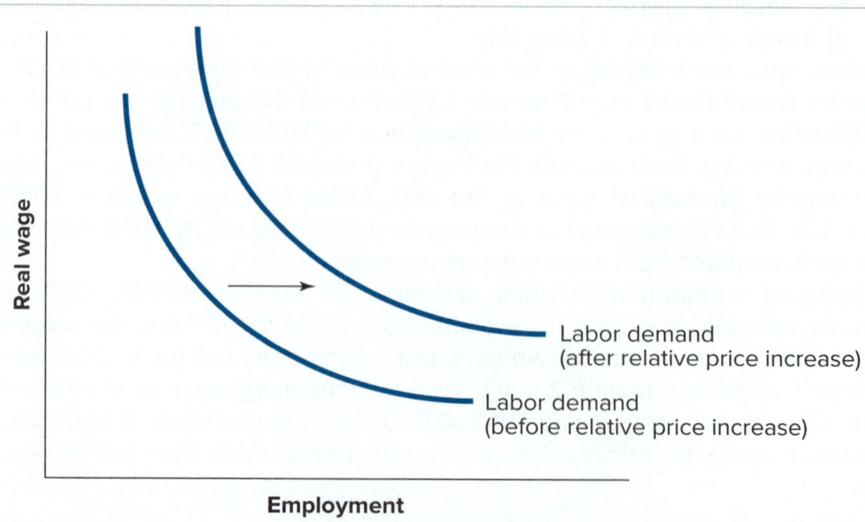

The second factor that affects the demand for labor is worker productivity. Since an increase in productivity increases the value of a worker's marginal product, it also increases the demand for labor, as Example 6.3 shows.

EXAMPLE 6.3 Worker Productivity and Demand for Labor

Will BCC hire more workers if their productivity rises?

Suppose BCC adopts a new technology that reduces the number of components to be assembled, permitting each technician to build 50 percent more machines per year. Assume that the relative price of computers is $3,000 per machine. How many technicians will BCC hire if the real wage is $60,000 per year?

Table 6.3 shows workers' marginal products and the value of their marginal products after the 50 percent increase in productivity, assuming that computers sell for $3,000 each.

Before the productivity increase, BCC would have demanded three workers at a wage of $60,000 (Table 6.1). After the productivity increase, however, the value of the marginal product of the first six workers exceeds $60,000 (see Table 6.3, column 4). So at a wage of $60,000, BCC's demand for labor increases from three workers to six.

TABLE 6.3
Production and Marginal Product for Banana Computers after an Increase in Worker Productivity

(1) Number of workers	(2) Computers produced per year	(3) Marginal product	(4) Value of marginal product (at $3,000/computer)
0	0		
		37.5	$112,500
1	37.5		
		34.5	103,500
2	72		
		31.5	94,500
3	103.5		
		28.5	85,500
4	132		
		25.5	76,500
5	157.5		
		22.5	67,500
6	180		
		19.5	58,500
7	199.5		
		16.5	49,500
8	216		

SELF-TEST 6.3

Refer to Example 6.3. How many workers will BCC hire after the 50 percent increase in productivity if the going real wage for technicians is $50,000 per year? Compare this figure to the demand for workers at a $50,000 wage before the increase in productivity.

In general, *an increase in worker productivity increases the demand for labor,* shifting the labor demand curve to the right, as in Figure 6.3.

FIGURE 6.3

Higher Productivity Increases the Demand for Labor.

An increase in productivity raises workers' marginal product and—assuming no change in the price of output—the value of their marginal product. Since a productivity increase raises the value of marginal product, employers will hire more workers at any given real wage, shifting the labor demand curve to the right.

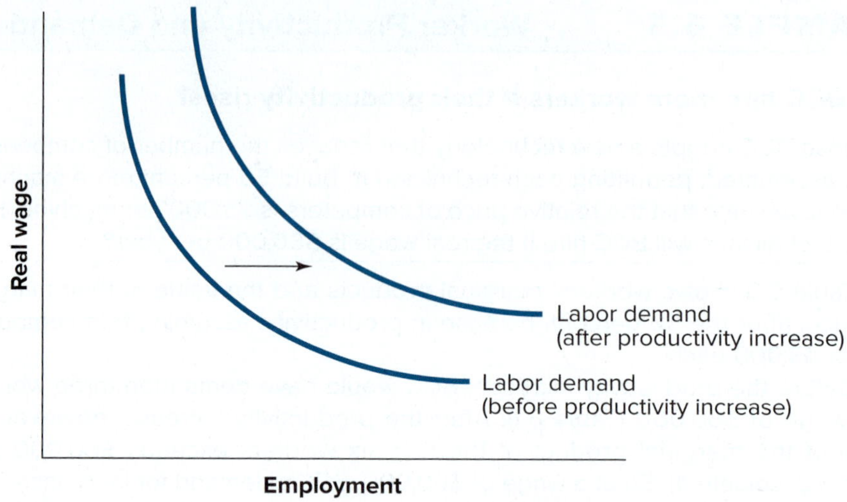

In Example 6.3, the increase in worker productivity that increases the demand for labor is due to the adoption of new technology. But sometimes, new technology can *reduce* the demand for certain workers, as we discuss in The Economic Naturalist 6.1.

The Economic Naturalist 6.1

Can new technology hurt workers?

Technological progress typically makes workers more productive. Examples are abundant. Electric hair dryers and hair clippers, invented more than a hundred years ago by individuals seeking to improve barber tools, make hairstylists more productive. The Global Positioning System (GPS), a satellite-based navigation system developed by the U.S. government a few decades ago, makes drivers more productive. Larger-scale examples include momentous breakthroughs like electricity, the engine, aviation, computing, mobile communication, modern medicine—and the list is still long.

But sometimes, automation and technical innovation can substitute certain types of workers, reducing the demand for such workers. From these workers' point of view, opposing new technology could be rational.

History is replete with examples of workers who opposed new technologies out of fear that their skills would become less valuable. In England in the early nineteenth century, rioting workers destroyed newly introduced labor-saving machinery. The name of the workers' reputed leader, Ned Ludd, has been preserved in the term *Luddite,* meaning a person who is opposed to the introduction of new technologies. The same theme appears in American folk history in the tale of John Henry, the mighty pile-driving man who died in an attempt to show that a human could tunnel into a rock face more quickly than a steam-powered machine.

More recently, some production and service workers have expressed concerns that automation, robotics, and artificial intelligence (AI) may "steal" their jobs. For example, some commercial drivers worry that autonomous cars may eliminate demand for their services. While many technologies unambiguously help drivers—GPS navigation and ride-sharing apps on smartphones, advanced driving-assistance systems in cars, and, of course, cars themselves—some technologies can hurt them.

Historically, the loss of jobs to new technologies has, on average, been compensated by new jobs created by technology. The overall demand for labor has not decreased, unemployment has remained low, and average real wages have risen. But while the average worker is typically much better off with new technology, not all workers are. Later in this chapter, we discuss the role of technology in increasing economic inequalities.

The Supply of Labor

We have discussed the demand for labor by employers; to complete the story we need to consider the supply of labor. The suppliers of labor are workers and potential workers. At any given real wage, potential suppliers of labor must decide if they are willing to work. The total number of people who are willing to work at each real wage is the supply of labor.[2]

EXAMPLE 6.4 Reservation Price for Labor

Will you clean your neighbor's basement or go to the beach?

You were planning to go to the beach today, but your neighbor asks you to clean out his basement. You like the beach a lot more than fighting cobwebs. Do you take the job?

Unless you are motivated primarily by neighborliness, your answer to this job offer would probably be "It depends on how much my neighbor will pay." You probably would not be willing to take the job for $10 or $20 unless you have a severe and immediate need for cash. But if your neighbor were wealthy and eccentric enough to offer you $500 (to take an extreme example), you would very likely say yes. Somewhere between $20 and the unrealistic figure of $500 is the minimum payment you would be willing to accept to tackle the dirty basement. This minimum payment, the *reservation price* you set for your labor, is the compensation level that leaves you just indifferent between working and not working.

In economic terms, deciding whether to work at any given wage is a straightforward application of the *cost-benefit principle*. The cost to you of cleaning out the basement is the opportunity cost of your time (you would rather be surfing) plus the cost you place on having to work in unpleasant conditions. You can measure this total cost in dollars simply by asking yourself, "What is the minimum amount of money I would take to clean out the basement instead of going to the beach?" The minimum payment that you would accept is the same as your reservation price. The benefit of taking the job is measured by the pay you receive, which will go toward that new smartphone you want. You should take the job only if the promised pay (the benefit of working) exceeds your reservation price (the cost of working).

[2]We are still holding the general price level constant, so any increase in the nominal wage also represents an increase in the real wage.

FIGURE 6.4

The Supply of Labor.

The labor supply curve is upward-sloping because, in general, the higher the real wage, the more people are willing to work.

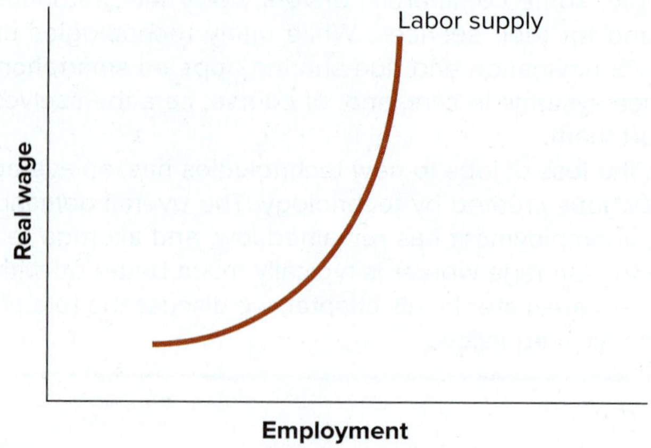

Might accepting a job that pays no salary ever be a good career move?

In this example, your willingness to supply labor is greater the higher the wage. In general, the same is true for the population as a whole. Certainly people work for many reasons, including personal satisfaction, the opportunity to develop skills and talents, and the chance to socialize with coworkers. Still, for most people, income is one of the principal benefits of working, so the higher the real wage, the more willing they are to sacrifice other possible uses of their time. The fact that people are more willing to work when the wage they are offered is higher is captured in the upward slope of the supply curve of labor (see Figure 6.4).

SELF-TEST 6.4

You want to make a career in broadcasting. The local radio station is offering an unpaid summer internship that would give you valuable experience. Your alternative to the internship is to earn $3,000 working in a car wash. How would you decide which job to take? Would a decision to take the internship contradict the conclusion that the labor supply curve is upward-sloping?

Shifts in the Supply of Labor

Any factor that affects the quantity of labor offered at a given real wage will shift the labor supply curve. At the macroeconomic level, the most important factor affecting the supply of labor is the size of the working-age population, which is influenced by factors such as the domestic birthrate, immigration and emigration rates, and the ages at which people normally first enter the workforce and retire. All else being equal, an increase in the working-age population raises the quantity of labor supplied at each real wage, shifting the labor supply curve to the right. Changes in the percentage of people of working age who seek employment—for example, as a result of social changes that encourage women to work outside the home—can also affect the supply of labor.

Now that we have discussed both the demand for and supply of labor, we are ready to apply supply and demand analysis to real-world labor markets. But first, try your hand at using supply and demand analysis to answer the following question.

SELF-TEST 6.5

Labor unions typically favor tough restrictions on immigration, while employers tend to favor more liberal rules. Why? (*Hint:* How is an influx of potential workers likely to affect real wages?)

RECAP

SUPPLY AND DEMAND IN THE LABOR MARKET

The Demand for Labor

The extra production gained by adding one more worker is the *marginal product* of that worker. The *value of the marginal product* of a worker is that worker's marginal product times the relative price of the firm's output. A firm will employ a worker only if the worker's value of marginal product, which is the same as the extra revenue the worker generates for the firm, exceeds the real wage that the firm must pay. The lower the real wage, the more workers the firm will find it profitable to employ. Thus the labor demand curve, like most demand curves, is downward-sloping.

For a given real wage, any change that increases the value of workers' marginal products will increase the demand for labor and shift the labor demand curve to the right. Examples of factors that increase labor demand are an increase in the relative price of workers' output and an increase in productivity.

The Supply of Labor

An individual is willing to supply labor if the real wage that is offered is greater than the opportunity cost of the individual's time. Generally, the higher the real wage, the more people are willing to work. Thus the labor supply curve, like most supply curves, is upward-sloping.

For a given real wage, any factor that increases the number of people available and willing to work increases the supply of labor and shifts the labor supply curve to the right. Examples of factors that increase labor supply include an increase in the working-age population or an increase in the share of the working-age population seeking employment.

EXPLAINING THE TRENDS IN REAL WAGES AND EMPLOYMENT

We are now ready to analyze the important trends in real wages and employment discussed earlier in the chapter.

Large Increases in Real Wages in Industrialized Countries

As we discussed, real annual earnings in the United States have increased more than fivefold since 1929, and other industrialized countries have experienced similar gains. These increases have greatly improved the standard of living of workers in these countries. Why have real wages increased by so much in the United States and other industrialized countries?

The large increase in real wages results from the sustained growth in productivity experienced by the industrialized countries during the twentieth century. (We mentioned this growth in productivity in Chapter 3, *Macroeconomics: The Bird's-Eye View of the Economy*, and discussed its determinants and consequences in Chapter 5,

FIGURE 6.5

An Increase in Productivity Raises the Real Wage.

An increase in productivity raises the demand for labor, shifting the labor demand curve from *D* to *D'*. The real wage rises from *w* to *w'*, and employment rises from *N* to *N'*.

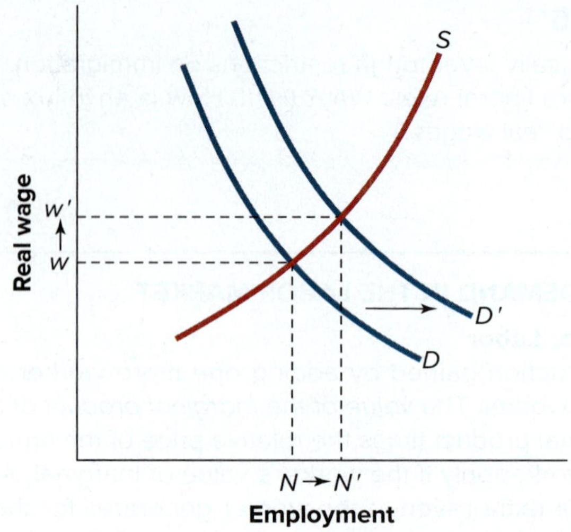

Economic Growth, Productivity, and Living Standards.) As illustrated by Figure 6.5, increased productivity raises the demand for labor, increasing employment and the real wage.

Of the factors contributing to productivity growth in the industrialized countries, two of the most important were (1) the dramatic technological progress that occurred during the twentieth century and (2) large increases in capital stocks, which provided workers with more and better tools with which to work. Labor supply increased during the century as well, of course (not shown in the diagram). However, the increases in labor demand, driven by rapidly expanding productivity, have been so great as to overwhelm the depressing effect on real wages of increased labor supply.

Real Wage Growth in the United States Has Stagnated since the Early 1970s, While Employment Growth Has Been Rapid

With the exception of the late 1990s, rates of real wage growth after 1973 in the United States have been significantly lower than in previous decades. But over much of the period, the economy has created new jobs at a record rate. What accounts for these trends?

Let's begin with the slowdown in real wage growth since the early 1970s. Supply and demand analysis tells us that a slowdown in real wage growth must result from slower growth in the demand for labor, more rapid growth in the supply of labor, or both. On the demand side, since the early 1970s the United States and other industrialized nations have experienced a slowdown in productivity growth. Thus, one possible explanation for the slowdown in the growth of real wages since the early 1970s is the decline in the pace of productivity gains.

Some evidence for a relationship between productivity and real wages is given in Table 6.4, which shows the average annual growth rates in labor productivity and real annual earnings for each decade since 1960. You can see that the growth in productivity decade by decade corresponds closely to the growth in real earnings. Particularly striking is the rapid growth of both productivity and wages during the 1960s. Since the 1970s, growth in both productivity and real wages has been significantly slower, although some improvement was apparent in the 1990s.

While the effects of the slowdown in productivity on the demand for labor are an important reason for declining real wage growth, they can't be the whole story. We

TABLE 6.4
Growth Rates in Productivity and Real Earnings

	Annual Growth Rate (%)	
	Productivity	Real earnings
1960–1970	2.4	2.9
1970–1980	0.8	0.6
1980–1990	1.5	1.3
1990–2000	2.0	2.2
2000–2010	1.6	0.8
2010–2018	0.8	0.9

Source: Federal Reserve Bank of St. Louis. Productivity is real GDP divided by civilian employment; real earnings equal total compensation of employees divided by civilian employment and deflated by the GDP deflator.

know this because, with labor supply held constant, slower growth in labor demand would lead to reduced rates of employment growth, as well as reduced growth in real wages. But job growth in the United States has been rapid in recent decades. Large increases in employment in the face of slow growth of labor demand can be explained only by simultaneous increases in the supply of labor (see Self-Test 6.6).

Labor supply in the United States does appear to have grown rapidly until recently. In particular, increased participation in the labor market by women increased the U.S. supply of labor from the mid-1970s to the late 1990s. Other factors, including the coming of age of the baby boomers and high rates of immigration, also help explain the increase in the supply of labor during those years. The combination of slower growth in labor demand (the result of the productivity slowdown) and accelerated growth in labor supply (the result of increased participation by women in the workforce, together with other factors) helps explain why real wage growth was sluggish for many years in the United States, even as employment grew rapidly.

What about the 2000s? Here the story is different. On the supply side, the participation rate of women in the workforce leveled off and then started slowly declining in the 2000s. This trend reversal, together with the aging population and other factors, slowed down the growth of labor supply. With tightening supply, why was earnings growth so disappointing? Part of the answer is slowing productivity gains. But again, productivity alone cannot be the whole story: As Table 6.4 shows, while increasing more slowly than in the 1990s, on average productivity still grew during the 2000s about twice as fast as real earnings, before slowing further in the 2010s. So another part of the answer must be that the demand for labor slowed more than the supply of labor for reasons other than productivity. One reason could be weak demand for the products of labor—namely, for goods and services. Consistent with this explanation, the 2000s started with a mild recession and ended with a severe one. (Recessions are periods of particularly weak demand, as we will see in later chapters.)

What about the 2010s and the future? As we have seen, labor supply growth is likely to continue slowing as the baby boomers retire. Productivity gains in the 2010s have so far been disappointing, in spite of the 2010s seeing the longest expansion on record. (Expansions, in contrast with recessions, are the periods of growth in demand.) If productivity starts accelerating again, perhaps reflecting the benefits of new technologies, among other factors, there seems a good chance that the more rapid increases in real wages that began around 1996 will return in years to come.

SELF-TEST 6.6

As we have just discussed, relatively weak growth in productivity and relatively strong growth in labor supply after about 1973 can explain (1) the slowdown in real wage growth and (2) the more rapid expansion in employment after about 1973. Show this point graphically by drawing two supply and demand diagrams of the labor market, one corresponding to the period 1960–1973 and the other to 1973–1995. Assuming that productivity growth was strong but labor supply growth was modest during 1960–1973, show that we would expect to see rapid real wage growth but only moderate growth in employment in that period. Now apply the same analysis to 1973–1995, assuming that productivity growth is weaker but labor supply growth stronger than in 1960–1973. What do you predict for growth in the real wage and employment in 1973–1995 relative to the earlier period? What could account for increased real wage growth in the late 1990s?

Increasing Wage Inequality: The Effects of Globalization and Technological Change

Another important trend in U.S. labor markets is increasing inequality in wages, especially the tendency for the wages of the less-skilled and less-educated to fall further and further behind those of better-trained workers. We next discuss two reasons for this increasing inequality: (1) globalization and (2) technological change.

Globalization

Many commentators have blamed the increasing divergence between the wages of skilled and unskilled workers on the phenomenon of "globalization." This term, which became popular in the late 1990s, refers to the fact that to an increasing extent, the markets for many goods and services are becoming international, rather than national or local, in scope. While Americans have long been able to buy products from all over the world, the ease with which goods and services can cross borders in recent decades has been increasing rapidly. In part, this trend is the result of international trade agreements, which reduced taxes on goods and services traded across countries. However, technological advances such as the Internet (which emerged in the 1990s) have also promoted globalization.

The main economic benefit of globalization is increased specialization and the efficiency that it brings. Instead of each country trying to produce everything its citizens consume, each can concentrate on producing those goods and services at which it is relatively most efficient. The result is that consumers of all countries enjoy a greater variety of goods and services, of better quality and at lower prices, than they would without international trade.

The effects of globalization on the *labor* market are mixed, however, which explains why many politicians oppose free-trade agreements. Expanded trade means that consumers stop buying certain goods and services from domestic producers and switch to foreign-made products. Consumers would not make this switch unless the foreign products were better, cheaper, or both, so expanded trade clearly makes them better off. But the workers and firm owners in the domestic industries that lose business may well suffer from the increase in foreign competition.

The effects of increasing trade on the labor market can be analyzed using Figure 6.6. The figure contrasts the supply and demand for labor in two different industries, (a) textiles and (b) computer software. Imagine that, initially, there is little or no international trade in these two goods. Without trade, the demand for workers in each industry is indicated by the curves marked D_{textiles} and D_{software}, respectively. Wages and employment in each industry are determined by the intersection of the demand curves and the labor supply curves in each industry. As we have drawn the

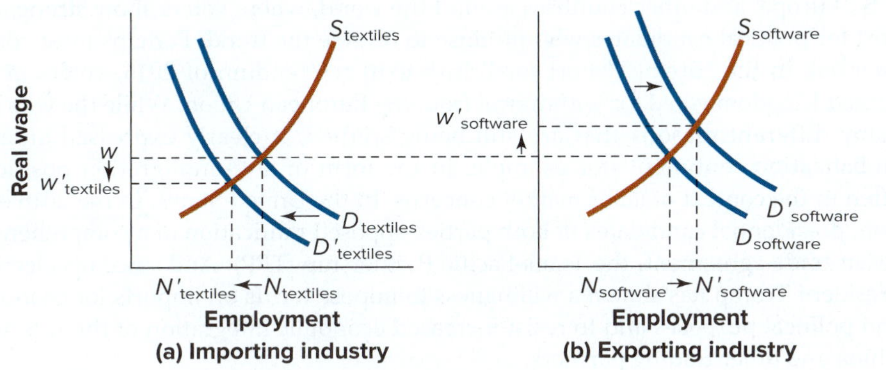

FIGURE 6.6

The Effect of Globalization on the Demand for Workers in Two Industries.

Initially, real wages in the two industries are equal at *w*. After an increase in trade, (a) demand for workers in the importing industry (textiles) declines, lowering real wages and employment, while (b) demand for workers in the exporting industry (software) increases, raising real wages and employment in that industry.

figure, initially, the real wage is the same in both industries, equal to w. Employment is N_{textiles} in textiles and N_{software} in software.

What will happen when this economy is opened up to trade, perhaps because of a free-trade agreement? Under the agreement, countries will begin to produce for export those goods or services at which they are relatively more efficient and to import goods or services that they are relatively less efficient at producing. Suppose the country in this example is relatively more efficient at producing software than manufacturing textiles. With the opening of trade, the country gains new foreign markets for its software and begins to produce for export as well as for domestic use. Meanwhile, because the country is relatively less efficient at producing textiles, consumers begin to purchase foreign-made textiles, which are cheaper or of higher quality, instead of the domestic product. In short, software becomes an exporting industry and textiles an importing industry.

These changes in the demand for domestic products are translated into changes in the demand for labor. The opening of export markets increases the demand for domestic software, raising its relative price. The higher price for domestic software, in turn, raises the value of the marginal products of software workers, shifting the labor demand curve in the software industry to the right, from D_{software} to D'_{software} in Figure 6.6(b). Wages in the software industry rise, from w to w'_{software}, and employment in the industry rises as well. In the textile industry the opposite happens. Demand for domestic textiles falls as consumers switch to imports. The relative price of domestic textiles falls with demand, reducing the value of the marginal product of textile workers and hence the demand for their labor, to D'_{textiles} in Figure 6.6(a). Employment in the textile industry falls, and the real wage falls as well, from w to w'_{textiles}.

In sum, Figure 6.6 shows how globalization can contribute to increasing wage inequality. Initially, we assumed that software workers and textile workers received the same wage. However, the opening up of trade raised the wages of workers in the "winning" industry (software) and lowered the wages of workers in the "losing" industry (textiles), increasing inequality.

In practice, the tendency of trade to increase wage inequality may be even worse than depicted in the example, because the great majority of the world's workers, particularly those in developing countries, have relatively low skill levels. Thus, when industrialized countries like the United States open up trade with developing countries, the domestic industries that are likely to face the toughest international competition are those that use mostly low-skilled labor. Conversely, the domestic industries that are likely to do the best in international competition are those that employ mostly skilled workers. Thus increased trade may lower the wages of those workers in the industrialized country who are already poorly paid and increase the wages of those who are well paid.

The fact that increasing trade may exacerbate wage inequality explains some of the political resistance to globalization. Such resistance is seen in recent years in the U.S., Europe, and other countries around the world, where voters show strong support for political candidates who promise to reverse the trend. Perhaps most consequential, in the "Brexit" (short for British exit) referendum of 2016, voters in the United Kingdom voted for withdrawal from the European Union. While the vote had many different reasons that are still being studied, it clearly expressed an anti-globalization sentiment–for example, in the form of anti-immigration positions, often in the context of labor market concerns. In the United States, in the 2016 election, presidential candidates of both parties opposed ratification of a comprehensive Asian trade agreement, the Trans-Pacific Partnership (TPP). And since his election, President Trump has shown a willingness to impose tariffs on imports for economic and political purposes and to resist increased economic integration of the U.S. with China and other trading partners.

But attempts to reverse the trend of globalization, if they succeed, would come with their own costs to society because increasing trade and specialization is a major source of improvement in living standards in the United States, Europe, the United Kingdom, and other countries. Indeed, the economic forces behind globalization–primarily, the desire of consumers for better and cheaper products and of producers for new markets–are so powerful that the process would be hard to stop even if government officials were determined to do so.

Rather than trying to stop globalization, helping the labor market adjust to the effects of globalization may be a better course. Indeed, our analysis of supply and demand in the labor market suggests that to a certain extent, *at least in theory,* the economy will adjust on its own. Figure 6.6 showed that, following the opening to trade, real wages and employment fall in (a) textiles and rise in (b) software. At that point, wages and job opportunities are much more attractive in the software industry than in textiles. Will this situation persist? Clearly, there is a strong incentive for workers who are able to do so to leave the textile industry and seek employment in the software industry.

worker mobility the movement of workers between jobs, firms, and industries

The movement of workers between jobs, firms, and industries is called **worker mobility.** In our example, worker mobility will tend to reduce labor supply in textiles and increase it in software, as workers move from the contracting industry to the growing one. This process will reverse some of the increase in wage inequality by raising wages in textiles and lowering them in software. It will also shift workers from a less competitive sector to a more competitive sector. To some extent, then, *in theory,* the labor market can adjust on its own to the effects of globalization.

Of course, *in practice,* the adjustment process is never quick, easy, or painless. While left outside our simple supply and demand model, in reality there are many barriers to a textile worker becoming a software engineer. Indeed, as reported in The Economic Naturalist 12.1, empirical evidence suggests that the reallocation of U.S. workers from less competitive sectors to more competitive ones can be painfully slow. In the case of opening up to trade with an economy like China, which has a large supply of low-skill workers, the adjustment of many U.S. workers could be difficult and could take many years.

As we discussed in Chapter 12, *International Trade and Trade Policy,* then, there may also be a need for *transition aid* to workers in the affected sectors. Ideally, such aid helps workers train for and find new jobs. If that is not possible or desirable–say, because a worker is nearing retirement–transition aid can take the form of government payments to help the worker maintain his or her standard of living. In addition, redevelopment aid may be needed in affected communities, as the slow adjustment process of affected workers may come with both economic and social problems. Transition aid and similar programs are also efficient because trade and specialization increase the total economic pie. The "winners" from globalization can afford the taxes necessary to finance aid and still enjoy a net benefit from increased trade. Developing effective aid programs is thus a priority.

Technological Change

A second source of increasing wage inequality is ongoing technological change that favors more highly skilled or educated workers. As we have seen, new scientific knowledge and the technological advances associated with it are a major source of improved productivity and economic growth. Increases in worker productivity are in turn a driving force behind wage increases and higher average living standards. In the long run and on average, technological progress is undoubtedly the worker's friend.

McGraw Hill connect

▶ Visit your instructor's Connect course and access your eBook to view this video.

Why have the salaries of top earners' been growing so much faster than everyone else's?

This sweeping statement is not true at all times and in all places, however. Whether a particular technological development is good for a particular worker depends on the effect of that innovation on the worker's value of marginal product and, hence, on his or her wage. For example, at one time the ability to add numbers rapidly and accurately was a valuable skill; a clerk with that skill could expect advancement and higher wages. However, the invention and mass production of the electronic calculator has rendered human calculating skills less valuable, to the detriment of those who have that skill. The Economic Naturalist 6.1 (on page 166) discussed more examples, from history and present.

How do these observations bear on wage inequality? According to some economists, many recent technological advances have taken the form of **skill-biased technological change**—that is, technological change that affects the marginal product of higher-skilled workers differently from that of lower-skilled workers. Specifically, technological developments in recent decades appear to have favored more-skilled and educated workers.

skill-biased technological change technological change that affects the marginal products of higher-skilled workers differently from those of lower-skilled workers

Developments in automobile production are a case in point. The advent of mass production techniques in the 1920s provided highly paid work for several generations of relatively low-skilled autoworkers. But in recent years automobile production, like the automobiles themselves, has become considerably more sophisticated. The simplest production jobs have been taken over by robots and computer-controlled machinery, which require skilled operatives and engineers who know how to use and maintain the new equipment. Consumer demand for luxury features and customized options has also raised the automakers' demand for highly skilled workers. Thus, in general, the skill requirements for jobs in automobile production have risen.

Figure 6.7 illustrates the effects of technological change that favors skilled workers. Figure 6.7(a) shows the market for unskilled workers; Figure 6.7(b) shows the market for skilled workers. The demand curves labeled $D_{\text{unskilled}}$ and D_{skilled} show the demand for each type of worker before a skill-biased technological change. Wages and employment for each type of worker are determined by the intersection of the demand and supply curves in each market. Figure 6.7 shows that, even before the

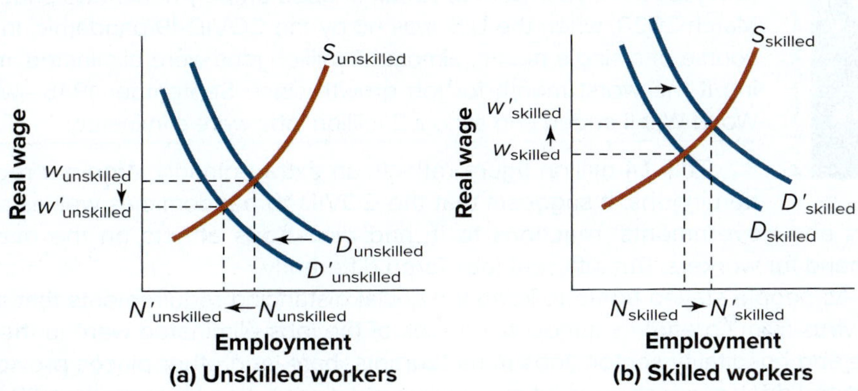

FIGURE 6.7

The Effect of Skill-Biased Technological Change on Wage Inequality.

The figure shows the effects of a skill-biased technological change that increases the marginal product of skilled workers and reduces the marginal product of unskilled workers. The resulting increase in the demand for skilled workers raises their wages (b), while the decline in demand for unskilled workers reduces their wages (a). Wage inequality increases.

technological change, unskilled workers received lower real wages than skilled workers ($w_{\text{unskilled}} < w_{\text{skilled}}$), reflecting the lower marginal products of the unskilled.

Now suppose that a new technology–computer-controlled machinery, for example–is introduced. This technological change is biased toward skilled workers, which means that it raises their marginal productivity relative to unskilled workers. We will assume in this example that the new technology also lowers the marginal productivity of unskilled workers, perhaps because they are unable to use the new technology, but all that is necessary for our conclusions is that they benefit less than skilled workers. Figure 6.7 shows the effect of this change in marginal products. In part (b) the increase in the marginal productivity of skilled workers raises the demand for those workers; the demand curve shifts rightward to D'_{skilled}. Accordingly, the real wages and employment of skilled workers also rise. In contrast, because they have been made less productive by the technological change, the demand for unskilled workers shifts leftward to $D'_{\text{unskilled}}$ [Figure 6.7(a)]. Lower demand for unskilled workers reduces their real wages and employment.

In summary, this analysis supports the conclusion that technological change that is biased in favor of skilled workers will tend to increase the wage gap between the skilled and unskilled. Empirical studies have confirmed the role of skill-biased technological change in recent increases in wage inequality.

Because new technologies that favor skilled workers increase wage inequality, should government regulators act to block them? As in the case of globalization, most economists would argue against trying to block new technologies since technological advances are necessary for economic growth and improved living standards. If the Luddites had somehow succeeded in preventing the introduction of labor-saving machinery in Great Britain, economic growth and development over the past few centuries might have been greatly reduced.

The remedies for the problem of wage inequalities caused by technological change are similar to those for wage inequalities caused by globalization. First among them is worker mobility. As the pay differential between skilled and unskilled work increases, unskilled workers will have a stronger incentive to acquire education and skills, to everyone's benefit. A second remedy is transition aid. Government policymakers should consider programs that will help workers retrain if they are able, or provide income support if they are not.

The Economic Naturalist 6.2

How did the COVID-19 pandemic affect the demand for U.S. jobs?

Terry Pierson/ZUMA Press/Newscom

The pandemic didn't reduce demand for these workers.

In the 10 years from February 2010 to February 2020, the U.S. economy created on average 190,000 new jobs each month, or almost 2.3 million new jobs each year. But the streak of good employment news ended in March 2020, when the U.S. was hit by the COVID-19 pandemic. In the course of a single month, almost 1.4 million jobs were eliminated, making it the worst month for job growth since September 1945—when World War II ended and almost 2 million jobs were eliminated.

This 1.4-million figure reflects an extraordinarily large *net* reduction in jobs. It suggests that the COVID-19 pandemic as well as people's and governments' reactions to it, had disastrous effects on the *overall* demand for workers. But different jobs fared differently.

As people stayed home to keep the social distancing requirements that stop the virus from spreading, almost two-thirds of the jobs eliminated were in the leisure and hospitality sector. Jobs in restaurants, bars, and other places providing food and drink services were hit especially hard, accounting for more than 90 percent of the lost jobs in that sector. Many of these jobs are low-skilled jobs.

At the same time, the economy created tens of thousands of jobs in other sectors. It is no surprise that new jobs were created in hospitals and outpatient care centers. In addition, as the economy was transitioning to dealing with the pandemic new jobs were added in finance and insurance, management, accounting, computer systems, technical consulting, scientific research and development, data processing, and other information services. Many of these added jobs require education, training, and experience, and some of them can be done from home. But thousands of new jobs were also added that require less skill, including in retail, warehousing, storage, and supermarkets.

These different trends in different parts of the economy continued later on. For example, as tourism plummeted, jobs in airlines and hotels were eliminated with unprecedented speed. At the same time, online shopping increased so dramatically that Amazon announced in mid-March that it was going to hire 100,000 new warehouse and delivery workers. Overall, though, the pandemic's *net* effect on the demand for jobs was unambiguously large and negative. Indeed, the destruction of 1.4 million jobs in March was dwarfed by the destruction of almost 21 million jobs in April. That's almost one in seven U.S. jobs, eliminated in a single month!

These shifts in the demand for labor could have important long-run effects even after the crisis is over. For example, there might be more teleworking and online shopping in the future at the expense of transportation and brick-and-mortar stores. In addition, small businesses that do not survive might result in some industries being more dominated by larger firms. All this remains to be seen.

RECAP

EXPLAINING THE TRENDS IN REAL WAGES AND EMPLOYMENT

- The long-term increase in real wages enjoyed by workers in industrial countries results primarily from large productivity gains, which have raised the demand for labor. Technological progress and an expanded and modernized capital stock are two important reasons for these long-term increases in productivity.
- The slowdown in real wage growth that began in the 1970s resulted in part from the slowdown in productivity growth (and, hence, the slower growth in labor demand) that occurred at about the same time. Increased labor supply, arising from such factors as the increased participation of women and the coming of age of the baby boom generation, depressed real wages further while also expanding employment. In the latter part of the 1990s, resurgence in productivity growth was accompanied by an increase in real wage growth. If such productivity growth returns in years to come, real wages are expected to resume their faster growth. The slower growth in labor supply since around 2000, resulting from a reversal in the earlier participation trends, is expected to further strengthen real wage growth.
- Both globalization and skill-biased technological change contribute to wage inequality. Globalization raises the wages of workers in exporting industries by raising the demand for those workers, while reducing the wages of workers in importing industries. Technological change that favors more-skilled workers increases the demand for such workers, and hence their wages, relative to the wages of less-skilled workers.
- Attempting to block either globalization or technological change is not the best response to the problem of wage inequality. To some extent, worker mobility (movement of workers from low-wage to high-wage industries) will offset the inequality created by these forces. Where mobility is not practical, or, as is often the case, is slow, transition aid—government assistance to workers whose employment prospects have worsened—may be the best solution. Developing effective assistance programs is thus a priority.

UNEMPLOYMENT

The concept of the unemployment rate was introduced in Chapter 4, *Measuring Economic Activity: GDP, Unemployment, and Inflation.* To review, government survey takers classify adults as employed (holding a job), unemployed (not holding a job, but looking for one), or not in the labor force (not holding a job and not looking for one—retirees, for example). The labor force consists of the employed and the unemployed. The unemployment rate is the percentage of the labor force that is unemployed.

Unemployment rates differ markedly from country to country. (Different countries measure their unemployment rates in slightly different ways; one should be careful to compare only unemployment rates that are either measured similarly or adjusted to be comparable.) Unemployment rates also vary with time. In the United States, unemployment rates reached historic lows in 2000—4 percent of the labor force—but were almost 2.5 times higher a decade later—reaching 9.6 percent in 2010—before gradually declining to become the lowest in 50 years—3.5 percent in late 2019. In many western European countries, unemployment rates for many years have been two to three times the U.S. rate (the years following the 2007–2009 recession were an exception). In Europe, unemployment is exceptionally high among young people.

A high unemployment rate has serious economic, psychological, and social costs. Understanding the causes of unemployment and finding ways to reduce it are therefore major concerns of macroeconomists. In the remainder of this chapter we discuss the causes and costs of three types of unemployment, and we will also consider some features of labor markets that may exacerbate the problem.

Types of Unemployment and Their Costs

Economists have found it useful to think of unemployment as being of three broad types: *frictional* unemployment, *structural* unemployment, and *cyclical* unemployment. Each type of unemployment has different causes and imposes different economic and social costs.

Frictional Unemployment

The function of the labor market is to match available jobs with available workers. If all jobs and workers were the same, or if the set of jobs and workers were static and unchanging, this matching process would be quick and easy. But the real world is more complicated. In practice, both jobs and workers are highly *heterogeneous*. Jobs differ in their location, in the skills they require, in their working conditions and hours, and in many other ways. Workers differ in their career aspirations, their skills and experience, their preferred working hours, their willingness to travel, and so on.

The real labor market is also *dynamic,* or constantly changing and evolving. On the demand side of the labor market, technological advances, globalization, and changing consumer tastes spur the creation of new products, new firms, and even new industries, while outmoded products, firms, and industries disappear. Thus CD players replaced record players and then were replaced by media-playing apps and streaming services. As a result of this upheaval, new jobs are constantly being created, while some old jobs cease to be viable. The workforce in a modern economy is equally dynamic. People move, gain new skills, leave the labor force for a time to rear children or go back to school, and even change careers.

Because the labor market is heterogeneous and dynamic, the process of matching jobs with workers often takes time. For example, a software engineer who loses or quits her job in Silicon Valley may take weeks or even months to find an appropriate new job. In her search, she will probably consider alternative areas of software development or even totally new challenges. She may also want to think about different regions of the country in which software companies are located, such as North Carolina's Research Triangle or New York City's Silicon Alley. During the period in which she is searching for a new job, she is counted as unemployed.

Short-term unemployment that is associated with the process of matching workers with jobs is called **frictional unemployment.** The *costs* of frictional unemployment are low and may even be negative; that is, frictional unemployment may be economically beneficial. First, frictional unemployment is short term, so its psychological effects and direct economic losses are minimal. Second, to the extent that the search process leads to a better match between worker and job, a period of frictional unemployment is actually productive, in the sense that it leads to higher output over the long run. Indeed, a certain amount of frictional unemployment seems essential to the smooth functioning of a rapidly changing, dynamic economy.

frictional unemployment the short-term unemployment associated with the process of matching workers with jobs

Structural Unemployment

A second major type of unemployment is **structural unemployment,** or the long-term and chronic unemployment that exists even when the economy is producing at a normal rate. Several factors contribute to structural unemployment. First, a *lack of skills, language barriers,* or *discrimination* keeps some workers from finding stable, long-term jobs. Migrant farmworkers and unskilled construction workers who find short-term or temporary jobs from time to time, but never stay in one job for very long, fit the definition of chronically unemployed.

structural unemployment the long-term and chronic unemployment that exists even when the economy is producing at a normal rate

Second, economic changes sometimes create a *long-term mismatch* between the skills some workers have and the available jobs. The U.S. steel industry, for example, has declined over the years, while the computer software industry has grown rapidly. Ideally, steelworkers who lose their jobs would be able to find new jobs in software firms (worker mobility), so their unemployment would be only frictional in nature. In practice, of course, many ex-steelworkers lack the education, ability, or interest necessary to work in the software industry. Since their skills are no longer in demand, these workers may drift into chronic or long-term unemployment.

Finally, structural unemployment can result from *structural features of the labor market* that act as barriers to employment. Examples of such barriers include laws that limit certain types of government help to people without jobs, thus discouraging people from taking a job (and losing their benefits as a result).

The *costs* of structural unemployment are much higher than those of frictional unemployment. Because structurally unemployed workers do little productive work over long periods, their idleness causes substantial economic losses both to the unemployed workers and to society. Structurally unemployed workers also lose out on the opportunity to develop new skills on the job, and their existing skills wither from disuse. Long spells of unemployment are also much more difficult for workers to handle psychologically than the relatively brief spells associated with frictional unemployment.

Cyclical Unemployment

The third type of unemployment occurs during periods of recession (that is, periods of unusually low production) and is called **cyclical unemployment.** Sharp peaks in unemployment reflect the cyclical unemployment that occurs during recessions. Increases in cyclical unemployment, although they are relatively short-lived, are associated with significant declines in real GDP and are therefore quite costly economically. We will study cyclical unemployment in more detail later in the chapters dealing with booms and recessions.

cyclical unemployment the extra unemployment that occurs during periods of recession

In principle, frictional, structural, and cyclical unemployment add up to the total unemployment rate. In practice, sharp distinctions often cannot be made between the different categories, so any breakdown of the total unemployment rate into the three types of unemployment is necessarily subjective and approximate.

Impediments to Full Employment

In discussing structural unemployment, we mentioned that structural features of the labor market may contribute to long-term and chronic unemployment. One such structural feature is the availability of *unemployment insurance,* or government transfer payments to unemployed workers. Unemployment insurance provides an important social benefit in that it helps the unemployed to maintain a decent standard of living while they are looking for a job. But because its availability allows the unemployed to search longer or less intensively for a job, it may lengthen the average amount of time the typical unemployed worker is without a job.

Most economists would argue that unemployment insurance should be generous enough to provide basic support to the unemployed but not so generous as to remove the incentive to actively seek work. Thus, unemployment insurance should last for only a limited time, and its benefits should not be as high as the income a worker receives when working.

Many other government regulations bear on the labor market. They include *health and safety regulations,* which establish the safety standards employers must follow, and rules that prohibit racial or gender-based discrimination in hiring. Many of these regulations are beneficial. In some cases, however, the costs of complying with regulations may exceed the benefits they provide. Further, to the extent that regulations increase employer costs and reduce productivity, they depress the demand for labor, lowering real wages and contributing to unemployment. For maximum economic efficiency, legislators should use *cost-benefit criterion* when deciding what regulations to impose on the labor market.

The points raised in this section can help us understand one of the important labor market trends discussed earlier in the chapter, namely, the persistence of high unemployment in western Europe. For several decades, unemployment has been exceptionally high in the major countries of western Europe, as Figure 6.8 shows. The figure shows "harmonized unemployment rates"—unemployment rates that are calculated by applying a uniform definition to data from different countries, facilitating comparisons. From 1995 to 2005, for example, the harmonized unemployment rate was roughly in the range of 8–11 percent in Germany, 9–12 percent in France, 8–11 percent in Italy, and 9–21 percent in Spain, compared with 5–6 percent in the U.S. In the 1950s, 1960s, and 1970s, western Europe consistently enjoyed very low unemployment rates. Why has European unemployment been so stubbornly high for the past decades?

One explanation for the high unemployment in major western European countries is the existence of structural "rigidities" in their labor markets. Relative to the United States, European labor markets have historically been highly regulated. European governments set rules in matters ranging from the number of weeks of vacation workers must receive to the reasons for which a worker can be dismissed. Minimum wages in Europe are historically high, and unemployment benefits are much more

FIGURE 6.8

Unemployment Rates in Western Europe, 1991–2018.

In the largest economies in continental western Europe, unemployment rates have been high in recent decades.

Source: Harmonized unemployment rates, Federal Reserve of St. Louis Economic Data, https://fred.stlouisfed.org.

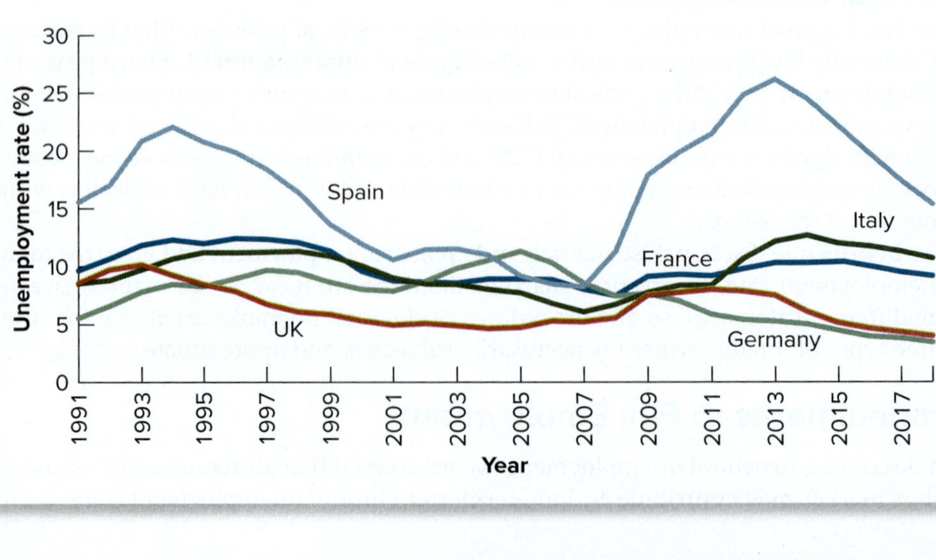

generous than in the United States. European unions are also more powerful than those in the United States; their wage agreements are often extended by law to all firms in the industry, whether or not they are unionized. This lack of flexibility in labor markets has caused higher frictional and structural unemployment.

If European labor markets are historically so dysfunctional, why has serious European unemployment emerged only in the past few decades? One explanation turns on the increasing pace of *globalization* and *skill-biased technological change.* As we saw, these two factors decrease the demand for less-skilled labor relative to the demand for skilled labor. In the United States, falling demand has depressed the wages of the less skilled, increasing wage inequality. But in western Europe, high minimum wages, union contracts, generous unemployment insurance, and other factors may have created a floor for the wage that firms could pay or that workers would accept. As the marginal productivity of the less skilled dropped below that floor, firms no longer found it profitable to employ those workers, swelling the ranks of the unemployed. Thus the combination of labor market rigidity and the declining marginal productivity of low-skilled workers may be responsible for the European unemployment problem.

Evidence for the idea that inflexible labor markets have contributed to European unemployment comes from the United Kingdom, where the government of Prime Minister Margaret Thatcher instituted a series of reforms beginning in the early 1980s. Britain has since largely deregulated its labor market so that it functions much more like that in the United States. Figure 6.8 shows that unemployment in Britain has gradually declined and is now lower than in other western European countries.

More recently, during 2003–2005, Germany enacted a series of labor market reforms (the "Hartz reforms") under the government of Chancellor Gerhard Schröder. Aimed at increasing the flexibility of Germany's labor markets, the reforms attempted, among other things, to make it easier for employers to hire for short periods and to make it harder for the unemployed to receive generous benefits for long periods. The reforms were controversial, and it is too early for a comprehensive assessment of their long-term impact. That said, as Figure 6.8 shows, the unemployment rate in Germany dropped sharply in the years since the reforms—from above 11 percent in 2005 to below 3.5 percent in 2018—setting Germany apart from the rest of continental Europe's large economies. Most recently, in the past decade (in the aftermath of the global recession following the 2008 financial crisis), countries in southern Europe have been implementing substantial labor market deregulation, including France, Spain, Italy, Greece, and Portugal. The effects of these reforms will be closely studied by economists in the next few years. Labor market reforms like those in Europe are examples of *structural policies*.

Finally, we note that on some metrics, Europe's labor market does better than the U.S. labor market. One example is female participation, where policies like greater support for child-care services make it easier for women in Europe to work in the formal labor market. Such policies, too, are examples of structural policies.

RECAP

UNEMPLOYMENT

Economists distinguish among three broad types of unemployment. *Frictional unemployment* is the short-term unemployment that is associated with the process of matching workers with jobs. *Structural unemployment* is the long-term or chronic unemployment that occurs even when the economy is producing at a normal rate. *Cyclical unemployment* is the extra unemployment that occurs during periods of recession. Frictional unemployment may be economically beneficial, as improved matching of workers and jobs may increase output in the long run. Structural and cyclical unemployment impose heavy economic costs on workers and society, as well as psychological costs on workers and their families.

Structural features of the labor market may cause structural unemployment. Examples of such features are unemployment insurance, which allows unemployed workers to search longer or less intensively for a job, and government regulations that impose extra costs on employers. Regulation of the labor market is not necessarily undesirable, but it should be subject to cost-benefit analysis. Heavy labor market regulation and high unionization rates in western Europe help explain the persistence, until recently, of high unemployment rates in some of those countries. At the same time, regulation that requires, for example, more comprehensive child-care and leave programs, could increase employment, in particular among women.

SUMMARY

- For the average person, the most tangible result of economic growth and increasing productivity is the availability of "good jobs at good wages." Over the long run, the U.S. economy has, for the most part, delivered on this promise as both real wages and employment have grown strongly. But while growth in employment has generally been rapid, two worrisome trends dog the U.S. labor market: a slowdown since the early 1970s in the growth of real wages and increasing wage inequality. Western Europe has experienced less wage inequality but significantly higher rates of unemployment than the United States. *(LO1)*

- Trends in real wages and employment can be studied using a supply and demand model of the labor market. The productivity of labor and the relative price of workers' output determine the demand for labor. Employers will hire workers only as long as the value of the marginal product of the last worker hired equals or exceeds the wage the firm must pay. Because of *diminishing returns to labor,* the more workers a firm employs, the less additional product will be obtained by adding yet another worker. The lower the going wage, the more workers will be hired; that is, the demand for labor curve slopes downward. Economic changes that increase the value of labor's marginal product, such as an increase in the relative price of workers' output or an increase in productivity, shift the labor demand curve to the right. Conversely, changes that reduce the value of labor's marginal product shift the labor demand curve to the left. *(LO2)*

- The supply curve for labor shows the number of people willing to work at any given real wage. Since more people will work at a higher real wage, the supply curve is upward-sloping. An increase in the working-age population, or a social change that promotes labor market participation (like increased acceptance of women in the labor force), will raise labor supply and shift the labor supply curve to the right. *(LO2)*

- Improvements in productivity, which raise the demand for labor, account for the bulk of the increase in U.S. real wages over the last century. The slowdown in real wage growth that has occurred in recent decades is the result of slower growth in labor demand, which was caused in turn by a slowdown in the rate of productivity improvement, and of more rapid growth in labor supply. Rapid growth in labor supply, caused by such factors as immigration and increased labor force participation by women, has until recently also contributed to the continued expansion of employment. Recently, however, overall labor force participation has been decreasing. *(LO3)*

- Two reasons for the increasing wage inequality in the United States are economic globalization and *skill-biased technological change*. Both have increased the demand for, and hence the real wages of, relatively skilled and educated workers. Attempting to block globalization and technological change is counterproductive, however, since both factors are essential to economic growth and increased productivity. To some extent, the movement of workers from lower-paying to higher-paying jobs or industries (*worker mobility*) will counteract the trend toward wage inequality. A policy of providing transition aid and training for workers with obsolete skills is a more useful response to the problem. *(LO3)*

- There are three broad types of unemployment: frictional, structural, and cyclical. *Frictional unemployment* is the short-term unemployment associated with the process of matching workers with jobs in a dynamic, heterogeneous labor market. *Structural unemployment* is the long-term and chronic unemployment that exists even when the economy is producing at a normal rate. It arises from a variety of factors, including language barriers, discrimination, structural features of the labor market, lack of skills, or long-term mismatches between the skills workers have and the available jobs. *Cyclical unemployment* is the extra unemployment that occurs during periods of recession. The costs of frictional unemployment are low, as it tends to be brief and to create more productive matches between workers and jobs. But structural unemployment, which is often long term, and cyclical unemployment, which is associated with significant reductions in real GDP, are relatively more costly. *(LO4)*

- Structural features of the labor market that may contribute to unemployment include unemployment insurance, which reduces the incentives of the unemployed to find work quickly, and other government regulations, which—although possibly conferring benefits—increase the costs of employing workers. The labor market "rigidity" created by government regulations and union contracts has historically been more of a problem in western Europe than in the United States, which may account for Europe's high unemployment rates. *(LO4)*

KEY TERMS

cyclical unemployment
diminishing returns to labor
frictional unemployment
skill-biased technological change
structural unemployment
worker mobility

REVIEW QUESTIONS

1. List and discuss the five important labor market trends given in the first section of the chapter. How do these trends either support or qualify the proposition that increasing labor productivity leads to higher standards of living? *(LO1)*
2. Acme Corporation is considering hiring Marisa Fabrizio. Based on her other opportunities in the job market, Marisa has told Acme that she will work for them for $40,000 per year. How should Acme determine whether to employ her? *(LO2)*
3. Why have real wages risen by so much in the United States in the past century? Why did real wage growth slow for 25 years beginning in the early 1970s? What has been happening to real wages recently? *(LO3)*
4. What are two major factors contributing to increased inequality in wages? Briefly, why do these factors raise wage inequality? Contrast possible policy responses to increasing inequality in terms of their effects on economic efficiency. *(LO3)*
5. List three types of unemployment and their causes. Which of these types is economically and socially the least costly? Explain. *(LO4)*

PROBLEMS

connect

1. Data on the average earnings of people of different education levels are available from the Bureau of the Census (try online at www.census.gov/population/socdemo/education/tableA-3.txt). Using these data, prepare a table showing the earnings of college graduates relative to high school graduates and of college graduates relative to those with less than a high school degree. Show the data for the latest year available and for every fifth year going back to the earliest data available. What are the trends in relative earnings? *(LO1)*
2. Production data for Bob's Bicycle Factory are as follows.

Number of workers	Bikes assembled/day
1	10
2	18
3	24
4	28
5	30

Other than wages, Bob has costs of $100 (for parts and so on) for each bike assembled. *(LO2)*

a. Bikes sell for $130 each. Find the marginal product and the value of the marginal product for each worker (don't forget about Bob's cost of parts).
b. Make a table showing Bob's demand curve for labor.
c. Repeat part b for the case in which bikes sell for $140 each.
d. Repeat part b for the case in which worker productivity increases by 50 percent. Bikes sell for $130 each.

3. The following table lists the marginal product per hour of workers in a lightbulb factory. Lightbulbs sell for $2 each, and there are no costs to producing them other than labor costs. *(LO2)*

Number of workers	Marginal product: lightbulbs/hr
1	24
2	22
3	20
4	18
5	16
6	14
7	12
8	10
9	8
10	6

a. The going hourly wage for factory workers is $24 per hour. How many workers should the factory manager hire? What if the wage is $36 per hour?
b. Graph the factory's demand for labor.
c. Repeat part b for the case in which lightbulbs sell for $3 each.
d. Suppose the supply of factory workers in the town in which the lightbulb factory is located is 8 workers (in other words, the labor supply curve is vertical at 8 workers). What will be the equilibrium real wage for factory workers in the town if lightbulbs sell for $2 each? If they sell for $3 each?

4. How would each of the following factors be likely to affect the economywide supply of labor? *(LO2)*
   a. The age at which people are eligible for Medicare is increased.
   b. Increased productivity causes real wages to rise.
   c. War preparations lead to the institution of a national draft, and many young people are called up.
   d. More people decide to have children (consider both short-run and long-run effects).
   e. Social Security benefits are made more generous.

5. How would each of the following likely affect the real wage and employment of unskilled workers on an automobile plant assembly line? *(LO3)*
   a. Demand for the type of car made by the plant increases.
   b. A sharp increase in the price of gas causes many commuters to switch to mass transit.
   c. Robots are introduced to do most basic assembly-line tasks.

6. Skilled or unskilled workers can be used to produce a small toy. Initially, assume that the wages paid to both types of workers are equal. *(LO3)*
   a. Suppose that electronic equipment is introduced that increases the marginal product of skilled workers (who can use the equipment to produce more toys per hours worked). The marginal products of unskilled workers are unaffected. Explain, using words and graphs, what happens to the equilibrium wages for the two groups.
   b. Suppose that unskilled workers find it worthwhile to acquire skills when the wage differential between skilled and unskilled workers reaches a certain point. Explain what will happen to the supply of unskilled workers, the supply of skilled workers, and the equilibrium wage for the two groups. In particular, what are the equilibrium wages for skilled workers relative to unskilled workers after some unskilled workers acquire training?

7. For each of the following scenarios, state whether the unemployment is frictional, structural, or cyclical. Justify your answer. *(LO4)*
   a. Ted lost his job when the steel mill closed down. He lacks the skills to work in another industry and so has been unemployed for over a year.
   b. Alice was laid off from her job at the auto plant because the recession reduced the demand for cars. She expects to get her job back when the economy picks up.
   c. Tao looked for a job for six weeks after finishing college. He turned down a couple of offers because they didn't let him use the skills he had acquired in college, but is now about to accept a job in the area that he trained for.

ANSWERS TO SELF-TESTS

6.1 The value of the marginal product of the seventh worker is $39,000, and the value of the marginal product of the eighth worker is $33,000. So the seventh but not the eighth worker is profitable to hire at a wage of $35,000. *(LO2)*

6.2 With the computer price at $5,000, it is profitable to hire three workers at a wage of $100,000 since the third worker's value of marginal product ($105,000) exceeds $100,000 but the fourth worker's value of marginal product ($95,000) is less than $100,000. At a computer price of $3,000, we can refer to Table 6.1 to find that not even the first worker has a value of marginal product as high as $100,000, so at that computer price BCC will hire no workers. In short, at a wage of $100,000, the increase in the computer price raises the demand for technicians from zero to three. *(LO2)*

6.3 The seventh but not the eighth worker's value of marginal product exceeds $50,000 (Table 6.3), so it is profitable to hire seven workers if the going wage is $50,000. From Table 6.1, before the increase in productivity, the first five workers have values of marginal product greater than $50,000, so the demand for labor at a given wage of $50,000 is five workers. Thus the increase in productivity raises the quantity of labor demanded at a wage of $50,000 from five workers to seven workers. *(LO2)*

6.4 Even though you are receiving no pay, the valuable experience you gain as an intern is likely to raise the pay you will be able to earn in the future, so it is an investment in human capital. You also find working in the radio station more enjoyable than working in a car wash, presumably. To decide which job to take, you should ask yourself, "Taking into account both the likely increase in my future earnings and my greater enjoyment from working in the radio station, would I be willing to pay $3,000 to work in the radio station rather than earn $3,000 working in the car wash?" If the answer is yes, then you should work in the radio station; otherwise you should go to the car wash.

A decision to work in the radio station does not contradict the idea of an upward-sloping labor supply curve, if we are willing to think of the total compensation for that job as including not just cash wages but such factors as the value of the training that you receive. Your labor supply curve is still upward-sloping in the sense that the greater the value you place on the internship experience, the more likely you are to accept the job. *(LO2)*

6.5 Immigration to a country raises labor supply—indeed, the search for work is one of the most powerful factors drawing immigrants in the first place. As shown in the accompanying figure, an increase in labor supply will tend to lower the wages that employers have to pay (from w to w'), while raising overall employment (from N to N'). Because of its tendency to reduce real wages, labor unions generally oppose large-scale immigration, while employers support it.

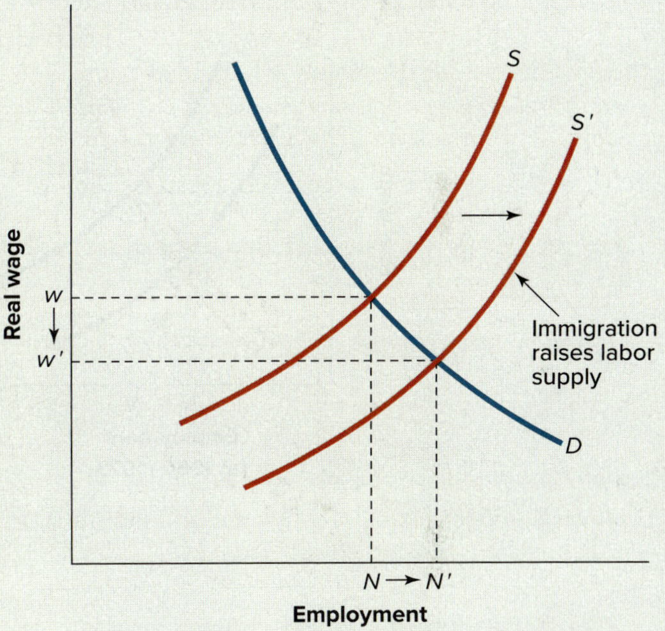

Although the figure shows the overall, or aggregate, supply of labor in the economy, the specific effects of immigration on wages depend on the skills and occupations of the immigrants. Current U.S. immigration policy makes the reunification of families the main reason for admitting immigrants, and for the most part immigrants are not screened for their education or skills. The U.S. also has a good deal of illegal immigration, made up largely of people looking for economic opportunity. These two factors create a tendency for new immigrants to the United States to be relatively low-skilled. Since immigration tends to increase the supply of unskilled labor by relatively more, it depresses wages of domestic low-skilled workers more than it does the wages of domestic high-skilled workers. Some economists, such as George Borjas of Harvard University, have argued that low-skilled immigration is another important factor reducing the wages of less-skilled workers relative to workers with greater skills and education. Borjas argues that the United States should adopt the approach used by Canada and give preference to potential immigrants with relatively higher levels of skills and education. *(LO2)*

6.6 Part (a) of the accompanying figure shows the labor market in 1960–1973; part (b) shows the labor market in 1973–1995. For comparability, we set the initial labor supply (*S*) and demand (*D*) curves the same in both parts, implying the same initial values of the real wage (*w*) and employment (*N*). In part (a), we show the effects of a large increase in labor demand (from *D* to *D*′), the result of rapid productivity growth, and a relatively small increase in labor supply (from *S* to *S*′). The real wage rises to *w*′ and employment rises to *N*′. In part (b), we observe the effects of a somewhat smaller increase in labor demand (from *D* to *D*″) and a larger increase in labor supply (from *S* to *S*″). Part (b), corresponding to the 1973–1995 period, shows a smaller increase in the real wage and a larger increase in employment than part (a), corresponding to 1960–1973. These results are consistent with actual developments in the U.S. labor market over these two periods. Since 1995, more rapid productivity growth, which raises labor demand more quickly, accounts for faster growth in real wages. *(LO3)*

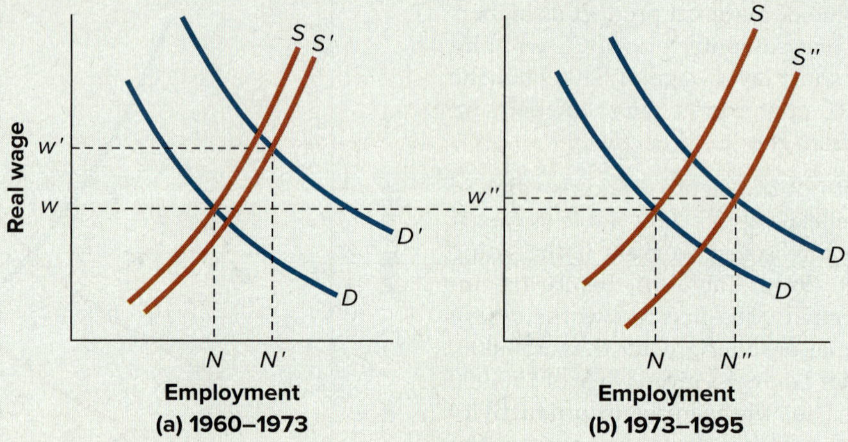

7

Saving and Capital Formation

LEARNING OBJECTIVES

After reading this chapter, you should be able to:

LO1 Explain the relationship between saving and wealth.

LO2 Discuss the reasons people save and how psychological factors influence saving.

LO3 Identify and apply the components of national saving.

LO4 Discuss the reasons firms choose to invest in capital.

LO5 Analyze financial markets using the tools of supply and demand.

You've probably heard Aesop's fable of the ant and the grasshopper. All summer the ant worked hard laying up food for the winter. The grasshopper mocked the ant's efforts and contented himself with basking in the sunshine, ignoring the ant's earnest warnings. When winter came the ant was well-fed, while the grasshopper starved. Moral: When times are good, the wise put aside something for the future.

Of course, there is also the modern ending to the fable, in which the grasshopper breaks his leg by tripping over the anthill, sues the ant for negligence, and ends up living comfortably on the ant's savings. (Nobody knows what happened to the ant.) Moral: Saving is risky; live for today.

The pitfalls of modern life notwithstanding, saving is important, both to individuals and to nations. People need to save to provide for their retirement and for other future needs, such as their children's education or a new home. An individual's or a family's savings can also provide a crucial buffer in the event of an economic emergency, such as the loss of a job or unexpected medical bills. At the national level, the production of new capital goods—factories, equipment, office buildings, and housing—is an important factor promoting economic growth and higher living standards. As we will see in this chapter, the resources necessary to produce new capital come primarily from a nation's collective saving.

Because adequate saving is so important to both ensuring families' financial security and creating new capital goods, many people have expressed concern about the low saving rate of American households. Never very high by international standards, the U.S. household saving rate—the percentage of after-tax household income that is saved—declined from around 13 percent of household disposable income in the early 1970s to around 7 to 8 percent in the past few years. (The household saving rate had reached a low of 3.2 percent in 2005, and then increased during and following the 2007–2009 recession to its current level.)

What is the significance of such a low and declining saving rate? Some see the data as evidence of "grasshopperish" behavior and a threat to Americans' future prosperity. The reality, as we will see, is more complex. Many American families do save very little, a fact that is likely to exact a toll on their economic well-being in the long run. Economists and policymakers are particularly concerned about the low rates among lower-income people (many of whom save little, or none at all). Low saving rates may mean that people fail to build wealth, have reserves for emergencies, or be adequately prepared for retirement. On the other hand, at the aggregate level, household saving is only one part of the total saving of the U.S. economy, as businesses and governments also save. In fact, the total saving of the U.S. economy, called *national saving,* is higher and has declined less dramatically than household saving during these years. Thus, if the United States is suffering a "savings shortfall," it is less severe than might be suggested by the figures on household saving only.

In this chapter, we will look at saving and its links to the formation of new capital. We begin by defining the concepts of saving and wealth and exploring the connection between them. We will consider why people choose to save, rather than spending all their income. We then turn to national saving—the collective saving of households, businesses, and government. Because national saving determines the capacity of an economy to create new capital, it is the more important measure of saving from a macroeconomic perspective.

We next discuss capital formation. Most decisions to invest in new capital are made by firms. As we will see, a firm's decision to invest is in many respects analogous to its decision about whether to increase employment; firms will choose to expand their capital stocks when the benefits of doing so exceed the costs. We end the chapter by showing how national saving and capital formation are related, using a supply and demand approach.

SAVING AND WEALTH

saving current income minus spending on current needs

saving rate saving divided by income

wealth the value of assets minus liabilities

assets anything of value that one *owns*

liabilities the debts one *owes*

balance sheet a list of an economic unit's assets and liabilities on a specific date

net worth an economic unit's wealth determined by subtracting liabilities from assets

In general, the **saving** of an economic unit—whether a household, a business, a university, or a nation—may be defined as its *current income* minus its *spending on current needs*. For example, if Consuelo earns $300 per week; spends $280 weekly on living expenses such as rent, food, clothes, and entertainment; and deposits the remaining $20 in the bank, her saving is $20 per week. The **saving rate** of any economic unit is its saving divided by its income. Since Consuelo saves $20 of her weekly income of $300, her saving rate is $20/$300, or 6.7 percent.

The saving of an economic unit is closely related to its **wealth,** or the value of its assets minus its liabilities. **Assets** are anything of value that one *owns,* either *financial* or *real*. Examples of financial assets that you or your family might own include cash, a checking account, stocks, and bonds. Examples of real assets include a home or other real estate, jewelry, consumer durables like cars, and valuable collectibles. **Liabilities,** on the other hand, are the debts one *owes*. Examples of liabilities are credit card balances, student loans, and mortgages.

Accountants list the assets and liabilities of a family, a firm, a university, or any other economic unit on a **balance sheet.** Comparing the values of the assets and liabilities helps them determine the economic unit's wealth, also called its **net worth.**

EXAMPLE 7.1 **Constructing a Balance Sheet**

What is Consuelo's wealth?

To take stock of her financial position, Consuelo lists her assets and liabilities on a balance sheet. The result is shown in Table 7.1. What is Consuelo's wealth?

TABLE 7.1
Consuelo's Balance Sheet

Assets		Liabilities	
Cash	$ 80	Student loan	$3,000
Checking account	1,200	Credit card balance	250
Shares of stock	1,000		
Car (market value)	3,500		
Furniture (market value)	500		
Total	**$6,280**		**$3,250**
		Net worth	**$3,030**

Consuelo's financial assets are the cash in her wallet, the balance in her checking account, and the current value of some shares of stock her parents gave her. Together her financial assets are worth $2,280. She also lists $4,000 in real assets, the sum of the market values of her car and her furniture. Consuelo's total assets, both financial and real, come to $6,280. Her liabilities are the student loan she owes the bank and the balance due on her credit card, which total $3,250. Consuelo's wealth, or net worth, then, is the value of her assets ($6,280) minus the value of her liabilities ($3,250), or $3,030.

SELF-TEST 7.1

What would Consuelo's net worth be if her student loan were for $6,500 rather than $3,000? Construct a new balance sheet for her.

Saving and wealth are related, because saving contributes to wealth. To understand this relationship better, we must distinguish between *stocks* and *flows*.

flow a measure that is defined *per unit of time*

stock a measure that is defined *at a point in time*

Stocks and Flows

Saving is an example of a **flow,** a measure that is defined *per unit of time*. For example, Consuelo's saving is $20 *per week*. Wealth, in contrast, is a **stock,** a measure that is defined *at a point in time*. Consuelo's wealth of $3,030, for example, is her wealth on a particular date—say, January 1, 2020.

To visualize the difference between stocks and flows, think of water running into a bathtub. The amount of water in the bathtub at any specific moment—for example, 40 gallons at 7:15 p.m.—is a stock because it is measured at a specific point in time. The rate at which the water flows into the tub—for example, 2 gallons per minute—is a flow because it is measured per unit of time. In many cases, a flow is the *rate of change* in a stock: If we know that there are 40 gallons of water in the tub at 7:15 p.m., for example, and that water is flowing in at 2 gallons per minute, we can easily determine that the stock of water will be changing at the rate of 2 gallons per minute and will equal 42 gallons at 7:16 p.m., 44 gallons at 7:17 p.m., and so on, until the bathtub overflows.

The flow of saving increases the stock of wealth in the same way that the flow of water through the faucet increases the amount of water in the tub.

SELF-TEST 7.2

Continuing the example of the bathtub: If there are 40 gallons of water in the tub at 7:15 p.m. and water is being *drained* at the rate of 3 gallons per minute, what will be the stock and flow at 7:16 p.m.? At 7:17 p.m.? Does the flow still equal the rate of change in the stock?

The relationship between saving (a flow) and wealth (a stock) is similar to the relationship between the flow of water into a bathtub and the stock of water in the tub in that the *flow* of saving causes the *stock* of wealth to change at the same rate. Indeed, as Example 7.2 illustrates, every dollar that a person saves adds a dollar to his or her wealth.

EXAMPLE 7.2 The Link between Saving and Wealth

What is the relationship between Consuelo's saving and her wealth?

Consuelo saves $20 per week. How does this saving affect her wealth? Does the change in her wealth depend on whether Consuelo uses her saving to accumulate assets or to pay down her liabilities?

Consuelo could use the $20 she saved this week to increase her assets—for example, by adding the $20 to her checking account—or to reduce her liabilities—for example, by paying down her credit card balance. Suppose she adds the $20 to her checking account, increasing her assets by $20. Since her liabilities are unchanged, her wealth also increases by $20, to $3,050 (see Table 7.1).

If Consuelo decides to use the $20 she saved this week to pay down her credit card balance, she reduces it from $250 to $230. That action would reduce her liabilities by $20, leaving her assets unchanged. Since wealth equals assets minus liabilities, reducing her liabilities by $20 increases her wealth by $20, to $3,050. Thus, saving $20 per week raises Consuelo's stock of wealth by $20 a week, regardless of whether she uses her saving to increase her assets or reduce her liabilities.

The close relationship between saving and wealth explains why saving is so important to an economy. Higher rates of saving today lead to faster accumulation of wealth, and the wealthier a nation is, the higher its standard of living. Thus a high rate of saving today contributes to an improved standard of living in the future.

Capital Gains and Losses

Though saving increases wealth, it is not the only factor that determines wealth. Wealth can also change because of changes in the values of the real or financial assets one owns. Suppose Consuelo's shares of stock rise in value, from $1,000 to $1,500. This increase in the value of Consuelo's stock raises her total assets by $500 without affecting her liabilities. As a result, Consuelo's wealth rises by $500, from $3,030 to $3,530 (see Table 7.2).

capital gains increases in the value of existing assets

capital losses decreases in the value of existing assets

Changes in the value of existing assets are called **capital gains** when an asset's value increases and **capital losses** when an asset's value decreases. Just as capital gains increase wealth, capital losses decrease wealth. Capital gains and losses are not counted as part of saving, however. Instead, the change in a person's wealth during any period equals the saving done during the period plus capital gains or minus capital losses during that period. In terms of an equation,

$$\text{Change in wealth} = \text{Saving} + \text{Capital gains} - \text{Capital losses}.$$

TABLE 7.2
Consuelo's Balance Sheet after an Increase in the Value of Her Stocks

Assets		Liabilities	
Cash	$ 80	Student loan	$3,000
Checking account	1,200	Credit card balance	250
Shares of stock	1,500		
Car (market value)	3,500		
Furniture (market value)	500		
Total	**$6,780**		**$3,250**
		Net worth	**$3,530**

SELF-TEST 7.3

How would each of the following actions or events affect Consuelo's *saving* and her *wealth*?

a. Consuelo deposits $20 in the bank at the end of the week as usual. She also charges $50 on her credit card, raising her credit card balance to $300.

b. Consuelo uses $300 from her checking account to pay off her credit card bill.

c. Consuelo's old car is recognized as a classic. Its market value rises from $3,500 to $4,000.

d. Consuelo's furniture is damaged and as a result falls in value from $500 to $200.

Capital gains and losses can have a major effect on one's overall wealth, as The Economic Naturalist 7.1 illustrates. Moreover, families' wealth, built through saving and capital gains, can persist over many generations, as The Economic Naturalist 7.2 illustrates.

The Economic Naturalist 7.1

How did many American households increase their wealth in the 1990s and 2000s while saving very little?

On the whole, Americans felt prosperous during the 1990s and, with a short pause around the relatively minor 2001 recession, the feeling of prosperity continued until the eve of the 2007–2009 recession. Measures of household wealth during this period showed enormous gains. Yet saving by U.S. households was quite low (and declining) throughout those years. How did many American households increase their wealth in the 1990s and early 2000s while saving very little?

During the 1990s, an increasing number of Americans acquired stocks, either directly through purchases or indirectly through their pension and retirement funds. At the same time, stock prices rose at record rates (see the blue line in Figure 7.1). The strongly rising "bull market," which increased the prices of most stocks, enabled many Americans to enjoy significant capital gains and increased wealth without saving much, if anything. Indeed, some economists argued that the low household saving rate of the 1990s is partially *explained* by the bull market; because capital gains increased household wealth by so much, many people saw no need to save. (Other proposed explanations include the increase in *government* saving during the 1990s, discussed below.)

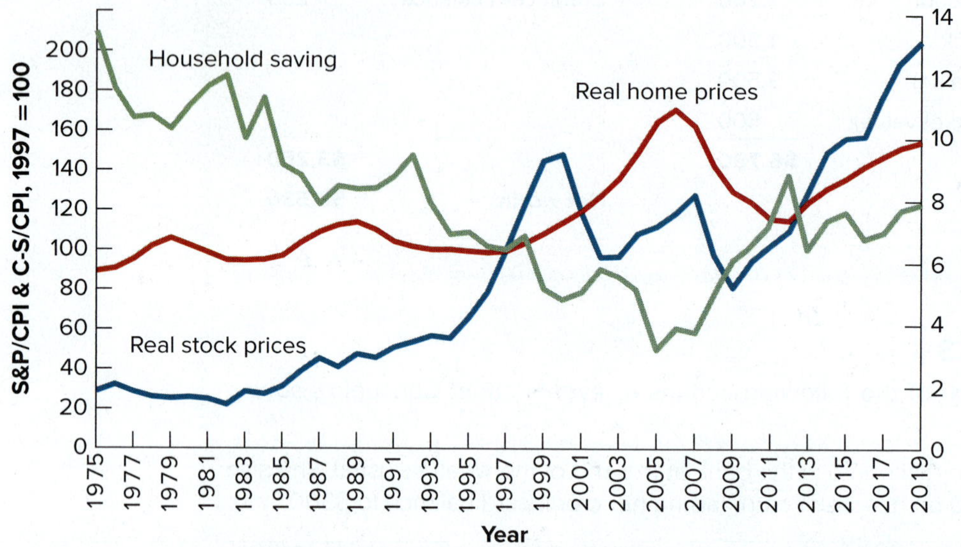

FIGURE 7.1

Household Saving versus Real Stock and Home Prices, 1975–2019.

Changes in household saving often accompany changes in the opposite direction in measures of household wealth such as stocks and homes. As both stock markets and home values started declining in the later part of the 2000s, the household saving rate reversed its trend and, for a few years, started increasing.

Sources: S&P CoreLogic Case-Shiller Home Price Indices, Federal Reserve Bank of St. Louis.

The stock market peaked in early 2000 and stock prices fell quite sharply over the following two years. It is interesting that U.S. households did not choose to save more in 2000 and the following years (see the green line in Figure 7.1), despite the decline in their stock market wealth. One explanation is that an even larger component of household wealth—the value of privately owned homes—rose significantly in 2000–2006, partly offsetting the effect of the decline in stock values on household wealth (see the red line in Figure 7.1).

More generally, as Figure 7.1 shows, changes in household saving often accompany changes in the opposite direction in measures of household wealth such as stocks and homes (for example, household saving and home prices during the 1970s and 1980s often moved in opposite directions). Indeed, the figure shows that as both stock markets and home values started declining in the later part of the 2000s, the household saving rate reversed its trend and started increasing.

Household saving then peaked in 2012 when the housing market bottomed, and has since declined only slightly, in spite of steep increases in both stock and home prices in recent years. With the steep declines of the global financial crisis still fresh in their memories, American households may not feel confident that these recent capital gains are here to last. Indeed, sharp stock market declines related to the COVID-19 pandemic in early 2020 provided a still fresher reminder of the instability of capital gains.

The Economic Naturalist 7.2

Why are racial and ethnic wealth disparities so persistent?

Wealth disparities between U.S. families in different racial and ethnic groups are substantial. Recent data and analyses show that in 2019, before the COVID-19 pandemic hit, the median white family had almost eight times the wealth of the median Black family and more than five times the wealth of the median Hispanic family.[1] Such disparities are long-standing, and have not changed much in recent years. Why are they so persistent?

Defining wealth as the difference between families' gross assets and their liabilities, in 2019, median family wealth among white families was $188,200, compared with $24,100 among Black families, and $36,100 among Hispanic families. Families from other racial and ethnic groups, including Asian, American Indian, Alaska Native, and others, had lower wealth than white families but higher wealth than Black and Hispanic families. (Of course, within each of these groups, wealth is not equally distributed; in fact it is highly concentrated at the top of each group.)

While current discrimination explains part of this difference in wealth, some of the difference is rooted in the legacy of past discrimination. Families transmit wealth from generation to generation through bequest (see next section, on bequest saving), gifts such as providing a down payment for home purchase, and paying for better, costlier education. Let's explore some of these channels.

Recent evidence suggests that bequest, which may account for at least half of aggregate wealth in the U.S., is the most important explanation for current racial wealth disparities. While 30 percent of white families report having received an inheritance or gift, only 10 percent of Black families, and 7 percent of Hispanic families, do. Among those who receive them, white families also receive larger inheritances. Current wealth disparities may therefore reflect a legacy of discrimination or unequal treatment in housing, education, and labor markets. Such disparities may also take generations to close even if discrimination and unequal treatment disappeared overnight.

Homeownership is a closely related reflection, cause, and consequence of this persistence of wealth disparities. In 2019, 46 percent of white young families (under the age of 35) owned their home, compared with only 17 percent of Black families, and 28 percent of Hispanic families. And among all white homeowner families, again the median home was worth significantly more ($219,000) than among all Black ($150,000) and Hispanic ($200,000) homeowner families. These gaps again reflect several persistent factors, including wealth and income gaps, residential segregation, and others. Moreover, for many homeowners, their home is their biggest asset. In periods when home prices are rising, homeownership can also be a way to build wealth (through capital gains). This makes homeownership a self-reinforcing component of wealth disparities.

Finally, Black and Hispanic families are also less likely to own retirement accounts than white families. Some of the gap is caused by greater access among white families to employer-sponsored retirement plans and the benefits they provide. Another part of the gap is explained by different take-up rates: 90 percent of white families with access to such plans do in fact participate in them, compared

[1]Neil Bhutta, Andrew C. Chang, Lisa J. Dettling, and Joanne W. Hsu with assistance from Julia Hewitt, "Disparities in Wealth by Race and Ethnicity in the 2019 Survey of Consumer Finances," FEDS Notes, September 28, 2020. The authors also provide many additional references for related data and studies on the topics mentioned in this Economic Naturalist.

with 80 percent of Black and 75 percent of Hispanic families. The factors that explain these take-up gaps include, for example, financial literacy, and whether a family has sufficient financial resources to be able to save through these plans. These factors again point to the cross-generational persistence of wealth gaps, through self-reinforcing gaps in resources such as education, inheritances, and housing.

We have seen how saving is related to the accumulation of wealth. To understand why people choose to save, however, we need to examine their motives for saving.

RECAP

SAVING AND WEALTH

In general, *saving* is current income minus spending on current needs. *Wealth* is the value of assets—anything of value that one owns—minus liabilities—the debts one owes. Saving is measured per unit of time (for example, dollars per week) and thus is a *flow*. Wealth is measured at a point in time and thus is a *stock*. In the same way the flow of water through the faucet increases the stock of water in a bathtub, the flow of saving increases the stock of wealth.

Wealth can also be increased by *capital gains* (increases in the value of existing assets) or reduced by *capital losses* (decreases in asset values). Capital gains by stockholders during bull markets and by homeowners during periods of home price increases allow families that own these assets to increase their wealth while doing little saving.

WHY DO PEOPLE SAVE?

Why do people save part of their income instead of spending everything they earn? Economists have identified at least three broad reasons for saving. First, people save to meet certain long-term objectives, such as a comfortable retirement. By putting away part of their income during their working years, they can live better after retirement than they would if they had to rely solely on Social Security and their company pensions, if they have one. Other long-term objectives might include college tuition for one's children and the purchase of a new home or car. Since many of these needs occur at fairly predictable stages in one's life, economists call this type of saving **life-cycle saving.**

life-cycle saving saving to meet long-term objectives such as retirement, college attendance, or the purchase of a home

A second reason to save is to protect oneself and family against unexpected setbacks—the loss of a job, for example, or a costly health problem. Personal financial advisors typically suggest that families maintain an emergency reserve (a "rainy-day fund") equal to three to six months' worth of income. Saving for protection against potential emergencies is called **precautionary saving.**

precautionary saving saving for protection against unexpected setbacks such as the loss of a job or a medical emergency

A third reason to save is to accumulate an estate to leave to one's heirs, usually one's children but possibly a favorite charity or other worthy cause. Saving for the purpose of leaving an inheritance, or bequest, is called **bequest saving.** Bequest saving is done primarily by people at the higher end of the income ladder. But because these people control a large share of the nation's wealth, bequest saving is an important part of overall saving.

bequest saving saving done for the purpose of leaving an inheritance

To be sure, people usually do not mentally separate their saving into these three categories; rather, all three reasons for saving motivate most savers to varying degrees. The Economic Naturalist 7.3 shows how the three reasons for saving can explain the high rate of household saving in China.

The Economic Naturalist 7.3

Why do Chinese households save so much?

A few years ago, economists estimated that Chinese households save more than 25 percent of their disposable income, an unusually high rate.[2] Although some suggested that the Chinese "are known to be thrifty," it is unlikely that cultural factors are a main reason for their propensity to save because the high saving rate is a relatively recent phenomenon. Chinese households saved well below 10 percent of their income until the late 1980s, and below 5 percent from the 1950s to the 1970s. Why do the Chinese save so much, then?

▶ Visit your instructor's Connect course and access your eBook to view this video.

Why do American households save so little while Chinese households save so much?

Among the reasons for saving we discussed, *life-cycle* and *precautionary saving* seem important in China. As we mentioned in Chapter 5, *Economic Growth, Productivity, and Living Standards,* the Chinese economy grew very quickly over the past several decades (Table 5.1 and Figure 5.2 in that chapter show the dramatic increase in China's real GDP per person from 1990 to 2010). In a very rapidly growing economy, younger people in their working years are richer on average than people in their retirement years, as the young's incomes are much higher than the incomes the retired had during their own working years. As a result, the saving of the young outweighs the dissaving of the retired. Moreover, China's limited "social safety net"—its version of Social Security, Medicare, and other social insurance schemes (discussed in The Economic Naturalist 7.4)—provides most people little in the way of retirement income or protection against health problems. That means that young households have to save both for their own retirement—life-cycle saving—and for unexpected expenses such as health-related ones—precautionary saving.

Another explanation for the high saving rates has to do with China's financial system, which is closely controlled by the government and does not afford the average consumer much opportunity to borrow. This again translates both to higher life-cycle saving—because, for example, paying for a house or for education requires saving much of the cost in advance—and to higher precautionary saving—because households know that their ability to borrow in the case of an unexpected need would be limited.

If these explanations are correct, why is the high saving rate a relatively recent phenomenon? Starting in the late 1970s, China has undergone extensive economic reforms (recall our discussion of structural macroeconomics policies in previous chapters). These reforms have gradually turned China from a centrally planned economy to a more market-oriented economy. Before the reforms, households had less ability as well as less perceived need to engage in life-cycle and precautionary saving, because the central government controlled many aspects of their economic behavior and was considered responsible for providing for their needs. As institutions changed, households' incentives changed, and they changed their saving behavior.

Note that the many uncertainties associated with changing economic institutions (indeed, with any big societal changes) could themselves provide another reason for relatively high precautionary saving. In particular, a transition to a more market-oriented economy could imply an increase in earnings uncertainty and unemployment risk. China's transition also meant that the prices of housing, education, and other life-cycle expenditures increased, increasing the need for life-cycle saving.

[2]For these estimates, and for detail on some of the explanations and evidence we discuss here, see, for example, Dennis Tao Yang, Junsen Zhang, and Shaojie Zhou, "Why Are Saving Rates So High in China?," in *Capitalizing China,* Joseph P. H. Fan and Randall Morck, eds. (Chicago: University of Chicago Press, 2013).

Although most people are usually motivated to save for at least one of the three reasons we have discussed, the amount they choose to save may depend on the economic environment. One economic variable that is quite significant in saving decisions is the real interest rate.

Saving and the Real Interest Rate

Most people don't save by putting cash in a mattress. Instead, they make financial investments that they hope will provide a good return on their saving. For example, a checking account may pay interest on the account balance. More sophisticated financial investments, such as government bonds or shares of stock in a corporation (see Chapter 8, *Money, the Federal Reserve, and Global Financial Markets*), also pay returns in the form of interest payments, dividends, or capital gains. High returns are desirable, of course, because the higher the return, the faster one's savings will grow.

The rate of return that is most relevant to saving decisions is the *real interest rate,* denoted *r.* The real interest rate is the rate at which the real purchasing power of a financial asset increases over time. The real interest rate equals the market, or *nominal,* interest rate (i) minus the inflation rate (π). An example will illustrate.

Suppose that there are two neighboring countries, Alpha and Beta. In Alpha, whose currency is called the alphan, the inflation rate is zero and is expected to remain at zero. In Beta, where the currency is the betan, the inflation rate is 10 percent and is expected to remain at that level. Bank deposits pay 2 percent annual interest in Alpha and 10 percent annual interest in Beta. In which countries are bank depositors getting a better deal?

You may answer "Beta," since interest rates on deposits are higher in that country. But if you think about the effects of inflation, you will recognize that Alpha, not Beta, offers the better deal to depositors. To see why, think about the change over a year in the real purchasing power of deposits in the two countries. In Alpha, someone who deposits 100 alphans in the bank on January 1 will have 102 alphans on December 31. Because there is no inflation in Alpha, on average prices are the same at the end of the year as they were at the beginning. Thus the 102 alphans the depositor can withdraw represent a 2 percent increase in buying power.

In Beta, the depositor who deposits 100 betans on January 1 will have 110 betans by the end of the year—10 percent more than she started with. But the prices of goods and services in Beta, we have assumed, will also rise by 10 percent. Thus the Beta depositor can afford to buy precisely the same amount of goods and services at the end of the year as she could at the beginning; she gets no increase in buying power. So the Alpha depositor has the better deal, after all.

real interest rate the annual percentage increase in the purchasing power of a financial asset; the real interest rate on any asset equals the nominal interest rate on that asset minus the inflation rate

nominal interest rate (or **market interest rate**) the annual percentage increase in the nominal value of a financial asset

Economists refer to the annual percentage increase in the *real* purchasing power of a financial asset as the **real interest rate,** or the *real rate of return,* on that asset. In our example, the real purchasing power of deposits rises by 2 percent per year in Alpha and by 0 percent per year in Beta. So the real interest rate on deposits is 2 percent in Alpha and 0 percent in Beta. The real interest rate should be distinguished from the more familiar market interest rate, also called the *nominal interest rate.* The **nominal interest rate** (or **market interest rate**) is the annual percentage increase in the nominal, or dollar, value of an asset.

As the example of Alpha and Beta illustrates, we can calculate the real interest rate for any financial asset, from a checking account to a government bond, by subtracting the rate of inflation from the market or nominal interest rate on that asset. So in Alpha, the real interest rate on deposits equals the nominal interest rate (2 percent) minus the inflation rate (0 percent), or 2 percent. Likewise in Beta, the real interest rate equals the nominal interest rate (10 percent) minus the inflation rate (10 percent), or 0 percent.

We can write this definition of the real interest rate in mathematical terms

$$r = i - \pi,$$

where r = the real interest rate,

i = the nominal, or market, interest rate,

π = the inflation rate.

The real interest rate is relevant to savers because it is the "reward" for saving. Suppose you are thinking of increasing your saving by $1,000 this year, which you can do if you give up your habit of eating out once a week. If the real interest rate is 5 percent, then in a year your extra saving will give you extra purchasing power of $1,050, measured in today's dollars. But if the real interest rate were 10 percent, your sacrifice of $1,000 this year would be rewarded by $1,100 in purchasing power next year. All else being equal, you would probably be more willing to save today if you knew the reward next year would be greater. In either case the *cost* of the extra saving–giving up your weekly night out–is the same. But the *benefit* of the extra saving, in terms of increased purchasing power next year, is higher if the real interest rate is 10 percent rather than 5 percent.

EXAMPLE 7.3 Saving versus Consumption

By how much does a high saving rate enhance a family's future living standard?

The Spends and the Thrifts are similar families, except that the Spends save 5 percent of their income each year and the Thrifts save 20 percent. The two families began to save in 1995 and plan to continue to save until their respective breadwinners retire in the year 2030. Both families earn $40,000 a year in real terms in the labor market, and both put their savings in a mutual fund that has yielded a real return of 8 percent per year, a return they expect to continue into the future. Compare the amount that the two families consume in each year from 1995 to 2030, and compare the families' wealth at retirement.

In the first year, 1995, the Spends saved $2,000 (5 percent of their $40,000 income) and consumed $38,000 (95 percent of $40,000). The Thrifts saved $8,000 in 1995 (20 percent of $40,000) and hence consumed only $32,000 in that year, $6,000 less than the Spends. In 1996, the Thrifts' income was $40,640, the extra $640 representing the 8 percent return on their $8,000 savings. The Spends saw their income grow by only $160 (8 percent of their savings of $2,000) in 1996. With an income of $40,640, the Thrifts consumed $32,512 in 1996 (80 percent of $40,640) compared to $38,152 (95 percent of $40,160) for the Spends. The consumption gap between the two families, which started out at $6,000, thus fell to $5,640 after one year.

Because of the more rapid increase in the Thrifts' wealth and hence interest income, each year the Thrifts' income grew faster than the Spends'; each year the Thrifts continued to save 20 percent of their higher incomes compared to only 5 percent for the Spends. Figure 7.2 shows the paths followed by the consumption spending of the two families. You can see that the Thrifts' consumption, though starting at a lower level, grows relatively more quickly. By 2010 the Thrifts had overtaken the Spends, and from that point onward, the amount by which the Thrifts outspent the Spends grew with each passing year. Even though the Spends continued to consume 95 percent of their income each year, their income grew so slowly that by 2015, they were consuming nearly $3,000 a year less than the Thrifts ($41,158 a year versus $43,957). And by the time the two families retire, in 2030, the Thrifts will be consuming more than $12,000 per year more than the

FIGURE 7.2

Consumption Trajectories of the Thrifts and the Spends.

The figure shows consumption spending in each year by two families, the Thrifts and the Spends. Because the Thrifts save more than the Spends, their annual consumption spending rises relatively more quickly. By the time of retirement in the year 2030, the Thrifts are both consuming significantly more each year than the Spends and also have a retirement nest egg that is five times larger.

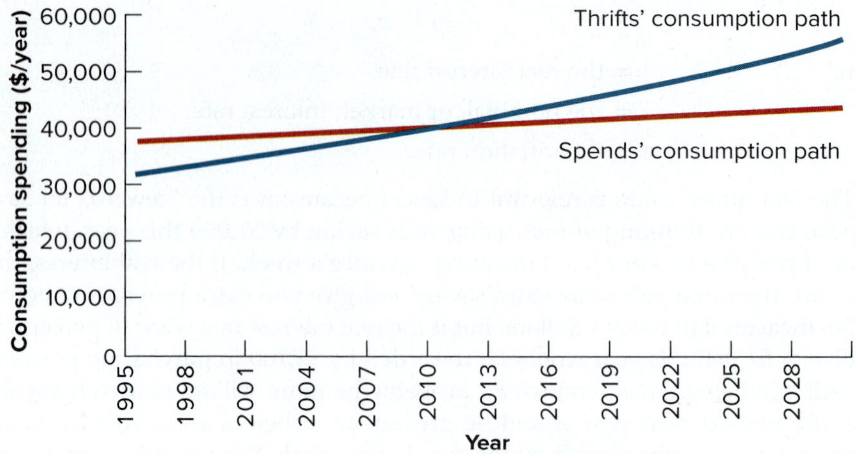

Spends ($55,774 versus $43,698). Even more striking is the difference between the retirement nest eggs of the two families. Whereas the Spends will enter retirement with total accumulated savings of just over $77,000, the Thrifts will have more than $385,000, five times as much.

These dramatic differences illustrated in Example 7.3 depend in part on the assumption that the real rate of return is 8 percent—around 1 percent higher than the actual real return to mutual funds tracking the S&P 500 (with dividends reinvested) since its inception in 1926. On the other hand, the Spend family in our example actually saves more than typical U.S. households, many of which carry $5,000 or more in credit card debt at high rates of interest and have no significant savings at all. The point of the example, which remains valid under alternative assumptions about the real interest rate and saving rates, is that, because of the power of compound interest, a high rate of saving pays off handsomely in the long run.

While a higher real interest rate increases the reward for saving, which tends to strengthen people's willingness to save, another force counteracts that extra incentive. Recall that a major reason for saving is to attain specific goals: a comfortable retirement, a college education, or a first home. If the goal is a specific amount—say, $25,000 for a down payment on a home—then a higher rate of return means that households can save *less* and still reach their goal, because funds that are put aside will grow more quickly. For example, to accumulate $25,000 at the end of five years, at a 5 percent interest rate a person would have to save about $4,309 per year. At a 10 percent interest rate, reaching the $25,000 goal would require saving only about $3,723 per year. To the extent that people are *target savers* who save to reach a specific goal, higher interest rates actually decrease the amount they need to save.

In sum, a higher real interest rate has both positive and negative effects on saving—a positive effect because it increases the reward for saving and a negative effect because it reduces the amount people need to save each year to reach a given target. Empirical evidence suggests that, in practice, higher real interest rates lead to modest increases in saving.

Saving, Self-Control, and Demonstration Effects

The reasons for saving we just discussed are based on the notion that people are rational decision makers who will choose their saving rates to maximize their welfare over the long run. Yet many psychologists, and some economists, have argued instead that people's saving behavior is based as much on psychological as on economic factors. For example, psychologists stress that many people lack the *self-control* to do what they know is in their own best interest. People smoke or eat greasy food, despite the known long-term health risks. Similarly, they may have good intentions about saving but lack the self-control to put aside as much as they ought to each month.

One way to strengthen self-control is to remove temptations from the immediate environment. A person who is trying to quit smoking will make a point of not having cigarettes in the house, and a person with a weight problem will avoid going to a bakery. Similarly, a person who is not saving enough might arrange to use a payroll savings plan, through which a predetermined amount is deducted from each paycheck and set aside in a special account from which withdrawals are not permitted until retirement. Making saving automatic and withdrawals difficult eliminates the temptation to spend all of current earnings or squander accumulated savings. Payroll savings plans have helped many people increase the amount that they save for retirement or other purposes.

An implication of the self-control hypothesis is that consumer credit arrangements that make borrowing and spending easier may reduce the amount that people save. For example, in recent years banks sometimes encouraged people to borrow against the *equity* in their homes—that is, the value of the home less the value of the outstanding mortgage. Such financial innovations, by increasing the temptation to spend, may have reduced the household saving rate. The increased availability of credit cards with high borrowing limits is another temptation.

Downward pressure on the saving rate may also occur when additional spending by some consumers stimulates additional spending by others. Such *demonstration effects* arise when people use the spending of others as a yardstick by which to measure the adequacy of their own living standards. For example, a family in an upper-middle-class American suburb in which the average house has 3,000 square feet of living space might regard a 1,500-square-foot house as being uncomfortably small—too cramped, for example, to entertain friends in the manner to which community members have become accustomed. In contrast, a similar family living in a low-income neighborhood might find the very same house luxuriously large.

The implication of demonstration effects for saving is that families who live among others who consume more than they do may be strongly motivated to increase their own consumption spending. When satisfaction or social status depends in part on *relative* living standards, an upward spiral may result in which household spending is higher, and saving lower, than would be best for either the individual families involved or for the economy as a whole.

The Economic Naturalist 7.4

Why do U.S. households save so little?

Household saving in the United States, which has always been comparatively low, has fallen even further in the past decades. (Figure 7.1 shows a long-term fall from 13.1 percent in 1975 to 7.9 percent in 2019.) Surveys show that a significant fraction of American households live from paycheck to paycheck with very little saving. Why do U.S. households save so little?

Economists do not agree on the reasons for low household saving in the United States, although many hypotheses have been suggested.

One possible reason for low saving is the availability of generous government assistance to older adults. From a *life-cycle* perspective, an important motivation for saving is to provide for retirement. In general, the U.S. government provides a less comprehensive "social safety net" than other industrialized countries; that is, it offers relatively fewer programs to assist people in need. To the extent that the U.S. government does provide income support, however, it is heavily concentrated on the older segment of the population. Together the Social Security and Medicare programs, both of which are designed primarily to assist retired people, constitute a major share of the federal government's expenditures. These programs have been very successful; indeed they have virtually wiped out poverty among older people. To the extent that Americans believe that the government will ensure them an adequate living standard in retirement, however, their incentive to save for the future is reduced.

Another important life-cycle objective is buying a home. We have seen that the Chinese must save a great deal to purchase a home because of high house prices and down payment requirements. The same is true in many other countries. But in the United States, with its highly developed financial system, people can buy homes with down payments of 15 percent or less of the purchase price. The ready availability of mortgages with low down payments reduces the need to save for the purchase of a home.

What about *precautionary saving*? Unlike Japan and Europe, which had to rebuild after World War II, and unlike China, which continued to suffer from major economic crises in the decades following the war, the United States has not known sustained economic hardship since the Great Depression of the 1930s (which fewer and fewer Americans are alive to remember). Perhaps the nation's prosperous past has led Americans to be more confident about the future and hence less inclined to save for economic emergencies than other people, even though the United States does not offer the level of employment security found in Japan or in Europe.

U.S. household saving is not only low by international standards; it has generally declined in recent decades. The good performance of the stock market in the 1990s along with continuing increases in the prices of family homes until the mid-2000s probably help explain this savings decline (see The Economic Naturalist 7.1). As long as Americans enjoy capital gains, they see their wealth increase almost without effort, and their incentive to save is reduced. Consistent with this explanation, U.S. household saving increased during and after the last recession as the value of stocks and homes declined, but stopped increasing in the last few years, as stocks and housing have been rising again.

Psychological factors may also explain Americans' saving behavior. For example, unlike in most countries, U.S. homeowners can easily borrow against their home equity. This ability, made possible by the highly developed U.S. financial markets, may exacerbate *self-control* problems by increasing the temptation to spend. Finally, *demonstration effects* may have depressed saving in recent decades. Chapter 6, *The Labor Market: Workers, Wages, and Unemployment,* discussed the phenomenon of increasing wage inequality, which has improved the relative position of more skilled and educated workers. Increased spending by households at the top of the earnings scale on houses, cars, and other consumption goods may have led those just below them to spend more as well, and so on. Middle-class families that were once content with medium-priced cars may now feel they need Volvos and BMWs to keep up with community standards. To the extent that demonstration effects lead families to spend beyond their means, they reduce their saving rate.

RECAP

WHY DO PEOPLE SAVE?

Motivations for saving include saving to meet long-term objectives, such as retirement (*life-cycle saving*), saving for emergencies (*precautionary saving*), and saving to leave an inheritance or bequest (*bequest saving*). The amount that people save also depends on macroeconomic factors, such as the real interest rate. A higher real interest rate stimulates saving by increasing the reward for saving, but it can also depress saving by making it easier for savers to reach a specific savings target. On net, a higher real interest rate appears to lead to modest increases in saving.

Psychological factors may also affect saving rates. If people have *self-control* problems, then financial arrangements (such as automatic payroll deductions) that make it more difficult to spend will increase their saving. People's saving decisions may also be influenced by *demonstration effects,* as when people feel compelled to spend at the same rate as their neighbors, even though they may not be able to afford to do so.

NATIONAL SAVING AND ITS COMPONENTS

Thus far, we have been examining the concepts of saving and wealth from the individual's perspective. But macroeconomists are interested primarily in saving and wealth for the country as a whole. In this section, we will study *national saving,* or the aggregate saving of the economy. National saving includes the saving of business firms and the government as well as that of households. Later in the chapter, we will examine the close link between national saving and the rate of capital formation in an economy.

The Measurement of National Saving

To define the saving rate of a country as a whole, we will start with a basic accounting identity that was introduced in Chapter 8, *Money, the Federal Reserve, and Global Financial Markets*. According to this identity, for the economy as a whole, production (or income) must equal total expenditure. In symbols, the identity is

$$Y = C + I + G + NX,$$

where Y stands for either production or aggregate income (which must be equal), C equals consumption expenditure, I equals investment spending, G equals government purchases of goods and services, and NX equals net exports.

For now, let's assume that net exports (NX) is equal to zero, which would be the case if a country did not trade at all with other countries or if its exports and imports were always balanced. (We discuss the case with NX being different from zero in the next chapter.) With net exports set at zero, the condition that output equals expenditure becomes

$$Y = C + I + G.$$

To determine how much saving is done by the nation as a whole, we can apply the general definition of saving. As for any other economic unit, a nation's saving equals its *current income* less its *spending on current needs*. The current income of the country as a whole is its GDP, or Y—that is, the value of the final goods and services produced within the country's borders during the year.

Identifying the part of total expenditure that corresponds to the nation's spending on current needs is more difficult than identifying the nation's income. The component of aggregate spending that is easiest to classify is investment spending I. We know that investment spending—the acquisition of new factories, equipment, and other capital goods, as well as residential construction—is done to expand the economy's future productive capacity or provide more housing for the future, not to satisfy current needs. So investment spending clearly is *not* part of spending on current needs.

Deciding how much of consumption spending by households, C, and government purchases of goods and services, G, should be counted as spending on current needs is less straightforward. Certainly most consumption spending by households—on food, clothing, utilities, entertainment, and so on—is for current needs. But consumption spending also includes purchases of long-lived *consumer durables,* such as cars, furniture, and appliances. Consumer durables are only partially used up during the current year; they may continue to provide service, in fact, for years after their purchase. So household spending on consumer durables is a combination of spending on current needs and spending on future needs.

As with consumption spending, most government purchases of goods and services are intended to provide for current needs. However, like household purchases, a portion of government purchases is devoted to the acquisition or construction of long-lived capital goods, such as roads, bridges, schools, government buildings, and military hardware. And like consumer durables, these forms of *public capital* are only partially used up during the current year; most will provide useful services far into the future. So, like consumption spending, government purchases are in fact a mixture of spending on current needs and spending on future needs.

Although in reality not all spending by households and the government is for current needs, in practice, determining precisely how much of such spending is for current needs and how much is for future needs is extremely difficult. For this reason, for a long time U.S. government statistics treated *all* of both consumption expenditures (C) and government purchases (G) as spending on current needs.[2] For simplicity's sake, in this book we will follow the same practice. But keep in mind that because consumption spending and government purchases do in fact include some spending for future rather than current needs, treating all of C and G as spending on current needs will understate the true amount of national saving.

If we treat all consumption spending and government purchases as spending on current needs, then the nation's saving is its income Y less its spending on current needs, $C + G$. So we can define **national saving** S as

national saving the saving of the entire economy, equal to GDP less consumption expenditures and government purchases of goods and services, or $Y - C - G$

$$S = Y - C - G. \tag{7.1}$$

Figure 7.3 shows the U.S. national saving rate (national saving as a percentage of GDP) for the years 1960 through 2019. The U.S. national saving rate fell from 18 to 20 percent in the 1960s to around 13 to 15 percent in recent years. Like household saving, national saving declined over time, though by comparing Figures 7.1 and 7.3, you can see that the decline in national saving has been more modest. Furthermore, unlike household saving, national saving recovered in the latter 1990s—indeed, in 1998 the national saving rate was above 16 percent, slightly higher than the rate in 1970. As we will see next, the reason for these differences between the behavior of national saving and household saving is that saving done by business firms and, in the late 1990s, by the government has been substantial.

FIGURE 7.3

U.S. National Saving Rate, 1960–2019.

U.S. national saving fell from 18 to 20 percent of GDP in the 1960s to 13 to 15 percent in recent years.

Source: Bureau of Economic Analysis, www.bea.gov.

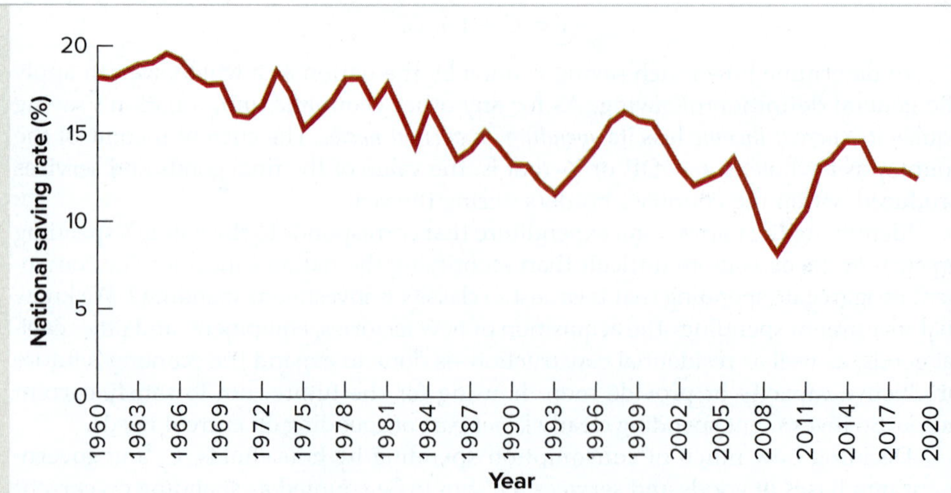

[3]Nowadays, the official data distinguish investment in public capital from the rest of government purchases.

Private and Public Components of National Saving

To understand national saving better, we will divide it into two major components: private saving, which is saving done by households and businesses, and public saving, which is saving done by the government.

To see how national saving breaks down into public and private saving, we work with the definition of national saving, $S = Y - C - G$. To distinguish private-sector income from public-sector income, we must expand this equation to incorporate taxes as well as payments made by the government to the private sector. Government payments to the private sector include both *transfer payments* and *interest* paid to individuals and institutions that hold government bonds. **Transfer payments** are payments the government makes to the public for which it receives no current goods or services in return. Social Security benefits, welfare payments, farm support payments, and pensions to government workers are transfer payments.

transfer payments payments the government makes to the public for which it receives no current goods or services in return

Let T stand for taxes paid by the private sector to the government *less* transfer payments and interest payments made by the government to the private sector:

$$T = \text{Total taxes} - \text{Transfer payments} - \text{Government interest payments}.$$

Since T equals private-sector tax payments minus the various benefits and interest payments the private sector receives from the government, we can think of T as *net taxes*. If we add and then subtract T from the definition of national saving, $S = Y - C - G$, we get

$$S = Y - C - G + T - T.$$

Rearranging this equation and grouping terms, we obtain

$$S = (Y - T - C) + (T - G). \quad (7.2)$$

This equation splits national saving S into two parts, *private saving*, or $Y - T - C$, and *public saving*, $T - G$.

Private saving, $Y - T - C$, is the saving of the private sector of the economy. Why is $Y - T - C$ a reasonable definition of private saving? Remember that saving equals current income minus spending on current needs. The income of the private (nongovernmental) sector of the economy is the economy's total income Y less net taxes paid to the government, T. The private sector's spending on current needs is its consumption expenditures C. So private-sector saving, equal to private-sector income less spending on current needs, is $Y - T - C$. Letting S_{private} stand for private saving, we can write the definition of private saving as

private saving the saving of the private sector of the economy is equal to the after-tax income of the private sector minus consumption expenditures ($Y - T - C$); private saving can be further broken down into household saving and business saving

$$S_{\text{Private}} = Y - T - C.$$

Private saving can be further broken down into saving done by households and business firms. *Household saving,* also called personal saving, is saving done by families and individuals. Household saving corresponds to the familiar image of families putting aside part of their incomes each month, and it is the focus of much attention in the news media. But businesses are important savers as well—indeed business saving makes up the bulk of private saving in the United States. Businesses use the revenues from their sales to pay workers' salaries and other operating costs, to pay taxes, and to provide dividends to their shareholders. The funds remaining after these payments have been made are equal to *business saving*. A business firm's savings are available for the purchase of new capital equipment or the expansion of its operations. Alternatively, a business can put its savings in the bank for future use.

Public saving, $T - G$, is the saving of the government sector, including state and local governments as well as the federal government. Net taxes T are the income of the government. Government purchases G represent the government's spending on current needs (remember that, for the sake of simplicity, we are ignoring the investment portion of government purchases). Thus $T - G$ fits our definition of saving, in

public saving the saving of the government sector is equal to net tax payments minus government purchases ($T - G$)

this case by the public sector. Letting S_{public} stand for public saving, we can write out the definition of public saving as

$$S_{\text{public}} = T - G.$$

Using Equation 7.2 and the definitions of private and public saving, we can rewrite national saving as

$$S = S_{\text{private}} + S_{\text{public}}. \tag{7.3}$$

This equation confirms that national saving is the sum of private saving and public saving. Since private saving in turn can be broken down into household and business saving, we see that national saving is made up of the saving of three groups: households, businesses, and the government.

Public Saving and the Government Budget

Although the idea that households and businesses can save is familiar to most people, the fact that the government can also save is less widely understood. Public saving is closely linked to the government's decisions about spending and taxing. Governments finance the bulk of their spending by taxing the private sector. If taxes and spending in a given year are equal, the government is said to have a *balanced budget*. If, in any given year, the government's spending exceeds its tax collections, the difference is called the **government budget deficit.** If the government runs a deficit, it must make up the difference by borrowing from the public through issuance of government bonds. Algebraically, the government budget deficit can be written as $G - T$, or government purchases minus net tax collections.

government budget deficit the excess of government spending over tax collections ($G - T$)

In some years, the government may spend less than it collects in taxes. The excess of tax collections over government spending is called the **government budget surplus.** When a government has a surplus, it uses the extra funds to pay down its outstanding debt to the public. Algebraically, the government budget surplus may be written as $T - G$, or net tax collections less government purchases.

government budget surplus the excess of government tax collections over government spending ($T - G$); the government budget surplus equals public saving

If the algebraic expression for the government budget surplus, $T - G$, looks familiar, that is because it is also the definition of public saving, as we saw earlier. Thus, *public saving is identical to the government budget surplus.* In other words, when the government collects more in taxes than it spends, public saving will be positive. When the government spends more than it collects in taxes so that it runs a deficit, public saving will be negative.

Example 7.4 illustrates the relationships among public saving, the government budget surplus, and national saving.

EXAMPLE 7.4 Government Saving

How do we calculate government saving?

Following are data on U.S. government revenues and expenditures for 2000, in billions of dollars. Find (a) the federal government's budget surplus or deficit, (b) the budget surplus or deficit of state and local governments, and (c) the contribution of the government sector to national saving.

Federal government:	
Receipts	2,068.4
Expenditures	1,912.9
State and local governments:	
Receipts	1,304.1
Expenditures	1,344.8

Source: Bureau of Economic Analysis, NIPA Tables 3.2 and 3.3.

The federal government's receipts minus its expenditures were 2,068.4 − 1,912.9 = 155.5, so the federal government ran a budget surplus of $155.5 billion in 2000. State and local government receipts minus expenditures were 1,304.1 − 1,344.8 = −40.7, so state and local governments ran a collective budget deficit of $40.7 billion. The budget surplus of the entire government sector—that is, the federal surplus minus the state and local deficit—was 155.5 − 40.7 = 114.8, or $114.8 billion. So the contribution of the government sector to U.S. national saving in 2000 was $114.8 billion.

SELF-TEST 7.4

Continuing Example 7.4, here are the analogous data on government revenues and expenditures for 2018, in billions of dollars. Again, find (a) the federal government's budget surplus or deficit, (b) the budget surplus or deficit of state and local governments, and (c) the contribution of the government sector to national saving.

Federal government:	
Receipts	3,497.7
Expenditures	4,507.4
State and local governments:	
Receipts	2,623.0
Expenditures	2,862.1

If you did Self-Test 7.4 correctly, you found that the government sector's contribution to national saving in 2018 was *negative*. The reason is that the federal, state, and local governments taken together ran a budget deficit in that year, reducing national saving by the amount of the budget deficit.

Figure 7.3 showed the U.S. national saving rate since 1960. Figure 7.4 shows the behavior since 1960 of the three components of national saving: household saving, business saving, and public saving, each measured as a percentage of GDP. Note that

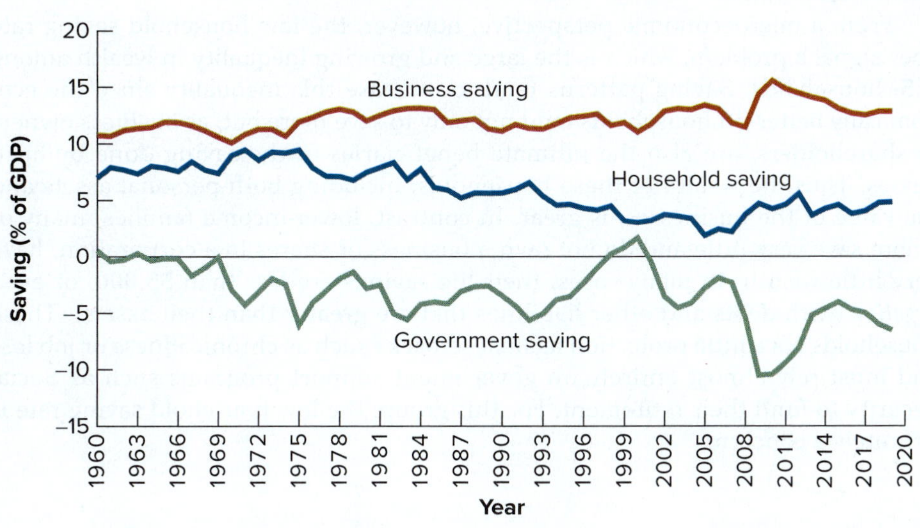

FIGURE 7.4

The Three Components of National Saving, 1960–2019.

Of the three components of national saving, business saving is the most important.

Source: Bureau of Economic Analysis, www.bea.gov.

business saving played a major role in national saving during these years, while the role of household saving was relatively modest. As we saw in Figure 7.1, household saving has declined since the mid-1970s.

The contribution of public saving has varied considerably over time. Until about 1970, the federal, state, and local governments typically ran a roughly balanced combined budget, making little contribution to national saving. But by the 1970s, public saving had turned negative, reflecting large budget deficits, particularly at the federal level. For the next two decades, the government was a net drain on national saving. During the late 1990s, government budgets moved closer to balance and, by the end of the decade, reached surplus, making a positive contribution to national saving. Government budgets dove again into deficits around the 2001 recession, and around the 2007–2009 recession, they reached deficits of historic scale. The relationship between government deficits and recessions was mentioned earlier in the text, and we will discuss it in more detail in future chapters.

In the years after the 2007–2009 recession, the government deficit returned more or less back to where it was from the mid-1970s to the mid-1990s. However, in the second half of the 2010s it started increasing again, and then it ballooned in 2020 due to the COVID-19 pandemic and the fight against it.

Is Low Household Saving a Problem?

In the opening to this chapter, and again in The Economic Naturalist 7.1 and 7.3, we mentioned that saving by U.S. households, never high by international standards, fell further during the past few decades. How big of a problem is the low (and declining) household saving rate in the United States? We will answer this question from both a macroeconomic and a microeconomic perspective.

From a macroeconomic perspective, the problem posed by low household saving may not be as big as it may first seem. The key point to remember is that national saving, not household saving, determines the capacity of an economy to invest in new capital goods and to achieve continued improvement in living standards. Although household saving is low, saving by business firms has been significant. Moreover, business saving has been increasing over the past few decades: As Figure 7.4 shows, business saving slowly increased from around 11 percent of GDP in the early 1960s to around 13 to 15 percent in the 2010s. Overall, the decline in the U.S. national saving rate shown in Figure 7.3 has been less dramatic than the decline in the household saving rate shown in Figure 7.1. Although U.S. national saving is somewhat low compared to that of other industrialized countries, it has been sufficient to allow the United States to become one of the world's most productive economies.[4]

From a microeconomic perspective, however, the low household saving rate does signal a problem, which is the large and growing inequality in wealth among U.S. households. Saving patterns tend to increase this inequality since the economically better-off households tend not only to save more but, as business owners or shareholders, are also the ultimate beneficiaries of the saving done by businesses. Thus the wealth of these households, including both personal assets and the value of the businesses, is great. In contrast, lower-income families, many of whom save very little and do not own a business or shares in a corporation, have very little wealth–in many cases, their life savings are less than $5,000, or even *negative* (with debts and other liabilities that are greater than their assets). These households have little protection against setbacks such as chronic illness or job loss and must rely almost entirely on government support programs such as Social Security to fund their retirement. For this group, the low household saving rate is definitely a concern.

[4]In addition to its domestic saving, the U.S. attracts savings from abroad, as we discuss in the next chapter.

RECAP

NATIONAL SAVING AND ITS COMPONENTS

National saving, the saving of the nation as a whole, is defined by $S = Y - C - G$, where Y is GDP, C is consumption spending, and G is government purchases of goods and services. National saving is the sum of public saving and private saving: $S = S_{\text{private}} + S_{\text{public}}$.

Private saving, the saving of the private sector, is defined by $S_{\text{private}} = Y - T - C$, where T is net tax payments. Private saving can be broken down further into household saving and business saving.

Public saving, the saving of the government, is defined by $S_{\text{public}} = T - G$. Public saving equals the government budget surplus, $T - G$. When the government budget is in surplus, government saving is positive; when the government budget is in deficit, public saving is negative.

INVESTMENT AND CAPITAL FORMATION

From the point of view of the economy as a whole, the importance of national saving is that it provides the funds needed for investment. Investment—the creation of new capital goods and housing—is critical to increasing average labor productivity and improving standards of living.

What factors determine whether and how much firms choose to invest? Firms acquire new capital goods for the same reason they hire new workers: they expect that doing so will be profitable. We saw in Chapter 6, *The Labor Market: Workers, Wages, and Unemployment,* that the profitability of employing an extra worker depends primarily on two factors: the cost of employing the worker and the value of the worker's marginal product. In the same way, firms' willingness to acquire new factories and machines depends on the expected *cost* of using them and the expected *benefit,* equal to the value of the marginal product that they will provide.

EXAMPLE 7.5 Investing in a Capital Good, Part 1

Should Lauren buy a riding lawn mower?

Lauren is thinking of going into the lawn care business. She can buy a \$4,000 riding mower by taking out a loan at 6 percent annual interest. With this mower and her own labor, Lauren can net \$6,000 per summer, after deduction of costs such as gasoline and maintenance. Of the \$6,000 net revenues, 20 percent must be paid to the government in taxes. Assume that Lauren could earn \$4,400 after taxes by working in an alternative job. Assume also that the lawn mower can always be resold for its original purchase price of \$4,000. Should Lauren buy the lawn mower?

To decide whether to invest in the capital good (the lawn mower), Lauren should compare the financial benefits and costs. With the mower she can earn revenue of \$6,000, net of gasoline and maintenance costs. However, 20 percent of that, or \$1,200, must be paid in taxes, leaving Lauren with \$4,800. Lauren could earn \$4,400 after taxes by working at an alternative job, so the financial benefit to Lauren of buying the mower is the difference between \$4,800 and \$4,400, or \$400; \$400 is the value of the marginal product of the lawn mower.

Since the mower does not lose value over time and since gasoline and maintenance costs have already been deducted, the only remaining cost Lauren should take into account is the interest on the loan for the mower. Lauren must pay 6 percent interest on \$4,000, or \$240 per year. Since this financial cost is less than the financial benefit of \$400, the value of the mower's marginal product, Lauren should buy the mower.

Lauren's decision might change if the costs and benefits of her investment in the mower change, as Example 7.6 shows.

EXAMPLE 7.6 Investing in a Capital Good, Part 2

How do changes in the costs and benefits affect Lauren's decision?

With all other assumptions the same as in Example 7.5, decide whether Lauren should buy the mower:

a. If the interest rate is 12 percent rather than 6 percent.

b. If the purchase price of the mower is $7,000 rather than $4,000.

c. If the tax rate on Lauren's net revenues is 25 percent rather than 20 percent.

d. If the mower is less efficient than Lauren originally thought so that her net revenues will be $5,500 rather than $6,000.

In each case, Lauren must compare the financial costs and benefits of buying the mower.

a. If the interest rate is 12 percent, then the interest cost will be 12 percent of $4,000, or $480, which exceeds the value of the mower's marginal product ($400). Lauren should not buy the mower.

b. If the cost of the mower is $7,000, then Lauren must borrow $7,000 instead of $4,000. At 6 percent interest, her interest cost will be $420—too high to justify the purchase, since the value of the mower's marginal product is $400.

c. If the tax rate on net revenues is 25 percent, then Lauren must pay 25 percent of her $6,000 net revenues, or $1,500, in taxes. After taxes, her revenues from mowing will be $4,500, which is only $100 more than she could make working at an alternative job. Furthermore, the $100 will not cover the $240 in interest that Lauren would have to pay. So again, Lauren should not buy the mower.

d. If the mower is less efficient than originally expected so that Lauren can earn net revenues of only $5,500, Lauren will be left with only $4,400 after taxes—the same amount she could earn by working at another job. So in this case, the value of the mower's marginal product is zero. At any interest rate greater than zero, Lauren should not buy the mower.

SELF-TEST 7.5

Repeat Example 7.5, but assume that, over the course of the year, wear and tear reduces the resale value of the lawn mower from $4,000 to $3,800. Should Lauren buy the mower?

The examples involving Lauren and the lawn mower illustrate the main factors firms must consider when deciding whether to invest in new capital goods. On the cost side, two important factors are the *price of capital goods* and the *real interest rate*. Clearly, the more expensive new capital goods are, the more reluctant firms will be to invest in them. Buying the mower was profitable for Lauren when its price was $4,000, but not when its price was $7,000.

Why is the real interest rate an important factor in investment decisions? The most straightforward case is when a firm has to borrow (as Lauren did) to purchase its new capital. The real interest rate then determines the real cost to the firm of paying back its debt. Since financing costs are a major part of the total cost of owning and operating a piece of capital, much as mortgage payments are a major part of the cost of owning a home, increases in the real interest rate make the purchase of capital goods less attractive to firms, all else being equal.

Even if a firm does not need to borrow to buy new capital—say, because it has accumulated enough profits to buy the capital outright—the real interest rate remains an important determinant of the desirability of an investment. If a firm does not use its profits to acquire new capital, most likely it will use those profits to acquire financial assets such as bonds, which will earn the firm the real rate of interest. If the firm uses its profits to buy capital rather than to purchase a bond, it forgoes the opportunity to earn the real rate of interest on its funds. Thus the real rate of interest measures the *opportunity cost* of a capital investment. Since an increase in the real interest rate raises the opportunity cost of investing in new capital, it lowers the willingness of firms to invest, even if they do not literally need to borrow to finance new machines or equipment.

On the benefit side, the key factor in determining business investment is the *value of the marginal product* of the new capital, which should be calculated net of both operating and maintenance expenses and taxes paid on the revenues the capital generates. The value of the marginal product is affected by several factors. For example, a technological advance that allows a piece of capital to produce more goods and services would increase the value of its marginal product, as would lower taxes on the revenues produced by the new capital. An increase in the relative price of the good or service that the capital is used to produce will also increase the value of the marginal product and, hence, the desirability of the investment. For example, if the going price for lawn-mowing services were to rise, then all else being equal, investing in the mower would become more profitable for Lauren.

RECAP

FACTORS THAT AFFECT INVESTMENT

Any of the following factors will increase the willingness of firms to invest in new capital:

1. A decline in the price of new capital goods.
2. A decline in the real interest rate.
3. Technological improvement that raises the marginal product of capital.
4. Lower taxes on the revenues generated by capital.
5. A higher relative price for the firm's output.

SAVING, INVESTMENT, AND FINANCIAL MARKETS

Saving and investment are determined by different forces. Ultimately, though, in an economy without international borrowing and lending, national saving must equal investment. The supply of savings (by households, firms, and the government) and the demand for savings (by firms that want to purchase or construct new capital) are equalized through the workings of *financial markets*. Figure 7.5 illustrates this process. Quantities of national saving and investment are measured on the horizontal axis; the real interest rate is shown on the vertical axis. As we will see, in the market for saving, the real interest rate functions as the "price."

In Figure 7.5, the supply of savings is shown by the upward-sloping curve marked *S*. This curve shows the quantity of national saving that households, firms, and the government are willing to supply at each value of the real interest rate. The saving curve is upward-sloping because empirical evidence suggests that increases in the real interest rate stimulate saving. The demand for saving is given by the downward-sloping curve marked *I*. This curve shows the quantity of investment in new capital that firms would choose and hence the amount they would need to borrow in financial markets, at each value of the real interest rate. Because higher real interest rates raise the cost of borrowing and reduce firms' willingness to invest, the demand for saving curve is downward-sloping.

FIGURE 7.5

The Supply of and Demand for Savings.

Savings are supplied by households, firms, and the government and demanded by borrowers wishing to invest in new capital goods. The supply of saving (*S*) increases with the real interest rate, and the demand for saving by investors (*I*) decreases with the real interest rate. In financial market equilibrium, the real interest rate takes the value that equates the quantity of saving supplied and demanded.

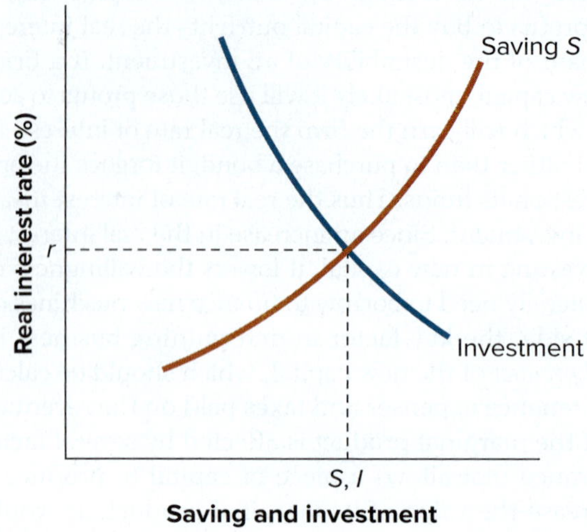

Putting aside the possibility of borrowing from foreigners (discussed in the next chapter), a country can invest only those resources that its savers make available. In equilibrium, then, desired investment (the demand for savings) and desired national saving (the supply of savings) must be equal. As Figure 7.5 suggests, desired saving is equated with desired investment through adjustments in the real interest rate, which functions as the "price" of saving. The movements of the real interest rate clear the market for saving in much the same way that the price of apples clears the market for apples. In Figure 7.5, the real interest rate that clears the market for saving is *r*, the real interest rate that corresponds to the intersection of the supply and demand curves.

The forces that push the real interest rate toward its equilibrium level are similar to the forces that lead to equilibrium in any other supply and demand situation. Suppose, for example, that the real interest rate exceeded *r*. At a higher real interest rate, savers would provide more funds than firms would want to invest. As lenders (savers) competed among themselves to attract borrowers (investors), the real interest rate would be bid down. The real interest rate would fall until it equaled *r*, the only interest rate at which both borrowers and lenders are satisfied, and no opportunities are left unexploited in the financial market. What would happen if the real interest rate were *lower* than *r*?

Changes in factors *other than the real interest rate* that affect the supply of or demand for saving will shift the curves, leading to a new equilibrium in the financial market. Changes in the real interest rate cannot shift the supply or demand curves, just as a change in the price of apples cannot shift the supply or demand for apples, because the effects of the real interest rate on savings are already incorporated in the slopes of the curves. A few examples will illustrate the use of the supply and demand model of financial markets.

EXAMPLE 7.7 The Effects of New Technology

How does the introduction of new technologies affect saving, investment, and the real interest rate?

The late 1990s saw the introduction and application of exciting new technologies, ranging from the Internet to new applications of genetics. A number of these technologies appeared at the time to have great commercial potential. How does the introduction of new technologies affect saving, investment, and the real interest rate?

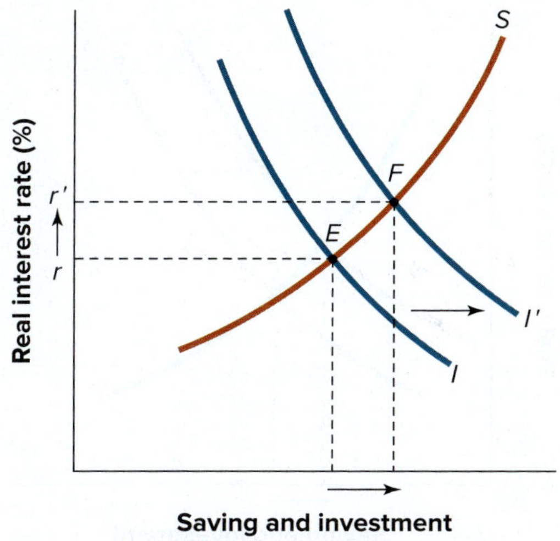

FIGURE 7.6

The Effects of a New Technology on National Saving and Investment.

A technological breakthrough raises the marginal product of new capital goods, increasing desired investment and the demand for savings. The real interest rate rises, as do national saving and investment.

The introduction of any new technology with the potential for commercial application creates profit opportunities for those who can bring the fruits of the technology to the public. In economists' language, the technical breakthrough raises the marginal product of new capital. Figure 7.6 shows the effects of a technological breakthrough, with a resulting increase in the marginal product of capital. At any given real interest rate, an increase in the marginal product of capital makes firms more eager to invest. Thus, the advent of the new technology causes the demand for saving to shift upward and to the right, from *I* to *I′*.

At the new equilibrium point *F*, investment and national saving are higher than before, as is the real interest rate, which rises from *r* to *r′*. The rise in the real interest rate reflects the increased demand for funds by investors as they race to apply the new technologies. Because of the incentive of higher real returns, saving increases as well. Indeed, the real interest rate in the United States was relatively high in the late 1990s, as was the rate of investment, reflecting the opportunities created by new technologies.

Example 7.8 examines the effect of changing fiscal policies on the market for saving.

EXAMPLE 7.8 The Effects of Changing Fiscal Policies

How does an increase in the government budget deficit affect saving, investment, and the real interest rate?

Suppose the government increases its spending without raising taxes, thereby increasing its budget deficit (or reducing its budget surplus). How will this decision affect national saving, investment, and the real interest rate?

National saving includes both private saving (saving by households and businesses) and public saving, which is equivalent to the government budget surplus. An increase in the government budget deficit (or a decline in the surplus) reduces public saving. Assuming that private saving does not change, the reduction in public saving will reduce national saving as well.

Figure 7.7 shows the effect of the increased government budget deficit on the market for saving and investment. At any real interest rate, a larger deficit reduces national saving, causing the saving curve to shift to the left, from *S* to *S′*. At the new equilibrium point *F*, the real interest rate is higher at *r′*, and both national

FIGURE 7.7

The Effects of an Increase in the Government Budget Deficit on National Saving and Investment.

An increase in the government budget deficit reduces the supply of saving, raising the real interest rate and lowering investment. The tendency of increased government deficits to reduce investment in new capital is called *crowding out*.

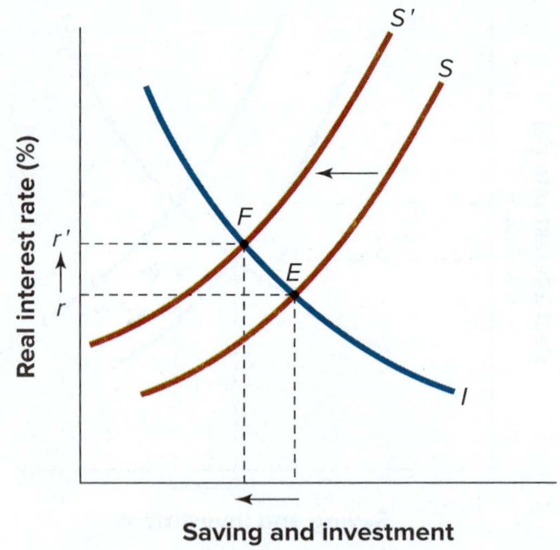

saving and investment are lower. In economic terms, the government has dipped further into the pool of private savings to borrow the funds to finance its budget deficit. The government's extra borrowing forces investors to compete for a smaller quantity of available saving, driving up the real interest rate. The higher real interest rate makes investment less attractive, ensuring that investment will decrease along with national saving.

crowding out the tendency of increased government deficits to reduce investment spending

The tendency of government budget deficits to reduce investment spending is called **crowding out.** Reduced investment spending implies slower capital formation, and thus lower economic growth. This adverse effect of budget deficits on economic growth is probably the most important cost of deficits, and a major reason why economists advise governments to minimize their deficits.

SELF-TEST 7.6

Suppose the general public becomes more "grasshopper-like" and less "ant-like" in their saving decisions, becoming less concerned about saving for the future. How will the change in public attitudes affect the country's rate of capital formation and economic growth?

At the national level, high saving rates lead to greater investment in new capital goods and thus higher standards of living. At the individual or family level, a high saving rate promotes the accumulation of wealth and the achievement of economic security. In this chapter we have studied some of the factors that underlie saving and investment decisions. The next chapter will look more closely at how savers hold their wealth and at how the financial system allocates the pool of available savings to the most productive investment projects.

The Economic Naturalist 7.5

Why have real interest rates declined globally in recent decades?

Real interest rates around the world have declined appreciably in the past few decades. In the U.S., the real interest rate on 10-year Treasury bonds—funds borrowed by the federal government for a term of 10 years—declined from around 7–8 percent in the early 1980s to around 0–2 percent in the 2010s. Such trends are found in all advanced economies. What can explain them?

In general, changes in the real interest rate can be caused by shifts in the supply of saving, shifts in the demand for new capital investment, or both. Because the decades-long decline in interest rates has been a global phenomenon, potential explanations have to consider shifts in *global* supply and demand. Indeed, both supply and demand have played an important role.

For simplicity, let's think of the world as a single market.[5] On the supply side, global saving has risen as global incomes have risen (recall our discussion of the rise in global incomes in Chapter 5, *Economic Growth, Productivity, and Living Standards*). Demographic factors, including aging populations and rising life spans, have also been important. Due to aging populations, more people are in the ages in which the need to save for retirement is greatest. And due to rising life spans, people expect to be retired for more years, causing them to save more.

On the demand side, slower global population growth has led to slower workforce growth, in turn reducing the need and thus the demand for new capital (recall our discussion in Chapter 6, *The Labor Market: Workers, Wages, and Unemployment*). In addition, many new industries, like social media companies, require less physical capital than traditional manufacturing industries, further reducing demand.

The combination of higher global saving and lower global investment helps explain the downward trend in real interest rates.[6]

RECAP

SAVING, INVESTMENT, AND FINANCIAL MARKETS

- Financial markets bring together the suppliers of savings (households, firms, and the government) and demanders for savings (firms that want to purchase or construct new capital).
- Putting aside the possibility of borrowing from foreigners, a country can invest only those resources that its savers make available. In equilibrium, then, desired investment (the demand for savings) must equal desired national saving (the supply of savings).
- In equilibrium, supply and demand are equated through adjustments in the real interest rate, which functions as the "price" of saving.
- Changes in factors other than the real interest rate that affect the supply of or demand for saving will shift the supply and demand curves, leading to a new equilibrium in the financial market.
- For example, any of the following factors will increase the willingness of firms to invest in new capital, and will therefore shift the demand curve outward:

  1. A decline in the price of new capital goods.
  2. Technological improvement that raises the marginal product of capital.
  3. Lower taxes on the revenues generated by capital.
  4. A higher relative price for the firm's output.

[5]In this chapter, we focused on *domestic* financial markets, putting aside the possibility of borrowing from foreigners and the possibility of investing abroad. These will be discussed in Chapter 8, *Money, the Federal Reserve, and Global Financial Markets*. Here we simply treat the entire world as a single country.

[6]The increase in global saving relative to global investment has been called *the global saving glut*. See "The Global Saving Glut and the U.S. Current Account Deficit," remarks by Governor Ben S. Bernanke at the Sandridge Lecture, Virginia Association of Economists, Richmond, Virginia, March 10, 2005, www.federalreserve.gov/boarddocs/speeches/2005/200503102/. Slower growth and lower demand for capital are aspects of *the secular stagnation hypothesis*. See "U.S. Economic Prospects: Secular Stagnation, Hysteresis, and the Zero Lower Bound," keynote address by Lawrence H. Summers at the NABE Policy Conference, February 24, 2014, *Business Economics* 49, pp. 65–73.

SUMMARY

- In general, *saving* equals current income minus spending on current needs; the *saving rate* is the percentage of income that is saved. *Wealth,* or net worth, equals the market value of assets (real or financial items of value) minus liabilities (debts). Saving is a *flow,* being measured in dollars per unit of time; wealth is a *stock,* measured in dollars at a point in time. As the amount of water in a bathtub changes according to the rate at which water flows in, the stock of wealth increases at the saving rate. Wealth also increases if the value of existing assets rises (*capital gains*) and decreases if the value of existing assets falls (*capital losses*). *(LO1)*
- Individuals and households save for a variety of reasons, including *life-cycle* objectives, such as saving for retirement or a new home; the need to be prepared for an emergency (*precautionary saving*); and the desire to leave an inheritance (*bequest saving*). The amount people save is also affected by the real interest rate, which is the "reward" for saving. Evidence suggests that higher real interest rates lead to modest increases in saving. Saving can also be affected by psychological factors, such as the degree of self-control and the desire to consume at the level of one's neighbors (demonstration effects). *(LO2)*
- The saving of an entire country is *national saving* S. National saving is defined by $S = Y - C - G$, where Y represents total output or income, C equals consumption spending, and G equals government purchases of goods and services. National saving can be broken up into private saving, or $Y - T - C$, and public saving, or $T - G$, where T stands for taxes paid to the government less transfer payments and interest paid by the government to the private sector. Private saving can be further broken down into household saving and business saving. In the United States, the bulk of private saving is done by businesses. *(LO3)*
- Public saving is equivalent to the government budget surplus, $T - G$; if the government runs a budget deficit, then public saving is negative. The U.S. national saving rate is low relative to other industrialized countries, but it is higher than U.S. household saving, and it declined less over the past few decades. *(LO3)*
- Investment is the purchase or construction of new capital goods, including housing. Firms will invest in new capital goods if the benefits of doing so outweigh the costs. Two factors that determine the cost of investment are the price of new capital goods and the real interest rate. The higher the real interest rate, the more expensive it is to borrow, and the less likely firms are to invest. The benefit of investment is the value of the marginal product of new capital, which depends on factors such as the productivity of new capital goods, the taxes levied on the revenues they generate, and the relative price of the firm's output. *(LO4)*
- In the absence of international borrowing or lending, the supply of and demand for national saving must be equal. The supply of national saving depends on the saving decisions of households and businesses and the fiscal policies of the government (which determine public saving). The demand for saving is the amount business firms want to invest in new capital. The real interest rate, which is the "price" of borrowed funds, changes to equate the supply of and demand for national saving. Factors that affect the supply of or demand for saving will change saving, investment, and the equilibrium real interest rate. For example, an increase in the government budget deficit will reduce national saving and investment and raise the equilibrium real interest rate. The tendency of government budget deficits to reduce investment is called *crowding out*. *(LO5)*

KEY TERMS

assets
balance sheet
bequest saving
capital gains
capital losses
crowding out
flow
government budget deficit
government budget surplus
liabilities
life-cycle saving
national saving
net worth
nominal interest rate (or market interest rate)
precautionary saving
private saving
public saving
real interest rate
saving
saving rate
stock
transfer payments
wealth

REVIEW QUESTIONS

1. Explain the relationship between saving and wealth, using the concepts of flows and stocks. Is saving the only means by which wealth can increase? Explain. *(LO1)*
2. Give three basic motivations for saving. Illustrate each with an example. What other factors would psychologists cite as being possibly important for saving? *(LO2)*
3. Define national saving, relating your definition to the general concept of saving. Why does the standard U.S. definition of national saving potentially understate the true amount of saving being done in the economy? *(LO3)*
4. Household saving rates in the U.S. are very low. Is this fact a problem for the U.S. economy? Why or why not? *(LO3)*
5. Why do increases in real interest rates reduce the quantity of saving demanded? (*Hint:* Who are the "demanders" of saving?) *(LO4, LO5)*
6. Name one factor that could increase the supply of saving and one that could increase the demand for saving. Show the effects of each on saving, investment, and the real interest rate. *(LO5)*

PROBLEMS

connect

1. Corey has a mountain bike worth $300, credit card debt of $150, $200 in cash, a Sandy Koufax baseball card worth $400, $1,200 in a checking account, and an electric bill due for $250. *(LO1)*
   a. Construct Corey's balance sheet and calculate his net worth. For each remaining part, explain how the event affects Corey's assets, liabilities, and wealth.
   b. Corey goes to a baseball card convention and finds out that his baseball card is a worthless forgery.
   c. Corey uses $150 from his paycheck to pay off his credit card balance. The remainder of his earnings is spent.
   d. Corey writes a $150 check on his checking account to pay off his credit card balance.

   Of the events in parts b–d, which, if any, correspond(s) to saving on Corey's part?
2. State whether each of the following is a stock or a flow, and explain. *(LO1)*
   a. The gross domestic product.
   b. National saving.
   c. The value of the U.S. housing stock on January 1, 2020.
   d. The amount of U.S. currency in circulation as of this morning.
   e. The government budget deficit.
   f. The quantity of outstanding government debt on January 1, 2020.
3. Ellie and Vince are a married couple, both with college degrees and jobs. How would you expect each of the following events to affect the amount they save each month? Explain your answers in terms of the basic motivations for saving. *(LO2)*
   a. Ellie learns she is pregnant.
   b. Vince reads in the paper about possible layoffs in his industry.
   c. Vince had hoped that his parents would lend financial assistance toward the couple's planned purchase of a house, but he learns that they can't afford it.
   d. Ellie announces that she would like to go to law school in the next few years.
   e. A boom in the stock market greatly increases the value of the couple's retirement funds.
   f. Vince and Ellie agree that they would like to leave a substantial amount to local charities in their wills.
4. Individual retirement accounts, or IRAs, were established by the U.S. government to encourage saving. An individual who deposits part of current earnings in an IRA does not have to pay income taxes on the earnings deposited, nor are any income taxes charged on the interest earned by the funds in the IRA. However, when the funds are withdrawn from the IRA, the full amount withdrawn is treated as income and is taxed at the individual's current income tax rate. In contrast, an individual depositing in a non-IRA account has to pay income taxes on the funds deposited and on interest earned in each year but does not have to pay taxes on withdrawals from the account. Another feature of IRAs that is different from a standard saving account is that funds deposited in an IRA cannot be withdrawn prior to retirement, except upon payment of a substantial penalty. *(LO2)*
   a. Sarah, who is five years from retirement, receives a $10,000 bonus at work. She is trying to decide whether to save this extra income in an IRA account or in a regular savings account.

Both accounts earn 5 percent nominal interest, and Sarah is in the 30 percent tax bracket in every year (including her retirement year). Compare the amounts that Sarah will have in five years under each of the two saving strategies, net of all taxes. Is the IRA a good deal for Sarah?

b. Would you expect the availability of IRAs to increase the amount that households save? Discuss in light of (1) the response of saving to changes in the real interest rate and (2) psychological theories of saving.

5. In each part that follows, use the economic data given to find national saving, private saving, public saving, and the national saving rate. *(LO3)*
   a. Household saving = 200 Business saving = 400
   Government purchases of goods and services = 260
   Government transfers and interest payments = 135
   Tax collections = 245 GDP = 3,000
   b. GDP = 6,400 Tax collections = 1,925
   Government transfers and interest payments = 400
   Consumption expenditures = 4,570
   Government budget surplus = 100
   c. Consumption expenditures = 4,800
   Investment = 1,000
   Government purchases = 1,000 Net exports = 16
   Tax collections = 1,700
   Government transfers and interest payments = 500

6. Ellie and Vince are trying to decide whether to purchase a new home. The house they want is priced at $200,000. Annual expenses such as maintenance, taxes, and insurance equal 4 percent of the home's value. If properly maintained, the house's real value is not expected to change. The real interest rate in the economy is 6 percent, and Ellie and Vince can qualify to borrow the full amount of the purchase price (for simplicity, assume no down payment) at that rate. Ignore the fact that mortgage interest payments are tax-deductible in the United States. *(LO4)*
   a. Ellie and Vince would be willing to pay $1,500 monthly rent to live in a house of the same quality as the one they are thinking about purchasing. Should they buy the house?
   b. Does the answer to part a change if they are willing to pay $2,000 monthly rent?
   c. Does the answer to part a change if the real interest rate is 4 percent instead of 6 percent?
   d. Does the answer to part a change if the developer offers to sell Ellie and Vince the house for $150,000?
   e. Why do home-building companies dislike high interest rates?

7. The builder of a new movie theater complex is trying to decide how many screens she wants. Below are her estimates of the number of patrons the complex will attract each year, depending on the number of screens available. *(LO4)*

Number of screens	Total number of patrons
1	40,000
2	75,000
3	105,000
4	130,000
5	150,000

After paying the movie distributors and meeting all other noninterest expenses, the owner expects to net $2.00 per ticket sold. Construction costs are $1,000,000 per screen.

   a. Make a table showing the value of marginal product for each screen from the first through the fifth. What property is illustrated by the behavior of marginal products?

   How many screens will be built if the real interest rate is
   b. 5.5 percent?
   c. 7.5 percent?
   d. 10 percent?
   e. If the real interest rate is 5.5 percent, how far would construction costs have to fall before the builder would be willing to build a five-screen complex?

8. For each of the following scenarios, use supply and demand analysis to predict the resulting changes in the real interest rate, national saving, and investment. Show all your diagrams. *(LO5)*
   a. The legislature passes a 10 percent investment tax credit. Under this program, for every $100 that a firm spends on new capital equipment, it receives an extra $10 in tax refunds from the government.
   b. A reduction in military spending moves the government's budget from deficit into surplus.
   c. A new generation of computer-controlled machines becomes available. These machines produce manufactured goods much more quickly and with fewer defects.
   d. The government raises its tax on corporate profits. Other tax changes are also made, such that the government's deficit remains unchanged.
   e. Concerns about job security raise precautionary saving.
   f. New environmental regulations increase firms' costs of operating capital.

ANSWERS TO SELF-TESTS

7.1 If Consuelo's student loan were for $6,500 instead of $3,000, her liabilities would be $6,750 (the student loan plus the credit card balance) instead of $3,250. The value of her assets, $6,280, is unchanged. In this case Consuelo's wealth is negative, since assets of $6,280 less liabilities of $6,750 equals −$470. Negative wealth or net worth means one owes more than one owns. *(LO1)*

7.2 If water is being drained from the tub, the flow is negative, equal to −3 gallons per minute. There are 37 gallons in the tub at 7:16 p.m. and 34 gallons at 7:17 p.m. The rate of change of the stock is −3 gallons per minute, which is the same as the flow. *(LO1)*

7.3 a. Consuelo has set aside her usual $20, but she has also incurred a new liability of $50. So her net saving for the week is *minus* $30. Since her assets (her checking account) have increased by $20 but her liabilities (her credit card balance) have increased by $50, her wealth has also declined by $30. *(LO1)*

b. In paying off her credit card bill, Consuelo reduces her assets by $300 by drawing down her checking account and reduces her liabilities by the same amount by reducing her credit card balance to zero. Thus there is no change in her wealth. There is also no change in her saving (note that Consuelo's income and spending on current needs have not changed).

c. The increase in the value of Consuelo's car raises her assets by $500. So her wealth also rises by $500. Changes in the value of existing assets are not treated as part of saving, however, so her saving is unchanged.

d. The decline in the value of Consuelo's furniture is a capital loss of $300. Her assets and wealth fall by $300. Her saving is unchanged.

7.4 The federal government had expenditures greater than receipts, so it ran a deficit. The federal deficit equaled expenditures of 4,507.4 minus revenues of 3,497.7, or $1,009.7 billion. Equivalently, the federal budget surplus was *minus* $1,009.7 billion. State and local governments had a deficit equal to expenditures of 2,862.1 minus receipts of 2,623.0, or $239.1 billion. The entire government sector ran a deficit of 1,009.7 + 239.1 = $1,248.8 billion. (You can also find this answer by adding federal to state and local expenditures and comparing this number to the sum of federal and state–local receipts.) The government sector's contribution to national saving in 2018 was negative, equal to −$1,248.8 billion. *(LO3)*

7.5 The loss of value of $200 over the year is another financial cost of owning the mower, which Lauren should take into account in making her decision. Her total cost is now $240 in interest costs plus $200 in anticipated loss of value of the mower (known as depreciation), or $440. This exceeds the value of marginal product, $400, and so now Lauren should not buy the mower. *(LO4)*

7.6 Household saving is part of national saving. A decline in household saving, and hence national saving, at any given real interest rate shifts the saving supply curve to the left. The results are as in Figure 7.7. The real interest rate rises and the equilibrium values of national saving and investment fall. Lower investment is the same as a lower rate of capital formation, which would be expected to slow economic growth. *(LO5)*

8

Money, the Federal Reserve, and Global Financial Markets

You have probably heard expressions such as “on the money,” “smart money,” “time is money,” “money talks,” and “put your money where your mouth is.” When people use the word *money,* they often mean something different than what economists mean when they use the word. For an economist, when you get a paycheck, you are receiving income, and any amount that you do not spend on current consumption is saving. Or think about someone who has done well in the stock market: Most people would say that they “made money” in the market. No, an economist would answer, their wealth increased. These terms don’t make for a catchy expression, but a good economic naturalist must use words like *income, saving, wealth,* and *money* carefully because each plays a different role in the financial system.

In the first part of this chapter, we discuss the role of money in modern economies: why it is important, how it is measured, and how it is created. Money plays a major role in everyday economic transactions but, as we will see, it is also quite important at the macro level. For example, as we mentioned in Chapter 3, *Macroeconomics: The Bird’s-Eye View of the Economy,* one of the three main types of macroeconomic policy, monetary policy, relates primarily to decisions about how much money should be allowed to circulate in the economy. In the United States, monetary policy is made by the Federal Reserve, the nation’s central bank. Because the Federal Reserve, or the Fed, determines the nation’s money supply, this chapter also introduces the Fed and discusses some of the policy tools at its disposal.

Having introduced money and the Fed, we are finally in a position to discuss the financial system in the second part of this chapter. We have discussed the importance of national saving in Chapter 7, *Saving and Capital Formation.* But a healthy economy not only saves adequately, it also invests those savings in a productive way. In market economies, like that of the United States, channeling society’s savings into the best possible capital investments is the role of the financial system: banks, stock markets, bond markets, and other financial markets and institutions as we will discuss in this chapter.

In the modern world, saving often flows across national boundaries, as savers purchase financial assets in countries other than their own and borrowers look

LEARNING OBJECTIVES

After reading this chapter, you should be able to:

LO1 Discuss the three functions of money and how the money supply is measured.

LO2 Analyze how the lending behavior of commercial banks affects the money supply.

LO3 Describe the structure and responsibilities of the Federal Reserve System.

LO4 Describe the role of financial intermediaries such as commercial banks in the financial system and differentiate between bonds and stocks.

LO5 Show how the financial market improves the allocation of saving to productive uses.

LO6 Analyze the factors that determine international capital flows to understand how domestic saving, the trade balance, and net capital flows are related.

abroad for sources of financing. Flows of funds between lenders and borrowers located in different countries are referred to as international capital flows. We discuss the international dimension of saving and capital formation in the last part of the chapter. As we will see, for many countries, including the United States, foreign savings provide an important supplement to domestic savings as a means of financing the formation of new capital.

MONEY AND ITS USES

money any asset that can be used in making purchases

What exactly is money? To the economist, **money** is any asset that can be used in making purchases. Common examples of money in the modern world are currency and coin. A checking account balance represents another asset that can be used in making payments (as when you write a check or use a debit card to pay for your weekly groceries) and so is also counted as money. In contrast, shares of stock, for example, cannot be used directly in most transactions. Stock must first be sold—that is, converted into cash or a checking account deposit—before further transactions, such as buying your groceries, can be made.

Historically, a wide variety of objects have been used as money, including cacao beans (used by the Aztec people, who dominated central Mexico until the coming of the Spanish in the sixteenth century), gold and silver coins, shells, beads, feathers, and, on the island of Yap, large, immovable boulders. Prior to the use of metallic coins, by far the most common form of money was the cowrie, a type of shell found in the South Pacific. Cowries were used as money in some parts of Africa until recently, being officially accepted for payment of taxes in Uganda until the beginning of the twentieth century. Today, money can be virtually intangible, as in the case of your checking account.

Why do people use money? Money has three principal uses: a *medium of exchange*, a *unit of account*, and a *store of value*.

medium of exchange an asset used in purchasing goods and services

barter the direct trade of goods or services for other goods or services

Money serves as a **medium of exchange** when it is used to purchase goods and services, as when you pay cash for a newspaper or write a check to cover your utilities bill. This is perhaps money's most crucial function. Think about how complicated daily life would become if there were no money. Without money, all economic transactions would have to be in the form of **barter**, which is the direct trade of goods or services for other goods or services.

Barter is highly inefficient because it requires that each party to a trade has something that the other party wants, a so-called *double coincidence of wants*. For example, under a barter system, a musician could get her dinner only by finding someone willing to trade food for a musical performance. Finding such a match of needs, where each party happens to want exactly what the other person has to offer, would be difficult to do on a regular basis. In a world with money, the musician's problem is considerably simpler. First, she must find someone who is willing to pay money for her musical performance. Then, with the money received, she can purchase the food and other goods and services that she needs. In a society that uses money, it is not necessary that the person who wants to hear music and the person willing to provide food to the musician be one and the same. In other words, there need not be a double coincidence of wants for trades of goods and services to take place.

Hill Street Studios/Blend Images LLC

In a world without money, she could eat only by finding someone willing to trade food for a musical performance.

By eliminating the problem of having to find a double coincidence of wants in order to trade, the use of money in a society permits individuals to specialize in producing particular goods or services, as opposed to having every family or village produce most of what it needs. Specialization greatly increases economic efficiency and material standards of living, as discussed in Chapter 12, *International Trade and Trade Policy* (the principle of comparative advantage). This usefulness of money in making transactions explains why savers hold money, even though money generally pays a low rate of return. Cash, for example, pays no interest at all, and the balances in checking accounts usually pay a lower rate of interest than could be obtained in alternative financial investments.

Money's second function is as a *unit of account.* As a **unit of account,** money is the basic yardstick for measuring economic value. In the United States, virtually all prices—including the price of labor (wages) and the prices of financial assets, such as shares of General Motors stock—are expressed in dollars. Expressing economic values in a common unit of account allows for easy comparisons. For example, grain can be measured in bushels and coal in tons, but to judge whether 20 bushels of grain is economically more or less valuable than a ton of coal, we express both values in dollar terms. The use of money as a unit of account is closely related to its use as a medium of exchange; because money is used to buy and sell things, it makes sense to express prices of all kinds in money terms.

unit of account a basic measure of economic value

As a **store of value,** its third function, money is a way of holding wealth. For example, the miser who stuffs cash in his mattress or buries gold coins under the old oak tree at midnight is holding wealth in money form. Likewise, if you regularly keep a balance in your checking account, you are holding part of your wealth in the form of money. Although money is usually the primary medium of exchange or unit of account in an economy, it is not the only store of value. There are numerous other ways of holding wealth, such as owning stocks, bonds, or real estate.

store of value an asset that serves as a means of holding wealth

For most people, money is not a particularly good way to hold wealth, apart from its usefulness as a medium of exchange. Unlike government bonds and other types of financial assets, most forms of money pay no interest, and there is always the risk of cash being lost or stolen. However, cash has the advantage of being anonymous and difficult to trace, making it an attractive store of value for smugglers, drug dealers, and others who want their assets to stay out of the view of the Internal Revenue Service.

The Economic Naturalist 8.1

From Ithaca Hours to Bitcoin: What is private money, communally created money, and open-source money?

Since money is such a useful tool, why is money usually issued only by governments? Are there examples of privately issued, or communally created, money?

connect

▸ Visit your instructor's Connect course and access your eBook to view this video.

Are all currencies issued by governments?

Money is usually issued by the government, not private individuals, but in part, this reflects legal restrictions on private money issuance. Where the law allows, private moneys do sometimes emerge.[1] For example, privately issued currencies circulate in several U.S. communities. In Ithaca, New York, a private currency famously known as "Ithaca Hours" has circulated since 1991. Instituted by town resident Paul Glover, each Ithaca Hour was originally equivalent to $10, the average hourly wage of workers in the county. The bills, printed with specially developed inks to prevent counterfeiting, honor local people and the environment. Many hundreds of individuals and businesses are estimated to have earned and spent Hours. The idea behind launching local currencies such as Ithaca Hours, which can't be spent elsewhere, is that they may induce people to do more of their shopping in the local economy.

A more recent development in private money was the emergence of the virtual currency known as "Bitcoin" in 2009. This is a peer-to-peer, open-source online payment system without a central administrator, where payments are recorded in a public ledger using Bitcoin as the unit of account. New bitcoins are created as a reward for payment-processing work, known as mining, in which users offer their computing power to verify and record payments into the public ledger. Already circulating bitcoins can be obtained in exchange for other currencies, products, and services. Users can send and receive bitcoins electronically using special wallet software on a personal computer, mobile device, or web application. As of mid-June, 2020, the value of one bitcoin was around US$9,300, with more than 18 million bitcoins in circulation.

bitcoin

[1]Barbara A. Good, "Private Money: Everything Old Is New Again," Federal Reserve Bank of Cleveland, *Economic Commentary,* April 1, 1998.

Despite its promise as a decentralized digital currency, Bitcoin has not been very successful as a money so far, and it is not widely accepted for most transactions. The relatively small commercial use of Bitcoin compared to its use by speculators has contributed to significant price volatility. In a famous episode, in November 2013 one bitcoin traded for more than $1,100—more than 10 times its price in dollars a few months earlier—before sharply declining and trading for less than $300 during much of 2015. More recently, during 2017, the digital currency's price climbed from below $1,000 on January 1 to above $20,000 on December 17. The currency subsequently lost around 85 percent of its value within a single year, and its price dipped below $3,200 on December 15, 2018. This volatility limits Bitcoin's ability to act as a stable store of value and as a reliable unit of account in which prices could be quoted—two of the three principal uses of money described earlier in this chapter.

What do Ithaca Hours and Bitcoin have in common? By functioning as a medium of exchange, each facilitates trade within a community.

Measuring Money

How much money, defined as financial assets usable for making purchases, is there in the U.S. economy at any given time? This question is not simple to answer because, in practice, it is not easy to draw a clear distinction between those assets that should be counted as money and those that should not. Dollar bills are certainly a form of money, and a van Gogh painting certainly is not. However, brokerage firms now offer accounts that allow their owners to combine financial investments in stocks and bonds with check-writing and credit card privileges. Should the balances in these accounts, or some part of them, be counted as money? It is difficult to tell.

Economists skirt the problem of deciding what is and isn't money by using several alternative definitions of money, which vary in how broadly the concept of money is defined. A relatively "narrow" definition of the amount of money in the U.S. economy is called **M1;** it is the sum of currency outstanding and balances held in checking accounts. A broader measure of money, called **M2,** includes all the assets in M1 plus some additional assets that are usable in making payments, but at greater cost or inconvenience than currency or checks. Table 8.1 lists the components of M1

M1 the sum of currency outstanding and balances held in checking accounts

M2 all the assets in M1 plus some additional assets that are usable in making payments but at greater cost or inconvenience than currency or checks

TABLE 8.1
Components of M1 and M2, January 2020

M1		**3,951.3**
Currency	1,717.7	
Demand deposits	1,564.2	
Other checkable deposits	669.4	
M2		**15,432.2**
M1	3,951.3	
Savings deposits	9,908.7	
Small-denomination time deposits	582.1	
Money market mutual funds	990.1	

Notes: Billions of dollars, adjusted for seasonal variations. In M1, currency refers to cash and coin. Demand deposits are non-interest-bearing checking accounts, and "other checkable deposits" includes checking accounts that bear interest. M2 includes all the components of M1, balances in savings accounts, "small-denomination" (under $100,000) deposits held at banks for a fixed term, and money market mutual funds (MMMFs). MMMFs are organizations that sell shares, use the proceeds to buy safe assets (like government bonds), and often allow their shareholders some check-writing privileges.

Source: Federal Reserve release H.6, www.federalreserve.gov/releases/h6/20200116.

and M2 and also gives the amount of each type of asset outstanding as of January 2020. For most purposes, however, it is sufficient to think of money as the sum of currency outstanding and balances in checking accounts, or M1.

Note that credit card balances are not included in either M1 or M2 even though people increasingly use credit cards to pay for many of their purchases, including food, clothing, and even college tuition. The main reason credit card balances are not included in the money supply is that they do not represent part of people's wealth. Indeed, a credit card charge of $1,000 represents an obligation to pay someone else $1,000.

RECAP

MONEY AND ITS USES

- *Money* is any asset that can be used in making purchases, such as currency or a checking account. Money serves as a *medium of exchange* when it is used to purchase goods and services. The use of money as a medium of exchange eliminates the need for *barter* and the difficulties of finding a "double coincidence of wants." Money also serves as a *unit of account* and a *store of value*.
- In practice, two basic measures of money are M1 and M2. M1, a narrower measure, is made up primarily of currency and balances held in checking accounts. The broader measure, M2, includes all the assets in M1 plus some additional assets usable in making payments.
- Credit card balances are never counted as or considered money because credit card balances are merely obligations to pay others.

COMMERCIAL BANKS AND THE CREATION OF MONEY

What determines the amount of money in the economy? If the economy's supply of money consisted entirely of currency, the answer would be simple: The supply of money would just be equal to the value of the currency created and circulated by the government. However, as we have seen, in modern economies the money supply consists not only of currency but also of deposit balances held by the public in commercial, that is, private, banks. The determination of the money supply in a modern economy thus depends in part on the behavior of commercial banks and their depositors.

To see how the existence of commercial banks affects the money supply, we will use the example of a fictional country, the Republic of Gorgonzola. Initially, we assume, Gorgonzola has no commercial banking system. To make trading easier and eliminate the need for barter, the government directs the central bank of Gorgonzola to put into circulation a million identical paper notes, called guilders. The central bank prints the guilders and distributes them to the populace. At this point, the Gorgonzolan money supply is a million guilders.

However, the citizens of Gorgonzola are unhappy with a money supply made up entirely of paper guilders since the notes may be lost or stolen. In response to the demand for safekeeping of money, some Gorgonzolan entrepreneurs set up a system of commercial banks. At first, these banks are only storage vaults where people can deposit their guilders. When people need to make a payment they can either physically withdraw their guilders or, more conveniently, write a check on their account.

Checks give the banks permission to transfer guilders from the account of the person paying by check to the account of the person to whom the check is made out. With a system of payments based on checks the paper guilders need never leave the banking system, although they flow from one bank to another as a depositor of one bank makes a payment to a depositor in

connect

▶ Visit your instructor's Connect course and access your eBook to view this video.

Why can it be more expensive to transfer funds between banks electronically than it is to send a check through the mail?

another bank. Deposits do not pay interest in this economy; indeed, the banks can make a profit only by charging depositors fees in exchange for safeguarding their cash.

Let's suppose for now that people prefer bank deposits to cash and so deposit all of their guilders with the commercial banks. With all guilders in the vaults of banks, the balance sheet of all of Gorgonzola's commercial banks taken together is as shown in Table 8.2.

TABLE 8.2
Consolidated Balance Sheet of Gorgonzolan Commercial Banks (Initial)

Assets		Liabilities	
Currency	1,000,000 guilders	Deposits	1,000,000 guilders

The *assets* of the commercial banking system in Gorgonzola are the paper guilders sitting in the vaults of all the individual banks. The banking system's *liabilities* are the deposits of the banks' customers, since checking account balances represent money owed by the banks to the depositors.

bank reserves cash or similar assets held by commercial banks for the purpose of meeting depositor withdrawals and payments

100 percent reserve banking a situation in which banks' reserves equal 100 percent of their deposits

Cash or similar assets held by banks are called **bank reserves.** In this example, bank reserves, for all the banks taken together, equal 1,000,000 guilders—the currency listed on the asset side of the consolidated balance sheet. Banks hold reserves to meet depositors' demands for cash withdrawals or to pay checks drawn on their depositors' accounts. In this example, the bank reserves of 1,000,000 guilders equal 100 percent of banks' deposits, which are also 1,000,000 guilders. A situation in which bank reserves equal 100 percent of bank deposits is called **100 percent reserve banking.**

Bank reserves are held by banks in their vaults, rather than circulated among the public, and thus are *not* counted as part of the money supply. However, bank deposit balances, which can be used in making transactions, *are* counted as money. So, after the introduction of "safekeeper" banks in Gorgonzola, the money supply, equal to the value of bank deposits, is 1,000,000 guilders, which is the same as it was prior to the introduction of banks.

To continue the story, after a while the commercial bankers of Gorgonzola begin to realize that keeping 100 percent reserves against deposits is not necessary. True, a few guilders flow in and out of the typical bank as depositors receive payments or write checks, but for the most part the stacks of paper guilders just sit there in the vaults, untouched and unused. It occurs to the bankers that they can meet the random inflow and outflow of guilders to their banks with reserves that are less than 100 percent of their deposits. After some observation, the bankers conclude that keeping reserves equal to only 10 percent of deposits is enough to meet the random ebb and flow of withdrawals and payments from their individual banks. The remaining 90 percent of deposits, the bankers realize, can be lent out to borrowers to earn interest.

So the bankers decide to keep reserves equal to 100,000 guilders, or 10 percent of their deposits. The other 900,000 guilders they lend out at interest to Gorgonzolan cheese producers who want to use the money to make improvements to their farms. After the loans are made, the balance sheet of all of Gorgonzola's commercial banks taken together has changed, as shown in Table 8.3.

TABLE 8.3
Consolidated Balance Sheet of Gorgonzolan Commercial Banks after One Round of Loans

Assets		Liabilities	
Currency (= reserves)	100,000 guilders	Deposits	1,000,000 guilders
Loans to farmers	900,000 guilders		

After the loans are made, the banks' reserves of 100,000 guilders no longer equal 100 percent of the banks' deposits of 1,000,000 guilders. Instead, the **reserve-deposit ratio,** which is bank reserves divided by deposits, is now equal to 100,000/1,000,000, or 10 percent. A banking system in which banks hold fewer reserves than deposits so that the reserve-deposit ratio is less than 100 percent is called a **fractional-reserve banking system.**

reserve-deposit ratio bank reserves divided by deposits

fractional-reserve banking system a banking system in which bank reserves are less than deposits so that the reserve-deposit ratio is less than 100 percent

Notice that 900,000 guilders have flowed out of the banking system (as loans to farmers) and are now in the hands of the public. But we have assumed that private citizens prefer bank deposits to cash for making transactions. So ultimately people will redeposit the 900,000 guilders in the banking system. After these deposits are made, the consolidated balance sheet of the commercial banks is as in Table 8.4.

TABLE 8.4
Consolidated Balance Sheet of Gorgonzolan Commercial Banks after Guilders Are Redeposited

Assets		Liabilities	
Currency (= reserves)	1,000,000 guilders	Deposits	1,900,000 guilders
Loans to farmers	900,000 guilders		

Note that bank deposits, and hence the economy's money supply, now equal 1,900,000 guilders. In effect, the existence of the commercial banking system has permitted the creation of new money. These deposits, which are liabilities of the banks, are balanced by assets of 1,000,000 guilders in reserves and 900,000 guilders in loans owed to the banks. The fractional-reserve commercial banking system has thus led to the creation of additional money over and above the initial 1,000,000 guilders in currency.

However, the story does not end here. On examining their balance sheets, the bankers are surprised to see that they once again have "too many" reserves. With deposits of 1,900,000 guilders and a 10 percent reserve-deposit ratio, they need only 190,000 guilders in reserves. But they have 1,000,000 guilders in reserves—810,000 too many. Since lending out their excess guilders is always more profitable than leaving them in the vault, the bankers proceed to make another 810,000 guilders in loans. Eventually these loaned-out guilders are redeposited in the banking system, after which the consolidated balance sheet of the banks is as shown in Table 8.5.

TABLE 8.5
Consolidated Balance Sheet of Gorgonzolan Commercial Banks after Two Rounds of Loans and Redeposits

Assets		Liabilities	
Currency (= reserves)	1,000,000 guilders	Deposits	2,710,000 guilders
Loans to farmers	1,710,000 guilders		

Now the money supply has increased to 2,710,000 guilders, equal to the value of bank deposits. Despite the expansion of loans and deposits, however, the bankers find that their reserves of 1,000,000 guilders *still* exceed the desired level of 10 percent of deposits, which are 2,710,000 guilders. And so yet another round of lending will take place.

SELF-TEST 8.1

Determine what the balance sheet of the banking system of Gorgonzola will look like after a third round of lending to farmers and redeposits of guilders into the commercial banking system. What is the money supply at that point?

The process of expansion of loans and deposits will end only when reserves equal 10 percent of bank deposits, because as long as reserves exceed 10 percent of deposits the banks will find it profitable to lend out the extra reserves. Since reserves at the end of every round equal 1,000,000 guilders, for the reserve-deposit ratio to equal 10 percent, total deposits must equal 10,000,000 guilders. Further, since the balance sheet must balance, with assets equal to liabilities, we know as well that at the end of the process loans to cheese producers must equal 9,000,000 guilders. If loans equal 9,000,000 guilders, then bank assets, the sum of loans and reserves (1,000,000 guilders), will equal 10,000,000 guilders, which is the same as bank liabilities (bank deposits). The final consolidated balance sheet is as shown in Table 8.6.

TABLE 8.6
Final Consolidated Balance Sheet of Gorgonzolan Commercial Banks

Assets		Liabilities	
Currency (= reserves)	1,000,000 guilders	Deposits	10,000,000 guilders
Loans to farmers	9,000,000 guilders		

The money supply, which is equal to total deposits, is 10,000,000 guilders at the end of the process. We see that the existence of a fractional-reserve banking system has multiplied the money supply by a factor of 10, relative to the economy with no banks or the economy with 100 percent reserve banking. Put another way, with a 10 percent reserve-deposit ratio, each guilder deposited in the banking system can "support" 10 guilders worth of deposits.

To find the money supply in this example more directly, we observe that deposits will expand through additional rounds of lending as long as the ratio of bank reserves to bank deposits exceeds the reserve-deposit ratio desired by banks. When the actual ratio of bank reserves to deposits equals the desired reserve-deposit ratio, the expansion stops. So ultimately, deposits in the banking system satisfy the following relationship

$$\frac{\text{Bank reserves}}{\text{Bank deposits}} = \text{Desired reserve-deposit ratio.}$$

This equation can be rewritten to solve for bank deposits as

$$\text{Bank deposits} = \frac{\text{Bank reserves}}{\text{Desired reserve-deposit ratio.}} \tag{8.1}$$

In Gorgonzola, since all the currency in the economy flows into the banking system, bank reserves equal 1,000,000 guilders. The reserve-deposit ratio desired by banks is 0.10. Therefore, using Equation 8.1, we find that bank deposits equal (1,000,000 guilders)/0.10, or 10 million guilders, the same answer we found in the consolidated balance sheet of the banks, Table 8.6.

SELF-TEST 8.2

Find deposits and the money supply in Gorgonzola if the banks' desired reserve-deposit ratio is 5 percent rather than 10 percent. What if the total amount of currency circulated by the central bank is 2,000,000 guilders and the desired reserve-deposit ratio remains at 10 percent?

The Money Supply with Both Currency and Deposits

In the example of Gorgonzola, we assumed that all money is held in the form of deposits in banks. In reality, of course, people keep only part of their money holdings in the form of bank accounts and hold the rest in the form of currency. Fortunately, allowing for the fact that people hold both currency and bank deposits does not greatly complicate the determination of the money supply, as Example 8.1 shows.

EXAMPLE 8.1 The Money Supply with Both Currency and Deposits

What is the money supply in Gorgonzola when there are both currency and bank deposits?

Suppose that the citizens of Gorgonzola choose to hold a total of 500,000 guilders in the form of currency and to deposit the rest of their money in banks. Banks keep reserves equal to 10 percent of deposits. What is the money supply in Gorgonzola?

The money supply is the sum of currency in the hands of the public and bank deposits. Currency in the hands of the public is given as 500,000 guilders. What is the quantity of bank deposits? Since 500,000 of the 1,000,000 guilders issued by the central bank are being used by the public in the form of currency, only the remaining 500,000 guilders are available to serve as bank reserves. We know that deposits equal bank reserves divided by the reserve-deposit ratio, so deposits are 500,000 guilders/0.10 = 5,000,000 guilders. The total money supply is the sum of currency in the hands of the public (500,000 guilders) and bank deposits (5,000,000 guilders), or 5,500,000 guilders.

We can write a general relationship that captures the reasoning of this example. First, let's write out the fact that the money supply equals currency plus bank deposits.

$$\text{Money supply} = \text{Currency held by the public} + \text{Bank deposits}.$$

We also know that bank deposits equal bank reserves divided by the reserve-deposit ratio that is desired by commercial banks (Equation 8.1). Using that relationship to substitute for bank deposits in the expression for the money supply, we get

$$\text{Money supply} = \text{Currency held by public} + \frac{\text{Bank reserves}}{\text{Desired reserve-deposit ratio}}. \quad (8.2)$$

We can use Equation 8.2 to confirm our answer to Example 8.1. In that example, currency held by the public is 500,000 guilders, bank reserves are 500,000 guilders, and the desired reserve-deposit ratio is 0.10. Plugging these values into Equation 8.2, we get that the money supply equals 500,000 + 500,000/0.10 = 5,500,000, the same answer we found before.

EXAMPLE 8.2 The Money Supply at Christmas

How does Christmas shopping affect the money supply?

During the Christmas season people choose to hold unusually large amounts of currency for shopping. With no action by the central bank, how would this change in currency holding affect the national money supply?

To illustrate with a numerical example, suppose that initially bank reserves are 500, the amount of currency held by the public is 500, and the desired reserve-deposit ratio in the banking system is 0.2. Inserting these values into Equation 8.2, we find that the money supply equals 500 + 500/0.2 = 3,000.

Now suppose that because of Christmas shopping needs, the public increases its currency holdings to 600 by withdrawing 100 from commercial banks. These withdrawals reduce bank reserves to 400. Using Equation 8.2 we find now that the money supply is 600 + 400/0.2 = 2,600. So the public's increased holdings of currency have caused the money supply to drop, from 3,000 to 2,600. The reason for the drop is that with a reserve-deposit ratio of 20 percent, every dollar in the vaults of banks can "support" $5 of deposits and hence $5 of money supply. However, the same dollar in the hands of the public becomes $1 of currency, contributing only $1 to the total money supply. So when the public withdraws cash from the banks, the overall money supply declines. (We will see in the next section, however, that in practice the central bank has means to offset the impact of the public's actions on the money supply.)

Later in this book, we discuss situations where an increase in bank reserves does not increase the money supply. Equation 8.2 shows that this will be the case when the reserve-deposit ratio desired by commercial banks increases together with bank reserves. For now, it is important to remember that whether an increase in bank reserves increases the money supply depends on what commercial banks do with their newly acquired reserves.

RECAP

COMMERCIAL BANKS AND THE CREATION OF MONEY

- Part of the money supply consists of deposits in private commercial banks. Hence the behavior of commercial banks and their depositors helps determine the money supply.
- Cash or similar assets held by banks are called *bank reserves*. In modern economies, banks' reserves are less than their deposits, a situation called *fractional-reserve banking*. The ratio of bank reserves to deposits is called the *reserve-deposit ratio;* in a fractional-reserve banking system, this ratio is less than 1.
- The portion of deposits not held as reserves can be lent out by the banks to earn interest. Banks will continue to make loans and accept deposits as long as the reserve-deposit ratio exceeds its desired level. This process stops only when the actual and desired reserve-deposit ratios are equal. At that point, total bank deposits equal bank reserves divided by the desired reserve-deposit ratio, and the money supply equals the currency held by the public plus bank deposits.

THE FEDERAL RESERVE SYSTEM

Federal Reserve System (or **the Fed**) the central bank of the United States

monetary policy determination of the nation's money supply

For participants in financial markets and the average citizen as well, one of the most important branches of the government is the **Federal Reserve System,** often called **the Fed.** The Fed is the *central bank* of the United States. Like central banks in other countries, the Fed has two main responsibilities.

First, it is responsible for **monetary policy,** which means that the Fed determines how much money circulates in the economy. As we will see in later chapters, changes in the supply of money can affect many important macroeconomic variables, including interest rates, inflation, unemployment, and exchange rates. Because of its ability to affect key variables, particularly financial variables such as interest rates, financial market participants pay close attention to Fed actions and announcements. As a necessary first step in understanding how Fed policies have the effects that they do, in this chapter we will focus on the basic question of how the Fed affects the supply of money, leaving for later the explanation of why changes in the money supply affect the economy.

Second, along with other government agencies, the Federal Reserve bears important responsibility for the oversight and regulation of financial markets. The Fed also plays a major role during periods of crisis in financial markets. To lay the groundwork for discussing how the Fed carries out its responsibilities, we first briefly review the history and structure of the Federal Reserve System.

The History and Structure of the Federal Reserve System

The Federal Reserve System was created by the Federal Reserve Act, passed by Congress in 1913, and began operations in 1914. Like all central banks, the Fed is a government agency. Unlike commercial banks, which are private businesses whose principal objective is making a profit, central banks like the Fed focus on promoting public goals such as economic growth, low inflation, and the smooth operation of financial markets.

The Federal Reserve Act established a system of 12 regional Federal Reserve banks, each associated with a geographical area called a Federal Reserve district. Congress hoped that the establishment of Federal Reserve banks around the country would ensure that different regions were represented in the national policymaking process. In fact, the regional Feds regularly assess economic conditions in their districts and report this information to policymakers in Washington. Regional Federal Reserve banks also provide various services, such as check-clearing services, to the commercial banks in their district.

At the national level, the leadership of the Federal Reserve System is provided by its **Board of Governors.** The Board of Governors, together with a large professional staff, is located in Washington, D.C. The Board consists of seven governors, who are appointed by the president of the United States to 14-year terms. The terms are staggered so that one governor comes up for reappointment every other year. The president also appoints one of these Board members to serve as chair of the Board of Governors for a term of four years. The Fed chair, along with the secretary of the Treasury, is probably one of the two most powerful economic policymakers in the United States government, after the president. Recent Fed chairs include Paul Volcker (1979–1987), Alan Greenspan (1987–2006), Ben Bernanke (2006–2014), Janet Yellen (2014–2018), and Jerome Powell (2018–present).

Board of Governors the leadership of the Fed, consisting of seven governors appointed by the president to staggered 14-year terms

Decisions about monetary policy are made by a 12-member committee called the **Federal Open Market Committee (FOMC).** The FOMC consists of the seven Fed governors, the president of the Federal Reserve Bank of New York, and four of the presidents of the other regional Federal Reserve banks, who serve on a rotating basis. The FOMC meets approximately eight times a year to review the state of the economy and to determine monetary policy.

Federal Open Market Committee (FOMC) the committee that makes decisions concerning monetary policy

Controlling the Money Supply: Open-Market Operations

The Fed's primary responsibility is making monetary policy, which involves decisions about the appropriate size of the nation's money supply. As we saw in the previous section, central banks in general, and the Fed in particular, do not control the money supply directly. However, they can control the money supply indirectly by changing the supply of reserves held by commercial banks.

The Fed has several ways of affecting the supply of bank reserves. Historically, the most important of these is *open-market operations.* Suppose that the Fed wants to increase bank reserves, with the ultimate goal of increasing bank deposits and the money supply. To accomplish this, the Fed buys financial assets, usually government bonds, from the public. The people who sell the bonds to the Fed will deposit the proceeds they receive as payment for their bonds in commercial banks. Thus, the reserves of the commercial banking system will increase by an amount equal to the value of the bonds purchased by the Fed. The increase in bank reserves will lead in turn, through the process of lending and redeposit of funds described in the previous section, to an expansion of bank deposits and the money supply, as summarized by Equation 8.2. The Fed's purchase of government bonds from the public, with the result that bank reserves and the money supply are increased, is called an **open-market purchase.**

open-market purchase the purchase of government bonds from the public by the Fed for the purpose of increasing the supply of bank reserves and the money supply

To reduce bank reserves and hence the money supply, the Fed reverses the procedure. It sells some of the government bonds that it holds (acquired in previous open-market purchases) to the public. Assume that the public pays for the bonds by writing checks on their accounts in commercial banks. Then, when the Fed presents the checks to the commercial banks for payment, reserves equal in value to the government bonds sold by the Fed are transferred from the commercial banks to the Fed. The Fed retires these reserves from circulation, lowering the supply of bank reserves and, hence, the overall money supply. The sale of government bonds by the Fed to the public for the purpose of reducing bank reserves and hence the money supply is called an **open-market sale.** Open-market purchases and sales together are called **open-market operations.**

open-market sale the sale by the Fed of government bonds to the public for the purpose of reducing bank reserves and the money supply

open-market operations open-market purchases and open-market sales

Open-market operations are the most convenient and flexible tool that the Federal Reserve has for affecting the money supply if we assume, as we have in this chapter, that banks always act to maintain a desired reserve-deposit ratio that never changes. In such a state of affairs, banks always attempt to avoid holding "too many" or "too few" reserves relative to that (never-changing) desired ratio. Changes in reserves caused by open-market operations are therefore immediately translated by banks into changes in lending conditions and the supply of money. Until the 2007–2008 financial crisis, things worked roughly this way, and open-market operations were employed on a regular basis for controlling the money supply. The details and purpose of open-market operations changed following the crisis, as we will discuss in later chapters. In that discussion, we will also introduce additional means by which the Fed can affect the money supply.

EXAMPLE 8.3 Increasing the Money Supply by Open-Market Operations

How do open-market operations affect the money supply?

In a particular economy, currency held by the public is 1,000 shekels, bank reserves are 200 shekels, and the desired reserve-deposit ratio is 0.2. What is the money supply? How is the money supply affected if the central bank prints 100 shekels and uses this new currency to buy government bonds from the public? Assume that the public does not wish to change the amount of currency it holds.

As bank reserves are 200 shekels and the reserve-deposit ratio is 0.2, bank deposits must equal 200 shekels/0.2, or 1,000 shekels. The money supply, equal to the sum of currency held by the public and bank deposits, is therefore 2,000 shekels, a result you can confirm using Equation 8.2.

The open-market purchase puts 100 more shekels into the hands of the public. We assume that the public continues to want to hold 1,000 shekels in currency, so they will deposit the additional 100 shekels in the commercial banking system, raising bank reserves from 200 to 300 shekels. As the desired reserve-deposit ratio is 0.2, multiple rounds of lending and redeposit will eventually raise the level of bank deposits to 300 shekels/0.2, or 1,500 shekels. The money supply, equal to 1,000 shekels held by the public plus bank deposits of 1,500 shekels, equals 2,500 shekels. So the open-market purchase of 100 shekels, by raising bank reserves by 100 shekels, has increased the money supply by 500 shekels. Again, you can confirm this result using Equation 8.2.

SELF-TEST 8.3

Continuing Example 8.3, suppose that instead of an open-market purchase of 100 shekels the central bank conducts an open-market sale of 50 shekels' worth of government bonds. What happens to bank reserves, bank deposits, and the money supply?

The Fed's Role in Stabilizing Financial Markets: Banking Panics

Besides controlling the money supply, the Fed also has the responsibility (together with other government agencies) of ensuring that financial markets operate smoothly. Indeed, the creation of the Fed in 1913 was prompted by a series of financial market crises that disrupted both the markets themselves and the U.S. economy as a whole. The hope of the Congress was that the Fed would be able to eliminate or at least control such crises.

Historically, in the United States, *banking panics* were perhaps the most disruptive type of recurrent financial crisis. In a **banking panic,** news or rumors of the imminent bankruptcy of one or more banks leads bank depositors to rush to withdraw their funds. Next, we will discuss banking panics and the Fed's attempts to control them.

banking panic a situation in which news or rumors of the imminent bankruptcy of one or more banks leads bank depositors to rush to withdraw their funds

Why do banking panics occur? An important factor that helps make banking panics possible is the existence of fractional-reserve banking. In a fractional-reserve banking system, like that of the United States and all other industrialized countries, bank reserves are less than deposits, which means that banks do not keep enough cash on hand to pay off their depositors if they were all to decide to withdraw their deposits. Normally this is not a problem, as only a small percentage of depositors attempt to withdraw their funds on any given day. But if a rumor circulates that one or more banks are in financial trouble and may go bankrupt, depositors may panic, lining up to demand their money. Since bank reserves are less than deposits, a sufficiently severe panic could lead even financially healthy banks to run out of cash, forcing them into bankruptcy and closure.

The Federal Reserve was established in response to a particularly severe banking panic that occurred in 1907. The Fed was equipped with two principal tools to try to prevent or moderate banking panics. First, the Fed was given the power to supervise and regulate banks. It was hoped that the public would have greater confidence in banks, and thus be less prone to panic, if people knew that the Fed was keeping a close watch on bankers' activities. Second, the Fed was allowed to make direct loans to banks through a new facility called the *discount window,* which we will discuss in a later chapter. The idea was that, during a panic, banks could borrow cash from the Fed with which to pay off depositors, avoiding the need to close.

No banking panics occurred between 1914, when the Fed was established, and 1930. However, between 1930 and 1933 the United States experienced the worst and most protracted series of banking panics in its history. Economic historians agree that much of the blame for this panic should be placed on the Fed, which neither appreciated the severity of the problem nor acted aggressively enough to contain it.

The Economic Naturalist 8.2

Why did the banking panics of 1930–1933 reduce the national money supply?

The worst banking panics ever experienced in the United States occurred during the early stages of the Great Depression, between 1930 and 1933. During this period, approximately one-third of the banks in the United States were forced to close. This near-collapse of the banking system was probably an important reason that the Depression was so severe. With many fewer banks in operation, it was very difficult for small businesses and consumers during the early 1930s to obtain credit. Another important effect of the banking panics was to greatly reduce the nation's money supply. Why should banking panics reduce the national money supply?

During a banking panic, people are afraid to keep deposits in a bank because of the risk that the bank will go bankrupt and their money will be lost (this was prior to the introduction of federal deposit insurance, discussed below). During the 1930–1933 period, many bank depositors withdrew their money from banks, holding currency instead. These withdrawals reduced bank reserves. Each extra dollar of currency held by the public adds $1 to the money supply; but each extra dollar of bank reserves translates into several dollars of money supply because in a fractional-reserve banking system, each dollar of reserves can "support" several dollars in bank deposits. Thus the public's withdrawals from banks, which increased currency holdings by the public but reduced bank reserves by an equal amount, led to a net decrease in the total money supply (currency plus deposits).

In addition, fearing banking panics and the associated withdrawals by depositors, banks increased their reserve-deposit ratios, which reduced the quantity of deposits that could be supported by any given level of bank reserves. This change in reserve-deposit ratios also tended to reduce the money supply.

Data on currency holdings by the public, the reserve-deposit ratio, bank reserves, and the money supply for selected dates are shown in Table 8.7. Notice the increase over the period in the amount of currency held by the public and in the reserve-deposit ratio, as well as the decline in bank reserves after 1930. The last column shows that the U.S. money supply dropped by about one-third between December 1929 and December 1933.

TABLE 8.7
Key U.S. Monetary Statistics, 1929–1933

	Currency held by public	Reserve-deposit ratio	Bank reserves	Money supply
December 1929	3.85	0.075	3.15	45.9
December 1930	3.79	0.082	3.31	44.1
December 1931	4.59	0.095	3.11	37.3
December 1932	4.82	0.109	3.18	34.0
December 1933	4.85	0.133	3.45	30.8

Note: Data on currency, the monetary base, and the money supply are in billions of dollars.

Source: Milton Friedman and Anna J. Schwartz, *A Monetary History of the United States, 1863–1960* (Princeton, NJ: Princeton University Press, 1963), Table A-1.

Using Equation 8.2, we can see that increases in currency holdings by the public and increases in the reserve-deposit ratio both tend to reduce the money supply. These effects were so powerful in 1930–1933 that the nation's money supply, shown in the fourth column of Table 8.7, dropped precipitously, even though currency holdings and bank reserves, taken separately, actually rose during the period.

SELF-TEST 8.4

Using the data from Table 8.7, confirm that the relationship between the money supply and its determinants is consistent with Equation 8.2. Would the money supply have fallen in 1931–1933 if the public had stopped withdrawing deposits after December 1930 so that currency held by the public had remained at its December 1930 level?

SELF-TEST 8.5

According to Table 8.7, the U.S. money supply fell from $44.1 billion to $37.3 billion over the course of 1931. The Fed did use open-market purchases during 1931 to replenish bank reserves in the face of depositor withdrawals. Find (a) the quantity of reserves that the Fed injected into the economy in 1931 and (b) the quantity of reserves the Fed would have had to add to the economy to keep the money supply unchanged from 1930, assuming that public currency holdings and reserve-deposit ratios for each year remained as reported in the table. Why has the Fed been criticized for being too timid in 1931?

When the Fed failed to stop the banking panics of the 1930s, policymakers decided to look at other strategies for controlling panics. In 1934 Congress instituted a system of deposit insurance. Under a system of **deposit insurance,** the government guarantees depositors—specifically, under current rules, those with deposits of less than $250,000—that they will get their money back even if the bank goes bankrupt. Deposit insurance eliminates the incentive for people to withdraw their deposits when rumors circulate that the bank is in financial trouble, which nips panics in the bud. Indeed, since deposit insurance was instituted, the United States has had no significant banking panics.

deposit insurance a system under which the government guarantees that depositors will not lose any money even if their bank goes bankrupt

Unfortunately, deposit insurance is not a perfect solution to the problem of banking panics. An important drawback is that when deposit insurance is in force, depositors know they are protected no matter what happens to their bank, and they become completely unconcerned about whether their bank is making prudent loans. This situation can lead to reckless behavior by banks or other insured intermediaries. For example, during the 1980s many savings and loan associations in the United States went bankrupt, in part because of reckless lending and financial investments. Like banks, savings and loans have deposit insurance, so the U.S. government had to pay savings and loan depositors the full value of their deposits. This action ultimately cost U.S. taxpayers hundreds of billions of dollars.

The Fed's role in stabilizing financial markets took center stage in more recent episodes of financial panic. During the global financial crisis of 2008 and, more recently, the financial disruptions related to the global COVID-19 pandemic of 2020, the Fed acted as a "lender of last resort." In this role, the Fed provided urgently needed credit lines to stressed financial institutions. To be able to lend to a set of institutions broader than commercial banks—to which the Fed can typically lend—the Fed revived a rarely used provision found in Section 13(3) of the Federal Reserve Act. The section, which was added in 1932 during the banking panics, allows the Fed to lend to nonbank institutions under certain "unusual and exigent" circumstances. Using this section for the first time since the 1930s, the Fed set up in 2008 special lending facilities for nonbank institutions. It further provided special assistance to specific firms that it considered "too big to fail." The Fed revived Section 13(3) lending in 2020, when it again found itself under unusual market conditions. We discuss monetary policy during the 2008 and 2020 episodes in later chapters.

RECAP

THE FEDERAL RESERVE SYSTEM

- The Fed is the central bank of the United States. Like central banks in other countries, it has two main responsibilities. First, it is in charge of monetary policy—that is, it determines how much money circulates in the economy. Second, it bears important responsibility for the oversight and regulation of financial markets. The Fed also plays a major role during periods of crisis in financial markets.
- An open-market purchase is the purchase of government bonds from the public by the Fed for the purpose of increasing the supply of bank reserves and the money supply. An open-market sale is the sale by the Fed of government bonds to the public for the purpose of reducing bank reserves and the money supply.
- Historically, such open-market operations are the most important among several ways that the Fed has of affecting the supply of bank reserves and the money supply.

THE FINANCIAL SYSTEM AND THE ALLOCATION OF SAVING TO PRODUCTIVE USES

Having discussed money, commercial banks, and the Fed, we are ready to introduce financial markets. These markets have an important role in the economy: putting saving to productive uses. In Chapter 7, *Saving and Capital Formation,* we emphasized the importance of high rates of saving and capital formation for economic growth and increased productivity. High rates of saving and investment by themselves are not sufficient, however. A successful economy not only saves, but also uses its savings wisely by applying these limited funds to the investment projects that seem likely to be the most productive. In a market economy like that of the United States, savings are allocated by means of a decentralized, market-oriented financial system. The U.S. financial system consists of both financial institutions, like banks, and financial markets, such as bond markets and stock markets.

The financial system improves the allocation of savings in at least two distinct ways. First, the financial system provides *information* to savers about which of the many possible uses of their funds are likely to prove most productive and hence pay the highest return. By evaluating the potential productivity of alternative capital investments, the financial system helps direct savings to its best uses. Second, financial markets help savers *share the risks* of individual investment projects. Sharing of risks protects individual savers from bearing excessive risk, while at the same time making it possible to direct savings to projects, such as the development of new technologies, which are risky but potentially very productive as well.

In this section, we briefly discuss three key components of the U.S. financial system: the banking system, the bond market, and the stock market. In doing so, we elaborate on the role of the financial system as a whole in providing information about investment projects and in helping savers share the risks of lending. In the next section, we add a global dimension and discuss international flows of financial assets through which savers in one country can invest in another country.

The Banking System

The banking system consists of commercial banks, of which there are thousands in the United States. Commercial banks, whose role in the creation of money was discussed earlier in this chapter, are privately owned firms that accept deposits from individuals and businesses and use those deposits to make loans. Banks are the most important example of a class of institutions called **financial intermediaries,** firms that extend credit to borrowers using funds raised from savers. Other examples of financial intermediaries are savings and loan associations and credit unions.

financial intermediaries firms that extend credit to borrowers using funds raised from savers

Why are financial intermediaries such as banks, which "stand between" savers and investors, necessary? Why don't individual savers just lend directly to borrowers who want to invest in new capital projects? The main reason is that, through specialization, banks and other intermediaries develop a *comparative advantage* in evaluating the quality of borrowers—the information-gathering function that we referred to a moment ago. Most savers, particularly small savers, do not have the time or the knowledge to determine for themselves which borrowers are likely to use the funds they receive most productively. In contrast, banks and other intermediaries have gained expertise in performing the information-gathering activities necessary for profitable lending, including checking out the borrower's background, determining whether the borrower's business plans make sense, and monitoring the borrower's activities during the life of the loan. Because banks specialize in evaluating potential borrowers, they can perform this function at a much lower cost, and with better results, than individual savers could on their own. Banks also reduce the costs of gathering information about potential borrowers by pooling the savings of many individuals to make large loans. Each large loan needs to be evaluated only once, by the bank, rather than separately by each of the hundreds of individuals whose savings may be pooled to make the loan.

Banks help savers by eliminating their need to gather information about potential borrowers and by directing their savings toward higher-return, more productive investments. Banks help borrowers as well, by providing access to credit that might otherwise not be available. Unlike a *Fortune* 500 corporation, which typically has many ways to raise funds, a small business that wants to buy equipment or remodel its offices will have few options other than going to a bank. Because the bank's lending officer has developed expertise in evaluating small-business loans, and may even have an ongoing business relationship with the small-business owner, the bank will be able to gather the information it needs to make the loan at a reasonable cost. Likewise, consumers who want to borrow to finish a basement or add a room to a house will find few good alternatives to a bank. In sum, banks' expertise at gathering information about alternative lending opportunities allows them to bring together small savers, looking for good uses for their funds, and small borrowers with worthwhile investment projects.

In addition to being able to earn a return on their savings, a second reason that people hold bank deposits is to make it easier to make payments. Most bank deposits allow the holder to write a check against them or draw on them using a debit card or ATM card. For many transactions, paying by check or debit card is more convenient than using cash. For example, it is safer to send a check through the mail than to send cash, and paying by check gives you a record of the transaction, whereas a cash payment does not; and it is faster (and often more convenient) to make an electronic transfer from your bank account to that of someone else. Moreover, for transactions such as online purchases from a laptop or a mobile device, cash is simply not an option.

The Economic Naturalist 8.3

What happens to national economies during banking crises?

The economists Carmen Reinhart and Kenneth Rogoff studied the relation between banking crises and several important economic outcomes, including real GDP growth, government finances, and housing prices.[2] They looked at dozens of historical banking crisis episodes, spanning many decades, in both emerging and advanced economies. They found that across countries and across time, bank

[2]C. Reinhart and K. Rogoff, *This Time Is Different: Eight Centuries of Financial Folly* (Princeton, NJ: Princeton University Press, 2009).

failures are associated with negative outcomes that include deep and prolonged recessions, dramatic increases in government debt, and drops in real estate values.

As Reinhart and Rogoff note, establishing causality from historical data is difficult. But even though most banking crises are not the sole causes of recessions, they certainly amplify them. When a country's economic growth slows—for example, due to a productivity slowdown—banks suffer because borrowers are less able to pay back their loans. The value of the banks' assets then deteriorates, confidence in the banks decreases, withdrawals of money increase, and, sometimes, banking panics and bank failures follow. Bank failures, in turn, make it difficult for households and businesses to borrow, further bringing down economic activity. This leads to further deterioration of banks' balance sheets, withdrawals, loss of confidence, shrinkage of credit, and so on, in a vicious cycle.

When a bank closes down, the expertise it developed as financial intermediary is lost. As discussed in this chapter, the lost expertise includes, for example, personalized knowledge regarding the bank's small-business customers—knowledge that the bank acquired during years of doing business together. It is therefore not easy for other banks, even if they are still in healthy financial condition, to step in and provide credit to the previous customers of banks that closed. Fixing a banking system that suffered bank failures can therefore be a slow and costly process. In addition to slower economic growth, during this process, many economies have also suffered asset value declines (due to the shortage of access to credit and financing options) and increased levels of government borrowing.

Bonds and Stocks

Large and well-established corporations that wish to obtain funds for investment will sometimes go to banks. Unlike the typical small borrower, however, a larger firm usually has alternative ways of raising funds, notably through the corporate bond market and the stock market. We first discuss some of the mechanics of bonds and stocks, and then return to the role of bond and stock markets in allocating saving.

Bonds

bond a legal promise to repay a debt, usually including both the principal amount and regular interest, or coupon, payments

principal amount the amount originally lent

coupon rate the interest rate promised when a bond is issued; the annual coupon payments are equal to the coupon rate times the principal amount of the bond

coupon payments regular interest payments made to the bondholder

A **bond** is a legal promise to repay a debt, usually including both the **principal amount,** which is the amount originally lent, and regular interest payments. The promised interest rate when a bond is issued is called the **coupon rate.** The regular interest payments made to the bondholder are called coupon payments. The **coupon payment** of a bond that pays interest annually equals the coupon rate times the principal amount of the bond. For example, if the principal amount of a bond is $1,000,000 and its coupon rate is 5 percent, then the annual coupon payment made to the holder of the bond is (0.05)($1,000,000), or $50,000.

Corporations and governments frequently raise funds by issuing bonds and selling them to savers. The coupon rate that a newly issued bond has to promise in order to be attractive to savers depends on a number of factors, including the bond's term, its credit risk, and its tax treatment. The *term* of a bond is the length of time before the debt it represents is fully repaid, a period that can range from 30 days to 30 years or more. Generally, lenders will demand a higher interest rate to lend for a longer term. *Credit risk* is the risk that the borrower will go bankrupt and thus not repay the loan. A borrower that is viewed as risky will have to pay a higher interest rate to compensate lenders for taking the chance of losing all or part of their financial investment. For example, so-called high-yield bonds, less formally known as "junk bonds," are bonds issued by firms judged to be risky by credit-rating agencies; these bonds pay higher interest rates than bonds issued by companies thought to be less risky.

Bonds also differ in their *tax treatment*. For example, interest paid on bonds issued by local governments, called *municipal bonds,* is exempt from federal taxes, whereas interest on other types of bonds is treated as taxable income. Because of this tax advantage, lenders are willing to accept a lower interest rate on municipal bonds.

Bondholders are not required to hold bonds until *maturity,* the time at which they are supposed to be repaid by the issuer, but are always free to sell their bonds in the *bond market,* an organized market run by professional bond traders. The market value of a particular bond at any given point in time is called the *price* of the bond. As it turns out, there is a close relationship between the price of a bond at a given point of time and the interest rate prevailing in financial markets at that time, illustrated by the following example.

EXAMPLE 8.4 Bond Prices and Interest Rates

What is the relationship between bond prices and interest rates?

On January 1, 2020, Tanya purchases a newly issued, two-year government bond with a principal amount of $1,000. The coupon rate on the bond is 5 percent, paid annually. Hence Tanya, or whoever owns the bond at the time, will receive a coupon payment of $50 (5 percent of $1,000) on January 1, 2021, and $1,050 (a $50 coupon payment plus repayment of the original $1,000 lent) on January 1, 2022.

On January 1, 2021, after receiving her first year's coupon payment, Tanya decides to sell her bond to raise the funds to take a vacation. She offers her bond for sale in the bond market. How much can she expect to get for her "used" bond if the prevailing interest rate in the bond market is 6 percent? If the prevailing interest rate is 4 percent?

As we mentioned, the price of a "used" bond at any point in time depends on the prevailing interest rate. Suppose first that, on January 1, 2021, when Tanya takes her bond to the bond market, the prevailing interest rate on newly issued one-year bonds is 6 percent. Would another saver be willing to pay Tanya the full $1,000 principal amount of her bond? No, because the purchaser of Tanya's bond will receive $1,050 in one year, when the bond matures; whereas if he uses his $1,000 to buy a new one-year bond paying 6 percent interest, he will receive $1,060 ($1,000 principal repayment plus $60 interest) in one year. So Tanya's bond is not worth $1,000 to another saver.

How much would another saver be willing to pay for Tanya's bond? Since newly issued one-year bonds pay a 6 percent return, he will buy Tanya's bond only at a price that allows him to earn at least that return. As the holder of Tanya's bond will receive $1,050 ($1,000 principal plus $50 interest) in one year, the price for her bond that allows the purchaser to earn a 6 percent return must satisfy the equation

$$\text{Bond price} \times 1.06 = \$1{,}050.$$

Solving the equation for the bond price, we find that Tanya's bond will sell for $1,050/1.06, or just under $991. To check this result, note that in one year the purchaser of the bond will receive $1,050, or $59 more than he paid. His rate of return is $59/$991, or 6 percent, as expected.

What if the prevailing interest rate had been 4 percent rather than 6 percent? Then the price of Tanya's bond would satisfy the relationship bond price $\times$ 1.04 = $1,050, implying that the price of her bond would be $1,050/1.04, or almost $1,010.

What happens if the interest rate when Tanya wants to sell is 5 percent, the same as it was when she originally bought the bond? You should show that in this case the bond would sell at its face value of $1,000.

This example illustrates a general principle, that *bond prices and interest rates are inversely related*. When the interest rate being paid on newly issued bonds rises, the price financial investors are willing to pay for existing bonds falls, and vice versa.

SELF-TEST 8.6

Three-year government bonds are issued at a face value (principal amount) of 100 and a coupon rate of 7 percent, interest payable at the end of each year. One year prior to the maturation of these bonds, a headline reads, "Bad Economic News Causes Prices of Bonds to Plunge," and the story reveals that these three-year bonds have fallen in price to 96. What has happened to interest rates? What is the one-year interest rate at the time of the story?

Issuing bonds is one means by which a corporation or a government can obtain funds from savers. Another important way of raising funds, but one restricted to corporations, is by issuing stock to the public.

Stocks

stock (or **equity**) a claim to partial ownership of a firm

dividend a regular payment received by stockholders for each share that they own

A share of **stock** (or **equity**) is a claim to partial ownership of a firm. For example, if a corporation has 1 million shares of stock outstanding, ownership of 1 share is equivalent to ownership of one-millionth of the company. Stockholders receive returns on their financial investment in two forms. First, stockholders receive a regular payment called a **dividend** for each share of stock they own. Dividends are determined by the firm's management and usually depend on the firm's recent profits. Second, stockholders receive returns in the form of *capital gains* when the price of their stock increases (we discussed capital gains and losses in Chapter 7, *Saving and Capital Formation*).

Prices of stocks are determined through trading on a stock exchange, such as the New York Stock Exchange. A stock's price rises and falls as the demand for the stock changes. Demand for stocks in turn depends on factors such as news about the prospects of the company. For example, the stock price of a pharmaceutical company that announces the discovery of an important new drug is likely to rise on the announcement, even if actual production and marketing of the drug is some time away, because financial investors expect the company to become more profitable in the future. Example 8.5 illustrates numerically some key factors that affect stock prices.

EXAMPLE 8.5 Buying Shares in a New Company

How much should you pay for a share of FortuneCookie.com?

You have the opportunity to buy shares in a new company called FortuneCookie .com, which plans to sell gourmet fortune cookies over the Internet. Your stockbroker estimates that the company will pay $1.00 per share in dividends a year from now and that in a year, the market price of the company will be $80.00 per share. Assuming that you accept your broker's estimates as accurate, what is the most that you should be willing to pay today per share of FortuneCookie.com? How does your answer change if you expect a $5.00 dividend? If you expect a $1.00 dividend but an $84.00 stock price in one year?

Based on your broker's estimates, you conclude that in one year, each share of FortuneCookie.com you own will be worth $81.00 in your pocket—the $1.00 dividend plus the $80.00 you could get by reselling the stock. Thus, finding the maximum price you would pay for the stock today boils down to asking how much would you invest today to have $81.00 a year from today. In turn, answering this question requires one more piece of information, which is the expected rate of return that you require in order to be willing to buy stock in this company.

How would you determine your required rate of return to hold stock in FortuneCookie.com? For the moment, let's imagine that you are not too worried about the potential riskiness of the stock, either because you think that it is a "sure thing" or because you are a devil-may-care type who is not bothered by risk. In that case, you can apply the Cost-Benefit Principle. Your required rate of return to hold FortuneCookie.com should be about the same as you can get on other financial investments, such as government bonds. The available return on other financial investments gives the *opportunity cost* of your funds. So, for example, if the interest rate currently being offered by government bonds is 6 percent, you should be willing to accept a 6 percent return to hold FortuneCookie.com as well. In that case, the maximum price you would pay today for a share of FortuneCookie satisfies the equation

$$\text{Stock price} \times 1.06 = \$81.00.$$

This equation defines the stock price you should be willing to pay if you are willing to accept a 6 percent return over the next year. Solving this equation yields stock price = \$81.00/1.06 = \$76.42. If you buy FortuneCookie.com for \$76.42, then your return over the year will be (\$81.00 − \$76.42)/\$76.42 = \$4.58/\$71.42 = 6 percent, which is the rate of return you required to buy the stock.

If, instead, the dividend is expected to be \$5.00, then the total benefit of holding the stock in one year, equal to the expected dividend plus the expected price, is \$5.00 + \$80.00, or \$85.00. Assuming again that you are willing to accept a 6 percent return to hold FortuneCookie.com, the price you are willing to pay for the stock today satisfies the relationship Stock price × 1.06 = \$85.00. Solving this equation for the stock price yields Stock price = \$85.00/1.06 = \$80.19. Comparing with the previous case, we see that a higher expected dividend in the future increases the value of the stock today. That's why good news about the future prospects of a company—such as the announcement by a pharmaceutical company that it has discovered a useful new drug—affects its stock price immediately.

If the expected future price of the stock is \$84.00, with the dividend at \$1.00, then the value of holding the stock in one year is once again \$85.00, and the calculation is the same as the previous one. Again, the price you should be willing to pay for the stock is \$80.19.

These examples show that an increase in the future dividend or in the future expected stock price raises the stock price today, whereas an increase in the return a saver requires to hold the stock lowers today's stock price. Since we expect required returns in the stock market to be closely tied to market interest rates, this last result implies that increases in interest rates tend to depress stock prices as well as bond prices.

Our examples also took the future stock price as given. But what determines the future stock price? Just as today's stock price depends on the dividend shareholders expect to receive this year and the stock price a year from now, the stock price a year from now depends on the dividend expected for next year and the stock price two years from now, and so on.

Ultimately, then, today's stock price is affected not only by the dividend expected this year but future dividends as well. A company's ability to pay dividends depends on its earnings. Thus, as we noted in the example of the pharmaceutical company that announces the discovery of a new drug, news about future earnings–even earnings quite far in the future–is likely to affect a company's stock price immediately.

SELF-TEST 8.7

As in Example 8.5, you expect a share of FortuneCookie.com to be worth \$80.00 per share in one year and also to pay a dividend of \$1.00 in one year. What should you be willing to pay for the stock today if the prevailing interest rate, equal to your required rate of return, is 4 percent? What if the interest rate is 8 percent? In general, how would you expect stock prices to react if economic news arrives that implies that interest rates will rise in the very near future?

In the examples we have studied, we assumed that you were willing to accept a return of 6 percent to hold FortuneCookie.com, the same return that you could get on a government bond. However, financial investments in the stock market are quite risky in that returns to holding stocks can be highly variable and unpredictable. For example, although you expect a share of FortuneCookie.com to be worth $80.00 in one year, you also realize that there is a chance it might sell as low as $50.00 or as high as $110.00 per share. Most financial investors dislike risk and unpredictability and thus have a higher required rate of return for holding risky assets like stocks than for holding relatively safe assets like government bonds. The difference between the required rate of return to hold risky assets and the rate of return on safe assets, like government bonds, is called the **risk premium.** The following example illustrates the effect of financial investors' dislike of risk on stock prices.

risk premium the rate of return that financial investors require to hold risky assets minus the rate of return on safe assets

EXAMPLE 8.6 Riskiness and Stock Prices

What is the relationship between risk and stock prices?

Continuing Example 8.5, suppose that FortuneCookie.com is expected to pay a $1.00 dividend and have a market price of $80.00 per share in one year. The interest rate on government bonds is 6 percent per year. However, to be willing to hold a risky asset like a share of FortuneCookie.com, you require an expected return four percentage points higher than the rate paid by safe assets like government bonds (a risk premium of 4 percent). Hence you require a 10 percent expected return to hold FortuneCookie.com. What is the most you would be willing to pay for the stock now? What do you conclude about the relationship between perceived riskiness and stock prices?

As a share of FortuneCookie.com is expected to pay $81.00 in one year and the required return is 10 percent, we have Stock price × 1.10 = $81.00. Solving for the stock price, we find the price to be $81.00/1.10 = $73.64, less than the price of $76.42 we found when there was no risk premium and the required rate of return was 6 percent. We conclude that financial investors' dislike of risk, and the resulting risk premium, lowers the prices of risky assets like stocks.

RECAP

THE FINANCIAL SYSTEM AND THE ALLOCATION OF SAVING

- The role of the financial system is allocating saving to productive uses. Three key components of the financial system are the banking system, the bond market, and the stock market.
- Commercial banks are financial intermediaries: they extend credit to borrowers using funds raised from savers.
- Bonds are legal promises to repay a debt. The prices of existing bonds decline when interest rates rise.
- Stocks (or equity) are claims to partial ownership of a firm. Factors affecting stock prices:
    1. An increase in expected future dividends or in the expected future market price of a stock raises the current price of the stock.
    2. An increase in interest rates, implying an increase in the required rate of return to hold stocks, lowers the current price of stocks.
    3. An increase in perceived riskiness, as reflected in an increase in the risk premium, lowers the current price of stocks.

BOND MARKETS, STOCK MARKETS, AND THE ALLOCATION OF SAVINGS

Like banks, bond markets and stock markets provide a means of channeling funds from savers to borrowers with productive investment opportunities. For example, a corporation that is planning a capital investment but does not want to borrow from a bank has two other options: it can issue new bonds, to be sold to savers in the bond market, or it can issue new shares in itself, which are then sold in the stock market. The proceeds from the sales of new bonds or stocks are then available to the firm to finance its capital investment.

How do stock and bond markets help ensure that available savings are devoted to the most productive uses? As we mentioned earlier, two important functions served by these markets are gathering information about prospective borrowers and helping savers share the risks of lending.

The Informational Role of Bond and Stock Markets

Savers and their financial advisors know that to get the highest possible returns on their financial investments, they must find the potential borrowers with the most profitable opportunities. This knowledge provides a powerful incentive to scrutinize potential borrowers carefully.

For example, companies considering a new issue of stocks or bonds know that their recent performance and plans for the future will be carefully studied by professional analysts on Wall Street and other financial investors. If the analysts and other potential purchasers have doubts about the future profitability of the firm, they will offer a relatively low price for the newly issued shares, or they will demand a high interest rate on newly issued bonds. Knowing this, a company will be reluctant to go to the bond or stock market for financing unless its management is confident that it can convince financial investors that the firm's planned use of the funds will be profitable. *Thus the ongoing search by savers and their financial advisors for high returns leads the bond and stock markets to direct funds to the uses that appear most likely to be productive.*

Risk Sharing and Diversification

Many highly promising investment projects are also quite risky. For example, the successful development of a new drug to lower cholesterol could create billions of dollars in profits for a drug company, but if the drug turns out to be less effective than some others on the market, none of the development costs will be recouped. An individual who lent his or her life savings to help finance the development of the anti-cholesterol drug might enjoy a handsome return but also takes the chance of losing everything. Savers are generally reluctant to take large risks, so without some means of reducing the risk faced by each saver, it might be very hard for the company to find the funds to develop the new drug.

Bond and stock markets help reduce risk by giving savers a means to *diversify* their financial investments. **Diversification** is the practice of spreading one's wealth over a variety of different financial investments to reduce overall risk. The idea of diversification follows from the adage that "you shouldn't put all your eggs in one basket." Rather than putting all of his or her savings in one very risky project, a financial investor will find it much safer to allocate a small amount of savings to each of a large number of stocks and bonds. That way, if some financial assets fall in value, there is a good chance that others will rise in value, with gains offsetting losses. The following example illustrates the benefits of diversification.

diversification the practice of spreading one's wealth over a variety of different financial investments to reduce overall risk

EXAMPLE 8.7 The Benefits of Diversification

What are the benefits of diversification?

Vikram has $1,000 to invest and is considering two stocks, the Smith Umbrella Company and the Jones Suntan Lotion Company. The price of Smith Umbrella stock will rise by 10 percent if it rains but will remain unchanged if the weather is sunny. The price of Jones Suntan stock is expected to rise by 10 percent if it is sunny but will remain unchanged if there is rain. The chance of rain is 50 percent, and the chance of sunshine is 50 percent. How should Vikram invest his $1,000?

If Vikram were to invest all his $1,000 in Smith Umbrella, he has a 50 percent chance of earning a 10 percent return, in the event that it rains, and a 50 percent chance of earning zero, if the weather is sunny. His average return is 50 percent times 10 percent plus 50 percent times zero, or 5 percent. Similarly, an investment in Jones Suntan yields 10 percent return half the time, when it's sunny, and 0 percent return the other half the time, when it rains, for an average return of 5 percent.

Although Vikram can earn an *average* return of 5 percent in either stock, investing in only one stock or the other is quite risky since the actual return he receives varies widely depending on whether there is rain or shine. Can Vikram *guarantee* himself a 5 percent return, avoiding the uncertainty and risk? Yes, all he has to do is put $500 into each of the two stocks. If it rains, he will earn $50 on his Smith Umbrella stock and nothing on his Jones Suntan. If it's sunny, he will earn nothing on Smith Umbrella but $50 on Jones Suntan. Rain or shine, he is guaranteed to earn $50—a 5 percent return—without risk.

The existence of bond markets and stock markets makes it easy for savers to diversify by putting a small amount of their savings into each of a wide variety of different financial assets, each of which represents a share of a particular company or investment project. From society's point of view, diversification makes it possible for risky but worthwhile projects to obtain funding, without individual savers having to bear too much risk.

mutual fund a financial intermediary that sells shares in itself to the public and then uses the funds raised to buy a wide variety of financial assets

For the typical person, a particularly convenient way to diversify is to buy bonds and stocks indirectly through *mutual funds*. A **mutual fund** is a financial intermediary that sells shares in itself to the public and then uses the funds raised to buy a wide variety of financial assets. Holding shares in a mutual fund thus amounts to owning a little bit of many different financial assets, which helps achieve diversification. The advantage of mutual funds is that it is usually less costly and time-consuming to buy shares in one or two mutual funds than to buy many different stocks and bonds directly. Over the past few decades mutual funds have become increasingly popular in the United States.

The Economic Naturalist 8.4

Why did the U.S. stock market rise sharply and fall sharply in the 1990s and again in the 2000s?

Stock prices soared during the 1990s in the United States. The Standard & Poor's (S&P) 500 index, which summarizes the stock price performance of 500 major companies, rose 60 percent between 1990 and 1995 and then more than doubled between 1995 and 2000. However, in the first two years of the new millennium, this index lost nearly half its value. Why did the U.S. stock market boom in the 1990s and then bust?

The prices of stocks depend on their purchasers' expectations about future dividends and stock prices and on the rate of return required by potential stockholders. The required rate of return in turn equals the interest rate on safe assets plus the risk premium. In principle, a rise in stock prices could be the result of increased optimism about future dividends, a fall in the required return, or some combination.

Probably both factors contributed to the boom in stock prices in the 1990s. Dividends grew rapidly in the 1990s, reflecting the strong overall performance of the U.S. economy. Encouraged by the promise of new technologies, many financial investors expected future dividends to be even higher.

There is also evidence that the risk premium that people required to hold stocks fell during the 1990s, thereby lowering the total required return and raising stock prices. One possible explanation for a decline in the risk premium in the 1990s is increased diversification. During that decade, the number and variety of mutual funds available increased markedly. Millions of Americans invested in these funds, including many who had never owned stock before or had owned stock in only a few companies. This increase in diversification for the typical stock market investor may have lowered the perceived risk of holding stocks, which in turn reduced the risk premium and raised stock prices.

After 2000, both of these favorable factors reversed. The growth in dividends was disappointing to stockholders, in large part because many high-tech firms did not prove as profitable as had been hoped. An additional blow was a series of corporate accounting scandals in 2002, in which it became known that some large firms had taken illegal or unethical actions to make their profits seem larger than in fact they were. A number of factors, including a recession, a major terrorist attack, and the accounting scandals, also increased stockholders' concerns about the riskiness of stocks, so that the risk premium they required to hold stocks rose from its 1990s lows. The combination of lower expected dividends and a higher premium for risk sent stock prices sharply downward.

As you already know, the stock boom and bust that ended around 2002 was by no means the last dramatic roller coaster in U.S. stock values. During the following five years, the S&P 500 almost doubled again, reaching all-time record levels in 2007 before collapsing again in the next 18 months to levels not seen since the 1990s. That latter collapse, of 2007–2008, arose in the context of a financial crisis and a deep recession, which both lowered expected dividends and increased the perceived riskiness of holding stocks. (The financial crisis and recession will be further discussed in later chapters.)

Since 2009, stocks have more than fully recovered, and on January 16, 2020, the S&P 500 pushed past the 3,300 milestone for the first time—more than double the previous records of 2000 and 2007. This recent rally reflects historically low interest rates on safe assets and considerable changes in recent years to stockholders' expectations and risk perceptions. Indeed, as these expectations and risk preferences suddenly reversed during February and March 2020—when the U.S. was hit by the COVID-19 pandemic—the S&P 500 declined sharply. As investors quickly updated downward their dividend expectations, and as they sought safer assets, the S&P dipped below 2,400 in late March—before again recovering and hitting an all-time record, 3,500, by August, as expectations recovered.

RECAP

BOND MARKETS, STOCK MARKETS, AND THE ALLOCATION OF SAVINGS

Two important functions served by bond and stock markets are gathering information about prospective borrowers and helping savers share the risks of lending through diversification. A convenient way to diversify is to buy bonds and stocks through mutual funds.

INTERNATIONAL CAPITAL FLOWS

Our discussion thus far has focused on financial markets operating within a given country, such as the United States. However, economic opportunities are not necessarily restricted by national boundaries. The most productive use of a U.S. citizen's savings might be located far from U.S. soil, such as helping build a factory in Thailand or starting a small business in Poland. Likewise, the best way for a Brazilian saver to diversify her assets and reduce her risks could be to hold bonds and stocks from a number of different countries. Over time, extensive financial markets have developed to permit cross-border borrowing and lending. Financial markets in which borrowers and lenders are residents of different countries are called **international financial markets.**

international financial markets financial markets in which borrowers and lenders are residents of different countries

International financial markets differ from domestic financial markets in at least one important respect: Unlike a domestic financial transaction, an international financial transaction is subject to the laws and regulations of at least two countries, the country that is home to the lender and the country that is home to the borrower. Thus the size and vitality of international financial markets depend on the degree of political and economic cooperation among countries. For example, during the relatively peaceful decades of the late nineteenth and early twentieth centuries, international financial markets were remarkably highly developed. Great Britain, at the time the world's dominant economic power, was a major international lender, dispatching its savings for use around the globe. However, during the turbulent years 1914–1945, two world wars and the Great Depression substantially reduced both international finance and international trade in goods and services. The extent of international finance and trade returned to the levels achieved in the late nineteenth century only in the 1980s.

In thinking about international financial markets, it is useful to understand that lending is economically equivalent to acquiring a real or financial asset, and borrowing is economically equivalent to selling a real or financial asset. For example, savers lend to companies by purchasing stocks or bonds, which are financial assets for the lender and financial liabilities for the borrowing firms. Similarly, lending to a government is accomplished in practice by acquiring a government bond—a financial asset for the lender, and a financial liability for the borrower, in this case the government. Savers can also provide funds by acquiring real assets such as land; if I purchase a parcel of land from you, though I am not making a loan in the usual sense, I am providing you with funds that you can use for consuming or investing. In lieu of interest or dividends from a bond or a stock, I receive the rental value of the land that I purchased.

Purchases or sales of real and financial assets across international borders (which are economically equivalent to lending and borrowing across international borders) are known as **international capital flows.** From the perspective of a particular country, say the United States, purchases of domestic (U.S.) assets by foreigners are called **capital inflows;** purchases of foreign assets by domestic (U.S.) households and firms are called **capital outflows.** To remember these terms, it may help to keep in mind that capital inflows represent funds "flowing in" to the country (foreign savers buying domestic assets), while capital outflows are funds "flowing out" of the country (domestic savers buying foreign assets). The difference between the two flows is expressed as *net capital inflows*—capital inflows minus capital outflows—or *net capital outflows*—capital outflows minus capital inflows. Note that capital inflows and outflows are *not* counted as exports or imports because they refer to the purchase of existing real and financial assets rather than currently produced goods and services. In the U.S., the Bureau of Economic Analysis (BEA)—which was mentioned earlier in the text as the government agency in charge of measuring exports, imports, and the other components of GDP—is also in charge of measuring capital inflows and outflows. Every quarter, the BEA publishes its most recent estimates of capital flows in the "Financial Account" section of its *International Transactions Accounts*.

international capital flows purchases or sales of real and financial assets across international borders

capital inflows purchases of domestic assets by foreign households and firms

capital outflows purchases of foreign assets by domestic households and firms

From a macroeconomic perspective, international capital flows play two important roles. First, they allow countries whose productive investment opportunities are greater than domestic savings to fill in the gap by borrowing from abroad. Second, they allow countries to run trade imbalances–situations in which the country's exports of goods and services do not equal its imports of goods and services. The rest of this chapter discusses these key roles. We begin by analyzing the important link between international capital flows and trade imbalances.

Capital Flows and the Balance of Trade

In Chapter 4, *Measuring Economic Activity: GDP, Unemployment, and Inflation,* we introduced the term **net exports** *(NX),* the value of a country's exports less the value of its imports. An equivalent term for the value of a country's exports less the value of its imports is the **trade balance.** Because exports need not equal imports in each quarter or year, the trade balance (or net exports) need not always equal zero. If the trade balance is positive in a particular period so that the value of exports exceeds the value of imports, a country is said to have a **trade surplus** for that period equal to the value of its exports minus the value of its imports. If the trade balance is negative, with imports greater than exports, the country is said to have a **trade deficit** equal to the value of its imports minus the value of its exports.

trade balance (or **net exports**) the value of a country's exports less the value of its imports in a particular period (quarter or year)

trade surplus when exports exceed imports, the difference between the value of a country's exports and the value of its imports in a given period

trade deficit when imports exceed exports, the difference between the value of a country's imports and the value of its exports in a given period

Figure 8.1 shows the components of the U.S. trade balance since 1960 (see Figure 3.5 for data extending back to 1929). The blue line represents U.S. exports as a percentage of GDP; the red line, U.S. imports as a percentage of GDP. When exports exceed imports, the vertical distance between the two lines gives the U.S. trade surplus as a percentage of GDP. When imports exceed exports, the vertical distance between the two lines represents the U.S. trade deficit. Figure 8.1 shows first that international trade has become an increasingly important part of the U.S. economy in the past several decades. In 1960, only 5 percent of U.S. GDP was exported, and the value of imports equaled 4.2 percent of U.S. GDP. In 2019, by comparison, 11.7 percent of U.S. production was sold abroad, and imports amounted to 14.6 percent of U.S. GDP. Second, the figure shows that since the late 1970s the United States has consistently run trade deficits, frequently equal to 2 percent or more of GDP. For a few years in the mid-2000s, these trade deficits ballooned to more than 5 percent of GDP. Why has the U.S. trade balance been in deficit for so long? We will answer that question later in this section.

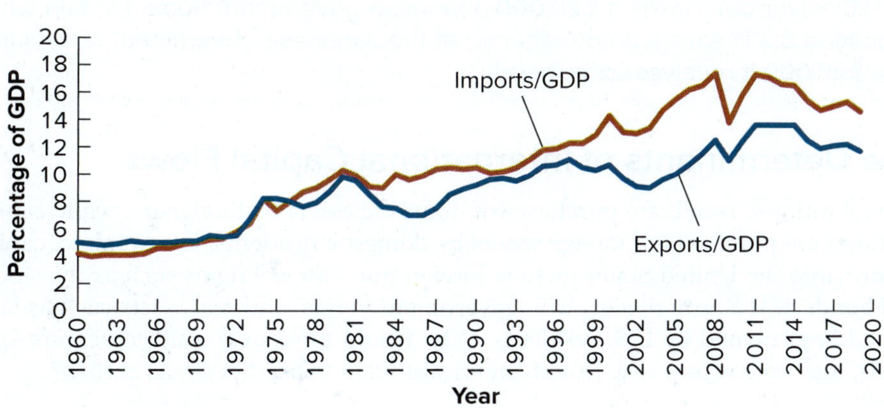

FIGURE 8.1

The U.S. Trade Balance, 1960–2019.

This figure shows U.S. exports and imports as a percentage of GDP. Since the late 1970s, the United States has run a trade deficit, with imports exceeding exports.

Source: Bureau of Economic Analysis, www.bea.gov.

The trade balance represents the difference between the value of goods and services exported by a country and the value of goods and services imported by the country. Net capital inflows represent the difference between purchases of domestic assets by foreigners and purchases of foreign assets by domestic residents. There is a precise and very important link between these two imbalances, which is that in any given period, *the trade balance and net capital inflows sum to zero*. For future reference, let's write this relationship as the equation

$$NX + KI = 0, \tag{8.3}$$

where NX is the trade balance (the same as net exports) and we use KI to stand for net capital inflows. The relationship given by Equation 8.3 is an identity, meaning that it is true by definition.[3]

To see why Equation 8.3 holds, consider what happens when (for example) a U.S. resident purchases an imported good—say, a Japanese automobile priced at $20,000. Suppose the U.S. buyer pays by check so that the Japanese car manufacturer now holds $20,000 in an account in a U.S. bank. What will the Japanese manufacturer do with this $20,000? Basically, there are two possibilities.

First, the Japanese company may use the $20,000 to buy U.S.-produced goods and services, such as U.S.-manufactured car parts or Hawaiian vacations for its executives. In this case, the United States has $20,000 in exports to balance the $20,000 automobile import. Because exports equal imports, the U.S. trade balance is unaffected by these transactions (for these transactions, $NX = 0$). And because no assets are bought or sold, there are no capital inflows or outflows ($KI = 0$). So under this scenario, the condition that the trade balance plus net capital inflows equals zero, as stated in Equation 8.3, is satisfied.

Alternatively, the Japanese car producer might use the $20,000 to acquire U.S. assets, such as a U.S. Treasury bond or some land adjacent to its plant in Tennessee. In this case, the United States compiles a trade deficit of $20,000, because the $20,000 car import is not offset by an export ($NX = -\$20{,}000$). But there is a corresponding capital inflow of $20,000, reflecting the purchase of a U.S. asset by the Japanese ($KI = \$20{,}000$). So once again the trade balance and net capital inflows sum to zero, and Equation 8.3 is satisfied.[4]

In fact, there is a third possibility, which is that the Japanese car company might swap its dollars to some other party outside the United States. For example, the company might trade its dollars to another Japanese firm or individual in exchange for Japanese yen. However, the acquirer of the dollars would then have the same two options as the car company—to buy U.S. goods and services or acquire U.S. assets—so that the equality of net capital inflows and the trade deficit would continue to hold.

SELF-TEST 8.8

A U.S. saver purchases a $20,000 Japanese government bond. Explain why Equation 8.3 is satisfied no matter what the Japanese government does with the $20,000 it receives for its bond.

The Determinants of International Capital Flows

Capital inflows, recall, are purchases of domestic assets by foreigners, while capital outflows are purchases of foreign assets by domestic residents. For example, capital inflows into the United States include foreign purchases of items such as the stocks and bonds of U.S. companies, U.S. government bonds, and real assets such as land or buildings owned by U.S. residents. Why would foreigners want to acquire U.S. assets, and, conversely, why would Americans want to acquire assets abroad?

[3]For simplicity, we do not discuss in this book the *current account balance* (CA), a measure that consists of the trade balance (NX) plus two additional components. The two components are net *primary income* (consisting mostly of investment income—that is, the net inflow of income on U.S.-owned assets abroad) and net *secondary income* (unilateral current transfers—that is, nonmarket transfers from foreigners to U.S. residents, such as foreign government grants and personal remittances). Technically, Equation 8.3 is not quite correct, and the precise relationship is $CA + KI = 0$. However, for the U.S., net primary plus secondary income is a relatively small share of the current account balance. Since it makes the discussion easier, we use net exports, rather than the current account balance, in Equation 8.3.

[4]If the Japanese company simply left the $20,000 in the U.S. bank, it would still count as a capital inflow, since the deposit would still be a U.S. asset acquired by foreigners.

The basic factors that determine the attractiveness of any asset, either domestic or foreign, are *return* and *risk*. Financial investors seek high real returns; thus, with other factors (such as the degree of risk and the returns available abroad) held constant, a higher real interest rate in the home country promotes capital inflows by making domestic assets more attractive to foreigners. By the same token, a higher real interest rate in the home country reduces capital outflows by inducing domestic residents to invest their savings at home. Thus, all else being equal, a higher real interest rate at home leads to net capital inflows. Conversely, a low real interest rate at home tends to create net capital outflows, as financial investors look abroad for better opportunities.

Figure 8.2 shows the relationship between a country's net capital inflows and the real rate of interest prevailing in that country. When the domestic real interest rate is high, net capital inflows are positive (foreign purchases of domestic assets exceed domestic purchases of foreign assets). But when the real interest rate is low, net capital inflows are negative (that is, the country experiences net capital outflows).

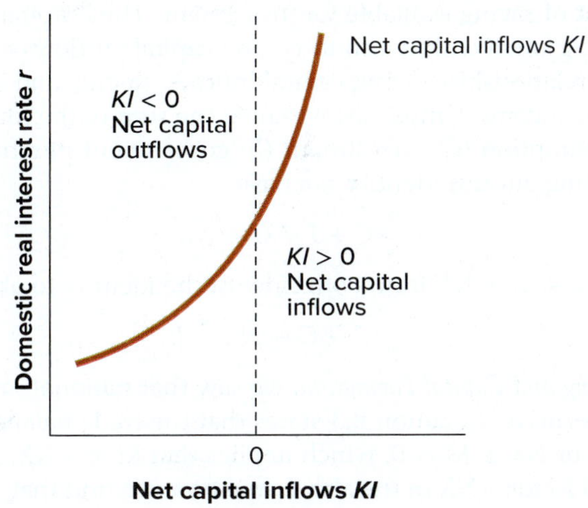

FIGURE 8.2

Net Capital Inflows and the Real Interest Rate.

Holding constant the degree of risk and the real returns available abroad, a high real interest rate in the home country will induce foreigners to buy domestic assets, increasing capital inflows. A high real rate in the home country also reduces the incentive for domestic savers to buy foreign assets, reducing capital outflows. Thus, all else being equal, the higher the domestic real interest rate *r*, the higher will be net capital inflows *KI*.

The effect of risk on capital flows is the opposite of the effect of the real interest rate. For a given real interest rate, an increase in the riskiness of domestic assets reduces net capital inflows, as foreigners become less willing to buy the home country's assets, and domestic savers become more inclined to buy foreign assets. For example, political instability, which increases the risk of investing in a country, tends to reduce net capital inflows. Figure 8.3 shows the effect of an increase in risk on

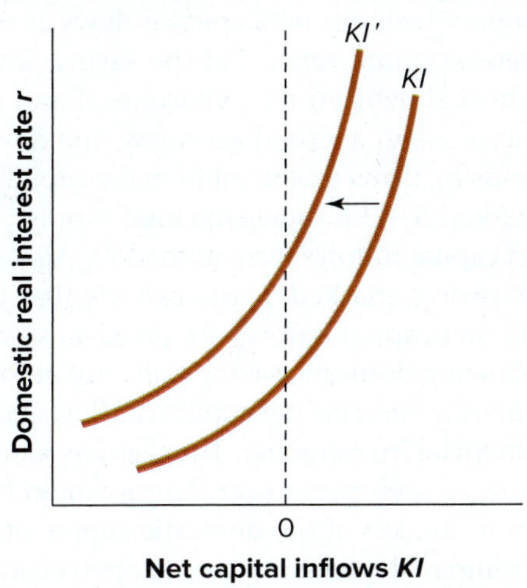

FIGURE 8.3

An Increase in Risk Reduces Net Capital Inflows.

An increase in the riskiness of domestic assets, arising, for example, from an increase in political instability, reduces the willingness of foreign and domestic savers to hold domestic assets. The supply of capital inflows declines at each value of the domestic real interest rate, shifting the *KI* curve to the left.

capital flows: at each value of the domestic real interest rate, an increase in risk reduces net capital inflows, shifting the capital inflows curve to the left.

SELF-TEST 8.9

For a given real interest rate and riskiness in the home country, how would you expect net capital inflows to be affected by an increase in real interest rates abroad? Show your answer graphically.

Saving, Investment, and Capital Inflows

International capital flows have a close relationship to domestic saving and investment. As we will see next, capital inflows augment the domestic saving pool, increasing the funds available for investment in physical capital, while capital outflows reduce the amount of saving available for investment. Thus capital inflows can help promote economic growth within a country, and capital outflows to restrain it.

To derive the relationship among capital inflows, saving, and investment, recall that total output or income Y must always equal the sum of the four components of expenditure: consumption (C), investment (I), government purchases (G), and net exports (NX). Writing out this identity, we have

$$Y = C + I + G + NX.$$

Next, we subtract $C + G + NX$ from both sides of the identity to obtain

$$Y - C - G - NX = I.$$

In Chapter 7, *Saving and Capital Formation,* we saw that national saving S is equal to $Y - C - G$. Furthermore, Equation 8.3 states that the trade balance plus capital inflows equals zero, or $NX + KI = 0$, which implies that $KI = -NX$. If we substitute S for $Y - C - G$ and KI for $-NX$ in the above equation, we find that

$$S + KI = I. \tag{8.4}$$

Equation 8.4, a key result, says that the sum of national saving S and capital inflows from abroad KI must equal domestic investment in new capital goods, I. In other words, in an open economy, the pool of saving available for domestic investment includes not only national saving (the saving of the domestic private and public sectors) but funds from savers abroad as well.

Chapter 7, *Saving and Capital Formation,* introduced the saving–investment diagram, which shows that in a closed economy, the supply of saving must equal the demand for saving. A similar diagram applies to an open economy, except that the supply of saving in an open economy includes net capital inflows as well as domestic saving. Figure 8.4 shows the open-economy version of the saving–investment diagram. The domestic real interest rate is shown on the vertical axis and saving and investment flows on the horizontal axis. As in a closed economy, the downward-sloping curve I shows the demand for funds by firms that want to make capital investments. The solid upward-sloping curve, marked $S + KI$, shows the total supply of saving, including *both* domestic saving S and net capital inflows from abroad KI. Also shown, for comparison, is the supply of domestic saving, marked S. You can see that for higher values of the domestic real interest rate, net capital inflows are positive, so the $S + KI$ curve falls to the right of the curve S showing domestic saving only. But at low enough values of the real interest rate r, the economy sustains net capital outflows, as savers look abroad for higher returns on their financial investments. Thus, at low values of the domestic real interest rate, the net supply of savings is lower than it would be in a closed economy, and the $S + KI$ curve falls to the left of the domestic supply of saving curve S. As Figure 8.4 shows, the equilibrium real interest rate in an open economy, r^*, is the level that

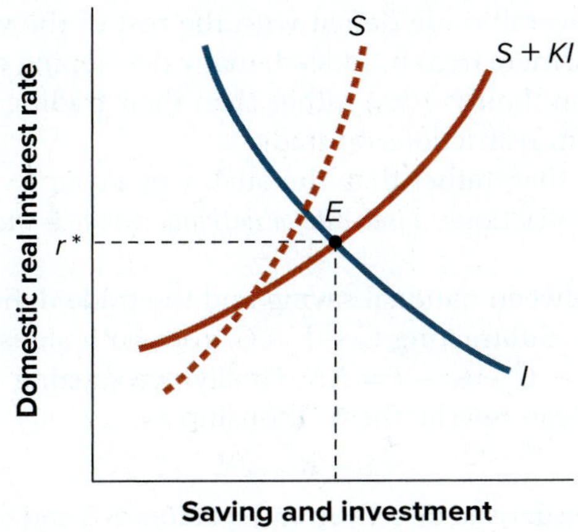

FIGURE 8.4

The Saving–Investment Diagram for an Open Economy. The total supply of savings in an open economy is the sum of national saving S and net capital inflows KI. The supply of domestic saving S is shown for comparison. Because a low real interest rate prompts capital outflows ($KI < 0$), at low values of the domestic interest rate the total supply of saving $S + KI$ is smaller than national saving S. The domestic demand for saving for purposes of capital investment is shown by the curve labeled I. The equilibrium real interest rate r^* sets the total supply of saving, including capital inflows, equal to the domestic demand for saving.

sets the total amount of saving supplied (including capital inflows from abroad) equal to the amount of saving demanded for purposes of domestic capital investment.

Figure 8.4 also indicates how net capital inflows can benefit an economy. A country that attracts significant amounts of foreign capital flows will have a larger pool of total saving and hence both a lower real interest rate and a higher rate of investment in new capital than it otherwise would. The United States and Canada both benefited from large inflows of capital in the early stages of their economic development, as do many developing countries today. Because capital inflows tend to react very sensitively to risk, an implication is that countries that are politically stable and safeguard the rights of foreign investors will attract more foreign capital and thus grow more quickly than countries without those characteristics.

Although capital inflows are generally beneficial to the countries that receive them, they are not costless. Countries that finance domestic capital formation primarily by capital inflows face the prospect of paying interest and dividends to the foreign financial investors from whom they have borrowed. A number of developing countries have experienced *debt crises,* arising because the domestic investments they made with foreign funds turned out poorly, leaving them insufficient income to pay what they owed their foreign creditors. An advantage to financing domestic capital formation primarily with domestic saving is that the returns from the country's capital investments accrue to domestic savers rather than flowing abroad.

The Saving Rate and the Trade Deficit

We have seen that a country's exports and imports do not necessarily balance in each period. Indeed, the United States has run a trade deficit, with its imports exceeding exports, for many years. What causes trade deficits? People sometimes think that trade deficits occur because a country produces inferior goods that no one wants to buy or because other countries impose unfair trade restrictions on imports. Despite the popularity of these explanations, however, there is little support for them in either economic theory or evidence. Economists acknowledge, of course, that trade restrictions can affect the overall levels of exports and imports—and that trade agreements can therefore increase gross trade flows. It is also true that trade barriers and agreements can affect a country's mix of imports, exports, and trading partners. So, for example, trade frictions between the United States and China, which, starting in 2018, included both countries imposing steep tariffs on imports from each other, reduced flows of trade in certain goods between the two countries. But as long as a country spends more than it produces—or, equivalently, saves less than it invests—it must be running an overall trade deficit with the rest of the world, no matter how fairly or unfairly its partners treat it. Indeed, many developing countries have significant trade deficits even though they, rather than their trading partners, tend to impose the more stringent restrictions on trade.

Economists argue that, rather than the quality of a country's exports or the existence of unfair trade restrictions, *a low rate of national saving is the primary cause of trade deficits.*

To see the link between national saving and the trade deficit, recall the identity $Y = C + I + G + NX$. Subtracting $C + I + G$ from both sides of this equation and rearranging, we get $Y - C - G - I = NX$. Finally, recognizing that national saving S equals $Y - C - G$, we can rewrite the relationship as

$$S - I = NX. \tag{8.5}$$

Equation 8.5 can also be derived directly from Equations 8.3 and 8.4. According to Equation 8.5, if we hold domestic investment (I) constant, a high rate of national saving S implies a high level of net exports NX, while a low level of national saving implies a low level of net exports. Furthermore, if a country's national saving is less than its investment, or $S < I$, then Equation 8.5 implies that net exports NX will be negative. That is, the country will have a trade deficit. The conclusion from Equation 8.5 is that, holding domestic investment constant, low national saving tends to be associated with a trade deficit ($NX < 0$), and high national saving is associated with a trade surplus ($NX > 0$).

Why does a low rate of national saving tend to be associated with a trade deficit? A country with a low national saving rate is one in which households and the government have high spending rates, relative to domestic income and production. Since part of the spending of households and the government is devoted to imported goods, we would expect a low-saving, high-spending economy to have a high volume of imports. Furthermore, a low-saving economy consumes a large proportion of its domestic production, reducing the quantity of goods and services available for export. With high imports and low exports, a low-saving economy will experience a trade deficit.

A country with a trade deficit must also be receiving capital inflows, as we have seen. (Equation 8.3 tells us that if a trade deficit exists so that $NX < 0$, then it must be true that $KI > 0$—net capital inflows are positive.) Is a low national saving rate also consistent with the existence of net capital inflows? The answer is yes. A country with a low national saving rate will not have sufficient savings of its own to finance domestic investment. Thus there likely will be many good investment opportunities in the country available to foreign savers, leading to capital inflows. Equivalently, a shortage of domestic saving will tend to drive up the domestic real interest rate, which attracts capital flows from abroad.

We conclude that a low rate of national saving tends to create a trade deficit, as well as to promote the capital inflows that must accompany a trade deficit. The Economic Naturalist 8.5 illustrates this effect for the case of the United States.

The Economic Naturalist 8.5

Why is the U.S. trade deficit so large?

As shown by Figure 8.1, U.S. trade was more or less in balance until the mid-1970s. Since the late 1970s, however, the United States has run large trade deficits, particularly in the mid-1980s and even more so since the latter part of the 1990s. Indeed, from 2004 to 2007, the trade deficit was 5 percent or more of U.S. GDP. Why is the U.S. trade deficit so large?

Figure 8.5 shows national saving, investment, and the trade balance for the United States from 1960 to 2019 (all measured relative to GDP). Note that the trade balance has been negative since the late 1970s, indicating a trade deficit. Note also that trade deficits correspond to periods in which investment exceeds national saving, as required by Equation 8.5.[5]

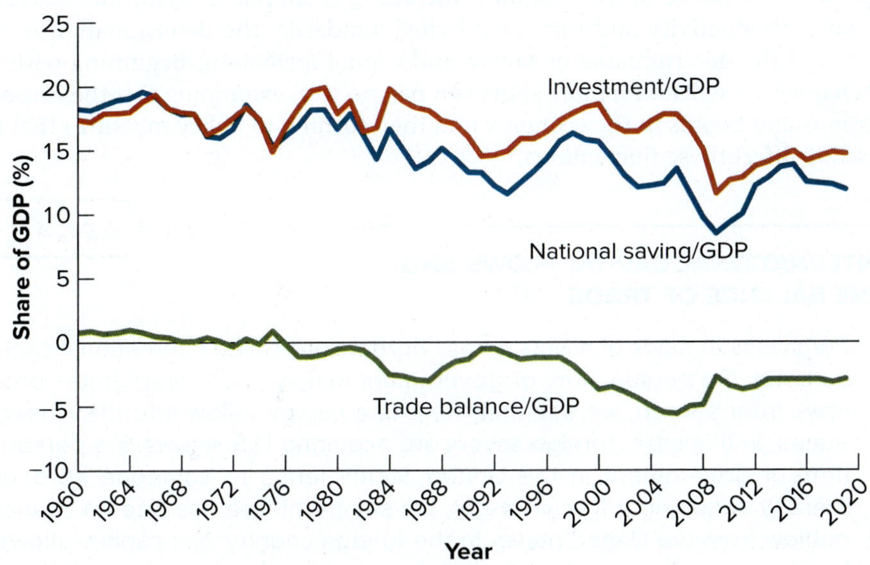

FIGURE 8.5

National Saving, Investment, and the Trade Balance in the United States, 1960–2019.

Since the 1970s, U.S. national saving has fallen below domestic investment, implying a significant trade deficit.

Source: Bureau of Economic Analysis, www.bea.gov.

U.S. national saving and investment were roughly in balance in the 1960s and early 1970s, and hence the U.S. trade balance was close to zero during that period. However, U.S. national saving fell during the late 1970s and 1980s. One factor that contributed to the decline in national saving was the large government deficits of the era. Because investment did not decline as much as saving, the U.S. trade deficit ballooned in the 1980s, coming under control only when investment fell during the recession of 1990–1991. Saving and investment both recovered during the 1990s, but in the latter part of the 1990s, national saving dropped again. This time the federal government was not at fault since its budget showed a healthy surplus. Rather, the fall in national saving reflected a decline in private saving, the result of a powerful upsurge in consumption spending. Much of the increase in consumption spending was for imported goods and services, which pushed the trade deficit to record levels.

Following the 2001 recession, large government deficits returned, and as household saving kept declining, by the mid-2000s the trade deficit broke the record again, reaching levels above 5 percent of GDP. The trade deficit changed course following the 2007–2009 recession, shrinking to about 3 percent of GDP, where it remained as of 2019. While saving declined dramatically during the recession as a result of large government deficits, and took years to recover, investment declined even faster, and has been recovering more slowly.

Is the U.S. trade deficit a problem? The trade deficit implies that the United States is relying heavily on foreign savings to finance its domestic capital formation

[5]If you look at Figure 8.5 very carefully, you may notice that in some years the gap between national saving and investment is slightly different from the trade balance. That difference, referred to as *statistical discrepancy,* results from imperfections in the measurement of these macroeconomic indicators. While typically much smaller, the statistical discrepancy in some years can reach around 2 percent of GDP.

(net capital inflows). These foreign loans must ultimately be repaid with interest. If the foreign savings are well invested and the U.S. economy grows, repayment will not pose a problem. However, if economic growth in the United States slackens, repaying the foreign lenders will impose an economic burden in the future.

To this point in the book we have discussed a variety of issues relating to the long-run performance of the economy, including economic growth, the sources of increasing productivity and improved living standards, the determination of real wages, and the determinants of saving and capital formation. Beginning with the next chapter, we will take a more short-run perspective, examining first the causes of recessions and booms in the economy and then turning to policy measures that can be used to affect these fluctuations.

RECAP

INTERNATIONAL CAPITAL FLOWS AND THE BALANCE OF TRADE

- Purchases or sales of assets across borders are called international capital flows. If a person, firm, or government in (say) the United States borrows from abroad, we say that there is a capital inflow into the United States. In this case, foreign savers are acquiring U.S. assets. If a person, firm, or government in the United States lends to someone abroad, thereby acquiring a foreign asset, we say that there has been a capital outflow from the United States to the foreign country. Net capital inflows to a given country equal capital inflows minus outflows.
- If a country imports more goods and services than it exports, it must borrow abroad to cover the difference. Likewise, a country that exports more than it imports will lend the difference to foreigners. Thus, as a matter of accounting, the trade balance NX and net capital inflows KI must sum to zero in every period.
- The funds available for domestic investment in new capital goods equal the sum of domestic saving and net capital inflows from abroad. The higher the return and the lower the risk of investing in the domestic country, the greater will be the capital inflows from abroad. Capital inflows benefit an economy by providing more funds for capital investment, but they can become a burden if the returns from investing in new capital goods are insufficient to pay back the foreign lenders.
- An important cause of a trade deficit is a low national saving rate. A country that saves little and spends a lot will tend to import a greater quantity of goods and services than it is able to export. At the same time, the country's low saving rate implies a need for more foreign borrowing to finance domestic investment spending.

SUMMARY

- *Money* is any asset that can be used in making purchases, such as currency and checking account balances. Money has three main functions: It is a *medium of exchange,* which means that it can be used in transactions. It is a *unit of account,* in that economic values are typically measured in units of money (for example, dollars). And it is a *store of value,* a means by which people can hold wealth. In practice, it is difficult to measure the money supply since many assets have some moneylike features. A relatively narrow measure of money is M1, which includes currency and checking accounts. A broader measure of money, M2, includes all the assets in M1 plus additional assets that are somewhat less convenient to use in transactions than those included in M1. *(LO1)*

- Because bank deposits are part of the money supply, the behavior of commercial banks and of bank depositors affects the amount of money in the economy. A key factor is the *reserve-deposit ratio* chosen by banks. *Bank reserves* are cash or similar assets held by commercial banks, for the purpose of meeting depositor withdrawals and payments. The reserve-deposit ratio is bank reserves divided by deposits in banks. A banking system in which all deposits are held as reserves practices *100 percent reserve banking*. Modern banking systems have reserve-deposit ratios less than 100 percent and are called *fractional-reserve banking systems*. *(LO2)*
- Commercial banks create money through multiple rounds of lending and accepting deposits. This process of lending and increasing deposits comes to an end when banks' reserve-deposit ratios equal their desired levels. At that point, bank deposits equal bank reserves divided by the desired reserve-deposit ratio. The money supply equals currency held by the public plus deposits in the banking system. *(LO2)*
- The central bank of the United States is called the *Federal Reserve System,* or the Fed for short. The Fed's two main responsibilities are making monetary policy, which means determining how much money will circulate in the economy, and overseeing and regulating financial markets, especially banks. Created in 1914, the Fed is headed by a *Board of Governors* made up of seven governors appointed by the president. One of these seven governors is appointed chair. The *Federal Open Market Committee,* which meets about eight times a year to determine monetary policy, is made up of the seven governors, the president of the Federal Reserve Bank of New York, and four of the presidents of the regional Federal Reserve banks. *(LO3)*
- One of the original purposes of the Federal Reserve was to help eliminate or control banking panics. A *banking panic* is an episode in which depositors, spurred by news or rumors of the imminent bankruptcy of one or more banks, rush to withdraw their deposits from the banking system. Because banks do not keep enough reserves on hand to pay off all depositors, even a financially healthy bank can run out of cash during a panic and be forced to close. The Federal Reserve failed to contain banking panics during the Great Depression, which led to sharp declines in the money supply. The adoption of a system of *deposit insurance* in the United States eliminated banking panics. A disadvantage of deposit insurance is that if banks or other insured intermediaries make bad loans or financial investments, the taxpayers may be responsible for covering the losses. *(LO3)*
- Corporations that do not wish to borrow from banks can obtain finance by issuing bonds or stocks. A *bond* is a legal promise to repay a debt, including both the *principal amount* and regular interest payments. The prices of existing bonds decline when interest rates rise. A share of *stock* is a claim to partial ownership of a firm. The price of a stock depends positively on the *dividend* the stock is expected to pay and on the expected future price of the stock and negatively on the rate of return required by financial investors to hold the stock. The required rate of return in turn is the sum of the return on safe assets and the additional return required to compensate financial investors for the riskiness of stocks, called the *risk premium*. *(LO4)*
- Besides balancing saving and investment in the aggregate, financial markets and institutions play the important role of allocating saving to the most productive investment projects. The financial system improves the allocation of saving in two ways: First, it provides information to savers about which of the many possible uses of their funds are likely to prove must productive, and hence pay the highest return. For example, *financial intermediaries* such as banks develop expertise in evaluating prospective borrowers, making it unnecessary for small savers to do that on their own. Similarly, stock and bond analysts evaluate the business prospects of a company issuing shares of stock or bonds, which determines the price the stock will sell for or the interest rate the company will have to offer on its bond. Second, financial markets help savers share the risks of lending by permitting them to *diversify* their financial investments. Individual savers often hold stocks through *mutual funds,* a type of financial intermediary that reduces risk by holding many different financial assets. By reducing the risk faced by any one saver, financial markets allow risky but potentially very productive projects to be funded. *(LO4, LO5)*
- The *trade balance,* or net exports, is the value of a country's exports less the value of its imports in a particular period. Exports need not equal imports in each period. If exports exceed imports, the difference is called a *trade surplus,* and if imports exceed exports, the difference is called a *trade deficit*. Trade takes place in assets as well as goods and services. Purchases of domestic assets (real or financial) by foreigners are called *capital inflows,* and purchases of foreign assets by domestic savers are called *capital outflows*. Because imports that are not financed by sales of exports must be financed by sales of assets, the trade balance and net capital inflows sum to zero. *(LO6)*
- The higher the real interest rate in a country, and the lower the risk of investing there, the higher its capital inflows. The availability of capital inflows expands a country's pool of saving, allowing for more domestic

investment and increased growth. A drawback to using capital inflows to finance domestic capital formation is that the returns to capital (interest and dividends) accrue to foreign financial investors rather than domestic residents. *(LO6)*

- A low rate of national saving is the primary cause of trade deficits. A low-saving, high-spending country is likely to import more than a high-saving country. It also consumes more of its domestic production, leaving less for export. Finally, a low-saving country is likely to have a high real interest rate, which attracts net capital inflows. Because the sum of the trade balance and capital inflows is zero, a high level of net capital inflows is consistent with a large trade deficit. *(LO6)*

KEY TERMS

bank reserves
banking panic
barter
Board of Governors
bond
capital inflows
capital outflows
coupon payments
coupon rate
deposit insurance
diversification
dividend
Federal Open Market Committee (FOMC)
Federal Reserve System (or the Fed)
financial intermediaries
fractional-reserve banking system
international capital flows
international financial markets
M1
M2
medium of exchange
monetary policy
money
mutual fund
100 percent reserve banking
open-market operations
open-market purchase
open-market sale
principal amount
reserve-deposit ratio
risk premium
stock (or equity)
store of value
trade balance (or net exports)
trade deficit
trade surplus
unit of account

REVIEW QUESTIONS

1. What is *money*? Why do people hold money even though it pays a lower return than other financial assets? *(LO1)*
2. Suppose that the public switches from doing most of its shopping with currency to using checks instead. If the Fed takes no action, what will happen to the national money supply? Explain. *(LO2, LO3)*
3. What is a *banking panic*? Prior to the introduction of deposit insurance, why might even a bank that had made sound loans have reason to fear a panic? *(LO3)*
4. Give two ways that the financial system helps improve the allocation of savings. Illustrate with examples. *(LO4)*
5. Arjay plans to sell a bond that matures in one year and has a principal value of $1,000. Can he expect to receive $1,000 in the bond market for the bond? Explain. *(LO4)*
6. Suppose you are much less concerned about risk than the typical person. Are stocks a good financial investment for you? Why or why not? *(LO4, LO5)*
7. How are capital inflows or outflows related to domestic investment in new capital goods? *(LO6)*
8. Explain with examples why, in any period, a country's net capital inflows equal its trade deficit. *(LO6)*

PROBLEMS

Mc Graw Hill connect

1. During World War II, an Allied soldier named Robert Radford spent several years in a large German prisoner-of-war camp. At times, more than 50,000 prisoners were held in the camp, with some freedom to move about within the compound. Radford later wrote an account of his experiences. He described how an economy developed in the camp, in which prisoners traded food, clothing, and other items. Services, such as barbering, were also exchanged. Lacking paper money, the prisoners

began to use cigarettes (provided monthly by the Red Cross) as money. Prices were quoted, and payments made, using cigarettes. *(LO1)*

a. In Radford's POW camp, how did cigarettes fulfill the three functions of money?
b. Why do you think the prisoners used cigarettes as money, as opposed to other items of value such as squares of chocolate or pairs of boots?
c. Do you think a nonsmoking prisoner would have been willing to accept cigarettes in exchange for a good or service in Radford's camp? Why or why not?

2. Redo the example of Gorgonzola in the text (see Tables 8.2 to 8.6), assuming that (1) initially, the Gorgonzolan central bank puts 5,000,000 guilders into circulation, and (2) commercial banks desire to hold reserves of 20 percent of deposits. As in the text, assume that the public holds no currency. Show the consolidated balance sheets of Gorgonzolan commercial banks for each of the following instances. *(LO2)*
   a. After the initial deposits (compare to Table 8.2).
   b. After one round of loans (compare to Table 8.3).
   c. After the first redeposit of guilders (compare to Table 8.4).
   d. After two rounds of loans and redeposits (Table 8.5).
   e. What are the final values of bank reserves, loans, deposits, and the money supply (compare to Table 8.6)?
3. Answer each of the following questions. *(LO2)*
   a. Bank reserves are 100, the public holds 200 in currency, and the desired reserve-deposit ratio is 0.25. Find deposits and the money supply.
   b. The money supply is 500, and currency held by the public equals bank reserves. The desired reserve-deposit ratio is 0.25. Find currency held by the public and bank reserves.
   c. The money supply is 1,250, of which 250 is currency held by the public. Bank reserves are 100. Find the desired reserve-deposit ratio.
4. Refer to Table 8.7. Suppose that the Fed had decided to set the U.S. money supply in December 1932 and in December 1933 at the same value as in December 1930. Assuming that the values of currency held by the public and the reserve-deposit ratio had remained as given in the table, by how much more should the Fed have increased bank reserves at each of those dates to accomplish that objective? *(LO3)*
5. The Federal Reserve System was created by the Federal Reserve Act, passed by Congress in 1913, and began operations in 1914. Like all central banks, the Fed is a government agency. Which of the following statements about the Fed is false? *(LO3)*
   a. The Fed has the power to supervise and regulate banks.
   b. The Fed's goals are to promote economic growth, maintain low inflation, and watch over a smooth operation of financial markets.
   c. The Fed is the "lender of last resort."
   d. The Fed is allowed to make a profit like commercial banks.
6. Simon purchases a bond, newly issued by the Amalgamated Corporation, for $1,000. The bond pays $60 to its holder at the end of the first and second years and pays $1,060 upon its maturity at the end of the third year. *(LO4)*
   a. What are the principal amount, the term, the coupon rate, and the coupon payment for Simon's bond?
   b. After receiving the second coupon payment (at the end of the second year), Simon decides to sell his bond in the bond market. What price can he expect for his bond if the one-year interest rate at that time is 3 percent? 8 percent? 10 percent?
   c. Can you think of a reason that the price of Simon's bond after two years might fall below $1,000, even though the market interest rate equals the coupon rate?
7. Shares in Brothers Grimm Inc., manufacturers of gingerbread houses, are expected to pay a dividend of $5.50 in one year and to sell for $99.00 per share at that time. How much should you be willing to pay today per share of Grimm if the safe rate of interest *(LO4)*
   a. is 5.1 percent and you believe that investing in Grimm carries no risk?
   b. is 10.1 percent and you believe that investing in Grimm carries no risk?
   c. is 5.1 percent but your risk premium is 2 percent?
   d. Repeat parts a–c, assuming that Grimm is not expected to pay a dividend but the expected price is unchanged.
8. You have $1,000 to invest and are considering buying some combination of the shares of two companies, DonkeyInc and ElephantInc. Shares of DonkeyInc will pay a 10 percent return if the Democrats are elected, an event you believe to have a 40 percent probability; otherwise, the shares pay a zero return. Shares of ElephantInc will pay 8 percent if the Republicans are elected (a 60 percent probability), zero otherwise. Either the Democrats or the Republicans will be elected. *(LO4, LO5)*
   a. If your only concern is maximizing your average expected return, with no regard for risk, how should you invest your $1,000?
   b. What is your expected return if you invest $500 in each stock? (*Hint:* Consider what your return will be if the Democrats win and if the Republicans win;

then weight each outcome by the probability that event occurs.)

c. The strategy of investing $500 in each stock does *not* give the highest possible average expected return. Why might you choose it anyway?
d. Devise an investment strategy that guarantees at least a 4.4 percent return, no matter which party wins.
e. Devise an investment strategy that is riskless—that is, one in which the return on your $1,000 does not depend at all on which party wins.

9. How do each of the following transactions affect (1) the trade surplus or deficit and (2) capital inflows or outflows for the United States? Show that in each case, the identity that the trade balance plus net capital inflows equals zero applies. *(LO6)*
   a. A U.S. exporter sells software to Israel. She uses the Israeli shekels received to buy stock in an Israeli company.
   b. A Mexican firm uses proceeds from its sale of oil to the United States to buy U.S. government debt.
   c. A Mexican firm uses proceeds from its sale of oil to the United States to buy oil drilling equipment from a U.S. firm.
10. Use a diagram like Figure 8.4 (solid lines only) to show the effects of each of the following on the real interest rate and capital investment of a country that is a net borrower from abroad. *(LO6)*
    a. Investment opportunities in the country improve owing to new technologies.
    b. The government budget deficit rises.
    c. Domestic citizens decide to save more.
    d. Foreign investors believe that the riskiness of lending to the country has increased.

ANSWERS TO SELF-TESTS

8.1 Table 8.5 shows the balance sheet of banks after two rounds of lending and redeposits. At that point, deposits are 2,710,000 guilders and reserves are 1,000,000 guilders. Since banks have a desired reserve-deposit ratio of 10 percent, they will keep 271,000 guilders (10 percent of deposits) as reserves and lend out the remaining 729,000 guilders. Loans to farmers are now 2,439,000 guilders. Eventually the 729,000 guilders lent to the farmers will be redeposited into the banks, giving the banks deposits of 3,439,000 guilders and reserves of 1,000,000 guilders. The balance sheet is as shown in the accompanying table.

Assets	
Currency (= reserves)	1,000,000 guilders
Loans to farmers	2,439,000 guilders
Liabilities	
Deposits	3,439,000 guilders

Notice that assets equal liabilities. The money supply equals deposits, or 3,439,000 guilders. Currency held in the banks as reserves does not count in the money supply. *(LO2)*

8.2 Because the public holds no currency, the money supply equals bank deposits, which in turn equal bank reserves divided by the reserve-deposit ratio (Equation 8.1). If bank reserves are 1,000,000 and the reserve-deposit ratio is 0.05, then deposits equal 1,000,000/0.05 = 20,000,000 guilders, which is also the money supply. If bank reserves are 2,000,000 guilders and the reserve-deposit ratio is 0.10, then the money supply and deposits are again equal to 20,000,000 guilders, or 2,000,000/0.10. *(LO2)*

8.3 If the central bank sells 50 shekels of government bonds in exchange for currency, the immediate effect is to reduce the amount of currency in the hands of the public by 50 shekels. To restore their currency holding to the desired level of 1,000 shekels, the public will withdraw 50 shekels from commercial banks, reducing bank reserves from 200 shekels to 150 shekels. The desired reserve-deposit ratio is 0.2, so ultimately deposits must equal 150 shekels in reserves divided by 0.2, or 750 shekels. (*Note:* To contract deposits, the commercial banks will have to "call in" loans, reducing their loans outstanding.) The money supply equals 1,000 shekels in currency held by the public plus 750 shekels in deposits, or 1,750 shekels. Thus the open-market purchase has reduced the money supply from 2,000 to 1,750 shekels. *(LO3)*

8.4 Verify directly for each date in Table 8.7 that

$$\text{Money supply} = \text{Currency} + \frac{\text{Bank reserves}}{\text{Desired reserve-deposit ratio}}.$$

For example, for December 1929 we can check that 45.9 = 3.85 + 3.15/0.075.

Suppose that the currency held by the public in December 1933 had been 3.79, as in

December 1930, rather than 4.85, and that the difference (4.85 − 3.79 = 1.06) had been left in the banks. Then bank reserves in December 1933 would have been 3.45 + 1.06 = 4.51, and the money supply would have been 3.79 + 4.51/0.133 = 37.7. So the money supply would still have fallen between 1930 and 1933 if people had not increased their holdings of currency, but only by about half as much. *(LO3)*

8.5 Over the course of 1931, currency holdings by the public rose by $0.80 billion but bank reserves fell overall by only $0.20 billion. Thus the Fed must have replaced $0.60 billion of lost reserves during the year through open-market purchases or discount window lending.

Currency holdings at the end of 1931 were $4.59 billion. To have kept the money supply at the December 1930 value of $44.1 billion, the Fed would have had to ensure that bank deposits equaled $44.1 billion − $4.59 billion, or $39.51 billion. As the reserve-deposit ratio in 1931 was 0.095, this would have required bank reserves of 0.095 × $39.51 billion, or $3.75 billion, compared to the actual value in December 1931 of $3.11 billion. Thus, to keep the money supply from falling, the Fed would have had to increase bank reserves by $0.64 billion more than it did. The Fed has been criticized for increasing bank reserves by only about half what was needed to keep the money supply from falling. *(LO3)*

8.6 Since bond prices fell, interest rates must have risen. To find the interest rate, note that bond investors are willing to pay only 96 today for a bond that will pay back 107 (a coupon payment of 7 plus the principal amount of 100) in one year. To find the one-year return, divide 107 by 96 to get 1.115. Thus, the interest rate must have risen to 11.5 percent. *(LO4)*

8.7 The share of stock will be worth $81.00 in one year—the sum of its expected future price and the expected dividend. At an interest rate of 4 percent, its value today is $81.00/1.04 = $77.88. At an interest rate of 8 percent, the stock's current value is $81.00/1.08 = $75.00. Recall from Example 8.5 that when the interest rate is 6 percent, the value of a share of FortuneCookie.com is $76.42. Since higher interest rates imply lower stock values, news that interest rates are about to rise should cause the stock market to fall. *(LO4)*

8.8 The purchase of the Japanese bond is a capital outflow for the United States, or $KI = -\$20{,}000$. The Japanese government now holds $20,000. What will it do with these funds? There are basically three possibilities. First, it might use the funds to purchase U.S. goods and services (military equipment, for example). In that case, the U.S. trade balance equals +$20,000, and the sum of the trade balance and capital inflows is zero. Second, the Japanese government might acquire U.S. assets—for example, deposits in U.S. banks. In that case, a capital inflow to the United States of $20,000 offsets the original capital outflow. Both the trade balance and net capital outflows individually are zero, and so their sum is zero.

Finally, the Japanese government might use the $20,000 to purchase non-U.S. goods, services, or assets—oil from Saudi Arabia, for example. But then the non-U.S. recipient of the $20,000 is holding the funds, and it has the same options that the Japanese government did. Eventually, the funds will be used to purchase U.S. goods, services, or assets, satisfying Equation 8.1. Indeed, even if the recipient holds onto the funds (in cash, or as a U.S. bank deposit), they would still count as a capital inflow to the United States, as U.S. dollars or accounts in a U.S. bank are U.S. assets acquired by foreigners. *(LO6)*

8.9 An increase in the real interest rate abroad increases the relative attractiveness of foreign financial investments to both foreign and domestic savers. Net capital inflows to the home country will fall at each level of the domestic real interest rate. The supply curve of net capital inflows will shift left, as in Figure 8.3. *(LO6)*

9

Short-Term Economic Fluctuations and Fiscal Policy

"Home Sales and Prices Continue to Plummet"
"As Jobs Vanish, Motel Rooms Become Home"
"Global Stock Markets Plummet"
"Steep Slide in Economy as Unsold Goods Pile Up"
"Fed Plans to Inject Another $1 Trillion to Aid the Economy"
"World Bank Says Global Economy Will Shrink in '09"

These headlines from *The New York Times* tell the story: From late 2007 to mid-2009, the U.S. economy passed through its worst economic downturn since the Great Depression of the 1930s. Average incomes fell; millions of Americans lost their jobs, many lost their health insurance, and even their homes; and governments at all levels struggled to deal with falling tax collections colliding with increased demands for public services like unemployment benefits and health care.

Other economic downturns between the Great Depression of the 1930s and the *Great Recession*—as the 2007–2009 downturn has come to be called—were generally milder. But they too inflicted great economic cost, most importantly lost jobs. And in some cases they had important political consequences.

The Great Recession of 2007–2009 was followed by almost 11 years without a downturn—the longest such period on record. Then, in early 2020, the U.S. was hit by the COVID-19 pandemic. The reaction to the pandemic caused sudden collapse in global and domestic travel, closure of many businesses, and sharp increase in unemployment (see The Economic Naturalist 6.2 in Chapter 6, *The Labor Market: Workers, Wages, and Unemployment*). How deep and long this most recent recession is remains to be seen.

In preceding chapters, we discussed the factors that determine long-run economic growth. Over the broad sweep of history, those factors determine the economic success of a society. Indeed, over a span of 30, 50, or 100 years, relatively small differences in the rate of economic growth can have an enormous effect on the

LEARNING OBJECTIVES

After reading this chapter, you should be able to:

LO1 List the four phases of the business cycle and explain the primary characteristics of recessions and expansions.

LO2 Use potential output and the output gap to analyze an economy's position in the business cycle.

LO3 Define the natural rate of unemployment and show how it is related to cyclical unemployment.

LO4 Discuss the basic differences between how the economy operates in the short run versus the long run.

LO5 Identify the key assumptions of Keynesian theory and explain their implications regarding the production decisions made by firms and the consumption decisions made by households.

LO6 Show how a change in aggregate expenditure can cause a change in short-run equilibrium output and how this is related to the income expenditure multiplier.

LO7 Explain why basic Keynesian theory suggests that fiscal policy is useful as a stabilization policy.

LO8 Discuss the qualifications that arise in applying fiscal policy to real-world situations.

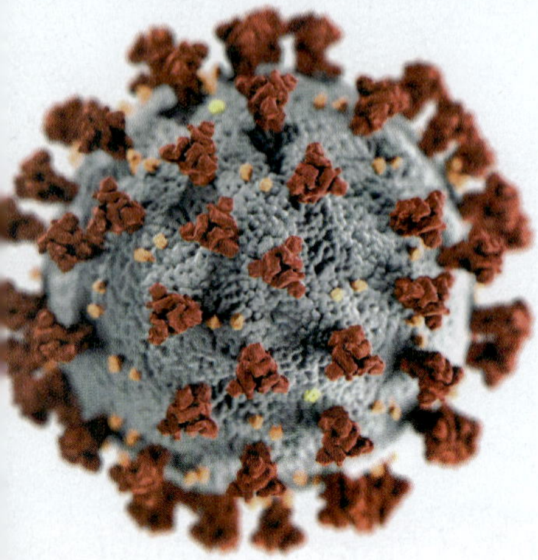
CDC/Alissa Eckert, MS; Dan Higgins, MAMS

average person's standard of living. But even though the economic "climate" (long-run economic conditions) is the ultimate determinant of living standards, changes in the economic "weather" (short-run fluctuations in economic conditions) are also important. A good long-run growth record is not much consolation to a worker who has lost her job due to a recession. The bearing that short-term macroeconomic performance has on election results is one indicator of the importance the average person attaches to it (see The Economic Naturalist 9.1).

In this chapter, we begin our study of short-term fluctuations in economic activity. Commonly known as *business cycles,* these fluctuations consist of *expansions* and *recessions*. We will start with some background on the history and characteristics of these economic ups and downs. We will then discuss some of the main ideas of the British economist John Maynard Keynes. The basic Keynesian account of the economic ups and downs focuses on the components of aggregate spending, such as consumption spending by households and investment spending by firms, and the effects of changes in spending on total real GDP. In the last part of the chapter we will discuss Keynes's proposed policy reaction to recessions, which is part of *fiscal stabilization policy*. We will close the discussion by noting important qualifications to using fiscal policy as a stabilization tool.

Though Keynes's account of the economy is a useful starting point, it does not address some key issues. First, and perhaps most important, it has little to say about the determinants of inflation. Second, because it focuses on the very short run, it does not give adequate attention to the economy's own natural tendency to eliminate deviations from full employment over the longer run. Because the basic Keynesian theory does not take into account the "self-correcting" tendencies of the economy, it tends to overstate the need for government intervention to offset fluctuations. These issues will be addressed in the two following chapters. By the end of these chapters, we will have discussed the major causes of short-term economic fluctuations, as well as the options policymakers have in responding to them.

The Economic Naturalist 9.1

Do economic fluctuations affect presidential elections?

In early 1991, following the defeat of Iraq in the Gulf War by the United States and its allies, one poll showed that 89 percent of the American public approved of the job George H. W. Bush was doing as president. Prior to Bush, the last U.S. president to enjoy such a high approval rating was Harry Truman in 1945, shortly after World War II ended with the U.S. a victorious global superpower. The Gulf War victory followed a number of other popular developments in the foreign policy sphere, including the ouster of the corrupt leader General Manuel Noriega from Panama in December 1989, improved relations with China, apparent progress in Middle East peace talks, and the end of apartheid in South Africa. The collapse of the Soviet Union in December 1991—a stunning event that signaled the end of the Cold War—also occurred during Bush's term. Yet despite these political pluses, in the months following the Gulf War, Bush's sky-high approval rating declined sharply. According to the same poll, by the time of the Republican National Convention in the summer of 1992, only 29 percent of the public approved of Bush's performance. Although the president's ratings improved during the campaign, Bush and his running mate, Dan Quayle, lost the 1992 general election to Bill Clinton and Al Gore, receiving only 39 million of the 104 million votes cast. A third-party candidate, Ross Perot, received nearly 20 million votes. What caused this turnaround in (the first) President Bush's political fortunes?

Despite his high marks from voters in foreign policy, the president's domestic economic policies were widely viewed as ineffective. Bush received much criticism for breaking his campaign pledge not to raise taxes. More important, the economy weakened significantly in 1990–1991 and then recovered only slowly. Although inflation was low, by mid-1992, unemployment had reached 7.8 percent of the labor force—2.5 percentage points higher than in the first year of Bush's term and the highest level since 1984. A sign in Democratic candidate Bill Clinton's campaign headquarters summarized Clinton's strategy for winning the White House: "It's the economy, stupid." Clinton realized the importance of the nation's economic problems and pounded away at the Republican administration's inability to pull the country out of the doldrums. Clinton's focus on the economy was the key to his election.

Clinton's ability to parlay criticism of economic conditions into electoral success is not unusual in U.S. political history. Weakness in the economy played a decisive role in helping Franklin D. Roosevelt beat Herbert Hoover in 1932, John F. Kennedy to best Richard Nixon in 1960, and Ronald Reagan to defeat Jimmy Carter in 1980. And in an echo of his father's experience, President George W. Bush found the political popularity he enjoyed after the 9/11 attacks in 2001—a record 90 percent approval rating—eroded by an economic downturn and a slow subsequent recovery. His approval rating as president hit a record low of 25 percent in October 2008, at the height of the financial crisis. A few weeks later, Barack Obama was elected president, defeating the Republican candidate (and war hero) John McCain.

On the other hand, strong economic conditions have often helped incumbent presidents (or the incumbent's party) retain office, including Nixon in 1972, Reagan in 1984, and Clinton in 1996. Indeed, a number of empirical studies have suggested that economic performance in the year preceding the election is among the most important determinants of whether an incumbent president is likely to win reelection.

Finally, it is important to remember that the economic conditions as measured by macroeconomic indicators (such as the rate of unemployment) do not necessarily reflect the economic conditions as perceived by all voters. For example, recall from Chapter 3, *Macroeconomics: The Bird's-Eye View of the Economy,* that the construction of macroeconomic indicators involves aggregation and averaging. These indicators can therefore hide economic differences and inequalities across regions, economic sectors, and demographic groups. Indeed, in spite of low and decreasing unemployment rate under Obama, frustration among populations that felt left behind economically was a frequent theme raised by Republican candidate Donald Trump in the 2016 elections and may help explain, among other reasons, why the Democrats lost the presidency.

RECESSIONS AND EXPANSIONS

As background to the study of short-term economic fluctuations, let's review the historical record of the fluctuations in the U.S. economy. Figure 9.1 shows the path of real GDP in the United States since 1929. As you can see, the growth path of real GDP is not always smooth; the bumps and wiggles correspond to short periods of faster or slower growth.

A period in which the economy is growing at a rate significantly below normal is called a **recession** or a **contraction.** An extremely severe or protracted recession is called a **depression.** You should be able to pick out the Great Depression in Figure 9.1, particularly the sharp initial decline between 1929 and 1933. But you can also see that the U.S. economy was volatile in the mid-1970s and the early 1980s, with serious recessions in 1973–1975 and 1981–1982. A moderate recession (but not moderate enough for the first President Bush) occurred in 1990–1991. The next recession began in March 2001, exactly 10 years after the end of the 1990–1991 recession, which

recession (or **contraction**) a period in which the economy is growing at a rate significantly below normal

depression a particularly severe or protracted recession

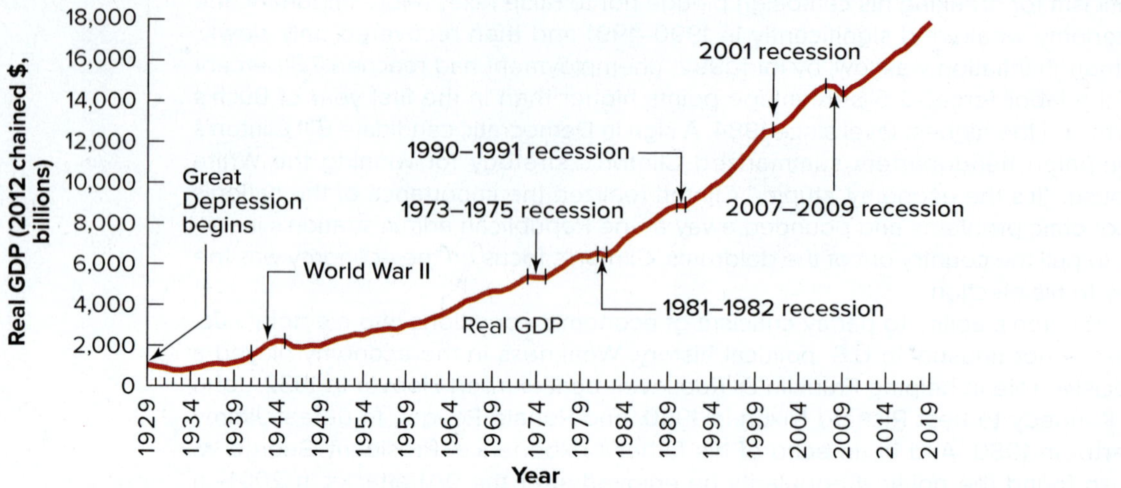

FIGURE 9.1

Fluctuations in U.S. Real GDP, 1929–2019.

Real GDP does not grow smoothly but has speedups (expansions or booms) and slowdowns (recessions or depressions).

Source: Federal Reserve of St. Louis Economic Data (FRED), https://fred.stlouisfed.org/series/GDPCA.

was declared over as of March 1991. This 10-year period without a recession was at that time the longest such period in U.S. history, and the 2001 recession that ended it was again short and relatively mild, lasting eight months. In contrast, the Great Recession was long and severe. Its beginning in 2007 and its end in 2009 are clearly visible in Figure 9.1. The Great Recession was followed by almost 11 years without a recession—a new U.S. record. That boom period ended in 2020 with the arrival of the coronavirus, when the most recent recession started.

A more informal definition of a recession, often cited by reporters, is a period during which real GDP falls for at least two consecutive quarters. This definition is not a bad rule of thumb because real GDP usually does fall during recessions. However, many economists would argue that periods in which real GDP growth is well below normal, though not actually negative, should be counted as recessions. Indeed, real GDP fell in only one quarter during the 2001 recession. Another problem with relying on GDP figures for dating recessions is that GDP data can be substantially revised, sometimes years after the fact. In practice, when trying to determine whether a recession is in progress, economists look at a variety of economic data, not just GDP.

Table 9.1 lists the beginning and ending dates of U.S. recessions since 1929, as well as the *duration* (length, in months) of each. The table also gives the highest unemployment rate recorded during each recession and the percentage change in real GDP. (Ignore the last column of the table for now.) The beginning of a recession is called the **peak,** because it represents the high point of economic activity prior to a downturn. The end of a recession, which marks the low point of economic activity prior to a recovery, is called the **trough.** The dates of peaks and troughs reported in Table 9.1 were determined by the National Bureau of Economic Research (NBER), a nonprofit organization of economists that has been a major source of research on short-term economic fluctuations since its founding in 1920 (see The Economic Naturalist 9.2). NBER is not a government agency, but it is usually treated by the news media and the government as the "official" arbiter of the dates of peaks and troughs.

peak the beginning of a recession, the high point of economic activity prior to a downturn

trough the end of a recession, the low point of economic activity prior to a recovery

Table 9.1 shows that since 1929, by far the longest and most severe recession in the United States was the 43-month economic collapse that began in August 1929 and lasted until March 1933, initiating what became known as the Great Depression. Between 1933 and 1937, the economy grew fairly rapidly, so technically the period was not a recession, although unemployment remained very high at close to 20 percent of

TABLE 9.1
U.S. Recessions since 1929

Peak date (beginning)	Trough date (end)	Duration (months)	Highest unemployment rate (%)	Change in real GDP (%)	Duration of subsequent expansion (months)
Aug. 1929	Mar. 1933	43	24.9	−26.3	50
May 1937	June 1938	13	19.0	−3.3	80
Feb. 1945	Oct. 1945	8	3.9	−11.6	37
Nov. 1948	Oct. 1949	11	5.9	−0.5	45
July 1953	May 1954	10	5.5	−0.6	39
Aug. 1957	Apr. 1958	8	6.8	−0.7	24
Apr. 1960	Feb. 1961	10	6.7	2.6	106
Dec. 1969	Nov. 1970	11	5.9	0.2	36
Nov. 1973	Mar. 1975	16	8.5	−0.7	58
Jan. 1980	July 1980	6	7.6	−0.2	12
July 1981	Nov. 1982	16	9.7	−1.9	92
July 1990	Mar. 1991	8	7.5	−0.1	120
Mar. 2001	Nov. 2001	8	6.0	1.0	73
Dec. 2007	June 2009	18	9.6	−3.1	128
Feb. 2020					

Notes: Unemployment rate is the annual rate for the trough year or the subsequent year, whichever is higher. Change in annual real GDP (chained 2009 dollars) is measured from the peak year to the trough year, except that the entry for the 1945 recession is the 1945–1946 change in real GDP, the entry for the 1980 recession is the 1979–1980 change, and the entry for 2001 is the 2000–2001 change.

Sources: Peak and trough dates: National Bureau of Economic Research; Unemployment: Bureau of Labor Statistics; Real GDP: Bureau of Economic Analysis.

the workforce. In 1937–1938, the nation was hit by another significant recession. Full economic recovery from the Depression did not come until U.S. entry into World War II at the end of 1941. The economy boomed from 1941 to 1945 (see Figure 9.1), reflecting the enormous wartime production of military equipment and supplies.

In sharp contrast to the 1930s, U.S. recessions since World War II have generally been short—between 6 and 18 months, from peak to trough. As Table 9.1 shows, the two most severe postwar recessions prior to 2007, 1973–1975 and 1981–1982, lasted just 16 months. And, though unemployment rates during those two recessions were quite high by today's standards, they were low compared to the Great Depression. During the quarter century (25 years) from 1982 to 2007, the U.S. economy has experienced only two relatively mild recessions, in 1990–1991 and in 2001. The decline in macroeconomic volatility during those years was dubbed the Great Moderation, and some economists and other observers wondered whether we were witnessing "the end of the business cycle." But then came the 2007–2009 recession, the longest and deepest since the end of World War II, lasting 18 months with annual real GDP falling 3.1 percent from peak year to trough year and the annual unemployment rate reaching 9.6 percent. And we are yet to see how long and deep the recession that started in 2020 will be. Such events warn us to guard against overconfidence. Prosperity and economic stability can never be guaranteed.

The opposite of a recession is an **expansion**—a period in which the economy is growing at a rate that is significantly *above* normal. A particularly strong and protracted expansion is called a **boom.** In the United States, strong expansions occurred during 1933–1937, 1961–1969, 1982–1990, and 1991–2001, with exceptionally strong growth during 1995–2000 (see Figure 9.1). On average, expansions have been much

expansion a period in which the economy is growing at a rate significantly above normal

boom a particularly strong and protracted expansion

longer than recessions. The final column of Table 9.1 shows the duration, in months, of U.S. expansions since 1929. As you can see in the table, the 1961–1969 expansion lasted 106 months; the 1982–1990 expansion, 92 months. The longest expansion before the most recent one began in March 1991, at the trough of the 1990–1991 recession. That expansion lasted 120 months, a full 10 years, until a new recession began in March 2001. And the longest expansion of all began in June 2009 and lasted 128 months, ending with the coronavirus recession that began in February 2020.

The Economic Naturalist 9.2

How was the 2020 recession called?

The Business Cycle Dating Committee of the National Bureau of Economic Research determined that a recession began in February 2020. What led the committee to choose that date?

The eight economists who form the Business Cycle Dating Committee met by conference call, and announced on Monday, June 8, 2020, that a recession had begun *in February*.

The determination of whether and when a recession has begun involves intensive statistical analysis, mixed in with a significant amount of human judgment. Indeed, it took four months' worth of economic data before the committee called the recession. The Business Cycle Dating Committee typically relies heavily on a small set of statistical indicators that measure the overall strength of the economy. The committee prefers indicators that are available monthly because they are available quickly and may provide relatively precise information about the timing of peaks and troughs. Three of the most important indicators used by the committee in its June 2020 meeting were

- Nonfarm employment (the number of people at work outside of agriculture), measured in two different ways: one based on a survey of employers, the other based on the BLS's survey of households.
- Real after-tax income received by households, excluding transfers like Social Security payments.
- Real personal consumption expenditures.

Each of these indicators measures a different aspect of the economy. Because their movements tend to coincide with the overall movements in the economy, they are called *coincident indicators*.

In its long and detailed statement calling the recession (available at www.nber.org/cycles/june2020.pdf), the committee included the following text:

> Because a recession is a broad contraction of the economy, not confined to one sector, the committee emphasizes economy-wide indicators of economic activity. The committee believes that domestic production and employment are the primary conceptual measures of economic activity.
>
> . . . The committee normally views the payroll employment measure, which is based on a large survey of employers, as the most reliable comprehensive estimate of employment. This series reached a clear peak in February.

The committee determined that the other monthly indicators listed above also supported a clear peak in February 2020. In its deliberations, the committee also looked at quarterly domestic production measures (including GDP), which, as the committee determined, provided consistent evidence with its announcement that a new recession began.

SELF-TEST 9.1

Using the National Bureau of Economic Research website (www.nber.org/cycles.html), is the U.S. economy currently in recession or expansion? How much time has elapsed since the last peak or trough? Explore the NBER website to find additional useful information about current conditions in the U.S. economy.

Some Facts about Short-Term Economic Fluctuations

Although Figure 9.1 and Table 9.1 show data starting only in 1929, periods of expansion and recession have been a feature of industrial economies since at least the late eighteenth century. Karl Marx and Friedrich Engels referred to these fluctuations, which they called "commercial crises," in their *Communist Manifesto* of 1848. In the United States, economists have been studying short-term fluctuations for at least a century. The traditional term for these fluctuations is **business cycles,** and they are still often referred to as **cyclical fluctuations.** Neither term is accurate though; as Figure 9.1 shows, economic fluctuations are not "cyclical" at all in the sense that they recur at predictable intervals, but instead are *irregular in their length and severity*. This irregularity makes the dates of peaks and troughs extremely hard to predict, despite the fact that professional forecasters have devoted a great deal of effort and brainpower to the task.

business cycles (or **cyclical fluctuations**) short-term fluctuations in GDP and other indicators of economic activity

Expansions and recessions usually are not limited to a few industries or regions but, as noted in The Economic Naturalist 9.2, are *felt throughout the economy*. Indeed, the largest fluctuations may have a *global impact*. For instance, the Great Depression of the 1930s affected nearly all the world's economies, and the 1973–1975 and 1981–1982 recessions were also widely felt outside the United States. When East Asia suffered a major slowdown in the late 1990s, the effects of that slowdown spilled over into many other regions (although not so much the United States). As you already know, the 2007–2009 recession quickly became worldwide in scope, and some of its effects are still being felt around the world today. And the recession that started in 2020 was a global phenomenon, hitting much of the world at the same time.

Recessions are very difficult to forecast.

But even a relatively moderate recession, like the one that occurred in 2001, can have global effects. Figure 9.2, which shows annual growth rates of real GDP over the period 1999–2014 for China, Germany, Japan, the United Kingdom, and the United States, illustrates this point. (The figure's shaded

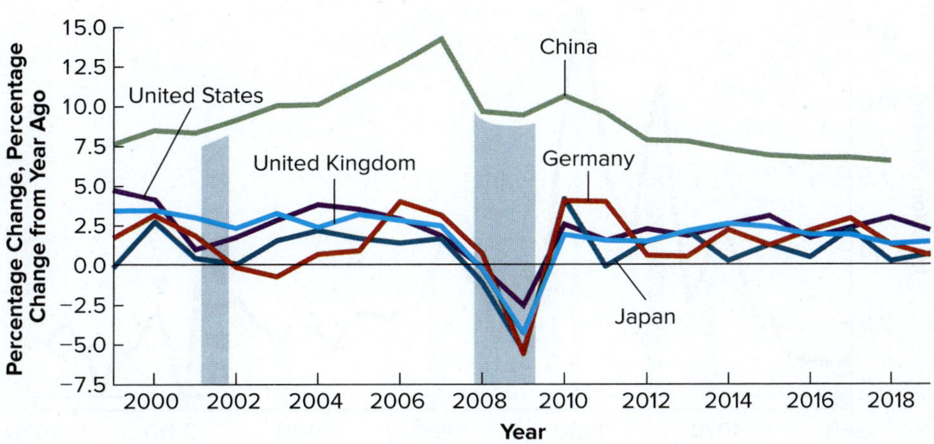

FIGURE 9.2

Real GDP Growth in Five Major Countries, 1999–2019.

Annual growth rates (measured as the change in real GDP over the past four quarters) for the world's five largest economies show that all the countries slowed somewhat in 2001—the year of a relatively mild recession—and slowed significantly in 2008 and 2009—during the much more severe Great Recession.

Source: Federal Reserve of St. Louis Economic Data (FRED), https://fred.stlouisfed.org.

areas show U.S. recession dates, taken from Table 9.1.) You can see that all five economies—the world's largest by GDP—slowed significantly in 2008 and, except for China, they all contracted rather significantly in 2009. All five economies also started recovering together, but after a promising 2010, they all slowed again in 2011 and have, in general, been growing more slowly in recent years than in the years just before the crisis. Figure 9.2 also shows that all five economies slowed at least somewhat from 2000 to 2001.

Unemployment is a key indicator of short-term economic fluctuations. The unemployment rate typically rises sharply during recessions and recovers (although more slowly) during expansions. Figure 4.4 showed the U.S. unemployment rate since 1965. You should be able to identify, most recently, the recessions that began in 1969, 1973, 1981, 1990, 2001, and 2007 by noting the sharp peaks in the unemployment rate in those or the following years. Recall that the part of unemployment that is associated with recessions is called *cyclical unemployment*. Beyond this increase in unemployment, labor market conditions generally worsen during recessions. For example, during recessions real wages grow more slowly, workers are less likely to receive promotions or bonuses, and new entrants to the labor force (such as college graduates) have a much tougher time finding attractive jobs.

durable goods goods that yield utility over time and are made to last for three years or more

nondurable goods goods that can be quickly consumed or immediately used, having a life span of less than three years

Generally, industries that produce **durable goods,** such as cars, houses, and capital equipment, are more affected than others by recessions and booms. In contrast, industries that provide *services* and **nondurable goods** like food are much less sensitive to short-term fluctuations. Thus an automobile worker or a construction worker is far more likely to lose his or her job in a recession than is a barber or a baker.

Like unemployment, *inflation* follows a typical pattern in recessions and expansions, though it is not so sharply defined. Figure 3.4 showed the U.S. inflation rate since 1929, and Figure 9.3 shows the rate since 1960 (periods of recession are again indicated by shaded vertical bars). As you can see, recessions tend to be followed soon after by a decline in the rate of inflation. For example, the recession of 1981–1982 was followed by a sharp reduction in inflation, and the recession of 2007–2009 ended with slightly negative inflation. Furthermore, many—though not all—postwar recessions have been preceded by increases in inflation, as Figure 9.3 shows. The behavior of inflation during expansions and recessions will be discussed more fully in the next two chapters.

FIGURE 9.3

U.S. Inflation, 1960–2019.

U.S. inflation since 1960 is measured by the change in the CPI, and periods of recession are indicated by the shaded vertical bars. Note that inflation declined during or following each of those recessions and rose prior to many of those recessions.

Source: U.S. Bureau of Labor Statistics, www.bls.gov.

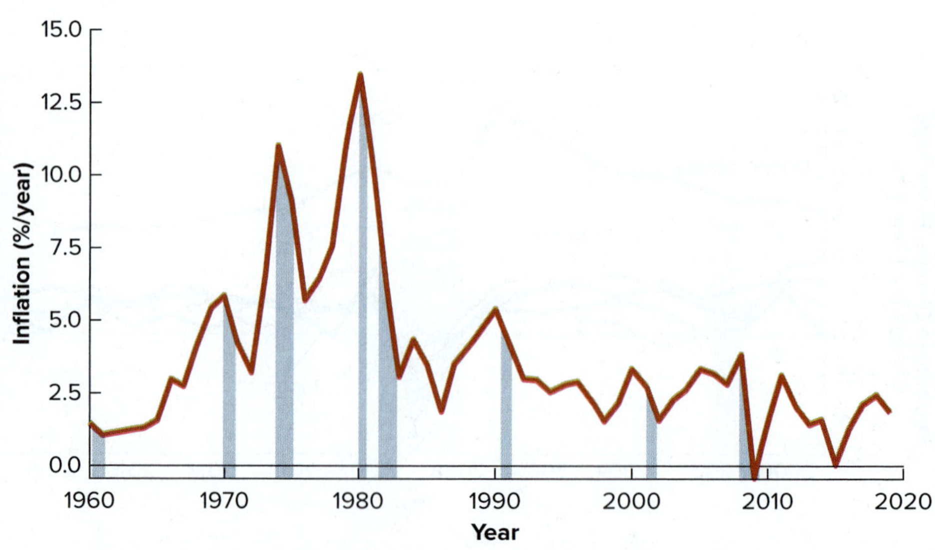

RECAP

RECESSIONS, EXPANSIONS, AND SHORT-TERM ECONOMIC FLUCTUATIONS

- A recession is a period in which output is growing more slowly than normal. An expansion, or boom, is a period in which output is growing more quickly than normal.
- The beginning of a recession is called the peak, and its end (which corresponds to the beginning of the subsequent expansion) is called the trough.
- The sharpest recession in the history of the United States was the initial phase of the Great Depression in 1929–1933. Severe recessions also occurred in 1973–1975, 1981–1982, and 2007–2009. Two relatively mild recessions occurred in 1990–1991 and 2001. The most recent recession started in 2020.
- Short-term economic fluctuations (recessions and expansions) are irregular in length and severity, and thus are difficult to predict.
- Expansions and recessions have widespread (and sometimes global) impacts, affecting most regions and industries.
- Unemployment rises sharply during a recession and falls, usually more slowly, during an expansion.
- Durable goods industries are more affected by expansions and recessions than other industries. Services and nondurable goods industries are less sensitive to ups and downs in the economy.
- Recessions tend to be followed by a decline in inflation and are often preceded by an increase in inflation.

OUTPUT GAPS AND CYCLICAL UNEMPLOYMENT

How can we tell whether a particular recession or expansion is "big" or "small"? The answer to this question is important to both economists who study business cycles and policymakers who must formulate responses to economic fluctuations. Intuitively, a "big" recession or expansion is one in which output and the unemployment rate deviate significantly from their normal or trend levels. In this section, we will attempt to be more precise about this idea by introducing the concept of the *output gap,* which measures how far output is from its normal level at a particular time. We will also revisit the idea of *cyclical unemployment,* or the deviation of unemployment from its normal level. Finally, we will examine how these two concepts are related.

Potential Output

The concept of potential output is a useful starting point for thinking about the measurement of expansions and recessions. **Potential output,** also called **potential GDP** or **full-employment output,** is the amount of output (real GDP) that an economy can produce when using its resources, such as capital and labor, at normal rates. The term *potential output* is slightly misleading, in that *potential* output is not the same as *maximum* output. Because capital and labor can be utilized at greater-than-normal rates, at least for a time, a country's actual output can exceed its potential output. These greater-than-normal utilization rates, however, cannot be sustained indefinitely, partly because workers cannot work overtime every week and machinery must occasionally be shut down for maintenance and repairs.

potential output, Y^* (or **potential GDP** or **full-employment output**) the amount of output (real GDP) that an economy can produce when using its resources, such as capital and labor, at normal rates

Potential output is not a fixed number but grows over time, reflecting increases in both the amounts of available capital and labor and their productivity. We discussed the sources of growth in potential output (the economy's productive capacity) in Chapter 5, *Economic Growth, Productivity, and Living Standards*. We will use the symbol $\mathbf{Y^*}$ to signify the economy's potential output at a given point in time.

Why does a nation's output sometimes grow quickly and sometimes slowly, as shown for the United States in Figure 9.1? Logically, there are two possibilities: First, changes in the rate of output growth may reflect *changes in the rate at which the country's potential output is increasing*. For example, unfavorable weather conditions, such as a severe drought, would reduce the rate of potential output growth in an agricultural economy, and a decline in the rate of technological innovation might reduce the rate of potential output growth in an industrial economy. Under the assumption that the country is using its resources at normal rates, so that actual output equals potential output, a significant slowdown in potential output growth would tend to result in recession. Similarly, new technologies, increased capital investment, or a surge in immigration that swells the labor force could produce unusually brisk growth in potential output, and hence an economic boom.

Undoubtedly, changes in the rate of growth of potential output are part of the explanation for expansions and recessions. In the United States, for example, the economic boom of the second half of the 1990s was propelled in part by new information technologies, such as the Internet. And the slow recovery in the first half of the 2010s from the financial crisis seems to reflect, at least in part, a slowdown in potential output caused by demographic changes and slow productivity growth. When changes in the rate of GDP growth reflect changes in the growth rate of potential output, the appropriate policy responses are those discussed in Chapter 5, *Economic Growth, Productivity, and Living Standards*. In particular, when a recession results from slowing growth in potential output, the government's best response is to try to promote saving, investment, technological innovation, human capital formation, and other activities that support growth.

The Output Gap

A second possible explanation for short-term economic fluctuations is that *actual output does not always equal potential output*. For example, potential output may be growing normally, but for some reason the economy's capital and labor resources may not be fully utilized, so that actual output is significantly below the level of potential output. This low level of output, resulting from underutilization of economic resources, would generally be interpreted as a recession. Alternatively, capital and labor may be working much harder than normal—firms may put workers on overtime, for example—so that actual output expands beyond potential output, creating a boom.

At any point in time, the difference between actual output and potential output is called the **output gap.** Recalling that Y^* is the symbol for potential output and that Y stands for actual output (real GDP), we can express the output gap as $Y - Y^*$. A negative output gap—when actual output is below potential, and resources are not being fully utilized—is called a **recessionary gap.** A positive output gap—when actual output is above potential, and resources are being utilized at above-normal rates—is referred to as an **expansionary gap.**

output gap the difference between the economy's actual output and its potential output at a point in time ($Y - Y^*$)

recessionary gap a negative output gap, which occurs when potential output exceeds actual output ($Y^* > Y$)

expansionary gap a positive output gap, which occurs when actual output is higher than potential output ($Y > Y^*$)

Policymakers generally view both recessionary gaps and expansionary gaps as problems. It is not difficult to see why a recessionary gap is bad news for the economy: When there is a recessionary gap, capital and labor resources are not being fully utilized, and output and employment are below normal levels (that is, they are below maximum sustainable levels). This is the sort of situation that poses problems for politicians' reelection prospects, as discussed in The Economic Naturalist 9.1. An expansionary gap is considered a problem by policymakers for a more subtle reason: What's wrong, after all, with having higher output and employment than normal? A prolonged expansionary gap is problematic because, when faced with a demand for their products that significantly exceeds their normal capacity, firms tend to raise prices. Thus an expansionary gap typically results in increased inflation, which reduces the efficiency of the economy in the longer run.

Thus, whenever an output gap exists, whether it is recessionary or expansionary, policymakers have an incentive to try to eliminate the gap by returning actual output to potential. In this and the next chapters we will discuss both how output gaps arise and the tools that policymakers have for *stabilizing* the economy—that is, bringing actual output into line with potential output.

The Natural Rate of Unemployment and Cyclical Unemployment

Whether recessions arise because of slower growth in potential output or because actual output falls below potential, they bring bad times. In either case, output falls (or at least grows more slowly), implying reduced living standards. Recessionary output gaps are particularly frustrating for policymakers, however, because they imply that the economy has the *capacity* to produce more, but for some reason available resources are not being fully utilized. Recessionary gaps are inefficient in that they unnecessarily reduce the total economic pie, making the typical person worse off.

An important indicator of the low utilization of resources during recessions is the unemployment rate. In general, a *high* unemployment rate means that labor resources are not being fully utilized so that output has fallen below potential (a recessionary gap). By the same logic, an unusually *low* unemployment rate suggests that labor is being utilized at a rate greater than normal so that actual output exceeds potential output (an expansionary gap).

To better understand the relationship between the output gap and unemployment, recall from Chapter 6, *The Labor Market: Workers, Wages, and Unemployment,* the three broad types of unemployment: frictional unemployment, structural unemployment, and cyclical unemployment. *Frictional unemployment* is the short-term unemployment that is associated with the matching of workers and jobs. Some amount of frictional unemployment is necessary for the labor market to function efficiently in a dynamic, changing economy. *Structural unemployment* is the long-term and chronic unemployment that occurs even when the economy is producing at its normal rate. Structural unemployment often results when workers' skills are outmoded and do not meet the needs of employers—so, for example, steelworkers may become structurally unemployed as the steel industry goes into a long-term decline, unless those workers can retrain to find jobs in growing industries. Finally, *cyclical unemployment* is the extra unemployment that occurs during periods of recession.

Unlike cyclical unemployment, which is present only during recessions, frictional unemployment and structural unemployment are always present in the labor market, even when the economy is operating normally. Economists call the part of the total unemployment rate that is attributable to frictional and structural unemployment the **natural rate of unemployment.** Put another way, the natural rate of unemployment is the unemployment rate that prevails when cyclical unemployment is zero, so that the economy has neither a recessionary nor an expansionary output gap. We will denote the natural rate of unemployment as u^*.

natural rate of unemployment, u^* the part of the total unemployment rate that is attributable to frictional and structural unemployment; equivalently, the unemployment rate that prevails when cyclical unemployment is zero, so that the economy has neither a recessionary nor an expansionary output gap

Cyclical unemployment, which is the difference between the total unemployment rate and the natural rate, can thus be expressed as $u - u^*$, where u is the actual unemployment rate and u^* denotes the natural rate of unemployment. In a recession, the actual unemployment rate u exceeds the natural unemployment rate u^*, so cyclical unemployment, $u - u^*$, is positive. When the economy experiences an expansionary gap, in contrast, the actual unemployment rate is lower than the natural rate, so that cyclical unemployment is negative. Negative cyclical unemployment corresponds to a situation in which labor is being used more intensively than normal, so that actual unemployment has dipped below its usual frictional and structural levels.

The Economic Naturalist 9.3

Why has the natural rate of unemployment in the United States declined?

According to the Congressional Budget Office, which regularly estimates the natural rate of unemployment in the United States, the long-term natural rate has been falling almost steadily since 1978, when it was 6.2 percent (this long-term trend reversed only briefly following the 2008 global financial crisis).[1] By 2020, it was estimated at 4.4 percent, and the CBO predicts that it will keep declining in the next 10 years. Why is the U.S. natural rate of unemployment apparently so much lower nowadays than it was in the late 1970s?

The natural rate of unemployment may have fallen because of reduced frictional unemployment, reduced structural unemployment, or both. A variety of ideas have been advanced to explain declines in both types of unemployment. One promising suggestion is based on the changing age structure of the U.S. labor force.[2] The average age of U.S. workers is rising, reflecting the aging of the baby boom generation. Indeed, over the past four decades, the share of the labor force aged 16–24 has fallen from about 25 percent to below 14 percent and is projected by the BLS to keep falling to about 12 percent by 2026. Since young workers are more prone to unemployment than older workers, the aging of the labor force may help explain the overall decline in unemployment.

Why are young workers more likely to be unemployed? Compared to teenagers and workers in their twenties, older workers are much more likely to hold long-term, stable jobs. In contrast, younger workers tend to hold short-term jobs, perhaps because they are not ready to commit to a particular career or because their time in the labor market is interrupted by schooling or military service. Because they change jobs more often, younger workers are more prone than others to frictional unemployment. They also have fewer skills, on average, than older workers, so they may experience more structural unemployment. As workers age and gain experience, however, their risk of unemployment declines.

Another possible explanation for the declining natural rate of unemployment is that labor markets have become more efficient at matching workers with jobs, thereby reducing both frictional and structural unemployment. For example, agencies that arrange temporary help have become much more commonplace in the United States in recent years. Although the placements these agencies make are intended to be temporary, they often become permanent when an employer and worker discover that a particularly good match has been made. Online job services, which allow workers to search for jobs nationally and even internationally, have also become increasingly important. By reducing the time people must spend in unemployment and by creating more lasting matches between workers and jobs, temporary help agencies, online job services, job-search apps, and similar innovations may have reduced the natural rate of unemployment.[3]

Technological change can also promote temporary job matches. For example, ride-sharing apps allow drivers to work on their own schedule, perhaps to supplement income from another job. Ride-sharing and other types of irregular work are known as the *gig economy.* Participants in the gig economy are officially counted as employed, even if they work only a few hours a week.

[1]U.S. Congressional Budget Office, *Natural Rate of Unemployment (Long-Term)* [NROU], FRED, Federal Reserve Bank of St. Louis, https://fred.stlouisfed.org/series/NROU (accessed June 15, 2020).

[2]See Robert Shimer, "Why Is the U.S. Unemployment Rate So Much Lower?," in *NBER Macroeconomics Annual 1998,* B. Bernanke and J. Rotemberg, eds. (Cambridge, MA: MIT Press, 1999).

[3]For a detailed analysis of factors affecting the natural rate, see Lawrence Katz and Alan Krueger, "The High-Pressure U.S. Labor Market of the 1990s," *Brookings Papers on Economic Activity* 1 (1999), pp. 1–88.

RECAP

OUTPUT GAPS AND CYCLICAL UNEMPLOYMENT

- Potential output is the amount of output (real GDP) that an economy can produce when using its resources, such as capital and labor, at normal rates. The output gap, $Y - Y^*$, is the difference between actual output Y and potential output Y^*.
- When actual output is below potential, the resulting output gap is called a recessionary gap. When actual output is above potential, the difference is called an expansionary gap.
- A recessionary gap reflects a waste of resources, while an expansionary gap threatens to ignite inflation; hence policymakers have an incentive to try to eliminate both types of output gaps.
- The natural rate of unemployment u^* is the sum of the frictional and structural unemployment rates. It is the rate of unemployment that is observed when the economy is operating at a normal level, with no output gap.
- Cyclical unemployment, $u - u^*$, is the difference between the actual unemployment rate u and the natural rate of unemployment u^*. Cyclical unemployment is positive when there is a recessionary gap, negative when there is an expansionary gap, and zero when there is no output gap.

WHY DO SHORT-TERM FLUCTUATIONS OCCUR? A PREVIEW AND A TALE

What causes periods of recession and expansion? In the preceding sections, we discussed two possible reasons for slowdowns and speedups in real GDP growth. First, growth in potential output itself may slow down or speed up, reflecting changes in the growth rates of available capital and labor and in the pace of technological progress. Second, even if potential output is growing normally, actual output may be higher or lower than potential output—that is, expansionary or recessionary output gaps may develop. Earlier in this book, we discussed some of the reasons that growth in potential output can vary, and the options that policymakers have for stimulating growth in potential output. But we have not yet addressed the question of how output gaps can arise or what policymakers should do in response. The causes and cures of output gaps will be a major topic of the next three chapters. Here is a brief preview of the main conclusions of these chapters:

1. In a world in which prices adjusted immediately to balance the quantities supplied and demanded for all goods and services, output gaps would not exist. However, for many goods and services, the assumption that prices will adjust immediately is not realistic. Instead, many firms adjust the prices of their output only periodically. In particular, rather than changing prices with every variation in demand, firms tend to adjust to changes in demand in the short run by varying the quantity of output they produce and sell. This type of behavior is known as "meeting the demand" at a preset price.
2. Because, in the short run, firms tend to meet the demand for their output at preset prices, changes in the amount that customers decide to spend will affect output. When total spending is low for some reason, output may fall below potential output; conversely, when spending is high, output may rise above potential output. In other words, *changes in economywide spending are*

the primary cause of output gaps. Thus government policies can help eliminate output gaps by influencing total spending. For example, the government can affect total spending directly simply by changing its own level of purchases.

3. Although firms tend to meet demand in the short run, they will not be willing to do so indefinitely. If customer demand continues to differ from potential output, firms will eventually adjust their prices to eliminate output gaps. If demand exceeds potential output (an expansionary gap), firms will raise their prices aggressively, spurring inflation. If demand falls below potential output (a recessionary gap), firms will raise their prices less aggressively or even cut prices, reducing inflation.
4. Over the longer run, price changes by firms eliminate any output gap and bring production back into line with the economy's potential output. Thus the economy is "self-correcting" in the sense that it operates to eliminate output gaps over time. Because of this self-correcting tendency, in the long run actual output equals potential output, so that output is determined by the economy's productive capacity rather than by the rate of spending. In the long run, total spending influences only the rate of inflation.

These ideas will become clearer as we proceed through the next chapters. Before plunging into the details of the analysis, though, let's consider an example that illustrates the links between spending and output in the short and long run.

Alice's Ice Cream Store: A Tale about Short-Run Fluctuations

Alice's ice cream store produces gourmet ice cream on the premises and sells it directly to the public. What determines the amount of ice cream that she produces on a daily basis? The productive capacity, or potential output, of the shop is one important factor. Specifically, Alice's potential output of ice cream depends on the amount of capital (number of ice cream makers) and labor (number of workers) that she employs and on the productivity of that capital and labor. Although Alice's potential output usually changes rather slowly, on occasion it can fluctuate significantly—for example, if an ice cream maker breaks down or Alice contracts the flu.

The main source of day-to-day variations in Alice's ice cream production, however, is not changes in potential output but fluctuations in the demand for ice cream by the public. Some of these fluctuations in spending occur predictably over the course of the day (more demand in the afternoon than in the morning, for example), the week (more demand on weekends), or the year (more demand in the summer). Other changes in demand are less regular—more demand on a hot day than a cool one, or when a parade is passing by the store. Some changes in demand are hard for Alice to interpret: For example, a surge in demand for rocky road ice cream on one particular Tuesday could reflect a permanent change in consumer tastes, or it might just be a random, one-time event.

How should Alice react to these ebbs and flows in the demand for ice cream? The basic supply and demand model that we introduced in Chapter 2, *Supply and Demand*, if applied to the market for ice cream, would predict that the price of ice cream should change with every change in the demand for ice cream. For example, prices should rise just after the movie theater next door to Alice's shop lets out on Friday night, and they should fall on unusually cold, blustery days, when most people would prefer a hot cider to an ice cream cone. Indeed, taken literally, the supply and demand model predicts that ice cream prices should change almost moment to moment. Imagine Alice standing in front of her shop like an auctioneer, calling out prices in an effort to determine how many people are willing to buy at each price!

Of course, we do not expect to see this behavior by an ice cream store owner. Price setting by auction does in fact occur in some markets, such as the market for grain or the stock market, but it is not the normal procedure in most retail markets, such as the market for ice cream. Why this difference? The basic reason is that sometimes the economic benefits of setting up an auction (including hiring an auctioneer, or implementing an automatic auction platform and having customers use it) exceed the costs of doing so, and sometimes they do not. In the market for grain, for example, many buyers and sellers gather together in the same place at the same time to trade large volumes of standardized goods (bushels of grain). In that kind of situation, an auction is an efficient way to determine prices and balance the quantities supplied and demanded. In an ice cream store, by contrast, customers come in by twos and threes at random times throughout the day. Some want shakes, some cones, and some sodas. With small numbers of customers and a low sales volume at any given time, the costs involved in selling ice cream by auction are much greater than the benefits of allowing prices to vary with demand.

So how does Alice the ice cream store manager deal with changes in the demand for ice cream? Observation suggests that she begins by setting prices based on the best information she has about the demand for her product and the costs of production. Perhaps she prints up a menu or makes a sign announcing the prices. Then, over a period of time, she will keep her prices fixed and serve as many customers as want to buy (up to the point where she runs out of ice cream or room in the store at these prices). This behavior is what we call "meeting the demand" at preset prices, and it implies that *in the short run,* the amount of ice cream Alice produces and sells is determined by the demand for her products.

However, *in the long run,* the situation is quite different. Suppose, for example, that Alice's ice cream earns a citywide reputation for its freshness and flavor. Day after day Alice observes long lines in her store. Her ice cream maker is overtaxed, as are her employees and her table space. There can no longer be any doubt that at current prices, the quantity of ice cream the public wants to consume exceeds what Alice is able and willing to supply on a normal basis (her potential output). Expanding the store is an attractive possibility, but not one (we assume) that is immediately feasible. What will Alice do?

Certainly one thing Alice can do is raise her prices. At higher prices, Alice will earn higher profits. Moreover, raising ice cream prices will bring the quantity of ice cream demanded closer to Alice's normal production capacity—her potential output. Indeed, when the price of Alice's ice cream finally rises to its equilibrium level, the shop's actual output will equal its potential output. Thus, over the long run, ice cream prices adjust to their equilibrium level, and the amount that is sold is determined by potential output.

This example illustrates, in a simple way, the links between spending and output—except, of course, that we must think of this story as applying to the whole economy, not to a single business. The key point is that there is an important difference between the short run and the long run. In the short run, producers often choose not to change their prices, but rather to meet the demand at preset prices. Because output is determined by demand, in the short run total spending plays a central role in determining the level of economic activity. Thus Alice's ice cream store enjoys a boom on an unusually hot day, when the demand for ice cream is strong, while an unseasonably cold day brings an ice cream recession. But in the long run, prices adjust to their market-clearing levels, and output equals potential output. Thus the quantities of inputs and the productivity with which they are used are the primary determinants of economic activity in the long run, as we saw in Chapter 5, *Economic Growth, Productivity, and Living Standards.* Although total spending affects output in the short run, in the long run its main effects are on prices.

RECESSIONS AND PROPOSED SOLUTIONS: KEYNES'S ANALYSIS

The idea that a decline in aggregate spending may cause output to fall below potential output was one of the key insights of John Maynard Keynes (pronounced "canes"), perhaps the most influential economist of the twentieth century.[4] He lived from 1883 to 1946 and was a remarkable individual who combined a brilliant career as an economic theorist with an active life in diplomacy, finance, journalism, and the arts. In the period between World War I and II, among his many other activities, Keynes was a Cambridge professor, developing an imposing intellectual reputation, editing Great Britain's leading scholarly journal in economics, writing articles for newspapers and magazines, advising the government, and playing a major role in the political and economic debates of the day.

Like other economists of the time, Keynes struggled to understand the Great Depression that gripped the world in the 1930s. His work on the problem led to the publication in 1936 of *The General Theory of Employment, Interest, and Money*. In *The General Theory,* Keynes tried to explain how economies can remain at low levels of output and employment for protracted periods. He stressed a number of factors, most notably that aggregate spending may be too low to permit full employment during such periods. Keynes recommended increases in government spending as the most effective way to increase aggregate spending and restore full employment.

The General Theory is a difficult book, reflecting Keynes's own struggle to understand the complex causes of the Depression. In retrospect, some of *The General Theory*'s arguments seem unclear or even inconsistent. Yet the book is full of fertile ideas, many of which had a worldwide impact and eventually led to what has been called the *Keynesian revolution*. Over the years, many economists have added to or modified Keynes's conception, to the point that Keynes himself, were he alive today, probably would not recognize much of what is now called Keynesian economics. But the ideas that insufficient aggregate spending can lead to recession and that government policies can help restore full employment are still critical to Keynesian theory.

In this section we explain Keynes's main ideas, but in order to keep the discussion easy, we leave out most of the technical detail. We keep the basic story simple: since in the short run firms meet demand at preset prices—just like Alice in her ice cream store—in the short run, the rate of aggregate spending helps to determine the level of output, which can be greater than or less than potential output. In other words, depending on the level of spending, the economy may develop an output gap. "Too little" spending leads to a recessionary output gap, while "too much" creates an expansionary output gap. Government policies that affect the level of spending can therefore be used to reduce or eliminate output gaps.

THE KEYNESIAN MODEL'S CRUCIAL ASSUMPTION: FIRMS MEET DEMAND AT PRESET PRICES

The basic Keynesian model is built on a key assumption: *In the short run, firms meet the demand for their products at preset prices.* Firms do not respond to every change in the demand for their products by changing their prices. Instead, they typically set a price for some period and then meet the demand at that price. By "meeting the demand," we mean that firms produce just enough to satisfy their customers at the prices that have been set.[5] As we will see, the assumption that firms vary their

[4]A brief biography of Keynes is available at www.bbc.co.uk/history/historic_figures/keynes_john_maynard.shtml.

[5]Obviously, firms can meet the forthcoming demand only up to the point where they reach the limit of their capacity to produce. For that reason, the Keynesian analysis of this chapter is relevant only when producers have unused capacity.

production in order to meet demand at preset prices implies that fluctuations in spending will have powerful effects on the nation's real GDP.

The assumption that, over short periods of time, firms meet the demand for their products at preset prices is generally realistic. Think of the stores where you shop. The price of a pair of jeans does not fluctuate from moment to moment according to the number of customers who enter the store or the latest news about the price of denim. Instead, the store posts a price and sells jeans to any customer who wants to buy at that price, at least until the store runs out of stock. Similarly, the corner pizza restaurant may leave the price of its large pie unchanged for months or longer, allowing its pizza production to be determined by the number of customers who want to buy at the preset price.

Firms do not normally change their prices frequently because doing so would be costly. Economists refer to the costs of changing prices as **menu costs.** In the case of the pizza restaurant, the menu cost is literally just that—the cost of printing up a new menu when prices change. Similarly, the clothing store faces the cost of remarking all its merchandise if the manager changes prices. But menu costs also may include other kinds of costs—for example, the cost of doing a market survey to determine what price to charge and the cost of informing customers about price changes. The Economic Naturalist 9.4 discusses how technology may affect menu costs in the future.

menu costs the costs of changing prices

Menu costs will not prevent firms from changing their prices indefinitely. As we saw in the case of Alice's ice cream store, too great an imbalance between demand and supply, as reflected by a difference between sales and potential output, will eventually lead firms to change their prices. If no one is buying jeans, for example, at some point the clothing store will mark down its jeans prices. Or if the pizza restaurant becomes the local hot spot, with a line of customers stretching out the door, eventually the manager will raise the price of a large pie.

Like many other economic decisions, the decision to change prices reflects a cost-benefit comparison: Prices should be changed if the benefit of doing so—the fact that sales will be brought more nearly in line with the firm's normal production capacity—outweighs the menu costs associated with making the change. As we have stressed, prices will eventually adjust; however, such adjustment will take time.

The Economic Naturalist 9.4

Will new technologies eliminate menu costs?

Thanks to new technologies, changing prices and informing customers about price changes is becoming increasingly less costly. Will technology eliminate menu costs as a factor in price setting?

connect

▸ Visit your instructor's Connect course and access your eBook to view this video.

Will new technologies eliminate menu costs?

Keynesian theory is based on the assumption that costs of changing prices, which economists refer to as *menu costs,* are sufficiently large to prevent firms from adjusting prices immediately in response to changing market conditions. However, in many industries, new technologies have eliminated or greatly reduced the direct costs of changing prices. For example, the use of bar codes to identify individual products, together with scanner technologies, allows a grocery store manager to change prices with just a few keystrokes, without having to change the price label on each can of soup or loaf of bread. Airlines use sophisticated computer software to implement complex pricing strategies, under which two travelers on the same flight to Milwaukee may pay very different fares, depending on whether they are business or vacation travelers and on how far in advance their flights were booked. Online retailers have the ability to vary their prices by type of customer and even by individual customer, while other Internet-based companies, such as eBay, allow for negotiation over the price of each individual purchase. Ride-sharing apps evaluate, in real time, customers' demand for rides and drivers' supply of rides; their pricing systems estimate the market-clearing price, and when supply does not meet demand, they send a notification of instant price increases that customers view on their phones and have to accept before they are connected to a driver.

Will these reductions in the direct costs of changing prices make the Keynesian theory, which assumes that firms meet demand at preset prices, less relevant to the real world? This is certainly a possibility that macroeconomists must take into account. However, it is unlikely that new technologies will completely eliminate the costs of changing prices anytime soon. In many sectors of the economy, gathering the information about market conditions needed to set the profit-maximizing price—including the prices charged by competitors, the costs of producing the good or service, and the likely demand for the product—will remain costly for firms. Another cost of changing prices is the use of valuable managerial time and attention needed to make informed pricing decisions. A more subtle cost of changing prices—particularly raising prices—is that doing so may lead regular customers to rethink their choice of suppliers and decide to search for a better deal elsewhere. Even when they do not switch suppliers, a price increase that is perceived by customers as unfair may cause antagonism toward the price-setting supplier.

Aggregate Output and Spending

Since, in the short run, firms meet the demand for their products at preset prices—that is, they produce just enough to satisfy their customers at the prices that have been set for some period—aggregate output in the economy at each point in time is determined by the amount that people throughout the economy want to spend. In other words, in Keynes's account of the economy, *short-run aggregate output is determined by aggregate spending*. As we discussed in previous chapters, aggregate spending (or **aggregate expenditure**) is the sum of four components: consumer expenditures (C), firms' investment (I), government purchases (G), and net exports (NX). Hence, in Keynes's theory, our accounting identity from Chapter 4, *Measuring Economic Activity: GDP, Unemployment, and Inflation*,

aggregate expenditure the sum of consumer expenditures, firms' investment, government purchases, and net exports

$$Y = C + I + G + NX, \tag{9.1}$$

gets a causal interpretation. As an accounting identity, Equation 9.1 says that everything that the economy produces is purchased by someone—be it households, firms, the government, or foreigners. The Keynesian causal interpretation adds that in the short run, demand from those purchasers *determines* how much the economy produces. In other words, according to Keynes, short-run aggregate output is not only *equal* to aggregate spending (or expenditure), as we stated earlier in the book; it is in fact *determined* by aggregate expenditure, as the economy produces just enough to meet the demand (at preset prices) from households, firms, the government, and foreigners. If that demand suddenly falls—for example, as consumers, firms, or foreigners decide to cut back on their expenditures—actual output Y will fall too. When actual Y falls short of potential output Y^*, the economy is in a recession.

Hey Big Spender! Consumer Spending and the Economy

In the U.S. economy, the largest component of aggregate expenditure—nearly two-thirds of total spending—is consumption spending, C. As already mentioned, consumer spending includes household purchases of goods, such as groceries and clothing; services, such as health care, concerts, and college tuition; and consumer durables, such as cars, furniture, and computers. Thus consumers' willingness to spend affects sales and profitability in a wide range of industries. (Households' purchases of new homes are classified as investment, rather than consumption; but home purchases represent another channel through which household decisions affect total spending.)

What determines how much people spend on consumer goods and services in a given period? While many factors are relevant, a particularly important determinant of the amount people consume is their after-tax, or *disposable,* income. All else being equal, households and individuals with higher **disposable incomes** will consume more than those with lower disposable incomes. Keynes himself stressed the importance of disposable income in determining household consumption decisions, claiming a "psychological law" that people would tie their spending closely to their incomes.

disposable income the after-tax amount of income that people are able to spend

Recall from Chapter 7, *Saving and Capital Formation,* that the disposable income of the private sector is the total production of the economy, Y, less net taxes (taxes minus transfers), or T. So we can assume that consumption spending (C) increases as disposable income ($Y - T$) increases. As already mentioned, other factors may also affect consumption, such as the real interest rate. For now we will ignore those other factors, returning to some of them later.

A general equation that captures the link between consumption and the private sector's disposable income is

$$C = \bar{C} + mpc(Y - T). \tag{9.2}$$

This equation, which we will dissect in a moment, is known as the *consumption function.* The **consumption function** relates consumption spending to its determinants, in particular, disposable (after-tax) income.

consumption function the relationship between consumption spending and its determinants, in particular, disposable (after-tax) income

Let's look at the consumption function, Equation 9.2, more carefully. The right side of the equation contains two terms, $\bar{C}$ and $mpc(Y - T)$. The first term, $\bar{C}$, is a constant term in the equation that is intended to capture factors *other than disposable income* that affect consumption, or **autonomous consumption**. For example, suppose consumers were to become more optimistic about the future, so that they desire to consume more and save less at any given level of their current disposable incomes. An increase in desired consumption at any given level of disposable income would be represented in the consumption function as an increase in the term $\bar{C}$.

autonomous consumption consumption spending that is not related to the level of disposable income

We can imagine other factors that may affect the term $\bar{C}$ in the consumption function. Suppose, for example, that there is a boom in the stock market or a sharp increase in home prices, making consumers feel wealthier and hence more inclined to spend, for a given level of current disposable income. This effect could be captured by assuming that $\bar{C}$ increases. Likewise, a fall in home prices or stock prices that made consumers feel poorer and less inclined to spend would be represented by a decrease in $\bar{C}$. Economists refer to the effect of changes in asset prices on households' wealth and hence their consumption spending as the **wealth effect** of changes in asset prices.

wealth effect the tendency of changes in asset prices to affect households' wealth and thus their spending on consumption goods

The second term on the right side of Equation 9.2, $mpc(Y - T)$, reflects the effect of disposable income, $Y - T$, on consumption. The parameter mpc, a fixed number, is called the *marginal propensity to consume.* The **marginal propensity to consume (*mpc*)** is the amount by which consumption rises when current disposable income rises by one dollar. Presumably, if people receive an extra dollar of income, they will consume part of the dollar and save the rest. In other words, their consumption will increase, but by less than the full dollar of extra income. Thus it is realistic to assume that the marginal propensity to consume is greater than 0 (an increase in income leads to an increase in consumption) but less than 1 (the increase in consumption will be less than the full increase in income). Mathematically, we can summarize these assumptions as $0 < mpc < 1$.

marginal propensity to consume (*mpc*) the amount by which consumption rises when disposable income rises by one dollar. We assume that $0 < mpc < 1$

The Multiplier

Together, Equations 9.1 and 9.2 tell much of Keynes's story about how recessions, or short-term drops in output, come about. Suppose that at first, the economy described by the two equations is in full-capacity equilibrium, so there is no output gap: $Y = Y^*$. The two equations tell us, first, that aggregate output equals aggregate spending and, second, that at the same time consumers (or households) spend a portion of their income described by the consumption function. Now suppose that expenditures suddenly drop. As discussed above, Equation 9.1 tells us that a drop in expenditures by households (C), firms (I), the government (G), or foreigners (NX) will lead to a drop in output—or, equivalently, in income—(Y). But Equation 9.2, the consumption function, tells us that the story does not end there; other things equal, the above drop in income (Y) will in turn lead to another drop, in household expenditures (C). This additional drop in C will be smaller than the original drop in Y, because the marginal propensity to consume, *mpc*, is smaller than 1. Back to Equation 9.1, the additional drop in C will lead to a "second-round" drop in Y which, according to Equation 9.2, will lead to a further drop in C, leading to a third-round drop in Y (Equation 9.1), and so on in a "vicious circle," until the system of two equations reaches a new equilibrium.

The intuition behind the vicious circle described by the two equations is simple. Equation 9.1 is just another way to say, using algebra, that in Keynes's account, short-run aggregate output is determined by aggregate spending. And Equation 9.2 is just another way to say that according to Keynes, household spending is determined by income (which equals aggregate output). Together, we have a cycle: an initial drop in expenditures leads to a drop in income, leading to a further (smaller) drop in expenditures, leading to a further drop in income, leading to a further (still smaller) drop in expenditures, and so on.

Specifically, a fall in consumer spending not only reduces the sales of consumer goods directly; it also reduces the incomes of workers and owners in the industries that produce consumer goods. As their incomes fall, these workers and capital owners reduce their spending, which reduces the output and incomes of *other* producers in the economy. And these reductions in income lead to still further cuts in spending. Ultimately, these successive rounds of declines in spending and income may lead to a decrease in **short-run equilibrium output** and aggregate expenditure that is significantly greater than the change in spending that started the process. Such short-run equilibrium output is the level of output at which Equations 9.1 and 9.2 hold true; that is, output Y equals aggregate expenditure and, at the same time, consumption spending C relates to output (or income) according to the consumption function. Short-run equilibrium output is thus the level of output that prevails during the period in which prices are predetermined.

short-run equilibrium output the level of output at which Equations 9.1 and 9.2 hold true; that is, output Y equals aggregate expenditure and, at the same time, consumption spending C relates to output (or income) according to the consumption function. Short-run equilibrium output is the level of output that prevails during the period in which prices are predetermined

The overall effect on short-run equilibrium output of an initial one-unit decrease or increase in expenditure is called the **income-expenditure multiplier**, or the ***multiplier*** for short. For example, if the multiplier is 2, then an initial \$1 change in expenditure leads, eventually (as a result of all the subsequent "rounds" described above), to a \$2 change in short-run equilibrium output in the same direction. For example, an initial \$50 billion decrease in expenditure reduces short-run equilibrium output by \$100 billion. The idea that a change in spending may lead to a significantly larger change in short-run equilibrium output is a key feature of Keynes's account of the economy.

income-expenditure multiplier (or **multiplier**) the effect of an initial one-unit decrease or increase in expenditure on short-run equilibrium output; for example, a multiplier of 2 means that an initial \$50 billion decrease in expenditure reduces short-run equilibrium output by \$100 billion

What determines how large the multiplier will be? An important factor is the marginal propensity to consume (*mpc*) out of disposable income, *mpc* in Equation 9.2. If the *mpc* is large, then falls in income will cause people to reduce their spending sharply, and the multiplier effect will then also be large. If the marginal propensity to consume is small, then people will not reduce spending so much when income falls, and the multiplier will also be small.

RECAP

KEYNES'S ANALYSIS OF RECESSIONS

- Keynes's crucial assumption is that *in the short run, firms meet the demand for their products at preset prices*. Thus, firms do not continuously change their prices as supply and demand conditions change; rather, over short periods, firms tend to keep their prices fixed and meet the demand that is forthcoming at those prices.
- The assumption that firms vary their production in order to meet demand at preset prices implies that in the short run, aggregate demand (or aggregate spending, or aggregate expenditure) affects aggregate output. Fluctuations in spending thus lead to fluctuations in output.
- But according to Keynes, aggregate expenditure (or spending) also *depends* on output, because output equals income, and aggregate expenditure depends on income. Specifically, the largest component of aggregate expenditure is consumer expenditure, or simply consumption. Consumption depends on disposable, or after-tax, income, according to a relationship known as the consumption function, stated algebraically as $C = \overline{C} + mpc(Y - T)$.
- The constant term in the consumption function, $\overline{C}$, captures factors other than disposable income that affect consumer spending. For example, an increase in housing or stock prices that makes households wealthier and thus more willing to spend—an effect called the wealth effect—could be captured by an increase in $\overline{C}$. The slope of the consumption function equals the marginal propensity to consume, *mpc*, where $0 < mpc < 1$. This is the amount by which consumption rises when disposable income rises by one dollar.
- That in the short run aggregate expenditure affects output and, at the same time, output (or income) affects aggregate expenditure creates a cycle. Generally, an initial one-unit change in expenditure leads to a larger eventual change in short-run equilibrium output, reflecting the working of the income-expenditure multiplier. The multiplier arises because, for example, a given initial decrease in spending reduces the incomes of producers and workers, which leads them to spend less, reducing the incomes and spending of other producers and workers, and so on.

STABILIZING SPENDING: THE ROLE OF FISCAL POLICY

According to Keynes, inadequate spending is an important cause of recessions. To fight recessions–at least, those caused by insufficient demand rather than slow growth of potential output–policymakers must find ways to stimulate spending. Policies that are used to affect aggregate expenditure, with the objective of eliminating output gaps, are called **stabilization policies**. Policy actions intended to increase spending and output are called **expansionary policies**; expansionary policy actions are normally taken when the economy is in recession. It is also possible, as we have seen, for the economy to be "overheated," with output greater than potential output (an expansionary gap). The risk of an expansionary gap, as we will see in more detail later, is that it may lead to an increase in inflation. To offset an expansionary gap, policymakers will try to reduce spending and output. **Contractionary policies** are policy actions intended to reduce spending and output.

stabilization policies government policies that are used to affect aggregate expenditure, with the objective of eliminating output gaps

expansionary policies government policy actions intended to increase spending and output

contractionary policies government policy actions designed to reduce spending and output

The two major tools of stabilization policy are *monetary policy* and *fiscal policy*. Recall that monetary policy refers to decisions about the size of the money supply, whereas fiscal policy refers to decisions about the government's budget—how much the government spends and how much tax revenue it collects. In the remainder of this chapter we will focus on how fiscal policy can be used to influence spending in the basic Keynesian model, as well as on some practical issues that arise in the use of fiscal policy in the real world. Monetary policy will be discussed in later chapters.

Government Purchases and Spending

Decisions about government spending represent one of the two main components of fiscal policy, the other being decisions about taxes and transfer payments. As was mentioned earlier, Keynes himself felt that changes in government purchases were probably the most effective tool for reducing or eliminating output gaps. His basic argument was straightforward: Government purchases of goods and services, being a component of aggregate expenditure, directly affect total spending. If output gaps are caused by too much or too little total spending, then the government can help guide the economy toward full employment by changing its own level of spending.

Keynes's argument can also be stated using Equation 9.1: An initial change in aggregate output resulting from a change in C, I, or NX can be offset by a change in the opposite direction in G. For example, if C initially dropped by \$50 billion due to a stock market crash, then the government could increase G by \$50 billion, offsetting the effect on aggregate demand of the initial drop in C. Moreover, suppose that the government did not respond promptly to the initial drop in C (this was arguably the case during the Great Depression). The initial drop in C (or in I, or in NX) would then lead, through the multiplier's vicious circle, to an even larger drop in short-run equilibrium output. According to Keynes, it is still not too late for the government to step in, increase G, and offset the resulting drop in output. The same multiplier effect that amplified the initial drop in expenditure will now work in the opposite direction, amplifying the government's increase in G, and help bring short-run equilibrium up by more than the increase in G.

Keynes's views seemed to be vindicated by the events of the 1930s, notably the fact that the Depression did not finally end until governments greatly increased their military spending in the latter part of the decade.

Example 9.1 shows how increased government purchases of goods and services can help eliminate a recessionary gap. (The effects of government spending on transfer programs, such as unemployment benefits, are a bit different. We will return to that case shortly.)

EXAMPLE 9.1 Recessionary Gap

By how much should the government increase its purchases in order to eliminate a recessionary gap?

Consider an economy that starts in equilibrium with $Y = Y^*$. Suppose, though, that consumers become more pessimistic about the future, so that they begin to spend less at every level of current disposable income. We can capture this change by assuming that $\bar{C}$, the constant term in the consumption function (Equation 9.2), falls to a lower level. To be specific, suppose that $\bar{C}$ falls by \$10 billion, which in turn implies an initial decline of \$10 billion in consumer expenditures C and hence in aggregate expenditure Y (Equation 9.1). Additionally, suppose that firms' managers also become more pessimistic about the future, and they too cut investment expenditures I by \$5 billion, leading to a further reduction in Y. By how much should the government increase its expenditures, G, to offset these initial drops and avoid a recession?

The initial drops of \$10 billion in C and \$5 billion in I lead to an initial drop of $\$5 + \$10 = \$15$ billion in aggregate spending (Equation 9.1). To fully offset this initial drop, the government would have to increase its expenditures, G, by the same amount, namely by \$15 billion.

What would happen if the government did not act quickly to offset the initial drops in consumer expenditures and investment? If the government waited, the effect of the initial drops would get amplified due to the multiplier's vicious circle. (According to Equation 9.2, the initial drop of \$15 billion in Y would lead consumers to further cut their expenditures as they see their incomes fall, in turn leading, according to Equation 9.1, to a further drop in Y, and so on.) For example, with a multiplier of 2, the initial drop would eventually lead to a new short-run equilibrium with a recessionary gap that is double the size of the initial drop: $Y - Y^* = -\$30$ billion. By how much would the government have to increase G now, to eliminate the recessionary gap? The answer is again \$15 billion.

This may sound counterintuitive at first, but it makes perfect sense once you remember that the multiplier works both ways: It amplifies *increases*, as well as decreases, in aggregate expenditure. With a multiplier of 2, a \$15 billion increase in government expenditures would eventually lead to a \$30 billion increase in short-run equilibrium, closing the output gap (so Y would again be equal to Y^*).

SELF-TEST 9.2

Consider the economy in Example 9.1, but now suppose that instead of becoming more pessimistic, consumers and investors become more optimistic about the future, leading to an initial *increase* of \$10 billion in C and \$5 billion in I. Discuss how a change in government purchases G could be used to offset this initial increase in aggregate demand. How would your answer change if the government did not act promptly, and by the time it considered changing G it had to eliminate an expansionary output gap that—due to a multiplier of 2—was double the size of the initial increase in aggregate expenditures?

In Example 9.1 and Self-Test 9.2, we saw how an increase in government purchases G can eliminate a recessionary gap, and how a decrease in G can eliminate an expansionary gap, but we did not discuss the components of G. The Economic Naturalist 9.5 focuses on changes in one specific component–military spending–and its links with recessions and expansions.

The Economic Naturalist 9.5

Does military spending stimulate the economy?

An antiwar poster from the 1960s bore the message "War is good business," referring to the uncomfortable fact that there are sectors in the economy that can do quite well during wars. War itself poses too many economic and human costs to be good business, but military spending could be a different matter. According to the basic Keynesian model, increases in aggregate expenditure resulting from stepped-up government purchases may help bring an economy out of a recession or depression. Does military spending stimulate aggregate demand?

Figure 9.4 shows U.S. military spending as a share of GDP from 1929 to 2019. The shaded areas in the figure correspond to periods of recession as shown in Table 9.1. Note the spike that occurred during World War II (1941–1945), when military spending exceeded 43 percent of U.S. GDP, as well as the surge during the

Korean War (1950–1953). Smaller increases in military spending relative to GDP occurred at the peak of the Vietnam War in 1967–1969, during the Reagan military buildup of the 1980s, and during the wars in Afghanistan and Iraq (which started in 2001 and 2003, respectively).

Figure 9.4 provides some support for the idea that expanded military spending tends to promote growth in aggregate demand. The clearest case is the World War II era, during which massive military spending helped the U.S. economy recover from the Great Depression. The U.S. unemployment rate fell from 17.2 percent of the workforce in 1939 (when defense spending was less than 2 percent of GDP) to 1.2 percent in 1944 (when defense spending was greater than 43 percent of GDP). Two brief recessions, in 1945 and 1948–1949, followed the end of the war and the sharp decline in military spending. At the time, though, many people feared that the war's end would bring a resumption of the Great Depression, so the relative mildness of the two postwar recessions was something of a relief.

FIGURE 9.4

U.S. Military Expenditures as a Share of GDP, 1929–2019.

Military expenditures as a share of GDP rose during World War II, the Korean War, the Vietnam War, the Reagan military buildup of the early 1980s, and during the wars in Afghanistan and Iraq. Increased military spending is often associated with an expanding economy and declining unemployment. The shaded areas indicate periods of recession.

Source: Bureau of Economic Analysis, NIPA Table 1.1.5, www.bea.gov.

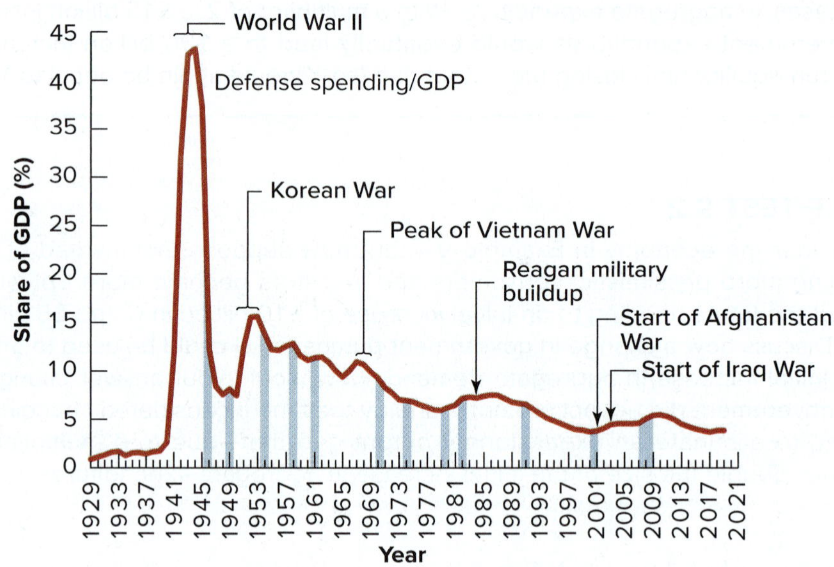

Increases in defense spending during the post–World War II period were also associated with economic expansions. The Korean War of 1950–1953 occurred simultaneously with a strong expansion, during which the unemployment rate dropped from 5.9 percent in 1949 to 2.9 percent in 1953. A recession began in 1954, the year after the armistice was signed, though military spending had not yet declined much. Economic expansions also occurred during the Vietnam-era military buildup in the 1960s and the Reagan buildup of the 1980s. Finally, on a smaller scale, increased government spending for military purposes and homeland security probably contributed to the relative mildness of the U.S. recession that began in 2001. These episodes support the idea that increases in government purchases—in this case, of weapons, other military supplies, and the services of military personnel—can help stimulate the economy.

Taxes, Transfers, and Aggregate Spending

Besides making decisions about government purchases of goods and services, fiscal policymakers also determine the level and types of taxes to be collected and transfer payments to be made. (Transfer payments, recall, are payments made by the government to the public, for which no current goods or services are received. Examples of transfer payments are unemployment insurance benefits, Social Security benefits, and income support payments to farmers. Once again, transfer payments are *not* included in government purchases of goods and services.) The basic Keynesian model implies that, like changes in government purchases, changes in the level of taxes or transfers can be used to affect aggregate expenditure and thus eliminate output gaps.

Unlike changes in government purchases, however, changes in taxes or transfers do not affect spending directly. Instead they work indirectly, by changing disposable income in the private sector. For example, either a tax cut or an increase in government transfer payments increases disposable income, equal to $Y - T$. According to the consumption function, when disposable income rises, households should spend more. Specifically, households should initially increase their expenditures by *mpc* times the increase in disposable income (Equation 9.2). Thus a tax cut or increase in transfers should increase aggregate expenditure. Likewise, an increase in taxes or a cut in transfers, by lowering households' disposable income, will tend to lower spending. The Economic Naturalist 9.6 discusses recent examples of changes in taxes and transfers that were aimed at stimulating aggregate spending.

The Economic Naturalist 9.6

Why did the federal government temporarily cut taxes in 2001, 2009, and 2020?

On May 25, 2001, Congress passed the Economic Growth and Tax Relief Reconciliation Act (EGTRRA) of 2001, which President George W. Bush signed on June 7. The EGTRRA made significant cuts in income tax rates and also provided for one-time tax rebate checks of up to $300 for individual taxpayers and up to $600 for married taxpayers filing a joint return. Millions of families received these checks in August and September of 2001, with payments totaling about $38 billion.

Almost eight years later, in February 2009, Congress passed the American Recovery and Reinvestment Act (ARRA) of 2009, which President Barack Obama signed on February 17, 2009. Among its provisions, the ARRA included $288 billion of tax relief, including a new payroll tax credit of $400 for individuals and $800 for couples in 2009 and 2010.

Most recently, in March 2020, Congress passed the Coronavirus Aid, Relief, and Economic Security (CARES) Act, which President Donald Trump signed into law on March 27, 2020. It was the largest economic relief bill in U.S. history, totaling around $2.2 trillion. It included hundreds of billions of dollars in tax-relief provisions, among them one-time checks of up to $1,200 for individuals and up to $2,400 for couples, with an additional $500 per child, as well as payroll tax credit for employers of up to $5,000 per employee.

Why did the federal government make these tax cuts?

Although the 2001 recession was not officially "declared" until November 2001 (when the National Bureau of Economic Research announced that the recession had begun in March), there was clear evidence by the spring of 2001 that the economy was slowing. Congress and the president hoped that by sending tax rebate checks to households, they could stimulate spending and perhaps avoid recession. In retrospect, the timing of the tax rebate was quite good since the economy and consumer confidence were further buffeted by the terrorist attacks on New York City and Washington on September 11, 2001.

Did the 2001 tax rebates have their intended effect of stimulating consumer spending? It is difficult to know with any certainty, since we do not know how much households would have spent if they had not received these extra funds. In a study published in 2006, economists found that households spent about two-thirds of their rebates within six months of receiving them.[6] This suggests that the rebate had a substantial effect on consumer spending, which held up remarkably well during the last quarter of 2001 and into 2002, assisting the economy's recovery substantially. Most economists would agree that fiscal policy generally—including not only the tax rebates, but also significantly increased spending for the military and for domestic security following September 11—was an important reason that the 2001 recession was relatively short and mild.

In contrast with the 2001 recession, the 2007–2009 recession was at the time the most severe recession since the end of World War II. By the time the ARRA was passed, not only had the beginning of the recession already been officially declared, but the recession's effects were already widely felt. For example, unemployment had already increased by around 3 percent since December 2007. Congress and the president hoped that a large tax cut, in addition to about half a trillion dollars of direct government spending and increased transfer payments, would stimulate the economy and help it recover from the recession.

Kena Betancur/Getty Images

Empty streets and frozen economic activity. Times Square, March 2020.

Finally, at the time CARES was passed, in late March 2020, the economic implications of the COVID-19 pandemic were only beginning to be felt in the U.S. However, it was already feared that the fast-spreading pandemic could trigger a global recession of historic proportions. Congress and the president hoped that by acting promptly and on an unprecedented scale, they could provide urgently needed stimulus to the economy.

RECAP

FISCAL POLICY AND PLANNED SPENDING

- Fiscal policy consists of two tools for affecting total spending and eliminating output gaps: (1) changes in government purchases and (2) changes in taxes or transfer payments.
- An increase in government purchases increases expenditure by an equal amount. A reduction in taxes or an increase in transfer payments increases expenditure by an amount equal to the marginal propensity to consume times the reduction in taxes or increase in transfers.
- The ultimate effect of a fiscal policy change on short-run equilibrium output equals the change in expenditure times the multiplier. Accordingly, if the economy is in recession, an increase in government purchases, a cut in taxes, or an increase in transfers can be used to stimulate spending and eliminate the recessionary gap.

FISCAL POLICY AS A STABILIZATION TOOL: THREE QUALIFICATIONS

The basic Keynesian model might lead you to think that precise use of fiscal policy can eliminate output gaps. But as is often the case, the real world is more complicated than economic models suggest. We close the chapter with three qualifications about the use of fiscal policy as a stabilization tool.

[6]David S. Johnson, Jonathan A. Parker, and Nicholas S. Souleles, "Household Expenditure and the Income Tax Rebates of 2001," *American Economic Review,* December 2006, pp. 1589–1610.

Fiscal Policy and the Supply Side

We have focused so far on the use of fiscal policy to affect aggregate expenditure. However, most economists would agree that *fiscal policy may affect potential output as well as aggregate expenditure*. On the spending side, for example, investments in public capital, such as roads, airports, and schools, can play a major role in the growth of potential output, as we discussed in Chapter 5, *Economic Growth, Productivity, and Living Standards*. On the other side of the ledger, tax and transfer programs may well affect the incentives, and thus the economic behavior, of households and firms. For example, a high tax rate on interest income may reduce the willingness of people to save for the future, while a tax break on new investment may encourage firms to increase their rate of capital formation. Such changes in saving or investment will in turn affect potential output. Many other examples could be given of how taxes and transfers affect economic behavior and thus possibly affect potential output as well.

Some critics of the Keynesian theory have gone so far as to argue that the *only* effects of fiscal policy that matter are effects on potential output. This was essentially the view of the so-called *supply-siders*, a group of economists and journalists whose influence reached a high point during the first Reagan term (1981–1985). Supply-siders focused on the need for tax cuts, arguing that lower tax rates would lead people to work harder (because they would be allowed to keep a larger share of their earnings), to save more, and to be more willing to innovate and take risks. Through their arguments that lower taxes would substantially increase potential output, with no significant effect on spending, the supply-siders provided crucial support for the large tax cuts that took place under the Reagan administration. Supply-sider ideas also were used to support the long-term income tax cut passed under President George W. Bush in 2001.

A more balanced view is that fiscal policy affects *both* spending *and* potential output. Thus, in making fiscal policy, government officials should take into account not only the need to stabilize aggregate expenditure but also the likely effects of government spending, taxes, and transfers on the economy's productive capacity.

The Problem of Deficits

A second consideration for fiscal policymakers thinking about stabilization policies is *the need to avoid large and persistent budget deficits*. Recall from Chapter 7, *Saving and Capital Formation*, that the government's budget deficit is the excess of government spending over tax collections. Sustained government deficits can be harmful because they reduce national saving, which in turn reduces investment in new capital goods—an important source of long-run economic growth. The need to keep deficits under control may make increasing spending or cutting taxes to fight a slowdown a less attractive option, both economically and politically.

Moreover, international lenders would not let a country run large and persistent deficits for too long even if at home deficits appeared politically attractive. As an extreme example, for many years Greece's government was running large budget deficits—estimated at more than 7 percent of GDP, on average, from 1995 to 2015. These large deficits eventually led to a government-debt crisis. As international lenders questioned the Greek government's ability to pay back any future loans, Greece's government became very limited in its ability to run further deficits to stimulate the economy and fight recessions. Indeed, in 2016, the Greek government was forced to run a small budget surplus in spite of no real GDP growth and a very high unemployment rate (more than 23 percent!). It kept running small surpluses in the following years. (By late 2019—before the COVID-19 pandemic—unemployment in Greece was still above 16 percent.)

The Relative Inflexibility of Fiscal Policy

The third qualification about the use of fiscal policy is that *fiscal policy is not always flexible enough to be useful for stabilization*. Our examples have implicitly assumed that the government can change spending or taxes relatively quickly in order to eliminate output gaps. In reality, changes in government spending or taxes must usually go through a lengthy legislative process, which reduces the ability of fiscal policy to respond in a timely way to economic conditions. For example, budget and tax changes proposed by the president must typically be submitted to Congress 18 months or more before they go into effect. Another factor that limits the flexibility of fiscal policy is that fiscal policymakers have many other objectives besides stabilizing aggregate spending, from ensuring an adequate national defense to providing income support to the poor. What happens if, say, the need to strengthen the national defense requires an increase in government spending, but the need to contain aggregate expenditure requires a decrease in government spending? Such conflicts can be difficult to resolve through the political process.

This lack of flexibility means that fiscal policy is less useful for stabilizing spending than the basic Keynesian model suggests. Nevertheless, most economists view fiscal policy as an important stabilizing force, for two reasons. The first is the presence of **automatic stabilizers,** provisions in the law that imply *automatic* increases in government spending or decreases in taxes when real output declines. For example, some government spending is earmarked as "recession aid"; it flows to communities automatically when the unemployment rate reaches a certain level. Taxes and transfer payments also respond automatically to output gaps: When GDP declines, income tax collections fall (because households' taxable incomes fall) while unemployment insurance payments and welfare benefits rise—all without any explicit action by Congress. These automatic changes in government spending and tax collections help increase planned spending during recessions and reduce it during expansions, without the delays inherent in the legislative process.

automatic stabilizers provisions in the law that imply *automatic* increases in government spending or decreases in taxes when real output declines

The second reason that fiscal policy is an important stabilizing force is that although fiscal policy may be difficult to change quickly, it may still be useful for dealing with prolonged episodes of recession, when other economic policies including monetary policy may prove insufficient. The Great Depression of the 1930s, the Japanese slump of the 1990s, the global recession of 2007–2009, and the COVID-19 recession that started in 2020 are four cases in point. However, because of the relative lack of flexibility of fiscal policy, in the absence of an unusual economic shock, in modern economies aggregate spending is more usually stabilized through monetary policy. The stabilizing role of monetary policy is the subject of the next chapter.

RECAP

FISCAL POLICY AS A STABILIZATION TOOL: THREE QUALIFICATIONS

- Changes in taxes and transfer programs may affect the incentives and economic behavior of households and firms.
- Governments must weigh the short-run effects of fiscal policy against the possibility of large and persistent budget deficits.
- Changes in spending and taxation take time and thus fiscal policy can be relatively slow and inflexible.

SUMMARY

- Real GDP does not grow smoothly. Periods in which the economy is growing at a rate significantly below normal are called *recessions;* periods in which the economy is growing at a rate significantly above normal are called *expansions*. A severe or protracted recession, like the long decline that occurred between 1929 and 1933, is called a *depression,* while a particularly strong expansion is called a *boom*. *(LO1)*
- The beginning of a recession is called the *peak* because it represents the high point of economic activity prior to a downturn. The end of a recession, which marks the low point of economic activity prior to a recovery, is called the *trough*. Since World War II, U.S. recessions have been much shorter on average than booms, lasting between 6 and 18 months. The two longest boom periods in U.S. history are pretty recent. The first began with the end of the 1990–1991 recession in March 1991, ending exactly 10 years later in March 2001 when a new recession began. The second began with the end of the 2007–2009 recession and lasted almost 11 years. *(LO1)*
- Short-term economic fluctuations are irregular in length and severity, and are thus hard to forecast. Expansions and recessions are typically felt throughout the economy and may even be global in scope. Unemployment rises sharply during recessions, while inflation tends to fall during or shortly after a recession. *Durable goods* industries tend to be particularly sensitive to recessions and booms, whereas services and *nondurable goods* industries are less sensitive. *(LO1)*
- *Potential output,* also called potential GDP or full-employment output, is the maximum sustainable amount of output (real GDP) that an economy can produce. The difference between the economy's actual output and its potential output is called the *output gap*. When output is below potential, the gap is called a *recessionary gap;* when output is above potential, the difference is called an *expansionary gap*. Recessions can occur either because potential output is growing unusually slowly or because actual output is below potential. Because recessionary gaps represent wasted resources and expansionary gaps threaten to create inflation, policymakers have an incentive to try to eliminate both types of gap. *(LO2)*
- The *natural rate of unemployment* is the part of the total unemployment rate that is attributable to frictional and structural unemployment. Equivalently, the natural rate of unemployment is the rate of unemployment that exists when the output gap is zero. Cyclical unemployment, the part of unemployment that is associated with recessions and expansions, equals the total unemployment rate less the natural unemployment rate. *(LO3)*
- If firms adjust prices only periodically, and in the meantime produce enough output to meet demand, then fluctuations in spending will lead to fluctuations in output over the short run. During that short-run period, government policies that influence aggregate spending may help eliminate output gaps. In the long run, however, firms' price changes will eliminate output gaps—that is, the economy will "self-correct"—and total spending will influence only the rate of inflation. *(LO4)*
- The basic Keynesian model shows how fluctuations in aggregate expenditure, or total planned spending, can cause actual output to differ from potential output. Too little spending leads to a recessionary output gap; too much spending creates an expansionary output gap. This model relies on the crucial assumption that firms do not respond to every change in demand by changing prices. Instead, they typically set a price for some period and then meet the demand forthcoming at that price. Firms do not change prices continually because changing prices entails costs, called *menu costs*. *(LO5)*
- *Aggregate expenditure* is total spending on final goods and services. The four components of total spending are consumption, investment, government purchases, and net exports. *(LO6)*
- Consumption is related to disposable, or after-tax, income by a relationship called the *consumption function*. The amount by which consumption rises when disposable income rises by one dollar is called the marginal propensity to consume (*mpc*). The marginal propensity to consume is always greater than zero but less than one (that is, $0 < mpc < 1$). *(LO6)*
- Changes in aggregate expenditure will lead to changes in short-run equilibrium output. In particular, if the economy is initially at full employment, a fall in aggregate expenditure will create a recessionary gap and a rise in aggregate expenditure will create an expansionary gap. The amount by which a one-unit increase in expenditure raises short-run equilibrium output is called the *multiplier*. An increase in expenditure not only raises spending directly; it also raises the incomes of producers, who in turn increase their spending, and so on. Hence the multiplier is greater than one; that is, a one-dollar increase in expenditure tends to raise short-run equilibrium output by more than one dollar. *(LO6)*

- To eliminate output gaps and restore full employment, the government employs *stabilization policies*. The two major types of stabilization policy are monetary policy and fiscal policy. Stabilization policies work by changing aggregate expenditure and hence short-run equilibrium output. For example, an increase in government purchases raises expenditure directly, so it can be used to reduce or eliminate a recessionary gap. Similarly, a cut in taxes or an increase in transfer payments increases the public's disposable income, raising consumption spending at each level of output by an amount equal to the marginal propensity to consume times the cut in taxes or increase in transfers. Higher consumer spending, in turn, raises short-run equilibrium output. *(LO7)*
- Three qualifications must be made to the use of fiscal policy as a stabilization tool. First, fiscal policy may affect potential output as well as aggregate spending. Second, large and persistent government budget deficits reduce national saving and growth; the need to keep deficits under control may limit the use of expansionary fiscal policies. Finally, because changes in fiscal policy must go through a lengthy legislative process, fiscal policy is not always flexible enough to be useful for short-run stabilization. However, *automatic stabilizers*—provisions in the law that imply automatic increases in government spending or reductions in taxes when output declines—can overcome the problem of legislative delays to some extent and contribute to economic stability. *(LO8)*

KEY TERMS

aggregate expenditure
automatic stabilizers
autonomous consumption
autonomous expenditure
boom
business cycles (or cyclical fluctuations)
consumption function
contractionary policies
depression
disposable income
durable goods
expansion
expansionary gap
expansionary policies
income-expenditure multiplier (or multiplier)
marginal propensity to consume (*mpc*)
menu costs
natural rate of unemployment, u^*
nondurable goods
output gap
peak
potential output, Y^* (or potential GDP or full-employment output)
recession (or contraction)
recessionary gap
short-run equilibrium output
stabilization policies
trough
wealth effect

REVIEW QUESTIONS

1. Define recession and expansion. What are the beginning and ending points of a recession called? In the postwar United States, which have been longer on average: recessions or expansions? *(LO1)*
2. Why is the traditional term *business cycles* a misnomer? How does your answer relate to the ease of difficulty of forecasting peaks and troughs? *(LO1)*
3. Which firm is likely to see its profits reduced the most in a recession: an automobile producer, a manufacturer of boots and shoes, or a janitorial service? Which is likely to see its profits reduced the least? Explain. *(LO1)*
4. How is each of the following likely to be affected by a recession: the natural unemployment rate, the cyclical unemployment rate, the inflation rate, the poll ratings of the president? *(LO1, LO3)*
5. Define potential output. Is it possible for an economy to produce an amount greater than potential output? Explain. *(LO2)*
6. True or false: All recessions are the result of output gaps. Explain. *(LO2)*
7. True or false: When output equals potential output, the unemployment rate is zero. Explain. *(LO3)*
8. What is the key assumption of the basic Keynesian theory? Explain why this assumption is needed if one is to accept the view that aggregate spending is a driving force behind short-term economic fluctuations. *(LO5)*
9. Give an example of a good or service whose price changes very frequently and one whose price changes relatively infrequently. What accounts for the difference? *(LO5)*
10. Define aggregate expenditure and list its components. Why does spending change when output changes? *(LO6)*
11. Define the multiplier. In economic terms, why is the multiplier greater than one? *(LO6)*
12. The government is considering two alternative policies, one involving increased government purchases of 50 units, the other involving a tax cut of 50 units. Which policy will stimulate aggregate expenditure by more? Why? *(LO7)*
13. Discuss three reasons why the use of fiscal policy to stabilize the economy is more complicated than suggested by the basic Keynesian model. *(LO8)*

PROBLEMS

1. Using Table 9.1, find the average duration, the minimum duration, and the maximum duration of expansions in the United States since 1929. Are expansions getting longer or shorter on average over time? Is there any tendency for long expansions to be followed by long recessions? *(LO1)*
2. From the home page of the Bureau of Economic Analysis (www.bea.gov), obtain quarterly data for U.S. real GDP from these recessions: 1981–1982, 1990–1991, 2001, and 2007–2009. *(LO1)*
   a. How many quarters of negative real GDP growth occurred in each recession?
   b. Which, if any, of the recessions satisfied the informal criterion that a recession must have two consecutive quarters of negative GDP growth?
3. Given below are data on real GDP and potential GDP for the United States for the years 2005–2016, in billions of 2009 dollars. For each year, calculate the output gap as a percentage of potential GDP and state whether the gap is a recessionary gap or an expansionary gap. Also calculate the year-to-year growth rates of real GDP. Identify the recessions that occurred during this period. *(LO2)*

Year	Real GDP	Potential GDP
2005	14,234.2	14,272.6
2006	14,613.8	14,578.7
2007	14,873.7	14,843.6
2008	14,830.4	15,098.3
2009	14,418.7	15,310.3
2010	14,783.8	15,457.0
2011	15,020.6	15,615.8
2012	15,354.6	15,815.5
2013	15,612.2	16,049.4
2014	16,013.3	16,305.7
2015	16,471.5	16,573.4
2016	16,716.2	16,832.8

Sources: Potential GDP, Federal Reserve Bank of St. Louis; real GDP, www.bea.gov.

4. From the home page of the Bureau of Labor Statistics (www.bls.gov), obtain the most recent available data on the unemployment rate for workers aged 16–19 and workers aged 20 or over. How do they differ? What are some of the reasons for the difference? How does this difference relate to the decline in the overall natural rate of unemployment since 1980? *(LO3)*
5. Of the following, identify the incorrect statement. *(LO4)*
   a. Output gaps are caused by inflationary pressures generated by the unintended side effects of government policy.
   b. Low aggregate spending can make output fall below potential output.
   c. When spending is high, output may rise above potential output.
   d. Government policies can help eliminate output gaps.
6. According to Keynes's assumption about the short run, firms that are experiencing a reduction in sales due to a recession will respond by *(LO5)*
   a. lowering pries to bring sales in line with their production capacity.
   b. reducing production to meet demand at the existing price.
   c. charging higher prices per unit to recoup their loss from selling fewer units.
   d. increasing production to lower the cost per unit.

   Explain your answer.
7. Data on before-tax income, taxes paid, and consumption spending for the Simpson family in various years are given below. *(LO6)*

Before-tax income ($)	Taxes paid ($)	Consumption spending ($)
25,000	3,000	20,000
27,000	3,500	21,350
28,000	3,700	22,070
30,000	4,000	23,600

   a. Find the Simpson household's marginal propensity to consume.
   b. How much would you expect the Simpsons to consume if their income was $32,000 and they paid taxes of $5,000?
   c. Homer Simpson wins a lottery prize. As a result, the Simpson family increases its consumption by $1,000 at each level of after-tax income. ("Income" does not include the prize money.) How does this change affect their consumption function? How does it affect their marginal propensity to consume?

   Explain your answer.
8. An economy is described by the following equations. *(LO7)*

$$C = 40 + 0.8(Y - T)$$
$$I = 70$$
$$G = 120$$
$$NX = 10$$
$$T = 150$$

a. What is aggregate expenditure when $Y = 600$?
b. Consumers and businesses alike become more pessimistic about the future and reduce their expenditures by 10 each. Immediately following this change, what is aggregate expenditure if Y is still 600? (In other words, what is the initial change in aggregate expenditure?)
c. What would you expect firms do in response to this change in expenditure? How will firms' response affect aggregate income, and how will households respond?
d. By how much should government purchases change in order to offset the initial drops and avoid a recession?
e. By how much more would government purchases have to change if the multiplier effect were allowed to take effect?

If the government instead decides to change taxes, determine if taxes would need to change by more, less, or the same as the answer in part d.

9. For each of these hyperbolized statements, identify the fiscal policy qualification to which it is related. *(LO8)*
   a. Fiscal policy is just as likely to impact a nation's actual GDP as its potential GDP.
   b. Given the average duration of recent recessions, fiscal policy is destined to provide help that arrives only after the problem is already fixed.
   c. While Keynesian economic theory states that fiscal policy is effective at addressing both types of output gaps, governments have a tendency to only use expansionary fiscal policy in real life at a cost to future generations.
10. Give three examples of automatic stabilizers of the economy. *(LO8)*

ANSWERS TO SELF-TESTS

9.1 Answers will vary, depending on when the data are obtained. As of mid-2020, the last recession started in February 2020. *(LO1)*

9.2 The initial increases of \$10 billion in C and \$5 billion in I would together imply an initial increase of \$15 billion in aggregate expenditure (or aggregate spending, or aggregate demand). To fully offset this initial increase in aggregate expenditure, the government could lower its purchases G by \$15 billion.

If the government did not act, however, the initial \$15 billion increase in aggregate expenditure would be amplified through the multiplier effect. With a multiplier of 2, the economy would eventually reach a new short-run equilibrium that is \$15 billion × 2 = \$30 billion above potential output. To close this expansionary gap, the government would *still* have to decrease G by "only" \$15 billion. Through the working of the multiplier, a \$15 billion decrease in G would eventually lead to a \$30 billion decrease in aggregate expenditure, closing the entire \$30 billion expansionary gap. *(LO7)*

*Problems marked by an asterisk (*) are more difficult.

10

Stabilizing the Economy: The Role of the Fed

Financial market participants and commentators go to remarkable lengths to try to predict the actions of the Federal Reserve. At the end of 2015, investors had been listening to every word uttered by Chair Janet Yellen to learn whether the Fed intended to raise interest rates for the first time in almost a decade. Then, in the summer of 2019, all eyes were on Chair Jerome Powell to learn whether—for the first time in *more* than a decade—interest rates were going to be *cut*. The close attention being paid to Fed chairs is not a new occurrence. For a while, the CNBC financial news program *Squawk Box* reported regularly on what the commentators called the Greenspan Briefcase Indicator. The idea was to spot Alan Greenspan, one of Yellen's and Powell's predecessors as Fed chair, on his way to meet with the Federal Open Market Committee (FOMC), the group that determines U.S. monetary policy. If Greenspan's briefcase was packed full, presumably with macroeconomic data and analyses, the guess was that the Fed planned to change interest rates. A slim briefcase meant no change in rates was likely.

"It was right 17 out of the first 20 times," the program's anchor Mark Haines noted, "but it has a built-in self-destruct mechanism, because Greenspan packs his [own] briefcase. He can make it wrong or right. He has never publicly acknowledged the indicator, but we have reason to believe that he knows about it. We have to consider the fact that he wants us to stop doing it because the last two times the briefcase has been wrong, and that's disturbing."[1]

The Briefcase Indicator is but one example of the close public scrutiny that the chair of the Federal Reserve and other monetary policymakers face. Every speech, every congressional testimony, every interview from a member of the Board of Governors is closely analyzed for clues about the future course of monetary policy. The reason for the intense public interest in the Federal Reserve's decisions about monetary policy—and especially the level of interest rates—is that those decisions have important implications both for financial markets and for the economy in general.

[1]Robert H. Frank, "Safety in Numbers," *New York Times Magazine,* November 28, 1999, p. 35.

LEARNING OBJECTIVES

After reading this chapter, you should be able to:

LO1 Show how the demand for money and the supply of money interact to determine the equilibrium nominal interest rate.

LO2 Explain how the Fed uses its ability to affect the money supply to influence nominal and real interest rates.

LO3 Discuss how the Fed uses its ability to affect bank reserves and the reserve-deposit ratio to affect the money supply.

LO4 Describe the additional monetary policy tools that the Fed can use when interest rates hit the zero lower bound.

LO5 Explain how changes in real interest rates affect aggregate expenditure and how the Fed uses changes in the real interest rate to fight a recession or inflation.

LO6 Discuss the extent to which monetary policy-making is an art or science.

In this chapter, we examine the workings of monetary policy, one of the two major types of *stabilization policy*. (The other type, fiscal policy, was discussed in the previous chapter.) As we have seen, stabilization policies are government policies that are meant to influence aggregate expenditure, with the goal of eliminating output gaps. Both types of stabilization policy, monetary and fiscal, are important and have been useful at various times. However, monetary policy, which can be changed quickly by a decision of the Federal Reserve's FOMC, is more flexible and responsive than fiscal policy, which can be changed only by legislative action by Congress. Under normal circumstances, therefore, monetary policy is used more actively than fiscal policy to help stabilize the economy.

We will begin this chapter by discussing how the Fed uses its ability to control the money supply to influence the level of interest rates. We then turn to the economic effects of changes in interest rates. Building on our analysis of the basic Keynesian theory in Chapter 9, *Short-Term Economic Fluctuations and Fiscal Policy,* we will see that, in the short run, monetary policy works by affecting planned spending and thus short-run equilibrium output. We will defer discussion of the other major effect of monetary policy actions, changes in the rate of inflation. The effects of monetary policy on inflation are addressed in the next chapter.

THE FEDERAL RESERVE AND INTEREST RATES: THE BASIC MODEL

When we introduced the Federal Reserve System in Chapter 8, *Money, the Federal Reserve, and Global Financial Markets,* we focused on the Fed's tools for controlling the *money supply*—that is, the quantity of currency and checking accounts held by the public. Determining the nation's money supply is the primary task of monetary policymakers. But if you follow the economic news regularly, you may find the idea that the Fed's job is to control the money supply a bit foreign because the news media nearly always focus on the Fed's decisions about *interest rates*. Indeed, the announcement the Fed makes after each meeting of the FOMC nearly always includes its plan for a particular short-term interest rate, called the *federal funds rate* (more on the federal funds rate later).

Actually, there is no contradiction between the two ways of looking at monetary policy—as control of the money supply or as the setting of interest rates. As we will see in this section, controlling the money supply and controlling the nominal interest rate are two sides of the same coin: any value of the money supply chosen by the Fed implies a specific setting for the nominal interest rate, and vice versa. The reason for this close connection is that the nominal interest rate is effectively the "price" of holding money (or, more accurately, its opportunity cost). So, by controlling the quantity of money supplied to the economy, the Fed also controls the "price" of holding money (the nominal interest rate).

In this section, we focus on the basic model of the market for money. To keep the discussion easy to follow, we will keep making two simplifying assumptions that we have made throughout the book. First, when discussing the money supply, we will keep assuming, as we did in Chapter 8, that the Fed can fully control the amount of money by controlling the amount of bank reserves. Second, when discussing interest rates, we will keep assuming that they all move more or less together. To better understand how the Fed determines interest rates, we will look first at the demand side of that market. We will see that given the demand for money by the public, the Fed can control interest rates by changing the amount of money it supplies. Having discussed the basics—that is, how the market for money works when our two simplifying assumptions hold—in the next section, we will discuss the market for money in more detail and highlight the changes that occurred in this market since 2008. In the last section of this chapter, we will show how the Fed uses control of interest rates to influence spending and the state of the economy.

The Demand for Money

Recall that *money* refers to the set of assets, such as cash and checking accounts, that are usable in transactions. Money is also a store of value, like stocks, bonds, or real estate–in other words, a type of financial asset. As a financial asset, money is a way of holding wealth.

Anyone who has some wealth must determine the *form* in which he or she wishes to hold that wealth. For example, if Louis has wealth of $10,000, he could–if he wished–hold all $10,000 in cash. Or he could hold $5,000 of his wealth in the form of cash and $5,000 in government bonds. Or he could hold $1,000 in cash, $2,000 in a checking account, $2,000 in government bonds, and $5,000 in rare stamps. Indeed, there are thousands of different real and financial assets to choose from, all of which can be held in different amounts and combinations, so Louis's choices are virtually infinite. The decision about the forms in which to hold one's wealth is called the **portfolio allocation decision.**

portfolio allocation decision the decision about the forms in which to hold one's wealth

What determines the particular mix of assets that Louis or another wealth holder will choose? All else being equal, people generally prefer to hold assets that they expect to pay a high *return* and do not carry too much *risk*. They may also try to reduce the overall risk they face through *diversification*–that is, by owning a variety of different assets.[2] Many people own some real assets, such as a car or a home, because they provide services (transportation or shelter) and often a financial return (an increase in value, as when the price of a home rises in a strong real estate market).

Here we do not need to analyze the entire portfolio allocation decision, but only one part of it–namely, the decision about how much of one's wealth to hold in the form of *money* (cash and checking accounts). The amount of wealth an individual chooses to hold in the form of money is that individual's **demand for money.** So if Louis decided to hold his entire $10,000 in the form of cash, his demand for money would be $10,000. But if he were to hold $1,000 in cash, $2,000 in a checking account, $2,000 in government bonds, and $5,000 in rare stamps, his demand for money would be only $3,000–that is, $1,000 in cash plus the $2,000 in his checking account.

demand for money the amount of wealth an individual or firm chooses to hold in the form of money

EXAMPLE 10.1 Consuelo's Demand for Money

What is Consuelo's demand for money, and how could she increase or reduce her money holdings?

Consuelo's balance sheet is shown in Table 10.1. What is Consuelo's demand for money? If she wanted to increase her money holdings by $100, how could she do so? What if she wanted to reduce her money holdings by $100?

TABLE 10.1
Consuelo's Balance Sheet

Assets		Liabilities	
Cash	$ 80	Student loan	$3,000
Checking account	1,200	Credit card balance	250
Shares of stock	1,000		
Car (market value)	3,500		
Furniture (market value)	500		
Total	**$6,280**		**$3,250**
		Net worth	**$3,030**

[2]We examined risk, return, and diversification in Chapter 8, *Money, the Federal Reserve, and Global Financial Markets.*

Looking at Table 10.1, we see that Consuelo's balance sheet shows five different asset types: cash, a checking account, shares of stock, a car, and furniture. Of these assets, the first two (the cash and the checking account) are forms of money. Consuelo's money holdings consist of $80 in cash and $1,200 in her checking account. Thus Consuelo's demand for money—the amount of wealth she chooses to hold in the form of money—is $1,280.

There are many different ways in which Consuelo could increase her money holdings, or demand for money, by $100. She could sell $100 worth of stock and deposit the proceeds in the bank. That action would leave the total value of her assets and her wealth unchanged (because the decrease in her stockholdings would be offset by the increase in her checking account) but would increase her money holdings by $100. Another possibility would be to take a $100 cash advance on her credit card. That action would increase both her money holdings and her assets by $100 but would also increase her liabilities—specifically, her credit card balance—by $100. Once again, her total wealth would not change, though her money holdings would increase.

To reduce her money holdings, Consuelo need only use some of her cash or checking account balance to acquire a nonmoney asset or pay down a liability.

For example, if she were to buy an additional $100 of stock by writing a check against her bank account, her money holdings would decline by $100. Similarly, writing a check to reduce her credit card balance by $100 would reduce her money holdings by $100. You can confirm that though her money holdings decline, in neither case does Consuelo's total wealth change.

How much money should an individual (or household) choose to hold? Application of the *Cost-Benefit Principle* tells us that an individual should increase his or her money holdings only so long as the benefit of doing so exceeds the cost. As we saw in Chapter 8, *Money, the Federal Reserve, and Global Financial Markets,* the principal *benefit* of holding money is its usefulness in carrying out transactions. Consuelo's shares of stock, her car, and her furniture are all valuable assets, but she cannot use them to buy groceries or pay her rent. She can make routine payments using cash or her checking account, however. Because of its usefulness in daily transactions, Consuelo will almost certainly want to hold some of her wealth in the form of money. Furthermore, if Consuelo is a high-income individual, she will probably choose to hold more money than someone with a lower income would, because she is likely to spend more and carry out more transactions than the low-income person.

Consuelo's benefit from holding money is also affected by the technological and financial sophistication of the society she lives in. For example, in the United States, developments such as credit cards, debit cards, ATMs, online and mobile payments, and electronic money transfers have generally reduced the amount of money people need to carry out routine transactions, decreasing the public's demand for money at given levels of income. In the United States in 1960, for example, money holdings in the form of cash and checking account balances (the monetary aggregate M1) were about 26 percent of GDP. By 2007, that ratio had fallen to less than 10 percent of GDP.

Although money is an extremely useful asset, there is also a cost to holding money—more precisely, an opportunity cost—that arises from the fact that most forms of money pay little or no interest. Cash pays zero interest, and most checking accounts pay either no interest or very low rates. For the sake of simplicity, we will just assume that *the nominal interest rate on money is zero*. In contrast, most alternative assets, such as bonds or stocks, pay a positive nominal return. A bond, for example, pays a fixed amount of interest each period to the holder, while stocks pay dividends and may also increase in value (capital gains).

The cost of holding money arises because, in order to hold an extra dollar of wealth in the form of money, a person must reduce by one dollar the amount of wealth held in the form of higher-yielding assets, such as bonds or stocks. The *opportunity cost* of holding money is measured by the interest rate that could have been earned if the person had chosen to hold interest-bearing assets instead of money. All else being equal, the higher the nominal interest rate, the higher the opportunity cost of holding money, and hence the less money people will choose to hold. Indeed, as the nominal interest rate fell dramatically during 2007–2008 and remained below 1 percent until mid-2017, M1 steadily increased from less than 10 percent of GDP in 2007 to more than 18 percent of GDP in 2017.

We have been talking about the demand for money by individuals, but businesses also hold money to carry out transactions with customers and to pay workers and suppliers. The same general factors that determine individuals' money demand also affect the demand for money by businesses. That is, in choosing how much money to hold, a business, like an individual, will compare the benefits of holding money for use in transactions with the opportunity cost of holding a non-interest-bearing asset. Although we will not differentiate between the money held by individuals and the money held by businesses in discussing money demand, you should be aware that in the U.S. economy, businesses hold a significant portion of the total money stock. Example 10.2 illustrates the determination of money demand by a business owner.

EXAMPLE 10.2 A Business's Demand for Money

How much money should Kim's restaurants hold?

Kim owns several successful restaurants. Her accountant informs her that on a typical day, her restaurants are holding a total of $50,000 in cash on the premises. The accountant points out that if Kim's restaurants reduced their cash holdings, Kim could use the extra cash to purchase interest-bearing government bonds.

The accountant proposes two methods of reducing the amount of cash Kim's restaurants hold. First, she could increase the frequency of cash pickups by her armored car service. The extra service would cost $500 annually but would allow Kim's restaurants to reduce their average cash holding to $40,000. Second, in addition to the extra pickups, Kim could employ a computerized cash management service to help her keep closer tabs on the inflows and outflows of cash at her restaurants. The service costs $700 a year, but the accountant estimates that, together with more frequent pickups, the more efficient cash management provided by the service could help Kim reduce average cash holdings at her restaurants to $30,000.

The interest rate on government bonds is 6 percent. How much money should Kim's restaurants hold? What if the interest rate on government bonds is 8 percent?

Kim's restaurants need to hold cash to carry out their normal business, but holding cash also has an opportunity cost, which is the interest those funds could be earning if they were held in the form of government bonds instead of zero-interest cash. Because the interest rate on government bonds is 6 percent, each $10,000 by which Kim can reduce her restaurants' money holdings yields an annual benefit of $600 (6 percent of $10,000).

If Kim increases the frequency of pickups by her armored car service, reducing the restaurants' average money holdings from $50,000 to $40,000, the benefit will be the additional $600 in interest income that Kim will earn. The cost is the $500 charged by the armored car company. Since the benefit exceeds the cost, Kim should purchase the extra service and reduce the average cash holdings at her restaurants to $40,000.

Should Kim go a step further and employ the cash management service as well? Doing so would reduce average cash holdings at the restaurants from $40,000 to $30,000, which has a benefit in terms of extra interest income of $600 per year. However, this benefit is less than the cost of the cash management service, which is $700 per year. So Kim should *not* employ the cash management service and instead should maintain average cash holdings in her restaurants of $40,000.

If the interest rate on government bonds rises to 8 percent, then the benefit of each $10,000 reduction in average money holdings is $800 per year (8 percent of $10,000) in extra interest income. In this case, the benefit of employing the cash management service, $800, exceeds the cost of doing so, which is $700. So Kim should employ the service, reducing the average cash holdings of her business to $30,000. The example shows that a higher nominal interest rate on alternative assets reduces the quantity of money demanded.

SELF-TEST 10.1

The interest rate on government bonds falls from 6 percent to 4 percent. How much cash should Kim's restaurants hold now?

Macroeconomic Factors That Affect the Demand for Money

In any household or business, the demand for money will depend on a variety of individual circumstances. For example, a high-volume retail business that serves thousands of customers each day will probably choose to have more money on hand than a legal firm that bills clients and pays employees monthly. But while individuals and businesses vary considerably in the amount of money they choose to hold, three macroeconomic factors affect the demand for money quite broadly: the nominal interest rate, real output, and the price level. As we see next, the nominal interest rate affects the cost of holding money throughout the economy, while real output and the price level affect the benefits of money.

- *The nominal interest rate (i).* We have seen that the interest rate paid on alternatives to money, such as government bonds, determines the opportunity cost of holding money. The higher the prevailing nominal interest rate, the greater the opportunity cost of holding money, and hence the less money individuals and businesses will demand.

What do we mean by *the* nominal interest rate? As we have discussed, there are thousands of different assets, each with its own interest rate (rate of return). So can we really talk about *the* nominal interest rate? The answer is that, while there are many different assets, each with its own corresponding interest rate, the rates on those assets tend to rise and fall together. This is to be expected, because if the interest rates on some assets were to rise sharply while the rates on other assets declined, financial investors would flock to the assets paying high rates and refuse to buy the assets paying low rates. So, although there are many different interest rates in practice, speaking of the general level of interest rates usually does make sense. In this book, when we talk about *the* nominal interest rate, what we have in mind is some average measure of interest rates. This simplification is one more application of the macroeconomic concept of *aggregation,* introduced in Chapter 3, *Macroeconomics: The Bird's-Eye View of the Economy.* (We will discuss post-2008 deviations from this simplifying assumption in the next section.)

The nominal interest rate is a macroeconomic factor that affects the cost of holding money. A macroeconomic factor that affects the *benefit* of holding money is

- *Real income or output (Y)*. An increase in aggregate real income or output—as measured, for example, by real GDP—raises the quantity of goods and services that people and businesses want to buy and sell. When the economy enters a boom, for example, people do more shopping and stores have more customers. To accommodate the increase in transactions, both individuals and businesses need to hold more money. Thus higher real output raises the demand for money.

A second macroeconomic factor affecting the benefit of holding money is

- *The price level (P)*. The higher the prices of goods and services, the more dollars (or yen, or euros) are needed to make a given set of transactions. Thus a higher price level is associated with a higher demand for money.

Today, when a couple of teenagers go out for a movie and snacks on Saturday night, they need about twice as much cash as their parents did 30 years ago. Because the prices of movie tickets and popcorn have risen steeply over 30 years, more money (that is, more dollars) is needed to pay for a Saturday night date than in the past. By the way, the fact that prices are higher today does *not* imply that people are worse off today than in the past, because nominal wages and salaries have also risen substantially. In general, however, higher prices do imply that people need to keep a greater number of dollars available, in cash or in a checking account.

The Money Demand Curve

For the purposes of monetary policymaking, economists are most interested in the aggregate, or economywide, demand for money. The interaction of the aggregate demand for money, determined by the public, and the supply of money, which is set by the Fed, determines the nominal interest rate that prevails in the economy.

The economywide demand for money can be represented graphically by the *money demand curve* (see Figure 10.1). The **money demand curve** relates the aggregate quantity of money demanded M to the nominal interest rate i. The quantity of money demanded M is a nominal quantity, measured in dollars (or yen, or euros, depending on the country). Because an increase in the nominal interest rate increases the opportunity

money demand curve a curve that shows the relationship between the aggregate quantity of money demanded M and the nominal interest rate i

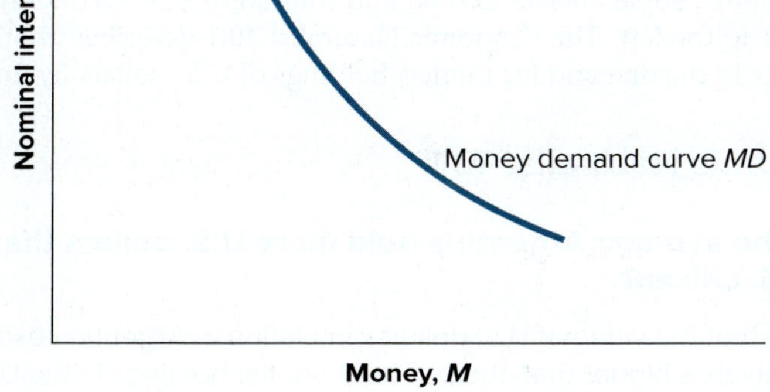

FIGURE 10.1

The Money Demand Curve. The money demand curve relates the economywide demand for money to the nominal interest rate. Because an increase in the nominal interest rate raises the opportunity cost of holding money, the money demand curve slopes downward.

FIGURE 10.2

A Shift in the Money Demand Curve.

At a given nominal interest rate, any change that makes people want to hold more money—such as an increase in the general price level or in real GDP—will shift the money demand curve to the right.

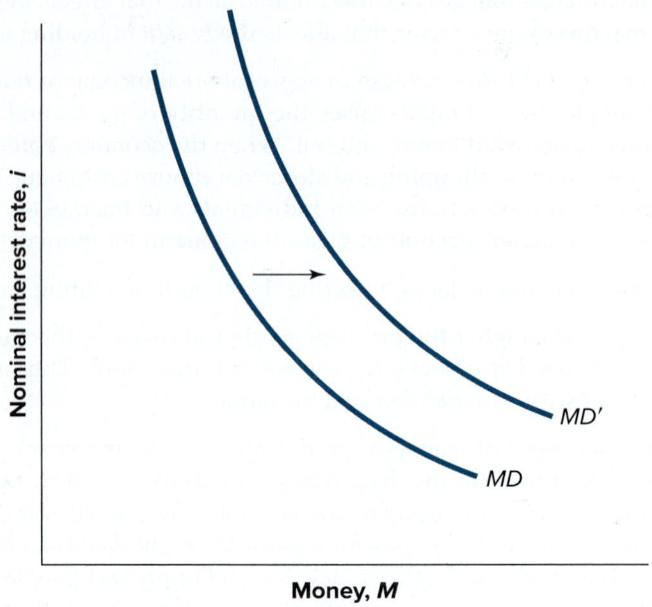

cost of holding money, which reduces the quantity of money demanded, the money demand curve slopes downward.

If we think of the nominal interest rate as the "price" (more precisely, the opportunity cost) of money and the amount of money people want to hold as the "quantity," the money demand curve is analogous to the demand curve for a good or service. As with a standard demand curve, the fact that a higher price of money leads people to demand less of it is captured in the downward slope of the demand curve. Furthermore, as in a standard demand curve, changes in factors other than the price of money (the nominal interest rate) can cause the demand curve for money to shift.

For a given nominal interest rate, any change that makes people want to hold more money will shift the money demand curve to the right, and any change that makes people want to hold less money will shift the money demand curve to the left. Thus, as in a standard demand curve, changes in factors other than the price of money (the nominal interest rate) cause the demand curve for money to shift. We have already identified two macroeconomic factors other than the nominal interest rate that affect the economywide demand for money: real output and the price level. Because an increase in either of these variables increases the demand for money, it shifts the money demand curve rightward, as shown in Figure 10.2. Similarly, a fall in real output or the general price level reduces money demand, shifting the money demand curve leftward.

The money demand curve may also shift in response to other changes that affect the cost or benefit of holding money, such as the technological and financial advances we mentioned earlier. For example, the introduction of ATMs reduced the amount of money people choose to hold and thus shifted the economywide money demand curve to the left. The Economic Naturalist 10.1 describes another potential source of shifts in the demand for money, holdings of U.S. dollars by foreigners.

The Economic Naturalist 10.1

Why does the average Argentine hold more U.S. dollars than the average U.S. citizen?

Estimates are that the value of U.S. dollars circulating in Argentina exceeds $1,000 per person, which is higher than the per capita dollar holdings in the United States. A number of other countries, including those that once belonged to the former Soviet Union, also hold large quantities of dollars. In all, as much as $600 billion in U.S. currency—about one-third of the total amount issued—may be circulating outside the borders of the United States. Why do Argentines and other non-U.S. residents hold so many dollars?

U.S. residents and businesses hold dollars primarily for transactions purposes, rather than as a store of value. As a store of value, interest-bearing bonds and dividend-paying stocks are a better choice for Americans than zero-interest money. But this is not necessarily the case for the citizens of other countries, particularly nations that are economically or politically unstable. Argentina, for example, endured many years of high and erratic inflation in the 1970s and 1980s, which sharply eroded the value of financial investments denominated in Argentine pesos. Lacking better alternatives, many Argentines began saving in the form of U.S. currency—dollar bills hidden in the mattress or plastered into the wall—which they correctly believed to be more stable in value than peso-denominated assets.

connect

▶ Visit your instructor's Connect course and access your eBook to view this video.

Why does the average Argentine citizen hold more U.S. dollars than the average U.S. citizen?

Argentina's use of dollars became officially recognized in 1990. In that year, the country instituted a new monetary system, called a currency board, under which U.S. dollars and Argentine pesos by law traded freely one for one. Under the currency board system, Argentines became accustomed to carrying U.S. dollars in their wallets for transaction purposes, along with pesos. However, in 2001 Argentina's monetary problems returned with a vengeance as the currency board system broke down, the peso plummeted in value relative to the dollar, and inflation returned. In the past few years, inflation in Argentina has been estimated to be between 25 and 55 percent. (For a while, the government's official inflation figures were not considered reliable.) The Argentine demand for dollars is thus likely only to increase in the next few years.

The African nation of Zimbabwe provides another example. After years of hyperinflation and price speculation, the Zimbabwean dollar was effectively abandoned as an official currency on April 12, 2009. This followed a year when the growth in the money supply rose from 81,143 percent to 658 billion percent from January to December, and an egg was reportedly selling for Z$50 billion. On January 29, 2014, the Zimbabwe central bank announced that the U.S. dollar would be one of several foreign currencies that would be accepted as legal currency within that country. (The central bank introduced a new Zimbabwean dollar in 2019.)

Feije Riemersma/Alamy Stock Photo

Some countries, including a number of those formed as a result of the breakup of the Soviet Union, have endured not only high inflation, but political instability and uncertainty as well. In a politically volatile environment, citizens face the risk that their savings, including their bank deposits, will be confiscated or heavily taxed by the government. Often they conclude that a hidden cache of U.S. dollars—an estimated $1 million in 100-dollar bills can be stored in a suitcase—is the safest way to hold wealth. Indeed, such wealth in a relatively small container is one reason international criminals, most notably drug dealers, allegedly hold so many $100 bills. Now that the European currency, the euro (€), which is worth more than $1, can be held in the form of a €500 banknote, it has been suggested that drug dealers and other cash-hoarders have been switching to holding €500 bills in even smaller suitcases. Concerned by this possibility, the European Central Bank announced in 2016 that it would phase out the €500 note and, since April 2019, the note has no longer been issued. This may further increase the demand for dollars.

In practice, changes in the foreign demand for U.S. dollars are an important source of fluctuation in the U.S. money demand curve. During periods of war, instability, or financial stress, foreign holdings of dollars tend to go up. Such increases in the demand for dollars shifts the U.S. money demand curve substantially to the right, as in Figure 10.2. Because policymakers at the Federal Reserve are concerned primarily with the number of dollars circulating in the U.S. economy, rather than in the world as a whole, they pay close attention to these international flows of greenbacks.

The Supply of Money and Money Market Equilibrium

Where there is demand, can supply be far behind? As we have discussed, for now we assume that the *supply* of money is determined by the supply of reserves, and hence is fully controlled by the central bank—in the United States, the Federal Reserve, or Fed. Historically, the Fed's primary tool for controlling the money supply is *open-market operations*. For example, to increase the money supply, the Fed can use newly created money to buy government bonds from the public (an open-market purchase), which puts the new money into circulation.

Figure 10.3 shows the demand for and the supply of money in a single diagram. The nominal interest rate is on the vertical axis, and the nominal quantity of money (in dollars) is on the horizontal axis. As we have seen, because a higher nominal interest rate increases the opportunity cost of holding money, the money demand curve slopes downward. And because the Fed fixes the supply of money, we have drawn the *money supply curve* as a vertical line that intercepts the horizontal axis at the quantity of money chosen by the Fed, denoted M.

As in standard supply and demand analysis, equilibrium in the market for money occurs at the intersection of the supply and demand curves, shown as point E in Figure 10.3. The equilibrium amount of money in circulation, M, is simply the amount of money the Fed chooses to supply. The equilibrium nominal interest rate i is the interest rate at which the quantity of money demanded by the public, as determined by the money demand curve, equals the fixed supply of money made available by the Fed.

To understand how the market for money reaches equilibrium, it may be helpful to recall the relationship between interest rates and the market price of bonds that was introduced in Chapter 8, *Money, the Federal Reserve, and Global Financial Markets.* As we saw in the earlier chapter, the prices of existing bonds are *inversely related* to the current interest rate. Higher interest rates imply lower bond prices, and lower interest rates imply higher bond prices. With this relationship between interest rates and bond prices in mind, let's ask what happens if, say, the nominal interest rate is initially below the equilibrium level in the market for money—for example, at a value such as i' in Figure 10.3. At that interest rate the public's demand for money is M', which is greater than the actual amount of money in circulation, equal to M. How will the public—households and firms—react if the amount of money they hold is less than they would like? To increase their

FIGURE 10.3

Equilibrium in the Market for Money.

Equilibrium in the market for money occurs at point *E*, where the demand for money by the public equals the amount of money supplied by the Federal Reserve. The equilibrium nominal interest rate, which equates the supply of and demand for money, is *i*.

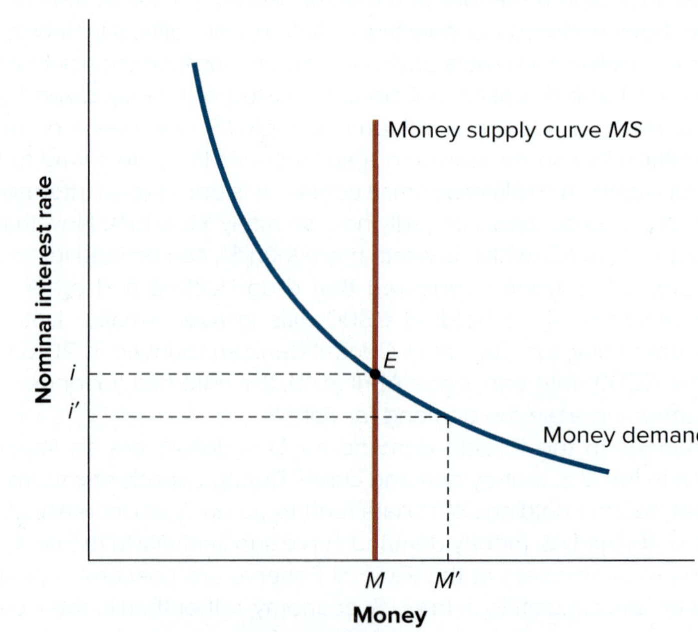

holdings of money, people will try to sell some of the interest-bearing assets they hold, such as bonds. But if everyone is trying to sell bonds and there are no willing buyers, then all the attempt to reduce bond holdings will achieve is to drive down the price of bonds, in the same way that a glut of apples will drive down the price of apples.

A fall in the price of bonds, however, is equivalent to an increase in interest rates. Thus the public's collective attempt to increase its money holdings by selling bonds and other interest-bearing assets, which has the effect of lowering bond prices, also implies higher market interest rates. As interest rates rise, the quantity of money demanded by the public will decline (represented by a right-to-left movement along the money demand curve), as will the desire to sell bonds. Only when the interest rate reaches its equilibrium value, *i* in Figure 10.3, will people be content to hold the quantities of money and other assets that are actually available in the economy.

SELF-TEST 10.2

Describe the adjustment process in the market for money if the nominal interest rate is initially above rather than below its equilibrium value. What happens to the price of bonds as the money market adjusts toward equilibrium?

RECAP

MONEY DEMAND AND SUPPLY

- For the economy as a whole, the demand for money is the amount of wealth that individuals, households, and businesses choose to hold in the form of money. The opportunity cost of holding money is measured by the nominal interest rate *i*, which is the return that could be earned on alternative assets such as bonds. The benefit of holding money is its usefulness in transactions.
- Increases in real GDP (*Y*) or the price level (*P*) raise the nominal volume of transactions and thus the economywide demand for money. The demand for money is also affected by technological and financial innovations, such as the introduction of ATMs, that affect the costs or benefits of holding money.
- The money demand curve relates the economywide demand for money to the nominal interest rate. Because an increase in the nominal interest rate raises the opportunity cost of holding money, the money demand curve slopes downward.
- Changes in factors other than the nominal interest rate that affect the demand for money can shift the money demand curve. For example, increases in real GDP or the price level raise the demand for money, shifting the money demand curve to the right, whereas decreases shift the money demand curve to the left.
- In the market for money, the money demand curve slopes downward, reflecting the fact that a higher nominal interest rate increases the opportunity cost of holding money and thus reduces the amount of money people want to hold. The money supply curve is vertical at the quantity of money that the Fed chooses to supply. The equilibrium nominal interest rate *i* is the interest rate at which the quantity of money demanded by the public equals the fixed supply of money made available by the Fed.

How the Fed Controls the Nominal Interest Rate

We began this chapter by noting that the public and the press usually talk about Fed policy in terms of decisions about the nominal interest rate rather than the money supply. Indeed, Fed policymakers themselves usually describe their plans in terms of

FIGURE 10.4

The Fed Lowers the Nominal Interest Rate.

The Fed can lower the equilibrium nominal interest rate by increasing the supply of money. For the given money demand curve, an increase in the money supply from *M* to *M′* shifts the equilibrium point in the money market from *E* to *F*, lowering the equilibrium nominal interest rate from *i* to *i′*.

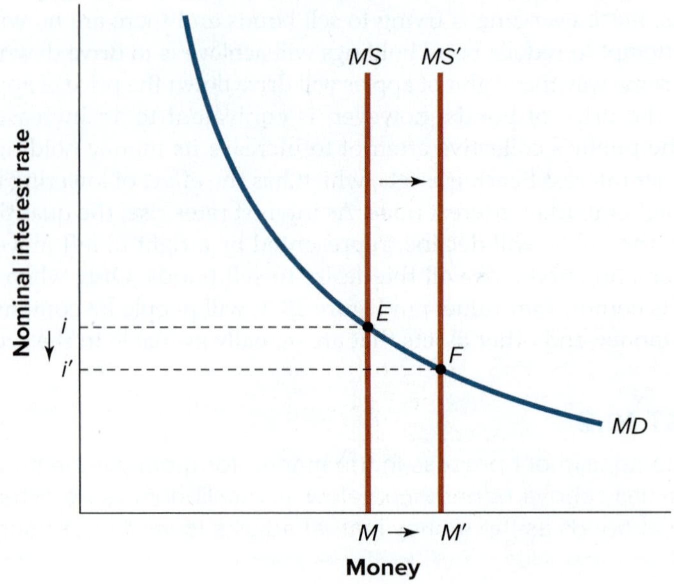

a target value (or a narrow target range) for the interest rate. We now have the necessary background to understand how the Fed translates the ability to determine the economy's money supply into control of the nominal interest rate.

Figure 10.3 showed that the nominal interest rate is determined by equilibrium in the market for money. Let's suppose that for some reason the Fed decides to lower the interest rate. As we will see, to lower the interest rate the Fed must increase the supply of money, which can be accomplished by using newly created money to purchase government bonds from the public (an open-market purchase).

Figure 10.4 shows the effects of such an increase in the money supply by the Fed. If the initial money supply is *M*, then equilibrium in the money market occurs at point *E* in the figure, and the equilibrium nominal interest rate is *i*. Now suppose the Fed, by means of open-market purchases of bonds, increases the money supply to *M′*. This increase in the money supply shifts the vertical money supply curve to the right, which shifts the equilibrium in the money market from point *E* to point *F* (see Figure 10.4). Note that at point *F* the equilibrium nominal interest rate has declined, from *i* to *i′*. The nominal interest rate must decline if the public is to be persuaded to hold the extra money that has been injected into the economy.

To understand what happens in financial markets when the Fed expands the money supply, recall once again the inverse relationship between interest rates and the price of bonds. To increase the money supply, the Fed must buy government bonds from the public. However, if households and firms are initially satisfied with their asset holdings, they will be willing to sell bonds only at a price that is higher than the initial price. That is, the Fed's bond purchases will drive up the price of bonds in the open market. But we know that higher bond prices imply lower interest rates. Thus the Fed's bond purchases lower the prevailing nominal interest rate.

A similar scenario unfolds if the Fed decides to raise interest rates. To raise interest rates, the Fed must *reduce* the money supply. Reduction of the money supply is accomplished by an open-market sale—the sale of government bonds to the public in exchange for money.[3] (The Fed keeps a large inventory of government bonds,

[3]The sale of existing government bonds by the Federal Reserve in an open-market sale should not be confused with the sale of newly issued government bonds by the Treasury when it finances government budget deficits. Whereas open-market sales reduce the money supply, Treasury sales of new bonds do not affect the money supply. The difference arises because the Federal Reserve does not put the money it receives in an open-market sale back into circulation, leaving less money for the public to hold. In contrast, the Treasury puts the money it receives from selling newly issued bonds back into circulation as it purchases goods and services.

acquired through previous open-market purchases, for use in open-market operations.) But in the attempt to sell bonds on the open market, the Fed will drive down the price of bonds. Given the inverse relationship between the price of bonds and the interest rate, the fall in bond prices is equivalent to a rise in the interest rate. In terms of money demand and money supply, the higher interest rate is necessary to persuade the public to hold less money.

As Figures 10.3 and 10.4 illustrate, control of the interest rate is not separate from control of the money supply. If Fed officials choose to set the nominal interest rate at a particular level, they can do so only by setting the money supply at a level consistent with the target interest rate. The Fed *cannot* set the interest rate and the money supply independently, since for any given money demand curve, a particular interest rate implies a particular size of the money supply, and vice versa.

Since monetary policy actions can be expressed in terms of either the interest rate or the money supply, why does the Fed (and almost every other central bank) choose to communicate its policy decisions to the public in terms of a target nominal interest rate rather than a target money supply? One reason, as we will see shortly, is that the main effects of monetary policy on both the economy and financial markets are exerted through interest rates. Consequently, the interest rate is often the best summary of the overall impact of the Fed's actions. Another reason for focusing on interest rates is that they are more familiar to the public than the money supply. Finally, interest rates can be monitored continuously in the financial markets, which makes the effects of Fed policies on interest rates easy to observe. By contrast, measuring the amount of money in the economy requires collecting data on bank deposits, with the consequence that several weeks may pass before policymakers and the public know precisely how Fed actions have affected the money supply.

The Role of the Federal Funds Rate in Monetary Policy

Although thousands of interest rates are used throughout the economy and are easily available, the interest rate that is perhaps most closely watched by the public, politicians, the media, and the financial markets is the *federal funds rate*.

The **federal funds rate** is the interest rate commercial banks charge each other for very short-term (usually overnight) loans. For example, a bank that has insufficient reserves to meet its legal reserve requirements might borrow reserves for a few days from a bank that has extra reserves (we return to the topic of reserve requirements in the next section). Despite its name, the federal funds rate is not an official government interest rate and is not connected to the federal government.

federal funds rate the interest rate that commercial banks charge each other for very short-term (usually overnight) loans

Because the market for loans between commercial banks is tiny compared to some other financial markets, such as the market for government bonds, one might expect the federal funds rate to be of little interest to anyone other than the managers of commercial banks. But enormous attention is paid to this interest rate, because over most of the past half-century, the Fed has expressed its policies in terms of a target value for it (since December 2008, the target is actually a narrow range of values). Indeed, at the close of every meeting of the Federal Open Market Committee, the Fed announces whether the federal funds rate will be increased, decreased, or left unchanged. The Fed may also indicate the likely direction of future changes in the federal funds rate. Thus more than any other financial variable, changes in the federal funds rate indicate the Fed's plans for monetary policy.[4]

Why does the Fed choose to focus on this particular nominal interest rate over all others? As we saw in Chapter 8, *Money, the Federal Reserve, and Global Financial Markets,* historically, the Fed affected the money supply through its control of bank reserves, which made the Fed's control over the federal funds rate particularly tight. Today, after decades of using this particular interest rate as the Fed's main policy

[4]The Federal Open Market Committee's announcements are available on the Federal Reserve's website, www.federalreserve.gov.

FIGURE 10.5

The Federal Funds Rate, 1970–2020.

The federal funds rate is the interest rate commercial banks charge each other for short-term loans. It is closely watched because the Fed expresses its policies in terms of a target for the federal funds rate. The Fed has allowed the federal funds rate to vary considerably in response to economic conditions.

Source: Federal Reserve Bank of St. Louis, https://fred.stlouisfed.org/series/FEDFUNDS.

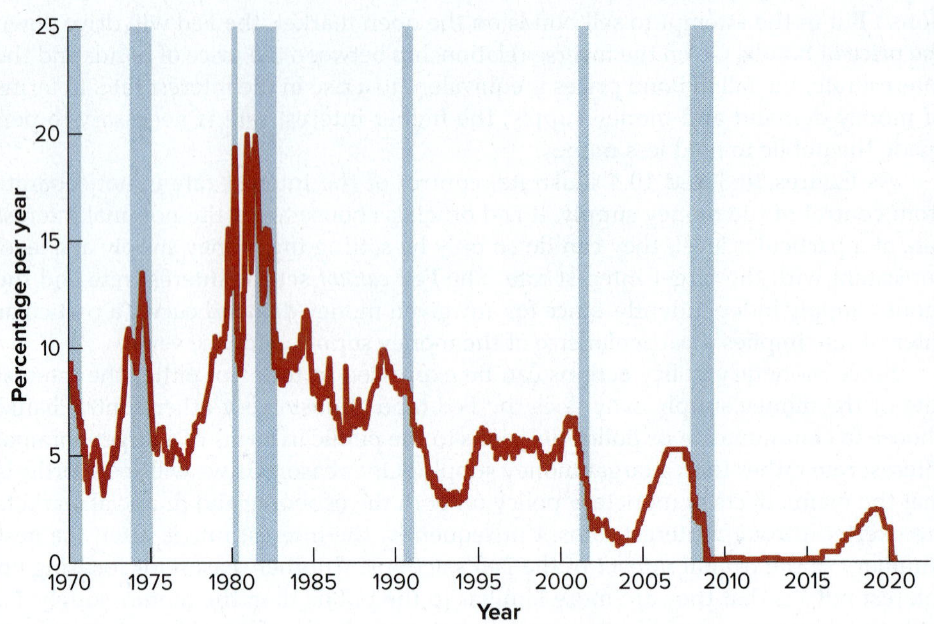

tool, the public has gotten used to it, which is one reason to keep using it. However, if Fed officials chose to do so, they could probably signal their intended policies just as effectively in terms of another short-term nominal interest rate, such as the rate on short-term government debt.

Figure 10.5 shows the behavior of the federal funds rate since 1970 (as usual, shaded areas correspond to recessions). As you can see, the Fed has allowed this interest rate to vary considerably in response to economic conditions. Note, however, how the federal funds rate has remained close to zero since the end of 2008—in fact, it has been effectively *at* zero in most years since. That is, it has remained both considerably lower and more stable than in the preceding four decades shown here. Later in the chapter we will consider two specific episodes in which the Fed changed the federal funds rate in response to an economic slowdown, and we will also discuss the situation since 2008.

Can the Fed Control the Real Interest Rate?

Through its control of the money supply the Fed can control the economy's *nominal* interest rate. But many important economic decisions, such as the decisions to save and invest, depend on the *real* interest rate. To affect those decisions, the Fed must exert some control over the real interest rate.

Most economists believe that the Fed can control the real interest rate, at least for some period. To see why, recall the definition of the real interest rate from Chapter 7, *Saving and Capital Formation*

$$r = i - \pi.$$

The real interest rate r equals the nominal interest rate i minus the rate of inflation π. As we have seen, the Fed can control the nominal interest rate quite precisely through its ability to determine the money supply. Furthermore, inflation appears to change relatively slowly in response to changes in policy or economic conditions, for reasons we will discuss in the next chapter. Because inflation tends to adjust slowly, actions by the Fed to change the nominal interest rate generally lead the real interest rate to change by about the same amount.

The idea that the Fed can set the real interest rate appears to contradict the analysis in Chapter 7, which concluded that the real interest rate is determined by the condition that national saving must equal investment in new capital goods. This apparent contradiction is rooted in a difference in the time frame being considered. Because inflation does not adjust quickly, the Fed can control the real interest rate over the short run. In the long run, however—that is, over periods of several years or more—the inflation rate and other economic variables will adjust, and the balance of saving and investment will determine the real interest rate. Thus the Fed's ability to influence consumption and investment spending through its control of the real interest rate is strongest in the short run.

In discussing the Fed's control over interest rates, we should also return to a point mentioned earlier in this chapter: In reality, not just one but many thousands of interest rates are seen in the economy. Because interest rates tend to move together (allowing us to speak of *the* interest rate), an action by the Fed to change the federal funds rate generally causes other interest rates to change in the same direction. However, the tendency of other interest rates (such as the long-term government bond rate or the rate on bonds issued by corporations) to move in the same direction as the federal funds rate is only a tendency, not an exact relationship. In practice, then, the Fed's control of other interest rates may be somewhat less precise than its control of the federal funds rate—a fact that complicates the Fed's policymaking. In the next section we will discuss what the Fed has been doing since 2008 to lower those other interest rates through channels other than the traditional channel of lowering the federal funds rate.

RECAP

THE FEDERAL RESERVE AND INTEREST RATES

- The Federal Reserve controls the nominal interest rate by changing the supply of money. An open-market purchase of government bonds increases the money supply and lowers the equilibrium nominal interest rate. Conversely, an open-market sale of bonds reduces the money supply and increases the nominal interest rate. The Fed can prevent changes in the demand for money from affecting the nominal interest rate by adjusting the quantity of money supplied appropriately. The Fed typically expresses its policy intentions in terms of a target for a specific nominal interest rate, the federal funds rate.
- Because inflation is slow to adjust, in the short run the Fed can control the real interest rate (equal to the nominal interest rate minus the inflation rate) as well as the nominal interest rate. In the long run, however, the real interest rate is determined by the balance of saving and investment.

THE FEDERAL RESERVE AND INTEREST RATES: A CLOSER LOOK

To this point in the book, we have discussed the basic market for money and how it works. We have seen how, by controlling the supply of money, the Fed controls the nominal interest rate (the nominal price of money) and hence, in the short run, the real interest rate (the real price of money). To keep the discussion simple, we assumed that the Fed has full control over the money supply, and we assumed that the different interest rates in the economy move more or less together, allowing us to talk about *the* interest rate. In this section we take a closer look at the market for money, and see how it works in times when these assumptions hold less well. As an important example of such times, we discuss the Fed's monetary policy since the 2008 peak of the financial crisis.

Can the Fed Fully Control the Money Supply?

We have seen that central banks in general, and the Fed in particular, do not control the money supply directly. But we assumed that central banks can control the money supply *indirectly* by changing the supply of reserves that commercial banks hold. We will now look at this assumption more closely. In Chapter 8, *Money, the Federal Reserve, and Global Financial Markets,* we introduced Equation 8.2, which says

$$\text{Money supply} = \text{Currency held by public} + \frac{\text{Bank reserves}}{\text{Desired reserve-deposit ratio}}. \quad (10.1)$$

The equation shows that given a certain amount of currency that the public wants to hold, and given a certain reserve-deposit ratio that the banks desire to maintain, the central bank can control the money supply by controlling the amount of bank reserves. Let's assume for now that the amount of currency that the public wants to hold and the reserve-deposit ratio that the banks desire to maintain are fixed at their present levels. Then, to increase the money supply, the central bank has to increase bank reserves; to decrease the money supply, the central bank has to decrease bank reserves. Moreover, the equation suggests a simple relationship between any change in reserves and the resulting change in the money supply: for every $1 of change (increase or decrease) in reserves, the money supply would change by $1/(Desired reserve-deposit ratio). For example, if the desired reserve-deposit ratio is 5 percent (that is, 0.05), then an increase in reserves by $1 (initiated by the central bank) would increase the money supply by $1/0.05 = $20.

The Fed can increase and decrease reserves using different methods, as we will now discuss. We will also see that the Fed can directly affect the desired reserve-deposit ratio.

Affecting Bank Reserves through Open-Market Operations

How can the Fed increase and decrease bank reserves? So far we have emphasized its main tool, open-market operations. In an open-market purchase, the Fed buys securities and, effectively, sells reserves. In an open-market sale, the Fed sells securities and, effectively, buys back reserves. Hence, as we have seen, the Fed can change the quantity of reserves in the banking system through open-market operations.

Affecting Bank Reserves through Discount Window Lending

Another tool by which the Fed can affect bank reserves is called *discount window lending*. Recall that the cash or assets held by a commercial bank for the purpose of meeting depositor withdrawals are called its reserves. Its desired amount of reserves is equal to its deposits multiplied by the desired reserve-ratio (as implied by Equation 8.1 in Chapter 8). When individual commercial banks are short of reserves, they may choose to borrow reserves from the Fed. For historical reasons, lending of reserves by the Federal Reserve to commercial banks is called **discount window lending.** The interest rate that the Fed charges commercial banks that borrow reserves is called the **discount rate.** The Fed offers three discount window programs (called primary credit, secondary credit, and seasonal credit), each with its own interest rate; different depository institutions qualify for different programs. Loans of reserves by the Fed directly increase the quantity of reserves in the banking system.[5]

discount window lending the lending of reserves by the Federal Reserve to commercial banks

discount rate the interest rate that the Fed charges commercial banks to borrow reserves

Setting and Changing Reserve Requirements

As we have shown, the economy's money supply depends on three factors: the amount of currency the public chooses to hold, the supply of bank reserves, and the reserve-deposit ratio maintained by commercial banks. The reserve-deposit ratio is equal to total bank reserves divided by total deposits. If banks kept all of their deposits as reserves,

[5]Be careful not to confuse the discount rate and the federal funds rate. The discount rate is the interest rate commercial banks pay to the Fed; the federal funds rate is the interest rate commercial banks charge each other for short-term loans.

the reserve-deposit ratio would be 100 percent (that is, 1.00), and banks would not make any loans. As banks lend out more of their deposits, the reserve-deposit ratio falls.

For given quantities of currency held by the public and of reserves held by the banks, an increase in the reserve-deposit ratio reduces the money supply. A higher reserve-deposit ratio implies that banks lend out a smaller share of their deposits in each of the rounds of lending and redeposit, limiting the overall expansion of loans and deposits.

Within a certain range, commercial banks are free to set the reserve-deposit ratio they want to maintain. However, Congress granted the Fed the power to set minimum values of the reserve-deposit ratio for commercial banks. The legally required values of the reserve-deposit ratio set by the Fed are called **reserve requirements.**

reserve requirements set by the Fed, the minimum values of the ratio of bank reserves to bank deposits that commercial banks are allowed to maintain

Changes in reserve requirements can be used to affect the money supply, although the Fed does not usually use them in this way. For example, suppose that commercial banks are maintaining the legally mandated minimum of 3 percent reserve-deposit ratio, and the Fed wants to contract the money supply. By raising required reserves to, say, 5 percent of deposits, the Fed could force commercial banks to raise their reserve-deposit ratio, at least until it reached 5 percent. As you can verify by looking at Equation 10.1, an increase in the reserve-deposit ratio lowers deposits and the money supply. Similarly, a reduction in required reserves by the Fed might allow at least some banks to lower their ratio of reserves to deposits. A decline in the economywide reserve-deposit ratio would in turn cause the money supply to rise.

Excess Reserves: The Norm since 2008

We have seen that the Fed can effectively control bank reserves through tools that include open-market operations and discount window lending. We have also seen that the Fed can set reserve requirements. This, however, gives the Fed only partial control over the desired reserve-deposit ratio, leaving some control in the hands of commercial banks. Specifically, while reserve requirements prevent banks from maintaining reserve-deposit ratios *below* a minimum level, reserve requirements do not prevent banks from maintaining reserve-deposit ratios that are well *above* that minimum level. By letting their reserve-deposit ratios increase when the Fed increases the quantity of reserves, commercial banks can "absorb" at least part of the increases in reserves without increasing bank deposits. Indeed, commercial banks could, in principle, absorb the entire increase in reserves initiated by the Fed, fully offsetting the effects of increases in reserves on the noncurrency component of the money supply.[6]

Up to this point, we assumed that banks would always translate an addition in reserves initiated by the Fed into an addition in their deposits (rather than into an increase in their reserve-deposit ratios). This is a reasonable assumption; banks generally do behave this way. But there are situations when banks prefer to let their reserve-deposit ratios (and excess reserves) increase in response to an increase in reserves. For example, to protect themselves from bank runs in times of economic or financial uncertainty, banks may prefer to respond to an increase in reserves by letting their reserve-deposit ratios increase to levels significantly above the minimum level mandated by official reserve requirements. Another reason for banks to let increases in reserves increase their reserve-deposit ratio rather than increasing deposits in times of uncertainty is that in such times banks may find only limited lending opportunities that seem sufficiently safe.

excess reserves bank reserves in excess of the reserve requirements set by the central bank

Bank reserves that exceed the reserve requirements set by the central bank are called **excess reserves.** Excess reserves are thus reserves that the central bank

[6]You can verify this by looking again at the second term of Equation 10.1. This second term represents the noncurrency component of the money supply. While the Fed controls its numerator (bank reserves), it only partially controls its denominator (desired reserve-deposit ratio) because the Fed can set only a legally binding *minimum,* but not a maximum, on the denominator. Indeed, banks can choose to let the denominator increase when the Fed increases the numerator, breaking the simple link from increased reserves to increased money supply. Banks could in principle even let the denominator increase at the same pace as the numerator, keeping the second term of Equation 10.1 constant, and thus preventing the increase in reserves from having any effect on the money supply.

makes available to commercial banks, but that do not add to the money supply because commercial banks do not use them for making additional loans. Because excess reserves do not add to the money supply, they allow for the possibility that the money supply will not change in spite of the central bank increasing or decreasing the supply of reserves.

During the 20 years that ended in August 2008, excess reserves in the U.S. banking system averaged less than $2 billion on most months—a negligible amount, considering the size of the U.S. banking system. The only notable exception was a short period in 2001, immediately following the events of 9/11, during which excess reserves increased temporarily as the financial industry was reeling from the effects of the terrorist attack on New York City. Since August 2008, however, things have changed dramatically. As the Fed injected unprecedented amounts of reserves into the system in its attempt to bring interest rates down, excess reserves grew to around $800 billion by the end of the year, and kept growing in the following years until they peaked in 2014 at more than $2.5 trillion, or almost 15 percent of GDP (for comparison, in 2014 the monetary aggregate M1 was about 16 percent of GDP). Excess reserves decreased in subsequent years, reaching around $1.3 trillion by late 2019—still a hefty sum. In early 2020, excess reserves shot up again, as the Fed injected large amounts of reserves into the system in its fight against the COVID-19 economic fallout.

The Fed's actions in 2008 and subsequent years were successful in reducing the price of money and increasing its supply, helping prevent another Great Depression (The Economic Naturalist 8.2 discussed the shrinking of the money supply during the Great Depression). As you can verify from Equation 10.1, for the money supply to increase as a result of the Fed-initiated increase in the quantity of reserves, the reserve-deposit ratio had to increase more slowly than the increase in the quantity of reserves. Indeed, while since 2008 banks absorbed much of the increase in reserves initiated by the Fed, they did not absorb it all, and some of it led to increases in the money supply.

We have seen, then, that the Fed does not always fully control the money supply. But even in times of great uncertainty, the Fed can still strongly *affect* the money supply through the Fed's control of the supply of reserves. The basic money-market model's assumption—that the Fed controls the money supply—should therefore be viewed as a useful simplifying assumption even in times when it does not hold exactly.

We now take a closer look at the other simplifying assumption made in the basic money-market model: that interest rates move together.

RECAP

CAN THE FED FULLY CONTROL THE MONEY SUPPLY?

- The Fed can effectively control the amount of bank reserves through tools that include open-market operations and discount window lending. The Fed can also set reserve requirements (a legally binding minimum on banks' reserve-deposit ratio). This however gives the Fed only partial control over the money supply. In particular, a Fed-initiated increase in bank reserves will not lead to an increase in the money supply if banks absorbed the increase in reserves by letting their reserve-deposit ratios increase at the same pace.
- In certain times banks may choose to let their reserve-deposit ratio increase substantially above the reserve requirements set by the Fed. Indeed, since 2008, banks have accumulated unprecedented amounts of excess reserves, that is, of reserves in excess of reserve requirements. While this broke the simple link between an increase in reserves and an increase in the money supply, the Fed was still successful in increasing the money supply.
- We conclude that the basic money-market model's assumption—that the Fed controls the money supply—should be viewed as a useful simplifying assumption even in times when it does not hold exactly.

Do Interest Rates Always Move Together?

To this point in the discussion, we have assumed that the many different nominal interest rates in the economy move more or less together, allowing us to speak of *the* interest rate. Like the assumption that banks do not hold significant amounts of excess reserves, the assumption that interest rates move more or less together is a reasonably accurate description of the market for money during most times, but not always. In particular, this assumption has held less well since 2008.

The Zero Lower Bound and the Need for "Unconventional" Monetary Policy

Earlier in this chapter, we presented Figure 10.5, which shows the federal funds rate from 1970 to 2020. Until December 2008, the Fed's main tool for conducting monetary policy was open-market operations aimed at increasing and decreasing the federal funds rate in accordance with the Fed's target rate. Other interest rates in the economy, which are typically higher than the federal funds rate due to a combination of higher risk and longer maturity, were expected to move up and down more or less together with the federal funds rate. But in December 2008 the Fed reduced its target for the federal funds rate to the range 0 to $\frac{1}{4}$ percent, effectively hitting what is called the **zero lower bound.** Attempting to stimulate the economy by reducing the federal funds rate further was no longer a viable option, because interest rates cannot in general be much below zero. (A negative nominal interest rate would mean that lending institutions pay borrowing institutions to hold their money—something lending institutions would not normally do.)

zero lower bound a level, close to zero, below which the Fed cannot further reduce short-term interest rates

The federal funds rate remained effectively zero in the years following December 2008 (Figure 10.5). But other interest rates in the economy remained significantly above zero during that period. For example, the nominal interest rate on 10-year debt issued by the U.S. government was in the range 1.5 to 4 percent between 2009 and 2015. After December 2008, the Fed could no longer effectively reduce the different interest rates in the economy that were still above zero by reducing the federal funds rate (which was already at its zero lower bound) and "pulling" other rates down with it. To keep stimulating the economy by making money cheaper, the Fed had to turn to less conventional methods: targeting such higher interest rates more directly. We now discuss some of these new methods the Fed used.

Quantitative Easing

You are already familiar with one way for making money more cheaply available: open-market operations. Following the financial crisis, the Fed engaged in a specific type of such operations, referred to as *large-scale asset purchase programs* (LSAPs). These programs, aimed to help in bringing down longer-term interest rates once the federal funds rate was already at (or close to) its zero lower bound, are examples of what is known as *quantitative easing*. **Quantitative easing (QE)** refers to a central bank buying specified amounts of financial assets from commercial banks and other private financial institutions, thereby lowering the yield or return of those assets while increasing the money supply. Quantitative easing basically includes the same steps as regular open-market purchases, but is distinguished from these regular purchases in the type and term of the financial assets purchased as well as in the overall goal of the policy. While conventional expansionary policy usually involves the purchase of short-term government bonds in order to keep interest rates at a specified target value, quantitative easing is used by central banks to stimulate the economy by purchasing assets of longer maturity, thereby lowering longer-term interest rates.

quantitative easing (QE) an expansionary monetary policy in which a central bank buys long-term financial assets, thereby lowering the yield or return of those assets while increasing the money supply

Since the peak of the financial crisis in 2008, the Federal Reserve has expanded its balance sheet dramatically, adding trillions of dollars' worth of longer-term treasury notes and mortgage-backed securities (MBS) through several rounds of quantitative easing. Under special emergency conditions, when credit markets are not working properly, the Fed's purchases have also included private debt and securities, as was the case when the Fed announced programs to lend to businesses during the coronavirus crisis of 2020.

In short, by purchasing *longer-term* assets (including bonds and other debt) the Fed increased the amount of bank reserves while exerting downward pressure on longer-term interest rates (recall that bond prices and interest rates are inversely related). And by purchasing specific *types* of assets—such as debt related to mortgages—the Fed could help decrease interest rates in specific markets—such as mortgage and housing markets that were hit particularly hard during the financial crisis.

Forward Guidance

forward guidance information that a central bank provides to the financial markets regarding its expected future monetary-policy path

Quantitative easing helps lower long-term interest rates in the economy through open-market purchases. Another means for lowering long-term rates is known as **forward guidance.** The idea behind it is simple: by guiding markets regarding the central bank's future intentions, the central bank can influence long-term interest rates because these rates are affected by what market participants believe the central bank will do in the future. To illustrate this, imagine that financial markets believe that short-term interest rates, currently at around zero, will remain close to zero for several more years. Then the market price of a three-year bond, for example, will be such that the implied interest rate (or yield, or return) on the bond is close to zero. But if financial markets believed that short-term interest rates, while currently at zero, were about to increase dramatically in the next few months and stay elevated for several years, then a three-year bond's current price would reflect these beliefs, and hence the implied interest rate on the bond would be much higher.

In its September 2015 meeting, for example, the Federal Open Market Committee (FOMC) decided to keep the federal funds rate at its 0 to $\frac{1}{4}$ percent target range—that is, effectively at its zero lower bound. The FOMC's statement following the meeting included sentences such as this: "The Committee currently anticipates that, . . . economic conditions may, for some time, warrant keeping the target federal funds rate below levels the Committee views as normal in the longer run." On the Fed's website, it was further explained how such forward guidance is expected to support economic recovery:[7]

> Through "forward guidance," the Federal Open Market Committee provides an indication to households, businesses, and investors about the stance of monetary policy expected to prevail in the future. By providing information about how long the Committee expects to keep the target for the federal funds rate exceptionally low, the forward guidance language can put downward pressure on longer-term interest rates and thereby lower the cost of credit for households and businesses and also help improve broader financial conditions.

The Fed returned to forward guidance in 2020, as part of its response to the COVID-19 pandemic. In its March 15, 2020, meeting statement, the FOMC announced that the federal funds rate was again cut to a 0-to-¼ percent target range. The statement then read: "The Committee expects to maintain this target range until it is confident that the economy has weathered recent events and is on-track to achieve its maximum employment and price stability goals." Six months later, in its September 16, 2020, statement, the FOMC extended its forward guidance still further into the future, citing more stringent conditions before it would raise its target range:

[7]"How Does Forward Guidance about the Federal Reserve's Target for the Federal Funds Rate Support the Economic Recovery?," updated September 17, 2015, www.federalreserve.gov/monetarypolicy/fomcminutes 20150917.htm.

"The Committee decided to keep the target range for the federal funds rate at 0-to-¼ percent and expects it will be appropriate to maintain this target range until labor market conditions have reach levels consistent with the Committee's assessments of maximum employment and inflation has risen to 2 percent and is on track to moderately exceed 2 percent for some time."

Interest on Reserves and the New Tools of Monetary Policy

We have seen that starting in 2008 and continuing in the following years, the Fed took unprecedented steps to support the economy and help it recover from a historically deep global recession. The close-to-zero federal funds rate, the several rounds of quantitative easing (or large-scale asset purchases) and the resulting massive amounts of excess reserves, and other policies such as forward guidance were an unusual combination, designed for unusual times. At the time, these policies were viewed as temporary, unconventional methods for addressing temporary, unusual problems. As time passed, however, the reality of low interest rates and large amounts of assets held by the Fed has been increasingly recognized as "a new normal"—a situation that is here to stay. Accordingly, many economists have changed their view of these methods, thinking of them less as "unconventional" and more simply as new tools of monetary policy.

In late 2015—after more than seven years with the federal funds rate at the zero lower bound (see Figure 10.5), and with around four times the amount of assets that the Fed held seven years earlier—the Fed concluded that it was time to start raising interest rates again, slowly and cautiously, as the recovery from the Great Recession was well under way. To raise the federal funds rate without first engaging in a large-scale asset sale, the Fed's main channel has been to increase the interest rate it pays banks on the reserves they hold with the Fed. These include banks' required reserves (reserves held with the Fed in order to meet the required reserve-deposit ratios) and banks' excess reserves. The Fed paid an interest rate of $\frac{1}{4}$ percent on required and excess reserve balances between 2008 and 2015. When the Fed started raising this interest rate in December 2015, the federal funds rate started rising with it, because banks have little incentive to lend their excess reserves to other banks at rates below the rate they get on these reserves from the Fed.[8]

Figure 10.5 shows that after several years of slow increases, the federal funds rate reached rates just above 2.25 percent in 2019. Then, in light of increasing uncertainties in the global economy during 2019, the Fed reversed its trend, and by year-end it had reduced the rate to below 1.75 percent. When COVID-19 hit the U.S. economy in early 2020, the Fed quickly cut the rate to close to zero. With the federal funds rate at its zero lower bound again, the Fed's new tools of monetary policy were again taking center stage—at an unprecedented scale and pace. As discussed above, in March 2020 the Fed announced new quantitative easing rounds and several new lending programs that were expected to increase its balance sheet by several trillion dollars. It also emphasized forward guidance.

As we discussed in the previous section, such movements in nominal interest rates translate, in the short run, to movements in real interest rates. We now turn to discuss how movements in real interest rates affect the economy. As in the rest of the book, we return to our simplifying assumption that the different interest rates in the economy move more or less together, as the basic money-market model assumes.

[8]The federal funds rate can be somewhat below the interest rate that the Fed pays on reserves because some nonbank financial institutions are not eligible to earn interest on the balances they keep with the Fed and, therefore, have incentives to lend reserves at rates below the Fed's interest rate on reserves. However, as banks can profit by borrowing from such institutions and then receiving interest from the Fed on the borrowed reserves, the price of these reserves—the federal funds rate—is bid up until it is closely below the Fed's interest rate on reserves. In addition, the Fed can offer to borrow directly from such institutions (through an arrangement called a reverse repurchase agreement), reducing their incentives to lend out reserves at rates below the rates offered by the Fed.

RECAP

DO INTEREST RATES ALWAYS MOVE TOGETHER?

- The zero lower bound is a level, close to zero, below which the Fed cannot further reduce short-term interest rates. After December 2008, the Fed could no longer reduce the different interest rates in the economy that were still above zero by reducing the federal funds rate, because the federal funds rate had reached its zero lower bound.
- To keep stimulating the economy after December 2008, the Fed had to turn to less conventional methods that are aimed at lowering higher interest rates more directly. These included quantitative easing (formally, large-scale asset purchase programs) and forward guidance.
- The federal funds rate remained effectively zero from 2008 to 2015. When the Fed concluded, in late 2015, that the time to start tightening monetary policy has come, the Fed started increasing the interest rate it pays banks on the reserves they hold with the Fed. These include banks' required reserves (reserves held with the Fed in order to meet the required reserve-deposit ratios) and banks' excess reserves. That is, the Fed's main policy tool from late 2015 to early 2020 was again moving the federal funds rate, a short-term interest rate.
- As the COVID-19 pandemic hit the U.S. economy, the Fed reacted promptly and decisively. In March 2020 the Fed quickly reduced both short-term interest rates (to the zero lower bound) and long-term interest rates (using its new tools such as quantitative easing and forward guidance). It also greatly expanded its lending facilities, and provided credit easing in several markets.

THE EFFECTS OF FEDERAL RESERVE ACTIONS ON THE ECONOMY

Now that we have seen how the Fed can influence interest rates (both nominal and real), we can consider how monetary policy can be used to eliminate output gaps and stabilize the economy. The basic idea is relatively straightforward. As we will see in this section, aggregate expenditure is affected by the level of real interest rate prevailing in the economy. Specifically, a lower real interest rate encourages higher planned spending by households and firms, while a higher real interest rate reduces spending. By adjusting the real interest rate, the Fed can move planned spending in the desired direction. Under the assumption of the basic Keynesian model that firms produce just enough goods and services to meet the demand for their output, the Fed's stabilization of planned spending leads to stabilization of aggregate output and employment as well. In this section we will first explain how aggregate expenditure is related to the real interest rate. Then we will show how the Fed can use changes in the real interest rate to fight a recession or inflation.

Aggregate Expenditure and the Real Interest Rate

In Chapter 9, *Short-Term Economic Fluctuations and Fiscal Policy,* we saw how spending is affected by changes in real output Y. Changes in output affect the private sector's disposable income ($Y - T$), which in turn influences consumption spending–a relationship captured by the consumption function.

A second variable that has potentially important effects on aggregate expenditure is the real interest rate r. In Chapter 8, *Money, the Federal Reserve, and Global*

Financial Markets, in our discussion of saving and investment, we saw that the real interest rate influences the behavior of both households and firms.

For households, the effect of a higher real interest rate is to increase the reward for saving, which leads households to save more.[9] At a given level of income, households can save more only if they consume less. Thus, saying that a higher real interest rate *increases* saving is the same as saying that a higher real interest rate *reduces* consumption spending at each level of income. The idea that higher real interest rates reduce household spending makes intuitive sense. Think, for example, about people's willingness to buy consumer durables, such as automobiles or furniture. Purchases of consumer durables, which are part of consumption spending, are often financed by borrowing from a bank, credit union, or finance company. When the real interest rate rises, the monthly finance charges associated with the purchase of a car or a piano are higher, and people become less willing or able to make the purchase. Thus a higher real interest rate reduces people's willingness to spend on consumer goods, holding constant disposable income and other factors that affect consumption.

When the real interest rate rises, financing a new car becomes more expensive and fewer cars are purchased.

Besides reducing consumption spending, a higher real interest rate also discourages firms from making capital investments. As in the case of a consumer thinking of buying a car or a piano, when a rise in the real interest rate increases financing costs, firms may reconsider their plans to invest. For example, upgrading a computer system may be profitable for a manufacturing firm when the cost of the system can be financed by borrowing at a real interest rate of 3 percent. However, if the real interest rate rises to 6 percent, doubling the cost of funds to the firm, the same upgrade may not be profitable and the firm may choose not to invest. We should also remember that residential investment—the building of houses and apartment buildings—is also part of investment spending. Higher interest rates, in the form of higher mortgage rates, certainly discourage this kind of investment spending as well.

The conclusion is that, at any given level of output, *both consumption spending and investment spending decline when the real interest rate increases*. Conversely, a fall in the real interest rate tends to stimulate consumption and investment spending by reducing financing costs. Example 10.3 is a numerical illustration of how aggregate expenditure can be related to the real interest rate and output.

EXAMPLE 10.3 Aggregate Expenditure, the Real Interest Rate, and Short-Run Equilibrium Output

How does the interest rate affect aggregate expenditure and short-run equilibrium output?

In a certain economy, the components of spending are given by

$$C = 640 + 0.8(Y - T) - 400r,$$
$$I = 250 - 600r,$$
$$G = 300,$$
$$NX = 20,$$
$$T = 250.$$

Find the relationship of aggregate expenditure and output Y to the real interest rate r in this economy.

In this example the real interest rate r is allowed to affect both consumption and investment. For example, the final term in the equation describing consumption,

[9]Because a higher real interest rate also reduces the amount households must put aside to reach a given savings target, the net effect of a higher real interest rate on saving is theoretically ambiguous. However, empirical evidence suggests that higher real interest rates have a modest positive effect on saving.

$-400r$, implies that a 1 percent (0.01) increase in the real interest rate, from 4 percent to 5 percent, for example, reduces consumption spending by $400(0.01) = 4$ units. Similarly, the final term in the equation for investment tells us that in this example, a 1 percent increase in the real interest rate lowers investment by $600(0.01) = 6$ units. Thus the initial overall effect of a 1 percent increase in the real interest rate is to lower aggregate expenditure by 10 units, the sum of the effects on consumption and investment. (Remember that this is only the *initial* overall effect. As we will see shortly, the *eventual* overall effect on short-run equilibrium spending and output would be larger, due to the multiplier effect discussed in Chapter 9, *Short-Term Economic Fluctuations and Fiscal Policy*.) In addition, in this example, disposable income $(Y - T)$ is assumed to affect consumption spending through a marginal propensity to consume of 0.8 (see the first equation), and government purchases G, net exports NX, and taxes T are assumed to be fixed numbers.

To find a numerical equation that describes the relationship of the real interest rate to aggregate expenditure and output, we can begin as in Chapter 9 with the general definition of aggregate expenditure:

$$Y = C + I + G + NX.$$

Substituting for the four components of expenditure, using the equations describing each type of spending, we get

$$Y = [640 + 0.8(Y - 250) - 400r] + [250 - 600r] + 300 + 20.$$

The first term in brackets on the right side of this equation is the expression for consumption, using the fact that taxes $T = 250$; the second bracketed term is investment; and the last two terms correspond to the given numerical values of government purchases and net exports. If we simplify this equation and group together the terms that do not depend on output Y and the terms that do depend on output, we get

$$Y = [(640 - 0.8 \times 250 - 400r) + (250 - 600r) + 300 + 20] + 0.8Y,$$

or, simplifying further,

$$Y = [1{,}010 - 1{,}000r] + 0.8Y.$$

Finally, subtracting $0.8Y$ from each side of the equation, we get

$$0.2Y = 1{,}010 - 1{,}000r,$$

and dividing each side by 0.2, we get

$$Y = 5{,}050 - 5{,}000r. \qquad (10.2)$$

In Equation 10.2, a 1 percent (0.01) increase in the real interest rate, from 4 percent to 5 percent, for example, reduces short-run equilibrium spending and output by $5{,}000(0.01) = 50$ units. Notice that this reduction of 50 units is five times larger than the initial reduction of 10 units discussed above. This means that in this economy, the multiplier is 5.

EXAMPLE 10.4 The Real Interest Rate and Short-Run Equilibrium Output

How does the interest rate translate to a specific level of short-run equilibrium output?

In the economy described in Example 10.3, the real interest rate r is set by the Fed to equal 0.05 (5 percent). Find short-run equilibrium output.

We found in Example 10.3 that, in this economy, short-run equilibrium spending and output are given by Equation 10.2. We are given that the Fed sets the real interest rate at 5 percent. Setting $r = 0.05$ in Equation 10.2 gives

$$Y = 5{,}050 - 5{,}000(0.05).$$

Simplifying, we get

$$Y = 4{,}800.$$

SELF-TEST 10.3

For the economy described in Example 10.4, suppose the Fed sets the real interest rate at 3 percent rather than at 5 percent. Find short-run equilibrium output.

The Fed Fights a Recession

We have seen that the Fed can control the real interest rate, and that the real interest rate in turn affects spending and short-run equilibrium output. Putting these two results together, we can see how Fed actions may help stabilize the economy.

Suppose the economy faces a recessionary gap—a situation in which real output is below potential output, and spending is "too low." To fight a recessionary gap, the Fed should reduce the real interest rate, stimulating consumption and investment spending. According to the theory we have developed, this increase in spending will cause output to rise, restoring the economy to full employment. Example 10.5 illustrates this point by extending Example 10.4.

EXAMPLE 10.5 The Fed Fights a Recession

How can monetary policy eliminate a recessionary gap?

For the economy described in Example 10.4, suppose potential output Y^* equals 5,000. As before, the Fed has set the real interest rate equal to 5 percent. At that real interest rate, what is the output gap? What should the Fed do to eliminate the output gap and restore full employment?

In Example 10.4 we showed that with the real interest rate at 5 percent, short-run equilibrium output for this economy is 4,800. We are now given that potential output is 5,000, so the output gap $(Y - Y^*)$ equals $5{,}000 - 4{,}800 = 200$. Because actual output is below potential, this economy faces a recessionary gap.

To fight the recession, the Fed should lower the real interest rate, raising aggregate expenditure until output reaches 5,000, the full-employment level. That is, the Fed's objective is to increase short-run equilibrium spending and output by 200. By how much should the Fed reduce the real interest rate to achieve that goal? When solving Example 10.3 we saw that a 1 percent increase in the real interest rate would translate to an initial decrease of 10 units in aggregate spending, and to an eventual decrease of 50 units in short-run equilibrium output (and spending), corresponding to a multiplier of 5. Of course, the opposite is also true: a 1 percent decrease in the real interest rate would translate to an initial *increase* of 10 units in aggregate spending and, as Equation 10.2 shows, to an eventual *increase* of 50 units in short-run equilibrium output. To increase output by 200 units (or 4 times 50 units) then, the Fed should lower the real interest rate by 4 percentage points, from 5 percent to 1 percent.

In summary, to eliminate the recessionary gap of 200, the Fed should lower the real interest rate from 5 percent to 1 percent. Notice that the Fed's decrease in the real interest rate increases short-run equilibrium output, as economic logic suggests.

SELF-TEST 10.4

Continuing Example 10.5, suppose that potential output is 4,850 rather than 5,000. By how much should the Fed cut the real interest rate to restore full employment? You may take as given that the multiplier is 5.

The Economic Naturalist 10.2

How did the Fed respond to recession and the terror attacks in 2001?

The U.S. economy began slowing in the fall of 2000, with investment in high-tech equipment falling particularly sharply. According to the National Bureau of Economic Research, a recession began in March 2001. To make matters worse, on September 11, 2001, terrorist attacks on New York City and Washington shocked the nation and led to serious problems in the travel and financial industries, among others. How did the Federal Reserve react to these events?

The Fed first began to respond to growing evidence of an economic slowdown at the end of the year 2000. At the time the federal funds rate stood at about 6.5 percent (see Figure 10.5). The Fed's most dramatic move was a surprise cut of 0.5 percentage point in the funds rate in January 2001, between regularly scheduled meetings of the Federal Open Market Committee. Further rate cuts followed, and by July the funds rate was below 4 percent. By summer's end, however, there was still considerable uncertainty about the likely severity of the economic slowdown.

The picture changed suddenly on September 11, 2001, when the terror attacks on the World Trade Center and the Pentagon killed more than 3,000 people. The terrorist attacks imposed great economic as well as human costs. The physical damage in lower Manhattan was in the billions of dollars, and many offices and businesses in the area had to close. The Fed, in its role as supervisor of the financial system, worked hard to assist in the restoration of normal operations in the financial district of New York City. (The Federal Reserve Bank of New York, which actually conducts open-market operations, is only a block from the site of the World Trade Center.) The Fed also tried to ease financial conditions by temporarily lowering the federal funds rate to as low as 1.25 percent, in the week following the attack.

In the weeks and months following September 11, the Fed turned its attention from the direct impact of the attack to the possible indirect effects on the U.S. economy. The Fed was worried that consumers, nervous about the future, would severely cut back their spending; together with the ongoing weakness in investment, a fall in consumption spending could sharply worsen the recession. To stimulate spending, the Fed continued to cut the federal funds rate. By January 2002, the funds rate was at 1.75 percent, nearly 5 percentage points lower than a year earlier. The Fed kept the interest rate at that low level until November 2002, when it lowered the federal funds rate another 0.5 percentage point, to 1.25 percent. Although the recession officially ended in late 2001, the recovery remained quite weak. Unemployment kept increasing, until it peaked at 6.3 percent in June 2003. That month, the Fed further lowered the federal funds rate to 1 percent, keeping it at that record low until June 2004.

A variety of factors helped the economy recover from the 2001 recession, including expansionary fiscal policy (see The Economic Naturalist 9.6). Most economists agree that expansionary actions by the Fed also played a constructive role in reducing the economic impact of the recession and the September 11 attacks.

The Fed Fights Inflation

To this point we have focused on the problem of stabilizing output, without considering inflation. In the next chapter we will see how ongoing inflation can be incorporated into our analysis. For now we will simply note that one important cause of inflation is an expansionary output gap—a situation in which spending, and hence actual output, exceeds potential output. When an expansionary gap exists, firms find that the demand for their output exceeds their normal rate of production. Although firms may be content to meet this excess demand at previously determined prices for some time, if the high demand persists, they will ultimately raise their prices, spurring inflation.

Because an expansionary gap tends to lead to inflation, the Fed moves to eliminate expansionary gaps as well as recessionary gaps. The procedure for getting rid of an expansionary gap—a situation in which output is "too high" relative to potential output—is the reverse of that for fighting a recessionary gap, a situation in which output is "too low." As we have seen, the cure for a recessionary gap is to reduce the real interest rate, an action that stimulates spending and increases output. The cure for an expansionary gap is to *raise* the real interest rate, which reduces consumption and investment by raising the cost of borrowing. The resulting fall in spending leads in turn to a decline in output and to a reduction in inflationary pressures.

EXAMPLE 10.6 The Fed Fights Inflation

How can monetary policy eliminate an expansionary gap?

For the economy studied in Examples 10.4 and 10.5, assume that potential output is 4,600 rather than 5,000. At the initial real interest rate of 5 percent, short-run equilibrium output is 4,800, so this economy has an expansionary gap of 200. How should the Fed change the real interest rate to eliminate this gap?

In Example 10.5, we saw that to eliminate a recessionary gap of 200, the Fed needed to lower the real interest rate by 4 percent—from 5 percent to 1 percent. You may correctly suspect, then, that to eliminate an *expansionary* gap of 200, the Fed would need to *increase* the real interest rate by 4 percent—from 5 percent to 9 percent. You could again use Equation 10.2 to verify that this indeed is the correct answer: replacing r in the equation with 0.09 and simplifying the equation, you will get that $Y = 4{,}600$. We conclude that to eliminate the inflationary gap, the Fed should raise the real interest rate by 4 percentage points (0.04), from 5 percent to 9 percent. The higher real interest rate will reduce aggregate expenditure and output to the level of potential output, 4,600, eliminating inflationary pressures.

The Economic Naturalist 10.3

Why did the Fed raise interest rates 17 times in a row between 2004 and 2006?

The Fed began tightening monetary policy in June 2004 when it increased the federal funds rate from 1.0 to 1.25 percent. (See Figure 10.5.) It continued to tighten by raising the federal funds rate by 0.25 percent at each successive meeting of the Federal Open Market Committee. By the end of June 2006, after more than two years of tightening, the federal funds rate was 5.25 percent. Why did the Fed begin increasing the funds rate in 2004?

Because the recovery that began in November 2001 was slower than normal and marked by weak job growth, the Fed kept reducing the funds rate until it reached

1.0 percent in June 2003. Once the recovery took hold, however, this very low rate was no longer necessary. While employment had not risen as much during the recovery as it had in previous recoveries, real GDP grew at a rate of nearly 6 percent during the second half of 2003 and nearly 4 percent in 2004. Furthermore, by June 2004, the unemployment rate had fallen to 5.6 percent, not far above most estimates of the natural rate of unemployment at the time. Although inflation began to rise in 2004, most of the increase was due to the sharp run-up in oil prices, and the rate of inflation excluding energy remained low. Nevertheless, the Fed began to raise the federal funds rate in order to prevent the emergence of an expansionary gap, which would result in higher inflation. Thus, the Fed's rate increases could be viewed as a preemptive strike against future inflation. Had the Fed waited until an expansionary gap appeared, a significant inflation problem could have emerged, and the Fed might have had to raise the federal funds rate by even more than it did.

The Fed's interest rate policies affect the economy as a whole, but they have a particularly important effect on financial markets. The introduction to this chapter noted the tremendous lengths financial market participants will go to in an attempt to anticipate Federal Reserve policy changes. The Economic Naturalist 10.4 illustrates the type of information financial investors look for, and why it is so important to them.

The Economic Naturalist 10.4

Why does news of inflation hurt the stock market?

Financial market participants watch data on inflation extremely closely. A report that inflation is increasing or is higher than expected often causes stock prices to fall sharply. Why does bad news about inflation hurt the stock market?

Investors in the financial markets worry about inflation because of its likely impact on Federal Reserve policy. Financial investors understand that the Fed, when faced with signs of an expansionary gap, is likely to raise interest rates in an attempt to reduce planned spending and "cool down" the economy. This type of contractionary policy action hurts stock prices in two ways. First, it slows down economic activity, reducing the expected sales and profits of companies whose shares are traded in the stock market. Lower profits, in turn, reduce the dividends those firms are likely to pay their shareholders.

Second, higher real interest rates reduce the value of stocks by increasing the required return for holding stocks. We saw in Chapter 8, *Money, the Federal Reserve, and Global Financial Markets,* that an increase in the return financial investors require in order to hold stocks lowers current stock prices. Intuitively, if interest rates rise, interest-bearing alternatives to stocks such as newly issued government bonds will become more attractive to investors, reducing the demand for, and hence the price of, stocks.

The Economic Naturalist 10.5

Should the Federal Reserve respond to changes in asset prices?

Many credit the Federal Reserve and its chair, Alan Greenspan, for effective monetary policymaking that set the stage for sustained economic growth and rising asset prices throughout the 1990s—in particular, in the second half of the decade. Between January 1995 and March 2000, the S&P 500 stock market index rose from a value of 459 to 1,527, a phenomenal 233 percent increase in just over five years, as the U.S. economy enjoyed a record-long business cycle expansion. Indeed, the stock market's strong, sustained rise helped fuel additional consumer spending, which in turn promoted further economic expansion.

However, as stock prices fell sharply in the two years after their March 2000 peak, some people questioned whether the Federal Reserve should have preemptively raised interest rates to constrain investors' "irrational exuberance."[10] Overly optimistic investor sentiment led to a speculative run-up in stock prices that eventually burst in 2000 as investors began to realize that firms' earnings could not support the stock prices that were being paid. Earlier intervention by the Federal Reserve, critics argued, would have slowed down the dramatic increase in stock prices and therefore could have prevented the resulting stock market "crash" and the resulting loss of consumer wealth.

Similar criticism was raised toward the Fed after the collapse of the housing bubble and the ensuing financial crisis of 2007–2008. Like stock prices, housing prices rose dramatically in the late 1990s, and they continued to rise into the early 2000s even as stock prices fell. Housing prices accelerated further during 2004–2005, increasing more than 15 percent a year. However, prices slowed in 2006, and fell sharply in the following years. In light of the severity of the financial crisis and the deep global recession that followed, some people again questioned whether the accommodative monetary policy of the Fed in the early 2000s (see The Economic Naturalist 10.2) contributed to the housing bubble.

Most recently, the Great Recession of 2007–2009 was followed by the longest economic expansion in U.S. history. The expansion was again accompanied by dramatic increases in stock and housing prices, interrupted only in early 2020 by the COVID-19 pandemic. If these asset prices again collapse, some observers are sure to criticize the Fed for inflating them by keeping interest rates "too low" from 2008 onward.

As this chapter makes clear, the Federal Reserve's primary focus is on reducing output gaps and keeping inflation low. Should the Fed also respond to changing asset prices when it makes decisions about monetary policy?

At a symposium in August 2002, Alan Greenspan defended the Fed's monetary policymaking performance in the late 1990s, pointing out that it is very difficult to identify asset bubbles—surges in prices of assets to unsustainable levels—"until after the fact—that is, when its bursting confirm(s) its existence."[11] Even if such a speculative bubble could be identified, Greenspan noted, the Federal Reserve could have done little—short of "inducing a substantial contraction in economic activity"—to prevent investors' speculation from driving up stock prices. Indeed, Greenspan claimed, "the notion that a well-timed incremental tightening could have been calibrated to prevent the late 1990s bubble is almost surely an illusion." Rather, the Federal Reserve was focusing as early as 1999 on policies that would "mitigate the fallout when it occurs and, hopefully, ease the transition to the next expansion."[12]

Seven years later, at the annual meeting of the American Economic Association in January 2010, then Fed chair Ben Bernanke delivered a speech defending the Fed's monetary policy during the early 2000s.[13] The evidence reviewed in his speech suggested that the links between the Fed's monetary policy and the rapid rise in housing prices that occurred at roughly the same time were, at best, weak. Rather,

[10]Fed chair Alan Greenspan mentioned the possibility of "irrational exuberance" driving investor behavior in a December 5, 1996, speech, which is available online at www.federalreserve.gov/boarddocs/speeches/1996/19961205.htm.

[11]The text of Greenspan's speech is available online at www.federalreserve.gov/boarddocs/speeches/2002/20020830/default.htm.

[12]*The Federal Reserve's Semiannual Report on Monetary Policy,* testimony of Chair Alan Greenspan before the Committee on Banking and Financial Services, U.S. House of Representatives, July 22, 1999. Available online at www.federalreserve.gov/boarddocs/hh/1999/July/Testimony.htm.

[13]The text of the speech is available online at www.federalreserve.gov/newsevents/speech/bernanke20100103a.htm.

the evidence pointed to increased use of "exotic" types of mortgages with very low down payment—in which both lenders and borrowers knew that the only way borrowers could afford making future payments would be a continued rise in home values—as a more likely cause of the housing bubble. This in turn suggested that the best response to the housing bubble would have been better regulation, such as tougher limits on risky mortgage lending, rather than tighter monetary policy.

Asset price bubbles can cause severe damage. The question of how we can improve our institutions and policymaking framework to reduce the risk of their occurrence is sure to remain an important topic for macroeconomists to study. While monetary policy cannot be ruled out as part of the answer, in general, regulation that is focused directly on the causes of bubbles is likely to be a more effective first line of defense.

The Fed's Policy Reaction Function

policy reaction function describes how the action a policymaker takes depends on the state of the economy

The Fed attempts to stabilize the economy by manipulating the real interest rate. When the economy faces a recessionary gap, the Fed reduces the real interest rate in order to stimulate spending. When an expansionary gap exists, so that inflation threatens to become a problem, the Fed restrains spending by raising the real interest rate. Economists sometimes find it convenient to summarize the behavior of the Fed in terms of a *policy reaction function*. In general, a **policy reaction function** describes how the action a policymaker takes depends on the state of the economy. Here, the policymaker's action is the Fed's choice of the real interest rate, and the state of the economy is given by factors such as the output gap or the inflation rate. The Economic Naturalist 10.6 describes one attempt to quantify the Fed's policy reaction function.

The Economic Naturalist 10.6

What is the Taylor rule?

In 1993, economist John Taylor proposed a "rule," now known as the Taylor rule, to describe the behavior of the Fed.[14] What is the Taylor rule? Does the Fed always follow it?

The rule Taylor proposed is not a rule in any legal sense but is, instead, an attempt to describe the Fed's behavior in terms of a quantitative policy reaction function. Taylor's "rule" can be written as

$$r = 0.01 + 0.5\left(\frac{Y - Y^*}{Y^*}\right) + 0.5\pi,$$

where r is the real interest rate set by the Fed, expressed as a decimal (for example, 5% = 0.05); $Y - Y^*$ is the current output gap (the difference between actual output and potential output); $(Y - Y^*)/Y^*$ is the output gap relative to potential output; and π is the inflation rate, expressed as a decimal (for example, a 2 percent inflation rate is expressed as 0.02). According to the Taylor rule, the Fed responds to both output gaps and the rate of inflation. For example, the formula implies that if a recessionary gap equal to a fraction 0.01 of potential output develops, the Fed will reduce the real interest rate by 0.5 percentage point (that is, 0.005). Similarly, if inflation rises by 1 percentage point (0.01), according to the Taylor rule the Fed will

[14]John Taylor, "Discretion versus Policy Rules in Practice," *Carnegie-Rochester Conference Series on Public Policy*, 1993, pp. 195–227.

increase the real interest rate by 0.5 percentage point (0.005). In his 1993 paper, Taylor showed that his rule did in fact describe the behavior of the Fed under Chair Alan Greenspan reasonably accurately between 1987 and 1992. Thus the Taylor rule is a real-world example of a policy reaction function.

Although the Taylor rule worked well as a description of the Fed's behavior in the five years preceding the publication of Taylor's 1993 paper, the rule has worked less well in describing the Fed's behavior in the years following its publication. Modified variants of the Taylor rule, in which the Fed reacts more strongly to output gaps than the original rule suggested, or in which the Fed reacts to inflation *forecasts* rather than to current inflation, appear to provide better descriptions of the Fed's behavior in the following decades. While different economists prefer different versions of the Taylor rule, we reiterate that it is not a rule in any legal sense. The Fed is perfectly free to deviate from it and does so when circumstances warrant. Still, variants of the Taylor rule provide a useful benchmark for assessing, and predicting, the Fed's actions.

SELF-TEST 10.5

This exercise asks you to apply the Taylor rule. Suppose inflation is 3 percent and the output gap is zero. According to the Taylor rule, at what value should the Fed set the real interest rate? The nominal interest rate? Suppose the Fed were to receive new information showing that there is a 1 percent recessionary gap (inflation is still 3 percent). According to the Taylor rule, how should the Fed change the real interest rate, if at all?

Notice that according to the Taylor rule, the Fed responds to two variables—the output gap and inflation. In principle, any number of economic variables, from stock prices to the value of the dollar in terms of the Japanese yen, could affect Fed policy and thus appear in the policy reaction function. For the sake of simplicity, in applying the policy reaction function idea in the next chapter, we will assume that the Fed's choice of the real interest rate depends on only one variable—the rate of inflation. This simplification will not change our main results in any significant way. Furthermore, as we will see, having the Fed react only to inflation captures the most important aspect of Fed behavior—namely, its tendency to raise the real interest rate when the economy is "overheating" (experiencing an expansionary gap) and to reduce it when the economy is sluggish (experiencing a recessionary gap).

Table 10.2 describes an example of a policy reaction function according to which the Fed reacts only to inflation. According to the policy reaction function given in the table, the higher the rate of inflation, the higher the real interest rate

TABLE 10.2
A Policy Reaction Function for the Fed

Rate of inflation, π	Real interest rate set by Fed, r
0.00 (= 0%)	0.02 (= 2%)
0.01	0.03
0.02	0.04
0.03	0.05
0.04	0.06

FIGURE 10.6

An Example of a Fed Policy Reaction Function.

This hypothetical example of a policy reaction function for the Fed shows the real interest rate the Fed sets in response to any given value of the inflation rate. The upward slope captures the idea that the Fed raises the real interest rate when inflation rises. The numerical values in the figure are from Table 10.2.

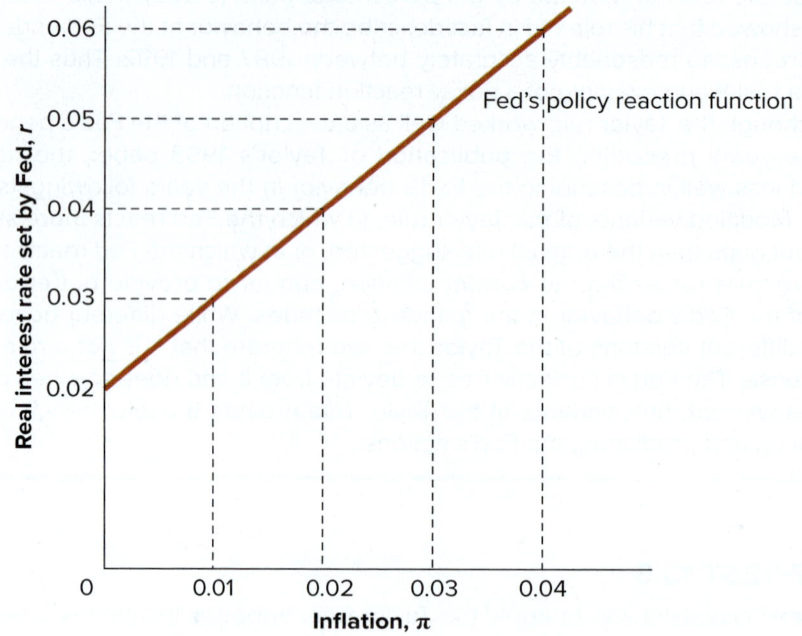

set by the Fed. This relationship is consistent with the idea that the Fed responds to an expansionary gap (which threatens to lead to increased inflation) by raising the real interest rate. Figure 10.6 is a graph of this policy reaction function. The vertical axis of the graph shows the real interest rate chosen by the Fed; the horizontal axis shows the rate of inflation. The upward slope of the policy reaction function captures the idea that the Fed reacts to increases in inflation by raising the real interest rate.

How does the Fed determine its policy reaction function? In practice, the process is a complex one, involving a combination of statistical analysis of the economy and human judgment. However, two useful insights into the process can be drawn even from the simplified policy reaction function shown in Table 10.2 and Figure 10.6. First, as we mentioned earlier in the chapter, though the Fed controls the real interest rate in the short run, in the long run the real interest rate is determined by the balance of saving and investment. To illustrate the implication of this fact for the Fed's choice of policy reaction function, suppose that the Fed estimates the long-run value of the real interest rate (as determined by the supply and demand for saving) to be 4 percent, or 0.04. By examining Table 10.2, we can see that the Fed's policy reaction function implies a long-run value of the real interest rate of 4 percent only if the inflation rate in the long run is 2 percent. Thus the Fed's choice of this policy reaction function makes sense only if the Fed's long-run target rate of inflation is 2 percent. We conclude that one important determinant of the Fed's policy reaction function is the policymakers' objective for inflation.

Second, the Fed's policy reaction function contains information not only about the central bank's long-run inflation target but also about how aggressively the Fed plans to pursue that target. To illustrate, suppose the Fed's policy reaction function was very flat, implying that the Fed changes the real interest rate rather modestly in response to increases or decreases in inflation. In this case we would conclude that the Fed does not intend to be very aggressive in its attempts to offset movements in inflation away from the target level. In contrast, if the reaction function slopes steeply upward, so that a given change in inflation elicits a large adjustment of the real interest rate by the Fed, we would say that the Fed plans to be quite aggressive in responding to changes in inflation.

RECAP

MONETARY POLICY AND THE ECONOMY

- An increase in the real interest rate reduces both consumption spending and investment spending. Through its control of the real interest rate, the Fed is thus able to influence spending and short-run equilibrium output. To fight a recession (a recessionary output gap), the Fed should lower the real interest rate, stimulating spending and output. Conversely, to fight the threat of inflation (an expansionary output gap), the Fed should raise the real interest rate, reducing spending and output.
- The Fed's policy reaction function relates its policy action (specifically, its setting of the real interest rate) to the state of the economy. For the sake of simplicity, we consider a policy reaction function in which the real interest rate set by the Fed depends only on the rate of inflation. Because the Fed raises the real interest rate when inflation rises, in order to restrain spending, the Fed's policy reaction is upward-sloping. The Fed's policy reaction function contains information about the central bank's long-run target for inflation and the aggressiveness with which it intends to pursue that target.

MONETARY POLICYMAKING: ART OR SCIENCE?

In this chapter, we analyzed the basic economics underlying real-world monetary policy. As part of the analysis, we worked through some examples showing the calculation of the real interest rate that is needed to restore output to its full-employment level. While those examples are useful in understanding how monetary policy works—as with our analysis of fiscal policy in Chapter 9, *Short-Term Economic Fluctuations and Fiscal Policy*—they overstate the precision of monetary policymaking. The real-world economy is highly complex, and our knowledge of its workings is imperfect. For example, though we assumed in our analysis that the Fed knows the exact value of potential output, in reality potential output can be estimated only approximately. As a result, at any given time the Fed has only a rough idea of the size of the output gap. Similarly, Fed policymakers have only an approximate idea of the effect of a given change in the real interest rate on spending, or the length of time before that effect will occur. Because of these uncertainties, the Fed tends to proceed cautiously. Fed policymakers avoid large changes in interest rates and rarely raise or lower the federal funds rate more than one-half of a percentage point (from 5.50 percent to 5.00 percent, for example) at any one time. Indeed, the typical change in the interest rate is one-quarter of a percentage point.

Is monetary policymaking an art or a science, then? In practice it appears to be both. Scientific analyses, such as the development of detailed statistical models of the economy, have proved useful in making monetary policy. But human judgment based on long experience—what has been called the "art" of monetary policy—plays a crucial role in successful policymaking and is likely to continue to do so.

SUMMARY

- Monetary policy is one of two types of stabilization policy, the other being fiscal policy. Although in the basic model of the market for money the Federal Reserve operates by controlling the money supply, the media's attention nearly always focuses on the Fed's decisions about interest rates, not the money supply. There is no contradiction between these two ways of looking at monetary policy, however, as the Fed's ability to control the money supply is the source of its ability to control interest rates. *(LO1)*

- The nominal interest rate is determined in the market for money, which has both a demand side and a supply side. For the economy as a whole, the *demand for money* is the amount of wealth households and businesses choose to hold in the form of money (such as cash or checking accounts). The demand for money is determined by a comparison of cost and benefits. The opportunity cost of holding money, which pays either zero interest or very low interest, is the interest that could have been earned by holding interest-bearing assets instead of money. Because the nominal interest rate measures the opportunity cost of holding a dollar in the form of money, an increase in the nominal interest rate reduces the quantity of money demanded. The benefit of money is its usefulness in carrying out transactions. All else being equal, an increase in the volume of transactions increases the demand for money. At the macroeconomic level, an increase in the price level or in real GDP increases the dollar volume of transactions, and thus the demand for money. *(LO1)*

- The *money demand curve* relates the aggregate quantity of money demanded to the nominal interest rate. Because an increase in the nominal interest rate increases the opportunity cost of holding money, which reduces the quantity of money demanded, the money demand curve slopes downward. Factors other than the nominal interest rate that affect the demand for money will shift the demand curve to the right or left. For example, an increase in the price level or real GDP increases the demand for money, shifting the money demand curve to the right. *(LO1)*

- In the basic model of the market for money, the Federal Reserve determines the supply of money through the use of open-market operations. The supply curve for money is vertical at the value of the money supply set by the Fed. Money market equilibrium occurs at the nominal interest rate at which money demand equals the money supply. The Fed can reduce the nominal interest rate by increasing the money supply (shifting the money supply curve to the right) or increase the nominal interest rate by reducing the money supply (shifting the money supply curve to the left). The nominal interest rate that the Fed targets most closely is the *federal funds rate,* which is the rate commercial banks charge each other for very short-term loans. *(LO2)*

- In the short run, the Fed can control the real interest rate as well as the nominal interest rate. Recall that the real interest rate equals the nominal interest rate minus the inflation rate. Because the inflation rate adjusts relatively slowly, the Fed can change the real interest rate by changing the nominal interest rate. In the long run, the real interest rate is determined by the balance of saving and investment. *(LO2)*

- The Fed can effectively control the amount of bank reserves through tools that include open-market operations and *discount window lending*. The Fed can also set *reserve requirements* (a legally binding minimum on banks' reserve-deposit ratio). This, however, gives the Fed only partial control over the money supply—something that the basic model of the market for money does not consider. In particular, a Fed-initiated increase in bank reserves will not lead to an increase in the money supply if banks absorb the increase in reserves by letting their reserve-deposit ratios increase at the same pace. *(LO3)*

- In December 2008 the federal funds rate effectively reached its *zero lower bound*. In the years that followed, the Fed used what started as unconventional methods to stimulate the economy. Such methods, including *quantitative easing* and *forward guidance,* go beyond the basic model of the market for money, which assumes that all the interest rates in the economy move together and that the Fed fully controls the money supply. These new methods used by the Fed directly aimed at lowering interest rates in the economy that were higher than the federal funds rate. Although the above two basic assumptions did not hold well after December 2008 (which explains why the Fed had to resort to the new methods to keep stimulating the economy), they still provide useful approximations. This in turn provides some justification for continuing to make these simplifying assumptions, in particular when speaking of the Fed's control of the interest rate. *(LO4)*

- The Federal Reserve's actions affect the economy because changes in the real interest rate affect spending. For example, an increase in the real interest rate raises the cost of borrowing, reducing consumption and investment. Thus, by increasing the real interest rate, the Fed can reduce spending and short-run equilibrium output. Conversely, by reducing the real interest rate, the Fed can stimulate aggregate expenditure and thereby raise short-run equilibrium output. The Fed's ultimate objective is to eliminate output gaps. To eliminate a recessionary output gap, the Fed will lower the real interest rate. To eliminate an expansionary output gap, the Fed will raise the real interest rate. *(LO5)*

- A *policy reaction function* describes how the action a policymaker takes depends on the state of the economy. For example, a policy reaction function for the Fed could specify the real interest rate set by the Fed for each value of inflation. *(LO5)*

- In practice, the Fed's information about the level of potential output and the size and speed of the effects of its actions is imprecise. Thus monetary policymaking is as much an art as a science. *(LO6)*

KEY TERMS

demand for money
discount rate
discount window lending
excess reserves
federal funds rate
forward guidance
money demand curve
policy reaction function
portfolio allocation decision
quantitative easing (QE)
reserve requirements
zero lower bound

REVIEW QUESTIONS

1. What is the *demand for money*? How does the demand for money depend on the nominal interest rate? On the price level? On income? Explain in terms of the costs and benefits of holding money. *(LO1)*
2. Show graphically how the Fed controls the nominal interest rate. Can the Fed control the real interest rate? *(LO2)*
3. What effect does an open-market purchase of bonds by the Fed have on nominal interest rates? Discuss in terms of (a) the effect of the purchase on bond prices and (b) the effect of the purchase on the supply of money. *(LO2)*
4. What other methods does the Fed have for affecting short-run interest rates besides open-market operations? Discuss whether these methods can be used for only lowering short-run interest rates, for only increasing them, or for both lowering and increasing them. *(LO3)*
5. In a situation where short-run interest rates have hit their zero lower bound, can the Fed still lower other, higher, longer-term interest rates? Discuss specific actions that the Fed can take and how they would work. *(LO4)*
6. Why does the real interest rate affect aggregate expenditure? Give examples. *(LO5)*
7. The Fed faces a recessionary gap. How would you expect it to respond? Explain step by step how its policy change is likely to affect the economy. *(LO5)*
8. The Fed decides to take a *contractionary* policy action. What would you expect to happen to the nominal interest rate, the real interest rate, and the money supply? Under what circumstances would this type of policy action most likely be appropriate? *(LO5)*
9. Discuss why the analysis of this chapter overstates the precision with which monetary policy can be used to eliminate output gaps. *(LO6)*

PROBLEMS

connect

1. During the heavy Christmas shopping season, sales of retail stores, online sales firms, and other merchants rise significantly. *(LO1)*
   a. What would you expect to happen to the money demand curve during the Christmas season? Show graphically.
   b. If the Fed took no action, what would happen to nominal interest rates around Christmas?
   c. In fact, nominal interest rates do not change significantly in the fourth quarter of the year, due to deliberate Fed policy. Explain and show graphically how the Fed can ensure that nominal interest rates remain stable around Christmas.
2. The following table shows Uma's estimated annual benefits of holding different amounts of money. *(LO1)*

Average money holdings ($)	Total benefit ($)
500	35
600	47
700	57
800	65
900	71
1,000	75
1,100	77
1,200	77

   a. How much money will Uma hold on average if the nominal interest rate is 9 percent? 5 percent? 3 percent? Assume that she wants her money holding to be a multiple of $100. (*Hint:* Make a table comparing the extra benefit of each additional \$100 in money holdings with the opportunity cost, in terms of forgone interest, of additional money holdings.)

b. Graph Uma's money demand curve for interest rates between 1 percent and 12 percent.

3. How would you expect each of the following to affect the economywide demand for U.S. money? Explain. *(LO1)*
   a. Competition among brokers forces down the commission charge for selling holdings of bonds or stocks.
   b. Grocery stores begin to accept credit cards in payment.
   c. Financial investors become concerned about increasing riskiness of stocks.

4. Using a supply and demand graph of the market for money, show the effects on the nominal interest rate if the Fed takes the following monetary policy actions: *(LO2, LO3)*
   a. The Fed lowers the discount rate and increases discount lending.
   b. The Fed increases the reserve requirements for commercial banks.
   c. The Fed conducts open-market sales of government bonds to the public.
   d. The Fed decreases the reserve requirements for commercial banks.

5. Assume that the central bank of a nation decides to lower the reserve requirements for commercial banks. What changes can one predict regarding the amount of: required reserves, excess reserves, the amount of loans generated by commercial banks, the economywide money supply, and finally interest rates in that nation? *(LO3)*

6. In August 2015, the Chinese central bank decided to reduce China's required reserve-deposit ratio from 18.5 percent to 18 percent. Assuming no change in the amount of cash held by the Chinese public, that commercial banks lend all their excess reserves, and that bank reserves was a constant 4,329 billion yuan both before and after the change, compute the maximum change in Chinese banks deposits as a consequence of the change in the reserve-deposit. *(LO3)*

7. Which of the following is not an example of an "unconventional" monetary policy tool available to the Fed when the federal funds rate is already at or close to zero: forward guidance, quantitative easing, or discount lending? *(LO4)*

8. Explain why an increase in interest that banks receive from the Fed on the required and excess reserves that banks hold with the Fed would also increase the interest rates that commercial banks charge their borrowers. *(LO4)*

9. An economy is described by the following information. *(LO5)*

$$C = 260 + 0.8(Y - T) - 1{,}000r,$$
$$I = 200 - 1{,}000r,$$
$$G = 180,$$
$$NX = 0,$$
$$T = 300.$$

   a. State the relationship between aggregate expenditure and output Y to the real interest rate r for this economy in the format of an equation. [*Hint:* it should follow the format $Y = a - b(r)$.]
   b. Assuming that the real interest rate is 0.10 (10%), compute the numerical value for aggregate expenditure and output Y.
   c. If the real interest rate increases to 0.12 (12%), compute the new numerical value for aggregate expenditure and output Y.
   d. If the real interest rate decreases to 0.08 (8%), compute the new numerical value for aggregate expenditure and output Y.

10. An economy with a potential output Y^* of 4,000 is described by the equation below. *(LO5)*

$$Y = 5{,}800 - 12{,}000r$$

   a. If real interest rate is 0.10 (10%), compute the numerical value for aggregate expenditure and output Y, and determine if the economy is at its potential or experiencing an output gap.
   b. If real interest rate is 0.20 (20%), compute the numerical value for aggregate expenditure and output Y, and determine if the economy is at its potential or experiencing an output gap.
   c. At what value should the Fed set the real interest rate to eliminate any output gap and achieve its potential?

11. Supposing that the Fed follows the Taylor rule (The Economic Naturalist 10.6), find the real interest rate and the nominal interest rate that the Fed will set in each of the following situations. *(LO5)*
   a. Inflation of 4 percent and an expansionary gap equal to 1 percent of potential output.
   b. Inflation of 2 percent and a recessionary gap equal to 2 percent of potential output.
   c. Inflation of 6 percent and no output gap.
   d. Inflation of 2 percent and a recessionary gap of 5 percent. (Can the Fed set a negative real interest rate? If so, how?)

12. In mid-2002, with inflation at 2 percent, some economists estimated the size of the recessionary gap to be about 2 percent of potential output. At that time, the Fed was holding the (nominal) federal funds rate

at 1.75 percent. How does the Fed's setting of the federal funds rate compare with what would be predicted by the Taylor rule? *(LO5)*

13. What are some of the uncertainties that Fed policymakers face, and how do these uncertainties affect monetary policymaking? *(LO6)*

ANSWERS TO SELF-TESTS

10.1 At 4 percent interest, the benefit of each \$10,000 reduction in cash holdings is \$400 per year (4% × \$10,000). In this case the cost of the extra armored car service, \$500 a year, exceeds the benefit of reducing cash holdings by \$10,000. Kim's restaurants should therefore continue to hold \$50,000 in cash. Comparing this result with Example 10.2, you can see that the demand for money by Kim's restaurants is lower, the higher the nominal interest rate. *(LO1)*

10.2 If the nominal interest rate is above its equilibrium value, then people are holding more money than they would like. To bring their money holdings down, they will use some of their money to buy interest-bearing assets such as bonds.

If everyone is trying to buy bonds, however, the price of bonds will be bid up. An increase in bond prices is equivalent to a fall in market interest rates. As interest rates fall, people will be willing to hold more money. Eventually interest rates will fall enough that people are content to hold the amount of money supplied by the Fed, and the money market will be in equilibrium. *(LO1)*

10.3 If $r = 0.03$, then the short-run equilibrium output Y equals 5,050 − 5,000 (0.03) = 5,050 − 150 = 4,900. Notice that the lower interest of 3 percent (0.03), compared to the original 5 percent (0.05) used in Example 10.4, has increased the short-run equilibrium output Y. In other words, lowering interest rates is an expansionary monetary policy. *(LO5)*

10.4 In Example 10.4, we saw that when the real interest rate is 5 percent, short-run equilibrium output is 4,800. If potential output is 4,850, we have a recessionary gap of 50 units. Equation 10.2 shows that each percentage point increase in the real interest rate reduces the short-run equilibrium by 50 units ($Y = 5{,}050 - 5{,}000r$). So if we instead need to increase the short-run equilibrium by 50 units, real interest rate should be cut by 1 percentage point, from 5 percent to 4 percent. Increasing output by 50 units, to 4,850, eliminates the output gap. *(LO5)*

10.5 If $\pi = 0.03$ and the output gap is zero, we can plug these values into the Taylor rule to obtain

$$r = 0.01 - 0.5(0) + 0.5(0.03) = 0.025 = 2.5\%.$$

So the real interest rate implied by the Taylor rule when inflation is 3 percent and the output gap is zero is 2.5 percent. The nominal interest rate equals the real rate plus the inflation rate, or 2.5% + 3% = 5.5%.

If there is a recessionary gap of 1 percent of potential output, the Taylor rule formula becomes

$$r = 0.01 - 0.5(0.01) + 0.5(0.03) = 0.02 = 2\%.$$

The nominal interest rate implied by the Taylor rule in this case is the 2 percent real rate plus the 3 percent inflation rate, or 5 percent. So the Taylor rule has the Fed lowering the interest rate when the economy goes into recession, which is both sensible and realistic. *(LO5)*

11

Aggregate Demand, Aggregate Supply, and Inflation

On October 6, 1979, the Federal Open Market Committee, the policymaking committee of the Federal Reserve, held a highly unusual—and unusually secretive—Saturday meeting. Fed chair Paul Volcker may have called the Saturday meeting because he knew the financial markets would be closed and thus would not be able to respond to any "leaks" to the press about the discussions. Or perhaps he hoped that the visit of Pope John Paul II to Washington on the same day would distract the news media from goings-on at the Fed. However unnoticed this meeting may have been at the time, in retrospect it marked a turning point in postwar U.S. economic history.

When Volcker called the October 6 meeting, he had been Fed chair for only six weeks. Six feet eight inches tall with a booming bass voice, and a chain-smoker of cheap cigars, Volcker had a reputation for financial conservatism and personal toughness. Partly for those qualities, President Carter had appointed Volcker to head the Federal Reserve in August 1979. Carter needed a tough Fed chair to restore confidence in both the economy and the government's economic policies. The U.S. economy faced many problems, including a doubling of oil prices following the overthrow of the Shah of Iran and a worrisome slowdown in productivity growth. But in the minds of the public, the biggest economic worry was an inflation rate that seemed to be out of control. In the second half of 1979, the annual rate of increase in consumer prices had reached 13 percent; by the spring of 1980, the inflation rate had risen to nearly 16 percent. Volcker's assignment: to bring inflation under control and stabilize the U.S. economy.

Volcker knew that getting rid of inflation would not be easy, and he warned his colleagues that a "shock treatment" might be necessary. His plan was couched in technical details, but in essence he proposed to reduce the rate of growth of the money supply sharply. Everyone in the room knew that slowing the growth of the money supply would cause interest rates to rise and aggregate spending to fall. Inflation might be brought down, but at what cost in terms of recession, lost output, and lost jobs? And how would the financial markets, which were already shaky, react to the new approach?

LEARNING OBJECTIVES

After reading this chapter, you should be able to:

LO1 Define the aggregate demand curve, explain why it slopes downward, and explain what may shift it.

LO2 Define the long-run and short-run aggregate supply curves, explain their orientation, and explain what may shift them. In particular, show how the curves capture the idea of inflation inertia and the link between inflation and the output gap.

LO3 Analyze how the economy is affected by aggregate spending shocks, inflation shocks, and shocks to potential output.

LO4 Discuss the short-run and long-run effects of an anti-inflationary monetary policy.

Dennis Brack/Newscom

Paul Volcker faced a tough assignment.

Officials in the room stirred nervously as Volcker spoke about the necessity of the move. Finally a vote was called. Every hand went up.

What happened next? We'll return to this story before the chapter ends, but first we need to introduce the basic framework for understanding inflation and the policies used to control it. In the previous two chapters, we made the assumption that firms are willing to meet the demand for their products at preset prices. When firms simply produce what is demanded, the level of aggregate expenditure determines the nation's real GDP. If the resulting level of short-run equilibrium output is lower than potential output, a recessionary output gap develops, and if the resulting level of output exceeds potential output, the economy experiences an expansionary gap. As we saw in the previous two chapters, policymakers can attempt to eliminate output gaps by taking actions that affect the level of autonomous expenditure, such as changing the level of government spending or taxes (fiscal policy) or using the Fed's control of the money supply to change the real interest rate (monetary policy).

The basic Keynesian account of the economy, or model, is useful for understanding the role of spending in the short-run determination of output, but it is too simplified to provide a fully realistic description of the economy. The main shortcoming of the basic Keynesian model is that it does not explain the behavior of *inflation*. Although firms may meet demand at preset prices for a time, as assumed in the basic Keynesian model, prices do *not* remain fixed indefinitely. Indeed, sometimes they may rise quite rapidly—the phenomenon of high inflation—imposing significant costs on the economy in the process. In this chapter, we will extend the basic Keynesian model to allow for ongoing inflation. As we will show, the extended model can be conveniently represented by a new diagram, called the *aggregate demand–aggregate supply diagram*. Using this extended analysis, we will be able to show how macroeconomic policies affect inflation as well as output, illustrating in the process the difficult trade-offs policymakers sometimes face.

aggregate demand (*AD*) curve shows the relationship between short-run equilibrium output Y and the rate of inflation π; it thus shows the amount of output consumers, firms, government, and foreign entities want to purchase at each inflation rate, holding all other factors constant

INFLATION, SPENDING, AND OUTPUT: THE AGGREGATE DEMAND CURVE

To begin incorporating inflation into the model, our first step is to introduce a new relationship, called the *aggregate demand curve,* which is shown graphically in Figure 11.1. The **aggregate demand (*AD*) curve** shows the relationship between short-run equilibrium output Y and the rate of inflation, denoted π. The name of

FIGURE 11.1

The Aggregate Demand (*AD*) Curve.

The *AD* curve shows the relationship between short-run equilibrium output Y and the rate of inflation π. Because short-run equilibrium output equals planned spending, the *AD* curve also shows the relationship between inflation and planned spending. The downward slope of the *AD* curve implies that an increase in inflation reduces short-run equilibrium output.

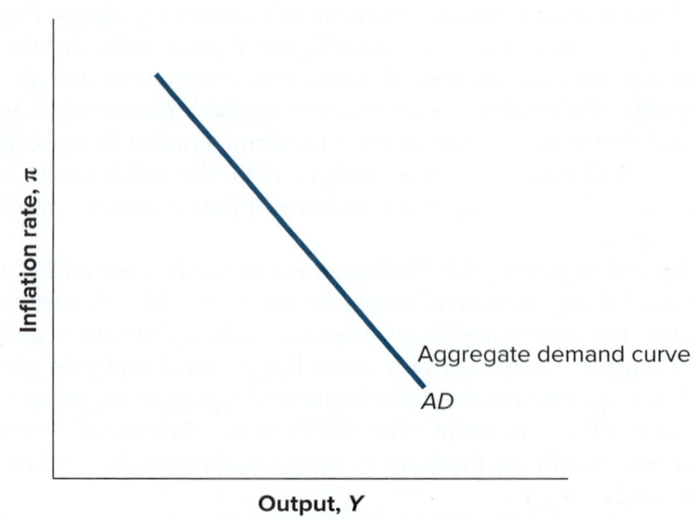

the curve reflects the fact that, as we have seen, short-run equilibrium output is determined by total spending, or demand, in the economy. Indeed, by definition, short-run equilibrium output *equals* aggregate expenditure, so that we could just as well say that the *AD* curve shows the relationship between inflation and spending.

We will see shortly that, all else being equal, *an increase in the rate of inflation tends to reduce short-run equilibrium output*. Therefore, in a diagram showing inflation π on the vertical axis and output Y on the horizontal axis (Figure 11.1), the aggregate demand curve is downward-sloping.[1] Note that we refer to the *AD* "curve," even though the relationship is drawn as a straight line in Figure 11.1. In general, the *AD* curve can be either straight or curving.

Why does higher inflation lead to a lower level of spending and short-run equilibrium output? As we will see next, one important reason is the Fed's response to increases in inflation.

Inflation, the Fed, and Why the *AD* Curve Slopes Downward

One of the primary responsibilities of the Fed, or any central bank, is to maintain a low and stable rate of inflation. For example, in recent years the Fed has tried to keep inflation in the United States at 2 percent over the long run. By keeping inflation low, the central bank tries to avoid the costs high inflation imposes on the economy.

What can the Fed do to keep inflation low and stable? As we have already mentioned, one situation that is likely to lead to increased inflation is an expansionary output gap, in which short-run equilibrium output exceeds potential output. When output is above potential output, firms must produce at above-normal capacity to meet the demands of their customers. Like Alice's ice cream store, described in Chapter 9, *Short-Term Economic Fluctuations and Fiscal Policy,* firms may be willing to do this for a time. But eventually they will adjust to the high level of demand by raising prices, contributing to inflation. To control inflation, then, the Fed needs to dampen spending and output when they threaten to exceed potential output.

How can the Fed avoid a situation of economic "overheating," in which spending and output exceed potential output? As we saw in the previous chapter, the Fed can act to reduce aggregate expenditure, and hence short-run equilibrium output, by raising the real interest rate. This behavior by the Fed is a key factor that underlies the link between inflation and output that is summarized by the aggregate demand curve. When inflation is high, the Fed responds by raising the real interest rate. Such response is implied by the Fed's *policy reaction function,* introduced in Chapter 10, *Stabilizing the Economy: The Role of the Fed* (also called a *monetary policy rule,* the reaction function describes how a central bank, like the Fed, takes action in response to changes in the state of the economy). The increase in the real interest rate reduces consumption and investment spending (aggregate expenditure) and hence reduces short-run equilibrium output. Because higher inflation leads, through the Fed's actions, to a reduction in output, the aggregate demand (*AD*) curve is downward-sloping, as Figure 11.1 shows. We can summarize this chain of reasoning symbolically as

$$\pi \uparrow \Rightarrow r \uparrow \Rightarrow \text{autonomous expenditure} \downarrow \Rightarrow Y \downarrow, \qquad (AD \text{ curve})$$

where, recall, π is inflation, r is the real interest rate, and Y is output.

[1]Economists sometimes define the aggregate demand curve as the relationship between aggregate demand and the *price level,* rather than inflation, which is the *rate of change* of the price level. The definition used here both simplifies the analysis and yields results more consistent with real-world data. For a comparison of the two approaches, see David Romer, "Keynesian Macroeconomics without the LM Curve," *Journal of Economic Perspectives,* Spring 2000, pp. 149–170. The graphical analysis used in this chapter follows closely the approach recommended by Romer.

Other Reasons for the Downward Slope of the *AD* Curve

Although we focus here on the behavior of the Fed as the source of the *AD* curve's downward slope, there are other channels through which higher inflation reduces spending and thus short-run equilibrium output. Hence the downward slope of the *AD* curve does not depend on the Fed behaving in the particular way just described.

One additional reason for the downward slope of the *AD* curve is the effect of inflation on the *real value of money* held by households and businesses. At high levels of inflation, the purchasing power of money held by the public declines rapidly. This reduction in the public's real wealth may cause households to restrain consumption spending, reducing short-run equilibrium output.

distributional effects changes in the distribution of income or wealth in the economy

A second channel by which inflation may affect spending is through **distributional effects.** Studies have found that people who are less well off are often hurt more by inflation than wealthier people are. For example, retirees on fixed incomes and workers receiving the minimum wage (which is set in dollar terms) lose buying power when prices are rising rapidly. Less affluent people are also likely to be relatively unsophisticated in making financial investments and hence less able than wealthier citizens to protect their savings against inflation.

People at the lower end of the income distribution tend to spend a greater percentage of their disposable income than do wealthier individuals. Thus, if a burst of inflation redistributes resources from relatively high-spending, less affluent households toward relatively high-saving, more affluent households, overall spending may decline.

A third connection between inflation and aggregate demand arises because higher rates of inflation generate *uncertainty* for households and businesses. When inflation is high, people become less certain about what things will cost in the future, and uncertainty makes planning more difficult. In an uncertain economic environment, both households and firms may become more cautious, reducing their spending as a result.

A final link between inflation and total spending operates through the *prices of domestic goods and services sold abroad*. As we will see in the next chapter, the foreign price of domestic goods depends in part on the rate at which the domestic currency, such as the dollar, exchanges for foreign currencies, such as the British pound. However, for constant rates of exchange between currencies, a rise in domestic inflation causes the prices of domestic goods in foreign markets to rise more quickly. As domestic goods become relatively more expensive to prospective foreign purchasers, export sales decline. Net exports are part of aggregate expenditure, and so once more we find that increased inflation is likely to reduce spending. All these factors contribute to the downward slope of the *AD* curve, together with the behavior of the Fed.

Factors That Shift the Aggregate Demand Curve

The downward slope of the aggregate demand, or *AD*, curve shown in Figure 11.1 reflects the fact that *all other factors held constant,* a higher level of inflation will lead to lower spending and thus lower short-run equilibrium output. Again, a principal reason higher inflation reduces spending and output is that the Fed tends to react to increases in inflation by raising the real interest rate, which in turn reduces consumption and investment, two important components of aggregate expenditure.

change in aggregate demand a shift of the *AD* curve

However, even if inflation is held constant, various factors can affect spending and short-run equilibrium output. Graphically, as we will see in this section, these factors will cause a **change in aggregate demand,** which causes the *AD* curve to

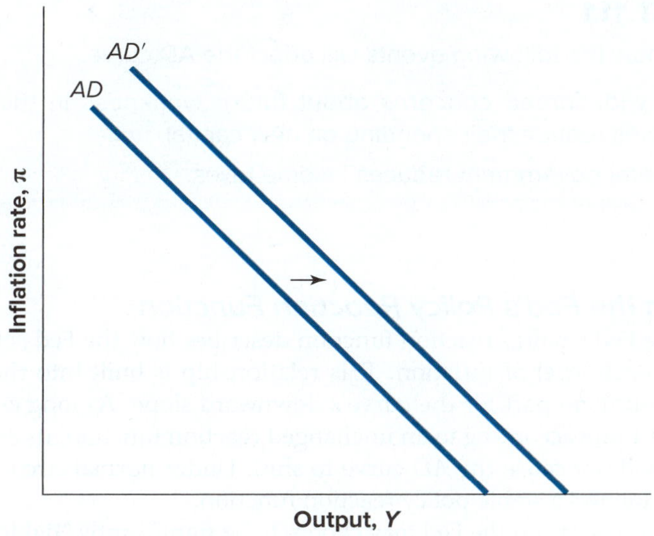

FIGURE 11.2

Effect of an Increase in Exogenous Spending.

The *AD* curve is seen both *before* (*AD*) and *after* (*AD′*) an increase in exogenous spending—specifically, an increase in consumption spending resulting from a rise in the stock market. If the inflation rate and the real interest rate set by the Fed are held constant, an increase in exogenous spending raises short-run equilibrium output. As a result, the *AD* curve will shift to the right, from *AD* to *AD′*.

shift. Specifically, for a given level of inflation, if there is a change in the economy that *increases* short-run equilibrium output, the *AD* curve will shift to the *right* (we provide an example in Figure 11.2). If, on the other hand, the change *reduces* short-run equilibrium output at each level of inflation, the *AD* curve will shift to the *left* [Figure 11.3(b) provides an example]. We will focus on two sorts of changes in the economy that shift the aggregate demand curve: (1) changes in spending caused by factors other than output or interest rates, which we will refer to as *exogenous* changes in spending; and (2) changes in the Fed's monetary policy, as reflected in a shift in the Fed's policy reaction function.

Changes in Spending

We have seen that aggregate expenditure depends both on output (through the consumption function) and on the real interest rate (which affects both consumption and investment). However, many factors other than output or the real interest rate can affect spending. For example, at given levels of output and the real interest rate, fiscal policy affects the level of government purchases, and changes in consumer confidence can affect consumption spending. Likewise, new technological opportunities may lead firms to increase their investment, and an increased willingness of foreigners to purchases domestic goods will raise net exports. We will refer to changes in spending unrelated to changes in output or the real interest rate as *exogenous* changes in spending.

For a given inflation rate (and thus for a given real interest rate set by the Fed), an exogenous increase in spending raises short-run equilibrium output, for the reasons we have discussed in the past two chapters. Because it increases output at each level of inflation, *an exogenous increase in spending shifts the AD curve to the right*. This result is illustrated graphically in Figure 11.2. Imagine, for example, that a rise in the stock market makes consumers more willing to spend (the wealth effect). Then, for each level of inflation, aggregate spending and short-run equilibrium output will be higher, a change which is shown as a shift of the *AD* curve to the right, from *AD* to *AD′*.

Similarly, at a given inflation rate, an exogenous decline in spending—for example, a fall in government purchases resulting from a more restrictive fiscal policy—causes short-run equilibrium output to fall. We conclude that *an exogenous decrease in spending shifts the AD curve to the left*.

SELF-TEST 11.1

Determine how the following events will affect the AD curve.

a. Due to widespread concerns about future weakness in the economy, businesses reduce their spending on new capital.

b. The federal government reduces income taxes.

Changes in the Fed's Policy Reaction Function

Recall that the Fed's policy reaction function describes how the Fed sets the real interest rate at each level of inflation. This relationship is built into the *AD* curve—indeed, it accounts in part for the curve's downward slope. As long as the Fed sets the real interest rate according to an unchanged reaction function, its adjustments in the real rate will not cause the *AD* curve to shift. Under normal circumstances, the Fed generally follows a stable policy reaction function.

However, on occasion the Fed may choose to be significantly "tighter" or "easier" than normal for a given rate of inflation. For example, if inflation is high and has stubbornly refused to decrease, the Fed might choose a tighter monetary policy, setting the real interest rate higher than normal at each given rate of inflation. This change of policy can be interpreted as an upward shift in the Fed's policy reaction function, as shown in Figure 11.3(a), where the real interest rate on the vertical axis is depicted as a function of inflation on the horizontal axis. A decision by the Fed to become more "hawkish" about inflation—that is, to set the real interest rate at a higher level for each given rate of inflation—reduces aggregate expenditure and thus short-run equilibrium output at each rate of inflation. Thus an upward shift of the Fed's policy reaction function leads the *AD* curve to shift to the left [Figure 11.3(b)]. Later in the chapter, we will interpret Chair Volcker's attack on inflation in 1979 as precisely such a policy shift.

FIGURE 11.3

A Shift in the Fed's Policy Reaction Function.

If inflation has remained too high for an extended period, the Fed may choose a "tighter" monetary policy by setting the real interest rate at a higher level than usual for each given rate of inflation. Graphically, this change corresponds to an upward movement in the Fed's policy reaction function (a). This change to a tighter monetary policy shifts the *AD* curve to the left (b). If a protracted recession led the Fed to decide to set a lower real interest rate at each level of inflation, the Fed's policy reaction function would shift downward, and the *AD* curve would shift to the right.

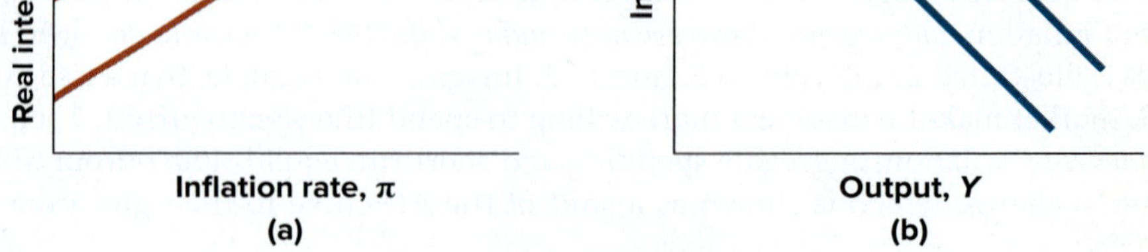

Similarly, if the nation is experiencing an unusually severe and protracted recession, the Fed may choose to change its policies and set the real interest rate lower than normal, given the rate of inflation. This change in policy can be interpreted as a downward shift of the Fed's policy reaction function. Given the rate of inflation, a lower-than-normal setting of the real interest rate will lead to higher levels of expenditure and short-run equilibrium output. Therefore, a downward shift of the Fed's policy reaction function causes the *AD* curve to shift to the right.

SELF-TEST 11.2

Explain why a shift in monetary policy like that shown in Figure 11.3 can be interpreted as a decline in the Fed's long-run "target" for the inflation rate. (*Hint:* In the long run, the real interest rate set by the Fed must be consistent with the real interest rate determined in the market for saving and investment.)

Shifts of the *AD* Curve versus Movements along the *AD* Curve

Let's end this section by reviewing and summarizing the important distinction between *movements along* the *AD* curve and *shifts* of the *AD* curve.

The downward slope of the *AD* curve captures the inverse relationship between inflation, on the one hand, and short-run equilibrium output, on the other. As we have seen, a rise in the inflation rate leads the Fed to raise the real interest rate, according to its policy reaction function. The higher real interest rate, in turn, depresses spending and hence lowers short-run equilibrium output. The downward slope of the *AD* curve embodies this relationship among inflation, spending, and output. Hence changes in the inflation rate, and the resulting changes in the real interest rate and short-run equilibrium output, are represented by *movements along* the *AD* curve. In particular, as long as the Fed sets the real interest rate in accordance with a fixed policy reaction function, changes in the real interest rate will *not* shift the *AD* curve.

However, any factor that changes the short-run equilibrium level of output *at a given level of inflation* will *shift* the *AD* curve—to the right if short-run equilibrium output increases or to the left if short-run equilibrium output decreases. We have identified two factors that can shift the *AD* curve: exogenous changes in spending (that is, changes in spending unrelated to output or the real interest rate) and changes in the Fed's policy reaction function. An exogenous increase in spending or a downward shift of the Fed's policy reaction function increases short-run equilibrium output at every level of inflation, hence shifting the *AD* curve to the right. An exogenous decline in spending or an upward shift in the Fed's policy reaction function decreases short-run equilibrium output at every level of inflation, shifting the *AD* curve to the left.

SELF-TEST 11.3

What is the difference, if any, between the following?

a. An upward shift in the Fed's policy reaction function.

b. A response by the Fed to higher inflation, for a given policy reaction function.

How does each scenario affect the *AD* curve?

RECAP

THE AGGREGATE DEMAND (*AD*) CURVE

- The *AD* curve shows the relationship between short-run equilibrium output and inflation. Higher inflation leads the Fed to raise the real interest rate, which reduces aggregate expenditure and thus short-run equilibrium output. Therefore, the *AD* curve slopes downward.
- The *AD* curve may also slope downward because (1) higher inflation reduces the real value of money held by the public, reducing wealth and spending; (2) inflation redistributes resources from less affluent people, who spend a high percentage of their disposable income, to more affluent people, who spend a smaller percentage of disposable income; (3) higher inflation creates greater uncertainty in planning for households and firms, reducing their spending; and (4) for a constant rate of exchange between the dollar and other currencies, rising prices of domestic goods and services reduce foreign sales and hence net exports (a component of aggregate spending).
- An exogenous increase in spending raises short-run equilibrium output at each value of inflation, and so shifts the *AD* curve to the right. Conversely, an exogenous decrease in spending shifts the *AD* curve to the left.
- A change to an easier monetary policy, as reflected by a downward shift in the Fed's policy reaction function, shifts the *AD* curve to the right. A change to a tighter, more anti-inflationary monetary policy, as reflected by an upward shift in the Fed's policy reaction function, shifts the *AD* curve to the left.
- Assuming no change in the Fed's reaction function, changes in inflation correspond to movements *along* the *AD* curve; they do not *shift* the *AD* curve.

INFLATION AND AGGREGATE SUPPLY

Thus far in this chapter, we have focused on how changes in inflation affect spending and short-run equilibrium output, a relationship captured by the *AD* curve. But we have not yet discussed how inflation itself is determined. In the rest of the chapter, we will examine the main factors that determine the inflation rate in modern industrial economies, as well as the options that policymakers have to control inflation. In doing so, we will introduce a useful diagram for analyzing the behavior of output and inflation, called the *aggregate demand–aggregate supply diagram.*

Physicists have noted that a body will tend to keep moving at a constant speed and direction unless it is acted upon by some outside force–a tendency they refer to as *inertia*. Applying this concept to economics, many observers have noted that inflation seems to be inertial, in the sense that it tends to remain roughly constant as long as the economy is at full employment and there are no external shocks to the price level. In the first part of this section, we will discuss why inflation behaves in this way.

However, just as a physical object will change speed if it is acted on by outside forces, so various economic forces can change the rate of inflation. Later in this chapter, we will discuss three factors that can cause the inflation rate to change. The first, which we will discuss in this section, is the presence of an *output gap:* Inflation tends to rise when there is an expansionary output gap and to fall when there is a recessionary output gap. The second factor that can affect the inflation rate is a shock that directly affects prices, which we will refer to as an *inflation shock*. A large increase in the price of imported oil, for example, raises the price of gasoline, heating oil, and other fuels, as well as of goods made with oil or services using oil, such as transportation. Finally, the third factor that directly affects the inflation rate is a *shock to potential output,* or a sharp change in the level of potential output—a natural disaster that destroyed a significant portion of a country's factories and businesses is one extreme example. Together, inflationary shocks and shocks to potential output are known as *aggregate supply shocks;* we postpone discussing them until the next section.

Inflation Inertia

In low-inflation industrial economies like that of the United States today, inflation tends to change relatively slowly from year to year, a phenomenon that is sometimes referred to as *inflation inertia*. If the rate of inflation in one year is 2 percent, it may be 3 percent or even 4 percent in the next year. But unless the nation experiences very unusual economic conditions, inflation is unlikely to rise to 6 percent or 8 percent or fall to −2 percent in the following year. This relatively sluggish behavior contrasts sharply with the behavior of economic variables such as stock or commodity prices, which can change rapidly from day to day. For example, oil prices might well rise by 20 percent over the course of a year and then fall 20 percent over the next year. Over the past 30 years or so, however, the U.S. inflation rate has generally remained in the range of 2–3 percent per year, with only small and short-lived deviations.

Why does inflation tend to adjust relatively slowly in modern industrial economies? To answer this question, we must consider two closely related factors that play an important role in determining the inflation rate: the behavior of the public's *inflation expectations* and the existence of *long-term wage and price contracts*.

Inflation Expectations

First, consider the public's expectations about inflation. In negotiating future wages and prices, both buyers and sellers take into account the rate of inflation they expect to prevail in the next few years. As a result, today's *expectations* of future inflation may help determine the future inflation rate. Suppose, for example, that office worker Fred and his boss Colleen agree that Fred's performance this past year justifies an increase of 2 percent in his real wage for next year. What *nominal,* or dollar, wage increase should they agree on? If Fred believes that inflation is likely to be 3 percent over the next year, he will ask for a 5 percent increase in his nominal wage to obtain a 2 percent increase in his real wage. If Colleen agrees that inflation is likely to be 3 percent, she should be willing to go along with a 5 percent nominal increase, knowing that it implies only a 2 percent increase in Fred's real wage. Thus the rate at which Fred and Colleen *expect* prices to rise affects the rate at which at least one price—Fred's nominal wage—*actually* rises.

A similar dynamic affects the contracts for production inputs other than labor. For example, if Colleen is negotiating with her office supply company, the prices she will agree to pay for next year's deliveries of copy paper and staples will depend on what she expects the inflation rate to be. If Colleen anticipates that the price of office supplies will not change relative to the prices of other goods and services, and that the general inflation rate will be 3 percent, then she should be willing to agree to a 3 percent increase in the price of office supplies. On the other hand, if she expects the general inflation rate to be 6 percent, then she will agree to pay 6 percent more for copy paper and staples next year, knowing that a nominal increase of 6 percent implies no change in the price of office supplies relative to other goods and services.

Economywide, then, the higher the expected rate of inflation, the more nominal wages and the cost of other inputs will tend to rise. But if wages and other costs of production grow rapidly in response to expected inflation, firms will have to raise their prices rapidly as well in order to cover their costs. Thus a high rate of expected inflation tends to lead to a high rate of actual inflation. Similarly, if expected inflation is low, leading wages and other costs to rise relatively slowly, actual inflation should be low as well.

SELF-TEST 11.4

Assume that employers and workers agree that real wages should rise by 2 percent next year.

a. If inflation is expected to be 2 percent next year, what will happen to nominal wages next year?

b. If inflation is expected to be 4 percent next year, rather than 2 percent, what will happen to nominal wages next year?

c. Use your answers from parts a and b to explain how an increase in expected inflation will tend to affect the following year's actual rate of inflation.

The conclusion that actual inflation is partially determined by expected inflation raises the question of what determines inflation expectations. To a great extent, people's expectations are influenced by their recent experience. If inflation has been low and stable for some time, people are likely to expect it to continue to be low. But if inflation has recently been high, people will expect it to continue to be high. If inflation has been unpredictable, alternating between low and high levels, the public's expectations will likewise tend to be volatile, rising or falling with news or rumors about economic conditions or economic policy.

Figure 11.4 illustrates schematically how low and stable inflation may tend to be self-perpetuating. As the figure shows, if inflation has been low for some time, people will continue to expect low inflation. Increases in nominal wages and other production costs will thus tend to be small. If firms raise prices only by enough to cover costs, then actual inflation will be low, as expected. This low actual rate in turn will promote low expected inflation, perpetuating the "virtuous circle." The same logic applies in reverse in an economy with high inflation: A persistently high inflation rate leads the public to expect high inflation, resulting in higher increases in nominal wages and other production costs. This in turn contributes to a high rate of actual inflation, and so on in a vicious circle. This role of inflation expectations in the determination of wage and price increases helps explain why inflation often seems to adjust slowly.

Long-Term Wage and Price Contracts

The role of inflation expectations in the slow adjustment of inflation is strengthened by a second key element, the existence of *long-term wage and price contracts*. Union wage contracts, for example, often extend for three years into the future. Likewise, contracts that set the prices manufacturing firms pay for parts and raw materials often cover several years. Long-term contracts serve to "build in" wage and price

FIGURE 11.4

A Virtuous Circle of Low Inflation and Low Expected Inflation.

Low inflation leads people to expect low inflation in the future. As a result, they agree to accept small increases in wages and in the prices of the goods and services they supply, which keeps inflation—and expected inflation—low. In a similar way, high inflation leads people to expect high inflation, which in turn tends to produce high inflation.

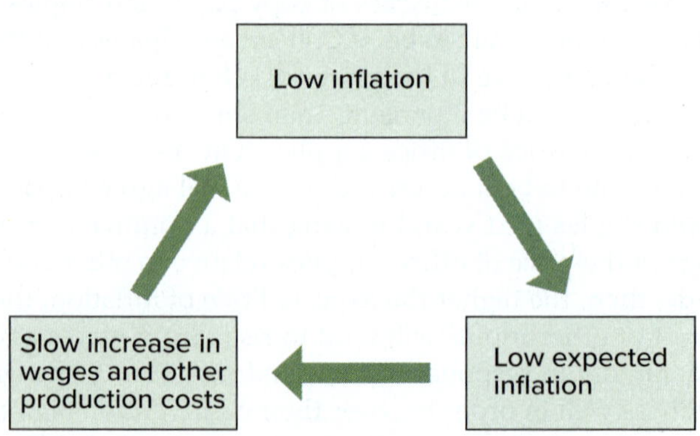

increases that depend on inflation expectations at the time the contracts were signed. For example, a union negotiating in a high-inflation environment is much more likely to demand a rapid increase in nominal wages over the life of the contract than would a union in an economy in which prices are stable.

To summarize, in the absence of external shocks, inflation tends to remain relatively stable over time—at least in low-inflation industrial economies like that of the United States. In other words, inflation is *inertial* (or as some people put it, "sticky"). Inflation tends to be inertial for two main reasons. The first is the behavior of people's expectations of inflation. A low inflation rate leads people to expect low inflation in the future, which results in reduced pressure for wage and price increases. Similarly, a high inflation rate leads people to expect high inflation in the future, resulting in more rapid increases in wages and prices. Second, the effects of expectations are reinforced by the existence of long-term wage and price contracts, which is the second reason inflation tends to be stable over time. Long-term contracts tend to build in the effects of people's inflation expectations.

Although the rate of inflation tends to be inertial, it does of course change over time. We next discuss a key factor causing the inflation rate to change.

SELF-TEST 11.5

Based on Figure 11.4, discuss why the Federal Reserve has a strong incentive to maintain a low inflation rate in the economy.

The Output Gap and Inflation

An important factor influencing the rate of inflation is the output gap, or the difference between actual output and potential output ($Y - Y^*$). We have seen that, in the short run, firms will meet the demand for their output at previously determined prices. For example, Alice's ice cream shop will serve ice cream to any customer who comes into the shop at the prices posted behind the counter. The level of output that is determined by the demand at preset prices is called short-run equilibrium output.

At a particular time the level of short-run equilibrium output may happen to equal the economy's long-run productive capacity, or potential output. But that is not necessarily the case. Output may exceed potential output, giving rise to an expansionary gap, or it may fall short of potential output, producing a recessionary gap. Let's consider what happens to inflation in each of these three possible cases: no output gap, an expansionary gap, and a recessionary gap. The resulting outcomes are summarized in Table 11.1.

TABLE 11.1
The Output Gap and Inflation

The table shows three possible situations. With no output gap, the rate of inflation will tend to remain the same. With expansionary gap, the rate of inflation will tend to increase. With recessionary gap, the rate of inflation will tend to decrease.

Relationship of output to potential output		Behavior of inflation
1. No output gap $Y = Y^*$	→	Inflation remains unchanged
2. Expansionary gap $Y > Y^*$	→	Inflation rises $\pi\uparrow$
3. Recessionary gap $Y < Y^*$	→	Inflation falls $\pi\downarrow$

No Output Gap: $Y = Y^*$

If actual output equals potential output, then by definition, there is no output gap. When the output gap is zero, firms are satisfied in the sense that their sales equal their normal production rates. As a result, firms have no incentive either to reduce or increase their prices *relative* to the prices of other goods and services. However, the fact that firms are satisfied with their sales does *not* imply that inflation—the rate of change in the overall price level—is zero.

To see why, let's go back to the idea of inflation inertia. Suppose that inflation has recently been steady at 3 percent per year, so that the public has come to expect an inflation rate of 3 percent per year. If the public's inflation expectations are reflected in the wage and price increases agreed to in long-term contracts, then firms will find their labor and materials costs are rising at 3 percent per year. To cover their costs, firms will need to raise their prices by 3 percent per year. Note that if all firms are raising their prices by 3 percent per year, the *relative* prices of various goods and services in the economy—say, the price of ice cream relative to the price of a taxi ride—will not change. Nevertheless, the economywide rate of inflation equals 3 percent, the same as in previous years. We conclude that, *if the output gap is zero, the rate of inflation will tend to remain the same.*

Expansionary Gap: $Y > Y^*$

Suppose instead that an expansionary gap exists so that most firms' sales exceed their normal production rates. As we might expect in situations in which the quantity demanded exceeds the quantity firms desire to supply, firms will ultimately respond by trying to increase their relative prices. To do so, they will increase their prices by *more* than the increase in their costs. If all firms behave this way, then the general price level will begin to rise more rapidly than before. Thus, *when an expansionary gap exists, the rate of inflation will tend to increase.*

Recessionary Gap: $Y < Y^*$

Finally, if a recessionary gap exists, firms will be selling an amount less than their capacity to produce, and they will have an incentive to cut their relative prices so they can sell more. In this case, firms will raise their prices less than needed to cover fully their increases in costs, as determined by the existing inflation rate. As a result, *when a recessionary gap exists, the rate of inflation will tend to decrease.*

EXAMPLE 11.1 Spending Changes and Inflation

How will a fall in consumer confidence affect the rate of inflation?

In Chapter 9, *Short-Term Economic Fluctuations and Fiscal Policy*, and Chapter 10, *Stabilizing the Economy: The Role of the Fed*, we saw that changes in spending can create expansionary or recessionary gaps. Therefore, based on the discussion above, we can conclude that changes in spending also lead to changes in the rate of inflation. If the economy is currently operating at potential output, what effect will a fall in consumer confidence that makes consumers less willing to spend at each level of disposable income have on the rate of inflation in the economy?

An exogenous decrease in consumption spending, C, for a given level of inflation, output, and real interest rates, reduces aggregate expenditures and short-run equilibrium output. If the economy was originally operating at potential output, the reduction in consumption will cause a recessionary gap since actual output, Y, will now be less than potential output, Y^*. As indicated above, when $Y < Y^*$, the rate of inflation will tend to fall because firms' sales fall short of normal production rates, leading them to slow down the rate at which they increase their prices.

SELF-TEST 11.6

Suppose that firms become optimistic about the future and decide to increase their investment in new capital. What effect will this have on the rate of inflation, assuming that the economy is currently operating at potential output?

The Aggregate Demand–Aggregate Supply Diagram

The adjustment of inflation in response to an output gap can be shown conveniently in a diagram. Figure 11.5, drawn with inflation π on the vertical axis and real output Y on the horizontal axis, is an example of an *aggregate demand–aggregate supply diagram,* or *AD-AS diagram* for short. The diagram has three elements, one of which is the downward-sloping *AD* curve, introduced earlier in the chapter. Recall that the *AD* curve shows how aggregate spending, and hence short-run equilibrium output, depends on the inflation rate. The second element is a vertical line marking the economy's potential output Y^*. Because potential output represents the economy's long-run productive capacity, we will refer to this vertical line as the **long-run aggregate supply (*LRAS*) line.** The third element in Figure 11.5, and a new one, is the *short-run aggregate supply line,* labeled *SRAS* in the diagram. The **short-run aggregate supply (*SRAS*) line** is a horizontal line that shows the current rate of inflation in the economy, which in the figure is labeled π. We can think of the current rate of inflation as having been determined by past expectations of inflation and past pricing decisions. The short-run aggregate supply line is horizontal because, in the short run, producers supply whatever output is demanded at preset prices.

long-run aggregate supply (*LRAS*) line a vertical line showing the economy's potential output Y^*

short-run aggregate supply (*SRAS*) line a horizontal line showing the current rate of inflation, as determined by past expectations and pricing decisions

The *AD-AS* diagram can be used to determine the level of output prevailing at any particular time. As we have seen, the inflation rate at any moment is given directly by the position of the *SRAS* line—for example, current inflation equals π in Figure 11.5. To find the current level of output, recall that the *AD* curve shows the level of short-run equilibrium output at any given rate of inflation. Since the inflation rate in this economy is π, we can infer from Figure 11.5 that short-run equilibrium output must equal Y, which corresponds to the intersection of the *AD* curve and the *SRAS* line (point *A* in the figure). Notice that in Figure 11.5, short-run equilibrium output Y is smaller than potential output Y^*, so there is a recessionary gap in this economy.

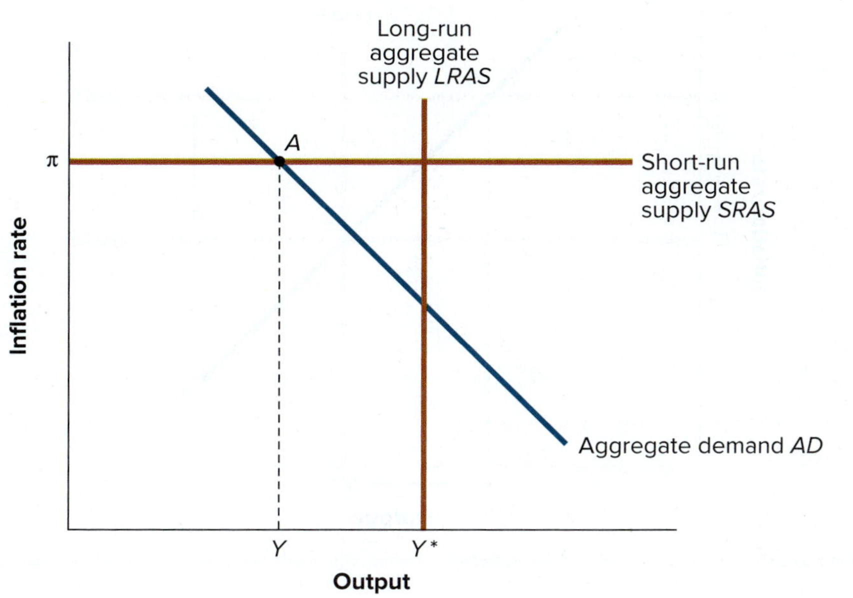

FIGURE 11.5

The Aggregate Demand–Aggregate Supply (*AD-AS*) Diagram.

This diagram has three elements: the *AD* curve, which shows how short-run equilibrium output depends on inflation; the long-run aggregate supply (*LRAS*) line, which marks the economy's potential output Y^*; and the short-run aggregate supply (*SRAS*) line, which shows the current value of inflation π. Short-run equilibrium output, which is equal to Y here, is determined by the intersection of the *AD* curve and the *SRAS* line (point *A*). Because actual output Y is less than potential output Y^*, this economy has a recessionary gap.

The intersection of the *AD* curve and the *SRAS* line (point *A* in Figure 11.5) is referred to as the point of *short-run equilibrium* in this economy. When the economy is in **short-run equilibrium,** inflation equals the value determined by past expectations and past pricing decisions, and output equals the level of short-run equilibrium output that is consistent with that inflation rate.

short-run equilibrium a situation in which inflation equals the value determined by past expectations and pricing decisions and output equals the level of short-run equilibrium output that is consistent with that inflation rate; graphically, short-run equilibrium occurs at the intersection of the *AD* curve and the *SRAS* line

Although the economy may be in short-run equilibrium at point *A* in Figure 11.5, it will not remain there. The reason is that at point *A*, the economy is experiencing a recessionary gap (output is less than potential output, as indicated by the *LRAS* line). As we have just seen, when a recessionary gap exists, firms are not selling as much as they would like to and so they slow down the rate at which they increase their prices. Eventually, the low level of aggregate demand that is associated with a recessionary gap causes the inflation rate to fall.

The adjustment of inflation in response to a recessionary gap is shown graphically in Figure 11.6. As inflation declines, the *SRAS* line moves downward, from *SRAS* to *SRAS′*. Because of inflation inertia (caused by the slow adjustment of the public's inflation expectations and the existence of long-term contracts), inflation adjusts downward only gradually. However, as long as a recessionary gap exists, inflation will continue to fall, and the *SRAS* line will move downward until it intersects the *AD* curve at point *B* in the figure. At that point, actual output equals potential output and the recessionary gap has been eliminated. Because there is no further pressure on inflation at point *B*, the inflation rate stabilizes at the lower level. A situation like that represented by point *B* in Figure 11.6, in which the inflation rate is stable and actual output equals potential output, is referred to as **long-run equilibrium** of the economy. Long-run equilibrium occurs when the *AD* curve, the *SRAS* line, and the *LRAS* line all intersect at a single point.

long-run equilibrium a situation in which actual output equals potential output and the inflation rate is stable; graphically, long-run equilibrium occurs when the *AD* curve, the *SRAS* line, and the *LRAS* line all intersect at a single point

Figure 11.6 illustrates the important point that when a recessionary gap exists, inflation will tend to fall. It also shows that as inflation declines, short-run equilibrium output rises, increasing gradually from *Y* to *Y** as the short-run equilibrium point moves down the *AD* curve. The source of this increase in output is the behavior of the Federal Reserve, which lowers the real interest rate as inflation falls, stimulating aggregate demand. Falling inflation stimulates spending and output in other ways, such as by reducing uncertainty.[2] As output rises cyclical unemployment, also

FIGURE 11.6

The Adjustment of Inflation When a Recessionary Gap Exists.

At the initial short-run equilibrium point *A*, a recessionary gap exists, which puts downward pressure on inflation. As inflation gradually falls, the *SRAS* line moves downward until it reaches *SRAS′*, and actual output equals potential output (point *B*). Once the recessionary gap has been eliminated, inflation stabilizes at π^*, and the economy settles into long-run equilibrium at the intersection of *AD*, *LRAS*, and *SRAS′* (point *B*).

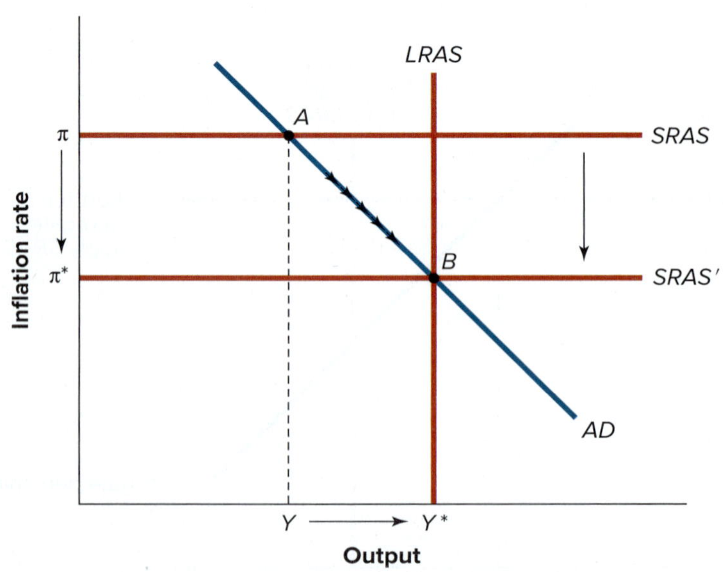

[2]Our explanation for the downward slope of the *AD* curve, earlier in the chapter, described some of these other factors.

declines. This process of falling inflation, falling real interest rates, rising output, and falling unemployment continues until the economy reaches full employment at point *B* in Figure 11.6, the economy's long-run equilibrium point.

What happens if instead of a recessionary gap, the economy has an expansionary gap, with output greater than potential output? An expansionary gap would cause the rate of inflation to *rise,* as firms respond to high demand by raising their prices more rapidly than their costs are rising. In graphical terms, an expansionary gap would cause the *SRAS* line to move upward over time. Inflation and the *SRAS* line would continue to rise until the economy reached long-run equilibrium, with actual output equal to potential output. This process is illustrated in Figure 11.7. Initially, the economy is in short-run equilibrium at point *A,* where $Y > Y^*$ (an expansionary gap). The expansionary gap causes inflation to rise over time; graphically, the short-run aggregate supply line moves upward, from *SRAS* to *SRAS′*. As the *SRAS* line rises, short-run equilibrium output falls—the result of the Fed's tendency to increase the real interest rate when inflation rises. Eventually the *SRAS* line intersects the *AD* curve *LRAS* and line at point *B,* where the economy reaches long-run equilibrium, with no output gap and stable inflation.

The Self-Correcting Economy

Our analysis of Figures 11.6 and 11.7 makes an important general point: The economy tends to be *self-correcting* in the long run. In other words, given enough time, output gaps tend to disappear without changes in monetary or fiscal policy (other than the change in the real interest rate embodied in the Fed's policy reaction function). Expansionary output gaps are eliminated by rising inflation, while recessionary output gaps are eliminated by falling inflation. This result contrasts sharply with the basic Keynesian model, which does not include a self-correcting mechanism. The difference in results is explained by the fact that the basic Keynesian model concentrates on the short-run period, during which prices do not adjust, and does not take into account the changes in prices and inflation that occur over a longer period.

Does the economy's tendency to self-correct imply that aggressive monetary and fiscal policies are not needed to stabilize output? The answer to this question depends crucially on the *speed* with which the self-correction process takes place. If self-correction takes place very slowly, so that actual output differs from potential for protracted periods, then active use of monetary and fiscal policy can help stabilize

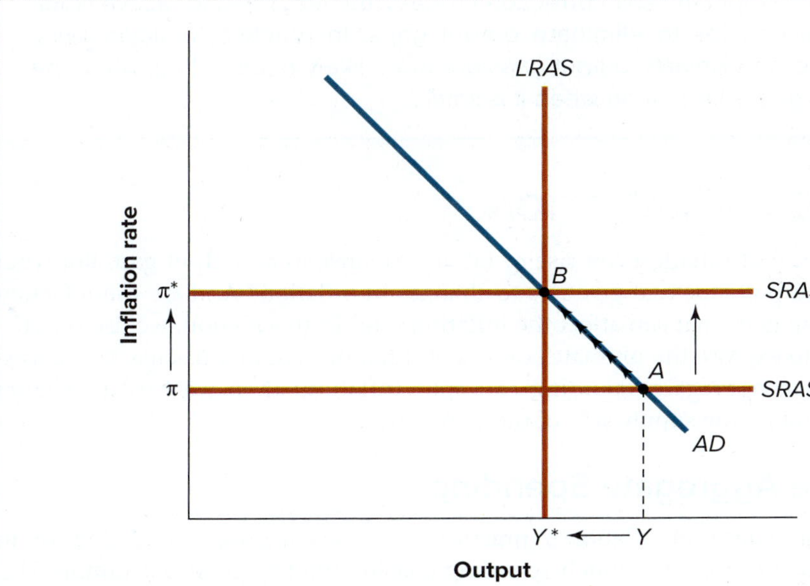

FIGURE 11.7

The Adjustment of Inflation When an Expansionary Gap Exists.

At the initial short-run equilibrium point *A*, an expansionary gap exists. Inflation rises gradually (the *SRAS* line moves upward) and output falls. The process continues until the economy reaches long-run equilibrium at point *B*, where inflation stabilizes and the output gap is eliminated.

output. But if self-correction is rapid, then active stabilization policies are probably not justified in most cases, given the lags and uncertainties that are involved in policymaking in practice. Indeed, if the economy returns to full employment quickly, then attempts by policymakers to stabilize spending and output may end up doing more harm than good, for example, by causing actual output to "overshoot" potential output.

The speed with which a particular economy corrects itself depends on a variety of factors, including the prevalence of long-term contracts and the efficiency and flexibility of product and labor markets. (For a case study, see the discussion of U.S. and European labor markets in Chapter 6, *The Labor Market: Workers, Wages, and Unemployment*.) However, a reasonable conclusion is that the greater the initial output gap, the longer the economy's process of self-correction will take. This observation suggests that stabilization policies should not be used actively to try to eliminate relatively small output gaps, but that they may be quite useful in remedying large gaps—for example, when the unemployment rate is exceptionally high.

RECAP

INFLATION, *AD-AS*, AND THE SELF-CORRECTING ECONOMY

- The economy is in short-run equilibrium when inflation equals the value determined by past expectations and pricing decisions, and output equals the level of short-run equilibrium output that is consistent with that inflation rate. Graphically, short-run equilibrium occurs at the intersection of the *AD* curve and the *SRAS* line. We refer to the fact that inflation is determined by past inflation (which affects past expectations and pricing decisions) as inflation inertia.
- The economy is in long-run equilibrium when actual output equals potential output (there is no output gap) and the inflation rate is stable. Graphically, long-run equilibrium occurs when the *AD* curve, the *SRAS* line, and the *LRAS* line intersect at a common point.
- Inflation adjusts gradually to bring the economy into long-run equilibrium (a phenomenon called the economy's self-correcting tendency). Inflation rises to eliminate an expansionary gap and falls to eliminate a recessionary gap. Graphically, the *SRAS* line moves up or down as needed to bring the economy into long-run equilibrium.
- The more rapid the self-correction process, the less need for active stabilization policies to eliminate output gaps. In practice, policymakers' attempts to eliminate output gaps are more likely to be helpful when the output gap is large than when it is small.

SOURCES OF INFLATION

We have seen that inflation can rise or fall in response to an output gap. But what creates the output gaps that give rise to changes in inflation? And are there factors besides output gaps that can affect the inflation rate? In this section, we use the *AD-AS* diagram to explore the ultimate sources of inflation. We first discuss how excessive growth in aggregate spending can spur inflation; then we turn to factors operating through the supply side of the economy.

Excessive Aggregate Spending

One important source of inflation in practice is excessive aggregate spending—or, in more colloquial terms, "too much spending chasing too few goods." Example 11.2 illustrates.

EXAMPLE 11.2 Military Buildups and Inflation

Can the Fed do anything to prevent inflation caused by wars or military buildups?

Wars and military buildups are sometimes associated with increased inflation. Explain why, using the *AD-AS* diagram. Can the Fed do anything to prevent the increase in inflation caused by a military buildup?

Wars and military buildups are potentially inflationary because increased spending on military hardware raises total demand relative to the economy's productive capacity. In the face of rising sales, firms increase their prices more quickly, raising the inflation rate.

The two panels of Figure 11.8 illustrate this process. Looking first at Figure 11.8(a), suppose that the economy is initially in long-run equilibrium at point *A*, where the aggregate demand curve *AD* intersects both the short-run and long-run aggregate supply lines, *SRAS* and *LRAS*, respectively. Point *A* is a long-run equilibrium point, with output equal to potential output and stable inflation. Now suppose that the government decides to spend more on armaments. Increased military spending is an increase in government purchases *G*, an exogenous increase in spending. We saw earlier that, for a given level of inflation, an exogenous increase in spending raises short-run equilibrium output, shifting the *AD* curve to the right. Figure 11.8(a) shows the aggregate demand curve shifting rightward, from *AD* to *AD′*, as the result of increased military expenditure. The economy moves to a new, short-run equilibrium at point *B*, where *AD′* intersects *SRAS*. Note that at point *B* actual output has risen above potential, to $Y > Y^*$, creating an expansionary gap. Because inflation is inertial and does not change in the short run, the immediate effect of the increase in government purchases is only to increase output, just as we saw in the Keynesian analysis in Chapter 9, *Short-Term Economic Fluctuations and Fiscal Policy.*

The process doesn't stop there, however, because inflation will not remain the same indefinitely. At point *B*, an expansionary gap exists, so inflation will gradually begin to increase. Figure 11.8(b) shows this increase in inflation as a shift of the *SRAS* line from its initial position to a higher level, *SRAS′*. When inflation has risen to π', enough to eliminate the output gap (point *C*), the economy is back in long-run

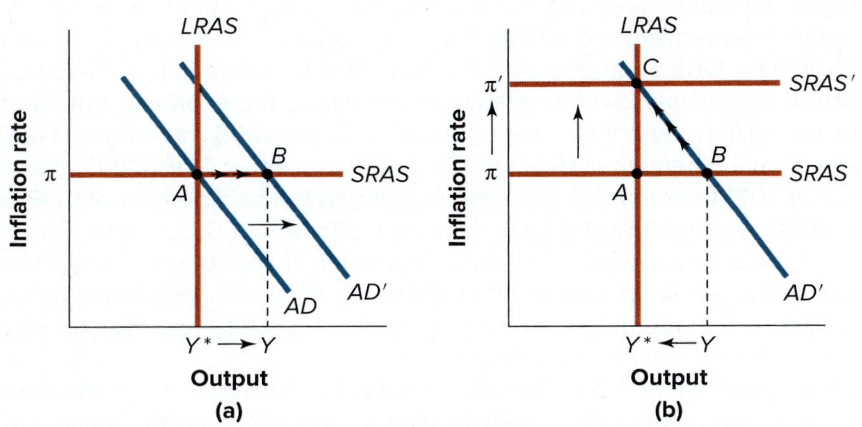

FIGURE 11.8

War and Military Buildup as a Source of Inflation.

(a) An increase in military spending shifts the *AD* curve to the right, from *AD* to *AD′*. At the new short-run equilibrium point *B*, actual output has risen above potential output Y^*, creating an expansionary gap. (b) This gap leads to rising inflation, shown as an upward movement of the *SRAS* line, from *SRAS* to *SRAS′*. At the new long-run equilibrium point *C*, actual output has fallen back to the level of potential output, but at π' inflation is higher than it was originally.

equilibrium. We see now that the increase in output created by the military buildup was only temporary. In the long run, actual output has returned to the level of potential output, but at a higher rate of inflation.

Does the Fed have the power to prevent the increased inflation that is induced by a rise in military spending? The answer is yes. We saw earlier that a decision by the Fed to set a higher real interest rate at any given level of inflation—an upward shift in the policy reaction function—will shift the *AD* curve to the left. So if the Fed aggressively tightens monetary policy (shifts its reaction function) as the military buildup proceeds, it can reverse the rightward shift of the *AD* curve caused by increased government spending. Offsetting the rightward shift of the *AD* curve in turn avoids the development of an expansionary gap, with its inflationary consequences. The Fed's policy works because the higher real interest rate it sets at each level of inflation acts to reduce consumption and investment spending. The reduction in private spending offsets the increase in demand by the government, eliminating—or at least moderating—the inflationary impact of the military purchases.

We should not conclude, by the way, that avoiding the inflationary consequences of a military buildup makes the buildup costless to society. As we have just noted, inflation can be avoided only if consumption and investment are reduced by a policy of higher real interest rates. Effectively, the private sector must give up some resources so that more of the nation's output can be devoted to military purposes. This reduction in resources reduces both current living standards (by reducing consumption) and future living standards (by reducing investment).

The Economic Naturalist 11.1

How did inflation get started in the United States in the 1960s?

In the United States from 1959 through 1963, inflation hovered around 1 percent per year. Beginning in 1964, however, inflation began to rise, reaching nearly 6 percent in 1970. Why did inflation become a problem in the United States in the 1960s?

Increases in government spending, plus the failure of the Federal Reserve to act to contain inflation, appear to explain most of the increase in inflation during the 1960s. On the fiscal side, military expenditures increased dramatically in the latter part of the decade as the war in Vietnam escalated. Annual defense spending, which hovered around $70 billion from 1962 to 1965, rose to more than $100 billion by 1968 and remained at a high level for some years. To appreciate the size of this military buildup relative to the size of the economy, note that the *increase* in military spending alone between 1965 and 1968 was about 1.3 percent of GDP—from 9.5 percent of GDP in 1965 to 10.8 percent of GDP in 1968. For comparison, in 2019 the *total* U.S. defense budget was below 4 percent of GDP, so its share of the economy would have to increase by about 33 percent over three years to have a similar relative increase. Moreover, at about the same time as the wartime military buildup, government spending on social programs—reflecting the impact of President Lyndon Johnson's Great Society and War on Poverty initiatives—also increased dramatically.

These government-induced increases in total spending contributed to an economic boom. Indeed, the 1961–1969 economic expansion was the longest in history at the time, being surpassed only 30 years later by the long expansion of the 1990s. However, an expansionary gap developed and eventually inflation began to rise, as would have been predicted by the analysis in Example 11.2.

An interesting contrast exists between these effects of the 1960s military buildup and those of the 1980s buildup under President Reagan, which did not lead to an increase in inflation. One important difference between the two eras was the behavior of the Federal Reserve. As we saw in Example 11.2, the Fed can offset the inflationary impact of increased government spending by fighting inflation more aggressively (shifting its policy reaction function upward). Except for a brief attempt in 1966, the Federal Reserve generally did not try actively to offset inflationary pressures during the 1960s. That failure may have been simply a miscalculation, or it may have reflected a reluctance to take the politically unpopular step of slowing the economy during a period of great political turmoil. But in the early 1980s, under Paul Volcker, the Federal Reserve acted vigorously to contain inflation. As a result, inflation actually declined in the 1980s, despite the military buildup.

SELF-TEST 11.7

In Example 11.1, we found that a decline in consumer spending tends to reduce the rate of inflation. Using the *AD-AS* diagram, illustrate the short-run and long-run effects of a fall in consumer spending on inflation. How does the decline in spending affect output in the short run and in the long run?

Whereas output gaps cause gradual changes in inflation, on occasion an economic shock can cause a relatively rapid increase or decrease in inflation. Such jolts to prices, which we call *inflation shocks,* are the subject of the next section.

Inflation Shocks

In late 1973, at the time of the Yom Kippur War between Israel and a coalition of Arab nations, the Organization of the Petroleum Exporting Countries (OPEC) dramatically cut its supplies of crude oil to the industrialized nations, quadrupling world oil prices. The sharp increase in oil prices was quickly transferred to the price of gasoline, heating oil, and goods and services that were heavily dependent on oil, such as air travel. The effects of the oil price increase, together with agricultural shortages that increased the price of food, contributed to a significant rise in the overall U.S. inflation rate in 1974.[3]

Everett Collection Historical/Alamy Stock Photo

OPEC's 1974 cutback in oil production created long lines, rising prices, and frayed tempers at the gas pump.

The increase in inflation in 1974 is an example of what is referred to as an *inflation shock*. An **inflation shock** is a sudden change in the normal behavior of inflation, unrelated to the nation's output gap. An inflation shock that causes an increase in inflation, like the large rise in oil prices in 1973, is called an *adverse* inflation shock. An inflation shock that reduces inflation is called a *favorable* inflation shock.

In contrast with the experience of the 1970s, when sharp increases in oil prices led to higher inflation, since the mid-1980s the effects of oil price changes on inflation have been much smaller. The Economic Naturalist 11.2 gives more details on the economic effects of inflation shocks, and discusses explanations for the smaller effects of oil price changes on inflation in more recent years.

inflation shock a sudden change in the normal behavior of inflation, unrelated to the nation's output gap

[3]In Chapter 4, *Measuring Economic Activity: GDP, Unemployment, and Inflation,* we distinguished between relative price changes (changes in the prices of individual goods) and inflation (changes in the overall price level). In the 1973–1974 episode, changes in the prices of individual categories of goods, such as energy and food, were sufficiently large and pervasive that the overall price level was significantly affected. Thus these relative price changes carried an inflationary impact as well.

The Economic Naturalist 11.2

Why did oil price increases cause U.S. inflation to escalate in the 1970s but not in the 2000s and 2010s?

Having risen in the second half of the 1960s, inflation continued to rise in the 1970s. Already at 6.2 percent in 1973, inflation jumped to 11.0 percent in 1974. After subsiding from 1974 to 1978, it began to rise again in 1979, to 11.4 percent, and reached 13.5 percent in 1980. Why did inflation increase so much in the 1970s?

We have already described the quadrupling of oil prices in late 1973 and the sharp increases in agricultural prices at about the same time, which together constituted an adverse inflation shock. A second inflation shock occurred in 1979, when the turmoil of the Iranian Revolution restricted the flow of oil from the Middle East and doubled oil prices yet again.

Figure 11.9 shows the effects of an adverse inflation shock on a hypothetical economy. Before the inflation shock occurs, the economy is in long-run equilibrium at point *A*, at the intersection of *AD*, *LRAS*, and *SRAS*. At point *A*, actual output is equal to potential output Y^*, and the inflation rate is stable at π. However, an adverse inflation shock directly increases inflation so that the *SRAS* line shifts rapidly upward to *SRAS*′. A new short-run equilibrium is established at point *B*, where *SRAS*′ intersects the aggregate demand curve *AD*. In the wake of the inflation shock, inflation rises to π' and output falls, from Y^* to Y'. Thus an inflation shock creates the worst possible scenario: higher inflation coupled with a recessionary gap. The combination of inflation and recession has been referred to as *stagflation*, or stagnation plus inflation. The U.S. economy experienced a stagflation in 1973–1975, after the first oil shock, and again in 1980, after the second oil shock.

An adverse inflation shock poses a difficult dilemma for macroeconomic policymakers. To see why, suppose monetary and fiscal policies were left unchanged

FIGURE 11.9

The Effects of an Adverse Inflation Shock.

Starting from long-run equilibrium at point *A*, an adverse inflation shock directly raises current inflation, causing the *SRAS* line to shift upward to *SRAS*′. At the new short-run equilibrium, point *B*, inflation has risen to π' and output has fallen to Y', creating a recessionary gap. If the Fed does nothing, eventually the economy will return to point *A*, restoring the original inflation rate but suffering a long recession in the process. The Fed could ease monetary policy by shifting down its policy reaction function, shifting the *AD* curve to *AD*′, and restoring full employment more quickly at point *C*. The cost of this strategy is that inflation remains at its higher level.

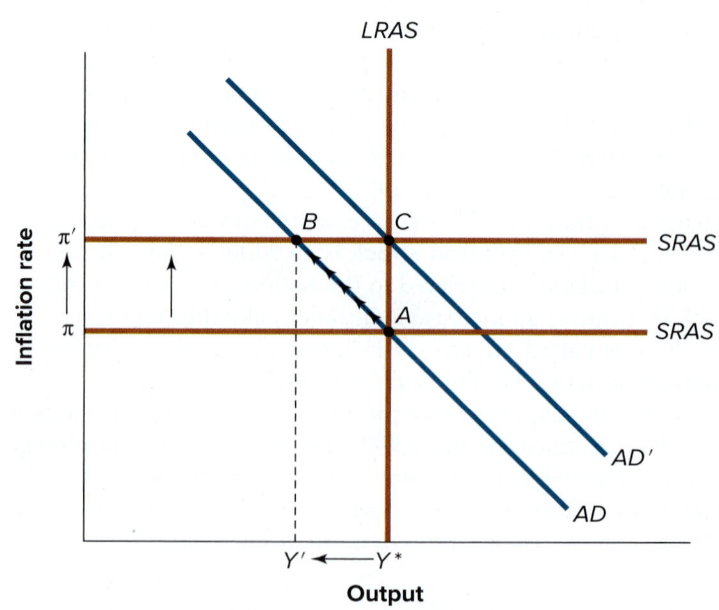

following an inflationary shock. In that case, inflation would eventually abate and return to its original level. Graphically, the economy would reach its short-run equilibrium at point *B* in Figure 11.9 soon after the inflation shock. However, because of the recessionary gap that exists at point *B*, eventually inflation would begin to drift downward, until finally the recessionary gap is eliminated. Graphically, this decline in inflation would be represented by a downward movement of the *SRAS* line, from *SRAS′* back to *SRAS*. Inflation would stop declining only when long-run equilibrium is restored, at point *A* in the figure, where inflation is at its original level of π and output equals potential output.

However, although a "do-nothing" policy approach would ultimately eliminate both the output gap and the surge in inflation, it would also put the economy through a deep and protracted recession, as actual output remains below potential output until the inflation adjustment process is completed. To avoid such an economically and politically costly outcome, policymakers might opt to eliminate the recessionary gap more quickly. By aggressively easing monetary policy (more precisely, by shifting down its policy reaction function), for example, the Fed could shift the *AD* curve to the right, from *AD* to *AD′*, taking the economy to a new long-run equilibrium, point *C* in Figure 11.9. This expansionary policy would help restore output to the full-employment level more quickly, but as the figure shows, it would also allow inflation to stabilize at the new, higher level.

In sum, inflation shocks pose a true dilemma for policymakers. If they leave their policies unchanged, inflation will eventually subside, but the nation may experience a lengthy and severe recession. If, instead, they act aggressively to expand aggregate spending, the recession will end more quickly, but inflation will stabilize at a higher level. In the 1970s, though U.S. policymakers tried to strike a balance between stabilizing output and containing inflation, the combination of recession and increased inflation hobbled the economy.

The 1970s were not the last time, however, that oil prices sharply increased. Since the late 1990s, oil prices have swung even more wildly than in the 1970s, yet inflation remained relatively stable. Why did the oil price increases of the 2000s and 2010s not lead to the effects analyzed in Figure 11.9?

Economists proposed different answers to this important question, and it appears that for a full explanation, several factors should be combined. For example, the economists Olivier Blanchard and Jordi Galí, who studied this question, focused on the following three explanations, and concluded that all three are likely to have played an important role.[4] First, labor markets have become more flexible, and wages less sticky, since the 1970s. If wages and prices adjust more quickly, the economy in Figure 11.9 would return to point *A* more quickly, even with a do-nothing policy by the Fed. Second, the share of oil in the economy has declined since the 1970s. With oil less important in both production and consumption, the effects of oil price changes on the economy are expected to be smaller.

Third, and most closely related to the discussion in this chapter, the public's expectations regarding the Fed's reaction to oil price increases were dramatically different in the 2000s and 2010s compared with those in the 1970s. Specifically, in the 1970s, people did not believe that the Fed would return inflation to a low level following an oil price increase. As a result, firms responded by increasing their prices more quickly, and workers demanded wage increases to reflect higher costs of living. But in the 2000s and 2010s, after Fed chairs Paul Volcker and his successor Alan Greenspan had brought inflation down and showed that the Fed was committed to keeping it low, expectations of inflation were much more stable and, as a result, the oil price shocks did not lead to extended periods of increases in wages and other prices.

[4]Olivier J. Blanchard and Jordi Galí, "The Macroeconomic Effects of Oil Price Shocks: Why Are the 2000s So Different from the 1970s?," in *International Dimensions of Monetary Policy* (Chicago: University of Chicago Press, 2010).

The Economic Naturalist 11.2 ended by returning to the idea that a central bank's credibility and perceived commitment to maintaining low inflation can by themselves help in achieving the goal of low inflation. This idea has already appeared on several occasions earlier in the chapter—for example, when we discussed Volcker's reputation of conservatism and toughness (in the introduction) and when we illustrated the virtuous cycle of low expected inflation and low inflation (in Figure 11.4). We will revisit this idea again later in the chapter, when mentioning some central banks' commitment to an explicit inflation target.

SELF-TEST 11.8

Inflation shocks can also be beneficial for the economy, such as when oil prices declined by 50 percent in late 2014. What effect would a decrease in oil prices have on output and inflation, if the public did not believe that the Fed would immediately act to keep inflation stable?

Shocks to Potential Output

In analyzing the effects of increased oil prices on the U.S. economy in the 1970s, we assumed that potential output was unchanged in the wake of the shock. However, the sharp rise in oil prices during that period probably affected the economy's potential output as well. As oil prices rose, for example, many companies retired less energy-efficient equipment or scrapped older "gas-guzzling" vehicles. A smaller capital stock implies lower potential output.

If the increases in oil prices did reduce potential output, their inflationary impact would have been compounded. Figure 11.10 illustrates the effects on the economy of a sudden decline in potential output. For the sake of simplicity, the figure includes only the effects of the reduction in potential output, and not the direct effect of the inflation shock. (Problem 7 at the end of the chapter asks you to combine the two effects.)

Suppose once again that the economy is in long-run equilibrium at point *A*. Then potential output falls unexpectedly, from Y^* to $Y^{*\prime}$, shifting the long-run

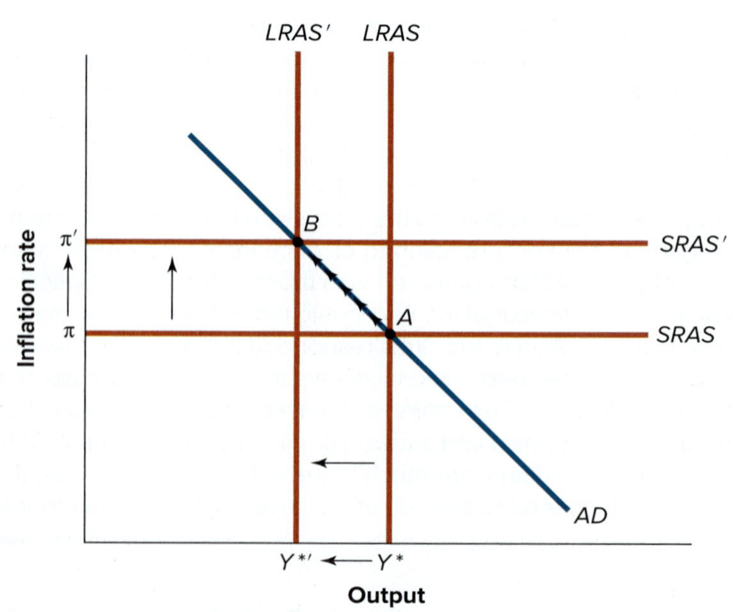

FIGURE 11.10

The Effects of a Shock to Potential Output.

The economy is in long-run equilibrium at point *A* when a decline in potential output, from Y^* to $Y^{*\prime}$, creates an expansionary gap. Inflation rises, and the short-run aggregate supply line shifts upward from *SRAS* to *SRAS′*. A new long-run equilibrium is reached at point *B*, where actual output equals the new, lower level of potential output, $Y^{*\prime}$, and inflation has risen to π'. Because it is the result of a fall in potential output, the decline in output is permanent.

aggregate supply line leftward from *LRAS* to *LRAS*′. After this decline in potential output, is the economy still in long-run equilibrium at point *A*? The answer is no, because output now exceeds potential output at that point. In other words, an expansionary gap has developed. This gap reflects the fact that although spending has not changed, the capacity of firms to supply goods and services has been reduced.

As we have seen, an expansionary gap leads to rising inflation. In Figure 11.10, increasing inflation is represented by an upward movement of the *SRAS* line. Eventually the short-run aggregate supply line reaches *SRAS*′, and the economy reaches a new long-run equilibrium at point *B*. (Why is point *B* a long-run, and not just a short-run, equilibrium?) At that point, output has fallen to the new, lower level of potential output, $Y^{*\prime}$, and inflation has risen to π'.

Sharp changes in potential output and inflation shocks are both referred to as **aggregate supply shocks.** As we have seen, an adverse aggregate supply shock of either type leads to lower output and higher inflation and, therefore, poses a difficult challenge for policymakers. A difference between the two types of aggregate supply shocks is that the output losses associated with an adverse inflation shock are temporary (because the economy self-corrects and will ultimately return to its initial level of potential output), but those associated with a fall in potential output are permanent (output remains lower even after the economy has reached a new long-run equilibrium).

aggregate supply shock either an inflation shock or a shock to potential output; adverse aggregate supply shocks of both types reduce output and increase inflation

The Economic Naturalist 11.3

Why was the United States able to experience rapid growth and low inflation in the latter part of the 1990s?

The second half of the 1990s was a boom period in the U.S. economy. As Table 11.2 shows, real GDP growth during the 1995–2000 period was 4.3 percent per year, significantly higher than the average growth rate over the previous decade; and unemployment averaged only 4.6 percent, also significantly better than the prior decade. Despite this rapid economic growth, inflation during 1995–2000 was contained, averaging only 2.5 percent per year. Why was the United States able to enjoy both rapid growth and low inflation in the latter 1990s?

During the latter part of the 1990s, the U.S. economy benefited from a positive shock to potential output. An important source of the faster-than-usual expansion of potential output was impressive technological advance, particularly in

TABLE 11.2
U.S. Macroeconomic Data, Annual Averages, 1985–2000

Years	% Growth in real GDP	Unemployment rate (%)	Inflation rate (%)	Productivity growth (%)
1985–1995	3.0	6.3	3.5	1.4
1995–2000	4.3	4.6	2.5	2.4

Sources: Bureau of Economic Analysis; Bureau of Labor Statistics. Real GDP is measured in 2012 dollars. The unemployment rate is the average civilian unemployment rate for the period. Inflation is measured by the CPI. Productivity is measured by real GDP per employed worker.

computers and software, as well as the application of these advances in areas ranging from automobile production to retail inventory management. One of the most prominent developments, the rapid growth of the Internet, not only made it possible for consumers to shop or find information online, but also helped companies improve their efficiency—for example, by improving coordination between manufacturers and their suppliers. These advances were reflected in more rapid productivity growth; as Table 11.2 shows, average annual growth of output per employed worker accelerated from 1.4 percent during the 1985–1995 period to a remarkable 2.4 percent during 1995–2000 (see The Economic Naturalist 5.5).

Graphically, the effects of a positive shock to potential output are just the reverse of those seen in Figure 11.10, which shows the effects of an adverse shock. A positive shock to potential output causes the *LRAS* line to shift right, leading in the short run to a recessionary gap (output is lower than the new, higher level of potential output). Inflation declines, reflected in a downward movement of the *SRAS* line. In the new, long-run equilibrium, output is higher and inflation lower than initially. These results are consistent with the U.S. experience of the latter part of the 1990s.

SELF-TEST 11.9

What if productivity hadn't increased in the late 1990s? How would the economy have been different in 2000?

RECAP

SOURCES OF INFLATION

- Inflation may result from excessive spending, which creates an expansionary output gap and puts upward pressure on inflation. An example is a military buildup, which raises government purchases. Monetary policy or fiscal policy can be used to offset excessive spending, preventing higher inflation from emerging.
- Inflation may also arise from an aggregate supply shock, either an inflation shock or a shock to potential output. An inflation shock is a sudden change in the normal behavior of inflation, unrelated to the nation's output gap. An example of an inflation shock is a run-up in energy and food prices large enough to raise the overall price level. In the absence of public beliefs that the central bank is committed to maintaining low inflation, an inflation shock would lead to stagflation, a combination of recession and higher inflation.
- Stagflation poses a difficult dilemma for policymakers. If they take no action, eventually inflation will subside and output will recover, but in the interim the economy may suffer a protracted period of recession. If they use monetary or fiscal policy to increase aggregate demand, they will shorten the recession but will also lock in the higher level of inflation.
- A shock to potential output is a sharp change in potential output. Like an adverse inflation shock, an adverse shock to potential output results in both higher inflation and lower output. Because lower potential output implies that productive capacity has fallen, however, output does not recover following a shock to potential output, as it eventually does following an inflation shock.

CONTROLLING INFLATION

High or even moderate rates of inflation can impose significant costs to the economy. Indeed, over the past several decades a consensus has developed among economists and policymakers that low and stable inflation is important and perhaps necessary for sustained economic growth. What, then, should policymakers do if the inflation rate is too high? As Example 11.3 will show, inflation can be slowed by policies that shift the aggregate demand curve leftward. Unfortunately, although they produce long-term gains in productivity and economic growth, such policies are likely to impose significant short-run costs in the form of lost output and increased unemployment.

EXAMPLE 11.3 The Effects of Anti-Inflationary Monetary Policy

How will output, unemployment, and inflation react to a monetary-policy tightening?

Suppose that, although the economy is at full employment, the inflation rate is 10 percent—too high to be consistent with economic efficiency and long-term economic growth. The Fed decides to tighten monetary policy to reduce the inflation rate to 3 percent. What will happen to output, unemployment, and inflation in the short run? Over the long run?

The economic effects of a monetary tightening are very different in the short and long run. Figure 11.11(a) shows the short-run effect. Initially, the economy is in long-run equilibrium at point *A*, where actual output equals potential output. But

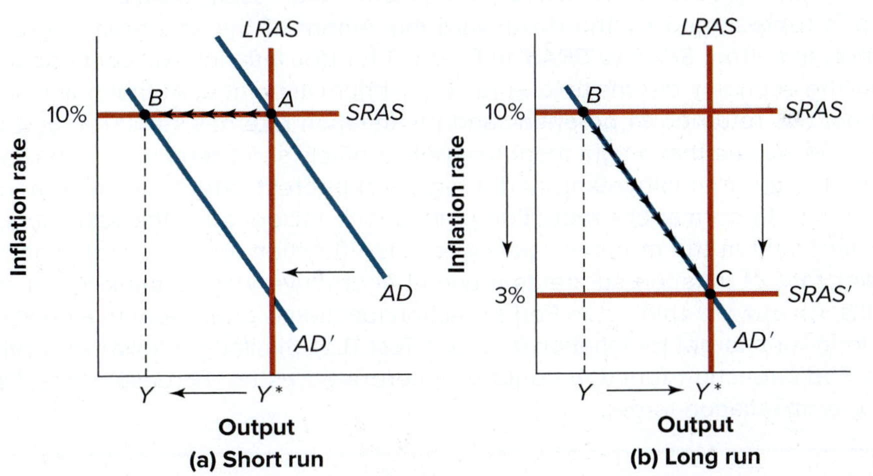

FIGURE 11.11

Short-Run and Long-Run Effects of an Anti-inflationary Monetary Policy.

(a) Initially the economy is in long-run equilibrium at point *A*, with actual output equal to potential and the inflation rate at 10 percent. If an anti-inflationary policy shift by the Fed shifts the *AD* curve to the left, from *AD* to *AD′*, the economy will reach a new short-run equilibrium at point *B*, at the intersection of *AD′* and *SRAS*. As short-run equilibrium output falls to *Y*, a recessionary gap opens up. The inflation rate does not change in the short run. (b) Following the tightening of monetary policy, a recessionary gap exists at point *B*, which eventually causes inflation to decline. The short-run aggregate supply line moves downward, from *SRAS* to *SRAS′*. Long-run equilibrium is restored at point *C*. In the long run, real output returns to potential and inflation stabilizes at a lower level (3 percent in this figure).

at point *A*, the inflation rate (10 percent) is high, as indicated by the aggregate supply line, *SRAS*.

To bring inflation down to 3 percent, what can policymakers do? To get "tough" on inflation, the Fed must set the real interest rate at a level higher than normal, given the rate of inflation. In other words, the Fed must shift its policy reaction function upward, as in Figure 11.11(a). At a constant rate of inflation, an increase in the real interest rate set by the Fed will reduce consumption and investment spending, lowering aggregate demand at every inflation rate. As we saw earlier in the chapter, this monetary tightening by the Fed causes the *AD* curve to shift leftward, from *AD* to *AD′* in Figure 11.11(a).

After the Fed's action, the *AD′* curve and the *SRAS* line intersect at point *B* in Figure 11.11(a), the new short-run equilibrium point. At point *B* actual output has fallen to *Y*, which is less than potential output Y^*. In other words, the Fed's action has allowed a recessionary gap to develop, one result of which will be that unemployment will exceed the natural rate. At point *B*, however, the inflation rate has not changed, remaining at 10 percent. We conclude that in the short run, a monetary tightening pushes the economy into recession but has little or no effect on the inflation rate, because of inflation inertia.

The short-run effects of the anti-inflationary shift in monetary policy—lower output, higher unemployment, and little or no reduction of inflation—are to say the least not very encouraging, and they explain why such policy shifts are often highly unpopular in their early stages. Fortunately, however, we have not reached the end of the story—because the economy will not remain at point *B* indefinitely. The reason is that the existence of a recessionary gap at that point eventually causes inflation to decline, as firms become more reluctant to raise their prices in the face of weak demand.

Graphically, the eventual decline in inflation that results from a recessionary gap is represented by the downward movement of the short-run aggregate supply line, from *SRAS* to *SRAS′* in Figure 11.11(b). Inflation will continue to fall until the economy returns to long-run equilibrium at point *C*. At that point, actual output has returned to potential, and the inflation rate has stabilized at 3 percent. So we see that a tight monetary policy inflicts short-term pain (a decline in output, high unemployment, and a high real interest rate) to achieve a long-term gain (a permanent reduction in inflation). Incidentally, the result that an upward shift in the monetary policy reaction function leads to a permanently lower rate of inflation suggests a useful alternative way to think about such shifts: An upward shift in the Fed's reaction function is equivalent to a decline in its long-term target for inflation (see Self-Test 11.2). Similarly, a downward shift in the Fed's reaction function could be interpreted as an increase in the Fed's long-term inflation target.

The Economic Naturalist 11.4 discusses the real-life episode of Fed tightening with which we began this chapter.

SELF-TEST 11.10

Show the typical time paths of output, inflation, and the real interest rate when the Fed employs an anti-inflationary monetary policy. Draw a separate graph for each variable, showing time on the horizontal axis. Be sure to distinguish the short run from the long run. Specific numerical values are not necessary.

The Economic Naturalist 11.4

How was inflation conquered in the 1980s?

After reaching double-digit levels in the late 1970s, inflation in the United States declined sharply in the 1980s. After peaking at 13.5 percent in 1980, the inflation rate fell all the way to 3.2 percent in 1983, and it remained in the 2–5 percent range for the rest of the decade. In the 1990s inflation fell even lower, in the 2–3 percent range in most years. How was inflation conquered in the 1980s?

The person who was most directly responsible for the conquest of inflation in the 1980s was the Federal Reserve's chair, Paul Volcker. Following the secret Saturday meeting he called on October 6, 1979 (described in the introduction to this chapter), the Federal Open Market Committee agreed to adopt a strongly anti-inflationary monetary policy. The results of this policy change on the U.S. economy are shown in Table 11.3, which includes selected macroeconomic data for the period 1978–1985.

The data in Table 11.3 fit our analysis of anti-inflationary monetary policy quite well. First, as our model predicts, in the short run the Fed's sharp tightening of monetary policy led to a recession. In fact, two recessions followed the Fed's action in 1979, a short one in 1980 and a deeper one in 1981–1982. Note that growth in real GDP was negative in 1980 and 1982, and the unemployment rate rose significantly, peaking at 9.7 percent in 1982. Nominal and real interest rates also rose, a direct effect of the shift in monetary policy. Inflation, however, did not respond much during the period 1979–1981. All these results are consistent with the short-run analysis in Figure 11.11.

By 1983, however, the situation had changed markedly. The economy had recovered, with strong growth in real GDP in 1983–1985 (see Table 11.3). In 1984, the unemployment rate, which tends to lag the recovery, began to decline. Interest rates remained relatively high, perhaps reflecting other factors besides monetary policy. Most significantly, inflation fell in 1982–1983 and stabilized at a much lower level. Inflation has remained low in the United States ever since.

TABLE 11.3
U.S. Macroeconomic Data, 1978–1985

Year	Growth in real GDP (%)	Unemployment rate (%)	Inflation rate (%)	Nominal interest rate (%)	Real interest rate (%)
1978	5.5	6.1	7.6	8.3	0.7
1979	3.2	5.8	11.3	9.7	−1.6
1980	−0.3	7.1	13.5	11.6	−1.9
1981	2.5	7.6	10.4	14.4	4.0
1982	−1.8	9.7	6.2	12.9	6.7
1983	4.6	9.6	3.2	10.5	7.3
1984	7.2	7.5	4.4	11.9	7.5
1985	4.2	7.2	3.5	9.6	6.1

Sources: Bureau of Economic Analysis; Bureau of Labor Statistics; Federal Reserve Bank of St. Louis. Real GDP is measured in 2012 dollars. Inflation is measured by the CPI. The nominal interest rate is the average annual value of the three-year Treasury bill rate. The real interest rate equals the nominal interest rate minus the inflation rate.

disinflation a substantial reduction in the rate of inflation

A substantial reduction in the rate of inflation, like the one the Fed engineered in the 1980s, is called a **disinflation.** But again, disinflation comes at the cost of a large recessionary gap and high unemployment like that experienced by the United States in the early 1980s. Is this cost worth bearing? This question is not an easy one to answer, because the costs of inflation are difficult to measure. Policymakers around the world appear to agree on the necessity of containing inflation, however, as many countries fought to bring their own inflation rates down to 2 percent or less in the 1980s and 1990s. Canada and Great Britain are among the many industrial countries that have borne the costs of sharp reductions in inflation.

Can the costs of disinflation be reduced? Unfortunately, no one has found a pain-free method of lowering the inflation rate. Accordingly, in recent decades central banks around the world have striven to keep inflation at manageable levels, to avoid the costs of disinflation. In the United States, under Alan Greenspan (Paul Volcker's immediate successor, who was chair of the Fed from 1987 to 2006), the Federal Reserve followed a strategy of *preemptive strikes,* raising interest rates at the first sign that inflation might soon begin to creep upward. This strategy appears to have been successful in keeping inflation low and avoiding the need for costly disinflation. Other countries—Canada, Great Britain, Sweden, Mexico, Brazil, Chile, Israel, and many others—have announced explicit numerical *targets* for the long-run inflation rate, usually in the range of 1–3 percent per year. More recently, the Fed announced that it views a 2 percent inflation rate as "most consistent over the longer run with the Federal Reserve's statutory mandate."[5] In its statement, the Fed added: "Communicating this inflation goal clearly to the public helps keep longer-term inflation expectations firmly anchored." The philosophy behind inflation targets is the same as that behind the preemptive approach to inflation: If inflation can be kept low, the economy can enjoy the resulting long-term benefits without having to incur the short-term costs of disinflationary policies like the ones followed by Chair Volcker.

The Economic Naturalist 11.5

Can inflation be too low?

connect

▸ Visit your instructor's Connect course and access your eBook to view this video.

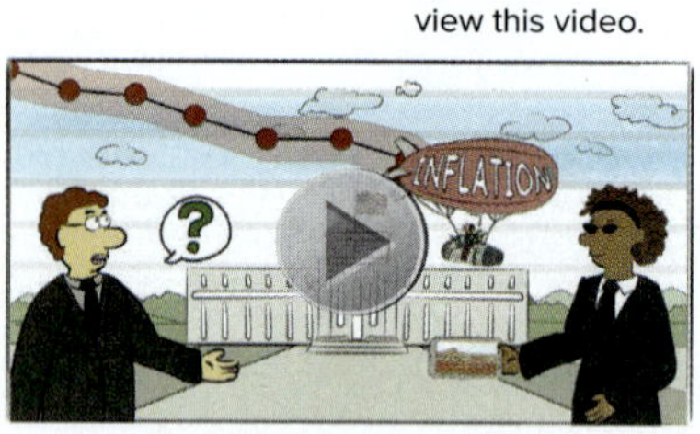

Can inflation be too low?

As the last section points out, the Federal Reserve is normally focused on keeping inflation from rising too fast, but by late 2002, some Fed policymakers began to worry that inflation might actually be too low. Why?

Minutes of the Federal Reserve's September 24, 2002, Federal Open Market Committee meeting, where Federal Reserve policymakers determine future monetary policy actions, indicate that committee members were concerned that continuing weakness in the U.S. economy was likely to lead to "quite low and perhaps declining inflation" well into 2003.[6] With prices of consumer goods rising only about 1.5 percent from September 2001 to September 2002, members noted that "further sizable disinflation that resulted in a nominal inflation rate near zero could create problems for the implementation of monetary policy through conventional means in the event of an adverse shock to the economy."

The potential for future monetary policymaking problems was raised by the combination of low inflation rates, low interest rates, and the possibility of further economic weakness. During 2001 and 2002, the Federal Reserve reduced its target for the federal funds rate to 1.75 percent, the lowest level in four decades, in an attempt to provide economic stimulus to an economy slowly emerging from recession. With an inflation rate of 1.5 percent, the resulting real rate of interest—the difference between the nominal interest rate and the inflation rate—was nearly zero percent by September 2002.

[5]"FOMC Statement of Longer-Run Goals and Policy Strategy," January 25, 2012, www.federalreserve.gov/newsevents/press/monetary/20120125c.htm.

[6]Minutes from the Federal Reserve's September 2002 FOMC meeting, www.federalreserve.gov/fomc/minutes/20020924.htm.

Why did this create a potential problem for the Federal Reserve? With inflation rates already low and possibly falling, if the Fed was forced in the future to further stimulate aggregate spending in response to a negative economywide spending shock—a real possibility given the concerns about a U.S. military confrontation with Iraq—it might need to reduce the real rate of interest below zero percent. As pointed out in Chapter 10, *Stabilizing the Economy: The Role of the Fed,* business and consumer spending respond to real interest rates, not nominal interest rates. However, in a period of declining inflation, the Federal Reserve needs to reduce nominal interest rates by more than the fall in inflation to reduce the real rate of interest. With the federal funds rate already at historic lows, Fed officials were worried that they would not be able to lower nominal interest rates enough to reduce real interest rates further. In particular, if the inflation rate fell to zero percent, the Fed would not be able to generate a negative real federal funds rate even if it pushed the (nominal) federal funds rate to its zero lower bound, thereby limiting the Fed's ability to conduct conventional expansionary monetary policy to offset a recessionary gap. Indeed, partly as a preemptive measure to prevent further economic weakening and declines in inflation, the Fed acted at its next meeting, in November 2002, to cut the federal funds rate to 1.25 percent.

However, Fed officials at the time also noted that, even if the federal funds rate were to be reduced all the way to zero percent, the Fed would still have a variety of options available to stimulate aggregate spending in the U.S. economy. For example, the Federal Reserve could buy long-term U.S. Treasury bonds (a form of quantitative easing), reducing long-term interest rates, in an effort to spur investment spending. As pointed out in the previous chapter, the Fed's monetary actions typically focus on the federal funds rate, a very short-term interest rate that may or may not move in concert with long-term interest rates that particularly influence mortgage lending. In addition, the Federal Reserve could increase its discount window lending to banks to promote increased consumer and business lending, intervene in foreign exchange markets to reduce the value of the dollar in an attempt to stimulate net exports, or finance a federal government tax cut by buying additional bonds, expanding the money supply in the process.

All of these nontraditional Fed policy actions have the effect of injecting more money into the economy, leading to increased aggregate spending and higher inflation rates over time. By using these monetary policy tools the Fed could, if necessary, generate negative real interest rates by inducing higher inflation, even if the federal funds rate is at zero percent. Thus, while low inflation rates, coupled with low interest rates, make monetary policymaking more complicated, interest rates can't ever really be "too low" to eliminate the Fed's ability to stimulate the economy. Indeed, as discussed in the previous chapter, six years after these late-2002 FOMC meetings the Fed would embark on a massive campaign of unconventional expansionary monetary policy to offset the recessionary gap of the 2007–2009 recession. Having successfully implemented some of these new tools of monetary policy during and following the 2007–2009 recession, the Fed and the public gained familiarity with them. In early 2020, when the COVID-19 pandemic struck, the Fed was therefore ready to move swiftly with new quantitative easing and other emergency lending programs on an unprecedented scale. These measures were aimed to help preemptively offset an expected large recessionary gap.

Too-low inflation has again been a recurring concern since 2015 not only in the U.S., but also in other major economies, including those of Europe and Japan, where inflation persists below central banks' targets. To try to get inflation up to target, both the European Central Bank (ECB) and the Bank of Japan (BOJ), following the example of the Fed from a few years earlier, introduced new tools such as quantitative easing programs.

RECAP

CONTROLLING INFLATION

Inflation can be controlled by policies that shift the aggregate demand curve leftward, such as a move to a "tighter" monetary policy (an upward shift in the monetary policy reaction function). In the short run, the effects of an anti-inflationary monetary policy are felt largely on output, so that a disinflation (a substantial reduction in inflation) may create a significant recessionary gap. According to the theory, in the long run output should return to potential and inflation should decline. These predictions appear to have been borne out during the Volcker disinflation of the early 1980s.

SUMMARY

- This chapter extended the basic Keynesian model to include inflation. First, we showed how spending and short-run equilibrium output are related to inflation, a relationship that is summarized by the aggregate demand curve. Second, we discussed how inflation itself is determined. In the short run, inflation is determined by past expectations and pricing decisions, but in the longer run inflation adjusts as needed to eliminate output gaps. *(LO1)*
- The *aggregate demand (AD) curve* shows the relationship between short-run equilibrium output and inflation. Because short-run equilibrium output is equal to spending, the aggregate demand curve also relates spending to inflation. Increases in inflation reduce spending and short-run equilibrium output, so the aggregate demand curve is downward-sloping. *(LO1)*
- The inverse relationship of inflation and short-run equilibrium output is the result, in large part, of the behavior of the Federal Reserve. To keep inflation low and stable, the Fed reacts to rising inflation by increasing the real interest rate. A higher real interest rate reduces consumption and investment, lowering aggregate expenditure and hence short-run equilibrium output. Other reasons that the aggregate demand curve slopes downward include the effects of inflation on the real value of money, *distributional effects* (inflation redistributes wealth from the poor, who save relatively little, to the more affluent, who save more), uncertainty created by inflation, and the impact of inflation on foreign sales of domestic goods. *(LO1)*
- For any given value of inflation, an exogenous increase in spending (that is, an increase in spending at given levels of output and the real interest rate) raises short-run equilibrium output, shifting the aggregate demand (*AD*) curve to the right. Likewise, an exogenous decline in spending shifts the *AD* curve to the left. The *AD* curve can also be shifted by a change in the Fed's policy reaction function. If the Fed gets "tougher," shifting up its reaction function and thus choosing a higher real interest rate at each level of inflation, the aggregate demand curve will shift to the left. If the Fed gets "easier," shifting down its reaction function and thus setting a lower real interest rate at each level of inflation, the *AD* curve will shift to the right. *(LO1)*
- In low-inflation industrial economies like the United States today, inflation tends to be inertial, or slow to adjust to changes in the economy. This inertial behavior reflects the fact that inflation depends in part on people's expectations of future inflation, which in turn depend on their recent experience with inflation. Long-term wage and price contracts tend to "build in" the effects of people's expectations for multiyear periods. In the aggregate demand–aggregate supply diagram, the *short-run aggregate supply (SRAS) line* is a horizontal line that shows the current rate of inflation, as determined by past expectations and pricing decisions. *(LO2)*
- Although inflation is inertial, it does change over time in response to output gaps. An expansionary gap tends to raise the inflation rate because firms raise their prices more quickly when they are facing demand that exceeds their normal productive capacity. A recessionary gap tends to reduce the inflation rate as firms become more reluctant to raise their prices. *(LO2)*
- The economy is in *short-run equilibrium* when the inflation rate equals the value determined by past expectations and pricing decisions and output equals the level of short-run equilibrium output that is consistent with that

inflation rate. Graphically, short-run equilibrium occurs at the intersection of the *AD* curve and the *SRAS* line. If an output gap exists, however, the inflation rate will adjust to eliminate the gap. Graphically, the *SRAS* line moves upward or downward as needed to restore output to its full-employment level. When the inflation rate is stable and actual output equals potential output, the economy is in *long-run equilibrium*. Graphically, long-run equilibrium corresponds to the common intersection point of the *AD* curve, the *SRAS* line, and the *long-run aggregate supply* (*LRAS*) *line*, a vertical line that marks the economy's potential output. *(LO2)*

- Because the economy tends to move toward long-run equilibrium on its own through the adjustment of the inflation rate, it is said to be self-correcting. The more rapid the self-correction process, the smaller the need for active stabilization policies to eliminate output gaps. In practice, the larger the output gap, the more useful such policies are. *(LO2)*
- One source of inflation is excessive spending, which leads to expansionary output gaps. Aggregate supply shocks are another source of inflation. *Aggregate supply shocks* include both *inflation shocks*—sudden changes in the normal behavior of inflation, created, for example, by a rise in the price of imported oil—and shocks to potential output. Adverse supply shocks both lower output and—in the absence of public beliefs that the central bank is committed to maintaining low inflation—increase inflation, creating a difficult dilemma for policymakers. *(LO3)*
- To reduce inflation, policymakers must shift the aggregate demand curve to the left, usually through a shift in monetary policy toward greater "tightness." In the short run, the main effects of an anti-inflationary policy may be reduced output and higher unemployment as the economy experiences a recessionary gap. These short-run costs of *disinflation* must be balanced against the long-run benefits of a lower rate of inflation. Over time, output and employment will return to normal levels and inflation declines. The disinflation engineered by the Fed under Chair Paul Volcker in the early 1980s followed this pattern. *(LO4)*

KEY TERMS

aggregate demand (*AD*) curve
aggregate supply shock
change in aggregate demand
disinflation
distributional effects
inflation shock
long-run aggregate supply (*LRAS*) line
long-run equilibrium
short-run aggregate supply (*SRAS*) line
short-run equilibrium

REVIEW QUESTIONS

1. What two variables are related by the aggregate demand (*AD*) curve? Explain how the behavior of the Fed helps determine the slope of this curve. List and discuss two other factors that lead the curve to have the slope that it does. *(LO1)*
2. State how each of the following affects the *AD* curve and explain. *(LO1)*
   a. An increase in government purchases.
   b. A cut in taxes.
   c. A decline in investment spending by firms.
   d. A decision by the Fed to lower the real interest rate at each level of inflation.
3. Why does the overall rate of inflation tend to adjust more slowly than prices of commodities, such as oil or grain? *(LO2)*
4. Discuss the relationship between output gaps and inflation. How is this relationship captured in the aggregate demand–aggregate supply diagram? *(LO2)*
5. Sketch an aggregate demand–aggregate supply diagram depicting an economy away from long-run equilibrium. Indicate the economy's short-run equilibrium point. Discuss how the economy reaches long-run equilibrium over a period of time. Illustrate the process in your diagram. *(LO2)*
6. True or false: The economy's self-correcting tendency makes active use of stabilization policy unnecessary. Explain. *(LO2)*
7. What factors led to increased inflation in the United States in the 1960s and 1970s? *(LO3)*
8. Why, in the absence of public beliefs that the central bank is committed to maintaining low inflation, does an adverse inflation shock pose a particularly difficult dilemma for policymakers? *(LO3)*

9. How does a tight monetary policy, like that conducted by the Volcker Fed in the early 1980s, affect output, inflation, and the real interest rate in the short run? In the long run? *(LO4)*

10. Most central banks place great value on keeping inflation low and stable. Why do they view this objective as so important? *(LO4)*

PROBLEMS

connect

1. We have seen that short-run equilibrium output falls when the Fed raises the real interest rate. Suppose the relationship between short-run equilibrium output Y and the real interest rate r set by the Fed is given by

$$Y = 1{,}000 - 1{,}000r.$$

Suppose also that the Fed's reaction function is the one shown in the following table. For whole-number inflation rates between 0 and 4 percent, find the real interest rate set by the Fed and the resulting short-run equilibrium output. Graph the aggregate demand curve numerically. *(LO1)*

Rate of inflation, π	Real interest rate, r
0.0	0.02
0.01	0.03
0.02	0.04
0.03	0.05
0.04	0.06

2. For the economy in Problem 1, suppose that potential output $Y^* = 960$. From the policy reaction function in the table in Problem 1, what can you infer about the Fed's objective for the inflation rate in the long term? *(LO1)*

3. An economy's relationship between short-run equilibrium output and inflation (its aggregate demand curve) is described by the equation

$$Y = 13{,}000 - 20{,}000\pi.$$

Initially, the inflation rate is 4 percent, or $\pi = 0.04$. Potential output Y^* equals 12,000. *(LO2)*
   a. Find the output in short-run equilibrium.
   b. Find the inflation rate in long-run equilibrium.
   Show your work.

4. This problem asks you to trace out the adjustment of inflation when the economy starts with an output gap. Suppose that the economy's aggregate demand curve is

$$Y = 1{,}000 - 1{,}000\pi,$$

where Y is short-run equilibrium output and π is the inflation rate, measured as a decimal. Potential output Y^* equals 950, and the initial inflation rate is 10 percent ($\pi = 0.10$). *(LO2)*
   a. Find output for this economy in short-run equilibrium and inflation in long-run equilibrium.
   b. Suppose that, each quarter, inflation adjusts according to the following rule.

$$\text{This quarter's inflation} = \text{Last quarter's inflation} - 0.0004(Y^* - Y).$$

   Starting from the initial value of 10 percent for inflation, find the value of inflation for each of the next five quarters. Remember, Y will continuously change as the current inflation rate change according to the given relationship $Y = 1{,}000 - 1{,}000\pi$. Does inflation come close to its long-run value?

5. For each of the following, use an *AD-AS* diagram to show the short-run and long-run effects on output and inflation. Assume the economy starts in long-run equilibrium. *(LO1, LO2, LO3)*
   a. An increase in consumer confidence that leads to higher consumption spending.
   b. A reduction in taxes.
   c. An easing of monetary policy by the Fed (a downward shift in the policy reaction function).
   d. A sharp drop in oil prices.
   e. A war that raises government purchases.

6. Suppose that the government cuts taxes in response to a recessionary gap, but because of legislative delays, the tax cut is not put in place for 18 months. Using an *AD-AS* diagram and assuming that the government's objective is to stabilize output and inflation, show how this policy action might actually prove to be counterproductive. *(LO2)*

7. Suppose that a permanent increase in oil prices both creates an inflationary shock and reduces potential output. Use an *AD-AS* diagram to show the effects of the oil price increase on output and inflation in the short run and the long run, assuming that there is no policy response. What happens if the Fed responds to the oil price increase by tightening monetary policy? *(LO3)*

8. An economy is initially in recession. Using the *AD-AS* diagram, show the process of adjustment. *(LO2, LO4)*
   a. If the Fed responds by easing monetary policy (moving its reaction function down).
   b. If the Fed takes no action.
   What are the costs and benefits of each approach, in terms of output loss and inflation?

ANSWERS TO SELF-TESTS

11.1 a. At the current level of inflation, output, and real interest rate, an exogenous reduction in business spending on new capital will reduce investment, causing a decline in overall aggregate expenditures (*AE*) and a reduction in short-run equilibrium output. Because output has fallen for a given level of inflation, the decrease in business spending leads to a leftward shift in the *AD* curve. *(LO1)*

b. At the current level of inflation, output, and real interest rate, a reduction in federal income taxes increases consumers' disposable income (*Y* − *T*), which leads to an exogenous increase in consumption at all income levels. The upward shift in the consumption function increases overall aggregate expenditures (*AE*) and leads to an increase in short-run equilibrium output. Because output has increased for a given level of inflation, the reduction in income taxes leads to a rightward shift in the *AD* curve. *(LO1)*

11.2 In the long run, the real interest rate set by the Fed must be consistent with the real interest rate determined in the market for saving and investment. To find the Fed's long-run inflation target, take as given the real interest rate determined in the long run by the market for saving and investment and read off the corresponding inflation rate from the Fed's policy reaction function. As the accompanying figure illustrates, a tightening of Fed policy (an upward shift of the policy reaction function) implies that, for any given long-run real interest rate, the Fed's inflation target must be lower. *(LO1)*

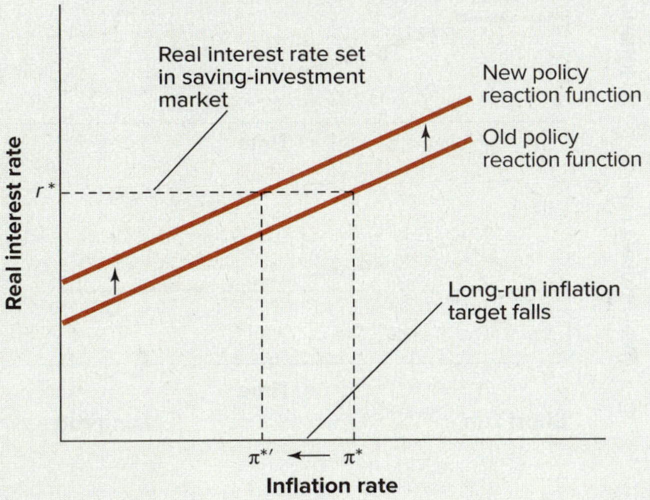

11.3 a. An upward shift in the Fed's policy reaction function means that the Federal Reserve is raising the real interest rate associated with a given level of inflation. An increase in the real interest rate causes both consumption and investment spending to fall, reducing overall aggregate expenditures and short-run equilibrium output. Thus, a shift in the Fed's policy reaction function causes the output level to fall for a given level of inflation, resulting in a leftward shift in the *AD* curve. *(LO1)*

b. The Federal Reserve's policy reaction function illustrates that the Federal Reserve responds to rising inflation rates by raising the real interest rate (a move *along* the policy reaction function), which causes a reduction in overall aggregate expenditures and short-run equilibrium output. However, in this case the Fed's response to higher inflation causes a *move along* a given *AD* curve.

Note that while the two actions appear to be similar, there is a key difference. In the first case the Fed is changing its policy rule for a *given inflation rate,* while in the second case the Fed is responding to a *changing inflation rate*. Changes in aggregate spending for a given inflation rate shift the *AD* curve, while changes in aggregate spending resulting from Fed policy responses to a rise or fall in inflation lead to moves along a given *AD* curve. *(LO1)*

11.4 a. If inflation is expected to be 2 percent next year and workers are expecting a 2 percent increase in their real wages, then they will expect, and ask for, a 4 percent increase in their nominal wages. *(LO2)*

b. If inflation is expected to be 4 percent next year, rather than 2 percent, workers will expect, and ask for, a 6 percent increase in their nominal wages. *(LO2)*

c. If wage costs rise, firms will need to increase the prices of their goods and services to cover their increased costs, leading to an increase in inflation. In part b, when expected inflation was 4 percent, firms will be faced with larger increases in nominal wages than in part a, when expected inflation was only 2 percent. Thus, we can expect firms to raise prices by more when expected inflation is 4 percent than when expected inflation is 2 percent. From this example, we can conclude that increased inflationary expectations lead to higher inflation. *(LO2)*

11.5 If the inflation rate is high, the economy will tend to stay in this high-inflation state due to expectations of high inflation and the existence of long-term wage and price contracts, while if the inflation rate is low, the economy will likewise tend to stay in this low-inflation state for similar reasons. However, since high inflation rates impose economic costs on society, the Federal Reserve has an incentive to avoid the high-inflation state by keeping inflation low, which helps maintain people's expectations of low inflation and leads to lower future inflation rates—perpetuating the "virtuous circle" illustrated in Figure 11.4. *(LO2)*

11.6 An increase in spending on new capital by firms for a given level of inflation, output, and real interest rate increases aggregate expenditures and short-run equilibrium output. Since the economy was originally operating at potential output, the increase in investment spending will lead to an expansionary gap; actual output, Y, will now be greater than potential output, Y^*. When $Y > Y^*$, the rate of inflation will tend to rise. *(LO2)*

11.7 The effects will be the opposite of those illustrated in Figure 11.8. Beginning in a long-run equilibrium with output equal to potential output and stable inflation [that is, where the aggregate demand (*AD*) curve intersects both the short-run and long-run aggregate supply lines (*SRAS* and *LRAS*, respectively)], the fall in consumption spending will initially lead to a leftward shift in the *AD* curve and the economy moves to a new, lower, short-run equilibrium output level at the same inflation rate. The shift in *AD* creates a recessionary gap, since Y is now less than Y^*. The immediate effect of the decrease in consumption spending is only to reduce output. However, over time inflation will fall because of the recessionary gap. As inflation falls the *SRAS* line will shift downward. The Federal Reserve responds to the fall in inflation by reducing real interest rates, leading to an increase in aggregate expenditure and output, a move down along the new *AD* curve. When inflation has fallen enough (and real interest rates have fallen enough) to eliminate the output gap the economy will be back in long-run equilibrium where output equals potential output but the inflation rate will be lower than before the fall in consumption spending. *(LO3)*

11.8 A decrease in oil prices is an example of a "beneficial" inflation shock and the economic effects of such a shock are the reverse of those illustrated in Figure 11.9. In this case, starting from a long-run equilibrium where output equals potential output, a beneficial inflation shock reduces current inflation, causing the *SRAS* line to shift downward. The downward shift in the *SRAS* curve leads to a short-run equilibrium with lower inflation and higher output, creating an expansionary gap. If the Fed does nothing, eventually the *SRAS* will begin to shift upward and the economy will return to its original inflation and output levels. However, the Fed may instead choose to tighten its monetary policy by shifting up its policy reaction function, raising the current real interest rate, shifting the *AD* curve to the left and restoring equilibrium at potential GDP, but at the new, lower inflation rate. *(LO3)*

11.9 If productivity growth hadn't increased in the last half of the 1990s the *LRAS* would not have shifted as far to the right as it actually did. As a consequence, the average inflation rate would not have fallen as much as illustrated in Table 11.2 and average real GDP growth would have been smaller. Similarly, if productivity growth slows in the future from its actual 1995–2000 rate, we can expect higher inflation and lower GDP growth than we otherwise would have experienced. *(LO3)*

11.10 See graphs below. *(LO4)*

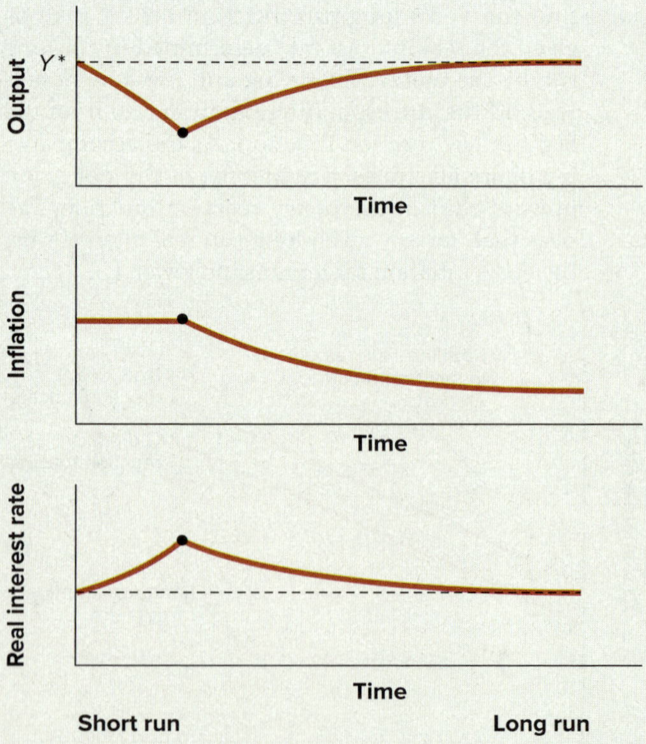

12

International Trade and Trade Policy

LEARNING OBJECTIVES

After reading this chapter, you should be able to:

LO1 Explain and apply the concept of comparative advantage and explain how it differs from absolute advantage.

LO2 Explain how the price of a tradable good is set in a closed versus an open economy, how the quantities of imports or exports are determined, and discuss who are the winners and losers from trade.

LO3 Illustrate why trade is often politically controversial, even though it promises to increase total income.

On April 13, 1861, Southern troops fired on Fort Sumter in Charleston harbor, initiating the American Civil War. Less than a week later, on April 19, President Lincoln proclaimed a naval blockade of the South. Code-named the Anaconda Plan (after the snake that squeezes its prey to death), the blockade required the Union navy to patrol the Southern coastline, stopping and boarding ships that were attempting to land or depart. The object of the blockade was to prevent the Confederacy from shipping cotton to Europe, where it could be traded for military equipment, clothing, foodstuffs, and other supplies.

Historians are divided on the effectiveness of the Union blockade in choking off Confederate trade. In the early years of the war, the North had too few ships to cover the 3,600-mile Southern coastline, so "running" the blockade was not difficult. But in the latter part of the war the number of Union ships enforcing the blockade increased from about 90 to more than 600, and sailing ships were replaced with faster, more lethal ironclad vessels. Still, private blockade runners attempted to elude the Union navy in small, fast ships. Because the price of raw cotton in Great Britain was between 10 and 20 times what it was in the Confederacy (a differential that indicated disruption in the normal flow of trade), blockade runners enjoyed huge profits when they were successful. But despite their efforts, by 1864 the Southern war effort was seriously hampered by a lack of military equipment and supplies, at least in part as a result of the blockade.

The use of a naval blockade as a weapon of war highlights a paradox in contemporary attitudes toward trade between nations. Presumably, an attempt by a foreign power to blockade U.S. ports today would be considered a hostile act that would elicit a strong response from the U.S. government. Yet one often hears politicians and others arguing that trade with other nations is harmful to the United States and should be restricted—in effect, that the United States should blockade its own ports! In the U.S. presidential election of 2016, for example, both candidates opposed the Trans-Pacific Partnership (TPP)—an agreement intended to increase trade between Australia, Canada, Japan, Mexico, the United States, and seven other, smaller economies—on the grounds that it would cost American jobs. As another example, politicians from both the Republican and Democratic Parties occasionally complain about China's exports to the United States. Some of them propose taking action against the Chinese government because, they say, it engages in unfair policies that cause Chinese products to sell in the U.S. for prices that are too *cheap*. So is trade a good thing or not? And if it is, why does it sometimes face determined opposition?

This chapter addresses international trade and its effects on the broader economy. We will begin by reviewing the idea of *comparative advantage*. We will show that everyone can enjoy more goods and services if nations specialize in those products in which they have a comparative advantage, and then trade freely among themselves. Furthermore, if trade is unrestricted, market forces will ensure that countries produce those goods in which they have a comparative advantage.

Having shown the potential benefits of trade, we will turn next to the reasons for opposition to trade. Although opening the economy to trade *can*, in our model, increase economic welfare overall, some groups—such as workers in industries that face competition from foreign producers—may in reality be made worse off. The fact that open trade may hurt some groups creates political pressure to enact measures restricting trade, such as taxes on imported goods (called tariffs) and limits on imports (called quotas). We will analyze the effects of these trade restrictions, along with other ways of responding to concerns about affected industries and workers through direct assistance programs.

Economists understand the frustrations with trade expressed by some groups. Indeed, economists recognize that for a displaced worker who does not expect effective direct government assistance to materialize—for example, because the worker does not expect the government to pass, implement, and sustain the relevant measures—opposing trade may appear a reasonable course of action. However, from an economic point of view that takes into account both the overall size of the economic pie and how it is distributed, providing direct assistance to those who are hurt by increased trade is preferable to blocking or restricting trade.

COMPARATIVE ADVANTAGE AS A BASIS FOR TRADE

One of the most important insights of modern economics is that when two people (or two nations) have different opportunity costs of producing different goods and services, they can always increase the total value of available goods and services by trading with one another. Recall from Chapter 1, *Thinking Like an Economist*, that the opportunity cost of spending more time (or other resources) on any one activity is having less time (or other resources) available to spend on others. To illustrate this insight, we will start with an example.

absolute advantage one person has an absolute advantage over another if he or she takes fewer hours to perform a task than the other person

comparative advantage one person has a comparative advantage over another if his or her opportunity cost of performing a task is lower than the other person's opportunity cost

In Example 12.1, economists would say that Wearstler has an **absolute advantage** at designing her web page but a **comparative advantage** at interior design. She has an absolute advantage at designing her web page because she can perform that task in less time than a web designer could. Even so, the web designer has a comparative advantage at designing web pages because his or her opportunity cost of performing that task is lower than Wearstler's.

Example 12.1 makes the implicit assumption that Wearstler would be equally happy to spend an hour designing her web page or working on an interior design project. But suppose she is tired of interior design work and feels it might be enjoyable to try her hand at web design. Designing her own web page might then make perfect sense! But unless she expects to gain extra satisfaction from performing that task, she almost certainly will do better to hire a web designer. The web designer will also benefit, or else he or she wouldn't have offered to design web pages for the stated price.

EXAMPLE 12.1 Scarcity Principle

Should Kelly Wearstler design her own web page?

Kelly Wearstler is among the most famous and influential interior designers in the United States today. She has received numerous accolades for her commercial and residential design work, has completed projects for top celebrities such as Cameron Diaz, Gwen Stefani, and Ben Stiller, and boasts more than 700,000 followers on Instagram.

Although Wearstler devotes most of her time and talent to interior design, she is well equipped to do a broad range of other design work. Suppose she could design her own web page in 300 hours, half the time it would take any other web designer. Does that mean that Wearstler should design her own web page?

Suppose that on the strength of her talents as an interior designer, Wearstler earns more than $1 million a year, implying that the opportunity cost of any time she spent designing her web page would be over $500 per hour. She would have little difficulty engaging a highly qualified web designer whose hourly wage is considerably less than $500 per hour. So even though Wearstler's substantial skills might enable her to design her web page more quickly than most web designers, it would not be in her interest to do so.

Amy Graves/Getty Images

Should Kelly Wearstler design her own web page?

In summary, this example demonstrates that by specializing in the activities at which they have comparative advantage (i.e., in the activities with lowest opportunity cost), Wearstler and another web designer could both gain. Indeed, the gains made possible from specialization based on comparative advantage constitute the rationale for market exchange. By concentrating on those tasks at which we are relatively most productive, together we can produce vastly more than if we all tried to be self-sufficient. (In addition, our relative productivity in those activities we concentrate on can itself increase, for example, through specialized training and experience—in turn further increasing our comparative advantage in those activities.) The next example illustrates more concretely how these productivity gains come about.

EXAMPLE 12.2 Comparative Advantage

Should Ana update her own web page?

Consider a small community in which Ana is the only professional bicycle mechanic and Xin is the only professional web designer. If the amount of time for each of them to update a web page and repair a bicycle is as shown in Table 12.1, and if each regards the two tasks as equally pleasant (or unpleasant), does the fact that Ana can update a web page faster than Xin imply that Ana should update her own web page?

TABLE 12.1
Productivity Information for Ana and Xin

	Time to update a web page	Time to complete a bicycle repair
Ana	20 minutes	10 minutes
Xin	30 minutes	30 minutes

The entries in the table show that Ana has an absolute advantage over Xin in both activities. While Ana, the mechanic, needs only 20 minutes to update a web page, Xin, the web designer, needs 30 minutes. Ana's advantage over Xin is even greater when the task is fixing bikes: She can complete a repair in only 10 minutes, compared to Xin's 30 minutes.

But the fact that Ana is a better web designer than Xin does *not* imply that Ana should update her own web page. Xin has a comparative advantage over Ana at web design: She is *relatively* more productive at updating a web page than Ana. Similarly, Ana has a comparative advantage in bicycle repair. (Remember that a person has a comparative advantage at a given task if his or her opportunity cost of performing that task is lower than another person's.)

What is Xin's opportunity cost of updating a web page? Because she takes 30 minutes to update each page—the same amount of time she takes to fix a bicycle—her opportunity cost of updating a web page is one bicycle repair. In other words, by taking the time to update a web page, Xin is effectively giving up the opportunity to do one bicycle repair. Ana, in contrast, can complete two bicycle repairs in the time she takes to update a single web page. For her, the opportunity cost of updating a web page is two bicycle repairs. Ana's opportunity cost to update a web page, measured in terms of bicycle repairs forgone, is twice as high as Xin's. Thus, Xin has a comparative advantage at web design.

The interesting and important implication of the opportunity cost comparison summarized in Table 12.2 is that the total number of bicycle repairs and web updates accomplished if Xin and Ana both spend part of their time at each activity will always be smaller than the number accomplished if each specializes in the activity in which she has a comparative advantage. Suppose, for example, that people in their community demand a total of 16 web page updates per day. If Ana spent half her time updating web pages and the other half repairing bicycles, an 8-hour workday would yield 12 web page updates and 24 bicycle repairs. To complete the remaining 4 updates, Xin would have to spend 2 hours web designing, which would leave her 6 hours to repair bicycles. And because she takes 30 minutes to do each repair, she would have time to complete 12 of them. So when the two women each try to be a jill of all trades, they end up completing a total of 16 web page updates and 36 bicycle repairs.

TABLE 12.2
Opportunity Costs for Ana and Xin

	Opportunity cost of updating a web page	Opportunity cost of a bicycle repair
Ana	2 bicycle repairs	0.5 web page update
Xin	1 bicycle repair	1 web page update

Consider what would have happened had each woman specialized in her activity of comparative advantage. Xin could have updated 16 web pages on her own and Ana could have performed 48 bicycle repairs. Specialization would have created an additional 12 bicycle repairs out of thin air.

When computing the opportunity cost of one good in terms of another, we must pay close attention to the form in which the productivity information is presented. In Example 12.2, we were told how many minutes each person needed to perform each task. Alternatively, we might be told how many units of each task each person can perform in an hour. Work through the following self-test to see how to proceed when information is presented in this alternative format.

SELF-TEST 12.1

Should Miguel update his own web page?

Consider a small community in which Miguel is the only professional bicycle mechanic and Monique is the only professional web designer. If their productivity rates at the two tasks are as shown in the table, and if each regards the two tasks as equally pleasant (or unpleasant), does the fact that Miguel can update a web page faster than Monique imply that Miguel should update his own web page?

	Productivity in web design	Productivity in bicycle repair
Monique	2 web page updates per hour	1 repair per hour
Miguel	3 web page updates per hour	3 repairs per hour

This insight, that specialization and trade among individuals can yield impressive gains in productivity, applies equally well to nations. Factors such as climate, natural resources, technology, workers' skills and education, and culture provide countries with comparative advantages in the production of different goods and services. For example, the large number of leading research universities in the United States gives that nation a comparative advantage in the design of technologically sophisticated computer and mobile hardware and software. Likewise, the wide international use of the English language endows the United States with a comparative advantage in producing popular films and TV shows. Similarly, France's climate and topography, together with the accumulated knowledge of generations of vintners, provides that country a comparative advantage in producing fine wines, while Australia's huge expanses of arable land give that country a comparative advantage in producing grain.

Climate and long experience give France a comparative advantage in producing fine wines.

We can all enjoy more goods and services when each country produces according to its comparative advantage, and then trades with other countries. So, while in reality software, films, TV shows, wines, and grain are all produced by each of the three countries, respectively (the U.S., France, and Australia), by concentrating on producing the specific products each country has a comparative at and then trading with other countries, consumers in each of these countries can enjoy a greater variety and quantity of these products.

However, there is an important difference between applying the principle of comparative advantage to individuals and applying it to nations: That a nation as a whole—in the aggregate—enjoys more goods and services does not imply that *everyone* in the nation enjoys more goods and services. Rather, it is possible that within the nation, some individuals will gain from opening up to trade, while others will lose. So when we say that in the transition from a **closed economy**—one that does not trade with the rest of the world—to a more **open economy**—one that does trade with other economies—everybody *can* gain, we are not saying that everybody *will* gain. For everybody to gain, or be better off, the winners from trade will have to share a sufficient amount of their gains with the losers. In itself, opening up trade does not guarantee that the gains will be shared. We return to these issues in the next section.

closed economy an economy that does not trade with the rest of the world

open economy an economy that trades with other countries

RECAP

COMPARATIVE ADVANTAGE AS A BASIS OF TRADE

Gains from exchange are possible if trading partners have comparative advantage in producing different goods and services. You have a comparative advantage in producing, say, web pages if your opportunity cost of producing a web page—measured in terms of other production opportunities forgone—is smaller than the corresponding opportunity costs of your trading partners. Maximum production is achieved if each person specializes in producing the good or service in which he or she has the lowest opportunity cost. This comparative advantage makes specialization worthwhile even if one trading partner is more productive than others, in absolute terms, in every activity.

A SUPPLY AND DEMAND PERSPECTIVE ON TRADE

In this section we will look more carefully at how international trade affects supply and demand in the markets for specific goods. We will see that when it is costly for workers and firms to change industries, opening up trade with other countries may create groups of winners and losers among producers, workers, and consumers.

Let's see how trade affects the markets for computers and coffee in a hypothetical economy that produces only these two goods. We will call this economy Costa Rica. Figure 12.1 shows the supply and demand for computers in that economy. As usual, the price is shown on the vertical axis and the quantity on the horizontal axis. For now, think of the price of computers as being measured in terms of coffee rather than in terms of dollars (in other words, we measure the price of computers *relative* to the price of the other good in the economy). As usual, the upward-sloping curve in Figure 12.1 is the supply curve of computers, in this case for computers produced in Costa Rica; and the downward-sloping curve is the demand curve for computers by Costa Rican residents. The supply curve for computers in Costa Rica reflects the opportunity cost of supplying computers (see Chapter 2, *Supply and Demand*). Specifically, at any level of computer production, the relative price at which Costa

FIGURE 12.1

The Market for Computers in Costa Rica.

If Costa Rica is closed to international trade, the equilibrium price and quantity of computers are determined by the intersection of the domestic supply and demand curves at point *E*. But if Costa Rica is open to trade, the domestic price of computers must equal the world price. At that price, Costa Ricans will demand q_D computers, but domestic producers will supply only q_S computers. Thus $q_D - q_S$ computers must be imported from abroad.

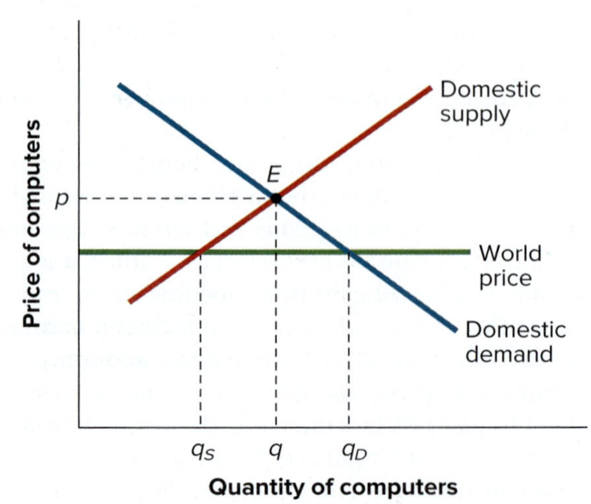

Rican firms are willing to supply an additional computer equals their opportunity cost of doing so. The demand curve, which tells us the number of computers Costa Ricans will purchase at each relative price, reflects the preferences and buying power of Costa Rican consumers.

If the Costa Rican economy is closed to international trade, then market equilibrium occurs where the domestic supply and demand curves intersect, at point E in Figure 12.1. The equilibrium price will be p and the equilibrium quantity, q.

If Costa Rica opens its market to trade, however, the relevant price for computers becomes the **world price** of computers, the price at which computers are traded internationally. The world price for computers is determined by the worldwide supply and demand for computers. If we assume that Costa Rica's computer market is too small to affect the world price for computers very much, the world price can be treated as fixed, and represented by a horizontal line in the figure. Figure 12.1 shows the world price for computers as being lower than Costa Rica's closed-economy price.

world price the price at which a good or service is traded on international markets

If Costa Ricans are free to buy and sell computers on the international market, then the price of computers in Costa Rica must be the same as the world price. (No one in Costa Rica will buy a computer at a price above the world price, and no one will sell one at a price below the world price.) Figure 12.1 shows that at the world price, Costa Rican consumers and firms demand q_D computers, but Costa Rican computer producers will supply only q_S computers. The difference between the two quantities, $q_D - q_S$, is the number of computers that Costa Rica must import from abroad. Figure 12.1 illustrates a general conclusion: *If the price of a good or service in a closed economy is greater than the world price, and that economy opens itself to trade, the economy will tend to become a net importer of that good or service.*

A different outcome occurs in Costa Rica's coffee market, shown in Figure 12.2. The price of coffee (measured relative to the price of computers) is shown on the vertical axis, and the quantity of coffee on the horizontal axis. The downward-sloping demand curve in the figure shows how much coffee Costa Rican consumers want to buy at each relative price, and the upward-sloping supply curve how much coffee Costa Rican producers are willing to supply at each relative price. If Costa Rica's economy is closed to trade with the rest of the world, then equilibrium in the market for coffee will occur at point E, where the domestic demand and supply curves intersect. The quantity produced will be q and the price p.

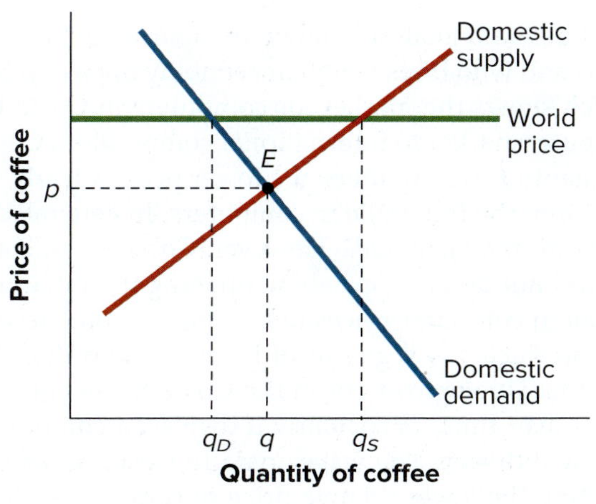

FIGURE 12.2

The Market for Coffee in Costa Rica.

With no international trade, the equilibrium price and quantity of coffee in Costa Rica are determined by the intersection of the domestic supply and demand curves (point E). But if the country opens to trade, the domestic price of coffee must equal the world price. At the higher world price, Costa Ricans will demand the quantity of coffee q_D, less than the amount supplied by Costa Rican producers, q_S. The excess coffee supplied by Costa Rican producers, $q_S - q_D$, is exported.

Now imagine that Costa Rica opens its coffee market to international trade. As in the case of computers, if free trade in coffee is permitted, then the prevailing price for coffee in Costa Rica must be the same as the world price. Unlike the case of computers, however, the world price of coffee as shown in Figure 12.2 is *higher* than the domestic equilibrium price. How do we know that the world price of coffee will be higher than the domestic price? Recall that the price of coffee is measured relative to the price of computers, and vice versa. If the price of computers relative to the price of coffee is higher in Costa Rica than in the world market, then the price of coffee relative to the price of computers must be lower, as each price is the reciprocal of the other. More generally, when two people or two countries trade with each other, neither can have a comparative advantage in *every* good and service. Thus, in an example with only two goods, if non–Costa Rican producers have a comparative advantage in computers, reflected in the lower cost of computers relative to coffee in the world market, then Costa Rican producers must have a comparative advantage in coffee. By definition, this comparative advantage implies that the opportunity cost of coffee in terms of computers must be lower in Costa Rica than in the rest of the world.

Figure 12.2 shows that at the world price for coffee, Costa Rican producers are willing to supply q_S coffee, while Costa Rican consumers want to purchase a smaller amount, q_D. The difference between domestic production and domestic consumption, $q_S - q_D$, is exported to the world market. The general conclusion of Figure 12.2 is this: *If the price of a good or service in a closed economy is lower than the world price, and that economy opens itself to trade, the economy will tend to become a net exporter of that good or service.*

These examples illustrate how the market translates comparative advantage into mutually beneficial gains from trade. If trade is unrestricted, then countries with a comparative advantage in a particular good will profit by supplying that good to the world market and using the revenue earned to import goods in which they do not have a comparative advantage. Thus the workings of the free market automatically ensure that goods will be produced where the opportunity cost is lowest, leading to the highest possible consumption possibilities for the world as a whole.

Winners and Losers from Trade

If trade is so wonderful, why do politicians so often resist free trade and "globalization"? The reason is that although free trade benefits the economy as a whole, specific groups may not benefit. Groups who are hurt by trade, and the politicians they elect, may support policies that restrict the free flow of goods and services across borders.

The supply and demand analyses shown in Figures 12.2 and 12.3 are useful in clarifying who gains and who loses when an economy opens up to trade. Look first at Figure 12.1, which shows the market for computers in Costa Rica. When Costa Rica opens its computer market to international competition, Costa Rican consumers enjoy a larger quantity of computers at a lower price. Clearly, Costa Rican computer users benefit from the free trade in computers. In general, *domestic consumers of imported goods benefit from free trade.* However, Costa Rican computer producers and their workers will not be so happy about opening their market to international competition. The fall in computer prices to the international level implies that less efficient domestic producers will go out of business, and that those who remain will earn lower profits. Unemployment in the Costa Rican computer industry will rise and may persist over time, particularly if displaced computer workers cannot easily move to a new industry. The wages paid to Costa Rican computer workers will also fall, reflecting the lower relative price of computers. We see that, in general, *domestic producers of imported goods, and workers in imported-good sectors, are hurt by free trade.*

Consumers are helped, while producers and workers are hurt, when imports increase. The opposite conclusions apply for an increase in exports (see Figure 12.3). In the example of Costa Rica, an opening of the coffee market raises the domestic price of coffee to the world price and creates the opportunity for Costa Rica to export coffee. Domestic producers of coffee benefit from the increased market (they can now sell coffee abroad as well as at home) and from the higher price of their product. Domestic workers in the coffee sector benefit too, as they are more in demand. In short, *domestic producers of exported goods, and workers in exported-good sectors, benefit from free trade.* Costa Rican coffee drinkers will be less enthusiastic, however, since they must now have to pay the higher world price of coffee, and can therefore consume less. *Thus domestic consumers of exported goods are hurt by free trade.*

Free trade is *efficient* in the sense that it increases the size of the pie available to the economy. Indeed, the efficiency of free trade is an application of the *equilibrium principle*: Markets in equilibrium leave no unexploited opportunities for individuals. Despite the efficiency of free trade, however, some groups may lose from trade, which generates political pressures to block or restrict trade. In the next section we will discuss the major types of policy used to restrict trade.

The Economic Naturalist 12.1

What is the China trade shock?

The China trade shock, a term most commonly associated with economists David Autor, David Dorn, and Gordon Hanson, is used to describe the dramatic change in international trade patterns that resulted from China's rise as a major player in the global economy over the past few decades.

In a series of influential studies, these economists and their collaborators investigated the costs of the shock to U.S. workers. They found that employment has fallen in U.S. industries and regions most exposed to import competition from China—something that our theory in this chapter helps explain. However, they did not find strong evidence of simultaneous offsetting employment increases in other sectors in the same regions, suggesting that the transition of workers into sectors in which the U.S. has comparative advantage has been neither quick nor easy—something that the theory does not emphasize.

Overall, these economists conclude that workers' adjustment to trade shocks is often a slow and difficult process, and that local labor force participation rates and unemployment rates in affected regions may take a decade or more to recover. Moreover, the slow adjustment means that trade shocks could lead to prolonged economic and social problems in affected communities.

While the research underlying these conclusions is still new and is still being examined, it serves as a reminder that for many workers, the short-term costs of trade may outweigh the short-term benefits. While opposition to trade among such workers is understandable, we should not conclude that the overall costs of trade outweigh the overall benefits. Rather, as these economists conclude in one of their studies:

> Better understanding when and where trade is costly, and how and why it may be beneficial, is a key item on the research agenda for trade and labor economists. Developing effective tools for managing and mitigating the costs of trade adjustment should be high on the agenda for policymakers and applied economists.[1]

[1]David Autor, David Dorn, and Gordon Hanson, "The China Shock: Learning from Labor Market Adjustment to Large Changes in Trade," *Annual Review of Economics* 8 (October 2016), pp. 205–240.

RECAP

A SUPPLY AND DEMAND PERSPECTIVE ON TRADE

- For a closed economy, the domestic supply and demand for a good or service determine the equilibrium price and quantity of that good or service.
- In an open economy, the price of a good or service traded on international markets equals the world price. If the domestic quantity supplied at the world price exceeds the domestic quantity demanded, the difference will be exported to the world market. If the domestic quantity demanded at the world price exceeds the domestic quantity supplied, the difference will be imported.
- Generally, if the price of a good or service in a closed economy is lower than the world price and the economy opens to trade, the country will become a net exporter of that good or service. If the closed-economy price is higher than the world price and the economy opens to trade, the country will tend to become a net importer of the good or service.
- Consumers of imported goods, producers of exported goods, and workers in exported-good sectors benefit from trade, whereas consumers of exported goods, producers of imported goods, and workers in imported-good sectors are hurt by trade. Those groups that are hurt, and the politicians they elect, may support enacting barriers to trade.

TRADE WINNERS AND LOSERS

Winners

- Consumers of imported goods
- Producers of exported goods
- Workers in exported-good sectors

Losers

- Consumers of exported goods
- Producers of imported goods
- Workers in imported-good sectors

PROTECTIONIST POLICIES: TARIFFS AND QUOTAS

protectionism the view that free trade is injurious and should be restricted

tariff a tax imposed on an imported good

quota a legal limit on the quantity of a good that may be imported

The view that free trade is injurious and should be restricted is known as **protectionism.** Supporters of this view believe the government should attempt to "protect" domestic markets by raising legal barriers to imports. (Interestingly, protectionists rarely attempt to restrict exports, even though they hurt consumers of the exported good.) Two of the most common types of such barriers are tariffs and quotas. A **tariff** is a tax imposed on an imported good. A **quota** is a legal limit on the quantity of a good that may be imported.

Tariffs

The effects of tariffs and quotas can be explained using supply and demand diagrams. Suppose that Costa Rican computer makers, dismayed by the penetration of "their" market by imported computers, persuade their government to impose a tariff—that is, a tax—on every computer imported into the country. Computers

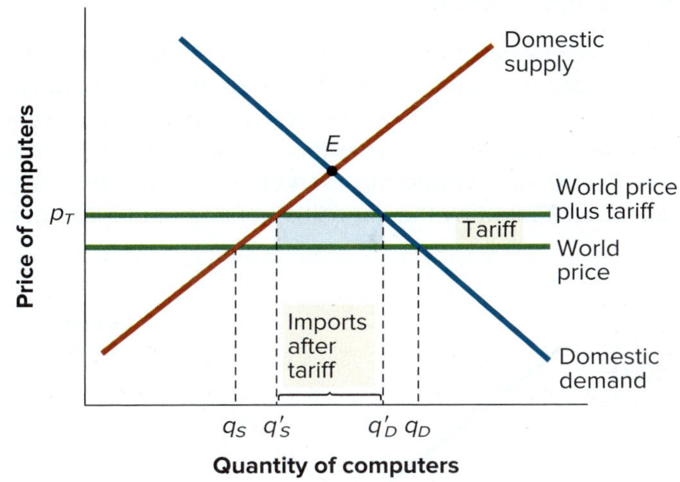

FIGURE 12.3

The Market for Computers after the Imposition of an Import Tariff.

The imposition of a tariff on imported computers raises the price of computers in Costa Rica to the world price plus tariff, p_T, represented by the upper horizontal line. Domestic production of computers rises from q_S to q'_S, domestic purchases of computers fall from q_D to q'_D, and computer imports fall from $q_D - q_S$ to $q'_D - q'_S$. Costa Rican consumers are worse off and Costa Rican computer producers are better off. The Costa Rican government collects revenue from the tariff equal to the area of the pale blue rectangle.

produced in Costa Rica will be exempt from the tax. Figure 12.3 shows the likely effects of this tariff on the domestic Costa Rican computer market. The lower of the two horizontal lines in the figure indicates the world price of computers, not including the tariff. The higher of the two lines indicates the price Costa Rican consumers will actually pay for imported computers, including the tariff. We refer to the price of computers including the tariff as p_T. The vertical distance between the two lines equals the amount of the tariff that is imposed on each imported computer.

connect

▶ Visit your instructor's Connect course and access your eBook to view this video.

Why do consumers in the United States often pay more than double the world price for sugar?

From the point of view of domestic Costa Rican producers and consumers, the imposition of the tariff has the same effects as an equivalent increase in the world price of computers. Because the price (including the tariff) of imported computers has risen, Costa Rican computer producers will be able to raise the price they charge for their computers to the world price plus tariff, p_T. Thus the price Costa Rican consumers must pay—whether their computers are imported or not—equals p_T, represented by the upper horizontal line in Figure 12.3.

The rise in the price of computers created by the tariff affects the quantities of computers supplied and the quantities demanded by Costa Ricans. Domestic computer producers, facing a higher price for computers, increase their production from q_S to q'_S (see Figure 12.3). Costa Rican consumers, also reacting to the higher price, reduce their computer purchases from q_D to q'_D. As a result, the number of imported computers—the difference between domestic purchases and domestic production—falls from $q_D - q_S$ to $q'_D - q'_S$.

Who are the winners and the losers from the tariff, then? Relative to an environment with free trade and no tariff, the winners are the domestic computer producers, who sell more computers and receive a higher price for them. The clearest losers are Costa Rican consumers, who must now pay more for their computers. Another winner is the government, which collects revenue from the tariff. The blue area in Figure 12.3 shows the amount of revenue the government collects, equal to the quantity of computer imports after the imposition of the tariff, $q'_D - q'_S$, times the amount of the tariff.

EXAMPLE 12.3 A Tariff on Imported Computers

What are the effects of a tariff on trade?

Suppose that the Costa Rican market for computers is represented by Figure 12.4. Thus, if the Costa Rican economy is closed to trade, the equilibrium price for computers would be $2,000, and 2,000 computers would be bought and sold in the Costa Rican computer market every year (point *E*). Assuming that the world price of computers is $1,400, how would this market be affected by opening to trade, and how would it be affected by the imposition of a tariff of $400 per computer?

FIGURE 12.4

The Market for Computers in Costa Rica after the Imposition of an Import Tariff.

A tariff of $400 per computer raises the price of computers by $400 and reduces imports by 400 computers per year.

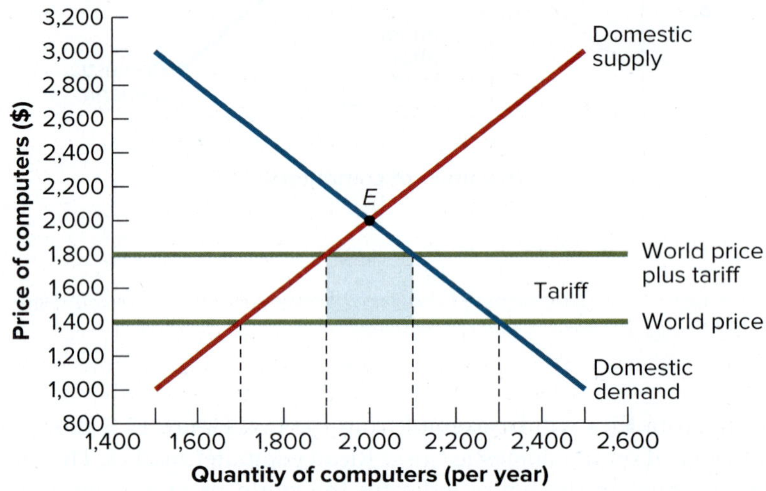

If the economy opens to trade, the domestic price of computers must equal the world price of $1,400. At this price, the domestic quantity demanded is 2,300 computers per year and the domestic quantity supplied is 1,700 computers per year. Imports equal the difference between the domestic quantities demanded and supplied, or 2,300 − 1,700 = 600 computers per year.

The imposition of a tariff of $400 per computer raises the price from $1,400 to $1,800. This price rise causes Costa Rican computer producers to increase their production from 1,700 to 1,900 computers per year, and it causes Costa Rican consumers to reduce their computer purchases from 2,300 to 2,100. As a result, the number of imported computers—the difference between domestic purchases and domestic production—falls from 600 to 200 (2,100 − 1,900).

Thus the tariff has raised the price of computers by $400 and reduced imports by 400 computers per year. The tariff revenue collected by the government is $400 per imported computer times 200 computers per year = $80,000 per year.

SELF-TEST 12.2

Repeat Example 12.3 under the assumption that the world price of computers is $1,200 (the tariff is still $400). What happens if the world price is $1,800?

Quotas

An alternative to a tariff is a quota, or legal limit, on the number or value of foreign goods that can be imported. One means of enforcing a quota is to require importers to obtain a license or permit for each good they bring into the country. The government then distributes exactly the same number of permits as the number of goods that may be imported under the quota.

How does the imposition of a quota on, say, computers affect the domestic market for computers? Figure 12.5, which is similar to Figure 12.3, illustrates the effect of a quota on imported computers. As before, assume that at first there are no restrictions on trade. Consumers pay the world price for computers, and $q_D - q_S$ computers are imported. Now suppose once more that domestic computer producers complain to the government about competition from foreign computer makers, and the government agrees to act. However, this time, instead of a tariff, the government imposes a quota on the number of computers that can be imported. For comparability with the tariff analyzed in Figure 12.3, let's assume that the quota permits the same level of imports as entered the country under the tariff: specifically, $q'_D - q'_S$ computers. What effect does this ruling have on the domestic market for computers?

After the imposition of the quota, the quantity of computers supplied to the Costa Rican market is the production of domestic firms plus the $q'_D - q'_S$ imported computers allowed under the quota. Figure 12.5 shows the quantity of computers supplied inclusive of the quota. The total supply curve, labeled "Domestic supply plus quota," is the same as the domestic supply curve shifted $q'_D - q'_S$ units to the right. The domestic demand curve is the same as in Figure 12.3. Equilibrium in the domestic market for computers occurs at point *F* in Figure 12.5, at the intersection of the supply curve including the quota and the domestic demand curve. The figure shows that, relative to the initial situation with free trade, the quota (1) raises the domestic price of computers above the world price, to the level marked p_T in Figure 12.5; (2) reduces domestic purchases of computers from q_D to q'_D; (3) increases domestic production of computers from q_S to q'_S; and (4) reduces imports to $q'_D - q'_S$, consistent with a quota. Like a tariff, the quota helps domestic producers by increasing their sales and the price they receive for their output, while hurting domestic consumers by forcing them to pay a higher price.

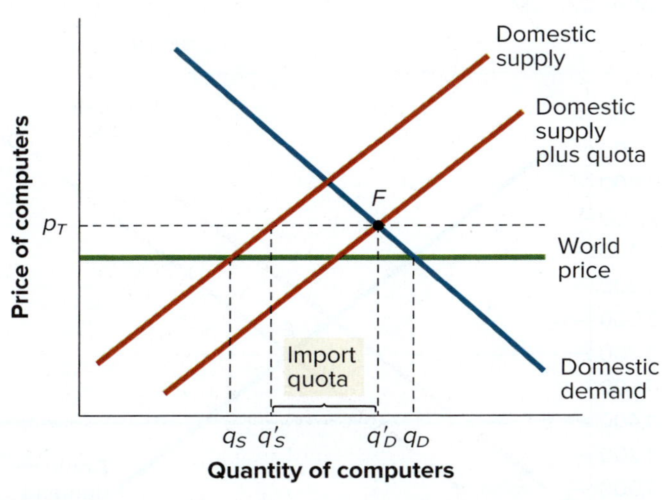

FIGURE 12.5

The Market for Computers after the Imposition of an Import Quota.

The figure shows the effects of the imposition of a quota that permits only $q'_D - q'_S$ computers to be imported. The total supply of computers to the domestic economy equals the domestic economy equals the domestic supply curve shifted to the right by $q'_D - q'_S$ units (the fixed amount of imports). Market equilibrium occurs at point *F*. The effects of the quota on the domestic market are identical to those of the tariff analyzed in Figure 12.3. The domestic price rises to p_T, domestic production of computers rises from q_S to q'_S, domestic purchases of computers fall from q_D to q'_D, and computer imports fall from $q_D - q_s$ to $q'_D - q'_S$. The quota differs from the tariff in that under a quota system the government collects no revenue.

Interestingly, under our assumption that the quota is set to permit the same level of imports as the tariff, the effects on the domestic market of the tariff (Figure 12.3) and the quota (Figure 12.5) are not only similar, they are *equivalent.* Comparing Figures 12.3 and 12.5, you can see that the two policies have identical effects on the domestic price, domestic purchases, domestic production, and imports.

Although the market effects of a tariff and a quota are the same, there is one important difference between the two policies, which is that a tariff generates revenue for the government, whereas a quota does not. With a quota, the revenue that would have gone to the government goes instead to those firms that hold the import licenses. A holder of an import license can purchase a computer at the world price and resell it in the domestic market at price p_T, pocketing the difference. Thus with a tariff the government collects the difference between the world price and the domestic market price of the good; with a quota, private firms or individuals collect that difference. Why then would the government ever impose a quota rather than a tariff? One possibility is that the distribution of import licenses is a means of rewarding the government's political supporters. Sometimes, international political concerns may also play a role (see The Economic Naturalist 12.2 for a possible example).

EXAMPLE 12.4 Effects of an Import Quota

What are the effects of an import quota on trade?

Suppose the supply of and demand for computers in Costa Rica, as well as the world price of computers, are as given in Figure 12.6. Suppose that the government imposes a quota of 200 on the number of computers that can be imported. What effect would this have on the domestic market for computers (relative to the free-trade alternative)?

FIGURE 12.6

The Market for Computers in Costa Rica after the Imposition of an Import Quota.

A quota of 200 computers per year raises the price of computers by $400 and reduces imports by 400 computers per year.

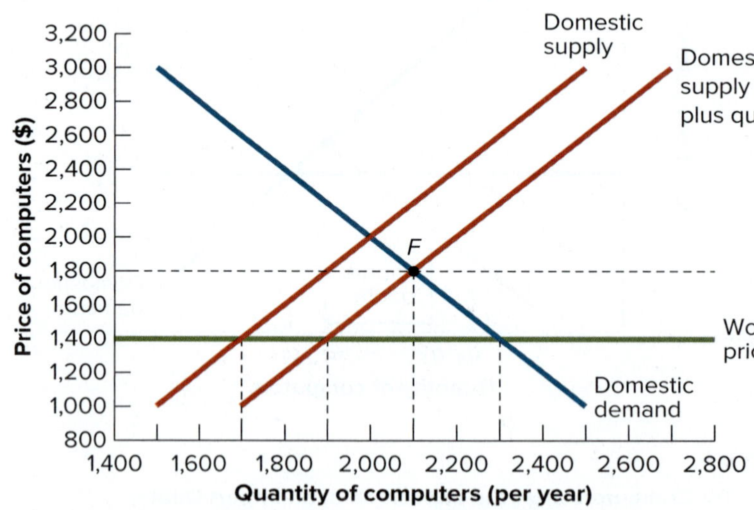

After the quota is imposed, the equilibrium in the domestic market occurs at point *F* in the figure. As the figure shows, relative to free trade, the domestic price increases to $1,800 per computer, domestic purchases of computers decrease to 2,100, domestic production of computers increases to 1,900, and imports decrease to 200 (the difference between the 2,100 computers demanded and the 1,900 computers domestically produced).

Note that the domestic price, domestic production, and domestic demand are the same in Examples 12.3 and 12.4. Thus, under the assumptions we made, the tariff and the quota have the same effects on the domestic market for computers. The only difference between the two policies is that with a quota, the government does not get the tariff revenue it got in Example 12.3. That revenue goes instead to the holders of import licenses, who can buy computers on the world market at $1,400 and sell them in the domestic market at $1,800.

The Economic Naturalist 12.2

Why did the U.S. start a trade war with China?

Starting in 2018 and continuing during 2019, the U.S. imposed several rounds of tariffs on commodities and products imported from China. The tariffs, ranging from 10 to 25 percent, were applied to imports worth hundreds of billions of dollars in total. In retaliation, China imposed tariffs of 5 to 25 percent on more than a hundred billion dollars' worth of goods imported from the United States.

As our analysis in this chapter predicts, studies show that the U.S. tariffs were largely reflected in higher prices for American consumers and for American producers who buy the affected goods.[2] The price of these goods increased not only when they were imported, but also, through reduced competition, when they were produced in the United States. The Chinese tariffs also hurt American producers who export to China. The overall costs of the trade war to Americans were thus substantial. Why did the United States start it?

Songquan Deng/Shutterstock

Why did the U.S. start a trade war with China?

One stated reason for imposing the tariffs was that U.S. trade negotiators were concerned that China was violating U.S. intellectual property rights, for example, by not enforcing patent laws or by requiring U.S. firms to share technology if they want to do business in China. Loss of intellectual property disadvantages U.S. producers in the long run. Concerns about worker protections, environmental protections, and regulatory differences have also historically influenced trade policy.

Another stated reason for the tariffs was national security. Traditionally, countries have emphasized maintaining food and defense independence through local production. Recently, the COVID-19 pandemic also has highlighted the vulnerability of countries that rely on trading partners for medications and medical equipment.

While the U.S.–China trade war is in principle still ongoing, a first ceasefire was reached in January 2020, when the United States and China signed a Phase One trade deal, and when some of the tariffs were reduced. At around the same time, the two countries turned to fighting the COVID-19 pandemic and its economic fallout—which shifted these governments' focus away from the trade war. While it remains to be seen how trade relations between the United States and China further develop, a range of political and economic issues between the two countries, going beyond those analyzed in this chapter, are likely to affect the negotiations.

Tariffs and quotas are not the only barriers to trade that governments erect. Importers may be subject to unnecessarily complex bureaucratic rules (so-called

[2]See, for example: Mary Amiti, Stephen J. Redding, and David Weinstein, "The Impact of the 2018 Trade War on U.S. Prices and Welfare," NBER Working Paper No. 25672 (March 2019); and Pablo D. Fajgelbaum, Pinelopi K. Goldberg, Patrick J. Kennedy, and Amit K. Khandelwal, "The Return to Protectionism," NBER Working Paper No. 25638 (October 2019).

red tape barriers), and regulations of goods that are nominally intended to promote health and safety sometimes have the side effect, whether intentionally or unintentionally, of restricting trade. One example is European restrictions on imports of genetically modified foods. Although these regulations were motivated in part by concerns about the safety of such foods, they also help protect Europe's politically powerful farmers from foreign competition.

The Inefficiency of Protectionism

Free trade is efficient because it allows countries to specialize in the production of goods and services in which they have the greatest comparative advantage. Conversely, protectionist policies that limit trade are inefficient—they reduce the total economic pie. Why, then, do governments adopt such policies? The reason is similar to why some city governments impose rent controls (see Chapter 2, *Supply and Demand*). Although rent controls reduce economic welfare overall, some people benefit from them—namely, the tenants whose rents are held artificially below market level. Similarly, as we have seen in this section, tariffs and quotas benefit certain groups. Those who benefit from these restrictions (such as firms facing import competition, and the workers in such firms) may support politicians who promise to enact the restrictions.

The fact that free trade is efficient suggests an alternative to trade restrictions, however. Because eliminating restrictions on trade increases the overall economic pie, in general the winners from free trade will be able to compensate the losers in such a way that everyone becomes better off. Government programs that assist workers displaced by import competition are an example of such compensation. They include programs to expand job training and retraining opportunities, especially for the less-educated, who are more likely to be hurt by competition from abroad; to provide transition assistance for displaced workers, including support for internal migration within the U.S. from regions with declining industries to regions with expanding industries; to mitigate residential and educational segregation and increase the access of those left behind to employment and educational opportunities; and to promote community redevelopment in regions with declining industries.

While by no means an easy task, developing and improving such programs, and making them widely available, could do a lot to help those who lose from trade. Spreading the benefits of free trade—or at least reducing its adverse effects on certain groups—reduces the incentives of those groups to oppose free trade.

Although we have focused on the winners and losers from trade, not all opposition to free trade is motivated by economic interest. For example, many who oppose further opening to trade cite environmental concerns. Protecting the environment is an important and laudable goal, but restricting trade may not be the most effective means of achieving that goal. Restricting trade lowers world income, reducing the resources available to deal with environmental problems. Furthermore, much of the income loss arising from barriers to trade is absorbed by poor nations trying to develop their economies. For this reason, leaders of developing countries are among the strongest advocates of free trade.

The Economic Naturalist 12.3

What is fast track authority?

In practice, trade agreements among countries are very complex. For example, agreements usually spell out in great detail the goods and services for which tariffs are being reduced or quotas are being expanded. Trade negotiators must also take into account barriers to trade other than explicit tariffs or quotas, such as rules that require a country's government to buy only from domestic suppliers.

Because trade negotiations can be so complex, having each country's legislature vote on each item in a proposed trade agreement is not practical.

In the United States, the solution to this problem has been for Congress to vote to give the president *fast track authority*. Under this authority, the executive branch is given discretion to negotiate the terms of a proposed trade agreement. Congress then has the opportunity to vote the agreement up or down, but it cannot amend the proposal or accept only certain parts of it.

Fast track authority has been successfully used by presidents of both parties to negotiate trade agreements. However, the granting of fast track authority itself can be contentious, reflecting political concerns about trade and globalization. In 2015, for example, Democrats strongly resisted President Obama's request for fast track authority to negotiate a trade agreement with a number of countries, and in 2018 some Congress members resisted a similar request by President Trump.

RECAP

PROTECTIONIST POLICIES: TARIFFS AND QUOTAS

- The view that free trade is injurious and should be restricted is called protectionism.
- The two most common types of trade barriers are tariffs, or taxes on imported goods, and quotas, legal limits on the quantity that can be imported. A tariff raises the domestic price to the world price plus the tariff. The result is increased domestic production, reduced domestic consumption, and fewer imports. A quota has effects on the domestic market that are similar to those of a tariff. The main difference is that under a quota, the government does not collect tariff revenue.
- Trade barriers are inefficient; they reduce the overall size of the economic pie. Thus, in general, the winners from free trade should be able to compensate the losers in such a way that everyone becomes better off. Government programs to help workers displaced by import competition are an example of such compensation. They are not easy to develop and implement. Without effective compensation, however, opposition to trade by those who are hurt by it may lead to the inefficiency brought by protectionism.

SUMMARY

- According to the principle of comparative advantage, the best economic outcomes occur when each nation specializes in the goods and services at which it is relatively most productive and then trades with other nations to obtain the goods and services its citizens desire. *(LO1)*
- In a closed economy, the relative price of a good or service is determined at the intersection of the supply curve of domestic producers and the demand curve of domestic consumers. In an open economy, the relative price of a good or service equals the *world price*—the price determined by supply and demand in the world economy. If the price of a good or service in a closed economy is greater than the world price and the country opens its market to trade, it will become a net importer of that good or service. But if the closed-economy price is below the world price and the country opens itself to trade, it will become a net exporter of that good or service. *(LO2)*
- Although free trade is beneficial to the economy as a whole, some groups—such as domestic producers of imported goods, and workers in imported-good

sectors—are hurt by free trade. Groups that are hurt by trade may support political candidates who promise to impose *protectionist* measures, such as tariffs or quotas. A *tariff* is a tax on an imported good that has the effect of raising the domestic price of the good. A higher domestic price increases domestic supply, reduces domestic demand, and reduces imports of the good. A *quota,* which is a legal limit on the amount of a good that may be imported, has the same effects as a tariff, except that the government collects no tax revenue. (The equivalent amount of revenue goes instead to those firms with the legal authority to import goods.) Because free trade is efficient, the winners from free trade should be able to compensate the losers so that everyone becomes better off. Thus policies to assist those who are harmed by trade, such as assistance and retraining for workers idled by imports, are usually preferable to trade restrictions. *(LO3)*

KEY TERMS

absolute advantage
closed economy
comparative advantage
open economy
protectionism
quota
tariff
world price

REVIEW QUESTIONS

1. Explain what "having a comparative advantage" at producing a particular good or service means. What does "having an absolute advantage" at producing a good or service mean? *(LO1)*
2. A small, open economy is equally productive in producing coffee and tea. What will this economy produce if the world price of coffee is twice that of tea? Half that of tea? What will the country produce if the world price of coffee happens to equal the world price of tea? *(LO2)*
3. True or false: If a country is more productive in every sector than a neighboring country, then there is no benefit in trading with the neighboring country. Explain. *(LO2)*
4. Suppose France has a comparative advantage in cheese production and Britain has a comparative advantage in bicycle manufacturing. How would you expect French bicycle manufacturers and British dairy farmers to react to a proposal to reduce trade barriers between Britain and France? *(LO1, LO2)*
5. Show graphically the effects of a tariff on imported automobiles on the domestic market for automobiles. Who is hurt by the tariff and why? Who benefits and why? *(LO3)*
6. Show graphically the effects of a quota on imported automobiles on the domestic market for automobiles. Who does the quota hurt and who benefits? Explain. *(LO3)*

PROBLEMS

1. Ted can wax a car in 20 minutes or wash a car in 60 minutes. Ishana can wax a car in 15 minutes or wash a car in 30 minutes. What is each person's opportunity cost of washing a car? Who has a comparative advantage in washing cars? *(LO1)*
2. Ted can wax 4 cars per day or wash 12 cars. Ishana can wax 3 cars per day or wash 6 cars. What is each person's opportunity cost of washing a car? Who has a comparative advantage in washing cars? *(LO1)*
3. Isa and Antonio are auto mechanics. Isa takes 4 hours to replace a clutch and 2 hours to replace a set of brakes. Antonio takes 6 hours to replace a clutch and 2 hours to replace a set of brakes. State whether anyone has an absolute advantage at either task and, for each task, identify who has a comparative advantage. *(LO1)*
4. An economy has two workers, Bella and Edward. Per day of work, Bella can pick 100 apples or 25 bananas, and Edward can pick 50 apples or

50 bananas. Bella and Edward each work 200 days per year. *(LO1)*

a. Which worker has an absolute advantage in apples? Which has a comparative advantage? Calculate each worker's opportunity cost of picking an additional apple.
b. Find the maximum number of each type of fruit that can be picked annually in this economy, assuming that none of the other type of fruit is picked. What is the most of each type that can be picked if each worker fully specializes according to his or her comparative advantage?

5. Suppose that a U.S. worker can produce 1,000 pairs of shoes or 10 industrial robots per year. For simplicity, assume there are no costs other than labor costs and firms earn zero profits. Initially, the U.S. economy is closed. The domestic price of shoes is \$30 a pair, so that a U.S. worker can earn \$30,000 annually by working in the shoe industry. The domestic price of a robot is \$3,000, so that a U.S. worker can also earn \$30,000 annually working in the robot industry.

   Now suppose that the U.S. opens trade with the rest of the world. Foreign workers can produce 500 pairs of shoes or 1 robot per year. The world price of shoes after the U.S. opens its markets is \$10 a pair, and the world price of robots is \$5,000. *(LO2, LO3)*

   a. What do foreign workers earn annually, in dollars?
   b. When it opens to trade, which good will the United States import and which will it export?
   c. Find the real income of U.S. workers after the opening to trade, measured in (1) the number of pairs of shoes annual worker income will buy and (2) the number of robots annual worker income will buy. Compare to the situation before the opening of trade. Does trading in goods produced by "cheap foreign labor" hurt U.S. workers?
   d. How might your conclusion in part c be modified in the short term, if it is costly for workers to change industries? What policy response might help with this problem?

6. The demand and supply for automobiles in a certain country is given in the following graph. *(LO2, LO3)*

   a. Assuming that the economy is closed, find the equilibrium price and production of automobiles.
   b. The economy opens to trade. The world price of automobiles is \$8,000. Find the domestic quantities demanded and supplied and the quantity of imports or exports. Who will favor the opening of the automobile market to trade, and who will oppose it?

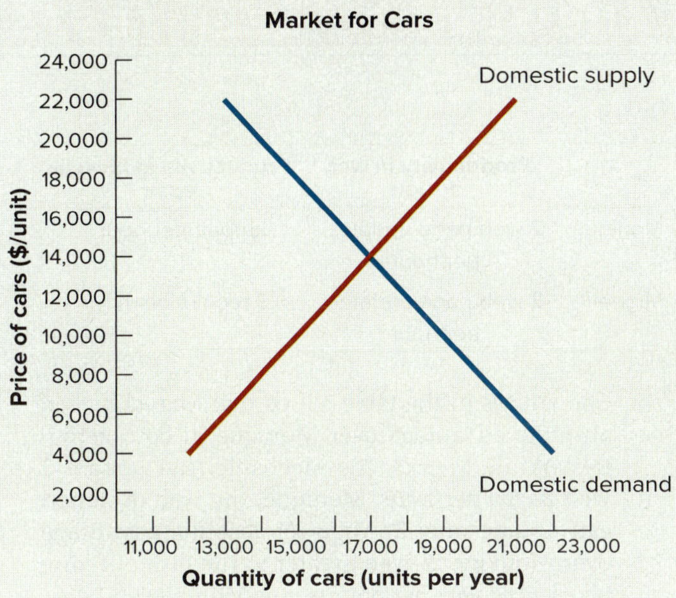

   c. The government imposes a tariff of \$2,000 per car. Find the effects on domestic quantities demanded and supplied.
   d. As a result of the tariff, what will happen to the quantity of imports or exports, and what is the revenue raised by the tariff? Who will favor the imposition of the tariff, and who will oppose it?

7. Suppose the domestic demand and supply for automobiles is as given in Problem 6. *(LO2, LO3)*

   a. The economy opens to trade. The world price of automobiles is \$10,000. Find the domestic quantities demanded and supplied and the quantity of imports or exports.
   b. Now assume that the government imposes a quota on automobile imports of 2,000 cars. What will happen to the quantity of imports or exports?
   c. Who will favor the imposition of the quota, and who will oppose it?

8. You are the president of Islandia, a small island nation that enjoys a comparative advantage in tourism. Trade representatives from the United States, which enjoys a comparative advantage in manufactured goods, have proposed a free-trade agreement between the two countries. Manufacturing workers have opposed the agreement, arguing that Islandia should maintain its steep tariff on American manufactured goods. In an election, the union representing these workers has more than enough votes to prevail over the union representing tourism workers. If you are determined to keep your job, how should you respond to the American proposal? *(LO3)*

ANSWERS TO SELF-TESTS

12.1

	Productivity in web design	Productivity in bicycle repair
Monique	2 web page updates per hour	1 repair per hour
Miguel	3 web page updates per hour	3 repairs per hour

The entries in the table tell us that Miguel has an absolute advantage over Monique in both activities. While Miguel, the mechanic, can update 3 web pages per hour, Monique, the web designer, can update only 2. Miguel's absolute advantage over Monique is even greater in the task of fixing bikes—3 repairs per hour versus Monique's 1.

But as in the second example in this chapter, the fact that Miguel is a better web designer than Monique does not imply that Miguel should update his own web page. Miguel's opportunity cost of updating a web page is 1 bicycle repair, whereas Monique must give up only half a bicycle repair to update a web page. Monique has a comparative advantage over Miguel at web design and Miguel has a comparative advantage over Monique at bicycle repair. *(LO1)*

12.2 If the world price of computers is $1,200, domestic demand for computers is 2,400 computers. Domestic supply is 1,600 computers. The difference between the quantity demanded and the quantity supplied, 800 computers, is imported.

A tariff of $400 raises the domestic price of computers to $1,600. Now domestic demand is 2,200 and domestic supply is 1,800. The difference, 400 computers, equals imports. Revenue for the government is ($400/computer) (400 imported computers) = $160,000.

If the world price of computers is $1,800 and there is no tariff, domestic demand is 2,100; domestic supply is 1,900; and imports are 200. A tariff of $400 raises the world price to $2,200, which is greater than the domestic price when there is no trade ($2,000). No computers are imported in this case and no tariff revenue is raised. *(LO3)*

13

Exchange Rates and the Open Economy

LEARNING OBJECTIVES

After reading this chapter, you should be able to:

LO1 Define the nominal exchange rate, fixed versus flexible exchange rates, and real exchange rates.

LO2 Summarize the law of one price and understand how purchasing power parity determines the long-run real exchange rate.

LO3 Use supply and demand to analyze how the nominal exchange rate is determined in the short run.

LO4 Explain how monetary policy impacts the exchange rate.

LO5 Detail how exchange rates can be fixed.

LO6 Discuss the advantages and disadvantages of flexible versus fixed exchange rates.

Two Americans discussing their foreign travels were commiserating over their problems understanding foreign currency. "Euro, yuan, yen, pounds, rubles, rupees, it's driving me crazy," said the first American. "They all look different and have different values. When I visit a foreign country, I can never figure out how much to pay the taxi driver."

The second American was more upbeat. "Actually," he said, "since I adopted my new system, I haven't had any problems at all."

The first American looked interested. "What's your new system?"

"Well," replied the second, "now, whenever I take a taxi abroad, I just give the driver all the local money I have. And would you believe it, I have got the fare exactly right every time!"

Dealing with unfamiliar currencies—and translating the value of foreign money into dollars—is a problem every international traveler faces. The traveler's problem is complicated by the fact that *exchange rates*—the rates at which one country's money trades for another—may change unpredictably. Thus the number of British pounds, Russian rubles, Japanese yen, or Australian dollars that a U.S. dollar can buy may vary over time, sometimes quite a lot.

The economic consequences of variable exchange rates are much broader than their impact on travel and tourism, however. For example, the competitiveness of U.S. exports depends in part on the prices of U.S. goods in terms of foreign currencies, which in turn depend on the exchange rate between the U.S. dollar and those currencies. Likewise, the prices Americans pay for imported goods depend in part on the value of the dollar relative to the currencies of the countries that produce those goods. Exchange rates also affect the value of financial investments made across national borders. For countries that are heavily dependent on trade and international capital flows—the majority of the world's nations—fluctuations in the exchange rate may have a significant economic impact.

Moreover, such impact has been increasing over time. One of the defining economic trends of recent decades is the "globalization" of national economies. From

the mid-1980s to 2008, the value of international trade has increased at nearly twice the rate of world GDP, and the volume of international financial transactions has expanded at many times that rate.[1] From a long-run perspective, the rapidly increasing integration of national economies we see today is not unprecedented: Before World War I, Great Britain was the center of an international economic system that was in many ways nearly as "globalized" as our own, with extensive international trade and lending. But even the most far-seeing nineteenth-century merchant or banker would be astonished by the sense of *immediacy* that recent revolutionary changes in communications and transportation have imparted to international economic relations. For example, ubiquitous cell phone–based videoconferencing now permits people on opposite sides of the globe to conduct "face-to-face" business negotiations and transactions.

This chapter discusses exchange rates and the role they play in open economies. We will start by distinguishing between the *nominal exchange rate*—the rate at which one national currency trades for another—and the *real exchange rate*—the rate at which one country's goods trade for another's. We will show how exchange rates affect the prices of exports and imports, and thus the pattern of trade.

Next we will turn to the question of how exchange rates are determined. Exchange rates may be divided into two broad categories, flexible and fixed. The value of a *flexible* exchange rate is determined freely in the market for national currencies, known as the *foreign exchange market*. Flexible exchange rates vary continually with changes in the supply of and demand for national currencies. In contrast, the value of a *fixed* exchange rate is set by the government at a constant level. Because most large industrial countries, including the United States, have a flexible exchange rate, we will focus on that case first. We will see that a country's monetary policy plays a particularly important role in determining the exchange rate. Furthermore, in an open economy with a flexible exchange rate, the exchange rate becomes a tool of monetary policy, in much the same way as the real interest rate.

Although most large industrial countries have a flexible exchange rate, many small and developing economies fix their exchange rates at least to some extent, so we will consider the case of fixed exchange rates as well. We will explain first how a country's government (usually, its central bank) goes about maintaining a fixed exchange rate at the officially determined level. Though fixing the exchange rate generally reduces day-to-day fluctuations in the value of a nation's currency, we will see that, at times, a fixed exchange rate can become severely unstable, with potentially serious economic consequences. We will close the chapter by discussing the relative merits of fixed and flexible exchange rates.

While this chapter focuses on the two extreme exchange rate approaches—fixed versus flexible—in today's world, most countries' exchange rates lie somewhere between the two extremes, with arrangements that combine the two approaches. Moreover, many countries constantly move between more flexible and more fixed exchange rate regimes. For example, for years China used to fix its currency, the renminbi (whose unit of account is the yuan), to the U.S. dollar. Since 2005, however, China has been switching between different exchange rate arrangements. In one recent arrangement, the People's Bank of China—China's central bank—let the renminbi float but only within a fixed band that shifts gradually over time or that is set by the central bank.

[1]Since the global financial crisis of 2008, trade has been growing at roughly the same rate as world GDP. The volume of international financial transactions declined dramatically during the financial crisis, but it is still several times higher today than in the mid-1980s.

EXCHANGE RATES

The economic benefits of trade between nations in goods, services, and assets are similar to the benefits of trade within a nation. In both cases, trade in goods and services permits greater specialization and efficiency, whereas trade in assets allows financial investors to earn higher or less volatile returns while providing funds for worthwhile capital projects. However, there is a difference between the two cases, which is that trade in goods, services, and assets *within* a nation normally involves a single currency—dollars, yen, pesos, or whatever the country's official form of money happens to be—whereas trade *between* nations usually involves dealing in different currencies. So, for example, if an American resident wants to purchase an automobile manufactured in South Korea, she (or more likely, the automobile dealer) must first trade dollars for the Korean currency, called the won. The Korean car manufacturer is then paid in won. Similarly, an Argentine who wants to purchase shares in a U.S. company (a U.S. financial asset) must first trade his Argentine pesos for dollars and then use the dollars to purchase the shares.

Nominal Exchange Rates

Because international transactions generally require that one currency be traded for another, the relative values of different currencies are an important factor in international economic relations. The rate at which two currencies can be traded for each other is called the **nominal exchange rate,** or more simply the *exchange rate,* between the two currencies. For example, if one U.S. dollar can be exchanged for 110 Japanese yen, the nominal exchange rate between the U.S. and Japanese currencies is 110 yen per dollar. Each country has many nominal exchange rates, one corresponding to each currency against which its own currency is traded. Thus the dollar's value can be quoted in terms of English pounds, Swedish kroner, Israeli shekels, Russian rubles, or dozens of other currencies. Table 13.1 gives exchange rates between the dollar and seven other important currencies as of the close of business in New York City on March 6, 2020.

nominal exchange rate the rate at which two currencies can be traded for each other

TABLE 13.1
Nominal Exchange Rates for the U.S. Dollar

Country	Foreign currency/dollar	Dollar/foreign currency
Canada (Canadian dollar)	1.3413	0.7455
China (yuan)	6.9320	0.1443
Mexico (peso)	20.1091	0.0497
Japan (yen)	105.29	0.00950
Euro area (euro)	0.8861	1.1286
South Korea (won)	1188.80	0.0008412
United Kingdom (pound)	0.7665	1.3047

Source: *The Wall Street Journal,* March 8, 2020, www.wsj.com/market-data/currencies/exchangerates.

As Table 13.1 shows, exchange rates can be expressed either as the amount of foreign currency needed to purchase one dollar (middle column) or as the number of dollars needed to purchase one unit of the foreign currency (right column). These two ways of expressing the exchange rate are equivalent: Each is the reciprocal of the other. For example, on March 6, 2020, the U.S.–Canadian exchange rate could have been expressed either as 1.3413 Canadian dollars per U.S. dollar or as 0.7455 U.S. dollars per Canadian dollar, where $0.7455 = 1/1.3413$.

EXAMPLE 13.1 Nominal Exchange Rates

What is the exchange rate between the British pound and Canadian dollar?

Based on Table 13.1, find the exchange rate between the British and Canadian currencies. Express the exchange rate in both Canadian dollars per pound and pounds per Canadian dollar.

From Table 13.1, we see that 0.7665 British pounds will buy a U.S. dollar, and that 1.3413 Canadian dollars will buy a U.S. dollar. Therefore, 0.7665 British pounds and 1.3413 Canadian dollars are equal in value

$$0.7665 \text{ pounds} = 1.3413 \text{ Canadian dollars.}$$

Dividing both sides of this equation by 1.3413 we get

$$0.5715 \text{ pounds} = 1 \text{ Canadian dollar.}$$

In other words, the British–Canadian exchange rate can be expressed as 0.5715 pounds per Canadian dollar. Alternatively, the exchange rate can be expressed as 1/0.5715 = 1.7498 Canadian dollars per pound.

SELF-TEST 13.1

From the business section of the newspaper or an online source (try *The Wall Street Journal*, www.wsj.com), find recent quotations of the value of the U.S. dollar against the British pound, the Canadian dollar, and the Japanese yen. Based on these data, find the exchange rate (a) between the pound and the Canadian dollar and (b) between the Canadian dollar and the yen. Express the exchange rates you derive in two ways (for example, both as pounds per Canadian dollar and as Canadian dollars per pound).

Figure 13.1 shows the nominal exchange rate for the U.S. dollar for 1973 to 2020. Rather than showing the value of the dollar relative to that of an individual foreign currency, such as the Japanese yen or the British pound, the figure expresses the value of the dollar as an average of its values against other major currencies. This average value of the dollar is measured relative to a base value of 100 in 2006. So, for example, a value of 120 for the dollar in a particular year implies that the dollar was 20 percent more valuable in that year, relative to other major currencies, than it was in 2006.

You can see from Figure 13.1 that the dollar's value has fluctuated over time, sometimes increasing (as in the periods 1980–1985 and 1995–2001) and sometimes decreasing (as in 1985–1987 and 2002–2004). An increase in the value of a currency relative to other currencies is known as an **appreciation;** a decline in the value of a currency relative to other currencies is called a **depreciation.** So we can say that the dollar appreciated in 1980–1985 and depreciated in 1985–1987. We will discuss the reasons a currency may appreciate or depreciate later in this chapter.

appreciation an increase in the value of a currency relative to other currencies

depreciation a decrease in the value of a currency relative to other currencies

In this chapter, we will use the symbol e to stand for a country's nominal exchange rate. Although the exchange rate can be expressed either as foreign currency units per unit of domestic currency or vice versa, as we saw in Table 13.1, let's agree to define e as *the number of units of the foreign currency that the domestic currency will buy*. For example, if we treat the United States as the "home" or "domestic" country and Japan as the "foreign" country, e will be defined as the number of Japanese yen that one dollar will buy. Defining the nominal exchange rate this way implies that an *increase* in e corresponds to an *appreciation,* or a strengthening, of the home currency, while a *decrease* in e implies a *depreciation,* or weakening, of the home currency.

FIGURE 13.1

The U.S. Nominal Exchange Rate, 1973–2020.

This figure expresses the value of the dollar from 1973 to 2020 as an average of its values against other major currencies, relative to a base value of 100 in January 2006.

Source: Federal Reserve Bank of St. Louis, FRED database, https://research.stlouisfed.org/fred2/series/TWEXMMTH (until January 2006) and https://fred.stlouisfed.org/series/TWEXAFEGSMTH (from January 2006).

Flexible versus Fixed Exchange Rates

As we saw in Figure 13.1, the exchange rate between the U.S. dollar and other currencies isn't constant but varies continually. Indeed, changes in the value of the dollar occur daily, hourly, minute by minute, and even within split seconds. Such fluctuations in the value of a currency are normal for countries like the United States, which have a *flexible* or *floating exchange rate*. The value of a **flexible exchange rate** is not officially fixed but varies according to the supply and demand for the currency in the **foreign exchange market**—the market on which currencies of various nations are traded for one another. We will discuss the factors that determine the supply and demand for currencies shortly.

flexible exchange rate an exchange rate whose value is not officially fixed but varies according to the supply and demand for the currency in the foreign exchange market

foreign exchange market the market on which currencies of various nations are traded for one another

fixed exchange rate an exchange rate whose value is set by official government policy

Some countries do not allow their currency values to vary with market conditions but instead maintain a *fixed exchange rate*. The value of a **fixed exchange rate** is set by official government policy. (A government that establishes a fixed exchange rate typically determines the exchange rate's value independently, but sometimes exchange rates are set according to an agreement among a number of governments.) Some countries fix their exchange rates in terms of the U.S. dollar (Hong Kong, for example), but there are other possibilities. Some French-speaking African countries have traditionally fixed the value of their currencies in terms of the French franc and then in terms of the euro since it was introduced as a new currency on January 1, 1999. Under the gold standard, which many countries used until its collapse during the Great Depression, currency values were fixed in terms of ounces of gold. In the next part of the chapter we will focus on flexible exchange rates, but we will return later to the case of fixed rates. We will also discuss the costs and benefits of each type of exchange rate.

The Real Exchange Rate

The nominal exchange rate tells us the price of the domestic currency in terms of a foreign currency. As we will see in this section, the *real exchange rate* tells us the price of the average domestic *good or service* in terms of the average foreign *good or service*. We will also see that a country's real exchange rate has important implications for its ability to sell its exports abroad.

To provide background for discussing the real exchange rate, imagine you are in charge of purchasing for a U.S. corporation that is planning to acquire a large number of new computers. The company's computer specialist has identified two models, one Japanese-made and one U.S.-made, that meet the necessary specifications. Since the two models are essentially equivalent, the company will buy the one with the lower price. However, since the computers are priced in the currencies of the countries of manufacture, the price comparison is not so straightforward. Your mission—should you decide to accept it—is to determine which of the two models is cheaper.

To complete your assignment you will need two pieces of information: the nominal exchange rate between the dollar and the yen and the prices of the two models in terms of the currencies of their countries of manufacture. Example 13.2 shows how you can use this information to determine which model is cheaper.

EXAMPLE 13.2 Purchasing a Domestic versus Imported Good

Which computer is the better buy, the import or the domestic computer?

A U.S.-made computer costs $2,400, and a similar Japanese-made computer costs 242,000 yen. If the nominal exchange rate is 110 yen per dollar, which computer is the better buy?

To make this price comparison, we must measure the prices of both computers in terms of the same currency. To make the comparison in dollars, we first convert the Japanese computer's price into dollars. The price in terms of Japanese yen is ¥242,000 (the symbol ¥ means "yen"), and we are told that ¥110 = $1. To find the dollar price of the computer, then, we observe that for any good or service,

$$\text{Price in yen} = \text{Price in dollars} \times \text{Value of dollar in terms of yen}.$$

Note that the value of a dollar in terms of yen is just the yen–dollar exchange rate. Making this substitution and solving, we get

$$\text{Price in dollars} = \frac{\text{Price in yen}}{\text{Yen–dollar exchange rate}}$$

$$= \frac{¥242{,}000}{¥110/\$1} = \$2{,}200.$$

Notice that the yen symbol appears in both the numerator and the denominator of the ratio, so it cancels out. Our conclusion is that the Japanese computer is cheaper than the U.S. computer at $2,200, or $200 less than the price of the U.S. computer, $2,400. The Japanese computer is the better deal.

SELF-TEST 13.2

Continuing Example 13.2, compare the prices of the Japanese and American computers by expressing both prices in terms of yen.

In Example 13.2, the fact that the Japanese computer was cheaper implied that your firm would choose it over the U.S.-made computer. In general, a country's ability to compete in international markets depends in part on the prices of its goods and services *relative* to the prices of foreign goods and services, when the prices are measured in a common currency. In the hypothetical example of the Japanese and U.S. computers, the price of the domestic (U.S.) good relative to the price of the foreign (Japanese) good is $2,400/$2,200, or 1.09. So the U.S. computer is 9 percent more expensive than the Japanese computer, putting the U.S. product at a competitive disadvantage.

real exchange rate the price of the average domestic good or service *relative* to the price of the average foreign good or service, when prices are expressed in terms of a common currency

More generally, economists ask whether *on average* the goods and services produced by a particular country are expensive relative to the goods and services produced by other countries. This question can be answered by the country's *real exchange rate*. Specifically, a country's **real exchange rate** is the price of the average domestic good or service *relative* to the price of the average foreign good or service, when prices are expressed in terms of a common currency.

To obtain a formula for the real exchange rate, recall that e equals the nominal exchange rate (the number of units of foreign currency per dollar) and that P equals the domestic price level, as measured, for example, by the consumer price index. We will use P as a measure of the price of the "average" domestic good or service. Similarly, let P^f equal the foreign price level. We will use P^f as the measure of the price of the "average" foreign good or service.

The real exchange rate equals the price of the average domestic good or service relative to the price of the average foreign good or service. It would not be correct, however, to define the real exchange rate as the ratio P/P^f because the two price levels are expressed in different currencies. As we saw in Example 13.2, to convert foreign prices into dollars, we must divide the foreign price by the exchange rate. By this rule, the price in dollars of the average foreign good or service equals P^f/e. Now we can write the real exchange rate as

$$\text{Real exchange rate} = \frac{\text{Price of domestic good}}{\text{Price of foreign good, in dollars}}$$

$$= \frac{P}{P^f/e}.$$

To simplify this expression, multiply the numerator and denominator by e to get

$$\text{Real exchange rate} = \frac{eP}{P^f}, \qquad (13.1)$$

which is the formula for the real exchange rate.

To check this formula, let's use it to re-solve the computer example, Example 13.2. (For this exercise, we imagine that computers are the only good produced by the United States and Japan, so the real exchange rate becomes just the price of U.S. computers relative to Japanese computers.) In that example, the nominal exchange rate e was ¥110/\$1, the domestic price P (of a computer) was \$2,400, and the foreign price P^f was ¥242,000. Applying Equation 13.1, we get

$$\text{Real exchange rate (for computers)} = \frac{(¥110/\$1) \times \$2{,}400}{¥242{,}000}$$

$$= \frac{¥264{,}000}{¥242{,}000}$$

$$= 1.09,$$

which is the same answer we got earlier.

The real exchange rate, an overall measure of the cost of domestic goods relative to foreign goods, is an important economic variable. As Example 13.2 suggests, when the real exchange rate is high, domestic goods are—on average—more expensive than foreign goods (when priced in the same currency). A high real exchange rate implies that domestic producers will have difficulty exporting to other countries (domestic goods will be "overpriced"), while foreign goods will sell well in the home country (because imported goods are cheap relative to goods produced at home). Since a high real exchange rate tends to reduce exports and increase imports, we conclude that *net exports will tend to be low when the real exchange rate is high*. Conversely, if the real exchange rate is low, then the home country will find it easier to export (because its goods are priced below those of foreign competitors), while domestic residents will buy fewer imports (because imports are expensive relative to domestic goods). *Thus net exports will tend to be high when the real exchange rate is low.*

Equation 13.1 also shows that the real exchange rate tends to move in the same direction as the nominal exchange rate e (since e appears in the numerator of the formula for the real exchange rate). To the extent that real and nominal exchange rates move in the same direction, we can conclude that net exports will be hurt by a high nominal exchange rate and helped by a low nominal exchange rate.

The Economic Naturalist 13.1

Does a strong currency imply a strong economy?

connect

▸ Visit your instructor's Connect course and access your eBook to view this video.

Does a strong currency imply a strong economy?

Politicians and the public sometimes take pride in the fact that their national currency is "strong," meaning that its value in terms of other currencies is high or rising. Likewise, policymakers sometimes view a depreciating ("weak") currency as a sign of economic failure. Does a strong currency necessarily imply a strong economy?

Contrary to popular impression, there is no simple connection between the strength of a country's currency and the strength of its economy. For example, Figure 13.1 shows that the value of the U.S. dollar relative to other major currencies was greater in the year 1973 than in the 1990s, though U.S. economic performance was considerably better in the 1990s than in 1973, a period of deep recession and rising inflation. Indeed, the one period shown in Figure 13.1 during which the dollar rose the most in value, 1980–1985, was a time of recession and high unemployment in the United States.

One reason a strong currency does not necessarily imply a strong economy is that an appreciating currency (an increase in e) tends to raise the real exchange rate (equal to eP/P^f), which may hurt a country's net exports. For example, if the dollar strengthens against the yen (that is, if a dollar buys more yen than before), Japanese goods will become cheaper in terms of dollars. The result may be that Americans prefer to buy Japanese goods rather than goods produced at home. Likewise, a stronger dollar implies that each yen buys fewer dollars, so exported U.S. goods become more expensive to Japanese consumers. As U.S. goods become more expensive in terms of yen, the willingness of Japanese consumers to buy U.S. exports declines. A strong dollar may therefore imply lower sales and profits for U.S. industries that export, as well as for U.S. industries (like automobile manufacturers) that compete with foreign firms for the domestic U.S. market.

RECAP

EXCHANGE RATES

- The nominal exchange rate between two currencies is the rate at which the currencies can be traded for each other. More precisely, the nominal exchange rate e for any given country is the number of units of foreign currency that can be bought for one unit of the domestic currency.
- An appreciation is an increase in the value of a currency relative to other currencies (a rise in e); a depreciation is a decline in a currency's value (a fall in e).
- An exchange rate can be flexible—meaning that it varies freely according to supply and demand for the currency in the foreign exchange market—or fixed—meaning that its value is established by official government policy. (While not our focus in this chapter, an exchange rate can also combine the two approaches.)
- The real exchange rate is the price of the average domestic good or service relative to the price of the average foreign good or service, when prices are expressed in terms of a common currency. A useful formula for the real exchange rate is eP/P^f, where e is the nominal exchange rate, P is the domestic price level, and P^f is the foreign price level.
- An increase in the real exchange rate implies that domestic goods are becoming more expensive relative to foreign goods, which tends to reduce exports and stimulate imports. Conversely, a decline in the real exchange rate tends to increase net exports.

THE DETERMINATION OF THE EXCHANGE RATE IN THE LONG RUN

Countries that have flexible exchange rates, such as the United States, see the international values of their currencies change continually. What determines the value of the nominal exchange rate at any point in time? In this section we will try to answer this basic economic question. Again, our focus for the moment is on flexible exchange rates, whose values are determined by the foreign exchange market. Later in the chapter we discuss the case of fixed exchange rates.

A Simple Theory of Exchange Rates: Purchasing Power Parity (PPP)

The most basic theory of how nominal exchange rates are determined is called *purchasing power parity,* or *PPP*. To understand this theory, we must first discuss a fundamental economic concept, called *the law of one price*. The **law of one price** states that if transportation costs are relatively small, the price of an internationally traded commodity must be the same in all locations. For example, if transportation costs are not too large, the price of a bushel of wheat ought to be the same in Mumbai, India, and Sydney, Australia. Suppose that were not the case—that the price of wheat in Sydney were only half the price in Mumbai. In that case, grain merchants would have a strong incentive to buy wheat in Sydney and ship it to Mumbai, where it could be sold at double the price of purchase. As wheat left Sydney, reducing the local supply, the price of wheat in Sydney would rise, while the inflow of wheat into Mumbai would reduce the price in Mumbai.

law of one price if transportation costs are relatively small, the price of an internationally traded commodity must be the same in all locations

The international market for wheat would return to equilibrium only when unexploited opportunities to profit had been eliminated—specifically, only when the prices of wheat in Sydney and in Mumbai became equal or nearly equal (with the difference being less than the cost of transporting wheat from Australia to India).

If the law of one price were to hold for all goods and services (which is not a realistic assumption, as we will see shortly), then the value of the nominal exchange rate would be determined as Example 13.3 illustrates.

EXAMPLE 13.3 The Law of One Price

How many Indian rupees equal 1 Australian dollar?

Suppose that a bushel of grain costs 5 Australian dollars in Sydney and 150 rupees in Mumbai. If the law of one price holds for grain, what is the nominal exchange rate between Australia and India?

Because the market value of a bushel of grain must be the same in both locations, we know that the Australian price of wheat must equal the Indian price of wheat, so that

$$5 \text{ Australian dollars} = 150 \text{ Indian rupees.}$$

Dividing by 5, we get

$$1 \text{ Australian dollar} = 30 \text{ Indian rupees.}$$

Thus the nominal exchange rate between Australia and India should be 30 rupees per Australian dollar.

SELF-TEST 13.3

The price of gold is $900 per ounce in New York and 7,500 kronor per ounce in Stockholm, Sweden. If the law of one price holds for gold, what is the nominal exchange rate between the U.S. dollar and the Swedish krona?

purchasing power parity (PPP) the theory that nominal exchange rates are determined as necessary for the law of one price to hold

Example 13.3 and Self-Test 13.3 illustrate the application of the purchasing power parity theory. According to the **purchasing power parity (PPP)** theory, nominal exchange rates are determined as necessary for the law of one price to hold.

A particularly useful prediction of the PPP theory is that in the long run, the *currencies of countries that experience significant inflation will tend to depreciate*. To see why, we will extend the analysis in Example 13.3.

EXAMPLE 13.4 Purchasing Power Parity

How does inflation affect the nominal exchange rate?

Suppose India experiences significant inflation so that the price of a bushel of grain in Mumbai rises from 150 to 300 rupees. Australia has no inflation, so the price of grain in Sydney remains unchanged at 5 Australian dollars. If the law of one price holds for grain, what will happen to the nominal exchange rate between Australia and India?

As in Example 13.3, we know that the market value of a bushel of grain must be the same in both locations. Therefore,

$$5 \text{ Australian dollars} = 300 \text{ rupees}.$$

Equivalently,

$$1 \text{ Australian dollar} = 60 \text{ rupees}.$$

The nominal exchange rate is now 60 rupees per Australian dollar. Before India's inflation, the nominal exchange rate was 30 rupees per Australian dollar (Example 13.3). So in this example, inflation has caused the rupee to depreciate against the Australian dollar. Conversely, Australia, with no inflation, has seen its currency appreciate against the rupee.

This link between inflation and depreciation makes economic sense. Inflation implies that a nation's currency is losing purchasing power in the domestic market. Analogously, exchange rate depreciation implies that the nation's currency is losing purchasing power in international markets.

Figure 13.2 shows annual rates of inflation and nominal exchange rate depreciation for the 10 largest South American countries from 1995 to 2004.[2] Inflation is measured as the annual rate of change in the country's consumer price index; depreciation is measured relative to the U.S. dollar. As you can see, inflation varied greatly among South American countries during the period. For example, Chile's inflation rate was within two percentage points of the inflation rate of the United States, while Venezuela's inflation was 33 percent per year.

[2]Since Ecuador adopted the U.S. dollar as its currency in 2000, the data for Ecuador refer to the period 1995–2000.

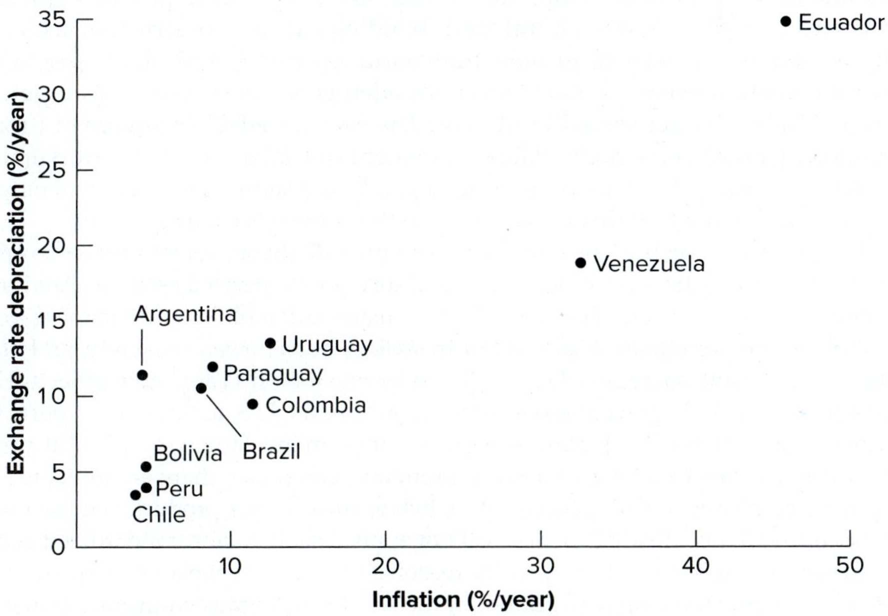

FIGURE 13.2

Inflation and Currency Depreciation in South America, 1995–2004.

The annual rates of inflation and nominal exchange rate depreciation (relative to the U.S. dollar) in the 10 largest South American countries varied considerably during 1995–2004. High inflation was associated with rapid depreciation of the nominal exchange rate. (Data for Ecuador refer to the period 1995–2000.)

Sources: International Monetary Fund, *International Financial Statistics;* authors' calculations.

Figure 13.2 shows that, as the PPP theory implies, countries with higher inflation during the 1995–2004 period tended to experience the most rapid depreciation of their currencies.

Shortcomings of the PPP Theory

Empirical studies have found that the PPP theory is useful for predicting changes in nominal exchange rates over the relatively long run. In particular, this theory helps explain the tendency of countries with high inflation to experience depreciation of their exchange rates, as shown in Figure 13.2. However, the theory is less successful in predicting short-run movements in exchange rates.

A particularly dramatic failure of the PPP theory occurred in the United States in the early 1980s. As Figure 13.1 indicates, between 1980 and 1985, the value of the U.S. dollar rose nearly 50 percent relative to the currencies of U.S. trading partners. This strong appreciation was followed by an even more rapid depreciation during 1986 and 1987. PPP theory could explain this roller-coaster behavior only if inflation were far lower in the United States than in U.S. trading partners from 1980 to 1985 and far higher from 1986 to 1987. In fact, inflation was similar in the United States and its trading partners throughout both periods.

Why does the PPP theory work less well in the short run than the long run? Recall that this theory relies on the law of one price, which says that the price of an internationally traded commodity must be the same in all locations. The law of one price works well for goods such as grain or gold, which are standardized commodities that are traded widely. However, *not all goods and services are traded internationally,* and *not all goods are standardized commodities.*

Many goods and services are not traded internationally because the assumption underlying the law of one price—that transportation costs are relatively small—does not hold for them. For example, for Indians to export haircuts to Australia, they would need to transport an Indian barber to Australia every time a Sydney resident desired a trim. Because transportation costs prevent haircuts from being traded internationally, the law of one price does not apply to them. Thus, even if the price of haircuts in Australia were double the price of haircuts in India, market forces would not necessarily force prices toward equality in the short run. (Over the long run, some Indian barbers might emigrate to Australia.) Other examples of nontraded goods and services are agricultural land, buildings, heavy construction materials (whose value is low relative to their transportation costs), and highly perishable foods. In addition, some products use nontraded goods and services as inputs: A McDonald's hamburger served in Moscow has both a tradable component (frozen hamburger patties) and a nontradable component (the labor of counter workers). In general, the greater the share of nontraded goods and services in a nation's output, the less precisely the PPP theory will apply to the country's exchange rate.[3]

The second reason the law of one price and the PPP theory sometimes fail to apply is that not all internationally traded goods and services are perfectly standardized commodities, like grain or gold. For example, U.S.-made automobiles and Japanese-made automobiles are not identical; they differ in styling, horsepower, reliability, and other features. As a result, some people strongly prefer one nation's cars to the other's. Thus if Japanese cars cost 10 percent more than American cars, U.S. automobile exports will not necessarily flood the Japanese market, since many Japanese will still prefer Japanese-made cars even at a 10 percent premium. Of course, there are limits to how far prices can diverge before people will switch to the cheaper product. But the law of one price, and hence the PPP theory, will not apply exactly to nonstandardized goods.

To summarize, the PPP theory works reasonably well as an explanation of exchange rate behavior over the long run, but not in the short run. Because transportation costs limit international trade in many goods and services, and because not all goods that are traded are standardized commodities, the law of one price (on which the PPP theory is based) works only imperfectly in the short run. To understand the short-run movements of exchange rates we need to incorporate some additional factors. In the next section, we will study a supply and demand framework for the determination of exchange rates.

RECAP

DETERMINING THE EXCHANGE RATE IN THE LONG RUN

- The most basic theory of nominal exchange rate determination, purchasing power parity (PPP), is based on the law of one price. The law of one price states that if transportation costs (and other costs and barriers to trade) are relatively small, the price of an internationally traded commodity must be the same in all locations. According to the PPP theory, the nominal exchange rate between two currencies can be found by setting the price of a traded commodity in one currency equal to the price of the same commodity expressed in the second currency.
- A useful prediction of the PPP theory is that the currencies of countries that experience significant inflation will tend to depreciate over the long run. However, the PPP theory does not work well in the short run. The fact that many goods and services are nontraded, and that not all traded goods are standardized, reduces the applicability of the law of one price, and hence of the PPP theory.

THE DETERMINATION OF THE EXCHANGE RATE IN THE SHORT RUN

Although the PPP theory helps explain the long-run behavior of the exchange rate, supply and demand analysis is more useful for studying its short-run behavior. As we will see, dollars are demanded in the foreign exchange market by foreigners who

[3]Trade barriers, such as tariffs and quotas, also increase the costs associated with shipping goods from one country to another. Thus trade barriers reduce the applicability of the law of one price in much the same way that physical transportation costs do.

seek to purchase U.S. goods and assets and are supplied by U.S. residents who need foreign currencies to buy foreign goods and assets. The equilibrium exchange rate is the value of the dollar that equates the number of dollars supplied and demanded in the foreign exchange market.

The Foreign Exchange Market: A Supply and Demand Analysis

In this section, we will discuss the factors that affect the supply and demand for dollars in the foreign exchange market, and thus the U.S. exchange rate.

One note before we proceed: In Chapter 10, *Stabilizing the Economy: The Role of the Fed,* we described how the supply of money by the Fed and the demand for money by the public help determine the nominal interest rate. However, the supply and demand for money in the domestic economy, as presented in that chapter, are *not* equivalent to the supply and demand for dollars in the foreign exchange market. As mentioned, the foreign exchange market is the market in which the currencies of various nations are traded for one another. The supply of dollars to the foreign exchange market is *not* the same as the money supply set by the Fed; rather, it is the number of dollars U.S. households and firms offer to trade for other currencies. Likewise, the demand for dollars in the foreign exchange market is *not* the same as the domestic demand for money, but the number of dollars holders of foreign currencies seek to buy. To understand the distinction, it may help to keep in mind that while the Fed determines the total supply of dollars in the U.S. economy, a dollar does not "count" as having been supplied to the foreign exchange market until some holder of dollars, such as a household or firm, tries to trade it for a foreign currency.

The Supply of Dollars

Anyone who holds dollars, from an international bank to a Russian citizen whose dollars are buried in the backyard, is a potential supplier of dollars to the foreign exchange market. In practice, however, the principal suppliers of dollars to the foreign exchange market are U.S. households and firms. Why would a U.S. household or firm want to supply dollars in exchange for foreign currency? There are two major reasons. First, a U.S. household or firm may need foreign currency *to purchase foreign goods or services*. For example, a U.S. automobile importer may need euros to purchase German cars, or an American tourist may need euros to make purchases in Paris, Rome, or Barcelona.[4] Second, a U.S. household or firm may need foreign currency *to purchase foreign assets*. For example, an American mutual fund may wish to acquire stocks issued by Dutch companies, or an individual U.S. saver may want to purchase Irish government bonds. Because these assets are priced in euros, the U.S. household or firm will need to trade dollars for euros to acquire these assets.

The supply of dollars to the foreign exchange market is illustrated in Figure 13.3. We will focus on the market in which dollars are traded for euros, but bear in mind that similar markets exist for every other pair of traded currencies. The vertical axis of the figure shows the U.S.–European exchange rate as measured by the number of euros that can be purchased with each dollar. The horizontal axis shows the number of dollars being traded in the euro–dollar market.

Note that the supply curve for dollars is upward-sloping. In other words, the more euros each dollar can buy, the more dollars people are willing to supply to the foreign exchange market. Why? At given prices for European goods, services, and assets, the more euros a dollar can buy, the cheaper those goods, services, and assets will be in dollar terms. For example, if a washing machine costs 200 euros in Germany and a dollar can buy 1 euro, the dollar price of the washing machine will be $200.

[4]The following 19 countries use euros as their local currency: Austria, Belgium, Cyprus, Estonia, Finland, France, Germany, Greece, Ireland, Italy, Latvia, Lithuania, Luxembourg, Malta, the Netherlands, Portugal, Slovakia, Slovenia, and Spain. See The Economic Naturalist 13.7 later in the chapter.

FIGURE 13.3

The Supply and Demand for Dollars in the Euro–Dollar Market.

The supply of dollars to the foreign exchange market is upward-sloping because an increase in the number of euros offered for each dollar makes European goods, services, and assets more attractive to U.S. buyers. Similarly, the demand for dollars is downward-sloping because holders of euros will be less willing to buy dollars the more expensive they are in terms of euros. The equilibrium exchange rate e*, also called the *fundamental value of the exchange rate*, equates the quantities of dollars supplied and demanded.

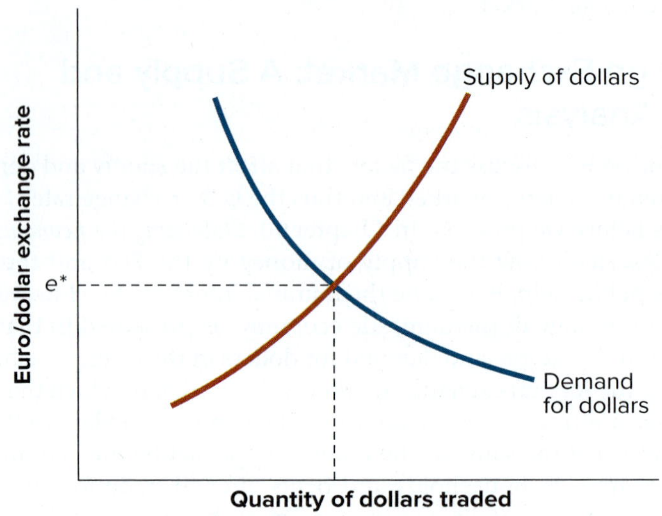

However, if a dollar can buy 2 euros, then the dollar price of the same washing machine will be $100. Assuming that lower dollar prices will induce Americans to increase their expenditures on European goods, services, and assets, a higher euro–dollar exchange rate will increase the supply of dollars to the foreign exchange market. Thus the supply curve for dollars is upward-sloping.

The Demand for Dollars

In the euro–dollar foreign exchange market, demanders of dollars are those who wish to acquire dollars in exchange for euros. Most demanders of dollars in the euro–dollar market are European households and firms, although anyone who happens to hold euros is free to trade them for dollars. Why demand dollars? The reasons for acquiring dollars are analogous to those for acquiring euros. First, households and firms that hold euros will demand dollars *so that they can purchase U.S. goods and services*. For example, a Portuguese firm that wants to license U.S.-produced software needs dollars to pay the required fees, and a Portuguese student studying in an American university must pay tuition in dollars. The firm or the student can acquire the necessary dollars only by offering euros in exchange. Second, households and firms demand dollars *in order to purchase U.S. assets*. The purchase of Hawaiian real estate by a Finnish company or the acquisition of Google stock by an Austrian pension fund are two examples.

The demand for dollars is represented by the downward-sloping curve in Figure 13.3. The curve slopes downward because the more euros a European person must pay to acquire a dollar, the less attractive U.S. goods, services, and assets will be. Hence the demand for dollars will be low when dollars are expensive in terms of euros and high when dollars are cheap in terms of euros.

The Equilibrium Value of the Dollar

As mentioned earlier, the United States maintains a flexible, or floating, exchange rate, which means that the value of the dollar is determined by the forces of supply and demand in the foreign exchange market. In Figure 13.3 the equilibrium value of the dollar is e^*, the euro–dollar exchange rate at which the quantity of dollars supplied equals the quantity of dollars demanded. The **fundamental value of the exchange rate** is also called the **equilibrium exchange rate**. In general, the equilibrium value of the dollar is not constant but changes with shifts in the supply of and demand for dollars in the foreign exchange market.

fundamental value of the exchange rate (or **equilibrium exchange rate**) the exchange rate that equates the quantities of the currency supplied and demanded in the foreign exchange market

Changes in the Supply of Dollars

Recall that people supply dollars to the euro–dollar foreign exchange market in order to purchase European goods, services, and assets. Factors that affect the desire of U.S. households and firms to acquire European goods, services, and assets will therefore affect the supply of dollars to the foreign exchange market. Some factors that will *increase* the supply of dollars, shifting the supply curve for dollars to the right, include:

- An increased preference for European goods. For example, suppose that European firms produce some popular new consumer electronics. To acquire the euros needed to buy these goods, American importers will increase their supply of dollars to the foreign exchange market.
- An increase in U.S. real incomes. An increase in the incomes of Americans will allow Americans to consume more goods and services (recall the consumption function, introduced in Chapter 9, *Short-Term Economic Fluctuations and Fiscal Policy*). Some part of this increase in consumption will take the form of goods imported from Europe. To buy more European goods, Americans will supply more dollars to acquire the necessary euros.
- An increase in the real interest rate on European assets. Recall that U.S. households and firms acquire euros in order to purchase European assets as well as goods and services. Other factors, such as risk, held constant, the higher the real interest rate paid by European assets, the more European assets Americans will choose to hold. To purchase additional European assets, U.S. households and firms will supply more dollars to the foreign exchange market.

Conversely, reduced demand for European goods, lower real U.S. incomes, or a lower real interest rate on European assets will *reduce* the number of euros Americans need, in turn reducing their supply of dollars to the foreign exchange market and shifting the supply curve for dollars to the left. Of course, any shift in the supply curve for dollars will affect the equilibrium exchange rate, as Example 13.5 shows.

EXAMPLE 13.5 Washing Machines and the Exchange Rate

How would increased demand for German washing machines affect the euro–dollar exchange rate?

Suppose German firms come to dominate the washing machine market, with washing machines that are more efficient and reliable than those produced in the United States. All else being equal, how will this change affect the relative value of the euro and the dollar?

The increased quality of German washing machines will increase the demand for the washing machines in the United States. To acquire the euros necessary to buy more German washing machines, U.S. importers will supply more dollars to the foreign exchange market. As Figure 13.4 shows, the increased supply of dollars will reduce the value of the dollar. In other words, a dollar will buy fewer euros than it did before. At the same time, the euro will increase in value: A given number of euros will buy more dollars than it did before.

FIGURE 13.4

An Increase in the Supply of Dollars Lowers the Value of the Dollar.

Increased U.S. demand for German washing machines forces Americans to supply more dollars to the foreign exchange market to acquire the euros they need to buy the machines. The supply curve for dollars shifts from *S* to *S*′, lowering the value of the dollar in terms of euros. The fundamental value of the exchange rate falls from e* to e*′.

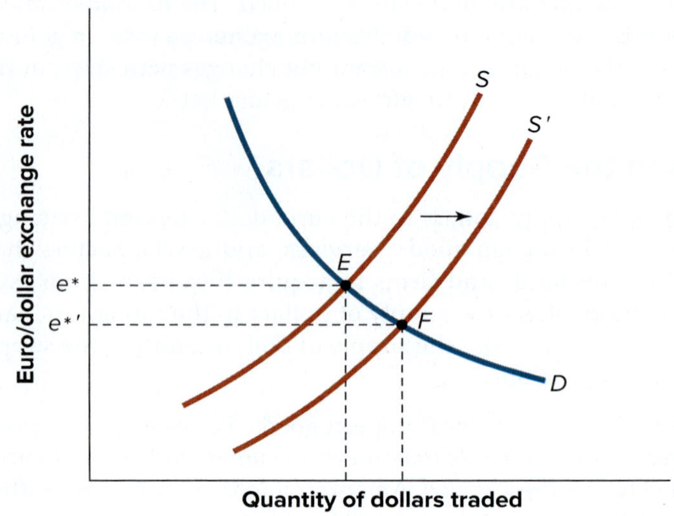

SELF-TEST 13.4

The U.S. goes into a recession, and real GDP falls. All else equal, how is this economic weakness likely to affect the value of the dollar?

Changes in the Demand for Dollars

The factors that can cause a change in the demand for dollars in the foreign exchange market, and thus a shift of the dollar demand curve, are analogous to the factors that affect the supply of dollars. Factors that will *increase* the demand for dollars include:

- An increased preference for U.S. goods. For example, European airlines might find that U.S.-built aircraft are superior to others and decide to expand the number of American-made planes in their fleets. To buy the American planes, European airlines would demand more dollars on the foreign exchange market.
- An increase in real incomes abroad and thus more demand for imports from the United States.
- An increase in the real interest rate on U.S. assets, which would make those assets more attractive to foreign savers. To acquire U.S. assets, European savers would demand more dollars.

The Economic Naturalist 13.2

What is a safe haven currency?

Certain currencies, such as the U.S. dollar, the Swiss franc, and the Japanese yen, are in high demand during times of global uncertainty. The tendency of individuals to "pull their wealth out" of other currencies (i.e., to sell assets denominated in other currencies) and "park their wealth in" certain currencies (e.g., by buying and holding cash or bonds denominated in dollar, Swiss franc, or yen) earned these currencies the name *safe haven currencies*.

What makes a currency a safe haven? In times of uncertainty, individuals seek safe and liquid assets. An asset such as cash or bond is considered safe when its issuing government has a good history of issuing assets that turned out to be safe—and is therefore considered financially reliable and stable. Governments that did not in the past default on their debt or suffer from high inflation make good candidates. A currency is considered liquid when it is widely recognized and used, and is therefore widely accepted and can be easily exchanged in global markets. Naturally, these features of currencies—safety and liquidity—help in making the countries that issue them global financial hubs, which, in turn, helps in making these currencies safer and even more liquid.

As a safe haven currency, the U.S. dollar's exchange rate spiked around the global financial crisis and again around the global coronavirus crisis. As Figure 13.1 shows, the dollar gained around 20 percent within a few months in late 2008. It also gained around 8 percent within two weeks in March 2020.

The Economic Naturalist 10.1 (in Chapter 10, *Stabilizing the Economy: The Role of the Fed*) discussed how the demand for the safety and liquidity of the dollar is an important source of demand for dollars in specific *countries*, such as Argentina, that have a history of financial instability. Similarly, the safety and liquidity of U.S. assets are a source of global demand for dollars in specific *times* of global uncertainty.

RECAP

DETERMINING THE EXCHANGE RATE IN THE SHORT RUN

- Supply and demand analysis is a useful tool for studying the short-run determination of the exchange rate. U.S. households and firms supply dollars to the foreign exchange market to acquire foreign currencies, which they need to purchase foreign goods, services, and assets. Foreigners demand dollars in the foreign exchange market to purchase U.S. goods, services, and assets. The equilibrium exchange rate, also called the fundamental value of the exchange rate, equates the quantities of dollars supplied and demanded in the foreign exchange market.
- An increased preference for foreign goods, an increase in U.S. real incomes, or an increase in the real interest rate on foreign assets will increase the supply of dollars on the foreign exchange market, lowering the value of the dollar. An increased preference for U.S. goods by foreigners, an increase in real incomes abroad, or an increase in the real interest rate on U.S. assets will increase the demand for dollars, raising the value of the dollar.
- Safe haven currencies, including the dollar, tend to appreciate in periods of uncertainty when investors look to hold safe and liquid assets.

MONETARY POLICY AND THE EXCHANGE RATE

Of the many factors that could influence a country's exchange rate, among the most important is the monetary policy of the country's central bank. As we will see, monetary policy affects the exchange rate primarily through its effect on the real interest rate.

Suppose the Fed is concerned about inflation and tightens U.S. monetary policy in response. The effects of this policy change on the value of the dollar are shown in Figure 13.5. Before the policy change, the equilibrium value of the exchange rate is e^*, at the intersection of supply curve S and the demand curve D (point E in the figure). The tightening of monetary policy raises the domestic U.S. real interest rate r, making U.S. assets more attractive to foreign financial investors. The increased willingness of foreign investors to buy U.S. assets increases the demand for dollars, shifting the demand curve rightward from D to D' and the equilibrium point from E to F. As a result of this increase in demand, the equilibrium value of the dollar rises from e^* to $e^{*\prime}$.

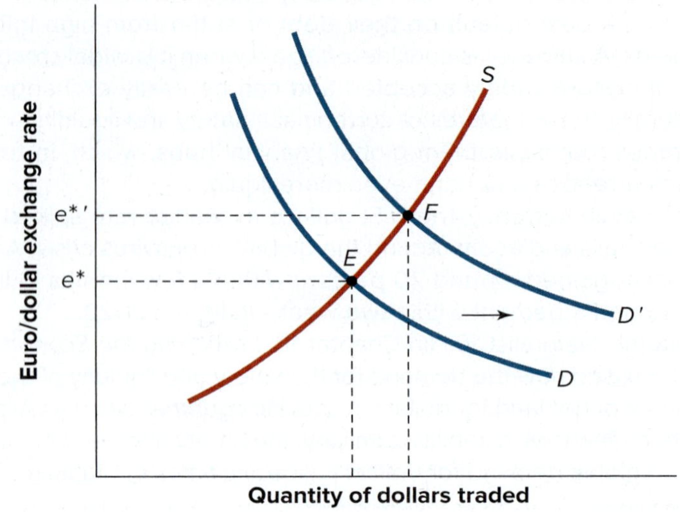

FIGURE 13.5

A Tightening of Monetary Policy Strengthens the Dollar.

Tighter monetary policy in the United States raises the domestic real interest rate, increasing the demand for U.S. assets by foreign savers. An increased demand for U.S. assets in turn increases the demand for dollars. The demand curve shifts from *D* to *D′*, leading the exchange rate to appreciate from e^* to $e^{*\prime}$.

In short, a tightening of monetary policy by the Fed raises the demand for dollars, causing the dollar to appreciate. By similar logic, an easing of monetary policy, which reduces the real interest rate, would weaken the demand for the dollar, causing it to depreciate.

The Economic Naturalist 13.3

Why did the dollar appreciate nearly 50 percent in the first half of the 1980s and nearly 40 percent in the second half of the 1990s?

Figure 13.1 showed the strong appreciation of the U.S. dollar in 1980–1985, followed by a sharp depreciation in 1986–1987. It also showed a strong appreciation in 1995–2001, followed by depreciation in 2002–2004. We saw earlier that the PPP theory cannot explain this roller-coaster behavior. What *can* explain it?

Tight monetary policy, and the associated high real interest rate, were important causes of the dollar's remarkable appreciation during 1980–1985. U.S. inflation peaked at 13.5 percent in 1980. Under the leadership of Chair Paul Volcker, the Fed responded to the surge in inflation by raising the real interest rate sharply in hopes of reducing aggregate demand and inflationary pressures. As a result, the real interest rate in the United States rose from negative values in 1979 and 1980 to more than 7 percent in 1983 and 1984. Attracted by these high real returns, foreign savers rushed to buy U.S. assets, driving the value of the dollar up significantly.

The Fed's attempt to bring down inflation was successful. By the middle of the 1980s the Fed was able to ease U.S. monetary policy. The resulting decline in the real interest rate reduced the demand for U.S. assets, and thus for dollars, at which point the dollar fell back almost to its 1980 level.

One reason for the dollar's appreciation in the late 1990s was the U.S. stock market boom and the generally strong pace of growth. These raised expected returns on U.S. assets, leading foreigners to want to buy these assets, increasing the demand for and thus appreciating the dollar. The relatively tight monetary policy during these years also played a role.

Stock markets peaked in the early 2000s before reversing course, and the U.S. economy was in recession during much of 2001, accompanied by a significant expansion in monetary policy starting early in 2001. While the dollar did not reverse its general upward trend until early 2002, when it eventually did, it started a long period of depreciation. By early 2004, with the federal funds rate at a historic low, the dollar fell back to its 1995 level.

The Exchange Rate as a Tool of Monetary Policy

In a closed economy, monetary policy affects aggregate demand solely through the real interest rate. For example, by raising the real interest rate, a tight monetary policy reduces consumption and investment spending. We will see next that in an open economy with a flexible exchange rate, the exchange rate serves as another channel for monetary policy, one that reinforces the effects of the real interest rate.

To illustrate, suppose that policymakers are concerned about inflation and decide to restrain aggregate demand. To do so, they increase the real interest rate, reducing consumption and investment spending. But, as Figure 13.5 shows, the higher real interest rate also increases the demand for dollars, causing the dollar to appreciate. The stronger dollar, in turn, further reduces aggregate demand. Why? As we saw in discussing the real exchange rate, a stronger dollar reduces the cost of imported goods, increasing imports. It also makes U.S. exports more costly to foreign buyers, which tends to reduce exports. Recall that net exports—or exports minus imports—is one of the four components of aggregate demand. Thus, by reducing exports and increasing imports, a stronger dollar (more precisely, a higher real exchange rate) reduces aggregate demand.[5]

In sum, when the exchange rate is flexible, a tighter monetary policy reduces net exports (through a stronger dollar) as well as consumption and investment spending (through a higher real interest rate). Conversely, an easier monetary policy weakens the dollar and stimulates net exports, reinforcing the effect of the lower real interest rate on consumption and investment spending. Thus, relative to the case of a closed economy we studied earlier, *monetary policy is more effective in an open economy with a flexible exchange rate*.

The tightening of monetary policy under Fed chair Volcker in the early 1980s illustrates the effect of monetary policy on net exports (the trade balance). As we saw in The Economic Naturalist 13.3, Volcker's tight-money policies were a major reason for the 50 percent appreciation of the dollar during 1980–1985. In 1980 and 1981, imports into the United States were only slightly above exports from the U.S., and the trade deficit did not exceed 0.5 percent of GDP. Largely in response to a stronger dollar, the U.S. trade deficit increased substantially after 1981. By the end of 1985 the U.S. trade deficit was about 3 percent of GDP, a substantial shift in less than half a decade.

RECAP

MONETARY POLICY AND THE EXCHANGE RATE

A tight monetary policy raises the real interest rate, increasing the demand for dollars and strengthening the dollar. A stronger dollar reinforces the effects of tight monetary policy on aggregate spending by reducing net exports, a component of aggregate demand. Conversely, an easy monetary policy lowers the real interest rate, weakening the dollar.

FIXED EXCHANGE RATES

So far we have focused on the case of flexible exchange rates, the relevant case for most large industrial countries like the United States. However, the alternative approach, fixing the exchange rate, has been quite important historically and is still used in many countries, especially small or developing nations. Furthermore, as mentioned earlier, even China—currently the world's second-largest economy—lets its currency float only within a fixed narrow band that shifts gradually over time or that is set by the central bank. (China kept its exchange rate fixed to the dollar throughout much of the 1990s and 2000s but has recently attempted to make its exchange rate somewhat more flexible.)

[5]We are temporarily assuming that the prices of U.S. goods in dollars and the prices of foreign goods in foreign currencies are not changing.

In this section, we will see how our conclusions change when the nominal exchange rate is fixed rather than flexible. One important difference is that when a country maintains a fixed exchange rate, its ability to use monetary policy as a stabilization tool is greatly reduced.

How to Fix an Exchange Rate

In contrast to a flexible exchange rate, whose value is determined solely by supply and demand in the foreign exchange market, the value of a fixed exchange rate is determined by the government (in practice, usually the finance ministry or treasury department, with the cooperation of the central bank). Today, the value of a fixed exchange rate is usually set in terms of a major currency (for instance, Hong Kong pegs its currency to the U.S. dollar at an exchange rate of HK$7.8 to US$1), or relative to a "basket" of currencies, typically those of the country's trading partners. Historically, currency values were often fixed in terms of gold or other precious metals, but in recent years, precious metals have rarely if ever been used for that purpose.

Once an exchange rate has been fixed, the government usually attempts to keep it unchanged for some time.[6] However, sometimes economic circumstances force the government to change the value of the exchange rate. A reduction in the official value of a currency is called a **devaluation;** an increase in the official value is called a **revaluation.** The devaluation of a fixed exchange rate is analogous to the depreciation of a flexible exchange rate; both involve a reduction in the currency's value. Conversely, a revaluation is analogous to an appreciation.

devaluation a reduction in the official value of a currency (in a fixed exchange rate system)

revaluation an increase in the official value of a currency (in a fixed exchange rate system)

The supply and demand diagram we used to study flexible exchange rates can be adapted to analyze fixed exchange rates. Let's consider the case of a country called Latinia, whose currency is called the peso. Figure 13.6 shows the supply and demand for the Latinian peso in the foreign exchange market. Pesos are *supplied* to the foreign exchange market by Latinian households and firms that want to acquire foreign currencies to purchase foreign goods and assets. Pesos are *demanded* by holders of foreign currencies who need pesos to purchase Latinian goods and assets. Figure 13.6 shows that the quantities of pesos supplied and demanded in the foreign exchange market are equal when a peso equals 0.1 dollar (10 pesos to the dollar). Hence

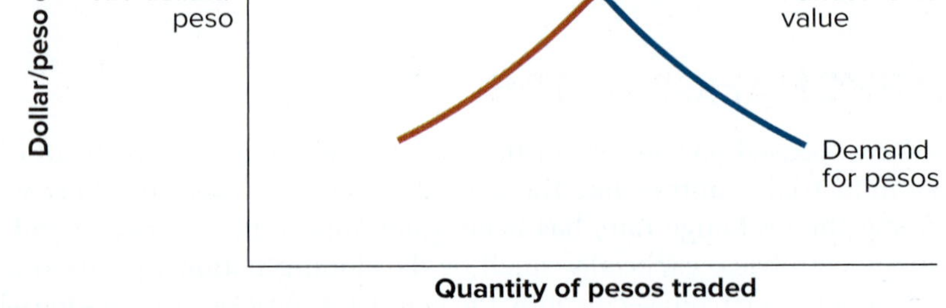

FIGURE 13.6

An Overvalued Exchange Rate. The peso's official value (0.125 dollars) is shown as greater than its fundamental value (0.10 dollars), as determined by supply and demand in the foreign exchange market. Thus the peso is overvalued. To maintain the fixed value, the government must purchase pesos in the quantity *AB* each period.

[6]There are exceptions to this statement. Some countries employ a *crawling peg* system, under which the exchange rate is fixed at a value that changes in a preannounced way over time. For example, the government may announce that the value of the fixed exchange rate will fall 2 percent each year. Other countries use a *target zone* system, in which the exchange rate is allowed to deviate by a small amount from its fixed value. To focus on the key issues, we will assume that the exchange rate is fixed at a single value for a protracted period.

0.1 dollar per peso is the *fundamental value* of the peso. If Latinia had a flexible exchange rate system, the peso would trade at 10 pesos to the dollar in the foreign exchange market.

But let's suppose that Latinia has a fixed exchange rate and that the government has decreed the value of the Latinian peso to be 8 pesos to the dollar, or 0.125 dollars per peso. This official value of the peso, 0.125 dollars, is indicated by the solid horizontal line in Figure 13.6. Notice that it is greater than the fundamental value, corresponding to the intersection of the supply and demand curves. When the officially fixed value of an exchange rate is greater than its fundamental value, the exchange rate is said to be **overvalued.** The official value of an exchange rate can also be lower than its fundamental value, in which case the exchange rate is said to be **undervalued.**

overvalued exchange rate an exchange rate that has an officially fixed value greater than its fundamental value

undervalued exchange rate an exchange rate that has an officially fixed value less than its fundamental value

In this example, Latinia's commitment to hold the peso at 8 to the dollar is inconsistent with the fundamental value of 10 to the dollar, as determined by supply and demand in the foreign exchange market (the Latinian peso is overvalued). How could the Latinian government deal with this inconsistency? There are several possibilities. First, Latinia could simply devalue its currency, from 0.125 dollars per peso to 0.10 dollars per peso, which would bring the peso's official value into line with its fundamental value. As we will see, devaluation is often the ultimate result of an overvaluation of a currency. However, a country with a fixed exchange rate will be reluctant to change the official value of its exchange rate every time the fundamental value changes. If a country must continuously adjust its exchange rate to market conditions, it might as well switch to a flexible exchange rate.

As a second alternative, Latinia could try to maintain its overvalued exchange rate by restricting international transactions. Imposing quotas on imports and prohibiting domestic households and firms from acquiring foreign assets would effectively reduce the supply of pesos to the foreign exchange market, raising the fundamental value of the currency. An even more extreme action would be to prohibit Latinians from exchanging the peso for other currencies without government approval, a policy that would effectively allow the government to determine directly the supply of pesos to the foreign exchange market. Such measures might help maintain the official value of the peso. However, restrictions on trade and capital flows are extremely costly to the economy, because they reduce the gains from specialization and trade and deny domestic households and firms access to foreign capital markets. Thus, a policy of restricting international transactions to maintain a fixed exchange rate is likely to do more harm than good.

The third and most widely used approach to maintaining an overvalued exchange rate is for the government to become a demander of its own currency in the foreign exchange market. Figure 13.6 shows that at the official exchange rate of 0.125 dollars per peso, the private-sector supply of pesos (point *B*) exceeds the private-sector demand for pesos (point *A*). To keep the peso from falling below its official value, in each period the Latinian government could purchase a quantity of pesos in the foreign exchange market equal to the length of the line segment *AB* in Figure 13.6. If the government followed this strategy, then at the official exchange rate of 0.125 dollars per peso, the total demand for pesos (private demand at point *A* plus government demand *AB*) would equal the private supply of pesos (point *B*). This situation is analogous to government attempts to keep the price of a commodity, like grain or milk, above its market level. To maintain an official price of grain that is above the market-clearing price, the government must stand ready to purchase the excess supply of grain forthcoming at the official price. In the same way, to keep the "price" of its currency above the market-clearing level, the government must buy the excess pesos supplied at the official price.

international reserves foreign currency assets held by a government for the purpose of purchasing the domestic currency in the foreign exchange market

To be able to purchase its own currency and maintain an overvalued exchange rate, the government (usually the central bank) must hold foreign currency assets, called **international reserves,** or simply *reserves*. For example, the Latinian central bank may hold dollar deposits in U.S. banks or U.S. government debt, which it can trade for pesos in the foreign exchange market as needed. In the situation shown in Figure 13.6, to keep

balance-of-payments deficit the net decline in a country's stock of international reserves over a year

balance-of-payments surplus the net increase in a country's stock of international reserves over a year

the peso at its official value, in each period the Latinian central bank will have to spend an amount of international reserves equal to the length of the line segment *AB*.

Because a country with an overvalued exchange rate must use part of its reserves to support the value of its currency in each period, over time its available reserves will decline. The net decline in a country's stock of international reserves over a year is called its **balance-of-payments deficit.** Conversely, if a country experiences a net increase in its international reserves over the year, the increase is called its **balance-of-payments surplus.**

EXAMPLE 13.6 Latinia's Balance-of-Payments Deficit

What is the balance-of-payments cost of keeping a currency overvalued?

The demand for and supply of Latinian pesos in the foreign exchange market are

$$\text{Demand} = 25{,}000 - 50{,}000e,$$
$$\text{Supply} = 17{,}600 + 24{,}000e,$$

where the Latinian exchange rate e is measured in dollars per peso. Officially, the value of the peso is 0.125 dollars. Find the fundamental value of the peso and the Latinian balance-of-payments deficit, measured in both pesos and dollars.

To find the fundamental value of the peso, equate the demand and supply for pesos

$$25{,}000 - 50{,}000e = 17{,}600 + 24{,}000e.$$

Solving for e, we get

$$7{,}400 = 74{,}000e$$
$$e = 0.10.$$

So the fundamental value of the exchange rate is 0.10 dollars per peso, as in Figure 13.6.

At the official exchange rate, 0.125 dollars per peso, the demand for pesos is $25{,}000 - 50{,}000(0.125) = 18{,}750$, and the supply of pesos is $17{,}600 + 24{,}000(0.125) = 20{,}600$. Thus the quantity of pesos supplied to the foreign exchange market exceeds the quantity of pesos demanded by $20{,}600 - 18{,}750 = 1{,}850$ pesos. To maintain the fixed rate, the Latinian government must purchase 1,850 pesos per period, which is the Latinian balance-of-payments deficit. Since pesos are purchased at the official rate of 8 pesos to the dollar, the balance-of-payments deficit in dollars is (1,850 pesos) × (0.125 dollars/peso) = \$(1,850/8) = \$231.25.

SELF-TEST 13.5

Repeat Example 13.6 under the assumption that the fixed value of the peso is 0.15 dollars per peso. What do you conclude about the relationship between the degree of currency overvaluation and the resulting balance-of-payments deficit?

Although a government can maintain an overvalued exchange rate for a time by offering to buy back its own currency at the official price, there is a limit to this strategy, since no government's stock of international reserves is infinite. Eventually the government will run out of reserves, and the fixed exchange rate will collapse. As we will see next, the collapse of a fixed exchange rate can be quite sudden and dramatic.

SELF-TEST 13.6

Diagram a case in which a fixed exchange rate is *undervalued* rather than overvalued. Show that to maintain the fixed exchange rate, the central bank must use domestic currency to purchase foreign currency in the foreign exchange market. With an undervalued exchange rate, is the country's central bank in danger of running out of international reserves? (*Hint:* Keep in mind that a central bank is always free to print more of its own currency.)

Speculative Attacks

A government's attempt to maintain an overvalued exchange rate can be ended quickly and unexpectedly by the onset of a *speculative attack*. A **speculative attack** involves massive selling of domestic currency assets by both domestic and foreign financial investors. For example, in a speculative attack on the Latinian peso, financial investors would attempt to get rid of any financial assets—stocks, bonds, deposits in banks—denominated in pesos. A speculative attack is most likely to occur when financial investors fear that an overvalued currency will soon be devalued since, in a devaluation, financial assets denominated in the domestic currency suddenly become worth much less in terms of other currencies. Ironically, speculative attacks, which are usually prompted by *fear* of devaluation, may turn out to be the *cause* of devaluation. Thus a speculative attack may actually be a self-fulfilling prophecy.

speculative attack a massive selling of domestic currency assets by financial investors

The effects of a speculative attack on the market for pesos are shown in Figure 13.7. At first, the situation is the same as in Figure 13.6: The supply and demand for Latinian pesos are indicated by the curves marked *S* and *D*, implying a fundamental value of the peso of 0.10 dollars per peso. As before, the official value of the peso is 0.125 dollars per peso—greater than the fundamental value—so the peso is overvalued. To maintain the fixed value of the peso, each period the Latinian central bank must use its international reserves to buy back pesos, in the amount corresponding to the line segment *AB* in the figure.

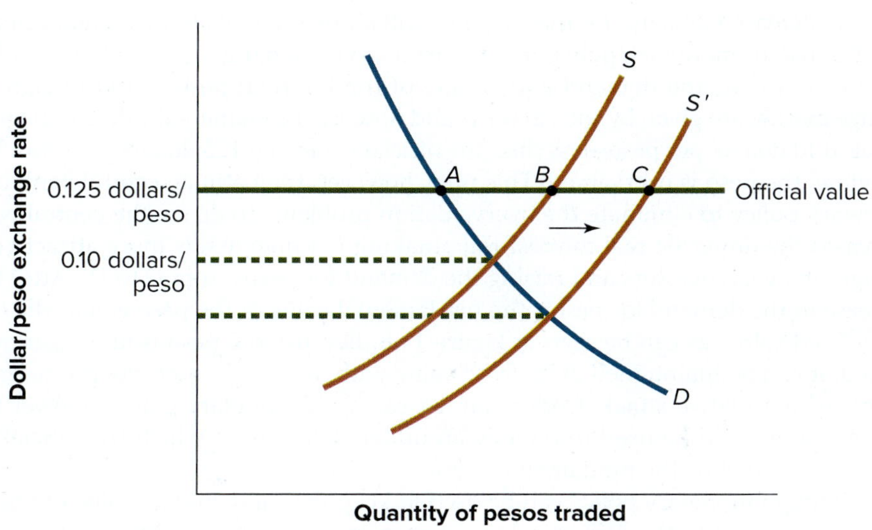

FIGURE 13.7

A Speculative Attack on the Peso.

Initially, the peso is overvalued at 0.125 dollars per peso. To maintain the official rate, the central bank must buy pesos in the amount *AB* each period. Fearful of possible devaluation, financial investors launch a speculative attack, selling peso-denominated assets and supplying pesos to the foreign exchange market. As a result, the supply of pesos shifts from *S* to *S'*, lowering the fundamental value of the currency still further and forcing the central bank to buy pesos in the amount *AC* to maintain the official exchange rate. This more rapid loss of reserves may lead the central bank to devalue the peso, confirming financial investors' fears.

Suppose, though, that financial investors fear that Latinia may soon devalue its currency, perhaps because the central bank's reserves are getting low. If the peso were to be devalued from its official value of 8 pesos to the dollar to its fundamental value of 10 pesos per dollar, then a 1 million peso investment, worth $125,000 at the fixed exchange rate, would suddenly be worth only $100,000. To try to avoid these losses, financial investors will sell their peso-denominated assets and offer pesos on the foreign exchange market. The resulting flood of pesos into the market will shift the supply curve of pesos to the right, from S to S' in Figure 13.7.

This speculative attack creates a serious problem for the Latinian central bank. Prior to the attack, maintaining the value of the peso required the central bank to spend each period an amount of international reserves corresponding to the line segment AB. Now suddenly the central bank must spend a larger quantity of reserves, equal to the distance AC in Figure 13.7, to maintain the fixed exchange rate. These extra reserves are needed to purchase the pesos being sold by panicky financial investors. In practice, such speculative attacks often force a devaluation by reducing the central bank's reserves to the point where further defense of the fixed exchange rate is considered hopeless. Thus a speculative attack ignited by fears of devaluation may actually end up producing the very devaluation that was feared.

Monetary Policy and the Fixed Exchange Rate

We have seen that there is no truly satisfactory way of maintaining a fixed exchange rate above its fundamental value for an extended period. A central bank can maintain an overvalued exchange rate for a time by using international reserves to buy up the excess supply of its currency in the foreign exchange market. But a country's international reserves are limited and may eventually be exhausted by the attempt to keep the exchange rate artificially high. Moreover, speculative attacks often hasten the collapse of an overvalued exchange rate.

An alternative to trying to maintain an overvalued exchange rate is to take actions that increase the fundamental value of the exchange rate. If the exchange rate's fundamental value can be raised enough to equal its official value, then the overvaluation problem will be eliminated. The most effective way to change the exchange rate's fundamental value is through monetary policy. As we saw earlier in the chapter, a tight monetary policy that raises the real interest rate will increase the demand for the domestic currency, as domestic assets become more attractive to foreign financial investors. Increased demand for the currency will in turn raise its fundamental value.

The use of monetary policy to support a fixed exchange rate is shown in Figure 13.8. At first, the demand and supply of the Latinian peso in the foreign exchange market are given by the curves D and S, so the fundamental value of the peso equals 0.10 dollars per peso—less than the official value of 0.125 dollars per peso. Just as before, the peso is overvalued. This time, however, the Latinian central bank uses monetary policy to eliminate the overvaluation problem. To do so, the central bank increases the domestic real interest rate, making Latinian assets more attractive to foreign financial investors and raising the demand for pesos from D to D'. After this increase in the demand for pesos, the fundamental value of the peso equals the officially fixed value, as can be seen in Figure 13.8. Because the peso is no longer overvalued, it can be maintained at its fixed value without loss of international reserves or fear of speculative attack. Conversely, an easing of monetary policy (a lower real interest rate) could be used to remedy an undervaluation, in which the official exchange rate is below the fundamental value.

Although monetary policy can be used to keep the fundamental value of the exchange rate equal to the official value, using monetary policy in this way has some drawbacks. In particular, *if monetary policy is used to set the fundamental value of the exchange rate equal to the official value, it is no longer available for stabilizing the domestic economy*. Suppose, for example, that the Latinian economy were suffering a recession due to insufficient aggregate demand at the same time that its exchange rate is

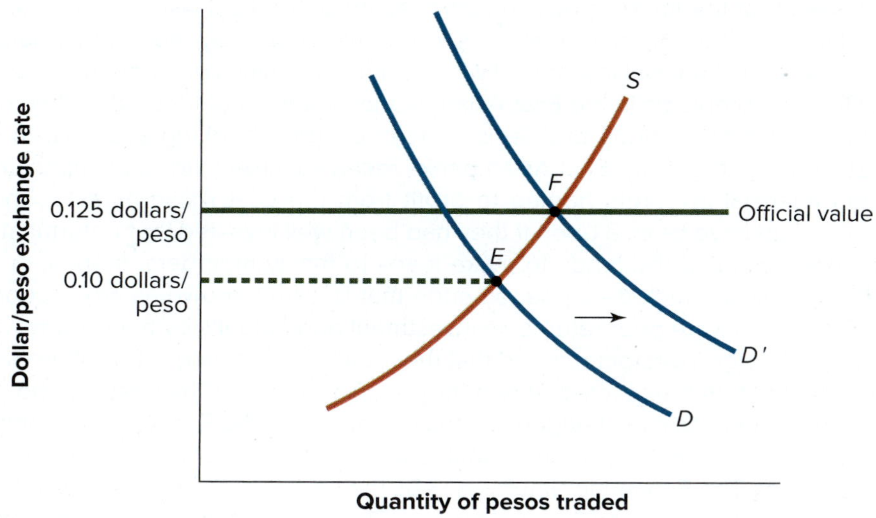

FIGURE 13.8

A Tightening of Monetary Policy Eliminates an Overvaluation.

With the demand for the peso given by *D* and the supply given by *S*, equilibrium occurs at point *E* and the fundamental value of the peso equals 0.10 dollars per peso—below the official value of 0.125 dollars per peso. The overvaluation of the peso can be eliminated by tighter monetary policy, which raises the domestic real interest rate, making domestic assets more attractive to foreign financial investors. The resulting increase in demand for the peso, from *D* to *D'*, raises the peso's fundamental value to 0.125 dollars per peso, the official value. The peso is no longer overvalued.

overvalued. The Latinian central bank could lower the real interest rate to increase spending and output, or it could raise the real interest rate to eliminate overvaluation of the exchange rate, *but it cannot do both*. Hence, if Latinian officials decide to maintain the fixed exchange rate, they must give up any hope of fighting the recession using monetary policy. The fact that a fixed exchange rate limits or eliminates the use of monetary policy for the purpose of stabilizing aggregate demand is one of the most important features of a fixed exchange rate system.

The conflict monetary policymakers face, between stabilizing the exchange rate and stabilizing the domestic economy, is most severe when the exchange rate is under a speculative attack. A speculative attack lowers the fundamental value of the exchange rate still further, by increasing the supply of the currency in the foreign exchange market (see Figure 13.7). To stop a speculative attack, the central bank must raise the fundamental value of the currency a great deal, which requires a large increase in the real interest rate. (In a famous episode in 1992, the Swedish central bank responded to an attack on its currency by raising the short-term interest rate to 500 percent!) However, because the increase in the real interest rate that is necessary to stop a speculative attack reduces aggregate demand, it can cause a severe economic slowdown. The Economic Naturalist 13.4 describes a real-world example of this phenomenon.

The Economic Naturalist 13.4

What were the causes and consequences of the East Asian crisis of 1997–1998?

During the last three decades of the twentieth century, the countries of East Asia enjoyed impressive economic growth and stability. But the "East Asian miracle" seemed to end in 1997, when a wave of speculative attacks hit the region's currencies. Thailand, which had kept a constant value for its currency in terms of the U.S. dollar for more than a decade, was the first to come under attack, but the crisis spread to other countries, including South Korea, Indonesia, and Malaysia. Each of these countries was ultimately forced to devalue its currency. What caused this crisis, and what were its consequences?

Because of the impressive economic record of the East Asian countries, the speculative attacks on their currencies were unexpected by most policymakers, economists, and financial investors. With the benefit of hindsight, however, we can identify some problems in the East Asian economies that contributed to the crisis. Perhaps the most serious problems concerned their banking systems. In the decade prior to the crisis, East Asian banks received large inflows of capital from foreign financial investors hoping to profit from the East Asian miracle. Those inflows would have been a boon if they had been well invested, but unfortunately, many bankers used the funds to make loans to family members, friends, or the politically well-connected—a phenomenon that became known as *crony capitalism*. The results were poor returns on investment and defaults by many borrowers. Ultimately, foreign investors realized that the returns to investing in East Asia would be much lower than expected. When they began to sell off their assets, the process snowballed into a full-fledged speculative attack on the East Asian currencies.

Despite assistance by international lenders such as the International Monetary Fund (see The Economic Naturalist 13.5), the effects of the speculative attacks on the East Asian economies were severe. The prices of assets such as stocks and land plummeted, and there were banking panics in several nations. (See Chapter 8, *Money, the Federal Reserve, and Global Financial Markets,* for a discussion of banking panics.) In an attempt to raise the fundamental values of their exchange rates and stave off additional devaluation, several of the countries increased their real interest rates sharply. However, the rise in real interest rates depressed aggregate demand, contributing to sharp declines in output and rising unemployment.

Fortunately, by 1999 most East Asian economies had begun to recover. Still, the crisis impressed the potential dangers of fixed exchange rates quite sharply in the minds of policymakers in developing countries. Another lesson from the crisis is that banking regulations need to be structured so as to promote economically sound lending rather than crony capitalism.

The Economic Naturalist 13.5

What is the IMF, and how has its mission evolved over the years?

The International Monetary Fund (IMF) was established after World War II. An international agency, the IMF is controlled by a 24-member executive board. Eight executive board members represent individual countries (China, France, Germany, Japan, Russia, Saudi Arabia, the United Kingdom, and the United States); the other 16 members each represent a group of countries.[7] A managing director oversees the IMF's operations and its approximately 2,700 staff (half of whom are economists).

The original purpose of the IMF was to help manage the system of fixed exchange rates, called the Bretton Woods system, put in place after the war. Under Bretton Woods, the IMF's principal role was to lend international reserves to member countries that needed them so that those countries could maintain their exchange rates at the official values. However, by 1973 the United States, the United Kingdom, Germany, and most other industrial nations had abandoned fixed exchange rates for flexible rates, leaving the IMF to find a new mission. Since 1973, the IMF has been involved primarily in lending to developing countries. For example, during the currency crises of the 1990s, it lent to Mexico, Russia, Brazil, and several East Asian countries. During the 2008 crisis, it again made loans to

[7]The Russian representative also represents Syria.

countries that saw their currencies under pressure. During the 2010s, the IMF joined European countries in making loans to Greece—a developed country—with the Europeans providing two-thirds of the money Greece needs to pay its government debts, and the IMF providing one-third. And in early 2020, the IMF made available $50 billion for low-income and emerging-market economies seeking loans related to addressing the global coronavirus epidemic.

The Economic Naturalist 13.6

How did policy mistakes contribute to the Great Depression?

We introduced the study of macroeconomics with the claim that policy mistakes played a major role in causing the Great Depression. Now that we are close to completing our study of macroeconomics, we can be more specific about that claim. How did policy mistakes contribute to the Great Depression?

Many policy mistakes (as well as a great deal of bad luck) contributed to the severity of the Depression. For example, U.S. policymakers, in an attempt to protect domestic industries, imposed the infamous Hawley-Smoot tariff in 1930. Other countries quickly retaliated with their own tariffs, leading to the virtual collapse of international trade.

However, the most serious mistakes by far were in the realm of monetary policy.[8] As we saw in Chapter 8, *Money, the Federal Reserve, and Global Financial Markets,* the U.S. money supply contracted by one-third between 1929 and 1933. Associated with this unprecedented decline in the money supply were sharply falling output and prices and surging unemployment.

At least three separate policy errors were responsible for the collapse of the U.S. money supply between 1929 and 1933. First, the Federal Reserve tightened monetary policy significantly in 1928 and 1929, despite the absence of inflation. Fed officials took this action primarily in an attempt to "rein in" the booming stock market, which they feared was rising too quickly. Their "success" in dampening stock market speculation was more than they bargained for, however, as rising interest rates and a slowing economy contributed to a crash in stock prices that began in October 1929.

The second critical policy error was allowing thousands of U.S. banks to fail during the banking panics of 1930 to 1933. Apparently officials believed that the failures would eliminate only the weakest banks, strengthening the banking system overall. However, the banking panics sharply reduced bank deposits and the overall money supply, for reasons discussed in Chapter 8.

The third policy error, related to the subject of this chapter, arose from the U.S. government's exchange rate policies. When the Depression began, the United States, like most other major countries, was on the gold standard, with the value of the dollar officially set in terms of gold.[9] By establishing a fixed value for the dollar, the United States effectively created a fixed exchange rate between the dollar and other currencies whose values were set in terms of gold. As the Depression worsened, Fed officials were urged by Congress to ease monetary policy to stop the fall in output and prices. However, as we saw earlier, under a fixed exchange rate, monetary policy cannot be used to stabilize the domestic economy. Specifically, policymakers of the early 1930s feared that if they eased monetary policy, foreign financial investors might perceive the dollar to be overvalued and launch a speculative attack, forcing a devaluation of the dollar or even the abandonment of the gold standard altogether. The Fed therefore made no serious attempt to arrest the collapse of the money supply.

[8]A classic 1963 book by Milton Friedman and Anna Schwartz, *A Monetary History of the United States: 1867–1960* (Princeton, NJ: Princeton University Press), was the first to provide detailed support for the view that poor monetary policy helped cause the Depression.

[9]The value of the dollar in 1929 was such that the price of 1 ounce of gold was fixed at $20.67.

With hindsight, we can see that the Fed's decision to put a higher priority on remaining on the gold standard than on stimulating the economy was a major error. Indeed, countries that abandoned the gold standard in favor of a floating exchange rate, such as Great Britain and Sweden, or that had never been on the gold standard (Spain and China) were able to increase their money supplies and to recover much more quickly from the Depression than the United States did. The Fed evidently believed, erroneously as it turned out, that stability of the exchange rate would somehow translate into overall economic stability.

Upon taking office in March 1933, Franklin D. Roosevelt reversed several of these policy errors. He took active measures to restore the health of the banking system, and he suspended the gold standard. The money supply stopped falling and began to grow rapidly. Output, prices, and stock prices recovered rapidly during 1933 to 1937, although unemployment remained high. However, ultimate recovery from the Depression was interrupted by another recession in 1937–1938.

RECAP

FIXED EXCHANGE RATES

- The value of a fixed exchange rate is set by the government. The official value of a fixed exchange rate may differ from its fundamental value, as determined by supply and demand in the foreign exchange market. An exchange rate whose officially fixed value exceeds its fundamental value is overvalued; an exchange rate whose officially fixed value is below its fundamental value is undervalued.
- For an overvalued exchange rate, the quantity of the currency supplied to the foreign exchange market at the official exchange rate exceeds the quantity demanded. The government can maintain an overvalued exchange rate for a time by using its international reserves (foreign currency assets) to purchase the excess supply of its currency. The net decline in a country's stock of international reserves during the year is its balance-of-payments deficit.
- Because a country's international reserves are limited, it cannot maintain an overvalued exchange rate indefinitely. Moreover, if financial investors fear an impending devaluation of the exchange rate, they may launch a speculative attack, selling domestic currency assets and supplying large amounts of the country's currency to the foreign exchange market—an action that exhausts the country's reserves even more quickly. Because rapid loss of reserves may force a devaluation, financial investors' fear of devaluation may prove a self-fulfilling prophecy.
- A tight monetary policy, which increases the real interest rate, raises the demand for the currency and hence its fundamental value. By raising a currency's fundamental value to its official value, tight monetary policies can eliminate the problem of overvaluation and stabilize the exchange rate. However, if monetary policy is used to set the fundamental value of the exchange rate, it is no longer available for stabilizing the domestic economy.

SHOULD EXCHANGE RATES BE FIXED OR FLEXIBLE?

Should countries adopt fixed or flexible exchange rates? In briefly comparing the two systems, we will focus on two major issues: (1) the effects of the exchange rate system on monetary policy and (2) the effects of the exchange rate system on trade and economic integration.

On the issue of monetary policy, we have seen that the type of exchange rate a country has strongly affects the central bank's ability to use monetary policy to stabilize the economy. A flexible exchange rate actually strengthens the impact of monetary policy on aggregate demand. But a fixed exchange rate prevents policymakers from using monetary policy to stabilize the economy because they must instead use it to keep the exchange rate's fundamental value at its official value (or else risk speculative attack).

In large economies like that of the United States, giving up the power to stabilize the domestic economy via monetary policy makes little sense. Thus large economies should nearly always employ a flexible exchange rate. However, in small economies, giving up this power may have some benefits. An interesting case is that of Argentina, which for the period 1991–2001 maintained a one-to-one exchange rate between its peso and the U.S. dollar. Although prior to 1991 Argentina had suffered periods of hyperinflation, while the peso was pegged to the dollar, Argentina's inflation rate essentially equaled that of the United States. By tying its currency to the dollar and giving up the freedom to set its monetary policy, Argentina attempted to commit itself to avoiding the inflationary policies of the past, and instead placed itself under the "umbrella" of the Federal Reserve. Unfortunately, early in 2002 investors' fears that Argentina would not be able to repay its international debts led to a speculative attack on the Argentine peso. The fixed exchange rate collapsed, the peso depreciated, and Argentina experienced an economic crisis. The lesson is that a fixed exchange rate alone cannot stop inflation in a small economy, if other policies are not sound as well. Large fiscal deficits, which were financed by foreign borrowing, ultimately pushed Argentina into crisis.

The second important issue is the effect of the exchange rate on trade and economic integration. Proponents of fixed exchange rates argue that fixed rates promote international trade and cross-border economic cooperation by reducing uncertainty about future exchange rates. For example, a firm that is considering building up its export business knows that its potential profits will depend on the future value of its own country's currency relative to the currencies of the countries to which it exports. Under a flexible exchange rate regime, the value of the home currency fluctuates with changes in supply and demand and is therefore difficult to predict far in advance. Such uncertainty may make the firm reluctant to expand its export business. Supporters of fixed exchange rates argue that if the exchange rate is officially fixed, uncertainty about the future exchange rate is reduced or eliminated.

One problem with this argument, which has been underscored by episodes like the East Asian crisis, the Argentine crisis, and, recently, the Greek crisis (see The Economic Naturalist 13.7), is that fixed exchange rates are not guaranteed to remain fixed forever. Although they do not fluctuate from day to day as flexible rates do, a speculative attack on a fixed exchange rate, or even a change in elected politicians' economic views, may lead suddenly and unpredictably to a large devaluation. Thus a firm that is trying to forecast the exchange rate 10 years into the future may face as much uncertainty if the exchange rate is fixed as if it is flexible.

The potential instability of fixed exchange rates caused by speculative attacks has led some countries to try a more radical solution to the problem of uncertainty about exchange rates: the adoption of a common currency. The Economic Naturalist 13.7 describes an important instance of this strategy.

The Economic Naturalist 13.7

Why have 19 European countries adopted a common currency?

Effective January 1, 1999, eleven western European nations, including France, Germany, and Italy, adopted a common currency, called the euro. In several stages, the euro replaced the French franc, the German mark, the Italian lira, and other national currencies. The process was completed in early 2002 when the old currencies were completely eliminated and replaced by euros. Since then, more

European nations, including eastern European ones, have joined the common currency. As of 2020, the last nation to join was Lithuania, which on January 1, 2015, became the 19th member of the *euro area* (or *eurozone*). Why have these nations adopted a common currency?

Since the end of World War II the nations of western Europe have worked to increase economic cooperation and trade among themselves. European leaders recognized that a unified and integrated European economy would be more productive and perhaps more competitive with the U.S. economy than a fragmented one. As part of this effort, these countries established fixed exchange rates under the auspices of a system called the European Monetary System (EMS). Unfortunately, the EMS did not prove stable. Numerous devaluations of the various currencies occurred, and in 1992, severe speculative attacks forced several nations, including Great Britain, to abandon the fixed exchange rate system.

In December 1991, in Maastricht in the Netherlands, the member countries of the European Community (EC) adopted a treaty popularly known as the Maastricht Treaty. One of the major provisions of the treaty, which took effect in November 1993, was that member countries would strive to adopt a common currency. This common currency, known as the euro, was formally adopted on January 1, 1999. The advent of the euro means that Europeans from eurozone countries no longer have to change currencies when trading with other eurozone countries, much as Americans from different states can trade with each other without worrying that a "New York dollar" will change in value relative to a "California dollar." The euro has helped promote European trade and cooperation while eliminating the problem of speculative attacks on the currencies of individual countries.

Because 19 European nations now have a single currency, they also must have a common monetary policy. The EC members agreed that European monetary policy would be put under the control of a new European Central Bank (ECB), a multinational institution located in Frankfurt, Germany. The ECB has in effect become "Europe's Fed." One potential problem with having a single monetary policy for so many different countries is that different countries may face different economic conditions, so a single monetary policy cannot respond to all of them. Indeed, in recent years countries in southern Europe like Spain and Italy have been in serious recessions (which requires an easing of monetary policy), while Germany has been close to full employment. With such a wide variation in economic conditions, the requirement of a single monetary policy has been creating conflicts of interest among the member nations of the European Community.

SUMMARY

- The *nominal exchange rate* between two currencies is the rate at which the currencies can be traded for each other. A rise in the value of a currency relative to other currencies is called an *appreciation;* a decline in the value of a currency is called a *depreciation. (LO1)*
- Exchange rates can be flexible or fixed. (Approaches that combine the two are not our focus in this chapter.) The value of a *flexible exchange rate* is determined by the supply and demand for the currency in the *foreign exchange market,* the market on which currencies of various nations are traded for one another. The government sets the value of a *fixed exchange rate. (LO1)*
- The *real exchange rate* is the price of the average domestic good or service *relative* to the price of the average foreign good or service, when prices are expressed in terms of a common currency. An increase in the real exchange rate implies that domestic goods and services are becoming more expensive relative to foreign goods and services, which tends to reduce exports and increase imports. Conversely, a decline in the real exchange rate tends to increase net exports. *(LO1)*

- A basic theory of nominal exchange rate determination, the *purchasing power parity* (*PPP*) theory, is based on the law of one price. The *law of one price* states that if transportation costs are relatively small, the price of an internationally traded commodity must be the same in all locations. According to the PPP theory, we can find the nominal exchange rate between two currencies by setting the price of a commodity in one of the currencies equal to the price of the commodity in the second currency. The PPP theory correctly predicts that the currencies of countries that experience significant inflation will tend to depreciate in the long run. However, the fact that many goods and services are not traded internationally, and that not all traded goods are standardized, makes the PPP theory less useful for explaining short-run changes in exchange rates. *(LO2)*
- Supply and demand analysis is a useful tool for studying the determination of exchange rates in the short run. The fundamental value of the exchange rate, also called the equilibrium exchange rate, equates the quantities of the currency supplied and demanded in the foreign exchange market. A currency is supplied by domestic residents who wish to acquire foreign currencies to purchase foreign goods, services, and assets. An increased preference for foreign goods, an increase in the domestic incomes, or an increase in the real interest rate on foreign assets will all increase the supply of a currency on the foreign exchange market and thus lower its value. A currency is demanded by foreigners who wish to purchase domestic goods, services, and assets. An increased preference for domestic goods by foreigners, an increase in real incomes abroad, or an increase in the domestic real interest rate will all increase the demand for the currency on the foreign exchange market and thus increase its value. *(LO3)*
- If the exchange rate is flexible, a tight monetary policy (by raising the real interest rate) increases the demand for the currency and causes it to appreciate. The stronger currency reinforces the effects of the tight monetary policy on aggregate demand by reducing net exports. Conversely, easy monetary policy lowers the real interest rate and weakens the currency, which in turn stimulates net exports. *(LO4)*
- The value of a fixed exchange rate is officially established by the government. A fixed exchange rate whose official value exceeds its fundamental value in the foreign exchange market is said to be *overvalued.* An exchange rate whose official value is below its fundamental value is *undervalued*. A reduction in the official value of a fixed exchange rate is called a *devaluation;* an increase in its official value is called a *revaluation*. *(LO5)*
- For an overvalued exchange rate, the quantity of the currency supplied at the official exchange rate exceeds the quantity demanded. To maintain the official rate, the country's central bank must use its *international reserves* (foreign currency assets) to purchase the excess supply of its currency in the foreign exchange market. Because a country's international reserves are limited, it cannot maintain an overvalued exchange rate indefinitely. Moreover, if financial investors fear an impending devaluation of the exchange rate, they may launch a *speculative attack,* selling their domestic currency assets and supplying large quantities of the currency to the foreign exchange market. Because speculative attacks cause a country's central bank to spend its international reserves even more quickly, they often force a devaluation. *(LO5)*
- A tight monetary policy, by raising the fundamental value of the exchange rate, can eliminate the problem of overvaluation. However, if monetary policy is used to set the fundamental value of the exchange rate equal to the official value, it is no longer available for stabilizing the domestic economy. Thus under fixed exchange rates, monetary policy has little or no power to affect domestic output and employment. *(LO5)*
- Because a fixed exchange rate implies that monetary policy can no longer be used for domestic stabilization, most large countries employ a flexible exchange rate. A fixed exchange rate may benefit a small country by forcing its central bank to follow the monetary policies of the country to which it has tied its rate. Advocates of fixed exchange rates argue that they increase trade and economic integration by making the exchange rate more predictable. However, the threat of speculative attacks greatly reduces the long-term predictability of a fixed exchange rate. *(LO6)*

KEY TERMS

appreciation
balance-of-payments deficit
balance-of-payments surplus
depreciation
devaluation
fixed exchange rate
flexible exchange rate
foreign exchange market
fundamental value of the exchange rate (or equilibrium exchange rate)
international reserves
law of one price
nominal exchange rate
overvalued exchange rate
purchasing power parity (PPP)
real exchange rate
revaluation
speculative attack
undervalued exchange rate

REVIEW QUESTIONS

1. Japanese yen trade at 110 yen per dollar and Mexico pesos trade at 10 pesos per dollar. What is the nominal exchange rate between the yen and the peso? Express in two ways. *(LO1)*
2. Define nominal exchange rate and real exchange rate. How are the two concepts related? Which type of exchange rate most directly affects a country's ability to export its goods and services? *(LO1)*
3. Would you expect the law of one price to apply to crude oil? To fresh milk? To taxi rides? To music produced in different countries by local recording artists? Explain your answer in each case. *(LO2)*
4. Why do U.S. households and firms supply dollars to the foreign exchange market? Why do foreigners demand dollars in the foreign exchange market? *(LO3)*
5. Under a flexible exchange rate, how does an easing of monetary policy (a lower real interest rate) affect the value of the exchange rate? Does this change in the exchange rate tend to weaken or strengthen the effect of the monetary ease on output and employment? Explain. *(LO4)*
6. Define overvalued exchange rate. Discuss four ways in which government policymakers can respond to an overvaluation. What are the drawbacks of each approach? *(LO5)*
7. Use a supply and demand diagram to illustrate the effects of a speculative attack on an overvalued exchange rate. Why do speculative attacks often result in a devaluation? *(LO5)*
8. Contrast fixed and flexible exchange rates in terms of how they affect (a) the ability of monetary policy to stabilize domestic output and (b) the predictability of future exchange rates. *(LO6)*

PROBLEMS

connect

1. Using the data in Table 13.1, find the nominal exchange rate between the Mexican peso and the Japanese yen. Express in two ways. How do your answers change if the peso appreciates by 10 percent against the dollar while the value of the yen against the dollar remains unchanged? *(LO1)*
2. A British-made automobile is priced at £20,000 (20,000 British pounds). A comparable U.S.-made car costs $26,000. One pound trades for $1.50 in the foreign exchange market. Find the real exchange rate for automobiles from the perspective of the United States and from the perspective of Great Britain. Which country's cars are more competitively priced? *(LO1)*
3. Between last year and this year, the CPI in Blueland rose from 100 to 120 and the CPI in Redland rose from 100 to 115. Blueland's currency unit, the blue, was worth 80 cents (U.S.) last year and is worth 60 cents (U.S.) this year. Redland's currency unit, the red, was worth 20 cents (U.S.) last year and is worth 15 cents (U.S.) this year.

   Find the percentage change from last year to this year in Blueland's *nominal* exchange rate with Redland and in Blueland's *real* exchange rate with Redland. (Treat Blueland as the home country.) Relative to Redland, do you expect Blueland's exports to be helped or hurt by these changes in exchange rates? *(LO1)*
4. The demand for U.S.-made cars in Japan is given by

   Japanese demand = 10,000 − 0.001(Price of U.S. cars in yen).

   Similarly, the demand for Japanese-made cars in the United States is

   U.S. demand = 30,000 − 0.2(Price of Japanese cars in dollars).

   The domestic price of a U.S.-made car is $20,000, and the domestic price of a Japanese-made car is ¥2,500,000. From the perspective of the United States, find the real exchange rate in terms of cars and net exports of cars to Japan, if *(LO1)*
   a. the nominal exchange rate is 100 yen per dollar.
   b. the nominal exchange rate is 125 yen per dollar.

   How does an appreciation of the dollar affect U.S. net exports of automobiles (considering only the Japanese market)?
5. a. Gold is $350 per ounce in the United States and 2,800 pesos per ounce in Mexico. What nominal exchange rate between U.S. dollars and Mexican pesos is implied by the PPP theory? *(LO2)*
   b. Mexico experiences inflation so that the price of gold rises to 4,200 pesos per ounce. Gold remains $350 per ounce in the United States. According to the PPP theory, what happens to the exchange rate? What general principle does this example illustrate? *(LO2)*

c. Gold is \$350 per ounce in the United States and 4,200 pesos per ounce in Mexico. Crude oil (excluding taxes and transportation costs) is \$30 per barrel in the United States. According to the PPP theory, what should a barrel of crude oil cost in Mexico? *(LO2)*

d. Gold is \$350 per ounce in the United States. The exchange rate between the United States and Canada is 0.70 U.S. dollars per Canadian dollar. How much does an ounce of gold cost in Canada? *(LO2)*

6. How would each of the following be likely to affect the value of the dollar, all else being equal? Explain. *(LO3)*
   a. U.S. stocks are perceived as having become much riskier financial investments.
   b. European computer firms switch from U.S.-produced software to software produced in India, Israel, and other nations.
   c. As East Asian economies recover, international financial investors become aware of many new, high-return investment opportunities in the region.

7. Suppose a French bottle of champagne costs 20.5 euros. *(LO3)*
   a. If the euro–dollar exchange rate is 0.8 euros per dollar, so that a dollar can buy 0.8 euros, how much will the champagne cost in the United States?
   b. If the euro–dollar exchange rate rises to 1.05 euro per dollar, how much will the champagne cost in the United States?
   c. If an increase in the euro–dollar exchange rate leads to an increase in Americans' dollar expenditures on French champagne, what will happen to the amount of dollars supplied to the foreign exchange market as the euro–dollar exchange rate rises?

8. Consider an Apple iPod that costs \$240. *(LO3)*
   a. If the euro–dollar exchange rate is 1 euro per dollar, so that it costs a European 1 euro to buy a dollar, how much will the iPod cost in France?
   b. If the euro–dollar exchange rate falls to 0.8 euros per dollar, how much will the iPod cost in France?
   c. Consequently, what will happen to French purchases of iPods and the amount of dollars demanded in the foreign exchange market as the euro–dollar exchange rate falls?

9. If the government follows an easy monetary policy and the exchange rate is flexible, which of the following will likely be the result? *(LO4)*
   a. A falling real interest rate but higher net exports.
   b. A higher real interest rate but lower net exports.
   c. A strong currency that helps stimulate exports.
   d. Increases in the demand for the currency and decreases in the supply of the currency.

10. The demand for and supply of shekels in the foreign exchange market are

$$\text{Demand} = 30{,}000 - 8{,}000e,$$
$$\text{Supply} = 25{,}000 + 12{,}000e,$$

where the nominal exchange rate is expressed as U.S. dollars per shekel. *(LO3, LO5)*
   a. What is the fundamental value of the shekel?
   b. The shekel is fixed at 0.30 U.S. dollars. Is the shekel overvalued, undervalued, or neither? Find the balance-of-payments deficit or surplus in both shekels and dollars. What happens to the country's international reserves over time?
   c. Repeat part b for the case in which the shekel is fixed at 0.20 U.S. dollars.

11. The annual demand for and supply of shekels in the foreign exchange market is as given in Problem 10. The shekel is fixed at 0.30 dollars per shekel. The country's international reserves are \$600. Foreign financial investors hold checking accounts in the country in the amount of 5,000 shekels. *(LO3, LO5)*
   a. Suppose that foreign financial investors do not fear a devaluation of the shekel and, thus, do not convert their shekel checking accounts into dollars. Can the shekel be maintained at its fixed value of 0.30 U.S. dollars for the next year?
   b. Now suppose that foreign financial investors come to expect a possible devaluation of the shekel to 0.25 U.S. dollars. Why should this possibility worry them?
   c. In response to their concern about devaluation, foreign financial investors withdraw all funds from their checking accounts and attempt to convert those shekels into dollars. What happens?
   d. Discuss why the foreign investors' forecast of devaluation can be considered a "self-fulfilling prophecy."

ANSWERS TO SELF-TESTS

13.1 Answers will vary, depending on when the data are obtained. *(LO1)*

13.2 The dollar price of the U.S. computer is \$2,400, and each dollar is equal to 110 yen. Therefore the yen price of the U.S. computer is (110 yen/dollar) × (\$2,400), or 264,000 yen. The price of the Japanese computer is 242,000 yen. Thus the conclusion that the Japanese model is cheaper does not depend on the currency in which the comparison is made. *(LO1)*

13.3 Since the law of one price holds for gold, its price per ounce must be the same in New York and Stockholm:

$$\$900 = 7{,}500 \text{ kronor}.$$

Dividing both sides by 900, we get

$$\$1 = 8.33 \text{ kronor}.$$

So the exchange rate is 8.33 kronor per dollar. *(LO2)*

13.4 A decline in U.S. GDP reduces consumer incomes and hence imports. As Americans are purchasing fewer imports, they supply fewer dollars to the foreign exchange market, so the supply curve for dollars shifts to the left. Reduced supply raises the equilibrium value of the dollar. *(LO3)*

13.5 At a fixed value for the peso of 0.15 dollars, the demand for the peso equals 25,000 − 50,000(0.15) = 17,500. The supply of the peso equals 17,600 + 24,000(0.15) = 21,200. The quantity supplied at the official rate exceeds the quantity demanded by 3,700. Latinia will have to purchase 3,700 pesos each period, so its balance-of-payments deficit will equal 3,700 pesos, or 3,700 × 0.15 = 555 dollars. This balance-of-payments deficit is larger than we found in Example 13.6. We conclude that the greater the degree of overvaluation, the larger the country's balance-of-payments deficit is likely to be. *(LO5)*

13.6 The figure shows a situation in which the official value of the currency is *below* the fundamental value, as determined by the supply of and demand for the currency in the foreign exchange market, so the currency is undervalued. At the official value of the exchange rate, the quantity demanded of the domestic currency (point *B*) exceeds the quantity supplied (point *A*). To maintain the official value, the central bank must supply domestic currency to the foreign exchange market each period in the amount *AB*. In contrast to the case of an overvalued exchange rate, here the central bank is providing its own currency to the foreign exchange market and receiving foreign currencies in return.

The central bank can print as much of its own currency as it likes, and so with an undervalued currency there is no danger of running out of international reserves. Indeed, the central bank's stock of international reserves increases in the amount *AB* each period as it receives foreign currencies in exchange for the domestic currency it supplies. *(LO5)*

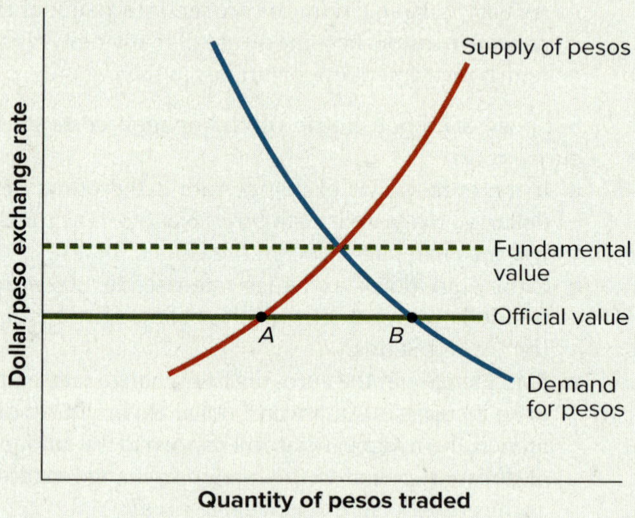

GLOSSARY

A

absolute advantage one person has an absolute advantage over another if he or she takes fewer hours to perform a task than the other person

aggregate demand (*AD*) curve a curve that shows the relationship between short-run equilibrium output Y and the rate of inflation π; it thus shows the amount of output consumers, firms, government, and entities abroad want to purchase at each inflation rate, holding all other factors constant

aggregate expenditure the sum of consumer expenditures, firms' investment, government purchases, and net exports

aggregate supply shock either an inflation shock or a shock to potential output; adverse aggregate supply shocks of both types reduce output and increase inflation

aggregation the adding up of individual economic variables to obtain economywide totals

appreciation an increase in the value of a currency relative to other currencies

assets anything of value that one *owns*

automatic stabilizers provisions in the law that imply *automatic* increases in government spending or decreases in taxes when real output declines

autonomous consumption consumption spending that is not related to the level of disposable income

autonomous expenditure the portion of planned aggregate expenditure that is independent of output

average benefit the total benefit of undertaking n units of an activity divided by n

average cost the total cost of undertaking n units of an activity divided by n

average labor productivity output per employed worker

B

balance sheet a list of an economic unit's assets and liabilities on a specific date

balance-of-payments deficit the net decline in a country's stock of international reserves over a year

balance-of-payments surplus the net increase in a country's stock of international reserves over a year

bank reserves cash or similar assets held by commercial banks for the purpose of meeting depositor withdrawals and payments

banking panic a situation in which news or rumors of the imminent bankruptcy of one or more banks leads bank depositors to rush to withdraw their funds

barter the direct trade of goods or services for other goods or services

bequest saving saving done for the purpose of leaving an inheritance

Board of Governors the leadership of the Fed, consisting of seven governors appointed by the president to staggered 14-year terms

bond a legal promise to repay a debt, usually including both the principal amount and regular interest, or coupon, payments

boom a particularly strong and protracted expansion

business cycles (or **cyclical fluctuations)** short-term fluctuations in GDP and other indicators of economic activity

buyer's reservation price the largest dollar amount the buyer would be willing to pay for a good

buyer's surplus the difference between the buyer's reservation price and the price he or she actually pays

C

capital gains increases in the value of existing assets

capital good a long-lived good that is used in the production of other goods and services

capital inflows purchases of domestic assets by foreign households and firms

capital losses decreases in the value of existing assets

capital outflows purchases of foreign assets by domestic households and firms

cash on the table an economic metaphor for unexploited gains from exchange

change in aggregate demand a shift of the entire *AD* curve

change in demand a shift of the entire demand curve

change in supply a shift of the entire supply curve

change in the quantity demanded a movement along the demand curve that occurs in response to a change in price

change in the quantity supplied a movement along the supply curve that occurs in response to a change in price

closed economy an economy that does not trade with the rest of the world

comparative advantage one person has a comparative advantage over another if his or her opportunity cost of performing a task is lower than the other person's opportunity cost

complements two goods are complements in consumption if an increase in the price of one causes a leftward shift in the demand curve for the other (or if a decrease causes a rightward shift)

compound interest the payment of interest not only on the original deposit, but on all previously accumulated interest

constant (or **parameter)** a quantity that is fixed in value

consumer price index (CPI) for any period, a measure of the cost in that period of a standard basket of goods and services relative to the cost of the same basket of goods and services in a fixed year, called the *base year*

consumption *See* **consumption expenditure**

consumption expenditure (or **consumption)** spending by households on goods and services such as food, clothing, and entertainment

consumption function the relationship between consumption spending and its determinants, in particular, disposable (after-tax) income

contraction *See* **recession**

contractionary policies government policy actions designed to reduce planned spending and output

coupon payments regular interest payments made to the bondholder

coupon rate the interest rate promised when a bond is issued; the annual coupon payments are equal to the coupon rate times the principal amount of the bond

crowding out the tendency of increased government deficits to reduce investment spending

cyclical fluctuations *See* **business cycles**

cyclical unemployment the extra unemployment that occurs during periods of recession

D

deflating (a nominal quantity) the process of dividing a nominal quantity by a price index (such as the CPI) to express the quantity in real terms

deflation a situation in which the prices of most goods and services are falling over time so that inflation is negative

demand curve a schedule or graph showing the quantity of a good that buyers wish to buy at each price

demand for money the amount of wealth an individual or firm chooses to hold in the form of money

dependent variable a variable in an equation whose value is determined by the value taken by another variable in the equation

deposit insurance a system under which the government guarantees that depositors will not lose any money even if their bank goes bankrupt

depreciation a decrease in the value of a currency relative to other currencies

depression a particularly severe or protracted recession

descriptive economic principle *See* **positive (descriptive) economic principle**

devaluation a reduction in the official value of a currency (in a fixed exchange rate system)

diminishing returns to capital if the amount of labor and other inputs employed is held constant, then the greater the amount of capital already in use, the less an additional unit of capital adds to production

diminishing returns to labor if the amount of capital and other inputs in use is held constant, then the greater the quantity of labor already employed, the less each additional worker adds to production

discount rate the interest rate that the Fed charges commercial banks to borrow reserves

discount window lending the lending of reserves by the Federal Reserve to commercial banks

discouraged workers people who say they would like to have a job but have not made an effort to find one in the past four weeks

disinflation a substantial reduction in the rate of inflation

disposable income the after-tax amount of income that people are able to spend

distributional effects changes in the distribution of income or wealth in the economy

diversification the practice of spreading one's wealth over a variety of different financial investments to reduce overall risk

dividend a regular payment received by stockholders for each share that they own

durable goods goods that yield utility over time and are made to last for three years or more

duration the length of an unemployment spell

E

economic efficiency *See* **efficiency**

economic surplus the benefit of taking an action minus its cost

economics the study of how people make choices under conditions of scarcity and of the results of those choices for society

efficiency (or **economic efficiency**) a condition that occurs when all goods and services are produced and consumed at their respective socially optimal levels

entrepreneurs people who create new economic enterprises

equation a mathematical expression that describes the relationship between two or more variables

equilibrium a balanced or unchanging situation in which all forces at work within a system are canceled by others

equilibrium exchange rate *See* **fundamental value of the exchange rate**

equilibrium price and equilibrium quantity the price and quantity at the intersection of the supply and demand curves for the good

equity *See* **stock**

excess demand (or **shortage**) the amount by which quantity demanded exceeds quantity supplied when the price of a good lies below the equilibrium price

excess reserves bank reserves in excess of the reserve requirements set by the central bank

excess supply (or **surplus**) the amount by which quantity supplied exceeds quantity demanded when the price of the good exceeds the equilibrium price

expansion a period in which the economy is growing at a rate significantly above normal

expansionary gap a positive output gap, which occurs when actual output is higher than potential output ($Y > Y^*$)

expansionary policies government policy actions intended to increase planned spending and output

F

federal funds rate the interest rate that commercial banks charge each other for very short-term (usually overnight) loans

Federal Open Market Committee (FOMC) the committee that makes decisions concerning monetary policy

Federal Reserve System (or **the Fed**) the central bank of the United States

final goods or services goods or services consumed by the ultimate user; because they are the end products of the production process, they are counted as part of GDP

financial intermediaries firms that extend credit to borrowers using funds raised from savers

fiscal policy decisions that determine the government's budget, including the amount and composition of government expenditures and government revenues

fixed exchange rate an exchange rate whose value is set by official government policy

flexible exchange rate an exchange rate whose value is not officially fixed but varies according to the supply and demand for the currency in the foreign exchange market

flow a measure that is defined *per unit of time*

foreign exchange market the market on which currencies of various nations are traded for one another

forward guidance information that a central bank provides to the financial markets regarding its expected future monetary-policy path

fractional-reserve banking system a banking system in which bank reserves are less than deposits so that the reserve-deposit ratio is less than 100 percent

frictional unemployment the short-term unemployment associated with the process of matching workers with jobs

full-employment output *See* **potential output, Y^***

fundamental value of the exchange rate (or **equilibrium exchange rate**) the exchange rate that equates the quantities of the currency supplied and demanded in the foreign exchange market

G

government budget deficit the excess of government spending over tax collections ($G - T$)

government budget surplus the excess of government tax collections over government spending ($T - G$); the government budget surplus equals public saving

government purchases purchases by federal, state, and local governments of final goods and services; government purchases do *not* include transfer payments, which are payments made by the government in return for which no current goods or services are received, nor do they include interest paid on the government debt

gross domestic product (GDP) the market value of the final goods and services produced in a country during a given period

H

human capital an amalgam of factors such as education, training, experience, intelligence, energy, work habits, trustworthiness, and initiative that affects the value of a worker's marginal product

I

income effect the change in the quantity demanded of a good that results because a change in the price of a good changes the buyer's purchasing power

income-expenditure multiplier (or **multiplier**) the effect of a one-unit increase in autonomous expenditure on short-run equilibrium output

independent variable a variable in an equation whose value determines the value taken by another variable in the equation

indexing the practice of increasing a nominal quantity each period by an amount equal to the percentage increase in a specified price index; indexing prevents the purchasing power of the nominal quantity from being eroded by inflation

inferior good a good whose demand curve shifts leftward when the incomes of buyers increase and rightward when the incomes of buyers decrease

inflation shock a sudden change in the normal behavior of inflation, unrelated to the nation's output gap

intermediate goods or services goods or services used up in the production of final goods and services and therefore not counted as part of GDP

international capital flows purchases or sales of real and financial assets across international borders

international financial markets financial markets in which borrowers and lenders are residents of different countries

international reserves foreign currency assets held by a government for the purpose of purchasing the domestic currency in the foreign exchange market

investment spending by firms on final goods and services, primarily capital goods

involuntary part-time workers people who say they would like to work full-time but are able to find only part-time work

L

labor force the total number of employed and unemployed people in the economy

law of one price if transportation costs are relatively small, the price of an internationally traded commodity must be the same in all locations

liabilities the debts one *owes*

life-cycle saving saving to meet long-term objectives such as retirement, college attendance, or the purchase of a home

long-run aggregate supply (*LRAS*) line a vertical line showing the economy's potential output Y^*

long-run equilibrium a situation in which actual output equals potential output and the inflation rate is stable; graphically, long-run equilibrium occurs when the *AD* curve, the *SRAS* line, and the *LRAS* line all intersect at a single point

M

M1 the sum of currency outstanding and balances held in checking accounts

M2 all the assets in M1 plus some additional assets that are usable in making payments but at greater cost or inconvenience than currency or checks

macroeconomic policies government actions designed to affect the performance of the economy as a whole

macroeconomics the study of the performance of national economies and the policies that governments use to try to improve that performance

marginal benefit the increase in total benefit that results from carrying out one additional unit of an activity

marginal propensity to consume (*mpc*) the amount by which consumption rises when disposable income rises by \$1; we assume that $0 < mpc < 1$

market the market for any good consists of all buyers or sellers of that good

market equilibrium occurs in a market when all buyers and sellers are satisfied with their respective quantities at the market price

market interest rate *See* **nominal interest rate**

market value the selling prices of goods and services in the open market

medium of exchange an asset used in purchasing goods and services

menu costs the costs of changing prices

microeconomics the study of individual choice under scarcity and its implications for the behavior of prices and quantities in individual markets

monetary policy determination of the nation's money supply

money any asset that can be used in making purchases

money demand curve a curve that shows the relationship between the aggregate quantity of money demanded M and the nominal interest rate i

multiplier *See* **income-expenditure multiplier**

mutual fund a financial intermediary that sells shares in itself to the public and then uses the funds raised to buy a wide variety of financial assets

N

national saving the saving of the entire economy, equal to GDP less consumption expenditures and government purchases of goods and services, or $Y - C - G$

natural rate of unemployment, u^* the part of the total unemployment rate that is attributable to frictional and structural unemployment; equivalently, the unemployment rate that prevails when cyclical unemployment is zero, so that the economy has neither a recessionary nor an expansionary output gap

net worth an economic unit's wealth determined by subtracting liabilities from assets

nominal exchange rate the rate at which two currencies can be traded for each other

nominal GDP a measure of GDP in which the quantities produced are valued at current-year prices; nominal GDP measures the *current dollar value* of production

nominal interest rate (or **market interest rate**) the annual percentage increase in the nominal value of a financial asset

nominal quantity a quantity that is measured in terms of its current dollar value

nondurable goods goods that can be quickly consumed or immediately used, having a life span of less than three years

normal good a good whose demand curve shifts rightward when the incomes of buyers increase and leftward when the incomes of buyers decrease

normative analysis addresses the question of whether a policy *should* be used; normative analysis inevitably involves the values of the person doing the analysis

normative economic principle one that says how people should behave

O

100 percent reserve banking a situation in which banks' reserves equal 100 percent of their deposits

open economy an economy that trades with other countries

open-market operations open-market purchases and open-market sales

open-market purchase the purchase of government bonds from the public by the Fed for the purpose of increasing the supply of bank reserves and the money supply

open-market sale the sale by the Fed of government bonds to the public for the purpose of reducing bank reserves and the money supply

opportunity cost the value of what must be forgone to undertake an activity

output gap, $Y - Y^*$ the difference between the economy's actual output and its potential output at a point in time

overvalued exchange rate an exchange rate that has an officially fixed value greater than its fundamental value

P

parameter *See* **constant**

participation rate the percentage of the working-age population in the labor force (that is, the percentage that is either employed or looking for work)

peak the beginning of a recession; the high point of economic activity prior to a downturn

physical capital equipment and tools (such as machines and factories) needed to complete one's work

policy reaction function describes how the action a policymaker takes depends on the state of the economy

portfolio allocation decision the decision about the forms in which to hold one's wealth

positive analysis addresses the economic consequences of a particular event or policy, not whether those consequences are desirable

positive (or **descriptive**) **economic principle** one that predicts how people will behave

potential GDP *See* **potential output, Y^***

potential output, Y^* (or **potential GDP** or **full-employment output**) the amount of output (real GDP) that an economy can produce when using its resources, such as capital and labor, at normal rates

precautionary saving saving for protection against unexpected setbacks such as the loss of a job or a medical emergency

price ceiling a maximum allowable price, specified by law

price index a measure of the average price of a given class of goods or services relative to the price of the same goods or services in a base year

price level a measure of the overall level of prices at a particular point in time as measured by a price index such as the CPI

principal amount the amount originally lent

private saving the saving of the private sector of the economy is equal to the after-tax income of the private sector minus consumption expenditures ($Y - T - C$); private saving can be further broken down into household saving and business saving

protectionism the view that free trade is injurious and should be restricted

public saving the saving of the government sector is equal to net tax payments minus government purchases ($T - G$)

purchasing power parity (PPP) the theory that nominal exchange rates are determined as necessary for the law of one price to hold

Q

quantitative easing (QE) an expansionary monetary policy in which a central bank buys long-term financial assets, thereby lowering the yield or return of those assets while increasing the money supply

quota a legal limit on the quantity of a good that may be imported

R

rate of inflation the annual percentage rate of change in the price level, as measured, for example, by the CPI

rational person someone with well-defined goals who tries to fulfill those goals as best he or she can

real exchange rate the price of the average domestic good or service *relative* to the price of the average foreign good or service, when prices are expressed in terms of a common currency

real GDP a measure of GDP in which the quantities produced are valued at the prices in a base year rather than at current prices; real GDP measures the actual *physical volume* of production

real interest rate the annual percentage increase in the purchasing power of a financial asset; the real interest rate on any asset equals the nominal interest rate on that asset minus the inflation rate

real quantity a quantity that is measured in physical terms—for example, in terms of quantities of goods and services

real wage the wage paid to workers measured in terms of purchasing power; the real wage for any given period is calculated by dividing the nominal (dollar) wage by the CPI for that period

recession (or **contraction**) a period in which the economy is growing at a rate significantly below normal

recessionary gap a negative output gap, which occurs when potential output exceeds actual output ($Y^* > Y$)

relative price the price of a specific good or service *in comparison to* the prices of other goods and services

reserve requirements set by the Fed, the minimum values of the ratio of bank reserves to bank deposits that commercial banks are allowed to maintain

reserve-deposit ratio bank reserves divided by deposits

revaluation an increase in the official value of a currency (in a fixed exchange rate system)

rise *See* **slope**

risk premium the rate of return that financial investors require to hold risky assets minus the rate of return on safe assets

run *See* **slope**

S

saving current income minus spending on current needs

saving rate saving divided by income

seller's reservation price the smallest dollar amount for which a seller would be willing to sell an additional unit, generally equal to marginal cost

seller's surplus the difference between the price received by the seller and his or her reservation price

short-run aggregate supply (*SRAS*) line a horizontal line showing the current rate of inflation, as determined by past expectations and pricing decisions

short-run equilibrium a situation in which inflation equals the value determined by past expectations and pricing decisions and output equals the level of short-run equilibrium output that is consistent with that inflation rate; graphically, short-run equilibrium occurs at the intersection of the *AD* curve and the *SRAS* line

short-run equilibrium output the level of output at which output Y equals planned aggregate expenditure *PAE*; the level of output that prevails during the period in which prices are predetermined

shortage *See* **excess demand**

skill-biased technological change technological change that affects the marginal products of higher-skilled workers differently from those of lower-skilled workers

slope in a straight line, the ratio of the vertical distance the straight line travels between any two points ***(rise)*** to the corresponding horizontal distance ***(run)***

socially optimal quantity the quantity of a good that results in the maximum possible economic surplus from producing and consuming the good

speculative attack a massive selling of domestic currency assets by financial investors

stabilization policies government policies that are used to affect planned aggregate expenditure, with the objective of eliminating output gaps

standard of living the degree to which people have access to goods and services that make their lives easier, healthier, safer, and more enjoyable

stock a measure that is defined *at a point in time*

stock (or **equity**) a claim to partial ownership of a firm

store of value an asset that serves as a means of holding wealth

structural policy government policies aimed at changing the underlying structure, or institutions, of the nation's economy

structural unemployment the long-term and chronic unemployment that exists even when the economy is producing at a normal rate

substitutes two goods are substitutes in consumption if an increase in the price of one causes a rightward shift in the demand curve for the other (or if a decrease causes a leftward shift)

substitution effect the change in the quantity demanded of a good that results because buyers switch to or from substitutes when the price of the good changes

sunk cost a cost that is beyond recovery at the moment a decision must be made

supply curve a graph or schedule showing the quantity of a good that sellers wish to sell at each price

surplus *See* **excess supply**

T

tariff a tax imposed on an imported good

the Fed *See* **Federal Reserve System**

total surplus the difference between the buyer's reservation price and the seller's reservation price

trade balance (or **net exports**) the value of a country's exports less the value of its imports in a particular period (quarter or year)

trade deficit when imports exceed exports, the difference between the value of a country's imports and the value of its exports in a given period

trade surplus when exports exceed imports, the difference between the value of a country's exports and the value of its imports in a given period

transfer payments payments the government makes to the public for which it receives no current goods or services in return

trough the end of a recession; the low point of economic activity prior to a recovery

U

undervalued exchange rate an exchange rate that has an officially fixed value less than its fundamental value

unemployment rate the number of unemployed people divided by the labor force

unemployment spell a period during which an individual is continuously unemployed

unit of account a basic measure of economic value

V

value added for any firm, the market value of its product or service minus the cost of inputs purchased from other firms

variable a quantity that is free to take a range of different values

vertical intercept in a straight line, the value taken by the dependent variable when the independent variable equals zero

W

wealth the value of assets minus liabilities

wealth effect the tendency of changes in asset prices to affect households' wealth and thus their consumption spending

worker mobility the movement of workers between jobs, firms, and industries

workers' compensation a government insurance system that provides benefits to workers who are injured on the job

world price the price at which a good or service is traded on international markets

Z

zero lower bound a level, close to zero, below which the Fed cannot further reduce short-term interest rates

Page numbers followed by n refer to notes.